Cultural Anthropology

AN APPLIED PERSPECTIVE

SEVENTH EDITION

Gary Ferraro

The University of North Carolina at Charlotte

THOMSON

WADSWORTH

Australia • Brazil • Canada • Mexico • Singapore • Spain • United Kingdom • United States

THOMSON

™

WADSWORTH

Cultural Anthropology: An Applied Perspective, Seventh Edition

Gary Ferraro

Editor in Chief: *Eve Howard*

Acquisitions Editor: *Lin Marshall*

Technology Project Manager: *David Lionetti*

Marketing Manager: *Caroline Concilla*

Marketing Assistant: *Teresa Jessen*

Marketing Communications Manager: *Shemika Britt*

Project Manager, Editorial Production: *Jerilyn Emori*

Creative Director: *Rob Hugel*

Art Director: *Maria Epes*

Print Buyer: *Rebecca Cross*

Permissions Editor: *Bob Kauser*

Production Service: *Joan Keyes, Dovetail Publishing Services*

Text Designer: *Jerry Wilke*

Photo Researcher: *Susan Kaprov*

Copy Editor: *Susan Gall*

Cover Designer: *Larry Didona*

Cover Image: © *Strauss/Curtis/Age Fotostock; background image:*
© *Sylvain Grandadam/Getty Images*

Text and Cover Printer: *Courier Corporation/Kendallville*

Compositor: *Newgen–Austin*

Printed in the United States of America
1 2 3 4 5 6 7 10 09 08 07

Library of Congress Control Number: 2006933466

ISBN 0-495-10008-0

Thomson Higher Education
10 Davis Drive
Belmont, CA 94002-3098
USA

For more information about our products, contact us at:
Thomson Learning Academic Resource Center
1-800-423-0563

For permission to use material from this text or product, submit a request online at **http://www.thomsonrights.com.**

Any additional questions about permissions can be submitted by e-mail to **thomsonrights@thomson.com.**

To Avery, Mitchell, Anna, and Greyson, with the hope that their generation will be the best intercultural communicators yet.

Brief Contents

Features Contents

APPLIED PERSPECTIVES

CONTEMPORARY ISSUES

CROSS-CULTURAL MISCUES

Detailed Contents

Preface

From the beginning, this text has had two major purposes. First, the book is designed to introduce university undergraduates to the field of cultural anthropology by drawing upon the rich ethnographic examples found within the discipline. With its comparative approach to the study of cultural diversity, the text provides a comprehensive overview of the discipline. Second, the text goes beyond the basic outline of introductory materials by applying the theory, insights, and methods of cultural anthropology to those contemporary situations that students, both majors and non-majors, are likely to encounter in their professional and personal lives. Most students enrolled in introductory anthropology courses will never take another course in anthropology during their undergraduate careers. It is, therefore, important that they be exposed to the relevance of the discipline at the introductory level, rather than expecting them to take additional courses in more applied areas of anthropology.

FEATURES THAT INTEGRATE THE APPLIED PERSPECTIVE

The text's applied orientation is integrated into each of the chapters by the features called Applied Perspectives and Cross-Cultural Miscues. The Applied Perspectives, which appear in boxed format in Chapters 2 through 16, demonstrate how cultural anthropology has been used to solve specific societal problems in such areas as medicine, education, government, architecture, business, and economic development. For example, in Chapter 5 of this Seventh Edition, students are shown how anthropological findings have been used to develop more efficient programs of AIDS education both at home and abroad. And an Applied Perspective in Chapter 8 illustrates how traditional anthropological interests in consumption patterns are now being used by major corporations in their market research.

Over the past decade, a number of leading introductory textbooks in the field have, to one degree or another, included some applied case studies in boxed format. I consider this imitation to be the sincerest form of flattery. Nevertheless, the Applied Perspective case studies in this text differ in some important respects. For example, each case study is selected to illustrate how certain understandings from each chapter have been applied to the solution of significant societal problems; there are a greater number of in-depth applied case studies in this text than in the others; and each of the case studies is followed by Questions for Further Thought, designed to encourage students to think critically about the broader implications of the applied case.

In addition to the Applied Perspective boxes, two Cross-Cultural Miscues also appear in boxed format in Chapters 2 through 16. These short scenarios illustrate the negative consequences of failing to understand cultural differences. To illustrate, one miscue from Chapter 4 tells how the deployment of tens of thousands of well-meaning, but culturally naïve, U.S. troops to Iraq in the aftermath of the 2003 invasion has led to a number of cross-cultural misunderstandings. And, in Chapter 16, students are able to see how differences in communication style lead to misunderstanding and even hostility between Koreans and African-American neighbors in Los Angeles.

Over the past decade, an increasing number of cultural anthropologists have agreed with our basic premise: that an introductory text with an applied focus was long overdue. Anthropology instructors at a number of different types of institutions, public and private, large and small, two-year and four-year, have adopted the first six editions of this book. However, as well received as the previous editions have been, there is always room for improvement. Responding to many helpful suggestions of reviewers, the following changes have been made in the Seventh Edition.

General

- A major feature introduced in the Fifth Edition of this text, and expanded upon since then, are the Contemporary Issues boxes. The Seventh Edition includes four new Contemporary Issues boxes, one dealing with a disciplinary issue and the remaining three addressing societal concerns. The new disciplinary issue, appearing in Chapter 3, examines the need for applied cultural anthropologists to find their public policy voice. Other new Contemporary Social Issue boxes focus on the culture specific disorder of young male shut-ins in Japan called *hikikomori* (Chapter 2) and the problems faced by disaster assistance personnel when they have an imperfect understanding of the cultural values of the people they are trying to assist (Chapter 16).

- Three new Applied Perspectives have been added to the Seventh Edition. One, appearing in

Chapter 9, shows how an applied educational anthropologist used the cultural patterns of Native Hawaiian students to help teachers better integrate them into the culture of the classroom. The second Applied Perspective (Chapter 10) shows how an applied anthropologist used data on local family and kinship systems to help redesign an agricultural development program in the West African country of Guinea. And the third new Applied Perspective illustrates how a cultural anthropologist hunted down stolen religious works of art from Kenya that had found their way into museums in the United States.

■ Six new Cross-Cultural Miscues have been added to this new edition, one each in Chapters 3, 7, 8, 11, 12, and 14.

■ The Suggested Reading sections at the end of the chapters have been updated with current works.

■ In keeping with the principle that well-chosen photographs can be highly instructive, this edition has more photo images than previous editions. Moreover, every effort has been taken to tie the photos to the text as explicitly as possible.

■ A new pedagogical feature of the Seventh Edition is the inclusion of locator maps, illustrating for students the geographic location of some of the peoples discussed in the text.

■ In addition to locator maps, the Seventh Edition includes a number of special issue maps, including the location of major language groups, religions, and concentrations of poverty.

■ Another feature appearing for the first time in this edition is a running glossary as well as the cumulative glossary at the book's end.

■ A deliberate effort has been made in this edition to make connections between the basic anthropological theories and insights and what is going on in the world around us as we begin the new millennium. The theme of globalization is discussed in a number of chapters including Chapter 1 (What Is Anthropology?), Chapter 7 (Making a Living), Chapter 8 (Economics), Chapter 13 (Political Organization and Social Control), Chapter 14 (Supernatural Beliefs), Chapter 15 (Art), and Chapter 16 (Culture Change and Globalization). Other contemporary events (from the twenty-first century) have also been integrated into the new edition. These include the "war on terrorism"; the T.V. series *Bones,* based on the life and work of forensic anthropologist Kathy Reichs; marriage brokers in Shanghai; the successful clone of the American Idol television program found in India called *Indian Idol;* disaster victims from both Katrina in New Orleans and the 2004 tsunami in South Asia; and the rapidly increasing influence of bloggers.

Chapter Changes

As with previous editions, all chapters have been revised with an eye toward streamlining, making materials more current, and reflecting recent trends in the discipline. For those familiar with previous editions of this book, a closer look at the specific changes made in each chapter will be helpful.

Chapter 1: What Is Anthropology? discusses the current debate of an integrated four-field approach to anthropology versus dividing the discipline into four separate sub-disciplines. The central concept of globalization is introduced in Chapter 1 so as to prepare the reader for more in-depth discussions of globalization in subsequent chapters. Two new tables appear for the first time: Table 1.2 dealing with the two facets of cultural anthropology (ethnography and ethnology) and Table 1.3 illustrating non-academic career opportunities in anthropology. In the section on ethnocentrism, a nineteenth-century British travel writer by the name of Mrs. Mortimer (who had something nasty to say about people from all cultures) is discussed as a vivid reminder of how we should not think in the twenty-first century. And finally, data is presented on how a University of Chicago archaeologist, Shannon Lee Dawdy, is helping post-Katrina New Orleans save some of its historic treasures.

Chapter 2: The Concept of Culture contains a new Contemporary Issues box dealing with young male shut-ins in Japan *(hikikomori),* a culture-specific problem analogous to anorexia among U.S. girls/women, caused by: (a) fierce competition to succeed, (b) prolonged interdependence between parents and children, and (c) enormous cultural emphasis on conformity. In the section on enculturation, there is a new discussion on how a growing number of parents in the United States are sending their children to special classes and summer camps to learn good manners and proper etiquette. And, a new table is introduced toward the end of the chapter that summarizes the major features of the concept of culture.

Chapter 3: Applied Anthropology includes a new table showing the essential differences between theoretical and applied anthropology in terms of objectives, methods, time frame, and extent of collaboration. A new case study of medical anthropology from South Africa has been added, and there is additional explanatory data on the federal legislation of the 1960s and 1970s supporting applied anthropology. And, finally, the chapter now contains a new Contemporary Issue box entitled "Can Cultural Anthropologists Find Their Public Policy Voice?" which discusses the need for anthropologists not just to engage in applied research, but to make their voices heard in the public policy arena.

Chapter 4: The Growth of Anthropological Theory contains new data on the numbers of women receiving PhDs in anthropology (62 percent of all degrees granted by 2003), a legacy of founding parent Franz Boas. The chapter also includes a more fully developed discussion of the methodological and theoretical implications of the Mead-Freeman debate. Despite these substantive additions, the chapter also reflects the author's relentless and continued efforts to edit down the considerable amount of information in this chapter.

Chapter 5: Methods in Cultural Anthropology includes a new discussion of a recent study of Native Americans who have become wealthy through the casino/gaming industry, new information on the role played by anthropologists in the HIV/AIDS pandemic, and additional information on the El Dorado controversy concerning anthropological ethics while conducting field research. The chapter also contains two new sections, one on field methods used primarily, if not exclusively, by applied cultural anthropologists; and the other on AnthroSource, the new database sponsored by the American Anthropological Association.

Chapter 6: Language and Communication has undergone extensive changes in the Seventh Edition. Specifically, new discussions have been added on how the governments of Mongolia, Chile, and South Korea are encouraging the use of English, with the ultimate long-term effect of discouraging traditional languages; how learning a second language leads to more positive attitudes and feelings about speakers of that language; and how Denglish (a combination of Deutsch and English) is becoming almost as common in Germany as Spanglish is becoming in the United States. New data is presented on the second language capabilities of English speakers in the United States as compared to Europeans, and a new table is included on the difficulties of learning the English language. In deference to the effects of modern technology on the process of communication, there are new discussions on (a) how people today fake cell phone conversations ("cell phonies") and (b) how the use of text messaging on cell phones is enabling people to communicate with a minimum of interpersonal intimacy. Also notice that the title of the chapter has changed from "Language" to "Language and Communication" in order to acknowledge that all human communication involves both language and nonverbal forms of discourse.

Chapter 7: Making a Living provides new information on the Inuit peoples of the Arctic regions in the twenty-first century. The good news is that the Inuits now own and operate their own cruise ship company, which runs ecotourist cruises to their self-governing territory of Nunavut. The bad news is that the Inuit are the first to experience the culture-altering consequences of global warming, including the migration of animals for areas farther north and the increasing number of instances of expensive snowmobiles falling through the ice. Moreover, the state of Nunavut, established in 1999, is struggling to establish itself as a viable administrative entity because it faces problems of high unemployment, low graduation rates, alcoholism, drug abuse, and suicide. To supplement the section "Human Adaptation," the chapter now contains an explanation of how the Moken people of Surin Island (off the coast of Thailand) were spared the wrath of the 2004 tsunami because of their intimate understanding of, and adaptation to, their physical environment. The chapter includes a new section on contemporary changes in the culture of the Ju/'hoansi of Namibia, how the cultural assumptions of some swidden farmers in Indonesia are diametrically opposed to those of developmental economists, and a new Cross-Cultural Miscue on how a British fertilizer salesperson misunderstood the culture of East African farmers.

Chapter 8: Economics now contains additional information on the dramatic rise of small (house-front) family businesses in Yucatan during times of economic transition away from cash crops. Because globalization is so prominently featured in Chapter 8, a new expanded discussion has been added on two radically different views of economic globalization (the optimistic views of Thomas Friedman are balanced against the more anthropological interpretation, which sees a number of deleterious effects on poor populations of the world). Also in keeping with the globalization theme, Chapter 8 now contains a discussion of how the fascination with blogs has hampered worker efficiency in offices in the United States and how a commitment to a free trade policy is sometimes constrained by more immediate political concerns. Finally, a new Cross-Cultural Miscue has been added dealing with gift giving in Columbia, South America.

Chapter 9: Marriage and the Family now contains a revised definition of marriage on the first page of the chapter so as to ensure that students are not left with the initial impression that marriages are always heterosexual unions. The chapter discusses the 38-percent rise in multigenerational families in the United States between 1990 and 2000, caused in part by high real estate costs and the desire of many retiring baby boomers to live with their children rather than go to a retirement community. Also included in Chapter 9 are new discussions on certain abuses of the practice of polygyny in the United States, marriage brokers for wealthy, fast-track executives in New York City and Shanghai, and emerging extended family living patterns among newly arrived immigrants to the United States. A new section on changing marital practices has been added illustrating how marriage ceremonies are changing rapidly in modern Japan and how those same forces for change are being counteracted in modern day Seoul, Korea. A new Applied Perspective from the field of educational anthropology has also been added, illustrating how positive changes in the classroom were made in Hawaiian schools after anthropologists studied child behavior within the home.

Chapter 10: Kinship and Descent   has a new Applied Perspective dealing with how a development anthropologist helped redesign an agricultural development program in Guinea by understanding the connections between local agricultural practices and kinship/family patterns. The discussion of the wife's view of the patrilineal family, formerly located in a Contemporary Issues box, has been moved into the section of the text dealing with patrilineages. In response to multiple suggestions by reviewers, the number of different kinship systems described has been reduced from six to four, and the accompanying diagrams have been made smaller. A new chart has been added summarizing the differences between patrilineal and matrilineal descent systems.

Chapter 11: Sex and Gender   contains new information on recent efforts by the Chinese government to correct sex imbalances (119 males for every 100 females) by providing incentives to have girl babies (such as free tuition for girls and annual pensions for elderly people who have only daughters). Moreover, new information is provided on "transgender" or "third gender" individuals found in traditional Native American cultures. Also new to Chapter 11 is a table on the division of labor by gender, an explanation of how gender differences influence workplace decisions in the United States, and information on the relationship between (relative) gender equality and the lack of HIV/AIDS. A new example of gender exploitation—the practice of "marriage abductions" in Kyrgyzstan—is included in Chapter 11 for the first time. Also appearing is a new Cross-Cultural Miscue dealing with the different meanings in Italy and the United States attached to the nonverbal gesture of tugging on one's own earlobe. Finally, the status of women in different countries throughout the world is illustrated by United Nations data called the Gender Empowerment Measure (2002).

Chapter 12: Social Stratification   examines the changing nature of social stratification in the United States by examining (1) how the U.S. consumer economy (everyone carrying a cell phone) makes identifying people from different classes more difficult than in earlier decades, (2) how Hurricane Katrina victims revealed the enormous class differences that are still very real in the United States, and (3) how the upper classes are not only more wealthy and powerful, but are also more healthy and actually live longer. In reference to the concept of race, the chapter now discusses how DNA testing in anthropology and sociology classes at Penn State University are showing students, in a very personal

way, that they are not who they think they are. Turning to global stratification, the chapter includes the latest data on GNI (gross national income) differences between the United States and other nations of the world and discusses how certain eastern European countries are cooperating to alleviate poverty and discrimination toward the Roma (gypsies). The chapter also includes a new Cross-Cultural Miscue involving how U.S. college students misunderstood why a Nigerian student wanted to carry his professor's books to class for him.

Chapter 13: Political Organization and Social Control   After updating the figures on the increasing number of "free" countries and the declining number of "not free" countries in the world between 1975 and 2005, a new discussion follows on the meaning of "freedom" depending on one's place in the social hierarchy. The chapter discusses the impact of the Internet on the political process in the United States as well as how certain U.S. information technology companies have assisted the Chinese government in quelling dissent over the Internet. Also new information is presented on the extent to which corporal punishment is used to socialize children (that is, teach them proper social behavior) in the Western world. Also new to this chapter is a discussion of the difference in legal objectives between the International Court of Justice (punishment) and certain local tribunals in Uganda (reconciliation). The chapter ends with a new major section on the "war on terrorism," which concludes that it is not only misleading, but wrong, to equate terrorist activities with Islamic fundamentalism.

Chapter 14: Supernatural Beliefs   includes a new discussion of religious fundamentalism throughout the world, and particularly the rise of Christian fundamentalism in such urban areas as New York City, which, unlike their rural counterparts, do not oppose such issues as stem cell research, abortion, or Darwinian evolution. A new table has been added to the Seventh Edition showing the relative numbers of adherents to the major religions of the world, as well as a new discussion of the shift in influence and power from Christians in Europe and North America to Christians living in Africa, South America, and south Asia. The chapter also contains a new Cross-Cultural Miscue illustrating how the apparently innocent remarks of a U.S. talk-show host could be taken as a verbal put-down of the religion of those victims of the 2004 tsunami in south Asia. And, as an illustration of twenty-first-century changes to Hinduism, the chapter discusses the concept of "yoga lite" (a more time-efficient, yet watered down, version of the traditional practice of Yoga), practiced by India's rapidly expanding middle class who are facing high-pressure jobs and a lack of time.

Chapter 15: Art   starts with a new discussion on the integration of art forms, showing how the paintings of

African-American artist Jonathan Green have been the subject matter of a fully staged ballet performed by the Columbia (SC) Ballet Company. The section on dance has been enhanced with a new discussion of the similarities between dance (as an art form) and nonverbal communication, the significant role of dance in Cuba, and the increasing popularity of the Brazilian dance form capoeira throughout the world. Also included is a new Applied Perspective on how a cultural anthropologist served as a sleuth to identify stolen religious works of art from Kenya. A new major section has been added on the art of humor and how it doesn't translate well from one culture to another. And, finally, there is a new discussion of *Indian Idol,* a competitive talent television show in India similar to *American Idol,* and how its popularity reflects certain deep-rooted Indian values.

Chapter 16: Culture Change and Globalization

Information concerning problems caused by the widespread use of cell phones has been transferred from a Contemporary Issues box in the previous edition directly into the text, and a new Contemporary Issues box has been added dealing with the need to understand the cultures of disaster victims before they can be given adequate disaster relief. The last section of this chapter on "globalization" has been extensively rewritten and expanded. Some of the information was moved to Chapters 1 and 8 so as to introduce the idea of globalization earlier in the book. The new information on globalization in Chapter 16 involves new "leading indicators of globalization," the growing influence of multinational corporations, how globalization is not homogenizing the world down into a single culture, and the need for a more "multicultural" approach to survival in the twenty-first century. The notion of global interdependence is illustrated by how an initial bank deposit in Chase Manhattan Bank influenced the lives of specific people around the world. And finally, Chapter 16 now contains a new discussion on how the "brain drain" of many Indian engineers coming to the United States in the 1980s and early 1990s has reversed itself to the extent that today many of those former residents of Silicon Valley are now living in Bangalore in California-like suburbs; and many recent U.S. college graduates are going to Bangalore for their first high-tech jobs, because that's where the growth industry is located.

In addition to the many changes—both additions and deletions—to the various chapters, the Glossary, and the References section have been revised to reflect the new content.

CHAPTER FEATURES

As with all previous editions, the Seventh Edition contains a number of pedagogical features designed to enhance student learning. These include introductory questions alerting the student to what will be learned in the chapter; concise chapter summaries; a running as well as a cumulative glossary; Applied Perspectives, Contemporary Issues, and Cross-Cultural Miscues, which appear in boxed format; Questions for Further Thought, designed to stimulate further thinking about the applied cases; and Suggested Readings, which provide relevant references for students who want to learn more about a particular topic discussed in the chapter.

SUPPLEMENTS FOR INSTRUCTORS
Instructor's Manual with Test Bank

Written by Gary Ferraro, this substantially revised supplement offers the instructor chapter outlines, learning objectives, lecture and classroom suggestions, student assignments, Internet and InfoTrac College Edition® exercises, as well as a film/video resource guide for each chapter. The test items consist of five to forty multiple choice questions and ten to fifteen true/false questions with page references, along with completion and essay questions for each chapter. A concise user guide for *InfoTrac College Edition* is included as an appendix.

A Guide to Visual Anthropology

Prepared by Jayasinhji Jhala of Temple University, this guide provides a compendium of fifty of the most outstanding classic and contemporary anthropological films. The guide describes the films, tells why they are important, and gives suggestions for their use in the classroom.

ExamView Computerized and Online Testing

Create, deliver, and customize tests and study guides (both print and online) in minutes with this easy-to-use assessment and tutorial system. ExamView offers both a Quick Test Wizard and an Online Test Wizard that guide you step-by-step throughout the process of creating tests, while its unique "WYSIWYG" capability allows you to see the test you are creating onscreen exactly as it will print or display online. You can build tests of up to 250 questions using up to twelve question types. Using ExamView's complete word processing capabilities, you can enter an unlimited number of new questions or edit existing questions.

Multimedia Manger for Anthropology: A Microsoft PowerPoint Link Tool

This new CD-ROM contains digital media and Microsoft® PowerPoint® presentations for all of Wadsworth's 2008 introductory anthropology texts, placing images, lectures, and video clips at your fingertips. This CD-ROM includes preassembled Microsoft PowerPoint presentations, as well as charts, graphs, maps, and line art from all Wadsworth anthropology texts. You can add your own lecture notes and images to create a customized lecture presentation. Also, an Earthwatch Institute Research Expedition feature offers even more images.

Wadsworth Anthropology Video Library

Qualified adopters may select full-length videos from an extensive library of offerings drawn from such excellent educational video sources as *Films for the Humanities and Sciences.*

ABC Anthropology Video Series

This exclusive video series was created jointly by Wadsworth and ABC for the anthropology course. Each video contains approximately sixty minutes of footage originally broadcast on ABC within the past several years. The videos are broken into short two- to seven-minute segments, perfect for classroom use as lecture launchers or to illustrate key anthropological concepts. An annotated table of contents accompanies each video, providing descriptions of the segments and suggestions for their possible use within the course.

AIDS in Africa DVD

Southern Africa has been overcome by a pandemic of unparalleled proportions. This documentary series focuses on the new democracy of Namibia and the many actions that are being taken to control HIV/AIDS. Included in this series are four documentary films created by the Periclean Scholars at Elon University: (1) *Young Struggles, Eternal Faith,* which focuses on caregivers in the faith community; (2) *The Shining Lights of Opuwo,* which shows how young people share their messages of hope through song and dance; (3) *A Measure of Our Humanity,* which describes HIV/AIDS as an issue related to gender, poverty, stigma, education, and justice; and (4) *You Wake Me Up,* a story of two HIV-positive women and their acts of courage helping other women learn to survive.

Thomson/Wadsworth is excited to offer these award-winning films to instructors for use in class. When presenting topics such as gender, faith, culture, poverty, and so forth, the films will be enlightening for students and will expand their global perspective of HIV/AIDS.

JoinIn on Turning Point

The anthropology discipline at Thomson/Wadsworth is pleased to offer **JoinIn**™ (clicker) content for Audience Response Systems tailored to this text. Use the program by posing your own questions and display students' answers instantly within the Microsoft® PowerPoint® slides of your existing lecture. Or, utilize any or all of the following content that will be included with your anthropology JoinIn product:

- **Opinion polls** on issues important to each anthropology chapter (five questions per chapter).

Students may feel uncomfortable talking about sensitive subjects such as sexuality or religion. JoinIn gives students complete anonymity and helps students feel connected to the issues.

- **Conceptual quiz questions** for each chapter give students a quick quiz during or after the chapter lecture and determine if they have understood the material.

- Plus, **preassembled PowerPoint lecture slides** for each chapter of your book are included with the aforementioned material integrated into the slides. All of the work integrating Click! questions into the chapter lecture slides has been done for you!

The program can be used to simply take roll, or it can assess your students' progress and opinions with in-class questions. Enhance how your students interact with you, your lecture, and one another. For college and university adopters only: *contact your local Thomson representative to learn more.*

Visual Anthropology Video

From Documentary Educational Resources and Wadsworth Publishing, this sixty-minute video features clips from more than thirty new and classic anthropological films. This video continues to be an engaging and effective lecture launcher. To accompany this valuable resource, Wadsworth also offers "A Guide to Visual Anthropology."

ONLINE RESOURCES FOR INSTRUCTORS AND STUDENTS
ThomsonNOW for *Cultural Anthropology: An Applied Perspective*

Instructors can empower students with ThomsonNOW, the online assessment-centered student tutorial system for *Cultural Anthropology: An Applied Perspective.* Seamlessly tied to the text, this web-based learning tool comes at no additional cost with every new copy of the book. This powerful and interactive resource helps students gauge their unique study needs for each chapter with a pretest, then gives them a personalized study plan that focuses their study time on the concepts they most need to master. Included in students' personalized study plans are learning modules, animations, map exercises, videos, and many more resources to help students better understand the chapter material. They then take a posttest to see if they are ready to move onto the next chapter. To get started with ThomsonNOW, students are directed to www.thomsonedu.com where they can create an account through 1Pass.

Anthropology Online: Book Companion Website

Go to http://thomsonedu.com/anthropology and click on *Cultural Anthropology: An Applied Perspective* to reach the website that accompanies this book. This website offers many study aids, including self-quizzes for each chapter and a practice final exam, crossword puzzles, and flash cards, as well as links to anthropology websites and information on the latest theories and discoveries in the field.

Anthropology Resource Center

This online center offers a wealth of information and useful tools for both instructors and students in all four fields of anthropology. It includes interactive maps, learning modules, video exercises, and breaking news in anthropology. For instructors, the Resource Center includes a gateway to timesaving teaching tools, such as image banks, sample syllabi, and more. To get started with the Anthropology Resource Center, students and instructors are directed to http://thomsonedu.com where they can create an account through 1Pass.

ThomsonInSite for Writing and Research with Turnitin Originality Checker

InSite features a full suite of writing, peer review, online grading, and e-portfolio applications. It is an all-in-one tool that helps instructors manage the flow of papers electronically and allows students to submit papers and peer reviews online. Also included in the suite is TurnItIn, an originality checker that offers a simple solution for instructors who want a strong deterrent against plagiarism, as well as encouragement for students to employ proper research techniques. Access is available for packaging with each copy of this book. For more information, visit http://insite.thomson.com.

Thomson Audio Study Products

Thomson Audio Study Products provide a quick, convenient way to master key concepts and prepare for exams using a personal computer or MP3 player. Created specifically for this book, they provide approximately ten minutes of up-beat audio content students can use to test their knowledge of the key concepts they need to learn for each chapter.

InfoTrac College Edition

InfoTrac College Edition is an online library that offers full-length articles from thousands of scholarly and popular publications. Among the journals available are *American Anthropologist, Current Anthropology,* and *Canadian Review of Sociology and Anthropology.* To get started with InfoTrac®, students are directed to http://thomsonedu.com where they can create an account through 1Pass.

SUPPLEMENTS FOR STUDENTS

Classic Readings in Cultural Anthropology

Brief, accessible, and inexpensive, this new reader has been carefully edited by Gary Ferraro to include those articles and excerpts from works that have been pivotal to the field of anthropology and that have endured over the decades. These eminently relevant selections allow students to further explore perspectives on key cultural anthropological topics such as culture, language and communication, ecology and economics, marriage and family, politics and social control, supernatural belief systems, and issues of culture change.

Case Studies in Cultural Anthropology, edited by George Spindler and Janice E. Stockard

Select from more than sixty classic and contemporary ethnographies representing geographic and topical diversity. Newer case studies focus on culture change and culture continuity, reflecting the globalization of the world.

Case Studies on Contemporary Social Issues, edited by John A. Young

Framed around social issues, these new contemporary case studies are globally comparative and represent the cutting-edge work of anthropologists today.

Globalization and Change in Fifteen Cultures: Born in One World, Living in Another, edited by George Spindler and Janice E. Stockard

In this volume, fifteen case study authors write about culture change in today's diverse settings around the world. Each original article provides insight into the dynamics and meanings of change, as well as the effects of globalization at the local level.

Cultural Anthropology Modules

Each free-standing module is actually a complete text chapter, featuring the same quality of pedagogy and illustration as are contained in Thomson/Wadsworth's anthropology texts. Coming Fall of 2007, Medical Anthropology module. Also, Human Environment Interactions *by Kathy Galvin. See your Thomson sales representative for more detailed information.*

ACKNOWLEDGMENTS

To one degree or another, many people have contributed to this textbook. Some have made very explicit suggestions for revisions, many of which have been incorporated into various editions over the past decade. Others have contributed less directly, yet their fingerprints are found throughout the text. I am particularly grateful to the many professors with whom I studied at Syracuse University including Aidan Southall, Bill Mangin, and Manfred Stanley. I owe a similar debt to the many colleagues over the years who have shared with me their thinking on anthropological research and teaching. While after thirty-plus years there are far too many names to fit into a small preface, they have had an important impact on my career as an anthropologist and, thus, on the content of this book. I am confident that they know who they are and will accept my most sincere gratitude. Moreover, all of the editions of this textbook have benefited from my longtime association with my colleagues at the University of North Carolina at Charlotte: Rachel Bonney, Jill Dubisch, Janet Levy, Jonathan Marks, Kathy Reichs, Dena Shenk, Gregg Starret, and Coral Wayland. They have always responded graciously to my requests for information in their various areas of expertise and have taught me a great deal about teaching introductory anthropology.

Since its first appearance in 1992, this textbook has benefited enormously from excellent editorial guidance and the comments of many reviewers. I want to thank my original editor at West Publishing, Peter Marshall, for encouraging me to write an introductory textbook with an applied focus before it was fashionable and for his support and advice on the first two editions. I also want to thank my present anthropology editor at Wadsworth, Lin Marshall (no relation to Peter), for her vision, counsel, and many excellent suggestions for improving the Seventh Edition.

Thanks are also extended to the entire Wadsworth editorial, marketing, and production team composed of: Eve Howard, Vice President and Editor-in-Chief; Leata Holloway, former Assistant Editor; Dave Lionetti, Technology Project Manager; Jessica Jang, Editorial Assistant; Caroline Concilla, Executive Marketing Manager; as well as Jerilyn Emori, Content Project Manager; and Maria Epes, Executive Art Director.

As with the previous editions of this book, many reviewers have made valuable and insightful suggestions for strengthening the text. For this Seventh Edition I would like to express my gratitude to the following colleagues:

Ivan Brady, State University of New York, Oswego

Alys Caviness-Gober, Ball State University

Jeffrey H. Cohen, Ohio State University

Meini Deng, Saddleback College

William Leons, The University of Toledo

Calvin Odhaimbo, Loras College

Frances E. Purifoy, University of Louisville

Michael J. Simonton, Northern Kentucky University

B. Jill Smith, University of Wisconsin, Eau Claire

Carolyn Smith-Morris, Southern Methodist University

Cassandra White, Georgia State University

I also want to thank the many unsolicited reviewers—both professors and students—who have commented on various aspects of the text over the years. I trust that these reviewers will see that many of their helpful suggestions have been incorporated into the Seventh Edition. I encourage any readers, professors, or students to send me comments, corrections, and suggestions for future improvements via e-mail at the following address: gpferrar@email.uncc.edu.

After more than three decades of teaching, I want to express my deepest gratitude to my many students, who have helped me define and refine my anthropological perspective and, consequently, the concepts and interpretations in this book.

And finally, I want to thank my wife, Lorne, for her patience, indulgence, and endless good humor during the preparation of this edition, along with her gentle reminders that I tend to take myself way too seriously.

About the Author

Gary Ferraro, Professor Emeritus of Anthropology at the University of North Carolina at Charlotte, received his BA in history from Hamilton College and his MA and PhD degrees from Syracuse University. He has been a Fulbright Scholar at the University of Swaziland in Southern Africa (1979–1980) and again at Masaryk University in the Czech Republic (2003), and has served twice as a visiting professor of anthropology in the University of Pittsburgh's Semester at Sea Program, a floating university that travels around the world. He has conducted research for extended periods of time in Kenya and Swaziland and has traveled widely throughout many other parts of the world. He has served as a consultant/trainer for such organizations as USAID, the Peace Corps, the World Bank, IBM, G.E. Plastics, and Georgia Pacific, among others. From 1996 to 2000 Dr. Ferraro served as the Director of the Intercultural Training Institute at UNC–Charlotte, a consortium of cross cultural trainers/educators from academia and business, designed to help regional organizations cope with cultural differences at home and abroad. He is the author of:

The Two Worlds of Kamau (1978)

The Cultural Dimension of International Business (1990, 1994, 1998, 2002, 2006)

Anthropology: An Applied Perspective (1994)

Applying Cultural Anthropology: Readings (1998)

Global Brains: Knowledge and Competencies for the 21st Century (2002)

Classic Readings in Cultural Anthropology (2004)

What Is Anthropology?

A nomadic Bopa gypsy woman from Rajasthan, India.

CHAPTER 1

WHEN MOST NORTH AMERICANS hear the word *anthropologist*, a number of images come to mind. They picture, for example,

- Dian Fossey devoting years of her life to making systematic observations of mountain gorillas in their natural environment in Rwanda
- A field anthropologist interviewing an exotic tribesman about his kinship system
- The excavation of a jawbone that will be used to demonstrate the evolutionary link between early and modern humans
- A linguist meticulously recording the words and sounds of a native informant speaking a language that has never been written down
- A cultural anthropologist studying the culture of hard-core unemployed men in Washington, DC
- A team of archaeologists in pith helmets unearthing an ancient temple from a rain forest in Guatemala

Each of these impressions—to one degree or another—accurately represents the concerns of scientists who call themselves anthropologists. Anthropologists do in fact travel to different parts of the world to study little-known cultures (cultural anthropologists) and languages (anthropological linguists), but they also study culturally distinct groups within their own cultures. Anthropologists also unearth fossil remains (physical anthropologists) and various artifacts (archaeologists) of people who lived thousands and, in some cases, millions of years ago. Even though these anthropological subspecialties engage in substantially different types of activities and generate different types of data, they are all directed toward a single purpose: the scientific study of humans, both biologically and culturally, in whatever form, time period, or region of the world they might be found.

Anthropology—derived from the Greek words *anthropos* for "human" and *logos* for "study"—is, if we take it literally, the study of humans. In one sense this is an accurate description to the extent that anthropology raises a wide variety of questions about the human condition. And yet this literal definition is not particularly illuminating because a number of other academic disciplines—including sociology, biology, psychology, political

What We Will Learn

- How does anthropology differ from other social and behavioral sciences?

- What is the four-field approach to the discipline of anthropology?

- How can anthropology help solve social problems?

- What is meant by "cultural relativism," and why is it important?

- What skills will students develop from the study of anthropology?

science, economics, and history—also study human beings. What is it that distinguishes anthropology from all of these other disciplines?

Anthropology is the study of people—their origins, their development, and contemporary variations, wherever and whenever they have been found. Of all the disciplines that study humans, anthropology is by far the broadest in scope. The subject matter of anthropology includes fossilized skeletal remains of early humans, artifacts and other material remains from prehistoric and historic archaeological sites, and all of the contemporary and historical cultures of the world. The task that anthropology has set for itself is an enormous one. Anthropologists strive for an understanding of the biological and cultural origins and evolutionary development of the species. They are concerned with all humans, both past and present, as well as their behavior patterns, thought systems, and material possessions. In short, anthropology aims to describe, in the broadest sense, what it means to be human (see Peacock 1986).

In their search to understand the human condition, anthropologists—drawing on a wide variety of data and methods—have created a diverse field of study. Many specialists in the field of anthropology often engage in research that is directly relevant to other fields. It has been suggested (Wolf 1964) that anthropology spans the gap between the humanities, the social sciences, and the natural sciences. To illustrate, anthropological investigations of native art, folklore, values, and supernatural belief systems are primarily humanistic in nature; studies of social stratification, comparative political systems, and means of distribution are common themes in sociology, political science, and economics, respectively; and studies of comparative anatomy and radiocarbon dating are central to the natural sciences of biology and chemistry.

The breadth of anthropology becomes apparent when looking at the considerable range of topics discussed in papers published in the *American Anthropologist* (the primary professional journal in the field). For example, following are just a few of the topics discussed in the *American Anthropologist* in recent years:

- Infant mortality, medicine, and colonial modernity in the U.S.-occupied Philippines

- The transition from hunting to animal husbandry
- The migration, education, and status of women in southern Nigeria
- The differences in overseas experiences among employees of General Motors
- Mobility, architectural investment, and food sharing among Madagascar's Mikea
- The emergence of multiracial neighborhood politics in Queens, New York City
- Status and power in classical Mayan society
- Men's and women's speech patterns among the Creek Indians of Oklahoma
- Gated communities in the United States and the discourse of urban fear
- Modern human emergence in western Asia
- The distribution and consumption of Islamic religious paraphernalia in Egypt and how it has transformed urban religious consciousness
- The biocultural factors in school achievement for Mopan children in Belize

The global scope of anthropological studies has actually increased over the past century. In the early 1900s, anthropologists concentrated on the non-Western, preliterate, and technologically simple societies of the world and were content to leave the study of industrial societies to other disciplines. In recent decades, however, anthropologists have devoted increasing attention to cultural and subcultural groups in industrialized areas while continuing their studies of more exotic peoples of the world. It is not uncommon today for anthropologists to apply their field methods to the study of the Hutterites of Montana, rural communes in California, or urban street gangs in Chicago. Only when the whole range of human cultural variation is examined will anthropologists be in a position to test the accuracy of theories about human behavior.

Traditionally, the discipline of anthropology is divided into four distinct branches or subfields: *physical anthropology*, which deals with humans as biological

Table 1.1 Branches of Anthropology

Physical Anthropology	Archaeology	Anthropological Linguistics	Cultural Anthropology
Paleoanthropology	Historical archaeology	Historical linguistics	Economic anthropology
Primatology	Prehistoric archaeology	Descriptive linguistics	Psychological anthropology
Human variation	Contract archaeology	Ethnolinguistics	Educational anthropology
Forensic anthropology	Applied archaeology	Sociolinguistics	Medical anthropology
Applied physical anthropology	Cultural resource management	Applied linguistics	Urban anthropology
			Political anthropology
			Applied anthropology

In 1991, construction workers in lower Manhattan unearthed a burial ground dating back to the seventeenth century, which turned out to be the final resting place of approximately ten thousand African slaves. Biological anthropologist Dr. Michael Blakey headed the African Burial Ground Project, which gathered valuable information on the biology and culture of early American slave populations by studying a sample of 419 skeletal remains.

organisms; *archaeology,* which attempts to reconstruct the cultures of the past, most of which have left no written records; *anthropological linguistics,* which focuses on the study of language in historical, structural, and social contexts; and *cultural anthropology,* which examines similarities and differences among contemporary cultures of the world (Table 1.1). In recent years each subfield has developed an applied (or more practical) component, which is directed more toward the solution of societal problems and less toward collecting knowledge purely for the sake of developing theory.

Despite this four-field division, the discipline of anthropology has a long-standing tradition of emphasizing the interrelations among these four subfields. One of the major sections of the American Anthropological Association is the General Anthropology Division (GAD), founded in 1984 to foster scholarly exchange on the central questions unifying the four subfields of the discipline. Moreover, in recent years there has been considerable blurring of the boundaries among the four branches. For example, the specialized area known as medical anthropology draws heavily from both physical and cultural anthropology; educational anthropology addresses issues that bridge the gap between cultural anthropology and linguistics; and sociobiology looks at the interaction between culture and biology.

Although a four-field approach to anthropology has prevailed in academic departments for the past century, a growing number of anthropologists are raising the question of dividing anthropology along sub-disciplinary lines. Some departments (such as those at Duke and Stanford) have already created separate departments of biological and cultural anthropology, while the biological wing of the anthropology department at Harvard, as of June 2005, has submitted a proposal to separate itself from the cultural anthropologists. On the other hand, other departments (such as at Emory and the Universities of Pennsylvania and Florida) have purposefully moved toward greater integration of cultural and biological anthropology. Whether a department divides or integrates will be determined by broad intellectual forces. Nevertheless, according to Shenk (2006:6), "Multiple paths appear to be both possible and desirable."

Although cultural anthropology is the central focus of this textbook, a brief discussion of the other three branches will provide an adequate description of the discipline as a whole.

PHYSICAL ANTHROPOLOGY

The study of humans from a biological perspective is called *physical anthropology*. Essentially, physical anthropologists are concerned with two broad areas of investigation. First, they are interested in reconstructing the evolutionary record of the human species; that is, they ask questions about the emergence of humans and how humans have evolved up to the present time. This area of physical anthropology is known as *paleoanthropology*. The second area of concern to physical anthropologists deals with how and why the physical traits of contemporary human populations vary throughout the world. This area of investigation is called human variation. Unlike comparative biologists, physical anthropologists study how culture and environment have influenced these

physical anthropology (biological anthropology) The subfield of anthropology that studies both human biological evolution and contemporary racial variations among peoples of the world.

paleoanthropology The study of human evolution through fossil remains.

© Marie-Reine Mattera

Dr. Kathy Reichs, a forensic anthropologist, works with police, the courts, medical examiners, and international organizations to help identify victims of crimes, disasters, and genocide. Also, a bestselling crime novelist, Dr. Reichs has inspired the primetime TV series *Bones*, featuring heroine Temperance Brennan.

two areas of biological evolution and contemporary variations.

Evolutionary Record of Humans

In their attempts to reconstruct human evolution, paleoanthropologists have drawn heavily on fossil remains (hardened organic matter such as bones and teeth) of humans, protohumans, and other primates. Once these fossil remains have been unearthed, the difficult job of comparison, analysis, and interpretation begins. To which species do the remains belong? Are the remains human or those of our prehuman ancestors? If not human, what do the remains tell us about our own species? When did these primates live? How did they adapt to their environment? To answer these questions, paleoanthropologists use the techniques of comparative anatomy. They compare such physical features as cranial capacity, teeth, hands, position of the pelvis, and shape of the head of the fossil remains with those of humans or other nonhuman primates. In addition to comparing physical features, paleoanthropologists look for signs of culture (such as tools) to help determine the humanity of the fossil remains. For example, if fossil remains are found in association with tools, and if it can be determined that the tools were made by these creatures, it is likely that the remains will be considered human.

The work of paleoanthropologists is often tedious and must be conducted with meticulous attention to detail. Even though the quantity of fossilized materials is growing each year, paleoanthropologists have few data to analyze. Much of the evolutionary record remains underground. Of the fossils that have been found, many are partial or fragmentary, and more often than not, they are not found in association with cultural artifacts. Consequently, to fill in the human evolutionary record, physical anthropologists need to draw on the work of a number of other specialists: paleontologists (who specialize in prehistoric plant and animal life), archaeologists (who study prehistoric material culture), and geologists (who provide data on local physical and climatic conditions).

In addition to reconstructing the human evolutionary record, paleoanthropology has led to various applications of physical anthropology. For example, forensic anthropology for years has used traditional methods and theories from physical anthropology to help identify the remains of crime and disaster victims for legal purposes. Forensic anthropologists can determine from skeletal remains the age, sex, and stature of the deceased as well as other traits such as physical abnormalities, traumas (such as broken bones), and nutritional history. In recent years, forensic anthropologists have been called on to testify in murder trials. On a larger scale, some applied forensic anthropologists have headed international teams to study the physical remains of victims of mass human rights abuses. For example, in 1984 forensic anthropologist Clyde Snow helped identify some of the nine thousand people murdered by the government of Argentina between 1976 and 1983. Snow's forensic research and subsequent testimony in an Argentinean court were crucial for convicting some of the perpetrators of these mass murders. Similarly, forensic anthropologists have been working in Bosnia and Kosovo to identify the victims of Slobodan Milosevich's programs of ethnic cleansing during the 1990s. More recently, the life and work of Dr. Kathy Reichs, a forensic anthropologist and bestselling crime novelist, has inspired the prime-time TV series *Bones,* featuring heroine Temperance Brennan.

Primatology

Since the 1950s, physical anthropologists have developed an area of specialization of their own that helps shed light on human evolution and adaptation over time and space. This field of study is known as *primatology*—the study of our nearest living relatives (apes, monkeys, and prosimians) in their natural habitats. Primatologists study the anatomy and social behavior of such nonhuman primate species as gorillas, baboons, and chimpanzees in an effort to gain clues about our own evolution as a

primatology   The study of nonhuman primates in their natural environments for the purpose of gaining insights into the human evolutionary process.

Primatologist Diane Brockman studies the behavior of Coquerel's sifaka at the Duke University Primate Center.

species. Because physical anthropologists do not have the luxury of observing the behavior of human ancestors several million years ago, we can learn how early humans could have responded to certain environmental conditions and changes in their developmental past by studying contemporary nonhuman primates (such as baboons and chimps) in similar environments. For example, the simple yet very real division of labor among baboon troops can shed light on role specialization and social stratification in early human societies, or the rudimentary tool-making skills found among chimpanzees in Tanzania may help explain early human strategies for adapting to the environment.

Sometimes the study of primatology leads to findings that are both startling and eminently practical. While studying chimps in their natural habitat in Tanzania, primatologist Richard Wrangham noticed that young chimps occasionally ate the leaves of plants that were not part of their normal diet. Because the chimps swallowed the leaves whole, Wrangham concluded that they were not ingesting these leaves primarily for nutritional purposes. Chemical analysis of the leaves by pharmacologist Eloy Rodriquez indicated that the plant contains substantial amounts of the chemical compound thiarubrine-A, which has strong antibiotic properties. Wrangham concluded that the chimps were medicating themselves, perhaps to control internal parasites. Seeing the potential for treating human illnesses, Rodriquez and Wrangham have applied for a patent. Interestingly, they use part of the proceeds from their new drug to help preserve the chimpanzee habitat in Tanzania. In Wrangham's words, "I like the idea of chimps showing us the medicine and then helping them to pay for their own conservation" (quoted in Howard 1991).

Physical Variations Among Humans

Although all humans are members of the same species and therefore are capable of interbreeding, considerable physical variation exists among human populations.

Some of these differences are based on visible physical traits, such as the shape of the nose, body stature, and color of the skin. Other variations are based on less visible biochemical factors such as blood type or susceptibility to diseases.

For decades, physical anthropologists attempted to document human physical variations throughout the world by dividing the world's populations into various racial categories. A *race* is a group of people who share a greater statistical frequency of genes and physical traits with one another than they do with people outside the group. Today, however, no anthropologists subscribe to the notion that races are fixed biological entities, the members of which all share the same physical features. Despite an enormous amount of effort devoted to classifying people into discrete racial categories during much of the twentieth century, most anthropologists do not consider these categories to be particularly useful. Today, we know that the amount of genetic variation is much greater *within* racial groups than *between* racial groups. Thus, most anthropologists view these early twentieth century racial typologies as largely an over simplification of our present state of genetic knowledge. (For more on race and racism, see Chapter 12.)

Although contemporary anthropologists continue to be interested in human physical variation, they have turned their attention to examining how human physical variations help people adapt to their environment. Physical anthropologists have found that populations with the greatest amount of melanin in their skin are found in tropical regions, whereas lighter-skinned populations generally reside in more northern latitudes. This suggests that natural selection has favored dark skin in tropical areas because it protects people from dangerous ultraviolet light. In colder climates people tend to have considerable body mass (less body surface), which is a natural protection from the deadly cold. And sickle cells, found widely in the blood of people living in sub-Saharan Africa, protect people against the ravages of malaria. These three examples illustrate how physical variations can help people adapt to their natural environments. In their investigations of how human biological variations influence adaptation, physical anthropologists draw on the work of three allied disciplines: *genetics* (the study of inherited physical traits), *population biology* (the study of the relationship between population characteristics and environment),

---

race A subgroup of the human population whose members share a greater number of physical traits with one another than they do with members of other subgroups.
genetics The study of inherited physical traits.
population biology The study of the interrelationship between population characteristics and environments.

Archaeologist Darius Arya works at the excavation of Caligula's house at Fori Imperiali in Rome.

© Tony Gentile/Reuters/Corbis

and *epidemiology* (the study of differential clusters of disease in populations over time).

ARCHAEOLOGY

Experts in the field of *archaeology* study the lifeways of people from the past by excavating and analyzing the material culture they have left behind. The purpose of archaeology is not to fill up museums by collecting exotic relics from prehistoric societies. Rather, it is to understand cultural adaptations of ancient peoples by at least partially reconstructing their cultures. Because archaeologists concentrate on societies of the past, they are limited to working with material culture including, in some cases, written records. From these material remains, however, archaeologists are able to infer many nonmaterial cultural aspects (ideas and behavior patterns) held by people thousands, and in some cases, millions of years ago.

Archaeologists work with three types of material remains: artifacts, features, and ecofacts. *Artifacts* are objects that have been made or modified by humans and that can be removed from the site and taken to the laboratory for further analysis. Tools, arrowheads, and fragments of pottery are examples of artifacts. *Features*, like artifacts, are made or modified by people, but they cannot be readily carried away from the dig site. Archaeological features include such things as house foundations, fireplaces, and postholes. *Ecofacts* include objects found in the natural environment (such as bones, seeds, and wood) that were not made or altered by humans but were used by them. Ecofacts provide archaeologists with important data concerning the environment and how people used natural resources.

The data that archaeologists have at their disposal are very selective. Not only are archaeologists limited to material remains, but also the overwhelming majority of material possessions that may have been part of a culture do not survive thousands of years under the ground. As a result, archaeologists search for fragments of material evidence (such items as projectile points, hearths, beads, and postholes) that will enable them to piece together a culture. A prehistoric garbage dump is particularly revealing, for the archaeologist can learn a great deal about how people lived from what they threw away. These material remains are then used to make inferences about the nonmaterial aspects of the culture (i.e., values, ideas, and behaviors) being studied. For example, the finding that all women and children are

epidemiology   The study of the occurrence, distribution, and control of disease in populations.
archaeology   The subfield of anthropology that focuses on the study of prehistoric and historic cultures through the excavation of material remains.
artifact   A type of material remain (found by archaeologists) that has been made or modified by humans, such as tools, arrowheads, and so on.

features   Archaeological remains that have been made or modified by people and cannot easily be carried away, such as house foundations, fireplaces, and post holes.
ecofacts   Physical remains—found by archaeologists—that were used by humans but not made or reworked by them (for example, seeds and bones).

buried with their heads pointing in one direction, whereas the heads of adult males point in a different direction, could lead to the possible explanation that the society practiced matrilineal kinship (that is, children followed their mother's line of descent rather than their father's).

Once the archaeologist has collected the physical evidence, the difficult work of analysis and interpretation begins. By studying the bits and pieces of material culture left behind (within the context of both environmental data and anatomical remains), the archaeologist seeks to determine how the people supported themselves, whether they had a notion of an afterlife, how roles were allocated between men and women, whether some people were more powerful than others, whether the people engaged in trade with neighboring peoples, and how lifestyles have changed over time.

Present-day archaeologists work with both historic and prehistoric cultures. Historic archaeologists help to reconstruct the cultures of people who used writing and about whom historical documents have been written. For example, historical archaeologists have contributed significantly to our understanding of colonial American cultures by analyzing material remains that can supplement such historical documents as books, letters, graffiti, and government reports.

Prehistoric archaeology, on the other hand, deals with the vast segment of the human record (several million years) that predates the advent of writing about 5,500 years ago. Archaeology remains the one scientific enterprise that systematically focuses on prehistoric cultures. Consequently, it has provided us with a much fuller time frame than written history for understanding the record of human development.

The relevance of studying ancient artifacts often goes beyond helping us better understand our prehistoric past. In some cases, the study of stone tools can lead to improvements in our own modern technology. To illustrate, while experimentally replicating the manufacture of stone tools, archaeologist Don Crabtree found that obsidian from the western part of the United States can be chipped to a very sharp edge. When examined under an electron microscope, the cutting edge of obsidian was found to be two hundred times sharper than modern surgical scalpels. Some surgeons now use these obsidian scalpels because the healing is faster and the scarring is reduced (Sheets 1993).

Another area of applied archaeology is called *cultural resource management*. During the 1960s and 1970s, a number of preservation and environmental protection laws were passed to identify and protect cultural and historic resources (for example, landmarks, historic buildings, and archaeological sites) from being bulldozed. The laws require environmental impact studies to be conducted prior to the start of federally funded projects such as dams, highways, airports, or office buildings. If the building project would destroy the cultural resource, then the law provides that archaeological research must be conducted to preserve the information from the site. In response to these laws, archaeologists have developed the applied area known as *cultural resource management* (also known as *public archaeology* or *contract archaeology*).

The goal of this form of applied archaeology is to ensure that the laws are properly followed, that high-quality research is conducted, and that the data from archaeological sites are not destroyed by federally funded building projects. Cultural resource management has grown so rapidly in recent years that by the turn of the millennium about half of all professionally trained archaeologists were working in this field.

Although we usually think of archaeology as focusing exclusively on history and prehistory, some archaeologists are finding ways to help people living in the twenty-first century. In the immediate aftermath of hurricanes Katrina and Rita, Shannon Lee Dawdy, an archaeologist from the University of Chicago, has served as the liaison between FEMA (the Federal Emergency Management Agency) and the state of Louisiana's historic preservation office. Her mission is to prevent the rebuilding of New Orleans from further destroying what remains of its past and current cultural heritage. One such urban treasure damaged during the hurricanes is the Holt cemetery, the final resting place for many poor residents of a city that has had strong ties with its dead. For generations Holt cemetery has been the gathering spot, particularly on All Souls' Day, for the living to pay their respects to the dead by decorating and adorning their grave sites with votive objects (everything from children's teddy bears to flowers to plastic jack-o'-lanterns). Dr. Dawdy is trying to convince FEMA and other officials that these votive objects, many of which have been scattered throughout the cemetery by the flood waters, should not be considered debris. Rather, she argues, every effort should be made to restore the damaged site by replacing as many of these votive objects as possible. If this very important place (which connects people to their dead ancestors and friends) is not restored, residents driven from New Orleans by the hurricanes will be much less likely to return and help rebuild their homes and their lives. Professor Jean Comaroff, chairperson of Chicago's Department of Anthropology, summed up the value of Dr. Dawdy's work: "The threat is great that much that was unique about New Orleans as a social and cultural world—qualities that are at once creative, poignant and fragile—will be lost in its reconstruction." (Schwartz 2006: D1).

cultural resource management   A form of applied archaeology that involves identifying, evaluating, and sometimes excavating sites before the construction of roads, dams, and buildings.

ANTHROPOLOGICAL LINGUISTICS

The branch of the discipline that studies human speech and language is called *anthropological linguistics*. Although humans are not the only species that has systems of symbolic communication, ours is by far the most complex form. In fact, some would argue that language is the most distinctive feature of being human, for without language we could not acquire and transmit our culture from one generation to the next.

Linguistic anthropology, which studies contemporary human languages as well as those of the past, is divided into four distinct branches: historical linguistics, descriptive linguistics, ethnolinguistics, and sociolinguistics.

Historical linguistics deals with the emergence of language in general and how specific languages have diverged over time. Some of the earliest anthropological interest in language focused on the historical connections between languages. For example, nineteenth-century linguists working with European languages demonstrated similarities in the sound systems between a particular language and an earlier parent language from which the language was derived. In other words, by comparing contemporary languages, linguists have been able to identify certain language families. Through techniques such as *glottochronology*, linguists can now approximate when two related languages began to diverge from each other.

Descriptive linguistics is the study of sound systems, grammatical systems, and the meanings attached to words in specific languages. Every culture has a distinctive language with its own logical structure and set of rules for putting words and sounds together for the purpose of communicating. In its simplest form, the task of the descriptive linguist is to compile dictionaries and grammar books for previously unwritten languages.

Cultural linguistics (also known as *ethnolinguistics*) is the branch of anthropological linguistics that examines the relationship between language and culture. In any language, certain cultural aspects that are emphasized (such as types of snow among the Inuit, cows among the pastoral Maasai, or automobiles in U.S. cul-

ture) are reflected in the vocabulary of that language. Moreover, cultural linguists explore how different linguistic categories can affect how people categorize their experiences, how they think, and how they perceive the world around them.

The fourth branch of anthropological linguistics, known as *sociolinguistics*, examines the relationship between language and social relations. For example, sociolinguists are interested in investigating how social class influences the particular dialect a person speaks. They also study the situational use of language—that is, how people use different forms of a language depending on the social situation they find themselves in at any given time. To illustrate, the words, and even grammatical structures, a U.S. college student would choose when conversing with a roommate would be significantly different from the linguistic style used when talking to a grandparent, a rabbi, or a potential employer during a job interview.

Anthropological linguists also engage in applied activities. After describing the structure of a language, descriptive linguists frequently take the next logical step and work with educators to plan effective strategies for teaching English as a second language. Some anthropological linguists serve as consultants to government and educational leaders responsible for setting language policy in a state or country. Anthropological linguists sometimes work with local (small-scale) minority groups whose languages are spoken by so few people that they are in danger of becoming extinct. Still other applied linguists help design foreign language and culture programs for people who are preparing to live and work abroad. Moreover, linguists like Deborah Tannen (see Chapter 11) apply their knowledge of gender differences in language to help men and women better understand one another. .

For most of the twentieth century, anthropological linguists documented the vocabularies, grammars, and phonetic systems of the many unwritten languages of the world. At this point, most of the hitherto unwritten languages have been recorded or have died out (that is, lost all of their native speakers). This has led some anthropologists to suggest that the field of anthropological linguistics has essentially completed its work and should no longer be regarded as one of the major branches of anthropology. Such a view, however, is shortsighted. Because languages are constantly changing, anthropological linguists will be needed to document these changes and to show how they reflect changes in the culture as a whole. Moreover, in recent years anthropological linguists have expanded their

---

anthropological linguistics   The scientific study of human communication within its sociocultural context.

historical linguistics   The study of how languages change over time.

glottochronology   The historical linguistic technique of determining the approximate date that two languages diverged by analyzing similarities and differences in their vocabularies.

descriptive linguistics   The branch of anthropological linguistics that studies how languages are structured.

ethnolinguistics   The study of the relationship between language and culture.

---

sociolinguistics   A branch of anthropological linguistics that studies how language and culture are related and how language is used in different social contexts.

Courtesy of Dr. Owen Sichone

Dr. Owen Sichone, an anthropologist at the University of Cape Town, conducts research on African migrants to Cape Town, issues of xenophobia, and emerging political structure in South Africa.

research interests to include television advertising, linguistic aspects of popular culture, and computer jargon.

CULTURAL ANTHROPOLOGY

The branch of anthropology that deals with the study of specific contemporary cultures (*ethnography*) and the more general underlying patterns of human culture derived through cultural comparisons (*ethnology*) is called *cultural anthropology*. Before cultural anthropologists can examine cultural differences and similarities throughout the world, they must first describe the features of specific cultures in as much detail as possible. These detailed descriptions (ethnographies) are the result of extensive field studies (usually a year or two in duration) in which the anthropologist observes, talks to, and lives with the people he or she is studying. The writing of large numbers of ethnographies over the course of the twentieth century has provided an empirical basis for the comparative study of cultures. In the process of developing these descriptive accounts, cultural anthropologists may provide insights into questions such as, How are the marriage customs of a group of people related to the group's economy? What effect

ethnography The anthropological description of a particular contemporary culture by means of direct fieldwork.
ethnology The comparative study of cultural differences and similarities.
cultural anthropology The scientific study of cultural similarities and differences wherever and in whatever form they may be found.

Table 1.2 Two Facets of Cultural Anthropology

Ethnography	Ethnology
Descriptive	Comparative
Based on direct fieldwork	Uses data collected by other ethnographers
Focuses on a single culture or subculture	Generalizes across cultures or subcultures

does urban migration have on the kinship system? In what ways have supernatural beliefs helped a group of people adapt more effectively to its environment? Thus, while describing the essential features of a culture, the cultural anthropologist may also explain why certain cultural patterns exist and how they may be related to one another.

Ethnology is the comparative study of contemporary cultures, wherever they may be found. (See Table 1.2) Ethnologists seek to understand both why people today and in the recent past differ in terms of ideas and behavior patterns and what all cultures in the world have in common with one another. The primary objective of ethnology is to uncover general cultural principles, the "rules" that govern human behavior. Because all humans have culture and live in groups called societies, there are no populations in the world today that are not viable subjects for the ethnologist. The lifeways of Inuit living in the Arctic tundra, Greek peasants, Maasai herdsmen in Tanzania, and the residents of a retirement home in southern California have all been studied by cultural anthropologists.

Cultural anthropologist Stacey Surla conducts participant-observation research in a kitchen hut in Cameroon.

Koons/Anthro-Photo

Ethnographers and ethnologists face a daunting task as they describe and compare the many peoples of the world today. A small number of cultural anthropologists must deal with enormous cultural diversity (thousands of distinct cultures where people speak mutually unintelligible languages), numerous features of culture that could be compared, and a wide range of theoretical frameworks for comparing them. To describe even the least complex cultures requires many months of interviewing people and observing their behavior. Even with this large expenditure of time, rarely do contemporary ethnographers describe total cultures. Instead, they usually describe only the more outstanding features of a culture, and then investigate a particular aspect or problem in greater depth.

Areas of Specialization

Because the description of a total culture is usually beyond the scope of a single ethnographer, in recent decades cultural anthropologists have tended to specialize, often identifying themselves with one or more of the following areas of specialization:

1. *Urban anthropology.* Cultural anthropologists during the first half of the twentieth century tended to concentrate their research on rural societies in non-Western areas. In the immediate post–World War II era, however, anthropologists in greater numbers turned their attention to the study of more complex urban social systems. With increases in rural-to-urban migration in many parts of the world, it was becoming increasingly difficult to think of rural populations as isolated, insulated entities. With this increase in

rural-urban interaction during the 1950s and 1960s, cultural anthropologists began to assess the impacts that cities were having on traditional rural societies. From that point it was a natural development to follow rural people into the cities to see how the two systems interacted. Thus was born the sub-discipline of urban anthropology.

By focusing on how factors such as size, density, and heterogeneity affect customary ways of behaving, urban anthropologists in recent decades have examined a number of important topics, including descriptive accounts of ethnic neighborhoods, rural-urban linkages, labor migration, urban kinship patterns, social network analysis, emerging systems of urban stratification, squatter settlements, and informal economies. Urban anthropology has also focused on social problems such as homelessness, race relations, poverty, social justice, unemployment, crime, and public health. Some recent studies have described the modern urban subcultures of truck drivers, cocktail waitresses, street gangs, drug addicts, skid row alcoholics, and prostitutes. Interestingly, few studies have been conducted in the middle-class suburbs, where various forms of social problems are also found.

2. *Medical anthropology.* Another recent area of specialization is medical anthropology, which studies the relationship of biological and sociocultural factors to health, disease, and illness—now and in the past. Medical anthropology includes a variety of perspectives and concerns, ranging from a biological pole at one end of the spectrum to a sociocultural pole at the other. Medical anthropologists with a more biological focus tend to

Manshan/Photodisc Red/Getty Images

This retirement community could be a possible subject of study for present day cultural anthropologists.

concentrate on interests such as the role of disease in human evolution, nutrition, growth and development, and *paleopathology* (the analysis of disease in ancient populations). Medical anthropologists with more social or cultural interests focus their studies on ethnomedicine (belief systems that affect sickness and health), medical practitioners, and the relationship between traditional and Western medical systems. Contemporary medical anthropology represents both the biological and the sociocultural approaches, but we should not think of them as separate and autonomous. In actual practice, theory and data from one approach are often used by the other.

Medical anthropology, like many other specialty areas, deals with both theoretical and applied questions of research. Because beliefs and practices about medicine and healing are part of any culture, they deserve study in much the same way as would other features of culture—such as economics or family patterns. However, many medical anthropologists are motivated by the desire to apply theories, methods, and insights to programs designed to improve health services at home and abroad.

3. *Educational anthropology.* In a general sense, educational anthropology involves the use of anthropological theory, data, and methods to study educational practices, institutions, and problems in their proper cultural contexts. The range of educational institutions studied varies from highly formal school systems in

industrialized societies to very informal systems in which important cultural knowledge is passed down from generation to generation by kin through such means as storytelling, experiential learning, and peer interaction.

The 1960s and 1970s witnessed a number of case studies in education and culture. For example, Thomas Williams (1969) wrote *A Borneo Childhood*, a study of how Dusun children learned what they needed to know at different stages of development; Margaret Read (1960) wrote *Children of Their Fathers*, an ethnography of growing up among the Ngoni of Malawi; and Bruce Grindal (1972), in his work *Growing Up in Two Worlds*, ethnographically examined how the Sisala children of northern Ghana were caught between traditional and more modern forms of education. At the same time, other educational anthropologists were working closer to home. For example, Gerry Rosenfeld (1971) studied school failure among Black children in Harlem schools, John Hostetler and Gertrude Huntington (1971) studied the process of education among the Amish in Ohio, and Martha Ward (1971) examined speech acquisition among Black children near New Orleans.

Today, some of the most interesting research is being done in ordinary classrooms where ethnographic methods are used to observe interaction among students, teachers, administrators, staff, parents, and visitors. And many contemporary studies are not confined to the classroom, but rather follow students into their homes and neighborhoods, because learning must be viewed within the wider cultural context of family and peers.

4. *Economic anthropology.* Economic anthropology studies how goods and services are produced, distributed, and consumed within the total cultural contexts of which they are a part. The variety of topics studied by

paleopathology The study of disease in prehistoric populations.

Table 1.3 Non-Academic Career Opportunities in Anthropology

Subfield	Examples
Physical Anthropology	Forensic specialists with law enforcement
	Museum curator
	Genetic counselor
	Human rights investigator
	Zoologist/primatologist
	Public health official
Archaeology	Cultural resource management
	Museum curator
	Environmental impact specialist
	Historical archaeologist
	Contract (salvage) archaeologist
Anthropological Linguistics	ESL teacher in public schools
	International business trainer
	Foreign language teacher
	Cross-cultural advertising/marketing
	Translator/interpreter
Cultural Anthropology	International business consultant
	Cross-cultural consultant in hospital
	Museum curator
	International economic development worker
	Cross-cultural trainer
	International human resources manager
	Public school educator
	Immigration/refugee counselor

economic anthropologists is wide, including patterns of work, division of labor, systems of exchange, and control of property. To illustrate, a collection of essays on economic anthropology might include a piece on traditional hunting patterns among the Hadza of Tanzania, a description of the decision-making process of a grandmother joining an economic cooperative in rural Bolivia, and an article on how the international price of cocoa beans affects the consumption patterns of a peasant farmer in Ghana. Early studies in economic anthropology during the late 1940s and early 1950s were largely descriptive in nature, but they have become more analytical in subsequent decades.

Like most cultural anthropologists, economic anthropologists have traditionally studied small-scale, non-Western societies that are not based on the profit motive. Economists, on the other hand, have examined institutions of production, distribution, and consumption primarily in large-scale capitalistic societies. Although over the years economic anthropologists have borrowed some concepts from the discipline of economics, most economic anthropologists feel that classical economic theories derived from modern Western economies are inappropriate for understanding small-scale, non-Western economies.

5. *Psychological anthropology.* Psychological anthropology, one of the largest subspecialty areas of cultural anthropology, looks at the relationship between culture and the psychological makeup of individuals and groups. Concerned with understanding the relationships between psychological processes and cultural factors, psychological anthropologists examine how culture may affect personality, cognition, attitudes, and emotions.

The early practitioners of psychological anthropology between the 1920s and 1950s—namely Benedict, Boas, and Sapir—were interested in the relationship between culture and personality. Many of these early theorists studied the effects of cultural features (such as feeding, weaning, and toilet training) on personality; but some, led by Abraham Kardiner, were interested in how group personality traits could be reflected in a culture. Stimulated by the need to know more about America's allies and enemies during World War II, some of the culture and personality anthropologists turned their attention to large, complex societies in what came to be known as national character studies. Geoffrey Gorer and John Rickman (1949), for example, studied Russia while Ruth Benedict wrote her classic study of the Japanese national character in 1946. Today, these studies are not taken very seriously because of the methodological difficulties involved in generalizing about large and diverse societies.

Since the 1960s, psychological anthropology has moved away from these broad national character studies and has focused on a more narrowly drawn set of problems. The early interest in large, global assessments of personality or character has been largely replaced by investigations of more particular psychocultural phenomena such as symbolism, cognition, and consciousness in specific societies. Methodologies have become more varied, statistics have been more widely used, and psychological anthropologists have been engaged in more collaborative research with those from other disciplines, such as psychology and linguistics.

These five areas are only a partial list of the specializations within cultural anthropology. Other specialties include agricultural anthropology, legal anthropology, development anthropology, environmental anthropology, political anthropology, the **anthropology of work**, and *nutritional anthropology*. To see the types of non-academic careers student of anthropology qualify for, see Table 1.3.

GUIDING PRINCIPLES

For the past century, cultural anthropology has distinguished itself from other disciplines in the humanities and social sciences by several guiding principles. Although other disciplines have adopted some of these major themes over the decades, they remain central to the discipline of cultural anthropology.

Holism

A distinguishing feature of the discipline of anthropology is its holistic approach to the study of human groups. Anthropological *holism* is evidenced in a number of important ways. First, the anthropological approach involves both biological and sociocultural aspects of humanity—i.e., people's genetic endowment as well as what they acquire from their environment after birth. Second, anthropology has the deepest possible time frame, from the earliest beginnings of humans several million years ago right up to the present. Third, anthropology is holistic to the extent that it studies all varieties of people wherever they may be found, from East African pastoralists to Korean factory workers. And, finally, anthropology studies many different aspects of human experience, including family structure, marital regula-

---

nutritional anthropology The study of the interface between social and cultural behavior and human nutrition.
holism A perspective in anthropology that attempts to study a culture by looking at all parts of the system and how those parts are interrelated.

---

tions, house construction, methods of conflict resolution, means of livelihood, religious beliefs, language, space usage, and art.

In the past, cultural anthropologists have made every effort to be holistic by covering as many aspects of a culture as possible in the total cultural context. More recently, however, the accumulated information from all over the world has become so vast that most anthropologists have needed to become more specialized or focused. This is called a problem-oriented research approach. To illustrate, one anthropologist may concentrate on marital patterns whereas another may focus on farming and land-use patterns. Despite the recent trend toward specialization, anthropologists continue to analyze their findings within a wider cultural context. Moreover, when all of the various specialties within the discipline are viewed together, they represent a very comprehensive or holistic view of the human condition.

Ethnocentrism

While waiting to cross the street in Mumbai, India, an American tourist stood next to a local resident, who proceeded to blow his nose, without handkerchief or Kleenex, into the street. The tourist's reaction was instantaneous and unequivocal: *How disgusting!* he thought to himself. He responded to this cross-cultural incident by evaluating the Indian's behavior on the basis of standards of etiquette established by his own culture. According to those standards, it would be considered proper to use a handkerchief in such a situation. But if the man from Mumbai were to see the American tourist blowing his nose into a handkerchief, he would be equally repulsed, thinking it strange indeed for the man to blow his nose into a handkerchief, and then put the handkerchief back into his pocket and carry it around for the rest of the day.

Both the American and the Indian are evaluating each other's behavior based on the standards of their own cultural assumptions and practices. This way of responding to culturally different behavior is known as *ethnocentrism:* the belief that one's own culture is superior to all others. In other words, it means viewing the rest of the world through the narrow lens of one's own culture.

Incidents of ethnocentrism are extensive. For example, we can see ethnocentrism operating in the historical accounts of the American Revolutionary War by both British and American historians. According to U.S. historians, George Washington was a folk hero of epic proportions. He led his underdog Continental Army successfully against the larger, better equipped redcoats, he threw a coin across the Potomac River, and he was

---

ethnocentrism The practice of viewing the customs of other societies in terms of one's own.

so incredibly honest that he turned himself in for chopping down a cherry tree. What a guy! But according to many British historians, George Washington was a thug and a hooligan. Many of Washington's troops were the descendants of debtors and prisoners who couldn't make it in England. Moreover, Washington didn't fight fairly. Whereas the British were gentlemanly about warfare (for example, standing out in open fields in their bright red coats, shooting at the enemy), Washington's troops went sneaking around ambushing the British. Even though the U.S. and British historians are describing the same set of historical events, their own biased cultural perspectives produce two very different interpretations.

In 2005 author Todd Pruzan published a compilation of writings of a nineteenth-century British travel writer, Mrs. Favell Lee Mortimer. This strangely cruel and prejudiced guidebook for world travelers, entitled *The Clumsiest People in Europe,* is perhaps the best single example of what it means to be ethnocentric. Even though her own travel outside of England was limited to two brief childhood trips to Europe, Mrs. Mortimer had almost nothing civil to say about any foreigners, be they civilized or uncivilized. The Spanish were "cruel, sullen, and revengeful," the Welsh were not very clean, and the Belgians were idol-worshipping Roman Catholics. As she got farther away from home, Mrs. Mortimer became even more disagreeable. Turks believed in a false prophet (Muhammed), who wrote a book (the Koran) filled with horrible lies and foolish stories; Afghans were cruel, covetous, and treacherous; and people from Bechuanaland in southwest Africa, despite covering their bodies in mutton fat, had the unmitigated gall to laugh at other peoples' customs while thinking that their own were superior. Even though this book was written more than 150 years ago, it has a good deal to say to us today. As Western countries like the United States become more immersed in the global economy, there appears to be a simultaneous rise in xenophobia (fear of things foreign). While it is easy to be horrified at the mid-nineteenth-century ethnocentrism of Mrs. Mortimer, how often have we heard or read similar sentiments from people in our own society?

It should be quite obvious why ethnocentrism is so pervasive throughout the world. Because most people are raised in a single culture and never learn another culture during their lifetime, it is only logical that their own way of life—their values, attitudes, ideas, and ways of behaving—would seem to be the most natural. Even though ethnocentrism is present in all cultures, it nevertheless serves as a major obstacle to the understanding of other cultures, which is, after all, the major objective of cultural anthropology. Although we cannot eliminate ethnocentrism totally, we can reduce it. By becoming aware of our own ethnocentrism, we can temporarily set aside our own value judgments long enough to learn how other cultures operate.

Cultural Relativism

Since the beginning of the twentieth century, the discipline of anthropology has led a vigorous campaign against the perils of ethnocentrism. As cultural anthropologists began to conduct empirical fieldwork among the different cultures of the world, they recognized a need for dispassionate and objective descriptions of the people they were studying. Following the lead of Franz Boas in the United States and Bronislaw Malinowski in Britain, twentieth-century anthropologists have participated in a tradition that calls on the researcher to strive to prevent his or her own cultural values from coloring the descriptive accounts of the people under study.

According to Boas, the father of modern anthropology in the United States, anthropologists can achieve that level of detachment by practicing *cultural relativism.* This is the notion that any part of a culture (such as an idea, a thing, or a behavior pattern) must be viewed in its proper cultural context rather than from the viewpoint of the observer's culture. Rather than asking, How does this fit into *my* culture? the cultural relativist asks, How does a cultural item fit into the rest of the cultural system of which it is a part? First formulated by Boas and later developed by one of his students, Melville Herskovits (1972), cultural relativism rejects the notion that any culture, including our own, possesses a set of absolute standards by which all other cultures can be judged. Cultural relativity is a cognitive tool that helps us understand why people think and act the way they do.

Perhaps a specific example of cultural relativity will help to clarify the concept. Anthropologists over the years have described a number of cultural practices from around the world that appear to be morally reprehensible to most Westerners. For example, the Dani of western New Guinea customarily cut off a finger from the hand of any close female relative of a man who dies, the Kikuyu of Kenya routinely remove part of the genitalia of teenage girls for the sake of suppressing their maleness, and the Dodoth of Uganda extract the lower front teeth of young girls in an attempt to make them more attractive. Some Inuit groups practice a custom that would strike the typical Westerner as inhumane at best: When aging parents become too old to contribute their share of the workload, they are left out in the cold to die. If we view such a practice by the standards of our Western culture (that is, ethnocentrically), we would have to conclude that it is cruel and heartless, hardly a way to treat those who brought you into the world. But the cultural relativist would look at this form of homicide in the context of the total culture of which it is a

cultural relativism   The idea that cultural traits are best understood when viewed within the cultural context of which they are a part.

part. John Friedl and John Pfeiffer (1977: 331) provide a culturally relativistic explanation of this custom:

> It is important to know . . . that this . . . [custom is not practiced] against the will of the old person. It is also necessary to recognize that this is an accepted practice for which people are adequately prepared throughout their lives, and not some kind of treachery sprung upon an individual as a result of a criminal conspiracy. Finally, it should be considered in light of the ecological situation in which the Eskimos [sic] live. Making a living in the Arctic is difficult at best, and the necessity of feeding an extra mouth, especially when there is little hope that the individual will again become productive in the food-procurement process, would mean that the whole group would suffer. It is not a question of Eskimos not liking old people, but rather a question of what is best for the entire group. We would not expect—and indeed we do not find—this practice to exist where there was adequate food to support those who were not able to contribute to the hunting effort.

For Boas, cultural relativism was an ethical mandate as well as a strategic methodology for understanding other cultures. In his attempt to counter the methodological abuses of his time and set anthropology on a more scientific footing, Boas perhaps overemphasized the importance of cultural relativism. If cultural relativism is taken to its logical extreme, we arrive at two indefensible positions. First, from a methodological perspective, if every society is a unique entity that can be evaluated only in terms of its own standards, then any type of cross-cultural comparison would be virtually impossible. Clearly, however, if cultural anthropology is to accomplish its major objective—that is, to scientifically describe and compare the world's cultures—it needs some basis for comparison.

A second difficulty with taking the notion of cultural relativism too literally is that, from an ethical standpoint, we would have to conclude that absolutely no behavior found in the world would be immoral provided that the people who practice it concur that it is morally acceptable or that it performs a function for the well-being of the society. Practicing cultural relativism, however, does not require that we view all cultural practices as morally equivalent. That is, not all cultural practices are equally worthy of tolerance and respect. To be certain, some cultural practices (such as genocide) are morally indefensible within any cultural context. Yet, if our goal is to *understand* human behavior in its myriad forms, then cultural relativism can help us identify the inherent logic behind certain ideas and customs. Sometimes cultural anthropologists have been criticized for being overly nonjudgmental about the customs they study, but as Richard Barrett (1991: 8) has suggested:

> The occasional tendency for anthropologists to treat other cultures with excessive approbation to the extent that they sometimes idealize them, is less cause

for concern than the possibility that they will misrepresent other societies by viewing them through the prism of their own culture.

Emic Versus Etic Approaches

Another feature of cultural anthropology that distinguishes it from other social science disciplines is its emphasis on viewing another culture from the perspective of an insider. For decades anthropologists have made the distinction between the *emic approach* and the *etic approach*, terms borrowed from linguistics. The emic approach (derived from the word *phonemic*) refers to the insider view, which seeks to describe another culture in terms of the categories, concepts, and perceptions of the people being studied. By contrast, the etic approach (derived from the word *phonetic*) refers to the outsider view, in which anthropologists use their own categories and concepts to describe the culture under analysis. For the last half century, there has been an ongoing debate among anthropologists as to which approach is the most valuable for the scientific study of comparative cultures.

A radically emic approach was taken by a group of U.S. anthropologists (known as ethnoscientists) during the 1950s and 1960s. In an attempt to obtain a more realistic understanding of another culture, the ethnoscientists insisted on the insider approach. More recently, the interpretive school of cultural anthropology has strongly supported the emic approach to research. This school, represented by the late Clifford Geertz and others, holds that because human behavior stems from the way people perceive and classify the world around them, then the only legitimate strategy is the emic, or insider, approach to cultural description. At the opposite end of the debate are the cultural materialists, best represented by the late Marvin Harris. Starting from the assumption that material conditions determine thoughts and behaviors (not the other way around), cultural materialists emphasize the viewpoint of the ethnographer, not the native informant. There is no consensus on this issue, and each cultural anthropologist must make a decision about which approach to take when doing research. (Fuller discussions of these three schools of anthropology can be found in Chapter 4.)

emic approach A perspective in ethnography that uses the concepts and categories that are relevant and meaningful to the culture under analysis.

etic approach A perspective in ethnography that uses the concepts and categories of the anthropologist's culture to describe another culture.

CONTRIBUTIONS OF ANTHROPOLOGY

One of the major contributions of anthropology to the understanding of the human condition stems from the very broad task it has set for itself. Whereas disciplines such as economics, political science, and psychology are considerably narrower in scope, anthropology has carved out for itself the task of examining all aspects of humanity for all periods of time and for all parts of the globe. Because of the magnitude of this task, anthropologists must draw on theories and data from a number of other disciplines in the humanities, the social sciences, and the physical sciences. As a result, anthropology is in a good position to integrate the various disciplines dealing with human physiology and culture.

Enhancing Understanding

In comparison with other countries, people from the United States do not stack up very well in terms of knowledge about other countries and other cultures. The level of knowledge about other parts of the world has been dismal for decades. In 1981 the Educational Testing Service (ETS) reported that college seniors in the United States got only half of the knowledge questions on international matters correct, and college freshmen got only 40 percent correct. A 1988 Gallup survey was equally discouraging, showing that compared with

© Reuters/Corbis

How much do you know about other parts of the world? Who is this, anyway?

citizens of eight other countries (Sweden, Germany, Japan, France, Canada, Mexico, Italy, and the United Kingdom), citizens from the United States had the lowest overall scores. Things have not gotten much better in the last few years. According to Hayward and Siaya (2001), fewer than seven out of ten U.S. citizens could identify the three terms *Farsi, Bengali,* and *Swahili* as languages. Fewer than 40 percent of Americans could identify Cuba as a socialist state. And fewer than two out of ten adults in the United States could name the Secretary General of the United Nations (Kofi Annan), the president of Mexico (Vincenze Fox), and the British prime minister (Tony Blair). Because it is inherently international and cross-cultural, the discipline of cultural anthropology is well positioned to help postsecondary students learn more about the sociocultural aspects of the world's people.

Knowledge about the rest of the world is particularly important today because the world has become increasingly interconnected. Thirty years ago it made relatively little difference whether North Americans spoke a second language, knew the name of the British prime minister, or held a passport. But now, in the twenty-first century, we are part of a nation whose actions send ripples throughout the rest of the world. When the U.S. Federal Reserve Bank cuts interest rates by a quarter of a point, it affects how much more it will cost a student in the Czech Republic to repay a student loan; when the U.S. government refuses to sign the Kyoto Protocol, it increases the likelihood that Italians will develop skin cancer; and when the U.S. government decides to invade Iraq, it heightens tensions between Christians and Muslims in Turkey. So, today, it is vitally important that we not only know something about other peoples of the world, but also grasp how our everyday decisions are influencing them in a multitude of ways.

For the past several decades, the world has experienced globalization, a process of rapidly increasing free market economies, the lowering of tariff barriers, and the worldwide use of high-speed information technology. This recent intensification of the flow of money, goods, and information to all parts of the globe has greatly accelerated culture change and has made the study of different cultures more complex. Increasing numbers of people today are moving, both geographically and through cyberspace, outside their own familiar cultural borders, causing dramatic increases in cross-cultural contact and the potential for culture change. Through its distinctive methodology of long-term, intensive, participant-observation research, cultural anthropology offers a unique perspective on how local cultural groups are engaging with the process of globalization. Although many pundits discuss the consequences of globalization by talking only to government and business leaders, cultural anthropologists are more likely to see what is actually occurring on the ground and how the local people themselves talk about their life experiences in a time of rapid globalization. In order to facilitate our understanding of both the continuity and change occurring in the diverse cultures of the world in the twenty-first century, this theme of *global interconnections* runs throughout this book, particularly in Chapters 8, 12, 14, and 16.

Because of its holistic approach, the data and theories of anthropology have served as a powerful corrective to deterministic thinking. That is, this broad, comparative perspective counterbalances oversimplified explanations concerning all of humanity based on evidence obtained from the Western world. A case in point is the revision of the notion of what a city is. Based largely on the study of American and European cities in the first several decades of the twentieth century, Western social scientists defined a *city* as a social system in which kinship ties were less elaborate than in rural communities. Although this was an accurate picture of cities in the industrialized areas of Europe and the United States, it was not accurate as a universal definition of *urbanism*. Since the 1950s, urban anthropologists studying cities in the non-Western world have called into question this "universal" characteristic of the city. For example, Horace Miner (1953) found substantial kinship interaction—in the form of joint activities, mutual assistance, and friendship ties—within the West African city of Timbuktu; Oscar Lewis (1952), in an article aptly titled "Urbanization Without Breakdown," found that extended kinship networks were every bit as real in Mexico City as they were in rural Tepoztlán; and more recent studies (Moock 1978–79; Keefe 1988) have found equally significant kinship ties in urban areas. Thus, urban anthropology, with its broad cross-cultural approach, has revised our thinking about the theory of urbanism.

This strong comparative tradition in cultural anthropology helps to reduce the possibility that our theories about human nature will be culture bound. For example, studies in cultural anthropology have revealed that great works of art are found in all parts of the world; that social order can be maintained without having centralized, bureaucratic governments; that reason, logic, and rationality did not originate solely in ancient Greece; and that all morality does not stem from Judeo-Christian ethics. Cultural anthropology, in other words, prevents us from taking our own cultural perspective too seriously. As Clifford Geertz (1984: 275) reminds us, one of the tasks of cultural anthropology is to "keep the world off balance; pulling out rugs, upsetting tea tables, setting off firecrackers. It has been the office of others to reassure; ours to unsettle."

Still another contribution of anthropology is that it helps us better understand ourselves. The early Greeks claimed that the educated person was the person with self-knowledge ("know thyself"). One of the best ways to gain self-knowledge is to know as much as possible about one's own culture—that is, to understand the forces that shape our thinking, values, and behaviors (see, for example, DeVita and Armstrong 2001). And the best way of learning about our culture is to learn something about other cultures. The anthropological perspective, with its emphasis on the comparative study of cultures, should lead us to the conclusion that our culture is just one way of life among many found in the world and that it represents one way (among many possible ways) to adapt to a particular set of environmental conditions. Through the process of contrasting and comparing, we gain a fuller understanding of other cultures and our own.

In this regard, the study of cultural anthropology can enhance personal development. Some students claim that their exposure to other cultures gives them a new perspective on both the world and themselves. For example, many traditional university undergraduates are undergoing their own rite of passage into the intellectual and social world of adulthood at the same time that they are reading about how people in other cultures are experiencing their own personal transformations. Thus, the immersion into the world of different cultures, provided by the study of cultural anthropology, broadens their perspective on issues of personal identity as these young adults learn to find their place in the world.

Anthropology's contribution to our understanding of other cultures became even more relevant after the tragic events of September 11, 2001. In the immediate aftermath of that horrifying day, the response of the United States has focused on (a) a military action against terrorism and (b) beefing up homeland security at airports, nuclear power facilities, and other likely targets of terrorists. Although these are understandable and necessary responses, they are inadequate if we are to preserve and protect our social and cultural institutions. We are seriously misrepresenting the situation if we attempt to explain the events of September 11 solely in terms of the evil acts of deranged terrorists. To do so focuses our attention on their evil nature rather than on the underlying social conditions that provide a fertile breeding ground for terrorism. To succeed in fighting terrorism, we will need to better understand people from other cultures and the conditions under which they live their lives (some of which Westerners may have contributed to). Only then will we, as a people, be in a position to distinguish between legitimate and illegitimate grievances and to take appropriate steps to address the legitimate ones.

Applications

Anthropology, with its holistic, cross-cultural perspective, has contributed in a number of important ways to the scientific understanding of humanity. Moreover, the study of anthropology is important because it enables the individual to better comprehend and appreciate his

The study of cultural anthropology prepares people for working in the global economy of the twenty-first century.

or her own culture. But, it may be asked, does anthropology have any practical relevance to our everyday lives? Apparently not, according to a recent nonscientific survey of one hundred undergraduates who had never taken an anthropology course. According to S. Elizabeth Bird and Carolena Von Trapp (1999), many of the common stereotypes about anthropology were confirmed. The majority of respondents associated anthropology with stones and bones, very few could cite the name of an anthropologist other than Indiana Jones, and the image of the anthropologist that emerged was drab, eccentric, elderly, bookish, unprofessional, disheveled (wearing shabby clothes), and having little or nothing to do with anything outside of academia.

As we hope to demonstrate in this book, however, anthropology has relevance for all of us, both personally and professionally. Because anthropology is concerned primarily with the scientific study of culture, and because our lives and our jobs are conducted within a cultural context, anthropologists do indeed have some practical things to say.

Anthropology, like other social science disciplines, engages in both basic and applied research. Basic research in anthropology is directed at gaining scientific understanding for its own sake, while applied research seeks to gain scientific knowledge for the sake of solving particular social problems. As discussed in greater depth in Chapter 3, interest in applying cultural anthropology has increased over the past several decades. Graduate and undergraduate courses in applied anthropology, as well as doctoral dissertations on applied topics, have become more numerous in recent years. Moreover,

there has been a noticeable increase in the number of anthropologists working outside universities and museums in capacities such as administrators, evaluators, planners, and research analysts. In response to the increasing interest in making anthropology practical, this textbook focuses on *applying* cultural anthropology. To demonstrate how widely cultural anthropology has been applied to the solution of practical societal problems, each of the remaining chapters includes applied case studies designed to show how the information from the chapter has been applied to the solution of practical problems.

Building Skills for the Twenty-First Century

As discussed in the previous section, the study of cultural anthropology has relevance to our everyday lives. The data, concepts, and insights derived from the study of other cultures can help us better meet our professional goals and lead more satisfying lives in a multicultural society. But the process of studying cultural anthropology is also valuable because of the skills and competencies that it helps develop. Activities such as taking courses about different cultures, participating in local internships with international organizations, living in the university's international dormitory, and participating in study abroad programs all combine to provide students with valuable carryover skills that go beyond the mere mastery of subject content.

Educators have written volumes concerning the behavioral traits, skills, and competencies needed for success in the twenty-first century. Although many of these writers have put a unique spin on their own list of competencies, there remains a basic core on which most can agree. These skills involve developing a broad perspective, appreciating other points of view, operating comfortably in ambiguous situations, working effectively as part of cross-cultural teams, and becoming emotionally resilient, open-minded, and perceptually aware. These traits have been identified as essential for coping with a world that has become increasingly interdependent. And, because the study of cultural anthropology involves immersing oneself in other cultures, it is perhaps the very best training ground for developing those competencies. How does the study of cultural anthropology help us develop skills and competencies needed for the twenty-first century?

Develop a Broad Perspective

This skill involves seeing the big picture and the interrelatedness of the parts. A basic anthropological strategy for understanding other cultures is to look at a cultural feature from within its original cultural context rather than looking at it from the perspective of one's own culture. In other words, the student of anthropology is continually being asked to analyze a part of a culture in relationship to the whole. What better way to develop this type of systems thinking?

Appreciate Other Perspectives

Being inquisitive, nonjudgmental, and open to new ways of thinking is vital if we are to adapt to ever-changing environments. This involves, essentially, willingness to learn and postpone making evaluations until more facts are known. Such a capacity also requires suppressing one's ego and letting go of old paradigms. It does not mean giving up one's cultural values in favor of others. But it does entail (at least temporarily) letting go of cultural certainty, learning how other cultures view us, and being willing to see the internal logic of another culture. This is exactly what students of cultural anthropology are encouraged to do in order to learn about other cultures.

Balance Contradictions

A major requirement for working and living effectively in a global society is to be able to balance contradictory needs and demands rather than trying to eliminate them. Contradictions and conflicts should be seen as opportunities, not as liabilities. Conflicting values, behaviors, and ideas are a fact of life in today's world. The study of cultural anthropology provides insights into the nature of the world's diversity and how each culture is a logical and coherent entity. When anthropology students are exposed to logical alternatives to their own way of thinking and behaving, they learn to cope with differences and contradictions and actually use these differences for the sake of achieving synergy.

Emphasize Global Teamwork

Success in the twenty-first century requires an emphasis on cultural awareness and cross-cultural teamwork, not just personal awareness and individual mastery. Both private and public institutions are becoming increasingly more global in focus. For example, foreign subsidiaries, joint ventures with foreign firms, and overseas facilities are commonplace in the world of business. If young adults are to be successful at working within and leading these culturally complex organizations, they will need to know the underlying cultural assumptions of the diverse people on those multicultural teams. There is no academic discipline in higher education today that addresses this competency better than cultural anthropology.

Develop Cognitive Complexity

Citizens of the new millennium need what is referred to as cognitive complexity, which is made up of the twin abilities of differentiating and integrating. Differentiation involves being able to see how a single entity is composed of a number of different parts; integration, on the other hand, involves the capacity to identify how the various parts are interconnected. The cognitively complex person is able to engage in both types of thinking and can move comfortably between the two. One must be able to focus on the unique needs of the local situation while at the same time understanding how it fits into the operations of the total organization. The study of cultural anthropology encourages one to examine another culture as well as one's own, compare the two, and understand the relationship of both cultures to the generalized concept of culture. Thus, the student of anthropology gets practice at becoming cognitively complex by moving from the specific parts to the whole and back again.

Develop Perceptual Acuity

Living and working in the twenty-first century requires people to be perceptually acute in a number of ways. We need to accurately derive meaning from interactions with others from a wide variety of cultures and subcultures. This involves being attentive to both verbal and nonverbal communication by being an active listener, deriving meaning from social context, and being sensitive to the feelings of others and to one's effect on others. Studying other cultures—and particularly living in other cultures—forces the anthropology student to derive meaning not only from the words exchanged in cross-cultural encounters but also from the nonverbal cues, the social context, and the assumptions embedded in the other culture.

Thus, a number of skills and capacities that are considered to be essential for effective living and working in the twenty-first century can be mastered while studying cultural anthropology. Although a mere exposure to cultural anthropology does not guarantee that these skills will be developed, the comparative study of the world's cultural diversity and shared heritage is the single best classroom for acquiring these competencies. And, an increasing number of college graduates (both anthropology and non-anthropology majors) are beginning to figure out the value of immersing oneself in a different culture. It has been estimated (Chura 2006) that approximately thirty-five thousand recent U.S. college graduates have taken a year or two off traveling and working in a culture different from their own. In most cases this is not frivolous "bumming around," but rather is a way of developing those global skills discussed previously. It has been for many a way to leverage their position in the job market when they return home.

THE BOTTOM LINE: UNDERSTANDING OTHER CULTURES

This book, and indeed cultural anthropology as a discipline, focuses on understanding other cultures, wherever they may be found. Although a large part of gaining this understanding involves acquiring accurate information on the world's cultures, it also involves learning about one's own culture. However, what we know, or think we know, about our own culture is not necessarily perceived in the same way by culturally different people. In other words, we may see ourselves as holding a particular value or cultural trait, but then describe that trait in only the most positive ways. Those looking at us from the outside, however, are more likely to see some of the negative implications as well. Thus, if cultural anthropology is to help us function more effectively in an increasingly interconnected world, we will have to focus on accomplishing three tasks: understanding culture-specific information about other cultures; understanding our own culture; and understanding how culturally different people view us and our cultural patterns. (For excellent ethnographic accounts of how foreign scholars view U.S. culture, see DeVita and Armstrong 2001 and Fujita and Sano 2001.)

Since the turn of the new millennium, relations between the United States and the European Economic Community have become increasingly strained, even though the United States is more culturally and politically compatible with Europe than with any other region of the world. While most middle-class North Americans and most western Europeans would agree on their shared value of individualism, Europeans generally view U.S. individualism as being quite different from their own. North Americans see themselves as strong individualists willing to protect their personal (individual) rights and freedoms at all costs. Such a vehement defense of individual liberties is necessary, most U.S. citizens would argue, to avoid a tyranny of the masses.

Residents of the United States also justify their individualism as a way of protecting the economic efficiency brought about when many individuals (all pursuing their own self-interests) are pitted against one another in a free market system. Both of these justifications for a strong ethic of individualism are positive, and are, no doubt, generally shared by most western Europeans.

Even though countries such as France, Great Britain, Germany, and Belgium have established long traditions of individualism, though, they often see that U.S individualism is taken to such an extreme that it produces negative social consequences often overlooked by North Americans. Many Europeans would argue that North Americans are so relentless in their pursuit of individualism that the common good is often neglected. To illustrate:

- The Second Amendment to the U.S. Constitution, guaranteeing citizens the right to bear arms and protect themselves from a repressive government, has led to a proliferation of all types of firearms (from handguns to military assault rifles) among the general population. This almost total lack of control of the sale of firearms (in the name of individual freedom) makes the United States the most dangerous (peacetime) country in the world in terms of the risk of being shot to death.

- The freedom to pursue one's individual dreams and fortunes in the United States has produced a widening gap between the "haves" and the "have-nots." According to Holly Sklar (2004, 2005), CEOs in the United States made forty-five times as much as the average worker in 1973 and three hundred times as much in 2004. At the same time, earnings of the middle class were growing slightly and those of the lower classes were actually shrinking. Many Europeans view this trend as working against the overall well-being of the general population, particularly in light of tax cuts for the wealthy during this same period.

- In the United States, there is a generalized suspicion of government and a desire to let the markets, rather than the government, take care of people. Those living in most western European countries, on the other hand, believe that government should take an active role in solving societal problems and ensuring a minimal quality of life for people. According to a recent study conducted by the Pew Global Attitudes Project, Americans and western Europeans were asked to choose between two contrasting values: the value of freedom of individuals to pursue their own interests without government interference and the value of a state guarantee that no one should be left in need. Nearly six out of every ten Americans (58 percent) opted for freedom from state interference, as compared to 39 percent in

Germany, 36 percent in France, 33 percent in the United Kingdom, and 24 percent in Italy (Berman 2004). Thus, European governments are much more concerned than the U.S. government is with reducing unemployment, ensuring universal health insurance, legislating for maternity-paternity leave in order to protect family values, and setting realistic minimum wage standards.

- The seemingly insatiable drive by some North Americans to further their own narrow self-interests (such as climbing to the top of one's field) has resulted in the neglect of those closest to them. Many Europeans, for example, cannot understand how some North Americans can entrust their aging parents to professional caregivers in an assisted living facility.

- In an attempt to protect the rights of the U.S. sugar industry to sell as much sugar as possible on world markets, the government of the United States has campaigned against the World Health Organization's (WHO) efforts to set world standards for healthy diets for children. Obesity and diabetes, caused largely but not exclusively by overindulgence in sugar, are major public health concerns of the WHO, which seeks to limit advertising of products

high in sugar to children around the world. The U.S. government, in its efforts to protect the *individual* interests of U.S. sugar producers, has argued that (a) there is no proof that advertising of products high in sugar content leads to more sugar consumption and (b) the WHO should rely on "individual responsibility" to control sugar intake among children of the world; that is, children should take the responsibility to restrain themselves by "just saying no" to sugar products. Some Europeans feel that this defense of one's individual rights to engage in unrestrained commerce works against the health interests of the world's children.

These are just some of the reservations expressed by peoples from other Western democracies who share our basic value of individualism. We mention these concerns not to suggest that Europeans are more rational individualists than are middle-class North Americans, or vice versa. Rather, the five points outlined previously should serve to remind us of the need to understand our own culture, to learn about other cultures, and to grasp how others view our culture. Then, and only then, will we be able to understand how other people view the world and why they think and behave the way they do. ■

Summary

1. The academic discipline of anthropology involves the study of the biological and cultural origins of humans. The subject matter of anthropology is wide-ranging, including fossil remains, nonhuman primate anatomy and behavior, artifacts from past cultures, past and present languages, and all of the prehistoric, historic, and contemporary cultures of the world.

2. As practiced in the United States, the discipline of anthropology follows an integrated four-field approach comprising physical anthropology, archaeology, anthropological linguistics, and cultural anthropology. All four sub-disciplines have both theoretical and applied components.

3. The subdiscipline of physical anthropology focuses on three primary concerns: paleoanthropology (deciphering the biological record of human evolution through the study of fossil remains), primatology (the study of nonhuman primate anatomy and behavior for the purpose of gaining insights into human adaptation to the environment), and studies in human physical variation (race) and how biological variations contribute to adaptation to one's environment.

4. The subfield of archaeology has as its primary objective the reconstruction of past cultures, both

historic and prehistoric, from the material objects the cultures leave behind.

5. Anthropological linguistics, which studies both present and past languages, is divided into four major subdivisions: historical linguistics (studying the emergence and divergence of languages over time), descriptive linguistics (structural analysis of phonetic and grammar systems in contemporary languages), ethnolinguistics (exploring the relationship between language and culture), and sociolinguistics (understanding how social relations affect language).

6. Cultural anthropology focuses on the study of contemporary cultures wherever they may be found in the world. One part of the task of cultural anthropology involves describing particular cultures (ethnography), and the other part involves comparing two or more cultures (ethnology). Cultural anthropologists tend to specialize in areas such as urban anthropology, medical anthropology, educational anthropology, economic anthropology, and psychological anthropology, among others.

7. A long-standing tradition in anthropology is the holistic approach. The discipline is holistic (or comprehensive) in four important respects: It looks at both the biological and the cultural aspects of

human behavior; it encompasses the broadest possible time frame by looking at contemporary, historic, and prehistoric societies; it examines human cultures in every part of the world; and it studies many different aspects of human cultures.

8. There are essentially two ways to respond to unfamiliar cultures. One way is ethnocentrically—that is, through the lens of one's own cultural perspective. The other way is from the perspective of a cultural relativist—that is, from within the context of the other culture. Cultural anthropologists strongly recommend the second mode, although they are aware of certain limitations.

9. Cultural anthropologists distinguish between the emic (insider) approach, which uses native categories, and the etic (outsider) approach, which describes a culture in terms of the categories, concepts, and perceptions of the anthropologist.

10. The study of anthropology is valuable from a number of different viewpoints. From the perspective of the social and behavioral sciences, cultural anthropology is particularly valuable for testing theories about human behavior within the widest possible cross-cultural context. For the individual, the study of different cultures provides a much better understanding of one's own culture and develops valuable leadership skills. From a societal point of view, the understanding of different cultures can contribute to the solution of pressing societal problems.

Key Terms

anthropological linguistics
archaeology
artifact
cultural anthropology
cultural relativism
cultural resource management
descriptive linguistics

ecofacts
emic approach
epidemiology
ethnocentrism
ethnography
ethnolinguistics
ethnology

etic approach
features
genetics
glottochronology
historical linguistics
holism
nutritional anthropology

paleoanthropology
paleopathology
physical anthropology
population biology
primatology
race
sociolinguistics

Suggested Readings

Barrett, Richard. *Culture and Conduct: An Excursion in Anthropology*, 2d ed. Belmont, CA: Wadsworth, 1991. By examining some of the questions, ideas, and issues facing modern anthropology, Barrett provides an interesting introduction to how cultural anthropologists investigate unfamiliar cultures.

Deutsch, Richard. *Perspectives: Anthropology*. St. Paul, MN: Coursewise, 1999. This selection of readings covering the field of cultural anthropology is a useful supplement to the broad-brush approach taken by most textbooks.

Ferraro, Gary, ed. *Classic Readings in Cultural Anthropology*. Belmont, CA: Wadsworth, 2004. This slim reader contains fifteen widely read articles by twentieth-century anthropologists dating back as early as Evans-Pritchard's study of witchcraft among the Azanda (1937) and as recently as Deborah Tannen's work on gender differences in language (1990).

Kluckhohn, Clyde. *Mirror for Man: Anthropology and Modern Life*. New York: McGraw-Hill, 1949. Although written in 1949, this classic study remains one of the best introductions to the discipline because it demonstrates in a number of concrete ways how the study of different cultures—both past and present—can contribute to the solution of contemporary world problems.

Nash, Dennison. *A Little Anthropology*, 3d ed. Upper Saddle River, NJ: Prentice-Hall, 1999. A brief and easy-to-read introduction to cultural anthropology designed to give students an overview of the discipline.

Peacock, James L. *The Anthropological Lens: Harsh Light, Soft Focus*, 2d ed. New York: Cambridge University Press, 2002. A very readable book that discusses the philosophical underpinnings of the discipline of anthropology, with special emphasis on cultural anthropology. Originally published in 1986, this clearly written book—of interest to both beginning students and professional anthropologists—deals with the substance, methods, philosophy, and significance of the discipline. The second edition includes updated coverage on such topics as gender, postmodernism, globalization, and public policy issues.

Welsch, Robert L. and Kirk M. Endicott, eds. *Taking Sides: Clashing Views on Controversial Issues in Cultural Anthropology*. Guilford, CT: McGraw-Hill/Dushkin, 2003. A debate-style reader designed to introduce students to controversies in anthropology such as whether sexually egalitarian societies really exist, whether anthropologists have a moral obligation to protect disadvantaged populations, and whether ethnic conflict is inevitable.

The Concept of Culture

Traditionally dressed water sellers in front of the Koutoubia Mosque in Marrakesh, Morocco.

2

ALTHOUGH THE TERM *culture* is used by most of the social sciences today, over the years it has received its most precise and thorough definition from the discipline of anthropology. Whereas sociology has concentrated on the notion of society; economics on the concepts of production, distribution, and consumption; and political science on the concept of power; anthropology has focused on the culture concept. From anthropology's nineteenth-century beginnings, culture has been central to both ethnology and archaeology and has been an important, if not major, concern of physical anthropology. Anthropology, through its constant examining of different lifeways throughout space and time, has done more than any other scientific discipline to refine our understanding of the concept of culture.

Culture Defined

In nonscientific usage, the term *culture* refers to personal refinements such as classical music, the fine arts, world philosophy, and gourmet cuisine. For example, according to this popular use of the term, the cultured person listens to Bach rather than Eminem, orders escargot rather than barbecued ribs when dining out, can distinguish between the artistic styles of Monet and Toulouse-Lautrec, prefers Grand Marnier to Kool-Aid, and attends the ballet instead of professional wrestling. The anthropologist, however, uses the term in a broader sense to include far more than just "the finer things in life." The anthropologist does not distinguish between cultured people and uncultured people. All people have culture, according to the anthropological definition. The Australian aborigines, living with a bare minimum of technology, are as much cultural animals as Yo-Yo Ma and Baryshnikov. Thus, for the anthropologist, projectile points, creation myths, and mud huts are as legitimate items of culture as a Beethoven symphony, a Warhol painting, and a Sondheim musical.

Over the past century, anthropologists have formulated a number of definitions of the concept of culture. In fact, in the often-cited work by Alfred Kroeber and Clyde Kluckhohn (1952), more than 160 different definitions of culture were identified. This proliferation of definitions should not lead to the conclusion that anthropology is a chaotic battleground where no consensus exists among practicing anthropologists. In

What We Will Learn

- What do anthropologists mean by the term *culture*?

- How do we acquire our culture?

- Despite the enormous variation in different cultures, are some common features found in all cultures of the world?

▶ Click!

For interactive exercises and study aids, Go to **www.ichapters.com**; enter the author name and select your text, then click the Study Help tab to purchase the following online resources:

- **ThomsonNOW** for chapter-specific online tutorials, quizzes, and a personalized study plan

- **Anthropology Resource Center** for interactive maps, modules, videos, and the Applied Anthropology site

- **Thomson Audio Study Products** for a brief overview of the major chapter themes and to test your knowledge with quiz questions

actuality, many of these definitions say essentially the same thing. One early definition was suggested by nineteenth-century British anthropologist Edward Tylor. According to Tylor, culture is "that complex whole which includes knowledge, belief, art, morals, law, custom, and any other capabilities and habits acquired by man as a member of society" (1871: 1). More recently, culture has been defined as "a mental map which guides us in our relations to our surroundings and to other people" (Downs 1971: 35), and perhaps most succinctly as "the way of life of a people" (Hatch 1985: 178).

Adding to the already sizable number of definitions, we will define the concept of culture as "everything that people have, think, and do as members of a society." This definition can be instructive because the three verbs (have, think, and do) correspond to the three major components of culture. That is, everything that people *have* refers to material possessions; everything that people *think* refers to the things they carry around in their heads, such as ideas, values, and attitudes; and everything that people *do* refers to behavior patterns. Thus, all cultures are composed of material objects; ideas, values, and attitudes; and patterned ways of behaving (see Figure 2.1).

Although we compartmentalize these components of culture, we should not conclude that they are unrelated. In fact, the components are so intimately connected that it is frequently hard to separate them in real life. To illustrate, a non-American anthropologist studying the mainstream culture of the United States would observe people engaged in writing in a wide number of contexts. Middle-class North Americans fill out job applications, pen letters to loved ones, scribble messages on Post-it notes, write books, and compose e-mail messages, to mention but a few examples. When we write, we are using a number of tangible *things* (or artifacts), such as pens, pencils, computers, word processing software, hard drives, and paper. Although these artifacts are both obvious and visible, they represent only one part of writing. If we are to understand the full significance of writing in U.S. culture, it is imperative that we look below the surface to those other components of culture, such as ideas, knowledge, attitudes, and behavior patterns. For example, in order for a New Yorker to use English in its written form, she must know the alphabet, how to spell, basic English grammar and syntax, and the rule that words are written from left to right and from top to bottom. She must know how to manipulate a writing implement (pen or pencil) or have basic computer skills. She needs to know a wealth of cultural information in order to communicate written messages coherently. In addition, she must follow certain

According to the anthropological perspective, this Australian aboriginal man playing the dijeridoo has as much culture as world famous cellist Yo-Yo Ma.

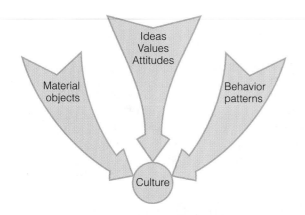

FIGURE 2.1   The Three Components of Culture

behavioral conventions, like not writing while sitting nude in a public library. Thus, the cultural process of writing involves an intimate knowledge of the three fundamental components of culture: things or artifacts, ideas and knowledge, and patterns of behavior.

Perhaps the most fundamental aspect of culture, and what makes humans unique in the animal world, is the capacity to symbolize. A *symbol* is something that stands for (represents) something else. When North Americans see a Nazi swastika, a multitude of images come to mind. These include the Holocaust, Adolf Hitler, concentration camps, and goose-stepping storm troopers. Also, most citizens of the United States have a generally positive feeling when they see the red, white, and blue stars and stripes. That particular arrangement of colors and shapes symbolizes, among other things, democracy, the Bill of Rights, due process, and the war on terrorism. Yet, as we have seen in recent years, the American flag represents a host of very different meanings for angry young men who delight in burning it in the streets of Tehran, Djakarta, and Karachi. Whether the U.S. flag symbolizes positive or negative images, it is true that all human behavior begins with the use of symbols.

As Leslie White (1959) stated so eloquently, the ability to symbolize is the single most important hallmark of humanity. It is this capacity to create and give meaning to symbols that helps people identify, sort, and classify things, ideas, and behaviors. When people symbolize by using language, they are able to express experiences that took place at an earlier time or suggest events that may happen in the future. Without symbols we would not be able to store the collective wisdom of past generations, and consequently we would be prone to repeating the mistakes of the past. Symbols tie together people who otherwise might not be part of a unified group. The power of our shared symbols becomes clear when we meet others from our own culture in a far-off country. We generally are drawn to them because we share a common set of symbols, such as language, nonverbal forms of communication, and material culture such as clothing. It is the shared meaning of our symbols that enables us to interact with one another with the least amount of ambiguity and misunderstanding.

In everyday terminology, the term *race* often is used as a synonym for *culture*. But anthropologists consider these to be two *very* different concepts. A *race* refers to an interbreeding population whose members share a number of important physical traits with one another, such as blood types, eye color and shape, skin color, and hair texture, to mention just a few (for a fuller discussion of race, see Chapter 13). By way of contrast, *culture* refers to our *nonbiological* and *nongenetic* characteristics. All people can be classified according to their physical traits and according to their acquired or cultural characteristics. And, even though many groups share both a common culture and a similar set of physical traits, these two concepts vary quite independently of each other.

Another popular misunderstanding involves the confusion between culture and civilization. Again, like the concept of race, the concepts of civilization and culture are not interchangeable. While all civilizations are cultures, not all cultures are civilizations.

The concept of *civilization*, as used by anthropologists, refers to a very specific type of culture that first appeared around 5,500 years ago in the Fertile Crescent (present-day Iraq). Civilizations are essentially cultures that have developed cities. Based largely on the definition of archaeologist V. Gordon Childe (1936), civilizations (or urban societies) are characterized by traits such as monumental architecture, centralized (hierarchical) governments, fully efficient food production systems, and writing. While we sometimes hear such statements as "Oh, how uncivilized!" modern anthropologists do not use the term *civilization* to designate a superior type of culture.

CULTURE IS SHARED

The last phrase in our working definition—*as members of a society*—should remind us that culture is a shared phenomenon. For a thing, idea, or behavior pattern to qualify as being cultural, it must have a meaning shared by most people in a society. It is this shared nature of culture that makes our lives less complicated. Because people share a common culture, they are able to predict, within limits, how others will think and behave. For example, when meeting someone for the first time in Toronto, it is customary to shake the person's hand. If both people grew up in Toronto, neither party will have to wonder what is meant by an outstretched hand. They will know, with nearly absolute certainty, that the extended hand is

symbol   Something, either verbal or nonverbal, that stands for something else.

civilization   A term used by anthropologists to describe any society that has cities.

Large, complex societies such as the United States and Canada are composed of a number of subcultural groups. One such group in the United States are Ravers, who congregate for late-night or all-night dance parties and have their own unique clothing styles and specialized vocabulary.

a nonverbal gesture signifying friendship rather than a sexual advance, a hostile attack, or an attempt to steal one's wallet. It is when we step outside our familiar cultural setting—where meanings are not shared with other people—that misunderstandings occur. In fact, the uncertainty one experiences when trying to operate in an unfamiliar culture often leads to *culture shock*, a form of psychological distress that can result in depression, overeating, or irritability (see Chapter 5).

The degree to which people within any given society share their culture varies from culture to culture. Even in small-scale, homogeneous societies, one can expect to find a certain amount of differentiation based on gender, class, age, religion, or ethnicity. The daughter of a wealthy physician in Athens, for example, is likely to have a somewhat different set of values and behavioral expectations than the daughter of a rural Greek farmer. Moreover, societal rules are never adhered to strictly. Although culture exerts a powerful influence, people continue to exercise free will either by reinterpreting rules, downplaying their consequences, or disregarding them altogether (such as the Catholic who practices birth control or the conscientious objector who flees the country rather than serve in a war).

In larger, highly complex societies, such as the United States or Canada, one is likely to find a number of subcultural groups in addition to the mainstream culture. The use of the terms *subculture* and *mainstream culture* should in no way imply that subcultures are inferior or any less worthy of study. Rather, subcultures are subsets of the wider culture. They share a number of cultural features with the mainstream, but they retain a certain level of cultural uniqueness that sets them apart. Often, however, sub-cultural groups within a society are not afforded all of the benefits enjoyed by the mainstream. The mainstream culture outnumbers the various subcultural groups and also controls the society's major institutional structures (government, economics, and education, for example).

An example of a long-standing subcultural group in the United States is the old-order Amish of Pennsylvania, Indiana, and Ohio. Originating in Switzerland and coming to the United States as early as 1727, the Amish people today number approximately sixty thousand. They have gone to considerable lengths to maintain the integrity of their traditional culture—no small feat in the United States, a country that emphasizes progress and change. The Amish value their religious beliefs, hard work, agrarian way of life, pacifism, simplicity, and neighborly cooperation. They are a clearly visible subcultural group in that they wear simple clothing, transport themselves by horse and buggy, and rarely send their children to public schools.

Although the Amish have been a long-standing subculture within the United States, there are others that have arisen more recently and are likely to have less staying power. Some excellent examples of such subcultural groups are found in American high schools. "Metalheads," "jocks," and "Ravers" are teen subcultures found in a number of secondary schools in North America that have distinct cultural traits setting them apart from the larger culture. To illustrate, Ravers are fans of a specific music style (Reynolds 1998). They engage in late-night or all-night parties held in large warehouses or open fields where laser light shows, music, and sometimes drugs such as ecstasy combine to create a feeling of euphoria. Alcohol and aggressive behavior are generally nonexistent at these parties, and devotees of this lifestyle are not likely to be aggressive in their personal lives. Clothing and personal adornment also serve to visually differentiate Ravers from the larger culture. Bright colors, flower rings, baby doll clothing, oversized pants, and other whimsical items set Ravers apart from their peers. Ravers maintain their group identity and cohesion through the use of specialized vocabulary, which further distinguishes them from those outside of this subculture.

Many societies, such as Canada and the United States, are called *pluralistic societies* because they are composed of a number of subcultural groups. Pluralistic societies are not without their difficulties. When different

culture shock A psychological disorientation experienced when attempting to operate in a radically different cultural environment.

subculture A subdivision of a national culture that shares some features with the larger society and also differs in some important respects.

pluralistic societies Societies composed of a number of different cultural or subcultural groups.

subcultural groups operate with different sets of values and behaviors, misunderstandings (or outright hostilities) are always possible. To illustrate the type of culture clash that can occur, Norine Dresser (1996) recounts an incident that took place in a sixth-grade classroom in the United States. The teacher noticed that one of his students, a Vietnamese girl, had strange red marks on her neck and forehead. Without giving the girl a chance to explain, the teacher notified local authorities, who accused the girl's parents of child abuse. What the teacher did not understand was that in many Asian countries, and in Vietnam in particular, rubbing a coin vigorously on the back, neck, and forehead is a common folk remedy for headaches, colds, and respiratory problems. Unfortunately, the resulting red marks from this remedy were misinterpreted by school officials as signs of child abuse.

CULTURE IS LEARNED

Culture is not transmitted genetically. Rather, it is acquired through the process of learning or interacting with one's cultural environment. This process of acquiring culture after we are born is called *enculturation*. We acquire our culture (ideas, values, and behavior patterns) by growing up in it. When an infant is born, he or she enters a cultural environment in which many solutions already exist to the universal problems facing all human populations. The child merely needs to learn or internalize those solutions in order to make a reasonable adjustment to his or her surroundings. A male child who is born in Kansas will probably watch a good deal of TV; attend schools with books, desks, and professionally trained teachers; eventually learn to drive a car; and marry one wife at a time. On the other hand, a male child who is born among the Jie of Uganda is likely to grow up playing with cows, learn most of what he knows from peers and elders rather than teachers, undergo an initiation ceremony into adulthood that involves being anointed with the undigested stomach contents of an ox slaughtered for the occasion, and look forward to having at least three or four wives at one time. Even though these children are born into radically different cultures, they have something important in common: both children are born into an already existing culture, and they have only to learn the ways of thinking and acting set down by their culture.

If we stop to think about it, a great deal of what we do during our waking hours is learned. Brushing our teeth, eating three meals a day, sweeping the floor, attending school, wearing a wristwatch, knowing to stop at a red light, sleeping on a mattress, and waving good-bye are all

enculturation   The process by which human infants learn their culture.

Courtesy of Preston O'Berry

Children learn their culture from their parents and others in their society.

learned responses to our cultural environment. To be certain, some aspects of our behavior are not learned but are genetically based or instinctive. For example, a newborn infant does not need to attend a workshop on the "art of sucking." Or, if someone throws a brick at your head, you do not have to be taught to duck or throw your hands up in front of your face. Nevertheless, the overwhelming majority of our behavioral responses are the result of complex learning processes.

Learning Versus Instincts

During the first half of the twentieth century, psychologists and other social scientists tended to explain human behavior in terms of various instincts or genetically based propensities. Gypsies traveled about because they were thought to have "wanderlust" in their blood; Black people were musical because they were believed to have natural rhythm; and some people, owing to their genetic makeup, were supposedly born criminals. Today, the discipline of anthropology has dismissed this type of biological determinism. Instead, although acknowledging the role of biology, most social scientists support the notion that humans are born with little predetermined behavior. If humans are to survive, they must learn most of their coping skills from others in their culture. This usually takes a number of years.

By the beginning of the twenty-first century, it is safe to say that, as a discipline, anthropology has taken a

APPLIED PERSPECTIVE

Cross-Cultural Coaching

An increasing number of organizations are beginning to use cultural anthropologists to help valued foreign employees adjust to the organization's culture. In 2000 your textbook author was hired by a U.S.-based multinational company to "coach" one of its foreign research scientists who was having difficulty becoming part of a research team located in rural Georgia. The researcher, whom we will call "Kwanda," grew up in French-speaking Zaire (today, the Democratic Republic of Congo), completed his undergraduate degree in France, and earned a Ph.D. from a Canadian university. Kwanda's supervisor described him as someone who, although highly competent, (a) was not a good "team player" (i.e., collaborative researcher), (b) did not take criticism well, and (c) was seen as aloof and arrogant by his colleagues. Your author, in his role as cross-cultural coach, met with Kwanda on five different occasions over a three-month period (with each session lasting three to four hours).

A major issue addressed in the coaching sessions was the "prima donna" factor. Arriving at his first job with a brand new Ph.D., Kwanda, no doubt, held his academic credentials (i.e., the highest level of training in his field) in very high esteem. He was not prepared, like most new Ph.D.s, for the fact that American society in general does not share his high opinion of a doctoral degree. Moreover, he was raised in Zaire (a country one-third the size of the United States), which when it gained its independence from Belgium in 1960 had a total of eight college graduates employed in its government. For youngsters growing up in Zaire, education of any type was limited and competition to get into school was fierce. Thus, anyone who managed to receive even a secondary education in Zaire was truly one of the very rare, fortunate, and highly competent students. To then go on to college and graduate school must have been a very heady experience. Clearly Kwanda had overcome enormous odds to achieve his high level of education. It is little wonder that he held his academic credentials in higher esteem than most people in corporate America.

Thus, part of the cross-cultural coaching challenge was to help Kwanda become more comfortable with the fact that his degrees did not automatically give him instant celebrity. Within the corporate culture of Kwanda's employer, people earned respect and credibility by *accomplishing* things, rather than by resting on their academic degrees. He eventually came to realize that he was not being discounted simply because his colleagues in Georgia did not want to bow down and kiss his ring. His view of education and the view of his colleagues are simply two different ways of approaching the world, and neither is better than the other. Through coaching, Kwanda came to understand that he could continue to feel pride in his educational accomplishments, but at the same time he would

strong stand in favor of the learned (rather than the biological) nature of human behavior. In a statement adopted in 1998 by its executive board, the American Anthropological Association weighed in on this topic:

> At the end of the twentieth century, we now understand that human cultural behavior is learned, conditioned into infants beginning at birth, and always subject to modification. No human is born with a built-in culture or language. Our temperaments, dispositions, and personalities, regardless of genetic propensities, are developed within a set of meanings and values that we call "culture." Studies of infant and early childhood learning and behavior attest to the reality of our cultures in forming who we are.

Learning Different Content

Even though there is an enormous range of variation in cultural behavior throughout the world, all people acquire their culture by the same process. People often assume erroneously that if a Hadza adult of Tanzania does not know how to solve an algebraic equation, then she or he must be less intelligent than we are. Yet there is no evidence to suggest that people from some cultures are fast learners and people from others are slow learners. The study of comparative cultures has taught us that people in different cultures learn *different* cultural content (attitudes, values, ideas, and behavioral patterns) and that they accomplish this with similar efficiency. The Hadza hunter has not learned algebra because such knowledge would not particularly enhance his adaptation to life in the East African grasslands. However, he would know how to track a wounded bush buck that he has not seen for three days, where to find groundwater, and how to build a house out of locally available materials. In short, people learn (with relatively equal efficiency) what they need to know to best adapt to their environment.

Some degree of learning is nearly universal among all animals. Yet, no other animal has a greater capacity

gain credibility and respectability within the organization only through his tangible accomplishments.

Another issue addressed in the coaching sessions dealt with communication, i.e., the sending and receiving of messages. Part of Kwanda's difficulty involved linguistic style (see Chapter 6). Growing up in French-speaking Zaire, Kwanda had learned not only the French language, but also the attitudes that go along with speaking French. French speakers, perhaps to a greater degree than any other linguistic group in the world, believe that their language is far more than just a mechanism for sending and receiving messages; rather, they perceive it as an art form and a thing of beauty. This is why the French do not appreciate *attempts* to speak their language. They feel that if you cannot speak their language eloquently, it is better not to speak it at all. Coming from such a linguistic tradition, Kwanda had difficulty with typically terse, functional American English. The function of language in the United States (other than in university English departments) is to communicate as quickly and effectively as possible. The words need not be beautifully constructed; they simply need to do the job efficiently. So, when Kwanda received a cryptic two-word e-mail message in the form of a question, he immediately interpreted this as a linguistic "slap in the face." Kwanda viewed this type of communication as offensive because it was interpreted as being sent by someone who did not care enough about the intended receiver to use the proper level of eloquence. Again, Kwanda needed to see that the American sender was not purposefully trying to be rude. It simply meant that Kwanda came from a very different linguistic tradition, one in which linguistic style communicates respect for the recipient of the message. Neither party, in other words, is right or wrong. Nevertheless, such cultural differences can cause communication breakdowns, hurt feelings, and hostility. Although Kwanda may never stop cringing at overly terse ways of communicating in the United States, he came to understand the nature of this linguistic difference and learned that he should not take it as a personal affront.

During the early coaching sessions, Kwanda came to understand the nature of the cross-cultural differences that were preventing him from making a smooth adjustment to his new work environment. After identifying behavioral changes that he could make to facilitate his adjustment, Kwanda was asked to keep a journal of his new behaviors in the workplace, as well as his thoughts and feelings about them. And because communicating across cultures is a two-way process, it was also recommended that Kwanda's supervisor and colleagues learn more about the cultural differences that were operating within their laboratory setting.

Questions for Further Thought

1. Can you think of any other cultural issues in this case that may have impeded Kwanda from making a smooth adjustment to the corporate culture?
2. Should Kwanda be solely responsible for modifying his attitudes and behavior so as to adjust to the corporate culture, or does the corporation have a responsibility to make certain accommodations?
3. In what other situations could you envision a cross-cultural coach working?

for learning than do humans; and no other animal relies as heavily on learning for its very survival. This is an extraordinarily important notion, particularly for people who are directly involved in the solution of human problems. If human behavior was largely instinctive (genetic), there would be little reason for efforts aimed at changing people's behavior—such as programs in agricultural development, family planning, or community health.

While the overwhelming majority of culture is learned by interacting with parents, peers, schools, and the media, some observers believe that people growing up in the United States may be missing some of the finer points of etiquette and getting along with people (Navarro 2005). Because twenty-first-century American life has become so rushed, parents simply are not taking the time to teach their children proper etiquette. Moreover, because our K-12 educational system is under increased pressure to teach more and more practical courses, there has been little time for teachers to instruct on how to get along in a civil society. The result is that we see an ever-increasing number of ill-groomed Americans, talking too loudly on their cell phones, drinking someone else's water at a business dinner, using sloppy grammar in their e-mails, failing to keep their nasal hair trimmed, or showing discomfort at making small talk at a cocktail party. As a result, U.S. society in recent years has witnessed a new growth industry: namely etiquette trainers, coaches, and consultants. Parents are sending their children to private etiquette classes and camps for the purpose of better preparing them for entering the job market; bookstores are selling a wider variety of books on the subject; colleges and universities are offering courses on how to comport oneself in the adult world; and adults in most walks of life are finding that a class or personal coaching in the social graces will give them an edge in their jobs and their love lives.

CULTURE IS TAKEN FOR GRANTED

Culture is so embedded in our psyche that we frequently take it for granted. We live out our lives without thinking too much about how our culture influences our thinking and behavior. How we act and what we think are often so automatic and habitual that we rarely give them any thought at all. Unfortunately, this leads to the uncritical conclusion that how we live out our lives is really no different from how people from other cultures live out theirs. The job of cultural anthropology is to heighten our awareness of other cultures, as well as our own, in hopes that we will be less likely to take our own culture for granted. Learning *not* to take our own culture for granted is the best way to combat ethnocentrism.

Perhaps an example of taking one's culture for granted would be helpful. Anthropologist Edward T. Hall has devoted much of his career to the study of time across cultures. He has identified a useful model for understanding how various cultures deal with time throughout the world. Hall distinguishes between two fundamentally different ways of dealing with time: monochronically and polychronically. People from *monochronic cultures*—such as the United States, Germany, and Switzerland—view time in a linear fashion, prefer to do one thing at a time, place a high value on punctuality, and keep very precise schedules. Most middle-class North Americans would never think of leaving the house without that little gadget strapped to their wrist that tells them, no matter where they may be, exactly what time it is.

Other cultures tend to be *polychronic*, preferring to do many things at the same time. Unlike Americans, they see no particular value in punctuality for its own sake. Rather than reacting to the hands of a clock, polychronic people strive to create and maintain social relationships. Their de-emphasis on schedules and punctuality should not be interpreted as being lazy. Rather, owing to their cultural values, they *choose* to place greater worth on social relationships instead of completing a particular task on time. In fact, polychronic people often interpret the typical North American's obsession with time as being antithetical to meaningful social relationships. Monochronic types are seen as wanting to rush through their personal encounters so they can move on to the next item on their list. In other words, this rigid adherence to schedules and the insistence on

© Dynamic Graphics Group/IT Stock Free/Alamy

North Americans place a high value on punctuality, schedules, and deadlines.

doing only one thing at a time are seen by polychronic people as being rude and dehumanizing.

How we deal with time varies greatly from culture to culture. Middle-class North Americans pay close attention to their watches, take deadlines very seriously, move rapidly, start their meetings on time, and eat because it is time to eat. Polychronic cultures, on the other hand, are much less attentive to the hands of a clock, view deadlines much less rigidly, build in a lot of socializing time before starting the business portion of their meetings, and eat because there are others with whom to share food. When we uncritically expect everyone to operate according to our sense of time, we are taking our own culture for granted.

CULTURE'S INFLUENCE ON BIOLOGICAL PROCESSES

Human existence, by its very nature, is biocultural (that is, the product of both biological and cultural factors). All animals, including humans, have certain biologically determined needs that must be met if they are to stay

monochronic culture   A culture whose people view time in a linear fashion, place great importance on punctuality and keeping on schedule, and prefer to work on one task at a time.
polychronic culture   A culture in which people typically perform a number of tasks at the same time and place a higher value on nurturing and maintaining social relationships rather than on punctuality for its own sake.

alive and well. We all need to ingest a minimal number of calories of food each day, protect ourselves from the elements, sleep, and eliminate wastes from our body, to mention a few. It is vital for us to distinguish between these needs and the ways in which we satisfy them. To illustrate, even though all people need to eliminate wastes from the body through defecation, how often, where, in what physical position, and under what social circumstances we defecate are all questions that are answered by our individual culture. Thus, to say that life is biocultural means that our bodies and their accompanying biological processes are heavily influenced by our cultures.

A dramatic example of how culture can influence or channel our biological processes was provided by anthropologist Clyde Kluckhohn (1949), who spent much of his career in the American Southwest studying the Navajo culture. Kluckhohn tells of a non-Navajo woman he knew in Arizona who took a somewhat perverse pleasure in causing a cultural response to food. At luncheon parties she often served sandwiches filled with a light meat that resembled tuna or chicken but had a distinctive taste. Only after everyone had finished lunch would the hostess inform her guests that what they had just eaten was neither tuna salad nor chicken salad but rather rattlesnake salad. Invariably, someone would vomit upon learning what they had eaten. Here, then, is an excellent example of how the biological process of digestion was influenced by a cultural idea. Not only was the process influenced, it was reversed! That is, the culturally based *idea* that rattlesnake meat is a despicable thing to eat triggered a violent reversal of the normal digestive process.

Our Bodies and Culture

The nonmaterial aspects of our culture, such as ideas, values, and attitudes, can have an appreciable effect on the human body. Culturally defined attitudes concerning male and female attractiveness, for example, have resulted in some dramatic effects on the body. Burmese women give the appearance of elongating their necks by depressing their clavicles and scapulas with heavy brass rings, Chinese women traditionally had their feet bound, men in New Guinea put bones through their noses, and scarification and tattooing are practiced in various parts of the world for the same reasons that women and men in the United States pierce their ear lobes (that is, because their cultures tell them that it looks good). People intolerant of different cultural practices often fail to realize that had they been raised in one of those other cultures, they would be practicing those allegedly disgusting or irrational customs.

Even our body stature is related to a large extent to our cultural ideas. In the Western world, people go to considerable lengths to become as slender as possible. They spend millions of dollars each year on running shoes, diet plans, appetite suppressants, and health spa

This Mursi woman from Ethiopia, with her colorful lip and earlobe plates, illustrates the principle that cultural ideas of beauty can affect our bodies.

memberships to help them take off "ugly pounds." However, our Western notion of equating slimness with physical beauty is hardly universally accepted. In large parts of Africa, for example, Western women are perceived as emaciated and considered to be singularly unattractive. This point was made painfully obvious to me when I was conducting fieldwork in Kenya during the 1970s. After months of living in Kenya, I learned that many of my male Kikuyu friends pitied me for having such an unattractive wife (five feet five inches tall and 114 pounds). Kikuyu friends often came by my house with a bowl of food or a chicken and discreetly whispered, "This is for your wife." Even though I considered my wife to be beautifully proportioned, my African friends thought she needed to be fattened up in order to be beautiful.

Altering the body for aesthetic purposes (what is known euphemistically as "plastic surgery") has become increasingly widespread in U.S. culture over the last decade. To illustrate, 1.8 million Americans submitted to plastic surgery in 2003, a 12 percent increase from the previous year, while 6.4 million Americans opted for nonsurgical procedures such as Botox injections, an increase of 22 percent from the previous year. In fact, surgical and nonsurgical altering of our physical appearance is becoming so widespread and routine that it has become a wildly popular form of entertainment. Such reality TV shows as ABC's *Extreme Makeover* and Fox network's *The Swan* feature seemingly unattractive people who voluntarily submit to a host of cosmetic surgical procedures and emerge at the end of the show transformed to enjoy rave reviews from friends, family members, and the sizeable viewing audience. After liposuction, nose jobs, forehead lifts, lip and breast augmentation, tooth veneering, and chin implants, the women begin to look like Barbie dolls or Pamela Anderson, while the men take on a number of physical traits of action heroes (Kuczynski 2004).

CULTURE CHANGES

Thus far, culture has been presented as a combination of things, ideas, and behavior patterns transmitted from generation to generation through the process of learning. Such a view of culture, focusing as it does on

Cultural diffusion, not independent invention, is responsible for the greatest amount of culture change in all societies.

continuity among the generations, tends to emphasize its static rather than dynamic aspects. And yet a fundamental principle underlying all cultures is that there is nothing as constant as change. Some cultures—those that remain relatively insulated from the global economy—change quite slowly, whereas for others, change occurs more rapidly. Despite the wide variation in the speed by which cultures change, one thing is certain: no culture remains completely static year after year.

The Processes of Change

Cultures change according to two basic processes: internal changes (innovations) and external changes (cultural diffusion). *Innovations*—the ultimate source of all culture change—can spread to other cultures. Those same innovations can also occur at different times and in different cultures independently. But not all innovations lead to culture change. An individual can come up with a wonderfully novel thing or idea, but unless it is accepted and used by the wider society, it will not lead to a change in the culture.

Some internal changes involve only slight variations in already existing cultural patterns. In other cases, the changes involve fairly complex reshuffling of a number of existing cultural features to form a totally new cultural feature. To be certain, internal culture changes involve creativity, ingenuity, and in some cases genius. To a large extent, however, the internal changes possible in any given culture are usually limited to what already exists in a culture. The automobile was invented in Europe because it was part of a cultural tradition that included many previous innovations, such as the internal combustion engine and the locomotive. Because innovations depend on the recombination of already existing elements in a culture, innovations are most likely to occur in societies with the greatest number of cultural elements. This is another way of saying that internal culture change occurs more often in technologically complex societies than it does in less developed ones.

The other source of culture change, which comes from outside the culture, is known as *cultural diffusion*: the spreading of a cultural element from one culture to another. As important as innovations are to the process of culture change, cultural diffusion is actually responsible for the greatest amount of change that occurs in any society. In fact, it has been estimated that the majority of cultural elements found in any society at any time got there through the process of cultural diffusion

innovations   Changes brought about by the recombination of already existing items within a culture.
cultural diffusion   The spreading of a cultural trait (that is, material object, idea, or behavior pattern) from one society to another.

rather than innovation. It is easier to borrow a thing, an idea, or a behavior pattern than it is to invent it. This is not to suggest that people are essentially uninventive, but only that cultural items can be acquired with much less effort by borrowing than by inventing them.

Causes of Cultural Change

Most anthropologists acknowledge that cultures change by means of both internal and external mechanisms, but there is no such agreement on the primary causes of culture change. Do cultures change in response to changing technologies and economies, or do these changes originate in values and ideologies? Some people argue that the prime mover of change is technology. They cite, for example, the introduction of the automobile and its many effects on all aspects of the American way of life. Others assert that ideas and values lead to culture change to the extent that they can motivate people to explore new ways of interacting with the environment, thereby inventing new items of technology. Still others suggest that cultures change in response to changes in the physical and social environment. For example, U.S. attitudes concerning mothers working outside the home have changed because of changing economic conditions and the need for two salaries; and the traditional Fulani pastoral culture has been drastically altered during the twentieth century by the encroachment of the Sahara desert.

The discipline of anthropology has not been able to make definitive statements about the actual causes of culture change. No doubt the truth resides within a combination of these factors. The forces of culture change are so complex, particularly in more technologically complex societies, that it is difficult, if not impossible, to identify any single factor as most important. The most reasonable way of viewing culture change, then, is as

CROSS-CULTURAL MISCUE

Eric Britt, the headmaster of a New Hampshire prep school for boys, was entertaining a group of Taiwanese parents and their sons who were interested in attending the school. As a recruiting tool, Eric made a point of presenting each father and son with a green baseball cap representing the school's colors. After receiving the caps, none of the male Taiwanese put the caps on their heads, and many of the fathers looked embarrassed when receiving their gift. Surprisingly, none of the Taiwanese boys applied for admission to the school.

Unfortunately, Britt failed to realize that in Taiwan the expression "He wears a green hat" conveys the meaning that a man's wife or girlfriend has been unfaithful. Clearly no self-respecting Taiwanese male would want to be seen in public wearing a green hat. Britt's choice of a gift was an unfortunate one.

a phenomenon brought about by the interaction of a number of different factors, such as ecology, technology, ideology, and social relationships. The topic of culture change is discussed in greater depth in Chapter 16.

CULTURAL UNIVERSALS

Since the early twentieth century, hundreds of cultural anthropologists have described the wide variety of cultures found in the contemporary world. As a result, the discipline of anthropology has been far more effective at documenting cultural differences than at showing similarities among cultures. This preoccupation with different forms of behavior and different ways of meeting human needs was the result, at least in part, of wanting to move away from the premature generalizing about human nature that was so prevalent a century ago.

This vast documentation of culturally different ways of behaving has been essential to our understanding of the human condition. The significant number of cultural differences illustrates how flexible and adaptable humans are in comparison with other animals, because each culture has developed its own set of solutions to the universal human problems facing all societies. For example, every society, if it is to survive as an entity, needs a system of communication enabling its members to send and receive messages. That there are thousands of mutually unintelligible languages in the world today certainly attests to human flexibility. Yet, when viewed from a somewhat higher level of abstraction, all of these different linguistic communities have an important common denominator—that is, they all have developed some form of language. Thus, it is important to bear in mind that despite their many differences, all cultures of the world share a number of common features (*cultural universals*) because they have all worked out solutions to a whole series of problems facing all human societies. We can perhaps gain a clearer picture of cultural universals by looking in greater detail at the universal societal problems or needs that give rise to them.

Basic Needs

As discussed by British anthropologist Bronislaw Malinowski (1944) as early as the 1940s, one of the most fundamental requirements of each society is to see that the basic physiological needs of its people are met. Clearly, people cannot live unless they receive a minimum amount of food, water, and protection from the elements. Because a society will not last without living people, every society needs to work out systematic ways of producing (or procuring from the environment) absolutely essential commodities and then distributing

cultural universals Those general cultural traits found in all societies of the world.

Although marriage practices in Africa and the United States differ in many respects, both sets of practices are responses to the universal need to have an orderly system of mating and child rearing.

them to its members. In the United States, goods and services are distributed according to the capitalistic principle of "to each according to his or her capacity to pay." In classic socialist countries of the mid-twentieth century, distribution took place according to the principle of "to each according to his or her need." The Hadza of Tanzania distribute meat according to how an individual is related to the person who killed the animal. The Mbuti of Central Africa engage in a system of distribution called silent barter, whereby they avoid having face-to-face interaction with their trading partners. Many societies distribute valuable commodities as part of the marriage system, sending considerable quantities of livestock from the family of the groom to the family of the bride. Even though the details of each of these systems of distribution vary greatly, every society has worked out systems of production and distribution ensuring that people get what they need for survival. As a result, we can say that every society has an *economic system.*

All societies face other universal needs besides the need to produce and distribute vital commodities to their members. For example, all societies need to make provisions for orderly mating and child-rearing that give rise to patterned *systems of marriage and family.* If a society is to endure, it will need to develop a systematic way of passing on its culture from one generation to the next. This universal societal need for cultural transmission leads to some form of *educational system* in all societies. A prerequisite for the longevity of any society is the maintenance of social order. That is, most of the people must obey most of the rules most of the time. This universal societal need to avoid chaos and anarchy leads to a set of mechanisms that coerce people to obey the social norms, which we call a *social control system.* Because people in all societies are faced with life occurrences that defy explanation or prediction, all societies have developed systems for

explaining the unexplainable, most of which rely on some form of supernatural beliefs such as religion, witchcraft, magic, or sorcery. Thus, all societies have developed a *system of supernatural beliefs* that serves to explain otherwise inexplicable phenomena. And because all societies, if they are to function, need their members to be able to send and receive messages efficiently, they all have developed *systems of communication,* both verbal and nonverbal.

Despite what may appear to be an overwhelming amount of cultural variety found in the world today, all cultures, because they must meet certain universal needs, have a number of traits in common. Those just mentioned are some of the more obvious cultural universals, but many more could be cited. Sixty years ago, anthropologist George Peter Murdock (1945: 124) compiled a list of cultural universals that our species has in common (see Table 2.1).

Sometimes the similarities (or universal aspects) of different cultural features are not obvious. To illustrate, in middle-class America it is customary to spend a certain proportion of one's income on various types of insurance policies, including life insurance, medical insurance, and fire insurance. In many parts of the world today, such as rural Swaziland, these forms of insurance are virtually unknown. This is not to suggest, however, that rural Swazis do not experience misfortunes such as death, illness, or accidents. Nor do they suffer misfortunes without any support or safety net. Whereas most North Americans view the insurance company as their first line of security against such calamities as death or serious illness, in contrast, Swazis have the extended family for support. If a husband dies prematurely, the widow and her children are provided for (financially, socially, and emotionally) by the relatives of the deceased. In Swaziland the extended family is the insurance company. Thus, the function of providing security and support in the face of

Table 2.1 Murdock's Cultural Universals

Are there any additional cultural universals you would add to Murdock's list?

Age grading	Etiquette	Joking	Postnatal care
Athletics	Faith healing	Kinship groups	Pregnancy usages
Bodily adornment	Family	Kin terminology	Property rights
Calendar	Feasting	Language	Propitiation of
Cleanliness training	Fire making	Law	supernatural beings
Community organization	Folklore	Luck/superstition	Puberty customs
Cooking	Food taboos	Magic	Religious rituals
Cooperative labor	Funeral rites	Marriage	Residence rules
Cosmology	Games	Mealtimes	Sexual restrictions
Courtship	Gestures	Medicine	Soul concepts
Dancing differentiation	Gift giving	Modesty	Status
Decorative arts	Government	Mourning	Surgery
Divination	Greetings	Music	Tool making
Division of labor	Hair styles	Mythology	Trade
Dream interpretation	Hospitality	Numerals	Visiting
Education	Housing	Obstetrics	Weaning
Eschatology	Hygiene	Penal sanctions	Weather control
Ethics	Incest taboos	Personal names	
Ethnobotany	Inheritance rules	Population policy	

SOURCE: George Peter Murdock, "The Common Denominator of Cultures," in Ralph Linton, ed. *The Science of Man in the World Crisis.* New York: Columbia University Press, 1945, p. 124. Reprinted by permission of Columbia University Press.

misfortune is performed in both Swazi and North American cultures. Indeed, such security systems are found in all cultures, and consequently are universal. What differs, of course, are the agencies that provide the systems of support—in this case, either insurance companies or extended families.

For much of the twentieth century, cultural anthropologists focused their efforts on explaining cultural differences. In an attempt to reestablish the discipline's focus that petered out with Murdock's list of cultural universals in the 1940s, Donald Brown (1991) has explored in considerable detail what is common to all cultures and societies. Of particular interest is Brown's description of "The Universal People," a composite culture of all peoples known to anthropologists. Drawing heavily from Murdock's 1945 list, as well as from Lionel Tiger and Robin Fox (1971) and Charles Hockett (1973), Brown makes a convincing case that cultural universals exist, are numerous, and are theoretically significant for carrying out the work of anthropology.

CULTURE: ADAPTIVE
AND MALADAPTIVE

Culture represents the major way by which human populations adapt or relate to their environments so that they can continue to reproduce and survive. Most living organisms other than humans adapt to their environments by developing physiological features that equip them to maximize their chances for survival. For example, certain species of predators such as wolves, lions, and leopards have developed powerful jaws and canine teeth to be used for killing animals and ripping the flesh of the animal. Humans, on the other hand, have relied more on cultural than on biological features for adapting to their environments. Through the invention and use of cultural tools such as spears, arrows, guns, and knives, humans are able to kill and butcher animals even more efficiently than an animal could with its massive jaws and teeth. The discovery of chemical substances such as penicillin, quinine, and the polio vaccine has provided the human species a measure of protection against disease and death. The proliferation of agricultural technology over the past century has dramatically increased humans' capacity to feed themselves. Because humans rely much more heavily on cultural adaptation than on biological adaptation, we are enormously flexible in our ability to survive and thrive in a wide variety of natural environments. Because of the *adaptive nature of culture*, people are now able to live in

adaptive nature of culture The implication that culture is the major way human populations adapt or relate to their specific habitat in order to survive and reproduce.

NASA

Culture enables humans to adapt to the most unusual conditions. Here astronaut Peggy Whitson and a fellow astronaut are eating a space meal on the International Space Station.

many previously uninhabitable places, such as deserts, the polar region, under the sea, and even in outer space.

Culture provides humans with an enormous adaptive advantage over all other forms of life. Biological adaptation depends on the Darwinian theory of natural selection. According to this theory, nature selects those members of a species that happen to already possess certain biologically based features that make them better adapted to a particular environment. But what if those adaptive characteristics do not exist in the gene pool? Then evolutionary change in the traits of the species will not happen over time, and as a result, the species may become extinct. Moreover, even when natural selection works, it works very slowly. But because culture is learned, humans can produce certain technological solutions to better adapt to the environment. For example, when one's environment becomes increasingly colder over a number of years, nonhumans (relying on Darwinian natural selection) must wait generations to develop more protective body hair. But humans with culture, on the other hand, need only to develop methods for making clothing and shelters to protect people from the elements. Thus, culture is a much quicker and more efficient means of adaptation than is a purely biological approach.

The notion that culture is adaptive should not lead us to the conclusion that every aspect of a culture is adaptive. It is possible for some features to be adaptively neutral, neither enhancing nor diminishing the capacity of a people to survive. Moreover, it is even possible for some features of a culture to be maladaptive or dysfunctional. To illustrate, the large-scale use of automobiles coupled with industrial pollutants is currently destroying the quality of the air in our environment. If this set of cultural behaviors continues unchecked, it will destroy our environment to such an extent that it will be unfit for human habitation. Thus, it is not likely that such a maladaptive practice will persist indefinitely. Either the practice will disappear when the people become extinct, or the culture will change so that the people will survive. Whichever outcome occurs, the maladaptive cultural feature will eventually disappear.

An understanding of the adaptive nature of culture is further complicated by its relativity. What is adaptive in one culture may be maladaptive or adaptively neutral in another culture. For example, the mastery of such skills as algebra, word analogies, and reading comprehension is necessary for a successful adaptation to life in the United States, for these skills contribute to academic success, landing a good job, and living in material comfort. However, such skills are of little value in helping the Nuer herdsman adapt to his environment in the Sudan. Furthermore, the adaptability of a cultural item varies over time within any particular culture. To illustrate, the survival capacity of traditional Inuit hunters living on the Alaskan tundra would no doubt be enhanced appreciably by the introduction of guns and snowmobiles. Initially, such innovations would be adaptive because they would enable the Inuit hunters to obtain caribou more easily, thereby enabling people to eat better, be more resistant to disease, and generally live longer. After several generations, however, the use of guns and snowmobiles would, in all likelihood, become maladaptive, for the newly acquired capacity to kill caribou more efficiently would eventually lead to the destruction and disappearance of a primary food supply.

CULTURES ARE GENERALLY INTEGRATED

To suggest that all cultures share a certain number of universal characteristics is not to imply that cultures comprise a laundry list of norms, values, and material objects. Instead, cultures should be thought of as integrated wholes, the parts of which, to some degree, are interconnected with one another. When we view cultures as integrated systems, we can begin to see how particular culture traits fit into the whole system and, consequently, how they tend to make sense *within that context.* Equipped with such a perspective, we can begin to better understand the "strange" customs found throughout the world.

One way of describing this integrated nature of cultures is by using the *organic analogy* made popular by some of the early functionalist anthropologists, most notably Herbert Spencer and Bronislaw Malinowski. This approach makes the analogy between a culture and a living organism such as the human body. The physical human body comprises a number of systems, all functioning to maintain the overall health of the organism; these include the respiratory, digestive, skeletal, excretory, reproductive, muscular, circulatory, endocrine, and lymphatic systems. Any anatomist or surgeon worth her or his salt knows where these systems are located in the body, what function each plays, and how parts of the body are interconnected. Surely no sane person would choose a surgeon to remove a malignant lung unless that surgeon knew how that organ was related to the rest of the body.

Cultural Interconnections

In the same way that human organisms comprise various parts that are both functional and interrelated, so too do cultures. When conducting empirical field research, the task of the cultural anthropologist is to describe the various parts of the culture, show how they function, and explain how they are interconnected. When describing cultures, anthropologists often identify such parts as the economic, kinship, social control, marriage, military, religious, aesthetic, technological, and linguistic systems—among others. These various parts of a culture are more than a random assortment of customs. Even though more often than not anthropologists fail to spell out clearly the nature and dimensions of these relationships, it is believed that many parts of a culture are to some degree interconnected (see Figure 2.2). Thus, we can speak of cultures as being logical and coherent systems.

organic analogy   Early functionalist idea that cultural systems are integrated into a whole cultural unit in much the same way that the various parts of a biological organism (such as a respiratory system or circulatory system) function to maintain the health of the organism.

The integrated nature of culture enables anthropologists to explain certain sociocultural facts on the basis of other sociocultural facts. When we say that cultures are integrated, we are suggesting that many parts are not only connected to one another, but in fact influence one another. To illustrate this point, consider the fact that Japan has the second largest economy in the world, yet Japanese scholars have received only six Nobel Prizes in the last fifty years—far fewer than most other indus-

CROSS-CULTURAL MISCUE

During the 1960s, a group of recent Cuban American immigrants in New York City were planning a peaceful demonstration, for which they had a permit, in front of the United Nations building. On the day of the demonstration, one of the leaders approached a New York City policeman to ask where the demonstrators could gather. As the two men were talking, the police officer became increasingly uncomfortable as the demonstrator moved closer to him. The officer told the demonstrator to "get out of my face," but owing to language differences, the demonstrator didn't understand what the policeman wanted. The Cuban American continued talking while standing closer to the officer than the officer felt was appropriate. Within minutes the Cuban American was arrested for threatening the safety of a law enforcement officer.

This incident illustrates a cross-cultural misunderstanding involving a subtle aspect of culture. According to Edward T. Hall (1969), people from different cultures adhere to predictable spatial distances when communicating; in other words, our culture dictates how much space we need from another when we talk. To illustrate, Hall has found that most middle-class North Americans choose a normal conversational distance of no closer than twenty-two inches from one mouth to the other. However, for certain South American and Caribbean cultures (such as that of Cubans), the distance is approximately fifteen inches, whereas Middle Eastern cultures maintain a distance of nine to ten inches. These culturally produced spatial patterns are extremely important when trying to communicate with culturally different people because they are so subtle, and thus, so frequently overlooked.

The conflict between the Cuban American and the New York City policeman occurred because their two cultures had different ideas about spatial distancing. The Cuban American was attempting to establish what for him was a comfortable conversational distance of approximately fifteen inches. Unfortunately, the policeman felt that his personal space, as defined by his culture, was being violated. Had either the policeman or the Cuban American demonstrator understood this aspect of cultural behavior, the breakdown in communication, and the arrest, could have been avoided.

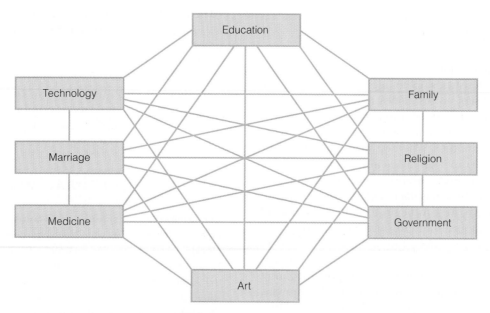

FIGURE 2.2   **Interconnectedness of the Parts of Culture**

trialized countries. If we want to explain or understand this phenomenon, it is important to seek answers in other parts of the culture. For example, Japanese culture is steeped in Confucianism, which emphasizes piety toward elders, age-graded promotions, and a general penchant for incremental advances rather than bold experimentation. Moreover, as a society that has always valued cooperation and harmony, Japanese scholars avoid the intense peer review that has stimulated creativity and experimentation in other industrialized nations. Professional advancement for Japanese scholars has been based more on seniority than on actual contributions, and relationships among scientists are cordial, friendly, and nonconfrontational. Thus, if we are to understand why the Japanese have received so few Nobel Prizes in science over the years, we need to look at other related parts of the Japanese culture that have influenced the behavior (and the creativity) of Japanese scientists.

The notion of integrated cultures has important implications for our understanding of culture change. If the parts of any given culture are integrated, then we might expect that a change in one part of the cultural system will bring about changes in other parts of the system. To illustrate, since Coca-Cola was introduced into the southern Mexican state of Chiapas in the 1950s, the soft drink has influenced (i.e., stimulated changes in) a number of other features of the local culture. The local power structure has been headed by a family that became the sole distributor of the soft drink nearly a half century ago. Because this enormously popular carbonated beverage plays such a prominent role in the total sales of local shopkeepers, this powerful family distributorship, for all practical purposes, determines who will or will not be a successful retailer in Chiapas. At the same time, Coke has become a major status

symbol in Chiapas at family celebrations such as baptisms. Serving Coca-Cola has replaced the local alcoholic beverage (called *pox*) as the highest form of hospitality. In fact, the number of servings of Coke offered to a guest is directly proportional to his or her social status. The introduction of Coke into Chiapas has even influenced the state government, which has over the past several decades used Coke in its campaign to curb the consumption of alcohol. Thus, as this example illustrates, a change in one part of the culture system (the introduction of Coke) has been responsible for changes in other parts of the system, namely the economic power structure, symbols of social status, and the operation of government programs (Borden 2004).

Although the organic analogy is a useful model for looking at culture, it should not lead us to believe that *all* parts of a culture are intimately interconnected with all other parts. If this were the case, every culture would be a smooth-running operation, like a well-oiled machine, with all of the parts working in harmony with one another. But cultures, like machines, often have parts that are out of sync and detract from the well-being of the whole. And yet the culture, or the machine, does not come to a grinding halt. There are, in other words, parts of culture that may not be mutually supportive, or may even be in conflict with one another. For example, the goals of a family are not always compatible with those of the workplace. Moreover, within the workplace itself, there are built-in conflicts between labor (interested in maximizing wages) and management (interested in maximizing profits). To be certain, cultures can be viewed as systems, but they also have certain parts that grind against one another. Thus, cultures are characterized by both harmony and conflict.

The concept of integrated cultures is directly related to the concept of cultural relativism (discussed

Table 2.2 Features of the Concept of Culture	
Culture defined	Everything that people *have*, *think*, and *do* as members of a society.
Culture is symbolic	The capacity to use such symbols as language and art (which is the hallmark of humanity) enables people to better understand the world around them.
Culture is shared	The shared meanings connected to things, ideas, and behavior patterns make life less ambiguous and more predictable for members of the same cultural group.
Culture is learned	Culture is transmitted not genetically but through interacting with one's cultural environment.
Culture is taken for granted	Our own culture is so ingrained into us that we are often unaware that it even exists.
Culture influences biological processes	Our bodies/biological processes are influenced by culture.
Cultures change	The things, ideas, and behavior patterns of some cultures change more rapidly than others, but all cultures experience change, both internally and externally.
Cultural universals	Despite variations in specific details, all cultures have certain common features such as systems of governing, patterns of producing and distributing food, forms of enculturation, and family patterns.
Culture is adaptive	Culture enables people to adapt to their environments and thus increase their chances of survival.
Cultures are integrated	The various parts of a culture (things, ideas, and behavior patterns) are interconnected to some degree. Thus, a change in one part of the culture is likely to bring about changes in other parts of the culture.

in Chapter 1), which involves viewing any item from within its proper cultural context rather than from the perspective of the observer's culture. The fact that all cultures are composed of interrelated parts prompts us to explore how a feature from a new and different culture fits into its original cultural context.

"PRIMITIVE" CULTURES

A fundamental feature of the discipline of cultural anthropology is its comparative approach. Whether studying religions, economic systems, ways of resolving conflicts, or art forms, cultural anthropologists look at these aspects of human behavior in the widest possible context, ranging from the most technologically simple foraging societies at one end of the continuum to the most highly industrialized societies at the other. Societies with simple technologies, once called "primitive," are described by contemporary cultural anthropologists as *preliterate, small-scale, egalitarian,* or *technologically simple.* Because of the misleading implication that something primitive is both inferior and earlier in a chronological sense, the term *primitive* will not be used in this book. Instead we will use the term small-scale society,

small-scale society A society that has a relatively small population, minimal technology, and little division of labor.

which refers to societies that have small populations, are technologically simple, are usually preliterate (that is, without a written form of language), have little labor specialization, and are not highly stratified. Making such a distinction between small-scale and more complex societies should not be taken to imply that all societies can be pigeonholed into one or the other category. Rather, it would be more fruitful to view all of the societies of the world along a continuum from most small-scale to most complex.

CULTURE AND THE INDIVIDUAL

Throughout this chapter we have used the term *culture* to refer to everything that people have, think, and do as members of a society. All cultures, both large and small, have shared sets of meanings that serve as a collective guide to behavior. Because people from the same culture learn essentially the same set of values, rules, and expected behaviors, their lives are made somewhat less complicated because they know, within broad limits, what to expect from one another. To illustrate, when walking down a crowded hallway in the United States, there is a general understanding that people will keep to the right. Because most people share that common understanding, the traffic flows without serious interruption. If, however, someone walks down the left-hand side of the hallway, traffic will slow down because people will be unsure how to cope

CONTEMPORARY ISSUES

Young Male Japanese Shut-Ins: A Culture-Specific Disorder

While *culture* enables people to adapt in a general sense to their environments, it is also possible for certain features of a culture to combine at a point in its history that causes some people to become socially dysfunctional. A particularly powerful example of a culture-specific syndrome is found in twenty-first-century Japan. Known as *hikikomori,* this culture-bound disorder refers to severe withdrawal found among an alarming numbers of teenage boys and young men in Japan. Those suffering from *hikikomori* sequester themselves in their rooms for months and years at a time, cutting themselves off socially from the rest of society. Occupying themselves with television, video games, and Internet surfing, they rarely leave their rooms other than for early morning visits to all-night convenience stores where they can avoid all but the most superficial social interaction. While many cases go undetected, is has been estimated that as many as a million Japanese males are shunning work and social contact by shutting themselves in their rooms (Jones 2006).

Medical and psychological experts see *hikikomori* largely as a social disease stemming from certain features of contemporary Japanese culture. First, for decades Japanese culture has put enormous pressure on Japanese youth, particularly males, to succeed in school and later on in the corporate structure. Highly competitive cram schools preparing students for high school and college entrance exams comprise a major industry in post–World War II Japan. Many Japanese believe that their sons will be failures if they are not admitted to a leading university and subsequently hired by a prestigious corporation. This social pressure on Japanese males to succeed is intensified by a second feature of Japanese society, namely conformity. In other words, a failure will "stick out like a sore thumb." With the economic downturn in the 1990s, many young Japanese men, having become

weary or fearful of the intensified competition, are dropping out, refusing to play the game, and withdrawing to their bedrooms. A third feature of Japanese culture that contributes to the rise of *hikikomori* is the normal relationship between parents and children. Because unmarried children normally live with their parents well into their twenties or thirties, parents often *enable* their children to drop out of society by continuing their economic support well into adulthood.

Young people in every culture experience difficulties adjusting to adult expectations. In Western cultures, the pressure of parental and societal expectations may cause teenagers to live on the streets (see Finkelstein, Applied Perspective, Chapter 10) or join a drug culture. In the United States, a serious (sometimes deadly) disorder among young women is anorexia nervosa, the relentless pursuit of thinness. Laboring under the culturally based assumption that beauty is directly proportional to slimness, young girls and women in the United States literally starve themselves in order to become as thin as possible. Unlike *hikikomori,* which affects mostly males, anorexia nervosa affects predominantly females between the ages of ten and twenty. What both of these disorders (*hikikomori* and anorexia nervosa) have in common is that (1) they both affect approximately 1 percent of the population and (2) they are both culture-specific disorders. *Hikikomori,* voluntarily taking oneself out of the game of life, results from the fear of failing to accomplish high levels of success in school and career, which Japanese values tend to encourage. Anorexia nervosa, on the other hand, is a potentially deadly eating disorder resulting from taking a basic U.S. value (i.e., that slimness equals female attractiveness) to its illogical conclusion. Both disorders remind us how an irrational reaction to one's own cultural values can lead to dysfunctional behavior.

with the oncoming person. Such an incident is disruptive and anxiety-producing for the simple reason that normal, expected, and predictable behavior has not occurred.

Our cultures exert a powerful influence on our conduct, often without our even being aware of it. However, to assert that culture influences our behavior is hardly the same as asserting that it determines our behavior. Deviance from the cultural norms is found in all societies. Because individual members of any society maintain, to varying degrees, a free will, they have the

freedom to say no to cultural expectations. Unlike the honeybee, which behaves according to its genetic programming, humans can make a range of behavioral choices. Of course, choosing an alternative may result in unpleasant consequences, but all people have the option of doing things differently from what is culturally expected. People sometimes choose to go against cultural conventions for a number of reasons. In some cases where adherence to a social norm involves a hardship, people may justify their noncompliance by stretching the meaning of the norm. Or sometimes people flout a social norm or custom in order to make a social statement. Whatever the reason, the fact remains that social norms rarely, if ever, receive total compliance. For this reason, cultural anthropologists distinguish between ideal behavior (what people are expected to do) and real behavior (what people actually do). ■

Summary

1. For the purposes of this book, we have defined the term *culture* as everything that people have, think, and do as members of a society.

2. Culture is something that is shared by members of the same society. This shared nature of culture enables people to predict—within broad limits—the behavior of others in the society. Conversely, people become disoriented when attempting to interact in a culturally different society because they do not share the same behavioral expectations as members of that society.

3. Rather than being inborn, culture is acquired through a learning process that anthropologists call enculturation. People in different cultures learn different things, but there is no evidence to suggest that people in some cultures learn more efficiently than do people in other cultures.

4. Certain aspects of culture—such as ideas, beliefs, and values—can affect our physical bodies and our biological processes. More specifically, certain culturally produced ideas concerning physical beauty can influence the ways in which people alter their bodies.

5. Cultures—and their three basic components of things, ideas, and behavior patterns—are constantly experiencing change. Although the pace of culture change varies from society to society, no culture is totally static. Cultures change internally (innovation) and by borrowing from other cultures (diffusion).

6. Although cultures found throughout the world vary considerably, certain common features (cultural universals) are found in all cultures. Cultural anthropology—the scientific study of cultures—looks at both similarities and differences in human cultures wherever they may be found.

7. Cultures function to help people adapt to their environments and consequently increase their chances for survival. It is also possible for cultures to negatively alter or even destroy their environments.

8. A culture is more than the sum of its parts. Rather, a culture should be seen as an integrated system with its parts interrelated to some degree. This cultural integration has important implications for the process of culture change because a change in one part of the system is likely to bring about changes in other parts.

9. Although culture exerts considerable influence on a person's thoughts and behaviors, it does not determine them.

Key Terms

adaptive nature of culture

civilization

cultural diffusion

cultural universals

culture shock

enculturation

innovations

monochronic culture

organic analogy

pluralistic society

polychronic culture

small-scale society

subculture

symbol

Suggested Readings

Brown, Donald E. *Human Universals.* New York: McGraw-Hill, 1991. Drawing on the works of earlier theorists, this work argues convincingly that cultural universals (the aspects of culture shared by all cultures) are numerous and theoretically significant.

DeVita, Philip R., and James D. Armstrong. *Distant Mirrors: America as a Foreign Culture.* Belmont, CA: Wadsworth, 1993. A readable collection of fourteen articles on American culture as seen through the eyes of foreign scholars who conducted field research in the United States. This slim volume, written from the critical perspective of foreign observers, should give American readers a different view of their own culture.

Gamst, Frederick C., and Edward Norbeck, eds. *Ideas of Culture: Sources and Uses.* New York: Holt, Rinehart Winston, 1976. This is a collection of writings over the past hundred years on the notion of culture, the concept that is central to the discipline of anthropology.

Hall, Edward T. *The Hidden Dimension.* Garden City, NY: Doubleday, 1969. Hall introduces the science of proxemics to show how a very subtle aspect of culture—how people use space—can have a powerful impact on international business relations, cross-cultural encounters, and the fields of architecture and urban planning.

Kuper, Adam. *Culture: The Anthropologists' Account.* Cambridge, MA: Harvard University Press, 1999. By drawing on the works of Parsons, Geertz, Schneider, and Sahlins, among others, Kuper thoughtfully traces the history of the concept of culture in American anthropology by showing its uses and limitations.

Middleton, DeWight. *The Challenge of Human Diversity: Mirrors, Bridges, and Chasms.* Prospect Heights, IL: Waveland, 1998. A readable look at the complex subject of human cultural diversity. By drawing on the personal narratives of anthropologists in the field, Middleton explores the origins of culture and culture's influence on the mind and emotions, while providing a model for understanding all forms of diversity.

Schlosser, Eric. *Fast Food Nation: The Dark Side of the All-American Meal.* Boston: Houghton Mifflin, 2001. A fascinating look at contemporary U.S. culture through the examination of the changes brought about in America's diet, economy, and workforce by the fast-food industry.

Spindler, George and Janice Stockard, eds. *Globalization and Change in 15 Cultures: Born in One World, Living in Another.* Belmont, CA: Wadsworth, 2007. New articles written by fifteen cultural anthropologists, all of whom have written original ethnographies in the Spindler case study series. Written from field sites from around the world, each article explores such dimensions of change as (a) migration and geographic mobility, (b) economic change, (c) challenges to identity and power, and (d) changing gender hierarchies.

Applied Anthropology

Applied anthropologists are often consulted by international development agencies on projects such as this well digging project in rural Ghana.

CHAPTER 3

A **DISTINGUISHING FEATURE OF** cultural anthropology is its direct, experiential approach to research through the technique known as *participant-observation*. By and large, cultural anthropologists conduct field research among populations experiencing serious societal problems, such as poor health, inadequate food production, high infant mortality, political repression, or rampant population growth, to mention but a few. The very nature of anthropological research—which involves living with people, sharing their lives, and often befriending them—makes it difficult for cultural anthropologists to ignore the enormity of the problems these societies face on an everyday basis. It should therefore come as no surprise that many cultural anthropologists feel a sense of responsibility for helping to solve—or at least alleviate—some of these pressing social problems.

Although anthropologists have always applied their findings to the solution of human problems, during the past fifty years an increasing number of anthropologists have conducted research aimed explicitly at practical applications. These practitioners represent a new and growing sub-discipline known as *applied anthropology*, which is characterized by *problem-oriented research* among the world's contemporary populations. These pragmatic anthropologists attempt to apply anthropological data, concepts, and strategies to the solution of social, economic, and technological problems, both at home and abroad. Specific examples of such applied projects would include lowering the incidence of obesity in certain populations, the amelioration of conflicts between police and immigrant populations in urban areas, and the development of sustainable economies in third world countries. In recent decades a number of terms have been given to these attempts to use anthropological research for the improvement of human conditions. They include *action anthropology, development anthropology, practical anthropology,* and *advocacy anthropology.*

participant-observation   A fieldwork method in which the cultural anthropologist lives with the people under study and observes their everyday activities.
applied anthropology   The application of anthropological knowledge, theory, and methods to the solution of specific societal problems.
problem-oriented research   A type of anthropological research designed to solve a particular societal problem rather than to test a theoretical proposition.

What We Will Learn

- How have cultural anthropologists applied their theories, methods, and insights to the solution of practical problems over the last century?

- What special contributions can cultural anthropology make as an applied science?

- How does applied anthropology differ from theoretical anthropology?

- What specialized roles do applied anthropologists play?

▶ Click!

For interactive exercises and study aids, Go to **www.ichapters.com**; enter the author name and select your text, then click the Study Help tab to purchase the following online resources:

- **ThomsonNOW** for chapter-specific online tutorials, quizzes, and a personalized study plan

- **Anthropology Resource Center** for interactive maps, modules, videos, and the Applied Anthropology site

- **Thomson Audio Study Products** for a brief overview of the major chapter themes and to test your knowledge with quiz questions

49

Applied cultural anthropologists study a wide variety of social settings, including this Chinese neighborhood in Toronto, Canada.

For purposes of this chapter, however, we will use the more widely accepted and generic term, *applied anthropology.*

Our use of this term requires some delineation because applied anthropology cuts across all of the traditional four fields. Most anthropologists who would identify with an applied perspective are cultural anthropologists, but the other three traditional sub-disciplines are certainly involved in their share of applied activities. Some examples of applied physical anthropology, archaeology, and linguistics have already been discussed briefly in Chapter 1.

Much of the applied anthropology carried out in recent decades has been supported by large public and private organizations seeking to better understand the cultural dimension of their sponsored programs. These organizations include international agencies such as the U.S. Agency for International Development (USAID), the World Bank, the World Health Organization (WHO), the Ford Foundation, and the Population Council; certain national organizations such as the National Institutes of Health (NIH), the Bureau of Indian Affairs, and the U.S. Department of Agriculture; and on a more local level, various hospitals, private corporations, school systems, urban planning departments, substance abuse programs, facilities for the aged, and family planning clinics. (For a listing of the types of applied anthropological studies discussed in this text, see Table 3.1.)

APPLIED VERSUS PURE ANTHROPOLOGY

For much of the past century, many anthropologists have distinguished applied anthropology from pure or academic anthropology. So-called pure anthropology was seen as being concerned only with the advancement of the discipline in terms of refining its methods and theories and providing increasingly more valid and reliable data. Applied anthropology, on the other hand, was characterized as being primarily aimed at changing human behavior in order to ameliorate contemporary problems. The two types of anthropology are not mutually exclusive enterprises, however.

In fact, unlike the traditional four subfields of anthropology, applied anthropology—which, some have argued, has become the fifth subfield—is considerably more difficult to define. Part of the difficulty of defining the applied subfield precisely is that it has always been a part of the discipline; in fact, both applied and theoretical anthropology have developed alongside each other. Throughout the history of anthropology, its practitioners have been concerned with the utility of their findings for solving social problems. For example, in the early 1930s the Applied Anthropology Unit of Indian Affairs was created by President Roosevelt's Commissioner of Indian Affairs, John Collier (an anthropologist himself). The aim of this unit was to study the progress of self-governing organizations among some Native American groups as called for in the 1934 Indian Reorganization Act. As part of the Interdisciplinary Committee on Human Relations at the University of Chicago, anthropologist W. Lloyd Warner, Burleigh Gardner, and others conducted applied research in the areas of industrial management, productivity, and working conditions. Moreover, World War II provided vast opportunities for anthropologists to apply their skills and insights to the war effort (see, for example, the Applied Perspective entitled "Rebuilding Japan After World War II" in Chapter 13). In the decades following World War II, cultural anthropologists conducted applied research in

© Rudy Sulgan/Corbis

Table 3.1 Types of Applied Anthropology

Forms of Applied Cultural Anthropology	Examples from Text (Chapters)
Agricultural Anthropology	1. Development in Guinea (10)
Architectural Anthropology	1. Park Restoration (12)
Business Anthropology	1. Cross-Cultural Coaching (2)
	2. Market Research (8)
	3. Baby Formula Controversy (3)
	4. Is Nepotism Always Bad? (8)
Development Anthropology	1. Trees in Haiti (4)
	2. Tibetan Rug Weaving (15)
Educational Anthropology	1. Ebonics (6)
	2. Schools in Hawaii (9)
Environmental Anthropology	1. Water Management in Mexico (7)
	2. Radiation on Marshall Island (3)
	3. Economic Development in Honduras (16)
Legal Anthropology	1. Minority Prison Inmates (3)
	2. Amish Case in Supreme Court (14)
	3. Anthropologist Tumed Detective (15)
Medical Anthropology	1. Diabetes in Mexican-Americans (12)
	2. AIDS Research (5)
	3. "Primitive Medicine" and Modern Drugs (7)
	4. Child Nutrition in Malawi (11)
	5. Family Planning in Ecuador (11)
	6. Public Health Among the Zulus (3)
Political Anthropology	1. Mediation with Trukese Villagers (3)
	2. Ruth Benedict in Post-War Japan (13)
Urban Anthropology	1. Homeless Youth (10)
	2. New Hope Anti-Poverty Program (4)
	3. Adolescent Drug Dealers/Florida (3)

Marni Finklestein

Participant-observation studies of homeless teenagers can lead to more realistic social programs to assist this misunderstood segment of the population.

Table 3.2 **Comparison of Theoretical and Applied Anthropology**

	Theoretical Anthropology	Applied Anthropology
Primary Objective	Test hypotheses and describe ethnographic reality	Help solve societal problems
Research Methods	Participant-observation and interviewing	Rapid Ethnographic Assessment (see Chapter 5)
Time Frame	A year or more	Several weeks to a month
Collaboration	Seldom collaborative	Usually collaborative

a wide variety of areas, including agriculture, medicine, criminal justice, alcohol and drug use, housing, tourism, geriatric services, education, and business, among many others. Thus, as we can see, many cultural anthropologists have very purposefully engaged in applied research throughout the twentieth century, others have applied secondary anthropological data to help solve certain social problems, and still others—engaging in the investigation of a theoretical problem—have taken the additional step of explaining the practical implications of their findings for policy makers.

If we take the pure/applied distinction too literally, we might conclude that applied anthropologists are devoid of any theoretical concerns and that academic purists have no concern for the practical implications of their work. In actual practice, neither of these is true. Applied anthropology, when it is done effectively, takes into account the theories, methods, and data that have been developed by the discipline as a whole. At the other polarity, the more theoretically oriented anthropologists are indebted to applied anthropologists for stimulating their interest in new areas of research and, in some cases, for contributing to the development of new theory. The beneficial consequences that can accrue from the interaction of theoretical and applied anthropologists have been well stated by Walter Goldschmidt (1979: 5): "The more a field is engaged in practical affairs, the greater the intellectual ferment; for programmatic activities

raise issues and often new approaches which would otherwise escape the attention of the discipline."

It is not surprising that the line between pure and applied anthropology is so murky, because both groups receive the same form of training and draw on the same methods—notably, participant-observation and ethnographic interviewing. The line is blurred still further by the fact that the two have experienced parallel development, have been mutually supportive, and often have claimed the same personnel. Thus, because of their common concerns and experiences, the task of distinguishing between applied and pure anthropologists is as elusive as trying to nail a custard pie to the wall.

RECENT HISTORY OF APPLIED ANTHROPOLOGY

Even though anthropologists have been applying their insights since the beginning of the twentieth century, the real stimulus came in the 1940s, when many of the leading cultural anthropologists of the time were asked to participate in efforts related to World War II.

Anthropologists were recruited by the National Research Council to examine national morale during wartime, to learn about food preferences and wartime rationing, and to perform national character studies on our adversaries—the Germans, Italians, and Japanese. After the war, many anthropologists left government service and returned to positions in colleges and universities. This trend, with a return to more theoretical concerns, continued through the 1950s and 1960s. Any applied anthropology that was conducted during the decades of the 1950s and 1960s was carried out by academic anthropologists engaged in short-term projects outside the university setting.

From the 1970s to the present, however, a new brand of applied anthropology has emerged. These new applied anthropologists are not university professors but full-time employees of the hiring agencies. Data from a recent survey conducted by the American Anthropological Association indicate that approximately 30 percent of all anthropology Ph.D.s work outside an academic setting for government organizations, nonprofits, or private sector firms. This trend is largely the result of two factors essentially external to the discipline of anthropology. First, over the past three decades, the market for most

Sometimes applied anthropologists serve as expert witnesses in court cases involving cultural issues.

© Michael Pole/Corbis

After WWII many anthropologists left government service and returned to colleges and universities. This trend, which continued through the 1960s, accompanied a return to more theoretical concerns.

academic jobs has declined dramatically. The abundance of jobs that marked the 1950s and 1960s turned into a shortage of jobs in the 1970s and afterward. A second factor contributing to the new applied anthropology has been increased federal legislation mandating policy research that can be accomplished effectively by cultural anthropologists. For example, the National Historic Preservation Act of 1966 (designed to preserve the historical and cultural foundations of the nation), the National Environmental Policy Act of 1969 (requiring impact assessments of federally funded construction projects on the cultural environment), and the Foreign Assistance Act of 1961 (establishing USAID, the foreign aid arm of the federal government), all provide for policy

research of a cultural nature. As a result of these two factors (fewer academic jobs coupled with more abundant applied research opportunities), more anthropology Ph.D.s are finding permanent employment outside academia. This trend has been paralleled by increases in the number of MA programs in applied anthropology and the membership of applied anthropology organizations such as the Society for Applied Anthropology (SFAA) and the National Association of Practicing Anthropologists (NAPA).

The extent to which an applied anthropologist becomes involved in any given project can vary considerably. At one extreme—the least interventionist end—are applied anthropologists who simply provide information for planners and decision makers. This information can range from very concrete observational data through low- and intermediate-level concepts and propositions, to the most abstract level of general theory. Moving along the continuum, there are applied anthropologists, either working alone or as members of an interdisciplinary team, who use the collected data to construct a plan for bringing about a desired change in a particular population. And finally, at the most interventionist extreme, applied anthropologists become involved in the actual implementation of particular projects. Although rare, these "action anthropologists" feel a professional responsibility not only to make their research findings available but also to propose, advocate, and carry out policy positions.

SPECIAL FEATURES OF ANTHROPOLOGY

What does the discipline of anthropology have to offer as an applied science? What unique contributions can anthropology make to social programs and agencies?

The understandings that emerge from applied anthropological studies of peasant farmers (such as these in Madagascar) can be helpful in agricultural development programs.

© Wolfgang Kaehler/Corbis

The answers to these questions rest largely in the unique approach to the study of humans that anthropology has taken from its earliest beginnings. Among some of the special features of anthropology that contribute to its potential as a policy science are the following: participant-observation, the holistic perspective, the development of regional expertise, the emic view, the value orientation of cultural relativism, and topical expertise.

Participant-observation: Direct field observation, a hallmark of twentieth-century anthropology, can lead to a fuller understanding of sociocultural realities than might be possible by relying on secondary sources alone. Also, the rapport developed while conducting participant-observation research can be drawn upon in the implementation stage of the applied project.

The holistic perspective: This distinctive feature of anthropology forces us to look at multiple variables and see human problems in their historical, economic, and cultural contexts. This conceptual orientation reminds us that the various parts of a sociocultural system are interconnected and therefore a change in one part of the system is likely to cause changes in other parts. The holistic perspective also encourages us to look at problems in terms of both the short run and the long run.

Regional expertise: Many anthropologists, despite recent trends toward specialization, continue to function as culture area specialists (such as Africanists and Micronesianists). The cultural anthropologist who has conducted doctoral research in Zambia, for example, often returns to that country for subsequent field studies. Thus, long-term association with a cultural region provides a depth of geographic coverage that most policy makers lack.

The emic view: Whatever the setting of a particular project—be it an agricultural development scheme in Zimbabwe, an inner-city hospital in Detroit, or a classroom in rural Peru—the applied anthropologist brings to the project the perspective of the local people—what anthropologists call the emic view. By describing the emic view (using the mental categories and assumptions of the local people) rather than their own technical/professional view (the etic view), anthropologists can provide program planners/administrators with strategic information that can seriously affect the outcome of programs of planned change.

Cultural relativism: The basic principle of cultural relativism (described in Chapter 1)—a vital part of every cultural anthropologist's training—tends to foster tolerance, which can be particularly relevant for applied anthropologists working in complex organizations. For example, tolerance stemming from the perspective of cultural relativism can help anthropologists cross class lines and relate to a wide range of people within a complex organization (such as a hospital or school system) in which they are working.

Topical expertise: It is generally recognized that the topical knowledge gleaned from fairly specific anthropological studies in one part of the world is likely to have policy relevance in other parts of the world. For example, cultural anthropologists who have studied pastoralism in East Africa have topical experience with and knowledge about pastoralism that can be applied not just elsewhere in Africa but also in the Middle East or Central Asia (Scudder 1999: 359).

These six features of anthropology can enhance the discipline's effectiveness as a policy science. Nevertheless, when compared with other disciplines, anthropology has some drawbacks that limit its effectiveness in solving societal problems. First, anthropologists have not, by and large, developed many time-effective research methods;

Applied anthropologists help medical personnel provide more efficient and culturally relevant services to people throughout the world. Here a Western doctor is innoculating children in Truk, Micronesia.

the premier anthropological data-gathering technique of participant-observation, which usually requires up to a year or more, is not particularly well suited to the accelerated time schedules of applied programs of change. Moreover, with their strong tradition of qualitative research methods, anthropologists have been relatively unsophisticated in their use of quantitative data, although recently anthropologists have begun to use more quantitative approaches.

Specialized Roles of Applied Anthropologists

Applied anthropologists also play a number of specialized roles, which are more thoroughly described by John Van Willigen (2002):

Policy Researcher: This role, perhaps the most common role for applied anthropologists, involves providing cultural data to policy makers so that they can make the most informed policy decisions.

Evaluator: In another role that is also quite common, evaluators use their research skills to determine how well a program or policy has succeeded in fulfilling its objectives.

Impact Assessor: This role entails measuring the effects of a particular project, program, or policy on local peoples. For example, impact assessors may determine the consequences, both intended and unintended, that a federal highway construction project might have on the community through which the highway runs.

Planner: In this fairly common role, applied anthropologists actively participate in the design of various programs and policies.

Needs Assessor: This role involves conducting research to determine ahead of time the need for a proposed program or project.

Trainer: Adopting what is essentially a teaching role, the applied anthropologist imparts cultural knowledge about certain populations to different professional groups working in cross-cultural situations (such as Peace Corps volunteers or international business people).

Advocate: This rare role involves becoming an active supporter of a particular group of people. Usually involving political action, this role is most often combined with other roles.

Expert Witness: This role involves the presentation of culturally relevant research findings as part of judicial proceedings through legal briefs, depositions, or direct testimony.

Administrator/Manager: An applied anthropologist who assumes direct administrative responsibility for a particular project is working in this specialized role.

Cultural Broker: This role may involve serving as a liaison between the program planner and administrators on one hand and local ethnic communities on the other, or between mainstream hospital personnel and their ethnically distinct patients.

These specialized roles are not mutually exclusive. In many cases, applied anthropologists play two or more of these roles as part of the same job. For example, an applied anthropologist who is working as a policy researcher may also conduct research as a needs assessor before a program is initiated and carry out an impact assessment and evaluation after the program has concluded.

The program that employs these three HIV/AIDS counselors in Chennai, India, can profit from cultural data provided by medical anthropologists.

Lorne Lassiter

APPLIED PERSPECTIVE

Environmental Impact of Radiation on Marshall Islands Population

After dropping atomic bombs on Japan in 1945 to end World War II, the U.S. government began large-scale nuclear testing to better understand the capacity of the weapons and the effects of radiation on human beings and their environments.

From 1946 to 1958, the government detonated sixty-seven atomic and thermonuclear devices in and around the Marshall Islands. For the people of the Marshall Islands, administered by the U.S. government as part of a United Nations trust territory, the consequences were profound. Many people were displaced because their land was made uninhabitable; others were exposed to high levels of radiation, causing illness, genetic damage, and death; and nearly everyone's relationship with their environment was severely altered.

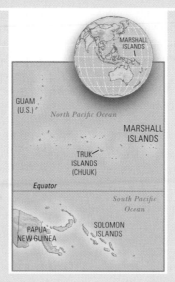

It wasn't until 1993—a half century after the U.S. government had collected data on the effects of radiation—that documents on the subject were declassified, allowing citizens of the Marshall Islands, and the rest of the world, to learn the magnitude of the damage and injury inflicted upon them. Using these government documents, coupled with extensive ethnographic research, applied anthropologist Holly Barker has been working with these involuntary victims of the Cold War for more than a decade. The core of Barker's ethnographic study is based on more than two hundred in-depth interviews with radiation survivors on the Marshall Islands. But Barker also supplements her Marshall Islands data with case studies of radiation exposure in other parts of the region (the results of French and British testing), studies of approximately three hundred thousand survivors of Hiroshima, studies of Scandinavians exposed to radiation from Chernobyl, and the radiation studies conducted by the U.S. government within the continental United States between 1940 and the 1970s.

Barker's findings in this decade-long environmental impact study of nuclear testing are both frightening and profound. In all cases of deliberate nuclear testing on the part of major governments, the populations affected were the least powerful and the most vulnerable. They were populations to which the governments felt no obligation to either seek their permission or inform them of the results of the research. The decisions of outsiders (government officials living far from the contaminated areas) resulted in illness and death to those present as well as to their future descendants. Property, either destroyed or contaminated, was made uninhabitable. People's relationships to their environments, their natural resources, and their communities were either severely altered or obliterated. Affected populations for decades harbored fears of invisible genetic damage that could affect future generations. Others interviewed by Barker expressed guilt and remorse over their very visible genetic abnormalities. Moreover, many Marshall Islanders developed a justifiable distrust of government officials who both undervalued their way of life, and then purposefully withheld important medical and environmental evidence because of political expediency.

Barker's applied anthropological research is significant on a number of levels. First, Barker's research demonstrates the enormity of the impact (environmental, economic, and social) that nuclear contamination can have on vulnerable populations. In this respect, it should be instructive to government policy makers when working with indigenous populations in the future. Second, the scope of the injury and damage inflicted on Marshall Islanders should serve as the basis for some type of compensation to those whose lives were so thoroughly disrupted by government decisions beyond their control. Third, Barker not only conducts research with survivors, but she also helps survivors go to Washington, DC, to seek medical assistance and environmental restoration for impacted communities. In this regard, Barker helps empower local communities to request the redress they seek. And finally, Barker's findings should be instructive to other applied anthropologists (including legal, environmental, medical, and political anthropologists) as a reminder of how to use scientific data to influence contemporary social problems and issues.

Questions for Further Thought

1. If Holly Barker sought employment in the federal government of the United States, what branch might be interested in hiring her?

2. What type of data did anthropologist Barker draw upon in her study of Marshall Islanders?

3. Based on what we now know about the environmental hazards of nuclear radiation, what advice would you give to the president of the United States about the proposed disposal of nuclear wastes at Yucca Mountain, Nevada?

EXAMPLES OF APPLIED ANTHROPOLOGY

The Nestlé Baby Formula Controversy

As mentioned previously, one of the roles played by applied anthropologists is that of advocate, whereby one's own research is used to support a public cause or protest movement. Applied anthropologist Penny Van Esterik (1989) played such a role during the late 1970s and early 1980s in the controversy surrounding the Nestlé Corporation's active marketing of baby formula in impoverished third world countries.

Because increasing numbers of new mothers in the United States and Europe were choosing breast feeding rather than bottle feeding during this period, Nestlé, a major manufacturer of baby formula, aggressively marketed its products to third world mothers in an effort to increase the company's worldwide market share.

Nestlé opponents argued that the company's aggressive marketing of baby formula in third world countries was highly irresponsible because of the increased health risks it posed to infants. The major problem was that the formula needed to be mixed with clean, potable water, which in many third world countries is in short supply. Moreover, the fuel needed to boil the local water to remove contaminants was often unavailable or unaffordable. Thus, more often than not, children in Africa, Asia, and South America were being fed instant formula made with contaminated water. The result was a marked increase in infant illness and mortality due to diarrhea, dehydration, and intestinal infections.

The scientific evidence supported the superiority of breast feeding over infant formula, because breast milk was safe, renewable, and free. Nevertheless, the Nestlé Corporation persisted in promoting its products to third world mothers for more than a decade. Spurred on by widespread international protests, the World Health Organization and UNICEF created a set of guidelines ensuring the ethical marketing of such products for infants. Interestingly, the United States was the only country that refused to endorse the guidelines owing to its insistence on unregulated worldwide trade. The protests, debates,

Courtesy of Elizabeth Briody

Industrial anthropologist Dr. Elizabeth Briody is a full-time employee of General Motors.

and boycotts lasted until 1984, when Nestlé finally agreed to comply with the internationally agreed-upon guidelines.

Throughout this period when Nestlé seemed to be thumbing its nose at the rest of the world, applied anthropologist Van Esterik played an important advocacy role in the debate. Having conducted fieldwork in Thailand, she brought her research on the deleterious health effects of baby formula to the public debate on this issue. She helped organize educational forums and local boycotts in the United States. She headed up a large-scale research project on the topic in Colombia, Kenya, Indonesia, and Thailand. And on three different occasions during the late 1970s and early 1980s, she participated in public debates on the topic, the last one of which involved official Nestlé spokespersons. Thus, Van Esterik provides an excellent example of the role of advocacy, whereby the applied anthropologist not only conducts research on a controversial topic but also takes the next step of directly advocating a particular position in the public debate.

Working with Minority Prison Inmates

In recent years some cultural anthropologists have found themselves in prison. That is, they have been applying their insights and skills to the area of prisons and corrections. For example, anthropologist Elizabeth Grobsmith has worked on behalf of Native American inmates in the Nebraska Department of Correctional Services, serving as a cultural broker, a program planner, and an expert witness in court cases.

Grobsmith's work began in 1975, when Native American inmates were granted a consent decree by a federal district court enabling them to practice their religion and culture within prison. The practice of traditional religions in prison created a number of opportunities for cross-cultural misunderstandings and thus increased tensions between the Native American inmates and prison guards. To illustrate, the burning of such substances as sage and sweet grass at religious ceremonies can be mistaken for the smell of marijuana, or the sacrificial cutting of skin with Exacto knives can make guards somewhat uneasy. Here Grobsmith played an important role as cultural broker in explaining the various aspects of traditional Native American religious practices, many of which appeared suspicious to the guards. Even though the inmates themselves could have explained these traditional practices, the use of a cultural anthropologist as expert outsider lent greater credibility and legitimacy to the practices.

Grobsmith's expertise in Native American cultures enabled her to make recommendations to the Department of Corrections on certain inmate programs. Based on her research on the history of substance abuse among inmates, she found that virtually 100 percent of her sample claimed to be chemically dependent prior to entering prison (1989: 285–98). As an applied anthro-

---

CROSS-CULTURAL MISCUE

Brad Hutchison, an applied anthropologist from California, was spending a semester as a visiting professor at Waseda University in Tokyo, Japan. Several days after arriving, Hutchison made an appointment to meet with one of his colleagues in the anthropology department, Todashi Kobayashi. In response to Hutchison's general question about his colleague's latest research project, Kobayashi-san proceeded to describe his research in considerable detail. Although Hutchison was interested in the topic, he was becoming increasingly annoyed with Kobayashi-san, who kept pausing to ask whether Hutchison understood him. Hutchison began to think that his Japanese colleague thought he was either inattentive or stupid.

This cross-cultural misunderstanding occurred because the role of the listener in Japan is substantially different from that in the United States. It is customary in Japan for listeners to use replies (*aizuchi*) such as "hai" ("yes") that indicate that one is listening and understanding what is being said. Americans also do this (by saying "yes" or grunting "mm-hmm"), but the Japanese use these to a much greater extent. Because Hutchison was not giving off any *aizuchi*, Kobayashi-san kept seeking reassurance that his message was getting through.

---

pologist familiar with Native American populations, Grobsmith understood the need to accommodate cultural practices into the design of substance abuse programs. For example, Native Americans are not likely to engage in emotional self-disclosure about their substance abuse unless they are in the relative safety of an exclusively Native American group. Moreover, Grobsmith knew that correctional programs would be more likely to succeed if the inmates could incorporate into them certain elements of traditional culture such as sweat lodges and smoking pipes.

Finally, Grobsmith served on seven occasions as a consultant in court proceedings involving Native American inmates. Occasionally, inmates sued the Department of Corrections for access to the rights granted them under the consent decree of 1975. During these cases, Grobsmith worked in three capacities: as a cross-cultural teacher/consultant to lawyers, as a liaison between lawyers and their inmate-clients, and as an expert witness to the court. In this last role of expert witness, Grobsmith's role was to inform the court of the content and validity of such Native American practices as sweat lodges, the ceremonial use of peyote, the Sun Dance, hand games, and general religious ideas, values, and practices. The role of expert witness to the courts is particularly significant because it enables the applied anthropologist, through his or her research-based testimony, to influence the outcome of a legal decision.

An Ethnographic Study of Adolescent Drug Dealers

Because of cocaine's high cost, cocaine addiction historically has been viewed as a rich person's problem. In the last several decades, however, the introduction of a cheaper variety of cocaine—crack—has made this drug accessible to all segments of the population. By and large, the appearance of crack cocaine has been a destructive force for both individuals and society as a whole. Increased trafficking in crack cocaine has been responsible, at least in part, for increases in crime, in the incidence of AIDS (sex-for-crack exchanges), and in the number of children born with drug addictions. One of the more disturbing aspects of the crack cocaine epidemic is the high rate of cocaine dealing among adolescents.

In an attempt to learn more about adolescent drug dealing, Richard Dembo and his colleagues (1993) conducted an ethnographic study of adolescent drug dealers in west central Florida. Dembo interviewed thirty-four drug-dealing youth and sixteen non-drug-dealing youth on topics such as the extent to which income from drugs was used to help meet family expenses, reasons for selling crack cocaine, the perceived risks of dealing in cocaine, and the negative effects of drug trafficking on the neighborhood. The adolescents who were dealing sold, on average, twenty-one weeks out of the year for an average weekly income of $672. The estimated mean financial worth of the adolescent dealers was $2,500. Most of the dealers said that they were not currently using cocaine. Two out of three adolescent dealers said they had killed or hurt someone through their association with cocaine. The great majority of the dealers reported that they spent most of their income on personal luxury items (such as clothes and jewelry) or business expenses such as guns or protection. It is estimated that they contributed less than 10 percent of their income to their families. Most adolescent dealers said that they sold cocaine to earn a lot of money (because legitimate jobs pay too little), which would give them higher status among their peers.

This ethnographic study of the culture of adolescent cocaine dealers has important policy implications because it suggests certain strategies for dealing with this problem. For example, because wanting to make money is the major reason for selling cocaine, intervention strategies must include ways of improving the vocational and educational skills of adolescents so they will have more access to legitimate work. Because most of the adolescent dealers were not using cocaine, there is little reason to treat the problem as one of drug dependency. Adolescent dealing is motivated by economics, not drug addiction. Knowing this fact about the culture of adolescent dealers suggests that the following would be a rational strategy for addressing the problem: former teenage dealers who have been successful in legitimate careers could serve as positive role models for adolescent dealers by encouraging and supporting those willing to enter legitimate career alternatives.

Medical Anthropology and Public Health in South Africa

For more than a half century, cultural anthropologists have been interested in the socio-cultural aspects of public health. During the 1940s the Polela Health Center, located in the Natal Province of South Africa, served the medical needs of approximately sixteen thousand local Zulus. Health conditions among the Zulus were extremely poor. In addition to widespread occurrences of such infectious diseases as typhoid, typhus, smallpox, and tuberculosis, the Zulus suffered from *kwashiorkor,* a form of protein malnutrition with debilitating consequences. There were particularly high rates of *kwashiorkor* among married women. Health officials at the clinic found this particularly puzzling because the Zulus are cattle keepers and thus should be able to use their milk supplies (a rich source of protein) to prevent the often deadly effects of *kwashiorkor.*

The key to understanding why *kwashiorkor* was so prevalent among married women rested with the understanding of a deeply held cultural belief that people are permitted to drink only the milk produced by the cows of their father's lineage. Although the dietary restrictions apply to all Zulus, the situation was particularly problematic for married women. Zulu society was patrilocal (that is, having a residence pattern in which a married couple lives with or near the husband's parents). When a woman married, she moved away from her father's extended family, and consequently, lost everyday access to the milk of her father's cows. The only way that a married woman could have access to milk was if her father gave her a cow of her own when she married, an unlikely occurrence. Thus, milk as a source of protein was, for all practical purposes, unavailable to Zulu wives.

Even though the reason for the dietary prohibition had long since been forgotten, the Zulu people

retained powerful feelings about maintaining it. Given such strong convictions, it would have served little purpose for the health professionals to have tried to argue the Zulus out of their belief. Much to their credit, the Polela health team overcame the cultural obstacle to improving the dietary intake of Zulu women by circumventing it. According to John Cassel:

> Fortunately, it was possible to overcome this difficulty to a considerable extent by introducing powdered milk into the area. Even though [they] knew that this powder was in fact milk, it was not called milk in Zulu but was referred to as "powder" or "meal" and accepted by all families without protest. Even the most orthodox of husbands and mothers-in-law had no objection to their wives or daughters-in-law using the powder. (1972: 308)

Because the Polela health staff, working like medical anthropologists, understood the essential features of Zulu culture, they were able to engage in some creative problem solving. All parties concerned were winners. The medical team was happy because it had improved the health of Zulu women. The Zulus themselves were happy because they were healthier. And it was all accomplished without having to do battle with a part of Zulu traditional culture. Not all public health problems are solved so painlessly. Nevertheless, this preventive health program would not have succeeded without a thorough understanding of traditional Zulu patterns of resource allocation and consumption.

Mediating Between the Government and Trukese Villagers

Whenever central governments initiate programs of planned change, problems are likely to emerge with the local target population because governments and local populations often have different cultural values and interests. In some cases, the plans and policies of the government are so much at odds with the needs of the local population that demonstrations, petitions, and other forms of popular protest may arise in opposition to the government's plans; hostilities and mistrust may be generated in both camps; and in some serious cases, the proposed project may come to a standstill. In such situations, cultural anthropologists have been recruited to serve as mediators or cultural brokers between the government and the local people whose lives are being affected by the projects.

During the late 1970s, the government of the Trust Territories for the Island of Truk (administered by the United States) made plans to expand the airport. The plans were drawn up, and the environmental impact study (required by U.S. law) was completed without any consultation with the local villagers. As originally proposed, the airport expansion would have created a number of problems for the local people. For example, proposed dredging operations would have destroyed certain local

fishing areas, the expanded runway would have prevented the villagers from mooring their boats near their homes, construction would have destroyed several cultural/ historical landmarks, and during construction, the project would have generated high levels of noise and dust. The people naturally objected. Protest demonstrations and the threat of a legal injunction to stop construction convinced the government that it had a serious problem.

In an attempt to address the local complaints, the government appointed Thomas King, an archaeological consultant in historic preservation, to mediate officially between the government and the local villagers on matters pertaining to the construction's impact. Although he had no official status in the mediation process, King's wife, Patricia Parker, a cultural anthropologist who was conducting ethnographic research on Trukese land law, played an important role by translating the villagers' concerns into language the government officials could understand (Parker and King 1987).

The first order of business facing this wife–husband mediating team was to work with the villagers to develop a list of specific grievances that could serve as the basis for negotiations. Meetings held in the various villages allowed the local people themselves to reach some consensus on the nature of their complaints against the proposed airport expansion. Parker, the cultural anthropologist, who was fluent in the local language, attended these meetings and provided detailed outlines of the villagers' concerns to King, who in turn brought the concerns to the responsible government officials.

Thus, Parker and King served as cultural mediators or cultural brokers between the government and the local Trukese villagers. Because they came to understand the constraints and interests on both sides of the controversy, they were able to mediate from a fairly strong knowledge base, thereby avoiding a hardening

CONTEMPORARY ISSUES

Can Cultural Anthropologists Find Their Public Policy Voice?

Before, and particularly during, World War II cultural anthropologists played prominent roles in setting governmental policy in a variety of areas including Native American affairs, food rationing programs, and how best to deal with our allies and our enemies during war time. Many of the biggest names in the field—such as Edward Spicer, Margaret Mead, Conrad Arensberg, and Ruth Benedict—were conducting research for the federal government for the specific purpose of informing public policy. After the war, however, most cultural anthropologists returned to university employment and lost their "public policy voice." Despite the growth of applied anthropology within the discipline over the last thirty-five years, cultural anthropologists are not widely sought out as public policy experts. Today, it is much more likely that when we hear an expert being interviewed on CNN or NPR news, it will be a sociologist or a political scientist, not a cultural anthropologist.

Will anthropologists be able to reclaim their public policy "mojo" in the twenty-first century? Cultural anthropology as a discipline—and the recent research by many of its practitioners—certainly has policy relevance for a number of issues facing the nation and the world. But, for whatever reason, most cultural anthropologists are not engaging (or are not being heard) on the pressing policy issues of our time. One very hopeful sign that cultural anthropologists may be reclaiming their place alongside sociologists and political scientists in public policy debates is the recent publication *Why America's Top Pundits Are Wrong: Anthropologists Talk Back* edited by Besteman and Gusterson (2005). By drawing on anthropological data and their own sharp analytical skills, a number of leading anthropologists take on, in this edited volume, many of America's leading pundits on some of the most controversial topics of the day. For example, most

domestic and foreign policy decisions made in the United States in recent years have been based on competition, the efficacy of free market economics, and the notion of "survival of the fittest." Although public policies based on free markets may work well for those at the top of the competitive hierarchy, anthropological studies of those at the middle and lower echelons of society paint a much different picture of the value of leaving everything up to the wisdom of the markets. Moreover, cultural anthropology, to a greater extent than any other social science, is in the best position to reframe the current debate on gay marriage and family life. As Gusterson and Besteman point out (2005: 31), it is cultural anthropologists who have collected "ethnographic information on the diversity of gender identities and marriage arrangements around the world—a diversity that would quickly puncture glib claims about what constitutes a 'natural' nuclear family."

Free market economies and the same sex marriage debate are just two areas in which anthropologists can contribute to public policy debate. They also have a good deal to say on other areas of public concern such as globalization, the culture wars, nation building and the spread of democracy, the biological roots of human behavior, the causes of war, family violence, the teaching of Darwinian evolution, issues of racism and social justice, the myth of I.Q. testing, poverty, and ethnic conflicts. Clearly, cultural anthropologists—with their cross-cultural perspective—are in a unique position to help people from all cultures navigate effectively and humanely through this twenty-first-century world—a world that is growing increasingly more interdependent each year. But before this can happen, there needs to be a considerably larger group of cultural anthropologists willing to re-engage in politically significant issues.

---

of positions on either side. As a result of their mediating efforts, the following modifications were made. First, dredging operations were changed so that local fishing areas were only minimally affected; where they were affected, the villagers received block grant compensation for the potential loss of food. Second, the government agreed to construct a new anchorage for local fishing boats. Third, construction plans were altered so that cultural/historic landmarks were not destroyed.

In the final analysis, the use of two anthropologists to mediate between the interests of the government and those of the local Trukese villagers worked out well for all parties concerned. The villagers were pleased with most of the modifications made in the original plans and the compensation they received. The govern-

ment now has an expanded airport. Although the cost of the airport was increased, its construction was not delayed by litigation.

THE GREATER USE OF ANTHROPOLOGICAL KNOWLEDGE

This book focuses on how anthropological knowledge can be used to solve problems of architects, government officials, business people, medical personnel, educators, foreign aid personnel, court officials, family planners, and others. Although this applied perspective demonstrates how anthropology has contributed to the solution of societal problems, much still needs to be done to

Federal law in the United States requires environmental impact studies to be conducted before the building of federally funded interstate highways. Applied anthropologists often conduct such studies to determine how local populations will be disrupted by highway construction.

© John Humble/Getty Images

Applied anthropologists can serve as consultants or cultural brokers to help businesspeople better understand the cultures of their international business partners.

© Charles Gupton/Getty images

increase the extent to which anthropological knowledge can actually be used by policy makers. It is one thing to point out the potential uses of anthropological information, and it is quite another to actually apply that information to make a difference in the quality of peoples' lives.

As applied anthropology continues to grow in prominence in the twenty-first century, more anthropologists will be ensuring that anthropological insights have an impact on the policy process. It is no longer enough for applied anthropologists to simply conduct their research and report their findings. Rather, applied anthropologists need to develop strategies that will maximize the likelihood that their findings will be used by policy makers and decision makers. This process involves collaborating in the research process with potential users, which would demystify the research, provide valuable feedback, and increase commitment to the research. Moreover, because policy makers often need cultural information quickly, applied anthropologists need to develop more time-efficient methods if their findings are to be useful. In short, applied anthropologists need to be astute in structuring their research with an eye toward practical application.

In addition to developing strategies for the use of applied research findings, there is an enormous potential for the use of existing anthropological data. As countries become more interconnected, people from around the world are being thrown together with increasing frequency. Businesspeople, diplomats, educators, technical assistance personnel, missionaries, scholars, and citizen-tourists are traveling throughout the world in greater numbers than ever before. Unhappily, our understanding of other cultures has not kept pace with advances in communications and transportation technology. Thus, a growing number of people are expected to perform their professional activities in an unfamiliar cultural environment. However, this situation can be changed.

For years cultural anthropologists have collected enormous quantities of data on the various cultures of the world. Although cultural information exists on most peoples of the world, it is not always accessible or understandable for non-anthropologists. The great bulk of cultural data is hidden away in obscure anthropological journals and written in language that would require a Ph.D. in anthropology to comprehend. Perhaps one of the greatest challenges facing anthropology at the start of the twenty-first century is to begin making existing anthropological data available and usable to non-anthropologists. In short, anthropologists must themselves become (or train others to become) cultural brokers who translate anthropological findings into terms that non-anthropologists can use to cope more effectively with the cultural environments in which they find themselves. ∎

Summary

1. Traditionally, many anthropologists have distinguished between pure anthropology (aimed at refining the discipline's theory, methods, and data) and applied anthropology (focusing on using anthropological insights to solve practical social problems).

2. World War II provided vast opportunities for anthropologists to turn their efforts to applied projects related to the war. The post-war boom in higher education lured many anthropologists back into academic positions during the 1950s and 1960s. But the decline in academic positions for anthropologists since the 1970s has resulted in an increase in applied types of employment outside the academic environment.

3. Cultural anthropology can make a number of unique contributions as a policy science. For example, anthropologists bring to a research setting their skills as participant-observers, the capacity to view sociocultural phenomena from a holistic perspective, their regional and topical expertise, a willingness to see the world from the perspective of the local people (emic view), and the value orientation of cultural relativism.

4. Applied anthropologists work in a wide range of settings, both at home and abroad. Moreover, they play a number of specialized roles, including policy researcher, impact assessor, expert witness, trainer, planner, and cultural broker.

5. Examples of applied anthropology include Penny Van Esterik's advocacy involvement in the Nestlé baby formula controversy, Elizabeth Grobsmith's work with Native American prison inmates, Richard Dembo's ethnographic research on teenage cocaine dealing in Florida, Cassel's work with public health among the Zulus of South Africa, and Parker and King's work as cultural brokers between the U.S. government and Trukese villagers.

6. Today, there is a growing need for applied anthropologists to develop strategies that will increase the likelihood of their research findings being used by policy makers.

Key Terms

applied anthropology   participant-observation   problem-oriented research

Suggested Readings

Besteman, Catherine and Hugh Gusterson, eds. *Why America's Top Pundits Are Wrong.* Berkeley, CA: University of California Press, 2005. This recent collection of essays by twelve prominent anthropologists shows how the conclusions of such popular "talking heads" as Samuel Huntington and Thomas Friedman are often simplistic and culturally misinformed. By offering an anthropological perspective on such topics as ethnic violence, globalization, and social justice, the contributors to this volume make a compelling case for the importance of anthropology to the public policy debate.

Bodley, John H. *Anthropology and Contemporary Human Problems.* New York: WCB/McGraw-Hill, 2000. Bodley argues that many of the problems facing the world today—overconsumption, resource depletion, hunger and starvation, overpopulation, violence, and war—are inherent in the basic cultural patterns of modern industrial civilization.

Ervin, Alexander M. *Applied Anthropology: Tools and Perspectives for Contemporary Practice.* Boston: Allyn & Bacon, 2000. One of the few comprehensive, readable, and up-to-date texts in applied cultural anthropology that deals with theory, methods, and a wide range of issues facing today's applied anthropologists.

Ferraro, Gary. *The Cultural Dimension of International Business,* 5th ed. Upper Saddle River, NJ: Prentice-Hall, 2006. This book demonstrates how the theory, methods, and insights of cultural anthropology can contribute to positive outcomes for global business. Cross-cultural scenarios in Chapters 2 through 8 encourage students to explore why a cultural conflict has arisen and how it could have been avoided.

Gwynne, Margaret A. *Applied Anthropology: A Career-oriented Approach.* Boston: Allyn & Bacon, 2003. This up-to-date and balanced introduction to the fast-growing field of applied cultural anthropology is particularly engaging for university undergraduates because of its emphasis on career possibilities.

Human Organization, a quarterly journal published by the Society for Applied Anthropology (www.sfaa.net), is a leading source of scholarly articles in the field of applied anthropology.

McDonald, James H., ed. *The Applied Anthropology Reader.* Boston: Allyn & Bacon, 2002. A selection of thirty-five readings from leading contemporary applied anthropologists organized around topics such as the anthropology of urban areas, medicine, development, the environment, education, and business.

Podolefsky, Aaron, and Peter Brown. *Applying Cultural Anthropology: An Introductory Reader,* 6th ed. New York: McGraw-Hill, 2003. An excellent collection of readings designed to expose students to how cultural anthropology is put to use in everyday life, including classic pieces such as Laura Bohannan's "Shakespeare in the Bush" and pieces written in the twenty-first century.

Van Willigen, John. *Applied Anthropology: An Introduction,* 3d ed. South Hadley, MA: Bergin & Garvey, 2002. An excellent introduction to the growing field of applied anthropology for students contemplating a non-academic career in anthropology. Topics covered include the history of applied anthropology, various intervention strategies, ethical issues, and anthropology as policy research.

Wulff, Robert, and Shirley Fiske, eds. *Anthropological Praxis: Translating Knowledge into Action.* Boulder, CO: Westview, 1987. A collection of writings by applied anthropologists especially for this volume on how they applied their trade to the solution of specific societal problems. Dealing with cases from both home and abroad, all of the case studies are written in the same format and discuss how anthropologists make a difference.

The Growth of Anthropological Theory

Woman and child in native costume from Ollantaytambo, Peru.

4

AS ANTHROPOLOGISTS BEGAN to accumulate data on different cultures during the mid-nineteenth century, they needed to be able to explain the cultural differences and similarities they found. This desire to account for vast cultural variations gave rise to anthropological theories. A *theory* is a statement that suggests a relationship among phenomena. Theories enable us to reduce reality to an abstract set of principles. These anthropological principles then allow us to make sense out of a variety of ethnographic information from different parts of the world. A good theory is one that can both explain and predict. In other words, theories as models of reality enable us to bring some measure of order to a vastly complex world.

Even when theories remain unproven, they are useful for research, for they can generate *hypotheses* (unproven propositions that can provide a basis for further investigation) to be tested in an empirical research investigation. In testing a hypothesis, it is possible to determine how close the actual findings are to the expected findings. If what is found is consistent with what was expected, the theory will be strengthened; if not, the theory will probably be revised or abandoned. But, either way, the original theory serves the important function of guiding empirical research. Anthropological theory changes as new data become available.

Anthropological theories attempt to answer such questions as "Why do people behave as they do?" and "How do we account for human diversity?" These questions guided nineteenth-century attempts to theorize, and they continue to be relevant today. We will explore—in roughly chronological order—the major theoretical schools of cultural anthropology that have developed since the mid-nineteenth century. Some of the earlier theoretical orientations, such as diffusionism, no longer attract much attention (although the concept of diffusion remains widely accepted today); others, such as evolutionism, have been refined and reworked into something new; and still others, such as functionalism, continue to command some popularity. It is easy, with the advantage of

---

theory   A general statement about how two or more facts are related to one another.

hypothesis   An educated hunch about the relationship among certain variables that guides a research project.

What We Will Learn

- What is a theory and how can it be useful?

- Who have been the important theorists in cultural anthropology since the mid-nineteenth century?

- What theories have anthropologists used to explain cultural differences and similarities among the peoples of the world?

- How can anthropological theory be used to help solve societal problems?

 Click!

For interactive exercises and study aids, Go to **www.ichapters.com**; enter the author name and select your text, then click the Study Help tab to purchase the following online resources:

- **ThomsonNOW** for chapter-specific online tutorials, quizzes, and a personalized study plan

- **Anthropology Resource Center** for interactive maps, modules, videos, and the Applied Anthropology site

- **Thomson Audio Study Products** for a brief overview of the major chapter themes and to test your knowledge with quiz questions

hindsight, to demonstrate the inherent flaws in some of the early theoretical orientations. We should keep in mind, however, that contemporary anthropological theories that appear plausible today have been built on what we learned from those older theories.

EVOLUTIONISM

Trying to account for the vast diversity in human cultures, the first group of early anthropologists, writing during the last half of the nineteenth century, suggested the theory of cultural *evolutionism*. Their basic premise was that all societies pass through a series of distinct evolutionary stages. We find differences in contemporary cultures because they are at different evolutionary stages of development. This theory, developed by Edward Tylor in England and Lewis Henry Morgan in the United States, placed Euro-American cultures at the top of the evolutionary ladder and "less-developed" cultures on the lower rungs. The evolutionary process was thought to progress from simpler (lower) forms to increasingly more complex (higher) forms of culture. Thus, the "primitive" societies at the bottom of the evolutionary ladder had only to wait an indeterminable length of time before eventually (and inevitably) rising to the top. It was assumed that all cultures would pass through the same set of preordained evolutionary stages.

Though this evolutionary scheme appears terribly ethnocentric by today's standards, we must remember that it replaced the prevailing theory that explained the existence of small-scale, preliterate societies by claiming that they were composed of people whose ancestors had fallen from God's grace. Hunters and gatherers, it had been argued previously, possessed simple levels of technology because their degeneration had made them intellectually inferior to peoples with greater technological complexity.

While Tylor (1832–1917) was writing in England, Morgan (1818–1881) was founding the evolutionary school in the United States. Morgan, who was a lawyer in Rochester, New York, was hired to represent the neighboring Iroquois Indians in a land grant dispute. After the lawsuit was resolved, Morgan conducted an ethnographic study of the Seneca Indians (an Iroquois group). Fascinated by the Senecas' matrilineal kinship system, Morgan circulated questionnaires and traveled around the United States gathering information about kinship systems among native North Americans and elsewhere in the world. This kinship research—which may

be Morgan's most enduring contribution to the comparative study of culture—was published in his *Systems of Consanguinity and Affinity* in 1871.

Six years later Morgan wrote his famous book, *Ancient Society* (1877). In keeping with the general tenor of the times, he developed a system of classifying cultures to determine their evolutionary niche. Morgan, like Tylor, used the categories of *savagery*, *barbarism*, and *civilization* but was more specific in defining them according to the presence or absence of certain technological features. Subdividing the stages of savagery and barbarism into three distinct subcategories (lower, middle, and upper), Morgan defined seven evolutionary stages—through which all societies allegedly passed—in the following way:

1. *Lower savagery:* From the earliest forms of humanity subsisting on fruits and nuts.

2. *Middle savagery:* Began with the discovery of fishing technology and the use of fire.

3. *Upper savagery:* Began with the invention of the bow and arrow.

4. *Lower barbarism:* Began with the advent of pottery making.

5. *Middle barbarism:* Began with the domestication of plants and animals in the Old World and irrigation cultivation in the New World.

6. *Upper barbarism:* Began with the smelting of iron and use of iron tools.

7. *Civilization:* Began with the invention of the phonetic alphabet and writing (1877: 12).

The theories of Tylor and Morgan have been criticized by succeeding generations of anthropologists for being ethnocentric, because they concluded that Western societies represented the highest levels of human achievement. Also, they have been criticized for being armchair speculators, putting forth grand schemes to explain cultural diversity based on fragmentary data at best. Although there is considerable substance to these criticisms, we must evaluate the nineteenth-century evolutionists with an eye toward the times in which they were writing. As David Kaplan and Robert Manners (1986: 39–43) remind us, Tylor and Morgan may have overstated their case somewhat because they were trying

---

evolutionism   The nineteenth-century school of cultural anthropology, represented by Tylor and Morgan, that attempted to explain variations in world cultures by the single deductive theory that they all pass through a series of evolutionary stages.

savagery   The first of three basic stages of cultural evolution in the theory of Lewis Henry Morgan; based on hunting and gathering.

barbarism   The middle of three basic stages of a nineteenth-century theory developed by Lewis Henry Morgan holding that all cultures evolve from simple to complex systems: savagery, barbarism, and civilization.

civilization   A term used by anthropologists to describe any society that has cities.

CROSS-CULTURAL MISCUE

Ethnographic research during the twentieth century demonstrated that people from different cultures have very different ways of conceptualizing and making sense of the world around them. These different ways of ordering the world can sometimes lead to cross-cultural misunderstandings.

Most North Americans typically have difficulty adjusting to living and working in other cultures. But when more than one hundred thousand mostly monolingual U.S. troops are deployed as a foreign occupation force in a radically different country such as Iraq, cross-cultural misunderstandings are likely to be rampant. In the aftermath of the 2003 war in Iraq, both American troops and civilian contractors expressed disdain for what they saw as blatant Iraqi dishonesty in their everyday dealings. Brought up to value honesty and straight talk, most Americans fail to appreciate that some other cultures, such as in Iraq, place a higher value on personal and family honor than on transparency. From an Iraqi perspective, if one's honor is threatened, it is far more desirable to preserve honor than to tell the unvarnished truth. Often Iraqis will tell Americans that they understand something when they do not. Americans see this as a lie, while Iraqis see it as a face-saving mechanism designed to preserve their personal honor and dignity. Moreover, many Iraqis learned very effectively during the repressive regime of Saddam Hussein that to express one's true feelings could be hazardous to one's health.

SOURCE: John Tierney, "Letter from the Middle East." *New York Times*, Oct. 22, 2003, p. A-4.

Brown Brothers

Lewis Henry Morgan, a nineteenth-century evolutionist, held that all societies pass through certain distinctive evolutionary stages.

■ Evolutionism was ethnocentric because evolutionists put their own societies at the top.

DIFFUSIONISM

During the late nineteenth and early twentieth centuries, the diffusionists, like the evolutionists, addressed the question of cultural differences in the world but came up with a radically different answer. Evolutionism may have overestimated human inventiveness by claiming that cultural features have arisen in different parts of the world independently of one another, due in large measure to the *psychic unity* of humankind. At the other extreme, *diffusionism* held that humans were essentially uninventive. According to the diffusionists, certain cultural features were invented originally in one or several parts of the world and then spread, through the process of diffusion, to other cultures.

Represented by Grafton Elliot Smith and William James Perry in England and Fritz Graebner and Wilhelm Schmidt in Germany and Austria, diffusionism eventually ran its course by the early part of the twentieth century. To be certain, the diffusionists started with a

to establish what Tylor called "the science of culture," whereby human behavior was explained in terms of secular evolutionary processes rather than supernatural causes.

In defense of Tylor and Morgan, we should acknowledge that they firmly established the notion (on which modern cultural anthropology now rests) that differences in human lifestyles are the result of certain identifiable cultural processes rather than biological processes or divine intervention. Moreover, Morgan's use of techno-economic factors to distinguish among fundamentally different types of cultures remains a viable concept.

Evolutionism in Brief

■ All cultures pass through the same developmental stages in the same order.

■ Evolution is unidirectional and leads to higher (better) levels of culture.

■ A deductive approach is used to apply general theories to explain specific cases.

psychic unity A concept popular among some nineteenth-century anthropologists who assumed that all people when operating under similar circumstances will think and behave in similar ways.

diffusion *See cultural diffusion (Chapter 2, page 36).*

particularly sound anthropological concept—that is, cultural diffusion—and either took it to its illogical extreme or left too many questions unanswered. Few cultural anthropologists today would deny the central role that diffusion plays in the process of culture change. But some of the early diffusionists, particularly Smith and Perry, took this essentially valid concept *ad absurdum* by suggesting that everything found in the world could ultimately be traced back to the early Egyptians. Moreover, even though they collected considerable historical data, the diffusionists were not able to prove primary centers of invention. Nor were the diffusionists able to answer a number of important questions concerning the process of cultural diffusion. For example, when cultures come into contact with one another, what accounts for the diffusion of some cultural items but not others? What conditions are required to bring about diffusion of a cultural item? What determines the rate at which a cultural item spreads throughout a geographic region? Furthermore, diffusionists failed to raise certain important questions, such as why certain traits have arisen in the first place. However, despite these limitations, the diffusionists made a major contribution to the study of comparative cultures: they were the first to point out the need to develop theories dealing with contact and interaction among cultures.

As we have seen, both evolutionists and diffusionists tried to explain why the world was inhabited by large numbers of highly diverse cultures. The evolutionists invoked the principle of evolution as the major explanatory variable. They claimed that the world's cultural diversity resulted from different cultures being at different stages of evolutionary development. The diffusionists proposed a different causal variable to explain the diversity, namely differential levels of cultural borrowing among societies. Although they offered different explanations for the diversity, both schools took a *deductive approach* to the discipline (reasoning from the general to the specific). Each started off with a general principle (either evolution or diffusion) and then used that principle to explain specific cases. The evolutionists and diffusionists based their theories on inadequate data at best. They seemed to be more interested in outlining universal history than in discovering how different people of the world actually lived their lives. This type of genteel armchair speculation was poignantly illustrated by evolutionist Sir James Frazer, who, when asked if he had ever seen any of the people about whom he had written, replied, "God forbid!" (Beattie 1964: 7).

Diffusionism in Brief

- All societies change as a result of cultural borrowing from one another.

- A deductive approach is used, with the general theory of diffusion being applied to explain specific cases of cultural diversity.

- The theory overemphasized the essentially valid idea of diffusion.

AMERICAN HISTORICISM

In the early twentieth century, *American historicism*, which was a reaction to the deductive approach, began under the leadership of Franz Boas (1858–1942). Coming from an academic background in physics and geography, Boas was appalled by what he saw as speculative theorizing masquerading as science. To Boas's way of thinking, anthropology was on the wrong path. Rather than dreaming up large, all-encompassing theories to explain why particular societies are the way they are, Boas wanted to put the discipline on a sound *inductive* footing. That is, Boas planned to start by collecting specific data and then move on to develop general theories. Boas felt that the enormous complexity of factors influencing the development of specific cultures rendered any type of sweeping generalization, such as those proposed by the evolutionists and diffusionists, totally inappropriate. Thus, Boas and his followers insisted on the collection of detailed ethnographic data through fieldwork and at the same time called for a moratorium on theorizing.

Some of Boas's more severe critics claimed that this antitheoretical stance was responsible for retarding the discipline of anthropology as a science. Yet, in retrospect, most commentators would agree that his experience in the areas of physics and mathematics enabled Boas to bring to the young discipline of anthropology both methodological rigor and a sense of how to define problems in scientific terms. Even though Boas himself did little theorizing, he left the discipline on a sound empirical footing so that those who followed him could develop cultural theories.

American historicism   Headed by Franz Boas, a school of anthropology prominent in the first part of the twentieth century that insisted upon the collection of ethnographic data (through direct fieldwork) prior to making cross-cultural generalizations.
inductive approach   The act or process of reasoning involving the development of general theories from the study of a number of specific cases. This approach was insisted on by Franz Boas.

deductive approach   The act or process of reasoning from general propositions to specific cases, used by the cultural anthropologists of the late nineteenth and early twentieth centuries.

The impact Boas had on anthropology is perhaps most eloquently demonstrated by the long list of anthropologists he trained. As the first anthropological guru in the United States, Boas trained virtually the entire first generation of American anthropologists. The list of Boas's students reads like a *Who's Who in Twentieth-Century U.S. Cultural Anthropology:* Margaret Mead, Robert Lowie, Alfred Kroeber, Edward Sapir, Melville J. Herskovits, Ruth Benedict, Paul Radin, Jules Henry, E. Adamson Hoebel, and Ruth Bunzel.

In recruiting graduate students to study anthropology with him at Columbia University, Boas, from the beginning, was very purposeful about attracting women to the discipline. Recognizing that male fieldworkers would be excluded from observing certain aspects of a culture because of their gender, Boas felt that the discipline needed both male and female ethnographers if total cultures were to be described. Today, compared to other academic disciplines, cultural anthropology has been producing more female professionals than males, a legacy that can be traced back to Boas's methodological concerns when the discipline was in its formative period. According to data provided by the American Anthropological Association, for every year since 1983, women have written more doctoral dissertations in cultural anthropology than men; and by 2003, women accounted for 62 percent of all new degrees granted in the discipline (Coates 2005: 29).

American Historicism in Brief

- Ethnographic facts must precede the development of cultural theories (induction).
- Any culture is partially composed of traits diffused from other cultures.
- Direct fieldwork is absolutely essential.
- Each culture is, to some degree, unique.
- Ethnographers should try to get the view of those being studied (emic), not their own view (etic).

FUNCTIONALISM

While Franz Boas was putting anthropology on a more empirical footing in the United States, Bronislaw Malinowski (1884–1942) was proceeding inductively by establishing a tradition of first-hand data collection in the United Kingdom. Like Boas, Malinowski was a strong advocate of fieldwork. Both men insisted on learning the local language and trying to understand a culture from an insider's perspective. They differed, however, in that Malinowski had no interest in asking how a cultural item got to be the way it is. Believing that little could be learned about the *origins* of small-scale societies,

Franz Boas, the teacher of the first generation of cultural anthropologists in the United States, put the discipline on a firm empirical basis.

During one of the longest uninterrupted fieldwork experiences on record, Bronislav Malinowski not only set the standard for conducting fieldwork but also developed an important new way of looking at cultures known as functionalism.

APPLIED PERSPECTIVE

Trees for Haiti

The Agroforestry Outreach Project (AOP), a reforestation program in Haiti, is an excellent example of how cultural anthropology can contribute to a multimillion-dollar development project (Murray 1984, 1986, 1987). Rapid population growth had created high market demands in Haiti for construction wood and charcoal. The cash-poor Haitian farmers have willingly met this demand by cutting down approximately 50 million trees per year. The effect of this deforestation has been devastating, as it not only denuded the country of trees but also significantly reduced agricultural productivity through soil erosion.

Faced with this rapid deforestation, the U.S. Agency for International Development (USAID) hired Gerald Murray, an anthropologist who had studied land tenure and population growth in Haiti, to direct a reforestation program. Previous reforestation projects in Haiti took a *conservationist* approach, whereby local farmers were rewarded for planting trees and penalized for cutting them down. Moreover, whatever trees were planted were defined as belonging to the general public, not the farmers. Murray, however, took a very unorthodox approach by suggesting that farmers be given seedlings to plant on a cash-crop basis. Wood trees, he argued, were meant to be harvested and sold in much the same way as corn or beans. Murray based this radical assumption on his previous research that showed Haitian farmers to be aggressive cash-croppers. Murray wanted to capitalize on this strong tradition of crop marketing by making wood trees just one more crop to be sold or traded.

Anthropologist Murray had three formidable barriers to overcome: He had to convince local farmers that the seedlings could mature in four years' time, that it was feasible to plant trees along with their food crops, and that whatever trees they grew on their land did, in fact, belong to them. Once he had convinced an initial group to participate in the tree-planting program, Murray's project

---

Malinowski concentrated on exploring how contemporary cultures operated or functioned. This theoretical orientation, known as *functionalism*, assumed that cultures provided various means for satisfying both societal and individual needs. According to Malinowski, no matter how bizarre a cultural item might at first appear, it had a meaning and performed some useful function for the well-being of the individual or the society. The job of the fieldworker is to become sufficiently immersed in the culture and language to be able to identify these functions.

Not only do all aspects of a culture have a function, but, according to Malinowski, they are also related to one another. This functionalist tenet is no better illustrated than in Malinowski's own description of the kula ring, a system of trade found among the Trobriand Islanders (see Chapter 8). The kula not only performs the function of distributing goods within the society but is related to many other areas of Trobriand culture—including political structure, magic, technology, kinship,

functionalism/functional theory A theory of social stratification holding that social stratification exists because it contributes to the overall well-being of a society.

Professor Gerald Murray, University of Florida, Gainsville

Working for USAID, anthropologist Gerald Murray applied what he knew about Haitian farmers to make the nationwide reforestation project wildly successful.

met with unprecedented success. The project, which lasted from 1981 to 1985, had set for itself the goal of having six thousand farmers plant 3 million trees. When the project ended, some 20 million trees had been planted by seventy-five thousand farmers! This reforestation project in Haiti was significant because it drew heavily on anthropological insights. That is, an understanding of the highly individualistic land tenure system of Haitian farmers, as well as their entrepreneurial nature, led to the decision to design a program based on a free enterprise (cash-cropping) model.

Murray admits that the project design was also directly affected by cultural evolutionary theory. Cultural evolutionists remind us that for the overwhelming majority of prehistory, humans, who were hunters and gatherers, faced food shortages. If hunters and gatherers became too efficient in exploiting their environments, they would eventually destroy their sources of food (wild plants and animals). The cultural evolutionists also remind us that this age-old problem of food shortages was not solved eventually by a conservationist's approach to the problem but rather by domesticating plants and animals. In other words, a quantum leap in the world's food supplies occurred when people began to produce food

(around ten thousand years ago) rather than rely on what nature had to offer.

Murray saw the connections between tree planting in Haiti and the evolutionary theory of the origins of agriculture. He rejected the conservationist approach, which would have called for raising the consciousness of peasant farmers about the ecological need for conserving trees. Instead, he reasoned that trees will reemerge in Haiti when people start planting them as a harvestable crop, in much the same way that food supplies were dramatically increased with the introduction of agriculture. Thus, the *theory* of plant domestication—arising from the anthropological study of the beginnings of agriculture—held the key to the solution of Haiti's tree problem.

Questions for Further Thought

1. How did an anthropologist contribute to the huge success of the reforestation project in Haiti?
2. What difficulties would the project have encountered if it had used a conservationist approach?
3. What applied anthropology role (discussed in the previous chapter) did Murray play?

social status, myth, and social control. To illustrate, the kula involves the exchange of both ceremonial necklaces and bracelets and everyday commodities between trading partners on a large number of islands. Even though the exchanges are based on the principle of reciprocity, usually long periods of time elapse between repayments made by trading partners. Alvin Gouldner (1960: 174) has suggested that during these periods debtors are morally obligated to maintain peaceful relationships with their benefactors. If this is the case, we can see how the kula ring maintains peace and thereby functions as a mechanism of social control as well as a medium of material exchange. Thus, by examining a cultural feature (such as the kula ring) in greater depth, the ethnographer, according to this functionalist perspective, will begin to see how it is related to many other aspects of the culture and what it contributes to individuals and society as a whole.

Another form of functionalism was developed by the British anthropologist Alfred Reginald Radcliffe-Brown (1881–1955). Like Malinowski, Radcliffe-Brown held that the various aspects of a society should be studied in terms of the functions they perform. Whereas Malinowski viewed functions mostly as meeting the needs of the individual, Radcliffe-Brown saw them in terms of contributions to the well-being of the society.

Because of this emphasis on social functions rather than individual functions, Radcliffe-Brown's theory has taken the name *structural functionalism*.

The functionalist approach, most closely associated with Malinowski and Radcliffe-Brown, is based on two fundamental principles. First, the notion of *universal functions* holds that every part of a culture has a function. For example, the function of a hammer is to drive nails into wood, the function of a belief in an omnipotent god is to control people's behavior, and the function of shaking hands in the United States is to communicate nonverbally one's intentions to be friendly. The second principle, known as *functional unity*, states that a culture is an integrated whole composed of

structural functionalism   A school of cultural anthropology, associated most closely with Radcliffe-Brown, that examines how parts of a culture function for the well-being of the society.

universal functions   A functionalist idea holding that every part of a culture has a particular function.

functional unity   A principle of functionalism stating that a culture is an integrated whole consisting of a number of interrelated parts.

a number of interrelated parts. As a corollary to this second principle, it follows that if the parts of a culture are interconnected, then a change in one part of the culture is likely to produce change in other parts.

Once functionalism was accepted into the discipline of anthropology, it appears that the functionalist anthropologists were distracted from reevaluating and revising their theory by the overwhelming demands of ethnographic field research. Even though anthropologists such as Malinowski and Radcliffe-Brown fought vigorously for the acceptance of the functionalist approach, the most effective revisions of functionalist theory have come from sociologists, most notably Robert Merton. For example, in his influential book *Social Theory and Social Structure* (1957), Merton suggests that although every cultural item may have a function, it would be premature to assume that every item *must* have a function. As a result, Merton proposed the notion of *dysfunction* as a source of stress or imbalance in a cultural system. According to Merton, whether a cultural trait is functional or dysfunctional can be resolved only by empirical research.

In addition, Merton took issue with the notion of functional unity. Although he fully recognized that all societies have some degree of functional integration, he could not accept the very high degree of interconnectedness suggested by the early British functionalists. Merton's more moderate views on the issue of functional unity are, at least in part, the result of his being a sociologist. Merton warns against applying extreme functionalist assumptions (which may be more valid for the small-scale, undifferentiated societies that anthropologists tend to study) to the large, complex societies that are most often studied by sociologists.

Functionalism in Brief

- Through direct fieldwork, anthropologists seek to understand how the parts of contemporary cultures contribute to the well-being of the individual and the society.

- Society is like a biological organism with many interconnected parts.

- With this high level of integration, societies tend to be in a state of equilibrium; a change in one part of the system brings change in other parts.

- Empirical fieldwork is absolutely essential.

- The existing institutional structure of any society performs indispensable functions without which the society could not continue.

dysfunction   The notion that some cultural traits can cause stress or imbalance within a cultural system.

© Laura Dwight/Corbis

Psychological anthropologists art interested in questions such as how the television-watching habits of children affect their personality structure, and how these personalities affect other parts of the culture.

PSYCHOLOGICAL ANTHROPOLOGY

As early as the 1920s, American anthropologists became interested in the relationship between culture and the individual. Radcliffe-Brown, warning against what he called psychological reductionism, looked almost exclusively to social structure for his explanations of human behavior. A number of Boas's students, however, were asking some theoretically powerful questions: What part do personality variables play in human behavior? Should personality be viewed as a part of the cultural system? If personality variables are part of culture, how are they causally related to the rest of the system? Wanting to relate some of the insights of Gestalt and Freudian psychology to the study of culture, the early psychological anthropologists looked at child-rearing practices and personality from a cross-cultural perspective. They held that child-rearing practices (which are an integral part of a culture) help shape the personality structure of the individual, which in turn influences the culture. Thus, they saw an interactive relationship among child-rearing practices, personality structure, and culture.

Although best known for his linguistic research, Edward Sapir (1884–1934) was very interested in the area of culture and personality. Individuals learn their cultural patterns unconsciously, Sapir suggested, in much the same way that they learn their language. Rejecting the notion that culture exists above the individual, Sapir believed that the true locus of culture could be found within the interaction of individuals. Even though Sapir did no direct fieldwork himself in this area of culture and personality, his writings and lectures stimulated interest in this topic among other anthropologists, most notably Ruth Benedict and Margaret Mead. Adherents of *psychological anthropology*, which studies the relationship between culture and personality, would be interested in such questions as "How do the TV-watching habits of U.S. children affect children's personality structures?" and "How do these personality structures, in turn, affect other parts of the culture?"

Margaret Mead (1901–1978), a student of both Benedict and Boas, was one of the earliest and most prolific writers in the field of culture and personality. After completing her graduate training under Boas at Columbia University, Mead became fascinated with the general topic of the emotional disruption that seemed to accompany adolescence in the United States. Psychologists at the time maintained that the stress and emotional problems found among American adolescents were a biological fact of life and occurred at puberty in all societies. But Mead wanted to know whether this emotional turbulence was the result of being an adolescent or of being an adolescent in the United States. In 1925 she left for Samoa to try to determine whether the strains of adolescence were universal (that is, biologically based) or varied from one culture to another. In her first book, *Coming of Age in Samoa* (1928), Mead reported that the permissive family structure and relaxed sexual patterns among Samoans were responsible for a calm adolescence. Thus, she concluded that the emotional turbulence found among adolescents in the United States was culturally rather than biologically based.

From the turbulence of adolescence, Mead next turned to the question of gender roles. Based on her research among the Arapesh, Tchambuli, and Mundugumor of New Guinea, she attempted to demonstrate that there were no universal temperaments that were exclusively masculine or feminine. More specifically, Mead reported that among the Arapesh, both men and women had what Westerners would consider feminine temperaments (that is, nurturing, cooperative, nonaggressive, maternal); both Mundugumor men and

© Ken Heyman/Woodfin Camp & Associates

Margaret Mead devoted much of her long and distinguished career in anthropology to the study of how culture affects the process of growing up.

women displayed exactly the opposite traits (that is, ruthless, aggressive, violent demeanors), whereas among the Tchambuli there was a complete reversal of the male–female temperaments found in North American culture. Based on these findings, Mead concluded in her *Sex and Temperament in Three Primitive Societies* (1935) that our own Western conception of masculine and feminine is not genetically based but rather is culturally determined.

Fifty years after its publication, and five years after her death, Mead's *Coming of Age in Samoa* was at the center of a major controversy in cultural anthropology. Australian anthropologist Derek Freeman, who had worked in other parts of Samoa since the 1940s, published a major factual, methodological, and theoretical challenge to Mead's findings in 1984. He claimed that, based on his findings, many of Mead's assertions were ideologically distorted at best or "preposterously false" at worst.

The controversy following the publication of Freeman's book (which continued for years and was at times deafening) put cultural anthropology in an embarrassing position. If, as anthropologists claim, direct

psychological anthropology   The sub-discipline of anthropology that looks at the relationships among cultures and such psychological phenomena as personality, cognition, and emotions.

(hands-on) fieldwork gives an accurate picture of reality, then how can we reconcile two such different interpretations of the same culture? Was one of the founding parents of modern cultural anthropology either incompetent or intellectually dishonest?

Despite the hundreds of thousands of words written and spoken on the controversy, the discipline of cultural anthropology learned some valuable lessons. It is possible that both Margaret Mead and Derek Freeman could be mostly correct, provided that we keep in mind some important anthropological principles. Because Mead collected her data in the 1920s and Freeman collected his in the 1960s, it is possible that both Samoan society and U.S. society had grown more similar in terms of sexual permissiveness during the intervening four decades. Mead was making a comparison between Samoans and middle-class North Americans at a time when extra-marital sex was uncommon in the United States. By the time Freeman came along in the 1960s, Samoa had been westernized and missionized while the United States was becoming more sexually liberated. Moreover, some of the differences in findings can be explained by the fact that Mead conducted her fieldwork in American Samoa while Freeman conducted his in Western Samoa. These variations in both time and location should serve as a reminder that we need to look more closely at the spatial and temporary contexts of our field research and the data derived from it.

Despite these criticisms leveled by Freeman, Mead's major contribution to anthropological theory was her demonstration of the importance of cultural rather than biological conditioning. Moreover, she popularized the discipline of cultural anthropology and served as a role model for many women who subsequently became anthropologists.

Psychological Anthropology in Brief

- Anthropologists need to explore the relationships between psychological and cultural variables.
- Personality is largely the result of cultural learning.
- Universal temperaments associated with males and females do not exist.

NEOEVOLUTIONISM

As we have seen, Franz Boas and others were extremely critical of the nineteenth-century evolutionists, in part because they were accustomed to making sweeping generalizations based on inadequate data. Despite these criticisms, however, no one, including Boas himself, was able to demonstrate that cultures do *not* develop or evolve in certain ways over time.

As early as the 1930s, Leslie White (1900–1975), a cultural anthropologist trained in the Boasian tradition, resurrected the theories of the nineteenth century-evolutionists. It was White's position that Tylor and

Morgan had developed a useful theory. Their major shortcoming was that they lacked the data to demonstrate it. Like Tylor and Morgan, White believed that cultures evolve from simple to increasingly more-complex forms and that cultural evolution is as real as biological evolution. White's unique contribution was to suggest the cause (or driving force) of evolution, which he called his "basic law of evolution." According to White (1959: 368–369), "Culture evolves as the amount of energy harnessed per capita per year increases or as the efficiency of the means of putting energy to work is increased."

According to White's *neoevolutionism*, culture evolves when people are able to increase the amount of energy under their control. For most of human prehistory, while people were hunters and gatherers, the major source of energy was human power. But with the invention of agriculture, animal domestication, the steam engine, the internal combustion engine, and nuclear power, humans have been able to dramatically increase the levels of energy at their disposal. To illustrate, the daily average energy output for a healthy man is a small fraction of a horsepower per day; the amount of energy produced from a kilo of uranium in a nuclear reactor is approximately 33 billion horsepower! For White, the significant equation was $C = E \times T$, where C is culture, E is energy, and T is technology. Cultural evolution, in other words, is caused by advancing levels of technology and a culture's increasing capacity to "capture energy."

Another anthropologist who rejected the particularist orientation of Franz Boas in the mid-twentieth century was Julian Steward. Like White, Steward was interested in the relationship between cultural evolution and adaptation to the environment. But White's approach—which focused on the whole of human culture—was far too general for Steward. Even though Steward rejected Boasian particularism, he was equally unaccepting of approaches that were overly abstract. For Steward the main problem with White's theory was that it cannot explain why some cultures evolve by "capturing energy" whereas others do not. One way of characterizing the difference between these two prominent neoevolutionists is that White was interested in the broad concept of culture and Steward was more interested in developing propositions about specific cultures or groups of cultures.

Steward distinguished among three different types of evolutionary thought. First, there is *unilinear evolution*

neoevolutionism   A twentieth-century school of cultural anthropology, represented by White and Steward, that attempted to refine the earlier evolutionary theories of Tylor and Morgan.

unilinear evolution   A theory held by anthropologists such as Tylor and Morgan attempting to place particular cultures into specific evolutionary phases.

According to the neoevolutionist theory of Leslie White, a society that produces nuclear power has reached an advanced stage of cultural evolution.

© Tim Wright/Corbis

(Tylor and Morgan), which attempts to place particular cultures into certain evolutionary stages. Second, Steward called White's approach *universal evolution* because it is concerned with developing laws that apply to culture as a whole. In contrast to these two earlier forms of evolutionism, Steward called his own form *multilinear evolution*, which focuses on the evolution of specific cultures without assuming that all cultures follow the same evolutionary process.

Steward held that by examining sequences of change in different parts of the world, one could identify paths of development and some limited causal principles that would hold true for a number of societies. To test out his formulation, Steward selected areas of the world that had produced complex societies (civilizations), such as Egypt and the Middle East in the Old World and Mexico and Peru in the New World. In all of these cases, Steward tried to show certain recurring developmental sequences from earliest agriculture up through large, complex urbanized societies. For example, in all of these areas, people were faced with dry environments that required them to develop methods of irrigation to obtain water for farming.

Steward's approach was based on analysis of the interaction between culture and environment. He argued that people who face similar environmental challenges (such as arid or semiarid conditions) are likely to develop similar technological solutions, which, in turn, lead to the parallel development of social and political institutions. Even though environment is a key variable in Steward's theory, he was not an environmental determinist, for he recognized the variety of human responses to similar environmental conditions. By focusing on the relationship among people, environment, and culture, Steward was the first and leading proponent of the study of *cultural ecology*.

Neoevolutionism in Brief

- Cultures evolve in direct proportion to their capacity to harness energy.
- Culture is shaped by environmental conditions.
- Through culture, human populations continuously adapt to techno-environmental conditions.
- Because technological and environmental factors shape culture, individual (personality) factors are de-emphasized.

universal evolution   White's approach to cultural evolution, which developed laws that apply to culture as a whole and argued that all human societies pass through similar stages of development.

multilinear evolution   Mid-twentieth-century anthropological theory of Julian Steward, who suggested that specific cultures can evolve independently of all others even if they follow the same evolutionary process.

cultural ecology   An approach to the study of anthropology that assumes that people who reside in similar environments are likely to develop similar technologies, social structures, and political institutions.

FRENCH STRUCTURALISM

No single theoretical orientation is as closely associated with a single person as *French structuralism* is associated with Claude Lévi-Strauss (1908–). Although both Radcliffe-Brown and Lévi-Strauss are called structuralists, their approaches to cultural analysis are vastly different. Whereas Radcliffe-Brown focused on identifying how the parts of a society function as a systematic whole, Lévi-Strauss concentrated on identifying the mental structures that undergird social behavior. For Lévi-Strauss, ethnology tends to be more psychological or cognitive than sociological.

The approach taken by Lévi-Strauss draws heavily on the science of linguistics. After assuming for decades that language is purely a learned response, many linguists in recent years have hypothesized that basic grammatical structures are preprogrammed in the human mind. Likewise, Lévi-Strauss argues that certain codes programmed into the human mind are responsible for shaping cultures. Cultural differences occur, according to Lévi-Strauss, because these inherent mental codes are altered by environment and history. Although he recognizes these surface differences, Lévi-Strauss suggests that in the final analysis the mental structure of all humans is essentially the same. Although the content of a cultural element may vary from one society to another, the structure of these elements is limited by the very nature of the human mind. In essence, Lévi-Strauss has reintroduced his own version of the psychic unity of humankind.

One of the basic characteristics of the human mind for Lévi-Strauss is that it is programmed to think in *binary oppositions*, or opposites. All people have a tendency to think in terms of pairs of opposites such as male–female, hot–cold, old–young, night–day, and right–left. It is these dichotomies that give shape to culture. Consider, for example, Lévi-Strauss's interpretation of totemism, a belief system found in many parts of the world that states a relationship between social groupings (such as clans or lineages) and aspects of the natural world (such as plants or animals). Lévi-Strauss suggests that totemic beliefs are complex mental devices that enable people to classify the units of their culture and relate them to the natural world.

Lévi-Strauss's structuralism has been criticized for being overly abstract. Because his theories, often brilliantly creative, are not susceptible to empirical testing, many anthropologists have rejected them. Even though

© Bassouls Sophie/Corbis Sygma

Claude Lévi-Strauss is closely associated with the theoretical orientation known as French Structuralism.

French structuralism does not appeal to the more empirically oriented anthropologists, Lévi-Strauss has made a major contribution by directing our attention to the relationship between culture and cognition. Moreover, he has focused on the grand questions that anthropologists, in their modern day quest for specialization, have largely abandoned: How does the human mind work? Even with the world's vast cultural variations, is there a psychic unity for all of humankind? In all likelihood, Lévi-Strauss will be remembered not for developing theories that help to explain the real world but rather for prodding other researchers to generate more imaginative hypotheses, which can then be tested through empirical research.

French Structuralism in Brief

- Human cultures are shaped by certain preprogrammed codes of the human mind.
- Theory focuses on the underlying principles that generate behavior rather than the observable empirical behavior itself.
- Theory emphasizes repetitive structures rather than sociocultural change.
- Rather than examining attitudes, values, and beliefs, structural anthropologists concentrate on what happens at the unconscious level.
- It is assumed that the human mind categorizes phenomena in terms of binary oppositions.

French structuralism   A theoretical orientation holding that cultures are the product of unconscious processes of the human mind.

binary oppositions   A mode of thinking found in all cultures, according to Claude Lévi-Strauss, based on opposites, such as old–young, hot–cold, and left–right.

ETHNOSCIENCE

The theoretical approach of Lévi-Strauss is similar in several significant respects to that of the ethnoscientists, a small but vocal group of American cultural anthropologists who gained fleeting recognition during the 1950s and 1960s. For example, both approaches draw on a linguistic model, seek explanations in the human mind, and view human behavior from a logical or rational perspective. However, the methods used are radically different. Whereas the French structuralists would infer mental structures or codes from cultural traits, ethnoscientists attempt to understand a culture from the point of view of the people themselves. Proponents of *ethnoscience* include Ward Goodenough (1956) and William Sturtevant (1964).

In an effort to make ethnographic description more accurate than in the past, ethnoscientists try to describe a culture in terms of how it is perceived, ordered, and categorized by the members of that culture (an emic approach) rather than by imposing the categories of the ethnographer (an etic approach). To illustrate, traditionally Western ethnographers used categories from their own cultures for describing another culture. Whereas most middle-class North Americans would divide all of the items in the fresh produce department of a supermarket into either fruits or vegetables, people from some other cultures would not. Whereas English speakers have different words for turquoise, aqua, and green, other cultures might include them all under a single color term, and still others would have thirty or more different words for various shades of blues and greens. Whereas some cultures have different linguistic categories for mother's brother's daughter and mother's sister's daughter, in the United States these two family members are lumped together under the single kinship category of *cousin*. Thus, the primary aim of ethnoscience is to identify the implicit rules, principles, and codes that people use to classify the things and events in their world.

Ethnoscientists have been criticized on several fronts. First, though admitting that it may be desirable to get the natives' viewpoint, some anthropologists feel that one's own conditioning and preconceptions make it impossible to get into the minds of culturally different people. Second, even if it is possible to understand another culture from the natives' point of view, how does one communicate one's findings to others in one's own linguistic/cultural group? Third, if every ethnographer described specific cultures using native categories, there would be little or no basis for comparing different societies. And fourth, ethnoscience is extremely time-consuming. To

---

ethnoscience A theoretical school popular in the 1950s and 1960s that tries to understand a culture from the point of view of the people being studied.

CROSS-CULTURAL MISCUE

A major legacy of the ethnoscientists is that they remind us to use the native categories (emic view) when trying to understand people from another culture. We can get ourselves into trouble if we assume that people from different cultures categorize the world around them exactly as we do. This point is well illustrated in the following cross-cultural misunderstanding.

Harold Josephson, an electronics engineer, had spent weeks negotiating with a Japanese parts distributor in Yokohama. The Japanese executive, Mr. Kushiro, was tough in the negotiations, so progress had been slow. Eventually, Josephson felt that they had found common ground and an equitable deal could be worked out to the advantage of both companies. On the final day of negotiations, Josephson was pleased to announce to Kushiro that their thinking on the contract negotiations was parallel. Kushiro pleasantly thanked Josephson for his time and left the meeting without further discussion.

What Josephson failed to realize is that the word *parallel* has a different meaning to Japanese than it does to Americans. We think of the word *parallel* as meaning compatible, proceeding on the same track, going in the same direction, or being in agreement. However, to the Japanese, *parallel* represents a lack of agreement—positions that will always remain apart, never to meet, as with two train tracks. When Josephson stated that their thinking was "parallel," Kushiro mistakenly thought that Josephson was saying that they would never come to agreement.

---

date, ethnoscientific studies have been completed on very limited domains of culture, such as kinship terms or color categories. The completion of an ethnoscientific study of a total culture would, no doubt, be beyond the time capabilities of a single ethnographer. Despite its impracticality, the ethnoscientific approach has served as a useful reminder of a fundamentally sound anthropological principle: People from different cultural and linguistic backgrounds organize and categorize their worlds in essentially different ways.

Ethnoscience in Brief

- This theory attempts to make ethnographic description more accurate and replicable.

- Ethnoscience describes a culture by using the categories of the people under study rather than by imposing categories from the ethnographer's culture.

- Because it is time-consuming, ethnoscience has been confined to describing very small segments of a culture.

- It is difficult to compare data collected by ethnoscientists.

APPLIED PERSPECTIVE

The New Hope Antipoverty Program

As pointed out in Chapter 3, it is misleading to think of all cultural anthropology as being either applied or pure. In reality, applied anthropologists use theoretical propositions to guide their research, while pure or academic anthropologists are informed by practical studies. A particularly good example of the use of theory to guide an applied study was a research project conducted by Christina Gibson and Tom Weisner (2002) evaluating the New Hope antipoverty program in Milwaukee, Wisconsin.

© Andrew Holbrooke/The ImageWorks

Based on the notion of "workfare" rather than "welfare," the New Hope program offered participants a package of benefits in exchange for a demonstrated work effort. If participants worked thirty hours per week, the program would make available to them wage subsidies, child-care subsidies, health insurance, and even temporary community service jobs. Like many welfare programs established since the mid-1990s, the Milwaukee program was predicated on "rational choice theory," which stipulates that people make decisions based on an objective cost-benefit analysis. In other words, people will avail themselves of the benefits offered by the program if the benefits outweigh the costs. Rational choice theory, however, rests on the assumptions of materialism, maximizing

one's financial gain, and self-interest; that is, a person will opt for health insurance or a child-care subsidy because it makes financial sense to do so. Gibson and Weisner, however, found that the extent to which program participants opted for the benefits package varied greatly from family to family. The purely economic incentives of the program were too narrow to motivate all of the participants.

Typically, evaluation research on social service programs such as New Hope is conducted by using survey methods. Although Gibson and Weisner used demographic and opinion surveys for both their experiment and control groups, they also used participant-observation as the basis for an ethnographic study of forty-six participating families. These urban ethnographers listened to parents tell their stories over meals, visited the children's schools, and accompanied the families to church, family visits, and shopping trips. By combining the quantitative survey data with the more qualitative information gained through participant-observation, Gibson and Weisner were able to use participants' own words to understand why they opted for some benefits and not others.

Testing of the rational choice theory in this program evaluation research led the researchers to suggest another theory to

FEMINIST ANTHROPOLOGY

Feminist anthropology developed alongside the wider women's movement in the 1960s and 1970s. Even though anthropology, since its beginnings, has been more gender equal than most academic disciplines, the feminist critique centered on the fact that anthropology has been androcentric (male-centered). They argued that, although some anthropologists were women, the women in those societies studied by anthropologists were often neglected as objects of study. Even when women were put under the anthropological lens, they were often portrayed as passive objects (such as in bridewealth transactions), rather than as prime players in the mainstream of social life.

As a long-overdue corrective to this neglect, marginalization, and misrepresentation of women in anthropology, *feminist anthropology* called for a systematic reanalysis of the role women play in the social structure. As recounted by Micaela di Leonardo (1991: 8), feminist anthropologists in the 1970s responded enthusiastically

to the challenge of reanalyzing and rewriting earlier ethnographies "as if gender really mattered." Feminist anthropologists such as Louise Lamphere (1974), Sherry Ortner (1974), and Michelle Zimbalist Rosaldo (1974), among others, tried to rectify this male bias by focusing on women's positions within society. Many of the early feminist studies concentrated on explaining female subordination (which some scholars saw as a cultural universal). More recent studies, however, have looked at the social construction of gender, variations between different groups of women, and how gender influences economic, political, and social power.

Although feminist anthropology is quite diverse in terms of areas of investigation and theoretical indebtedness, a number of basic features are generally agreed upon. First, feminist anthropology takes as a given that gender is an important, albeit previously neglected, variable when studying any aspect of cultural life. That is, just as economics, politics, and religion vary according to status, class, power, and age, they also vary according to gender. Second, the feminist critique rejects *positivism*,

---

feminist anthropology   A theoretical approach that seeks to describe and explain cultural life from the perspective of women.

positivism   A philosophical system based on observable scientific facts and their relationship to one another.

partially explain their findings, which they call an "ecocultural theory." Rational choice theory does not take into account beliefs, emotions, or other cultural factors. Availing oneself of program benefits is not just a matter of maximizing one's material benefits, as the rational choice theory would suggest. Instead, Gibson and Weisner found that some people made choices on program benefits based on whether they thought the benefit would sustain their daily routine. Others used a cost-benefit analysis but didn't define costs in largely materialistic or financial terms. For them, costs included nonfinancial factors such as family well-being, their children's mental health, or the effects on other social relationships. The researchers concluded that if we are to understand why participants opted for some program features and not others, it is imperative that we use a wider theoretical model than the rational choice theory. They acknowledge that rational choice is involved in the decision-making process of low-income families but argue that the rational choice model does not account for all of the choices made. What is needed, according to Gibson and Weisner, is to use both rational choice theory (based largely on financial cost-benefit analysis) and ecocultural theory (based on the need to sustain a familiar daily routine).

This study is significant on two levels: theoretical and applied. First, it tested the utility of the widely used rational choice theory to explain behavioral choices in a social service program for low-income families. That the theory, although viable, did not explain all of the behavioral data provides us with an excellent example of how theories can be refined and reworked by means of applied anthropology. On the other hand, this research project also demonstrates the utility of social theory for the applied enterprise of program evaluation. If the New Hope program (or others like it) is to continue to provide services to the poor, administrators will need to know why some people opt for program benefits and others do not. Program implementers should avoid overemphasizing financial motivation and pay closer attention to the sociocultural circumstances of their target populations.

Questions for Further Thought

1. What data-gathering techniques did Gibson and Weisner use in their evaluation research of the New Hope project? In what ways did the different techniques yield different types of information for the researchers?
2. Compare and contrast the two theories used in this study: the rational choice theory and the ecocultural theory.
3. What other government-sponsored programs might benefit by using both theories to evaluate why some people participate and others do not?

because the language of science (i.e., hypotheses, objective measures, generalizations, etc.) is seen as repressive and serving the interests of the elites. Instead, feminist ethnographies are more subjective and collaborative, with the line between the researcher and the subject becoming less distinct. Third, this anti-positivist approach leads to a preference for qualitative methods (based on empathy, subjectivity, and a dialogue between the anthropologist and the informant), so as to eventually better understand the inner world of women. In fact, most feminists would avoid the term *informant* because it implies an unequal relationship between the anthropological "expert" and the subordinate "lay person." Instead, the feminist methodology seeks to eliminate status and power differences between the researcher and the subject, thereby creating a more equal and collaborative relationship. And finally, there is little or no attempt in feminist anthropology to assume a value-neutral position; it is aimed at consciousness-raising and empowerment of women and, in the words of Stanley Barrett (1996: 164), "unapologetically promotes the interests of women."

Annette Weiner (1976) serves as an excellent example of a feminist anthropologist who returned to restudy none other than Malinowski's Trobriand Islanders. According to Malinowski's (1922) original ethnography,

Trobriand men gave gifts of yams at harvest time to their sisters' husbands. Malinowski viewed these gifts as a type of tribute from the girl's family to her husband's family, and thus as a way of consolidating male power, but Weiner (1976) had a very different interpretation. She found that, because the yams are given *in the wife's name*, the gift is as much a symbol of the high value placed on women as it is a symbol of power and status for men. Moreover, because Malinowski paid limited attention to the world of women, he failed to record that this gift of yams had to be reciprocated. Rather than reciprocating to his wife's brother, however, the recipient of the yams was expected to give *directly to his own wife* a unique form of wealth consisting of women's skirts made from banana leaves, which she used in important funeral ceremonies. If the husband failed to provide his wife with these skirts, his own brother-in-law might reduce or eliminate altogether his gift of yams, which would negatively affect the husband's chances of ever becoming a big man (see Chapter 8 for explanation of big men). Thus, in her restudy of Trobriand culture, Annette Weiner was able to show that men were much more dependent on women for their status and power than Malinowski's earlier description would have us believe.

Courtesy of Dr. William E. Mitchell

Anthropologist Annette Weiner with two Trobriand Islanders and harvested yams.

Feminist Anthropology in Brief

- All aspects of culture have a gender dimension that must be considered in any balanced ethnographic description.

- Theory represents a long-overdue corrective to male bias in traditional ethnographies.

- Feminist anthropologists are more subjective and collaborative than objective and scientific.

- Generally, feminist anthropologists do not embrace a value-free orientation.

CULTURAL MATERIALISM

Most closely associated with Marvin Harris (1968, 1979b, 1999), *cultural materialism* is the theoretical position based on the concept that material conditions or modes of production determine human thoughts and behavior. According to this approach, the primary task of anthropology is to provide causal explanations for the similarities and differences in thought and behavior found among human groups. Cultural materialists accomplish this task by studying material constraints that arise from the universal needs of producing food, technology, tools, and shelter. These material con-

cultural materialism A contemporary orientation in anthropology that holds that cultural systems are most influenced by such material things as natural resources and technology.

straints are distinguished from mental constraints, which include such human factors as values, ideas, religion, and aesthetics. Harris and the cultural materialists see the material constraints as the primary causal factors accounting for cultural variations.

Harris has been criticized for devaluing the importance of ideas and political activities as sources of cultural change. But rather than ignoring these nonmaterial factors, Harris suggests that they have a secondary, or less important, role in causing cultural changes and variations: ideas and political ideologies can either accelerate or retard the process of change but are not themselves causes of the change.

Cultural materialists rely heavily on an etic research methodology—that is, one that assumes the viewpoint of the anthropologist rather than the native informant. This research strategy utilizes the scientific method, logical analysis, the testing of hypotheses, measurement, and quantification. Using these scientific methods, cultural materialists attempt to explain the similarities and differences among various sociocultural structures by focusing on the material and economic factors.

Although cultural materialism has much in common with the ideas of Karl Marx (in particular, a materialist interpretation), the two schools should not be equated. Cultural materialists reject the Marxist notion of dialectical materialism, which calls for destroying capitalism and empowering the working class. Cultural materialism, which doesn't have a particular political agenda, is committed to the scientific study of culture. At the same time, Harris is equally critical of cultural idealists, anthropologists who rely on an emic approach (native's

© Jerry Bauer

Marvin Harris, the most prominent advocate of cultural materialism, argued that material conditions determine thoughts and behaviors.

point of view) and use ideas, values, and ideologies as the major explanatory factors. As Harris (1979b) has argued, codes and rules (à la ethnoscientists) are not at all helpful in explaining phenomena such as poverty, underdevelopment, imperialism, population explosions, minorities, ethnic and class conflict, exploitation, taxation, private property, pollution, the military-industrial complex, political repression, crime, urban blight, unemployment, and war.

Cultural Materialism in Brief

- Material conditions determine human thoughts and behavior.
- Theorists assume the viewpoint of the anthropologist, not the native informant.
- Anthropology is seen as scientific, empirical, and capable of generating causal explanations.
- Cultural materialism de-emphasizes the role of ideas and values in determining the conditions of social life.

POSTMODERNISM

For much of the twentieth century, anthropology saw itself as essentially a scientific enterprise. The nineteenth- and early twentieth-century founders of the discipline attempted to put anthropology on a solid scientific footing by offering an alternative to a theological explanation of human behavior. Although many

of the schools of anthropology discussed so far varied between hard and soft scientific approaches, they never abandoned such scientific canons as gathering empirical data, testing hypotheses, looking for cause-and-effect relationships, and adhering to the scientific method. However, in the 1970s and 1980s a number of anthropologists, collectively referred to as postmodernists, questioned the scientific nature of anthropology itself.

Although *postmodernism* means different things to different people, it grew out of the traditions of the structuralists, interpretative anthropology, and feminist anthropology. Essentially, postmodernists dispute the possibility that anthropology can construct a grand theory of human behavior. A basic tenet of postmodernism is that the "modernists" (scientific anthropologists) are extraordinarily arrogant to think that they can describe, interpret, and give meaning to the lives of people from other cultures. The modernists' enterprise for much of the twentieth century, they claim, was based on the privileged status of science (held by most developed countries) and reflected the basic power imbalances between the wealthy, colonial countries and those developing countries where much anthropological research was conducted. It is impossible, they contend, for predominantly White, male, Euro-American anthropologists to step outside of their own culture so as to produce an objective view of another culture.

Rather than attempting to discover the truth about how the world works through empirical investigations, the postmodernists hold that all ethnographic accounts are subjective because they are conditioned by the experiences and personal histories of the ethnographer. Instead of the ethnographer being the sole authority, postmodernists call for a more collaborative approach to the study of culture. Written ethnography should consist of multiple authors, creating a dialogue between the anthropologist and the people being studied. This call for dialogue rather than monologue goes further than the attempts of the ethnoscientists to describe the culture using native categories (emic approach). Rather, it involves relinquishing sole authorship to include the voice of the research subjects themselves. Postmodernists contend that only through this dialogical process will meaning and interpretation emerge.

Another tenet of the postmodernist philosophy involves the rejection of generalizing and developing predictable theories. By emphasizing the uniqueness of every culture, postmodernists view culture as a changing set of individual meanings that require continual reinterpretation. For anthropologists to think that they can single-handedly develop generalizable theories of cul-

postmodernism A school of anthropology that advocates the switch from cultural generalization and laws to description, interpretation, and the search for meaning.

ture that have any level of predictability is both misguided and unethical. It is misguided because it cannot be done. It is unethical because grand theories tend to support the dominant ideology (usually that of the anthropologist) by promoting order and consistency at the expense of individual autonomy and variation. Whereas many of the twentieth-century schools of anthropology assume a scientific posture in which they are searching for generalizations, the postmodernists are more interested in describing and interpreting particular cultures. The postmodernists see cultural anthropology as more of a humanistic enterprise than a scientific one, having more in common with art and literature than with biology or psychology.

Interpretive anthropology, led by Clifford Geertz (1926–2006), is a major force in postmodernism. Rather than searching for general propositions about human behavior, Geertz (1973, 1983) and the interpretive anthropologists take a more descriptive approach by examining how the people themselves interpret their own values and behaviors. Cultures can best be understood by listening and recording the ways in which the natives explain their own customary behavior. Thus, like ethnoscientists, interpretive anthropologists are strongly wedded to the emic, rather than the etic, approach to the discipline. According to Geertz, the job of the anthropologist is not to generate laws or models that will predict human behavior, for these predictive devices tend to ignore the complexity and living qualities of human cultures. Rather, Geertz would have anthropology concentrate on cultural description, literature, folklore, myths, and symbols.

The interpretive orientation is admittedly relativistic and is designed to sensitize anthropologists to their own views and values as well as those of the informant. Geertz advocates combining self-knowledge with knowledge of the people under study so that anthropologists learn something about themselves as they are learning about the culture of the informant. In fact, a reading of a postmodernist ethnography usually reveals as much about the anthropologist as it does about the people being studied. The recent writings of Cuban American anthropologist Ruth Behar of the University of Michigan are an excellent example of what Geertz had in mind for interpretive anthropology.

In her book *Translated Woman: Crossing the Border with Esperanza's Story* (1993), Behar tells how she started her research by listening to the life story of Esperanza, a Mexican woman she had befriended. Before long Behar found that learning about Esperanza's life history was

Professor Clifford Geertz, Institute of Advanced Study, Princeton

Interpretive anthropologist Clifford Geertz advocates a more descriptive approach by examining how the people themselves interpret their own values and behaviors, rather than trying to generate theories about human behavior.

causing her to reflect on her own life. Anthropologist Behar began to question aspects of her own life and work, including the role of the ethnographer, the validity of comparing her life with Esperanza's, and her achievements as an affluent and successful academic. The book, written from an interpretive perspective, turned out to be two life stories rather than one.

The most radical postmodernists contend that because objectivity is impossible and all interpretations are relative, generalizations are unwarranted and anthropology should be treated as literature rather than as science. Very few anthropologists today hold such an extreme view, which would, in effect, reject all of the past attempts to make generalizations about cultural differences and similarities. As one can well imagine, postmodernists have generated many heated discussions with their more traditional, scientifically oriented colleagues. However, even their strongest critics should realize that the postmodernists have raised the consciousness of all anthropologists to consider issues such as how we generate knowledge, how we come to know what we think we know, and whose story we are telling in ethnographic accounts—theirs or ours.

interpretive anthropology A contemporary theoretical orientation holding that the critical aspects of cultural systems are subjective factors such as values, ideas, and worldviews.

Table 4.1 Anthropological Theories and Their Proponents

School	Major Assumption	Advocates
Evolutionism	All societies pass through a series of stages.	Tylor, Morgan
Diffusionism	All societies change as a result of cultural borrowing from one another.	Graebner, Smith
American historicism	Fieldwork must precede cultural theories.	Boas, Kroeber
Functionalism	Task of anthropology is to understand how parts of contemporary cultures contribute to the well-being of individuals.	Malinowski
Structural functionalism	Anthropology's task is to determine how cultural elements function for the well-being of the society.	Radcliffe-Brown
Psychological anthropology	Anthropology's task is to show relationships among psychological and cultural variables.	Benedict, Mead
Neoevolutionism	Cultures evolve in direct proportion to their capacity to harness energy.	White, Steward
French structuralism	Human cultures are shaped by certain preprogrammed codes in the human mind.	Lévi-Strauss
Ethnoscience	Cultures must be described in terms of native categories.	Sturtevant, Goodenough
Feminist anthropology	Social relationships should be viewed as being gendered.	Lamphere, Ortner, and Rosaldo
Cultural materialism	Material conditions determine human consciousness and behavior.	Harris
Postmodernism	Human behavior stems from the way people perceive and classify the world around them.	Geertz

Postmodernism in Brief

- Postmodernism calls on anthropologists to switch from cultural generalization and laws to description, interpretation, and the search for meaning.

- Ethnographies should be written from several voices—that of the anthropologist along with those of the people under analysis.

- Postmodernism involves a distinct return to cultural relativism.

CONCLUDING THOUGHTS ON ANTHROPOLOGICAL THEORY

This chapter was written with distinct subheadings dividing the field of anthropological theory into discrete schools. Table 4.1 summarizes the primary anthropological theories and their proponents. These divisions can serve as a useful device to help track, in general terms, the various emphases that anthropologists have taken since the mid-nineteenth century. However, these schools of anthropology are not particularly relevant categories for distinguishing among the different approaches used by contemporary anthropologists. Few anthropologists today would tie themselves to a single school or theoretical orientation such as neoevolutionist, structuralist, or functionalist.

Contemporary anthropologists tend to be more eclectic and problem oriented, focusing on explaining cultural phenomena while drawing on a wide variety of theories, research methods, and sources of data. Today, it is generally recognized that many of these theoretical schools are not mutually exclusive. It is evident that anthropology is maturing as a discipline when its practitioners reject hard-drawn lines among themselves and thereby enrich one another's thinking. ■

Summary

1. Anthropological theory, which arose from the desire to explain the great cultural diversity in the world, enables us to reduce reality to an abstract, yet manageable, set of principles.

2. The first group of anthropologists used the notion of evolution to account for differences in human cultures. Nineteenth-century evolutionists such as Tylor and Morgan suggested that all societies pass through a series of distinct evolutionary stages. Although they have been criticized by their successors for being overly speculative and ethnocentric in their formulations, these early evolutionists fought and won the battle to establish that human behavior was the result of certain cultural processes rather than biological or supernatural processes.

3. The diffusionists explained cultural differences and similarities in terms of the extent of contact cultures had with one another. The British diffusionists, represented by Smith and Perry, held that all cultural features, wherever they may be found, had their origins in Egypt. The German/Austrian diffusionists, Graebner and Schmidt, took a more methodologically sound approach by examining the diffusion of entire complexes of culture.

4. In contrast to the evolutionists and diffusionists, Boas took a more inductive approach to anthropology, insisting on the collection of firsthand empirical data on a wide range of cultures before developing anthropological theories. Although he has been criticized for not engaging in much theorizing himself, the meticulous attention Boas gave to methodology put the young discipline of anthropology on a solid scientific footing.

5. The British functionalists Malinowski and Radcliffe-Brown, who, like Boas, were strong advocates of fieldwork, concentrated on how contemporary cultures functioned to meet the needs of the individual and perpetuate the society. Not only do all parts of a culture serve a function (universal functions), but they are interconnected (functional unity) so that a change in one part of the culture is likely to bring about change in other parts.

6. The early psychological anthropologists, most notably Benedict and Mead, were interested in exploring the relationships between culture and the individual. By examining the configuration of traits, Benedict described whole cultures in terms of individual personality characteristics. Mead's early research efforts brought her to Samoa to study the emotional problems associated with adolescence and later to New Guinea to study male and female gender roles.

7. The theory of evolution was brought back into fashion during the twentieth century by White and Steward. White, like Tylor and Morgan before him, held that cultures evolve from simple to complex forms, but for White, the process of evolution was driven by his "basic law of evolution" ($C = E \times T$). Steward's major contribution was to introduce the concept of multilinear evolution, a form of evolution of specific cultures that did not assume that all cultures passed through the same stages.

8. Drawing heavily on the models of linguistics and cognitive psychology, Lévi-Strauss maintained that certain codes or mental structures preprogrammed in the human mind are responsible for culture and social behavior. A fundamental tenet of Lévi-Strauss's theory is that the human mind thinks in binary oppositions—opposites that enable people to classify the units of their culture and relate them to the world around them.

9. Like the French structuralism of Lévi-Strauss, the theoretical approach known as ethnoscience is cognitive in that it seeks explanations in the human mind. By distinguishing between the emic and the etic approaches to research, ethnoscientists attempt to describe a culture in terms of how it is perceived, ordered, and categorized by members of that culture rather than by the codes or categories of the ethnographer's culture.

10. As a corrective to a long-standing male bias in anthropological theory, feminist anthropologists call for a systematic analysis of the role women play in the social structure. The feminist critique, by and large, does not embrace positivism, quantitative methods, or a value-neutral orientation.

11. Led by Harris, cultural materialists believe that tools, technology, and material well-being are the most critical aspects of cultural systems.

12. Diametrically opposed to the cultural materialists are the postmodernists, who advocate cultural description and interpretation rather than a search for generalizations and explanatory theories. A major debate in anthropological theory today is taking place between the cultural materialists and the postmodernists.

Key Terms

American historicism

barbarism

binary oppositions

civilization

cultural ecology

cultural materialism

deductive approach

diffusionism

dysfunction

ethnoscience

evolutionism

feminist anthropology

French structuralism

functionalism

functional unity

hypothesis

inductive approach

interpretive anthropology

multilinear evolution

neoevolutionism

postivism

postmodernism

psychic unity

pyschological anthropology

savagery

structural functionalism

theory

unilinear evolution

Suggested Readings

Barnard, Alan. *History and Theory in Anthropology.* Cambridge, U.K.: Cambridge University Press, 2000. A clear and concise discussion of the rise of anthropological theory, complete with a glossary of terms, an extensive bibliography, and an appendix of key theorists.

Barrett, Stanley R. *Anthropology: A Student's Guide to Theory and Method.* Toronto: University of Toronto Press, 1996. Starting with the foundations of anthropology during the nineteenth century, Barrett brings the reader up to date with the current trends of postmodernism and feminist criticism. This is one of the few books that attempts to integrate both anthropological theory and methods.

Bohannan, Paul, and Mark Glazer, eds. *High Points in Anthropology.* 2d ed. New York: Knopf, 1988. This collection of writings dating back to Spencer, Morgan, and Tylor traces the history and development of cultural anthropological thought up to the present time. Each selection is prefaced by editorial background notes on the theorists and their works.

Erickson, Paul A., and Liam Murphy. *A History of Anthropological Theory.* Peterborough, Ontario, Canada: Broadview, 1998. A readable introduction to the history of anthropological thought from ancient times to the postmodernists.

Ferraro, Gary. *Classic Readings in Cultural Anthropology.* Belmont, CA: Wadsworth, 2004. A collection of fifteen classic articles written by some of the founding figures in modern cultural anthropology, including E. E. Evans-Pritchard, Ernestine Friedl, Marvin Harris, Clyde Kluckhohn, and Horace Miner.

Harris, Marvin. *Theories of Culture in Postmodern Times.* Walnut Creek, CA: Altamira, 1999. This is Harris's most recent defense of his cultural materialist orientation in light of the challenges from the postmodernists.

McGee, Jon, and Richard Warms. *Anthropological Theory: An Introductory History.* 3d ed. New York: McGraw-Hill, 2003. A comprehensive collection of nineteenth- and twentieth-century anthropological theories containing excellent introductions and annotations that will be helpful to students.

Methods in Cultural Anthropology

© Tronick/Anthro-Photo

Cultural anthropologist Ed Tronick studies child development among the Efe people of the Ituri Forest, Zaire.

5

A DISTINCTIVE FEATURE OF present-day cultural anthropology is the reliance on fieldwork as the primary way of conducting research. To be certain, cultural anthropologists carry out their research in other contexts as well—such as libraries and museums—but they rely most heavily on experiential fieldwork. Like professionals from any other discipline, cultural anthropologists want to describe the basic subject matter of their discipline. They are interested in documenting the enormous variety of lifeways found among the peoples of the world today. How do people feed themselves? What do they believe? How do they legitimize marriages? In addition to learning the "what" and the "how" of different cultures, cultural anthropologists are interested in explaining why people in different parts of the world behave and think the way they do. To answer these questions by providing both description and explanation, cultural anthropologists collect their data and test their hypotheses by means of *fieldwork*.

As a research strategy, fieldwork is eminently experiential. That is, cultural anthropologists collect their primary data by throwing themselves into the cultures they are studying. This involves living with the people they study, learning their language, asking them questions, surveying their environments and material possessions, and spending long periods of time observing their everyday behaviors and interactions in their natural setting. Doing first-hand fieldwork has become a necessary rite of passage for becoming a professional anthropologist. In fact, it is unusual to receive a Ph.D. in cultural anthropology in the United States without first having conducted fieldwork in a culture or subculture other than one's own.

The strong insistence on direct fieldwork has not always been an integral part of the discipline. Much of the theorizing of nineteenth-century anthropology was based on second-hand data at best, and often on superficial and impressionistic writings of untrained observers. For example, Morgan's classic work *Ancient Society* (1877), discussed in Chapter 4, was based largely on data collected by ships' captains, missionaries, explorers, and others who inadvertently came across cultures in

fieldwork   The practice in which an anthropologist is immersed in the daily life of a culture in order to collect data and test cultural hypotheses.

What We Will Learn

- How do cultural anthropologists conduct fieldwork?

- What types of data-gathering techniques do cultural anthropologists use?

- What are some of the problems faced by cultural anthropologists that make fieldwork somewhat less than romantic?

- What ethical dilemmas do applied anthropologists face when conducting fieldwork?

▶ Click!

The study of everyday life in the state of Bahia in Brazil (above) presents different problems and challenges to the field anthropologist than does the study of village life in Namibia (below).

Cultural anthropologist Steve Winn conducts participant-observation fieldwork in central Africa among the Efe of Zaire.

their travels around the world. It wasn't until the early twentieth century—largely at the suggestion of Boas and Malinowski—that fieldwork became the norm for collecting cultural data. Even though anthropologists have routinely conducted fieldwork for most of the twentieth century, they have not explicitly discussed their field techniques until quite recently.

Before the 1960s, it was usual for an anthropologist to produce a book on "his" or "her" people several years after returning from a fieldwork experience. Nowhere in these books was there an explanation of field methods or of the fieldwork experience itself. The reader had no way of knowing, for instance, how long the investigator stayed in the field, how many people were interviewed and observed, how samples were selected, what data-gathering techniques were used, what problems were encountered, or how the data were analyzed. Because the credibility of any ethnographic study depends on its methodology, cultural anthropologists since the 1960s have been producing some excellent accounts of their own fieldwork experiences. In addition, a number of books and articles have appeared in recent decades

that explore the methodological issues involved in designing a fieldwork study, collecting the data, and analyzing the results.

Whereas early twentieth-century cultural anthropologists concentrated their fieldwork studies on small-scale, non-Western cultures, more recently anthropologists have studied cultures or subcultures closer to home. In recent decades cultural anthropologists have conducted fieldwork in urban ethnic neighborhoods, retirement homes, industrial plants, hospitals, elementary schools, prisons, administrative bureaucracies, and among recreational vehicle owners, to mention but a few. One such ethnographic study, entitled *New Capitalists* (Darian-Smith 2004), explores the emerging cultural identity of Native Americans who have become wealthy in recent years through the casino/gaming industry. Proceeds from the casinos located on reservations throughout the country have resulted in some dramatic improvements in housing, health care, education, and self-esteem among many Native Americans. Moreover, it has led to a new breed of Native American, one that no longer fits the stereotype of poverty, isolation, and marginality. Darian-Smith points out, however, that this new form of Native American capitalism is not a carbon copy of traditional capitalism, nor has it always been graciously accepted on an equal footing with its mainstream counterpart.

Even though cultural anthropologists in recent decades have studied larger, more-complex societies such as our own, they have not abandoned the essential features of ethnographic research. In fact, they have often blended their traditional ethnographic methods with the *survey methods* used by other social sciences, particularly sociology, economics, psychology, and political science. Ethnographic and survey methods differ in a number of important ways. First, ethnographies take a holistic view (see Chapter 1) by studying complete, functioning societies (e.g., an urban neighborhood or a retirement community), while survey research focuses on a representative sampling of a larger population—such as the city of Boston. Second, ethnographies use first-hand, experiential methods, whereas survey researchers have indirect (not face-to-face) contact with their subjects. Third, survey researchers, who work almost exclusively in literate societies, have the luxury of mailing questionnaires to the intended respondents. And finally, because survey researchers are using much larger sample sizes, they rely much more heavily upon statistical analysis than do ethnographers.

Any general discussion of how to do fieldwork is difficult because no two fieldwork situations are the same. The problems encountered while studying the reindeer-herding Chukchee of Siberia would be quite different from those faced when studying hard-core unemployed street people in Philadelphia or rural peasant farmers in Greece. Even studies of the same village by the same anthropologist at two different times involve different experiences because, in the period between the two studies, both the anthropologist and the people being studied have changed.

Despite these differences, all fieldworkers have a number of concerns, problems, and issues in common. For example, everyone entering fieldwork must make many preparations before leaving home, gain acceptance into the community, select the most appropriate data-gathering techniques, understand how to operate within the local political structure, take precautions against investigator bias, choose knowledgeable *informants* (also known as "cultural consultants"), cope with culture shock, learn a new language, and be willing to reevaluate his or her findings in light of new evidence. In this

chapter, we will explore these and other common concerns of the fieldworker, while recognizing that every fieldwork situation has its own unique set of concerns, problems, and issues.

PREPARING FOR FIELDWORK

The popular image of the field anthropologist tends to be overly romanticized. Field anthropologists are often envisioned working in idyllic settings, reclining in their hammocks while being served noncarcinogenic foods by beautiful native people. In reality, conducting anthropological fieldwork bears little resemblance to a carefree vacation. Like any scientific enterprise, it makes serious demands on one's time, patience, and sense of humor and requires a lot of hard work and thoughtful preparation. Although luck can be a factor, the success of a fieldwork experience is usually directly proportional to the thoroughness of one's preparations.

Any fieldwork project lasting a year or more may well require a minimum of a year's preparation. If a fieldwork project is to be successful, the anthropologist must attend to a number of essential matters during this preparatory period. First, because doing fieldwork is expensive, it is necessary to obtain funding from a source that supports anthropological research, such as the Social Science Research Council, the National Science Foundation, or the Wenner-Gren Foundation. Financial support (covering living expenses, transportation, and various research-related costs) is awarded on a highly competitive basis to the proposals that have the greatest merit. Even though a proposal may require months of preparation, there is no guarantee that it will be funded.

Second, preparation for fieldwork involves taking the proper health precautions. Before leaving home, it is imperative to obtain all relevant immunizations. A fieldworker traveling to a malaria-infested area must take the appropriate (region-specific) malarial suppressants before leaving home. It is also prudent to obtain information about available health facilities ahead of time in case the anthropologist or a family member becomes ill while in the field.

Third, if the field research is to be conducted in a foreign country (as is usually the case), permission or clearance must be obtained from the host government. Because field projects usually last a year or longer, no foreign government will allow an anthropologist to conduct research without prior approval. Some parts of the world are simply off-limits to U.S. citizens because of travel restrictions established by either U.S. officials or the governments of the particular countries. Even countries that are hospitable to Westerners require that the researcher spell out the nature of the proposed research in considerable detail. The host government officials often want to make sure that the research will not be embarrassing or politically sensitive, that the findings

survey methods The use of large samples, impersonal data-gathering techniques, and statistical analysis to study sociocultural groups.

informant A person who provides information about his or her culture to the ethnographic fieldworker.

will be useful, and that the researcher's presence in the host country will not jeopardize the safety, privacy, or jobs of any local citizens. Moreover, host governments often require cultural anthropologists to affiliate with local academic institutions in order to share their research experiences with local scholars and students. Sometimes—particularly in developing countries—the approval process can be very slow.

A fourth concern that must be addressed before leaving for the field is proficiency in the local language. An important part of the tradition of anthropological fieldwork is that it must be conducted using the native language. If the fieldworker is not fluent in the language of the culture to be studied, she or he should learn the language before leaving home. That may not always be possible, however, depending on the language. Dictionaries and grammar books may not even exist for some of the more esoteric languages, and finding a native speaker to serve as a tutor while still at home may not be possible. In such cases, the ethnographer will have to learn the language after arriving in the field.

Finally, the soon-to-be fieldworker must take care of a host of personal details before leaving home. Arrangements must be made for care of personal possessions such as houses, cars, and pets while out of the country; decisions have to be made about what to ship and what to purchase abroad; if families are involved, arrangements must be made for children's education; equipment such as cameras and recording devices must be purchased, insured, and protected against adverse environmental conditions; up-to-date passports must be obtained; and a schedule for transferring money must be worked out between one's bank at home and a convenient bank in the host country. These and other pre-departure details should put an end to the illusion that fieldwork is a romantic holiday.

STAGES OF FIELD RESEARCH

Although no two fieldwork experiences are the same, every study should progress through the same basic stages:

1. Selecting a research problem
2. Formulating a research design
3. Collecting the data
4. Analyzing the data
5. Interpreting the data

Rather than describing these five stages in abstract terms, it will perhaps be more meaningful to discuss them within the framework of an actual fieldwork project: the Kenya Kinship Study, a comparative analysis of rural and urban kinship interaction in Kenya, which was conducted by the author during the 1970s.

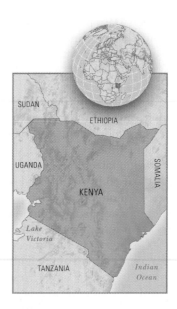

Stage 1: Selecting a Research Problem

In the early twentieth century, the major aim of fieldwork was to describe a culture in as much ethnographic detail as possible. In recent decades, however, fieldworkers have moved away from general ethnographies to research that is focused, specific, and problem oriented. Rather than studying all the parts of a culture with equal attention, contemporary cultural anthropologists are more likely to examine specific theoretical issues dealing with relationships among various phenomena, such as the relationship between matrilineal kinship and high levels of divorce, or the relationship between nutrition and food-getting strategies. This shift to a problem-oriented approach results in the formulation of hypotheses (statements of the predicted relationship between two or more variables) that are then tested in a fieldwork setting.

The theoretical issue that gave rise to the Kenya Kinship Study (KKS) was the relationship between family interaction and urbanization. What happens to family patterns in the face of rapid urbanization? Throughout most of Western social thought, there has been general agreement concerning the effects of urbanization on the family. The general proposition—which has been stated in one form or another since the mid-nineteenth century—sees a "nuclearization" of the family when confronted with urbanization. This relationship is perhaps best stated by William Goode, who held that urbanization brings with it "fewer kinship ties with distant relatives and a greater emphasis on the 'nuclear' family unit of couple and children" (1963: 1). The purpose of the KKS was to see whether this alleged relationship between family interaction and urbanization held up in Kenya, a country that has been experiencing rapid urbanization since gaining independence in the early 1960s. The general research problem thus generated the following hypothesis: as Kenya becomes more urbanized, extended family interaction will be replaced by more nuclear family interaction.

Stage 2: Formulating a Research Design

In the *research design* stage, the would-be fieldworker must decide how to measure the two major variables in the hypothesis: urbanization and family interaction. In this hypothesis, urbanization is the *independent variable* (i.e., the variable that is capable of effecting change in the other variable) and family interaction is the *dependent variable* (i.e., the variable whose value is dependent on the other variable). In our research design, the dependent variable (family interaction) is the variable we wish to explain, whereas the independent variable (urbanization) is the hypothesized explanation.

Both the dependent and the independent variable in our hypothesis must be made less abstract and more concrete and measurable so as to test the validity of the relationship. One way to do this with regard to the concept of urbanization is to design the study in a comparative fashion. This involves selecting two different populations in Kenya—one rural and one urban. The urban sample selected was from Nairobi, by far the largest city in Kenya and indeed in all of East Africa; the rural sample was selected from a small village very isolated from Nairobi and having none of the major features of a city, such as a large population, industrialization, or labor specialization. If we find that rural people interact with extended family members to a greater extent than urban people, the hypothesis is supported. If we find no appreciable differences in patterns of family interaction between rural and urban populations, the hypothesis will be rejected.

The dependent variable in our hypothesis (family interaction) must be defined more specifically so that it can be measured quantitatively. The task, in other words, is to identify certain concrete measures of family interaction. The KKS identified several such measures:

1. *Residence patterns:* Who lives with whom in the same house or compound? How close do people live to various types of family members?

2. *Visitation patterns:* How often do people have face-to-face interaction with various types of family members?

3. *Mutual assistance:* How often and to what extent do people exchange gifts or money with various types of family members?

4. *Formal family gatherings:* How often and to what extent do people get together for formal family meetings or ceremonies?

When designing a research project, it is important to control for any extraneous factors that might interfere with the testing of the hypothesis. If we are examining differences in kinship interaction between rural and urban residents, we must try to eliminate any variable (other than degree of urbanism) that might explain the differences. For example, if we select the rural sample from among the Kikuyu and the urban sample from a neighborhood comprising Luo and Nandi, the differences in family interaction may be the result of tribal affiliation (ethnicity) rather than degree of urbanization. Consequently, to control for this ethnic variable, only one ethnic group (the Kikuyu) was used for both rural and urban samples.

Stage 3: Collecting the Data

Once the hypothesis has been made concrete, the next step, *collecting data*, involves selecting the appropriate data-gathering techniques for measuring the variables. The KKS used three principal data-gathering techniques: participant-observation, structured interviews, and day histories, a type of biographical interview that focuses on what a person did and with whom he or she interacted during a twenty-four-hour period.

Participant-observation and interviewing—two primary field techniques used by cultural anthropologists—are discussed in the next section. Because the day history technique was developed (or at least modified) especially for this study, it is described here in detail. Day histories were designed to answer questions such as, Whom were you with? What relationship is this person to you? How much time did you spend with this person? How long have you known this person? How often do you see this person? What did you do while you were together?

Day histories were collected from fifty-three informants from the rural sample and eighty-six from the urban sample. Although there are obvious limitations to the usefulness of this technique, the KKS day histories generated specific quantitative data on family interaction. Moreover, the day histories proved beneficial as an initial device for gathering general sociocultural data that were later helpful in constructing questions used in the structured interviews.

Stage 4: Analyzing the Data

Once the day histories have been collected, the process of *analyzing data* begins. The content of the day histories was analyzed, and the various time segments

---

research design Overall strategy for conducting research.
independent variable The variable that can cause change in other variables.
dependent variable A variable that is affected by the independent variable.

collecting data Stage of fieldwork involving selection of data-gathering techniques and gathering of information pertinent to the hypothesis being studied.
analyzing data One of five stages of fieldwork in which the cultural anthropologist determines the meaning of data collected in the field.

were categorized into one of nine types of social inter-action (such as interaction with nonrelatives, nuclear family members, and extended family members). Because every hour of the twenty-four-hour period was accounted for, it was a straightforward matter to code the various time segments according to one of the nine categories.

The next step in the analysis involved simply count-ing the number of minutes per twenty-four-hour period that each interviewee spent in nuclear family interaction and the number of minutes spent in extended family interaction. From there, it was a routine mathematical exercise to determine the mean number of minutes spent in each type of family interaction for both rural and urban samples.

When all of the data were coded and analyzed, no significant differences in family interaction emerged between urban and rural samples. In fact, part of the urban sample (those having resided in Nairobi for five years or longer) showed greater involvement with ex-tended family members than did those in the rural sam-ple. These data generated from the day histories were supported by data collected from 298 structured inter-views and thirteen months of participant-observation. The KKS concluded that living and working within the highly differentiated, industrial urban complex of Nairobi does not in itself lead to the truncation of extended kinship ties.

Stage 5: Interpreting the Data

Like any science, the discipline of anthropology does more than simply describe specific cultures. *Interpreting data*—perhaps the most difficult step—involves explain-ing the findings. Has the original hypothesis been con-firmed or rejected? What factors can be identified that will help explain the findings? How do these findings compare with the findings of other similar studies? How generalizable are the findings to wider populations? Have these findings raised methodological or theoretical issues that have bearing on the discipline? These are the types of questions anthropologists must answer, usually after returning home from the fieldwork experience.

The significant lack of fit between the data and the so-called nuclearization hypothesis in the KKS requires an explanation. The key to understanding these data lies in the general socioeconomic status of the people under study. Kenya, like most other African nations in the 1970s, was a nation with a dual economy comprising two quite distinct categories of people. On one hand was a small elite with secure, well-paying jobs and po-

---

interpreting data The stage of fieldwork, often the most difficult, in which the anthropologist searches for meaning in the data collected while in the field.

CROSS-CULTURAL MISCUE

While conducting urban fieldwork in Kuala Lumpur, Malay-sia, medical anthropologist Jennifer Roberts was devoting the first several weeks of her research time to establishing her credibility, building social networks, and getting to know the local people. Her research assistant introduced Roberts to a woman who was accompanied by her five-year-old daughter. Roberts was so taken by the girl's beauty that she patted the girl on the head while comment-ing to the mother what a gorgeous child she had. Much to Roberts' surprise, the mother responded by saying that the girl was not very pretty at all and then abruptly left. What had Roberts done? She was simply trying to pay the woman and her daughter a compliment.

In fact, Roberts had inadvertently committed two cross-cultural gaffes. First, in this part of the world, the head is considered to be the most sacred part of the body, where one's spiritual power resides. Although patting a child on the head in North America is a gesture of endearment, in Malaysia it is viewed as a violation of the most sacred part of the body. Second, complimenting a child on her beauty or health is regarded in Malaysia as inviting bad fortune for the child. If evil people or evil spirits believe that a child is particularly healthy or beautiful, they might become jeal-ous and want to harm the child.

So, unlike parents in North America who often boast of their children's beauty, health, and intelligence, parents in Malaysia will downplay those traits to protect their chil-dren from harm.

---

tential for further upward mobility; on the other hand was everyone else, with either poor-paying jobs or no jobs at all and little or no economic mobility. The critical dimension, then, is between the haves and the have-nots, and with few exceptions, all of the people in both rural and urban samples clearly qualify for have-not status.

The wide range of family interaction found among both rural and urban populations in Kenya can be understood largely in terms of a lack of money and economic security. For example, in the absence of a public welfare system protecting workers against acci-dents, illness, old age, and unemployment, it is reason-able to expect that welfare will continue to take place along already established lines of kinship. Moreover, family ties between rural and urban areas remain high in Kenya because of two important economic facts of life: the instability of employment in Kenya and the Kikuyu land tenure system, whereby most land remains in the hands of the lineage (extended family). Urban migrants who neglect their rural kinship obligations are, in effect, relinquishing their rights to a portion of their lineage land, which for most impoverished migrants remains their sole retreat from the insecurities of urban

Alan Rumsey listens to a warrior from Highland New Guinea while collecting linguistic anthropological data.

Iven DeVore/Anthro-Photo

employment. Thus, given the national economy within which all Kikuyu are operating, the maintenance of strong kinship ties for both rural and urban residents is the most rational choice they can make.

In describing these five stages of field research, we run the risk of portraying the research process as a neat, precise, and systematic process. In reality, doing ethnographic fieldwork is messier than we often admit. There are many personal and intellectual issues that often interfere with this idealized scheme. To illustrate, using certain data-gathering techniques may prove to be inappropriate among a particular group of people; representative samples may be impossible to achieve because the ethnographer is not the correct gender, age, or race; and, there is always the problem of observer bias. The books and articles reporting on ethnographic research that finally emerge are usually cleaned up to the extent that the orderly, systematic, and scientific aspects of the research are emphasized and the chaotic aspects are downplayed.

Data-Gathering Techniques

A central problem facing any anthropological fieldworker is determining the most appropriate methods for collecting data. Data-collection methods that might work in one culture may be totally inappropriate for a neighboring culture. Given the wide variety of cultures in the world, it is important that anthropologists have a number of options so that they can match the appropriate set of data-gathering techniques to each fieldwork situation. There is a need to be flexible, however, for the techniques originally planned in the *research proposal* may prove to be inappropriate when actually used in the field. Whatever techniques are finally chosen, a variety of methods will be needed so that the findings from one technique can be used to check the findings from others.

Participant-Observation

It seems only fitting to start a discussion of data-gathering techniques with participant-observation because anthropologists use this technique more than any other single technique and more extensively than any other social science discipline. Participant-observation—as the name implies—means becoming involved in the culture under study while making systematic observations of what people actually do. When fieldworkers participate, they become as immersed in the culture as the local people permit. They share activities, attend ceremonies, eat together, and generally become part of the rhythm of everyday life. H. Russell Bernard captured the complexity of participant-observation:

> It involves establishing rapport in a new community; learning to act so that people go about their business as usual when you show up; and removing yourself every day from cultural immersion so you can intellectualize what you've learned, put it into perspective, and write about it convincingly. If you are a successful participant-observer, you will know when to laugh at what your informant thinks is funny; and when

research proposal   A written proposal required for funding of anthropological research that spells out in detail a research project's purpose, hypotheses, methodology, and significance.

informants laugh at what you say, it will be because you meant it to be a joke. (1988: 148)

From the very first day of fieldwork, gaining entry into the community presents a major problem for the participant-observer. Cultural anthropologists in the field can hardly expect to be accepted as soon as they walk into the local community. Under the best of circumstances, the fieldworker, as an outsider, will be an object of curiosity. More often, however, the beginning fieldworker encounters a wide variety of fears, suspicions, and hostilities of the local people that must be overcome. There is no reason whatsoever for traditional Samoan fishermen or Pygmy hunters to understand who the fieldworker is or what he or she is doing in their midst. In his classic study of the Nuer of the Sudan, E. E. Evans-Pritchard stated that the Nuer were so suspicious and reluctant to cooperate with him that after just several weeks of fieldwork "one displays, if the pun be allowed, the most evident symptoms of Nuerosis" (1940: 13).

Guidelines for Participant-Observation Fieldwork

By and large, the anthropologist conducting participant-observation fieldwork for the first time has probably received little instruction in how to cope with these initial problems of resistance. For most of the twentieth century, cultural anthropology was notorious for its sink-or-swim approach to preparing doctoral candidates for fieldwork. In a sense, it is not really possible to prepare the first-time fieldworker for every eventuality for the obvious reason that no two fieldwork situations, cultures, or ethnographers are ever the same. Nevertheless, it is possible to offer some general guidelines applicable to most fieldwork situations.

First, because the participant-observer is interested in studying people at the grassroots level, it is always advisable to work one's way down the political hierarchy. Before entering a country on a long-term visa, the fieldworker must obtain *research clearance* from a high level of the national government. In the case of the KKS, research clearance came in the form of a brief letter from the office of the president of the country. Starting with this letter from the top of the political pyramid, courtesy calls were made on each descending rung of the administrative ladder (from the provincial commissioner, through the district commissioner, location chief, sub-location chief, and finally to the two local headmen in the areas where the study was to be conducted). Because the study had the approval of the president, it was not likely that any of the administrators down the line would oppose it.

research clearance Permission of the host country in which fieldwork is to be conducted.

Second, when introducing oneself, it is important to select one role and use it consistently. There are a number of ways that a field anthropologist could answer the question "Who are you?" (a question, incidentally, that will be asked frequently and requires an honest and straightforward answer). In my own case when conducting the KKS, I could have said, with total honesty, that I was a student (I was finishing my Ph.D.), an anthropologist (my research was funded by NIMH), Pam's husband, a visiting research associate at the University of Nairobi, Kathryn's father, a teacher, a former basketball player, Charles's son, a Catholic, and a member of the Democratic Party. Yet many of these roles, though accurate, were not particularly understandable to the people asking the question. Even though the reason for my being there was that I was an anthropologist, that particular role has little meaning to people with little formal education. So I selected a role that was comprehensible: the role of teacher, a role that was both well known and, much to my advantage, well respected. Even though I wasn't teaching at the time, I had taught professionally before doing fieldwork, and I had planned on a career in teaching at the college level upon returning to the States. So, when asked who I was and what was I doing there, I always said that I was a teacher collecting information about the Kikuyu culture so that I could teach my students about it. Had I not standardized my introductions, but instead told one person that I was an anthropologist, another that I was a student, and still another that I was a teacher, the local people would have thought that I was lying or, perhaps equally bad, that I didn't know who I was.

A third general piece of advice for most fieldworkers is to proceed slowly. Coming from a society that places a high value on time, most U.S. anthropologists do not take kindly to the suggestion to slow down. After all, because they will be in the field for a limited amount of time, most Western anthropologists feel that they must make the best use of that time by collecting as much data as possible. The natural tendency for most Westerners is to want to hit the ground running. There seems to be so much to learn and so little time.

There are compelling reasons for not rushing into asking highly specific questions from day one. First, because most fieldworkers have such an imperfect understanding of the culture during the initial weeks and months, they often do not know enough to even ask the right types of specific questions. And, second, the very quality of one's data will vary directly with the amount of social groundwork the fieldworker has been able to lay. In other words, ethnographers must invest a considerable amount of time and energy establishing their credibility by allowing the local people to get to know them. For example, in the KKS, I spent the first three months engaging in a number of activities that didn't seem particularly scientific, including helping

Anthropologist Marjorie Shostak conducting anthropological fieldwork among the indigenous peoples of the Kalahari Desert in Botswana, southern Africa.

Konner/Anthro-Photo

people with their tax forms, showing teenage boys how to shoot a fifteen-foot jump shot, taking people for rides in my car, sharing large quantities of food, and talking about life in the United States. None of these activities involved the deliberate gathering of cultural data about the Kikuyu, but they did help to demonstrate that I was interested in them as people rather than merely as sources of information. Once the local people got to know and trust me, they were far more willing to give me the type of cultural information I was looking for.

Fourth, the fieldworker must communicate to the local people, in a genuine way, that she or he is a student, wanting to learn more about a subject on which *they* are the experts. For example, fieldworkers are not interested in simply studying the physical environment (rivers, grasslands, livestock, homes, and so on) of a pastoral people; instead they try to discover how the people define and value these aspects of their physical surroundings. They don't attempt to study marriage and kinship by superimposing already existing notions of how relatives deal with one another; rather, they are interested in the insider's view of how different categories of kin are expected to relate to one another in that society. To assume a student's role, while putting the local informant in the role of the teacher/resident expert, is more than just a cynical way of enticing people to give you information. The reason the fieldworker is there is to gather information on the local culture, a subject on which he or she has a very imperfect understanding at best. The local people, on the other hand, certainly know their own culture better than anyone else. When people are put in their well-deserved position of teacher/expert, they are likely to be most willing to share the knowledge that is near and dear to their hearts.

Advantages of Participant-Observation

Using participant-observation has certain methodological advantages for enhancing the quality of the data obtained. For example, people in most cultures appreciate any attempt on the part of the anthropologist to live according to the rules of their culture. No matter how ridiculous one might appear at first, the very fact that the fieldworker takes an interest in the local culture is likely to enhance rapport. And as trust levels increase, so do the quantity and quality of the data.

Another major advantage of participant-observation is that it enables the fieldworker to distinguish between normative and real behavior—that is, between what people *should do* and what people *actually do*. When conducting an interview, there is no way to know for certain whether people behave as they say they do. The participant-observer, however, has the advantage of seeing actual behavior rather than relying on hearsay. To illustrate, as part of the KKS, urban informants were asked how often they traveled to their rural homelands to visit family. A number of male informants who lived up to ninety-five miles away said that they went home every weekend to visit family. Through participant-observation, however, it became apparent that many of the men remained in the city for a number of consecutive weekends. When confronted with this discrepancy between what they said they did and what they actually did, the men claimed that their families wanted them to come home every weekend, but it was too costly and time-consuming to do so. In actual fact, they traveled home on an average of once a month. The difference between once a week and once a month is a 400-percent error in the data. Thus, the participant-observer gains a more accurate picture of the culture by observing what

APPLIED PERSPECTIVE

Anthropological Research and AIDS

In the early 1980s, very few Americans had ever heard of acquired immune deficiency syndrome (AIDS). By the start of the new millennium, however, AIDS had become the leading infectious cause of death in the world. Since its inception several decades ago, more than 60 million people worldwide have been infected with HIV. In 2003 alone AIDS claimed 3 million lives, or more than 8,200 people each day. This death toll is equivalent to twenty fully loaded 747s crashing every day! Tragically, 95 percent of all new AIDS cases are occurring in the poorest countries that are least equipped to handle the epidemic. The situation is most grim on the continent of Africa, where AIDS is erasing decades of progress in life expectancy. For example, the life expectancy in sub-Saharan Africa is currently forty-seven years, but without the AIDS epidemic, life expectancy would be sixty-two years. The future for many African countries is particularly bleak. It has been estimated by the Joint United Nations Program on HIV/AIDS that a person in Lesotho who turned fifteen years of age in 2000 has a 74 percent chance of contracting HIV before he or she turns fifty. And while the death rate from AIDS has slowed down in wealthy countries that can afford expensive drugs, the disease remains the fifth leading cause of death in the United States among people between the ages of twenty-five and forty-four.

The AIDS epidemic is particularly difficult to get under control for several reasons. First, the disease attacks the human immune system, one of the most complex and inadequately understood systems of the body. Second, the group of viruses thought to cause the disease is so poorly understood that a chemical cure is not likely to be found in the immediate future. Thus, the biological factors in solving the AIDS threat are highly complex. Efforts to stem the epidemic are further complicated by cultural factors. That is, the high-risk populations (intravenous drug users and prostitutes) are not visible subcultures. This creates additional problems for programs of AIDS prevention.

Until a vaccine for AIDS is developed, education remains the best strategy for reducing the spread of the disease. Because AIDS is sexually transmitted, the world's populations must learn as much as possible about how to avoid contracting the disease. Yet before public health officials can design effective educational programs, they need a good deal of cultural and behavioral information on high-risk populations. Cultural anthropologists have made significant contributions to programs of preventive education by conducting ethnographic research on the cultural patterns of sexual behavior among these high-risk groups.

One such study was conducted by anthropologist Michelle Renaud (1993, 1997), who worked with registered (legal) prostitutes in Kaolack, Senegal. Because Kaolack is a crossroads town with a steady flow of truck drivers and rural migrants, this particular town has a thriving sexual trade and a

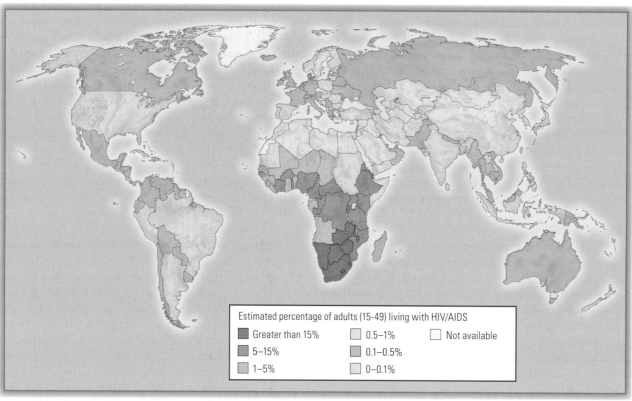

Estimated percentage of adults (15-49) living with HIV/AIDS		
Greater than 15%	0.5–1%	Not available
5–15%	0.1–0.5%	
1–5%	0–0.1%	

Distribution of HIV/AIDS

correspondingly high rate of sexually transmitted diseases. It was estimated that approximately four of every ten of Kaolack's registered prostitutes were HIV positive, as compared to 10 percent of prostitutes nationally. Renaud worked out of a local health clinic where registered prostitutes came for their bimonthly examinations as well as for treatment of sexually transmitted diseases.

Drawing on structured and unstructured interviews, as well as participant-observation, Renaud gathered valuable data on the lifestyles, worldviews, and decision making of these legal prostitutes. A primary finding of the study was that almost all prostitutes enforced condom use among their clients. However, in their roles as girlfriends, these same prostitutes required their partners to use condoms only 71 percent of the time. Similarly, nonprostitutes in Renaud's sample were reluctant to insist that their sexual partners use condoms. Renaud concluded that both prostitutes and nonprostitutes did "not want to risk losing their partners by implying that one of them might be HIV positive" (1993: 28). Armed with this empirical finding, she could then recommend to the Senegalese health officials that future AIDS education programs target groups other than just the prostitutes, including the clients of the prostitutes and particularly their boyfriends.

Applied anthropological studies such as Renaud's have limitations. The collection of behavioral data on sexual practices among any group of people will always be difficult because of its highly personal nature. When seeking such sensitive information from a subgroup often stigmatized by the wider society, problems of data validity are greatly magnified. Nevertheless, cultural anthropologists such as Renaud have an important role to play in the monumental effort it will take to eradicate this disease; that is, they can contribute to the design of successful prevention programs by providing both attitudinal and behavioral data from the ethnographic study of at-risk communities at home and abroad. In fact, a study released in March 2006 (Donnelly 2006: 8) suggests that new HIV infections have peaked in most areas of the world. Even though HIV has stabilized at very high levels, the findings raise hope that the types of preventive programs designed by anthropologists are having a positive impact on the fight against the pandemic.

Questions for Futher Thought

1. Why is the AIDS epidemic so difficult to control?
2. How could culture be a factor in the spread of a disease such as AIDS?
3. What other areas concerning the AIDS epidemic must be investigated by anthropologists?

people actually do rather than merely relying on what they say they do.

Disadvantages of Participant-Observation

On the other hand, participant-observation poses certain methodological problems that can diminish the quality of the data. For example, the very nature of participant-observation precludes a large sample size. Because participant-observation studies are both in-depth and time-consuming, fewer people are actually studied than would be using questionnaires or surveys. A second problem with participant-observation is that the data are often hard to code or categorize, which makes synthesizing and comparing the data difficult. Third, participant-observers face special problems when recording their observations because it may be difficult, if not impossible, to record notes while attending a circumcision ceremony, participating in a feast, or chasing through the forest after a wild pig. The more time that passes between the event and its recording, the more details are forgotten. And, finally, a major methodological shortcoming of participant-observation is that it has an obtrusive effect on the very thing that is being studied. Inhibited by the anthropologist's presence, many people are likely to behave in a way they would not behave if the anthropologist were not there. Table 5.1 lists the methodological advantages and disadvantages of participant-observation.

It is interesting to note that participant-observation as a data-gathering technique is being used outside of anthropological research. During the 1990s, the

Table 5.1 Methodological Advantages and Disadvantages of Participant-Observation	
Advantages	**Disadvantages**
■ Generally enhances rapport	■ Practical only for small sample size
■ Enables fieldworkers to distinguish actual from expected behavior	■ Difficult to obtain standardized comparable data
■ Permits observation of nonverbal behavior	■ Incomplete data due to problems recording information
	■ Obtrusive effect on subject matter

Jenike/Anthro-Photo

Anthropologist Mark Jenike weighs a duiker that was caught by a Lese hunter in Zaire, central Africa.

Samsung Group, the largest company in South Korea, took a very anthropological approach to preparing its employees for overseas assignments. After recruits had gone through a month-long international "boot camp," they then spent the next year in a Western culture engaged not in any particular functional area of business, but rather in "participant-observation." These junior managers were expected to immerse themselves in the host culture, make systematic observations of how the "natives" lived, and develop local tastes and sensibilities. In short, they were expected to become cultural anthropologists for the year. Although some corporate leaders considered the Samsung program to be frivolous, it was based on educating an entire cadre of future corporate leaders by helping them to acquire first-hand knowledge of the lifeways of the company's future customers.

Interviewing

In addition to using participant-observation, cultural anthropologists in the field rely heavily on ethnographic interviewing. This technique is used for obtaining infor-

mation on what people think or feel (*attitudinal data*) as well as on what they do (*behavioral data*). Even though interviewing is used widely by a number of different disciplines (including sociology, economics, political science, and psychology), the ethnographic interview is unique in several important respects. First, in the ethnographic interview, the interviewer and the subject almost always speak different first languages. Second, the ethnographic interview is often much broader in scope because it elicits information on the entire culture. Third, the ethnographic interview cannot be used alone but must be used in conjunction with other data-gathering techniques.

Structured and Unstructured Interviews

Ethnographic interviews can be unstructured or structured, depending on the level of control retained by the interviewer. In *unstructured interviews*, which involve a minimum of control, the interviewer asks open-ended questions on a general topic and allows interviewees to respond at their own pace using their own words. At the other extreme, in *structured interviews*, the interviewer asks all informants exactly the same set of questions, in the same sequence, and preferably under the same set of conditions. If we can draw an analogy between interviews and school examinations, structured interviews would be comparable to short-answer tests whereas unstructured interviews would be more like open-ended essay tests.

Structured and unstructured interviews have advantages that tend to complement each other. Unstructured interviews, which are most often used early in the data-gathering process, have the advantage of allowing informants to decide what is important to include in their information. In an unstructured interview, for example, an informant might be asked to describe all of the steps necessary for getting married in her or his culture. Structured interviews, on the other hand, have the advantage of producing large quantities of data that are comparable and thus lend themselves well to statistical descriptions. Because structured interviews ask questions based on highly specific cultural information, they are used most commonly late in the fieldwork, only

attitudinal data Information collected in a fieldwork situation that describes what a person thinks, believes, or feels.
behavioral data Information collected in a fieldwork situation that describes what a person does.
unstructured interview An ethnographic data-gathering technique—most often used in early stages of one's fieldwork—in which interviewees are asked to respond to broad, open-ended questions.
structured interview An ethnographic data-gathering technique in which large numbers of respondents are asked a set of specific questions.

after the anthropologist knows enough about the culture to ask highly specific questions.

It is important to be aware of the social situation in which the interview takes place. In other words, what effect does the presence of other people have on the answers given? The social context of the interview became an issue when I was collecting day history interviews as part of the KKS. Early in the interview stage of the research, a single adult male, who was being interviewed in the presence of two of his single male friends, mentioned that he spent the night with his girlfriend. When the two friends were interviewed the next day, they mentioned that they too had spent the night with their girlfriends. It seemed fairly transparent that the two friends, in order to preserve their reputations as sexually active bachelors, had at least the motivation to fabricate that part of their day history. After throwing out all three of these day histories, I decided to conduct each day history privately, rather than in groups. Table 5.2 offers guidelines for conducting ethnographic interviews.

Validity of the Data Collected

The cultural anthropologist in the field must devise ways to check the validity of interview data. One way to validate data is to ask a number of different people the same question; if all people independently of one another answer the question in essentially the same way, it is safe to assume that the data are valid. Another method of checking the validity of interview data is to ask a person the same question over a certain period of time. If the person answers the question differently, there is

reason to believe that one of the responses might not be truthful. A third way to determine validity is to compare the responses with people's actual behavior. As we saw in the discussion on participant-observation, what people do is not always the same as what they say they do.

Additional Data-Gathering Techniques

Even though participant-observation and interviewing are the mainstays of anthropological fieldwork, cultural anthropologists use other techniques for collecting cultural data at various stages of the field study. These techniques include census taking, mapping, document analysis, collection of genealogies, and photography—although this list is hardly exhaustive.

Census Taking

Early on in the fieldwork, anthropologists usually conduct a census of the area under investigation. Because *census taking* involves the collection of basic demographic data—such as age, occupation, marital status, and household composition—it is generally nonthreatening to the local people. It is important for the fieldworker to update the census data continuously as he or she learns more about the people and their culture.

Mapping

Another data-gathering tool used in the early stages of fieldwork is *ethnographic mapping*: attempting to locate people, material culture, and environmental features in space. To illustrate, anthropologists are interested in mapping where people live, where they pasture their livestock, where various public and private buildings are located, how people divide up their land, and how the people position themselves in relation to environmental features such as rivers, mountains, or oceans. We can learn a good deal about a culture by examining how people interact with their physical environment. Aerial and panoramic photography are particularly useful techniques for mapping a community's ecology.

Document Analysis

Cultural anthropologists may do *document analysis* to supplement the information collected through interviewing and observation. For example, some anthropol-

---

Table 5.2 Guidelines for Ethnographic Interviewing

- Obtain informed consent before interviewing.
- Maintain neutrality by not conveying to the interviewee what may be the "desired" answer.
- Pretest questions to make sure they are understandable and culturally relevant.
- Keep the recording of an interview as unobtrusive as possible.
- Make certain that the conditions under which the interviews are conducted are consistent for all interviews.
- Use simple, unambiguous, and jargon-free language.
- Phrase questions positively ("Do you smoke cigarettes?") rather than negatively ("You don't smoke cigarettes, do you?")
- Keep the questions and the interview itself short.
- Avoid two-pronged (having two parts to the answer) questions.
- Save controversial questions for the end of the interview.

---

census taking   The collection of demographic data about the culture being studied.

ethnographic mapping   A data-gathering tool that locates where the people being studied live, where they keep their livestock, where public buildings are located, and so on, in order to determine how that culture interacts with its environment.

document analysis   Examination of data such as personal diaries, newspapers, colonial records, and so on to supplement information collected through interviewing and participant-observation.

© Lawrence Manning/Corbis

Ethnographers in the field are interested in studying all segments of a population. They would include these children from Guizhou Province in China as well as their parents.

Collecting Genealogies

Another technique used to collect cultural data is the *genealogical method*, which involves writing down all of the relatives of a particular informant. Collecting this type of information is especially important in the small-scale, preliterate societies that anthropologists often study, because kinship relationships tend to be the primary ones in those societies. Whereas in Western societies much of our lives are played out with people who are not family members—such as teachers, employers, co-workers, and friends—in small-scale societies people tend to interact primarily with their family. When using the genealogical method, the fieldworker asks each informant to state the name and relationship of all family members and how they are referred to, addressed, and treated. From this information the anthropologist can deduce how family members interact with one another and what behavioral expectations exist among different categories of kin.

Photography

A particularly important aid to the fieldworker's collection of data is *photography*, both still photography and videography. Recent decades have witnessed a proliferation of ethnographic videos portraying a wide variety of cultures from all parts of the globe. Although videos are valuable for introducing anthropology students to different cultures, they also have more specific uses for anthropological research. To illustrate, videos can be extremely helpful in *proxemic analysis* (that is, studying how people in different cultures distance themselves from one another in normal interaction) or *event analysis* (that is, documenting who participates in events such as circumcision ceremonies, marriages, or funerals).

Photography has become such an important part of anthropological research that it is hard to imagine an anthropologist in the field without a camera. As a research tool, the camera can be put to many uses. First, as mentioned previously, the camera can produce a lasting record of land-use patterns and the general ecological arrangements in the community under study. Second, as the adage suggests, a picture is worth a thousand words. Photography can document the technology of the culture (tools, weapons, machines, utensils), how these

ogists use personal diaries, colonial administrative records, newspapers, marriage registration data, census information, and various aspects of popular culture, such as song lyrics, television programs, and children's nursery rhymes. As an illustration of how anthropologists can use already existing documents, consider how tax records in Swaziland from the 1920s and 1930s can shed light on the changing practice of polygyny (a man having more than one wife at a time). For example, an anthropologist might be interested in determining how the incidence of polygyny has changed over time. The present practice of polygyny can be assessed by using direct methods such as interviewing and participant-observation. To compare the present practice of polygyny with the practice in the 1930s, one needs only to consult the tax rolls, because during the decade of the 1930s (when Swaziland was under colonial rule), Swazi men were taxed according to the number of wives they had. A man with three wives paid three times as much tax as a man with one wife. The advantages of using this type of historical tax data are obvious: it provides large quantities of data, it is neither expensive nor time-consuming, and it is totally unobtrusive.

genealogical method   A technique of collecting data in which the anthropologist writes down all the kin relationships of informants in order to study the kinship system.
photography   The use of a camera or video camera to document the ecology, material culture, and even social interaction of people when conducting ethnographic fieldwork.
proxemic analysis   The study of how people in different cultures use space.
event analysis   Photographic documentation of events such as weddings, funerals, and festivals in the culture under investigation.

Within the first several weeks of conducting fieldwork in rural Kenya, anthropologist Peter Sutton decided to photograph the physical surroundings of the village he was studying. He wanted to visually document the location of houses and fields so as to better understand how the people used space. But within minutes of his photographing the environment (which unavoidably also included some people), several men in the village began shaking their fists and shouting angrily at him. Sutton retreated and rarely used his camera again during his eighteen months of fieldwork.

Sutton learned an important lesson from this incident: photography has different meanings in different cultures. Even though cameras can be useful for documenting cultural features, they must be used with caution. In addition to being an invasion of privacy—as may be true in our own society—there are additional reasons why East Africans are reluctant to have their pictures taken. For example, because some East Africans (particularly in the coastal region) are Islamic, they feel strongly about not violating the Koranic prohibition against making images of the human form. Moreover, people who do not understand the nature of photography may believe that having one's picture taken involves the entrapment of their souls in the camera. In those societies where witchcraft is practiced, the prospect of having one's soul captured, particularly by a witch, can be terrifying.

items are used (by whom, where, when, in what combinations, and so on), the sequences in a craft process, and the sex roles associated with different items of technology. Third, photography can be used to probe in the interview process. Because the photograph becomes the object of discussion, the informant feels less like a subject and more like an expert commentator. And finally, still photography can be used for *sociometric tracking*. If enough photos are taken of people interacting over a period of time, it is possible to quantify which members spend time with whom.

As an example of the use of still photography for sociometric tracking, a study of voluntary interaction was conducted in the cafeteria of the author's university by anthropology students. They were interested in determining the extent to which people from different segments of the university actually chose to interact with one another during lunchtime. The students took a series of still photographs of the same set of tables at

---

sociometric tracking   A data-gathering method that social scientists use to measure different types of interaction among people.

---

the university cafeteria over a two-week period. Then, by identifying the people who chose to sit together for lunch (commuter students, international students, jocks, fraternity and sorority members, minority students, and so forth), they were able to determine the extent to which university social life was either segregated or integrated. Their findings—that the various groups of students stayed very much to themselves—made a dramatic statement about the nature of the university, which, by definition, should be a place where diverse people from different backgrounds can share their ideas with one another.

Applied Field Methods

As was pointed out in Chapter 3, there are some fundamental differences in the research conducted by traditional (theoretical) and applied cultural anthropologists. When compared to more traditional anthropological research, applied research is characterized as (a) more collaborative and interdisciplinary, (b) more inclusive of local people in all stages of the research, and (c) faced with real-time limitations (weeks or months rather than years). In the previous sections we have described data-gathering techniques that have been developed over the last century by traditional cultural anthropologists. While all of these techniques can, and have been, used by both traditional and applied anthropologists, the latter have also developed some additional fieldwork techniques that are particularly well suited for applied research projects.

- *Rapid Ethnographic Assessment (REA):* As its name implies, REA requires much less time than traditional ethnographic fieldwork. The usual steps in an applied research project (such as problem identification, needs assessment, designing research plan, data collection, intervention, and program evaluation) do not typically require long term, total immersion into the culture. Applied anthropologists are, in most cases, familiar with the culture, speak the local language, and are experts in the problems being investigated. The scope of the research tends to be more narrowly focused toward just the problem area and the sample size is smaller. Not all applied anthropologists use REA, as is discussed in the Contemporary Issues feature in this chapter).

- *Surveys:* While surveys are more closely associated with the discipline of sociology, some applied anthropologists use survey methods in order to gather a large amount of attitudinal and behavioral data in a relatively short time frame. Surveys are particularly useful to applied anthropologists working in complex communities where there is not a single "native" point of view. Moreover, if the survey questions are standardized and "close ended," the data will have the additional advantage of being statistically comparable.

CONTEMPORARY ISSUES

Rapid Ethnographic Assessment Procedures: How Rapid Is Too Rapid?

As this chapter on methods points out, conducting fieldwork in cultural anthropology is not completed in a matter of days—or even weeks. Ethnographic fieldwork typically lasts at least a year and often longer. Although fieldwork findings have utility for formulating public policy, policy makers often do not have the luxury of waiting several years for the findings. In an attempt to resolve this dilemma—and to ensure that research data are actually used for policy making—some anthropologists have developed rapid ethnographic assessment procedures (REAP).

Time Life Pictures/Getty Images

Rapid assessment techniques originated in two areas of applied anthropology: rural agricultural development programs in third world countries (Hildebrand 1982) and public health programs (Scrimshaw and Hurtado (1987). Since the early 1980s, rapid research techniques have been used in the field of social forestry, irrigation projects, and even historic restoration of parklands. Rapid assessment is typically collaborative and multidisciplinary, including researchers, service providers, and local people. It is applied rather than theoretical research, for it is not aimed at generating new theories but rather at assisting with a rational decision-making process for policy makers. Rapid assessment concentrates on delivering timely, focused, and qualitative information at the expense of more laborious and time-consuming scientific research with large probability samples. Specific research strategies are selected from a wide range of data-gathering techniques (for example, semi-structured interviews, group interviews, focus groups, and participant-observation) and adapted to the local situation. Research findings are constantly reevaluated as new data come in and, in fact, incoming data may lead to the formulation of new research questions during the course of the research. Because policy makers need cultural information quickly, REAP is conducted in two to six weeks rather than twelve to twenty-four months.

Because rapid assessment procedures are compressed into a relatively short period of time, they raise issues concerning the quality of the information generated. For example, how accurate are the data in comparison with data collected by more traditional ethnographers? How much social and cultural context is overlooked in the interest of saving time? Do the observations accurately measure the cultural realities? Whose reality is being measured: that of the researcher or that of the local people? Can the research findings be replicated and generalized beyond the local community?

Beyond questions involving validity and reliability of data, REAP need to be evaluated on the basis of other criteria. For example, how useful are the findings for all of the stakeholders? If informants are not selected from all segments of the population, then the findings will not be representative of the total community and, as such, will sacrifice some of their usefulness. Also, are the rapid assessment procedures feasible in terms of cost effectiveness? And do the assessment procedures create any ethical problems, such as violation of confidentiality or any other rights of the human subjects involved? To be certain, these questions need to be asked when using *any* type of research methods. But, given the compression of time from several years to several months, these questions become all the more critical when dealing with rapid assessment techniques.

Some anthropologists have questioned whether REAP has any place in the fieldworker's tool kit. Rapid appraisal methods efficiently combine a number of data-gathering strategies and can be useful in situations when information is needed quickly to help solve problems that cannot wait. But, in many other situations, REAP is not a substitute for in-depth, long-term studies drawing on considerably larger samples. To quote James Beebe (1995), "Rapid appraisal provides relatively quick qualitative results that are likely to be *vaguely right*, [and] ... when applied with care and caution, it can help a decision maker avoid being *precisely wrong*."

■ *Focus groups:* These are small groups (composed of six to ten people) convened by an applied anthropologist to discuss a particular topic. Topics might include what people living with HIV/AIDS need in terms of community assistance, what homeless people think of available homeless shelters, or what negative effects the construction of a large highway might have on members of a local community. While popular for conducting public opinion polls and commercial product marketing, applied anthropologists use focus groups to both save time and also generate insights not always possible by merely interviewing individuals.

techniques, the investigator can collect different types of data around the same set of issues, using the different sets of data to cross-check their validity.

The Pains and Gains of Fieldwork

It should be clear by now that the process of direct fieldwork is central to doing cultural anthropology. Unlike many other scientific endeavors, anthropological fieldwork inevitably has a powerful impact on the life of the practitioner. Spending a year or more living and working in an unfamiliar culture is bound to have life-altering consequences in most cases. The anthropologist is never quite the same after completing a fieldwork project (see DeVita 1992, 2000).

The anthropologist in the field is faced with a number of anxiety-producing situations that can be both stressful and growth inducing. In other words, both pains and gains are associated with doing anthropological fieldwork. For example, cultural anthropologists in the field rarely, if ever, follow their research design step by step in cookbook fashion. Despite the most meticulous research design and predeparture preparations, fieldwork is fraught with unanticipated difficulties. From day one, the fieldworker can expect to be surprised. Napoleon Chagnon's initial encounter with the Yanomamo Indians of Venezuela and Brazil was hardly what he had anticipated:

> I looked up and gasped when I saw a dozen burly, naked, sweaty, hideous men staring at us down the shafts of their drawn arrows! I am not ashamed to admit that had there been a diplomatic way out, I would have ended my fieldwork then and there.... I wondered why I ever decided to switch from physics and engineering in the first place. (1983: 10–11)

The initial desire to flee the fieldwork situation is more common than most anthropologists are willing to admit. And one does not have to travel to the remote parts of the world to feel that way. One American anthropology student who was preparing to do fieldwork among homeless people in Charlotte, North Carolina, experienced an initial rude awakening. During his first hour of fieldwork, while waiting to speak to the director of a homeless shelter, the budding anthropologist encountered a number of situations that made him question his sanity. In his own words:

> During the first five minutes of being in the shelter, a child tried to steal my knapsack. Both the homeless people in the waiting room and the staff kept looking at me with (what I can only describe as) disgust in their eyes. I overheard two Black men talking to each other. I couldn't for the life of me understand a word they were saying, although they seemed to be communicating just fine. Well, here it is—the old language barrier of

Photographs taken in the field can serve as probes during an interview as well as useful sources of information.

Choosing a Technique

Which of the variety of data-gathering techniques will be used depends largely on the nature of the problem being investigated. Kinship studies are likely to draw heavily on the genealogical method, studies of child-rearing practices rely on observation of parent–child relationships, and studies of values will probably use the interview (a technique particularly well suited to generating attitudinal data).

Another significant factor influencing the choice of techniques is the receptivity of the people being studied. It is important that the fieldworker carefully plan which techniques will be appropriate to use and what types of data to collect, as well as the segments of the population to study. If, after entering the field, the anthropologist finds that a technique is not working, he or she must be sufficiently flexible to revise the research design and creative enough to come up with a workable alternative. Whatever technique is selected, it should be used in conjunction with other techniques. By using multiple

anthropological fieldwork. So I decided to keep quiet and just listen and observe. Before long a White woman entered the waiting room with a 5-year-old boy, whereupon another woman yelled out, "We don't want that little rat in here." OK, I thought, we have a fight on our hands. But in fact, it turned out that the two women were friends. . . . Another small child approached me and pushed his head under my hand, as if he was a dog and wanted me to pat his head in approval. I did. Then I noticed that all of the staff wore plastic gloves and only had physical contact with the homeless people when wearing them. I then decided that I had contracted head lice from the boy. My head started to itch, as if, oh I don't know, like I had lice or something. Despite the fact that I had just touched the child's head, I was convinced that I had head lice. . . . Then the director of the shelter came out to greet me. She was very cordial—perhaps she was trying to console me because she sensed that I had a head lice problem. Once in her office, I settled down somewhat and began to tell her about my research project, discussing theories and hypotheses as if I knew what I was talking about. But as we talked about research, my mind was on the lice in my head. Oh, to hell with anthropology. I'm going home to take a bath! (Frank Vagnone 1989, personal communication)

Sometimes cultural anthropologists in the field can be in life-threatening situations, not just uncomfortable ones. By conducting fieldwork in remote parts of the world, anthropologists expose themselves to dangers from the physical environment that can be fatal. Contagious disease, another major risk factor, has resulted in the serious illness or even death of anthropologists in the field. And, in certain situations, anthropologists are exposed to various forms of social violence, including civil wars, intergroup warfare, muggings, and other forms of crime. To illustrate, anthropologist Philippe Bourgois, who studied the drug culture of East Harlem, New York, witnessed shootings, muggings, bombings, machine-gunnings, fire bombings, and numerous fistfights, and was manhandled by New York City police who mistook him for a drug dealer. These risks, some of which can be fatal, make the conduct of fieldwork serious business. Ethnographers who study and experience violence have to cope with what Antonius Robben and Carolyn Nordstrom (1995: 13) refer to as "existential shock," "a disorientation about boundaries between life and death, which appear erratic rather than discrete." Those with higher safety needs might want to consider becoming a historian who rarely has to stray from the safe, yet less interesting, stacks of the university library.

Culture Shock

Not all introductions to fieldwork are as unsettling as these, of course. But even anthropologists whose fieldwork experience is less traumatic undergo some level of stress from culture shock, the psychological disorientation caused by trying to adjust to major differences in lifestyles

and living conditions. *Culture shock*, a term introduced by anthropologist Kalervo Oberg (1960), ranges from mild irritation to out-and-out panic. This general psychological stress occurs when the anthropologist tries to play the game of life with little or no understanding of the basic rules. The fieldworker, struggling to learn what is meaningful in the new culture, never really knows when she or he may be committing a serious social indiscretion that might severely jeopardize the entire fieldwork project.

When culture shock sets in, everything seems to go wrong. You often become irritated over minor inconveniences. The food is strange, people don't keep their appointments, no one seems to like you, everything seems so unhygienic, people don't look you in the eye, and on and on. Even though culture shock manifests itself in a number of symptoms, it is usually characterized by the following:

- A sense of confusion over how to behave
- A sense of surprise, even disgust, after realizing some of the features of the new culture
- A sense of loss of old familiar surroundings (such as friends, possessions, and ways of doing things)
- A sense of being rejected (or at least not accepted) by members of the new culture
- A loss of self-esteem because you don't seem to be functioning very effectively
- A feeling of impotence at having so little control over the situation
- A sense of doubt when your own cultural values are brought into question.

Table 5.3 lists twenty-two symptoms of culture shock. One would hope that undergoing the training to become an anthropologist and making specific preparations for entering the field would help to prevent anyone from experiencing extreme culture shock. Nevertheless, every anthropologist should expect to suffer, to some extent, from the discomfort of culture shock. Generally, the negative effects of culture shock subside as time passes, but it is unlikely that they will go away completely. The very success or failure of an anthropological field project depends largely on how well the ethnographer can make the psychological adjustment to the new culture and overcome the often debilitating effects of culture shock.

Biculturalism

Not all of the consequences of fieldwork are negative. To be certain, culture shock is real and should not be taken lightly. Yet, despite the stress of culture shock—or

culture shock A psychological disorientation experienced when attempting to operate in a radically different cultural environment.

Table 5.3 Symptoms of Culture Shock	
Homesickness	Chauvinistic excesses
Boredom	Stereotyping of host nationals
Withdrawal (for example, spending excessive amounts of time reading, only seeing other Americans, and avoiding contact with host nationals)	Hostility toward host nationals
	Loss of ability to work effectively
	Unexplainable fits of weeping
Need for excessive amounts of sleep	Physical ailments (psychosomatic illnesses)
Compulsive eating	Feelings of isolation
Compulsive drinking	Weight loss
Irritability	Feelings of helplessness
Exaggerated cleanliness	Tenseness, moodiness, and irritability
Marital stress	Loss of confidence
Family tension and conflict	Fear of the worst happening

SOURCE: L Robert Kohls, *Survival Kit for Overseas Living* (Yarmouth, ME: Intercultural Press, 1984), p. 65; Elizabeth Marx, *Breaking Through Culture Shock: What You Need to Succeed in International Business* (London: Nicholas Brealey Publishing, 1999), p. 32.

perhaps because of it—the total immersion experience of fieldwork provides opportunities for personal growth and increased understanding. Spending weeks and months operating in a radically different culture can provide new insights into how the local people think, act, and feel. In the process of learning about another culture, however, we unavoidably learn a good deal about our own culture as well (Gmelch 1994a). When we become bicultural, which can be a consequence of successful fieldwork, we develop a much broader view of human behavior. Richard Barrett captures the essence of this *bicultural perspective*, which he claims enables cultural anthropologists

> to view the world through two or more cultural lenses at once. They can thus think and perceive in the categories of their own cultures, but are able to shift gears, so to speak, and view the same reality as it might be perceived by members of the societies they have studied. This intellectual biculturalism is extremely important to anthropologists. It makes them continually aware of alternative ways of doing things and prevents them from taking the customs of our own society too seriously. (1991: 20–21)

When we speak of achieving biculturalism, we should not assume that the anthropologist, no matter how much fieldwork he or she does, will ever become a native. Anthropologist Roger Keesing (1992) reminds us that after many fieldwork encounters with the Malaita Kwaio of the Solomon Islands he still considered himself little more than an informed outsider. Keesing relates a story of his unsuccessful attempts to convince the Malaita Kwaio not to eat a dolphin they had caught

because, he argued, it was not a fish but a mammal like us. He used the argument that dolphins, like humans, were warm-blooded and red-blooded, but they were unimpressed. He got their rapt attention when he informed the locals that dolphin should not be eaten because they actually communicate with one another, just as humans do. Keesing was then asked a series of questions he could not answer to their satisfaction: How do you talk to a dolphin? What language do they speak? How can they talk under water? Finally, as his informants were cooking the dolphin steaks on the fire, Keesing came to realize a basic fact about anthropological fieldwork: no matter how long one spends studying another culture, the anthropologist is little more than "an outsider who knows something of what it is to be an insider" (Keesing 1992: 77).

RECENT TRENDS IN ETHNOGRAPHIC FIELDWORK

Much of this chapter on ethnographic field research has taken an essentially scientific approach. We have explored the various stages of the ethnographic process as exemplified by the KKS. We have talked about generating hypotheses, dependent and independent variables, ways of maximizing the validity and reliability of the data, minimizing observer bias, and a fairly wide range of data-gathering techniques. The point of this chapter has been to demonstrate that cultural anthropology, like any scientific discipline, must strive toward objectivity by being sensitive to methodological issues.

Reflexive Methods

Despite the quest for scientific objectivity, conducting ethnographic fieldwork is quite different from doing research in a chemistry or biology laboratory. To reflect the native's point of view, the observer must interact

bicultural perspective The capacity to think and perceive in the categories of one's own culture as well as in the categories of a second culture.

THE FAR SIDE® BY GARY LARSON

"Anthropologists! Anthropologists!"

Cultural anthropologists often have an obstructive effect on the people they study.

with her or his subjects, thereby introducing a powerful element of subjectivity. Nowhere is the coexistence of subjectivity and objectivity more evident than in the widely used data-gathering technique of participant-observation. Participation implies a certain level of emotional involvement in the lives of the people being studied. Making systematic observations, on the other hand, requires emotional detachment. Participant-observers are expected to be emotionally engaged participants while at the same time being dispassionate observers. Thus, by its very nature, participant-observation carries with it an internal source of tension, because it is incompatible to sympathize with those people whom you are trying to describe with scientific objectivity.

Since the 1970s, however, the postmodernists (see Chapter 4) have ushered in a new type of ethnography that has become known as *reflexive* or *narrative ethnography*. Being less concerned with scientific objectivity,

reflexive or **narrative ethnography**   A type of ethnography, associated with postmodernism, which focuses more on the interaction between the ethnographer and the informant than on scientific objectivity.

narrative ethnographers are interested in coproducing ethnographic knowledge by focusing on the interaction between themselves and their informants (Michrina and Richards 1996). In fact, many ethnographers today use the term *research collaborator* rather than *informant*. These narrative ethnographers are no longer interested in producing descriptive accounts of another culture written with scientific detachment. Rather, their ethnographies are conscious reflections on how their own personalities and cultural influences combine with personal encounters with their informants to produce cultural data. Nancy Lundgren (2002: 38) speaks of how her form of participant-observation has taken on a new dimension:

> Now I am engaged in what I would call a reflexive anthropology with a local expert as my guide. He is interested in telling the story of his village, and together we gather much of the data for this work. We have interviewed elders of the village, both men and women. We have collected stories and drawings from the children. Together we have participated in rituals, both public and private, have conversed for hours, experienced family exchanges, and had encounters with almost every aspect of village life we call culture. He is the insider; he is the one who has the culture in his land, his compound, his family, and his bones. He corrects me and guides me, and together we sort out the meaning of what is now our collective culture.

The narrative or reflexive approach to ethnography involves a dialogue between informant and ethnographer. Such a postmodern approach, it is argued, is needed because the traditional ethnographer can no longer presume to be able to obtain an objective description of other cultures. In an effort to reclaim a more "scientific" methodology, these reflexive methods have come under harsh attack by Lawrence Kuznar (1996) and Marvin Harris (1999) in recent years. If we take these often ferocious debates on methods too literally, we are led to believe that the discipline is in turmoil because it cannot agree on which methodology is the correct one. But, as Ivan Brady (1998) has noted, we should avoid drawing absolute lines between subjective and objective ethnographic methods. Instead, ethnography of the twenty-first century is moving toward a "methodological pluralism," whereby all forms of information and all methods are considered legitimate, provided they help us produce a richer and more accurate description of ethnographic reality.

Statistical Cross-Cultural Comparisons

During the first half of the twentieth century, anthropologists, following the lead of Boas in the United States and Malinowski in Britain, amassed considerable descriptive data on a wide variety of cultures throughout the world. Because of the many first-hand ethnographic field studies conducted by the students of Boas and

Malinowski, by 1945 sufficient data existed to begin testing hypotheses and building theory inductively.

The emergence of statistical, cross-cultural comparative studies was made possible in the 1940s by George Peter Murdock and his colleagues at Yale University, who developed a coded data retrieval system known as the *Human Relations Area Files (HRAF)*. The largest anthropological data bank in the world, HRAF has vast amounts of information about more than three hundred different cultures organized into more than seven hundred different cultural subject headings. The use of the simple coding system enables the cross-cultural researcher to access large quantities of data within minutes for the purpose of testing hypotheses and drawing statistical correlations.

The creation of HRAF has opened up the possibility for making statistical comparisons among large numbers of cultures. Murdock himself used HRAF as the basis for his groundbreaking book *Social Structure* (1949), in which he compiled correlations and generalizations on family and kinship organization. John Whiting and Irvin Child (1953) used HRAF as the database for studying the relationship between child-rearing practices and adult attitudes toward illness. More recently, a host of studies using HRAF data have appeared in the literature, including studies on the adoption of agriculture, sexual division of labor, female political participation, reproduction rituals, and magicoreligious practitioners. Such cross-cultural studies are significant, for they allow us to test the universality of anthropological theories by using large numbers of ethnographic cases.

The HRAF data bank must be used carefully and with full recognition of some potential methodological pitfalls. For example:

- Much of the data contained in HRAF varies considerably in quality.

- The coverage is uneven, with a greater amount of material coming from non-Western cultures.

- Because the data describe a wide range of types of social systems (such as tribes, clans, nations, and ethnic groups), one can question whether the units of analysis are comparable.

- And, if, as the functionalists remind us, all parts of a culture are to some degree interconnected, how legitimate is it to pull a cultural trait from its original context and compare it to other cultural traits that have been similarly ripped from their contexts?

In the past several decades, however, largely through the efforts of Murdock and Raoul Naroll, most of these criticisms and objections to using HRAF for cross-cultural research have been adequately answered. Because many of these methodological shortcomings can now be overcome by thoughtful researchers, HRAF remains a powerful tool for testing universal theories and identifying causal relationships among cultural phenomena.

Although HRAF has been around, in either its paper or electronic form since the 1940s, *AnthroSource* is a communication and data retrieval system with its roots squarely in the twenty-first century. Initiated in 2005, AnthroSource is the American Anthropological Association's (AAA's) Internet portal designed to enable its members to share information with one another as well as have access to a wide range of online literature. Initially, this information technology tool will provide a complete full-text database containing all peer-reviewed journal articles, newsletters, and bulletins (approximately 230,000 pages) published by AAA since its beginnings. Like many other electronic databases, AnthroSource can search (by using keywords and phrases) everything ever published in such journals as the *American Anthropologist*, *Ethos*, and the *American Ethnologist*, among many others. To be certain, this ambitious project will be of considerable use to scholars needing access to data going back to the late nineteenth century. However, any good research library, irrespective of whether it subscribes to AnthroSource, has a number of other web portals that can search full-text copies of more recent literature from a much wider set of holdings than are available presently through AnthroSource.

THE ETHICS OF CULTURAL ANTHROPOLOGY

All field anthropologists—both applied and theoretical—find themselves in social situations that are varied and complex because they work with people in a number of different role relationships. They are involved with and have responsibilities to their subjects, their discipline, their colleagues (both in and outside anthropology), their host governments, their own governments, and their sponsoring agencies.

Under such socially complex conditions, it is likely that the anthropologist, having to choose between conflicting values, will be faced with a number of ethical dilemmas. For example, how do you make your findings public without jeopardizing the anonymity of your informants? Can you ever be certain that the data your informants gave you will not eventually be used to harm them? How can you be certain that the project you are working on will be beneficial for the target population?

Human Relations Area Files (HRAF) The world's largest anthropological data retrieval system, used to test cross-cultural hypotheses.

AnthroSource A twenty-first-century communication and data retrieval system sponsored by the American Anthropological Association.

© AP Photo/Greg Gibson

Herman Shaw, 94, a Tuskegee Syphilis Study victim, smiles after receiving an official apology from President Clinton Friday, May 16, 1997, in Washington. Making amends for a shamefully unethical U.S. experiment, Clinton apologized to black men whose syphilis went untreated by government doctors.

To what extent should you become personally involved in the lives of the people you are studying? Should you intervene to stop illegal activity? These are just a few of the ethical questions that arise in anthropological research. Although recognizing that anthropologists continually face such ethical decisions, the profession has made it clear that each member of the profession is ultimately responsible for anticipating these ethical dilemmas and for resolving them in such a way as to avoid causing harm to their subjects or to other scholars.

Today, U.S. federal law and policies at most research-oriented universities require that any faculty research (in which human beings are subjects) must comply with accepted ethical and professional standards. Generally, anthropologists are required to submit a description of their research to their university's Committee on Human Subjects and obtain approval for conducting the research. Many granting agencies will refuse to fund anthropological research unless the proposed research has been reviewed for potential ethical pitfalls.

Concern for professional ethics is hardly a recent phenomenon among anthropologists. As early as 1919, Franz Boas, the guru of the first generation of anthropologists in the United States, spoke out adamantly against the practice of anthropologists engaging in spying activ-

ities while allegedly conducting scientific research. Writing in *Nation*, Boas (1919: 797) commented, "A person who uses science as a cover for political spying … prostitutes science in an unpardonable way and forfeits the right to be classed as a scientist." While anthropologists have been aware of ethical dilemmas since the beginning, the profession did not adopt a comprehensive code of behavioral standards until the 1970s. In 1971 the AAA adopted its "Principles of Professional Responsibility" and established its Committee on Ethics; and the SFAA (Society for Applied Anthropology) published its "Statement on Professional and Ethical Responsibilities" in 1975. The AAA revised its code of ethics in 1998.

The publication of these professional codes of ethics in the 1970s was, to a large degree, precipitated by several controversial events that occurred in the 1960s. One such controversy revolved around the allegation that U.S. anthropologists secretly had engaged in counterinsurgency research for the Pentagon during the Vietnam War. Another ethical crisis arose around *Project Camelot*, a $6 million research project funded by the U.S. Army to gather data on counterinsurgency that would enable the U.S. Army to cope more effectively with internal revolutions in foreign countries. Project Camelot, which had hired the services of a number of prominent anthropologists, was canceled by the secretary of defense shortly after the project director was hired. Word about this clandestine operation in Chile was brought to the attention of the Chilean senate, which reacted with outrage over the apparent U.S. interference in its internal affairs.

Although the project never really got under way, it had enormous repercussions on the discipline of anthropology. The heated debate among anthropologists that followed revolved around two important questions. First, was Project Camelot a legitimately objective attempt to gather social science data, or was it a cover for the U.S. Army to intervene in the internal political affairs of sovereign nations? And second, were the participating anthropologists misled into thinking that scientific research was the project's sole objective, while they were really (and perhaps unwittingly) serving as undercover spies?

One of the very practical and immediate consequences of the alleged activities of U.S. anthropologists in both Vietnam and Project Camelot was the cloud of suspicion that fell over all legitimate anthropological research. For years afterward, many U.S. anthropologists experienced difficulties trying to prove that they were not engaged in secret research sponsored by the CIA or the Department of Defense. On a personal note, five years

Project Camelot An aborted U.S. Army research project designed to study the cause of civil unrest and violence in developing countries; created a controversy among anthropologists as to whether the U.S. government was using them as spies.

after the demise of Project Camelot in Chile, this author was questioned on several occasions by his Kikuyu informants in Kenya (who were aware of Project Camelot) about his possible links with the U.S. government.

The discipline of anthropology learned an important but costly lesson from Vietnam and Project Camelot: Anthropologists have a responsibility to their subjects, their profession, their colleagues, and themselves to become much more aware of the motives, objectives, and assumptions of the organizations sponsoring their research. All anthropologists have an ethical responsibility to avoid employment or the receipt of funds from any organization that would use their research findings in morally questionable ways.

In 2000, ethical questions were raised anew with the publication of Patrick Tierney's book *Darkness in El Dorado: How Scientists and Journalists Devastated the Amazon*. A cultural anthropologist and an ethnographic filmmaker were accused of staging events for the camera and inciting men to warfare in order to support their claims that the local people were naturally violent. Moreover, Tierney claimed that other anthropologists, working in the same area, had purposefully introduced measles into a remote Amazon community in order to test their genetic theories. While the charges and countercharges may never be resolved definitively, the book and the ensuing controversy surrounding it have stimulated much discussion and perhaps some ethical education for anthropologists concerning issues such as informed consent, deception in research, and the protection of human rights of those being studied.

Anthropologists' Major Areas of Responsibility

The codes of professional ethics adopted by the American Anthropological Association (AAA) or the Society for Applied Anthropology (SFAA) are not appreciably different. Both codes cover the major areas of responsibility for practicing anthropologists, including the following:

■ *Responsibility to the people studied:* According to the AAA, the anthropologist's paramount responsibility is to the people he or she studies. Every effort must be made to protect the physical, psychological, and social well-being of the people under study. The aims and anticipated consequences of the research must be clearly communicated to the research subjects so that they can be in the best position to decide for themselves whether they wish to participate in the research. Participation is to be voluntary and should be based on the principle of informed consent. Informants should in no way be exploited, and their rights to remain anonymous must be protected.

■ *Responsibility to the public:* Anthropologists have a fundamental responsibility to respect the dignity, integrity, and worth of the communities that will be directly affected by the research findings. In a more general sense, anthropologists have a responsibility to the general public to disseminate their findings truthfully and openly. They are also expected to make their findings available to the public for use in policy formation.

■ *Responsibility to the discipline:* Anthropologists bear responsibility for maintaining the reputation of the discipline and their colleagues. They must avoid engaging in any research of which the results or sponsorship cannot be freely and openly reported. Anthropologists must refrain from any behavior that will jeopardize future research for other members of the profession.

■ *Responsibility to students:* Anthropologists should be fair, candid, and non-exploitive when dealing with their students. They should alert students to the ethical problems of research and should acknowledge in print the contributions that students make to anthropologists' professional activities, including both research and publications.

■ *Responsibility to sponsors:* Anthropologists have a professional responsibility to be honest about their qualifications, capabilities, and purposes. Before accepting employment or research funding, an anthropologist is obligated to reflect sincerely on the purposes of the sponsoring organizations and the potential uses to which the findings will be put. Anthropologists must retain the right to make all ethical decisions in their research while at the same time reporting the research findings accurately, openly, and completely.

■ *Responsibility to one's own and the host governments:* Anthropologists should be honest and candid in their relationships with both their own and the host governments. They should demand assurances that they will not be asked to compromise their professional standards or ethics as a precondition for research clearance. They should not conduct clandestine research or write secret reports.

With the growth in applied anthropology in recent decades, a number of cultural anthropologists are working for private-sector companies. Cultural anthropologists are now conducting market research on a wide variety of products and studying how cultural minorities can best be integrated into corporate cultures. This raises a number of important ethical dilemmas because, as employees, this new breed of applied anthropologists may not have control over their own research. To illustrate, it is possible that an employer could ask the applied anthropologist to engage in research that could be harmful to the target population, such as how best to market cigarettes or alcohol. Or, even in cases where the products are not harmful, it is possible that anthropological research can be applied not to developing better products, but rather to devise new ways to dupe consumers into buying one product rather than a competitor's. Also, suppose an applied anthropologist was prohibited from publishing important scientific findings based on his or her proprietary research because the employing firm felt it might give an advantage to a competitor. Unfortunately, these, and many other, potential conflicts of interest are not explicitly covered by the general guidelines of either the AAA or the SFAA.

Sometimes, particularly when conducting potentially risky research, a fieldworker can be faced with conflicting ethical responsibilities. One such recent case involved Rik Scarce, an ethnographer from Washington State University, who conducted a study of the radical environmental movement. Among the groups Scarce examined were Greenpeace, Earth First!, and the Animal Liberation Front (ALF). A year after the publication of his findings, one of the groups studied, the ALF, raided a federally funded animal research laboratory at Washington State University. Because some of the defendants in the case had been his informants, Scarce was subpoenaed to testify

against the ALF defendants. Even though the aforementioned ethical guidelines call for dealing honestly with governmental officials, to do so in this case would have violated another ethical principle—that is, protecting the confidentiality of one's sources of information. Scarce argued before the court that, if coerced to testify against his research subjects, he would be violating his own promise and obligation to maintain their anonymity. He further argued that to testify would jeopardize his own career as a social scientist because future research subjects would refuse to talk to him and academic/research institutions would be reluctant to hire him. Clearly, Scarce found himself at the horns of an ethical dilemma. His eventual choice not to violate the confidence of his research subjects resulted in his being jailed for 159 days for contempt of court. Scarce tells of his ethical stance and his subsequent jailing in a recent book entitled *Contempt of Court* (2005). This case illustrates that field ethnographers in the United States have little legal protection in maintaining the confidentiality of their sources. ∎

Summary

1. Since the beginning of the twentieth century, cultural anthropologists have conducted their research in a first-hand manner by means of direct fieldwork. Explicit discussion of how anthropologists actually do their fieldwork is a much more recent phenomenon, however.

2. A number of preparations must be made before any fieldwork experience is begun, including the securing of research funds; taking adequate health precautions, such as getting immunizations; obtaining research clearance from the host government; gaining proficiency in the local language; and attending to a host of personal matters, such as making provisions for accompanying family members, securing passports and visas, purchasing equipment and supplies, and making sure that one's affairs at home are in order.

3. Although every fieldwork project in cultural anthropology has its own unique character, all projects go through the same basic stages: selecting a research problem, formulating a research design, collecting the data, analyzing the data, and interpreting the data.

4. Because no two fieldwork experiences are identical, it is important that cultural anthropologists match the appropriate data-gathering techniques to their own fieldwork situations. Among the tools at the fieldworker's disposal are participant-observation, interviewing, ethnographic mapping, census taking, document analysis, the collection of genealogies, and photography.

5. Some general guidelines are applicable to most fieldwork situations. First, when attempting to gain entry into a small community, it is advisable to work one's way down, rather than up, the political hierarchy. Second, when introducing oneself to the local population, it is important to select a single role for oneself and use it consistently. Third, to firmly establish one's credibility with the local people, it is best to proceed slowly.

6. The use of the participant-observation technique has certain methodological advantages, including increasing rapport and allowing the researcher to distinguish between real and normative behavior. Participant-observation is not without its methodological shortcomings, however. It is time-consuming, poses problems of data comparability, presents difficulties in recording data, and may interfere with the very thing that is being studied.

7. Ethnographic interviewing, which is particularly useful for collecting both attitudinal and behavioral data, is of two basic types: unstructured and structured interviews. In unstructured interviews, interviewers ask open-ended questions and permit interviewees to respond at their own pace. In contrast, in structured interviews, interviewers ask the same questions of all respondents, in the same order, and under the same set of social conditions.

8. When cultural anthropologists conduct field research in cultures different from their own, they need to be personally flexible and should always expect the unexpected. Like anyone else trying to operate in an unfamiliar cultural setting, cultural anthropologists are susceptible to culture shock.

9. Since the 1980s, postmodernists have conducted fieldwork as a collaborative learning experience

between themselves and their informants rather than as an objective, scientific discovery of how the culture works.

10. Largely through the efforts of Murdock, the Human Relations Area Files (HRAF)—the world's largest anthropological database—was developed for the purpose of testing hypotheses and building theory. The files include easily retrievable ethnographic data on more than three hundred different cultures organized according to more than seven hundred different subject headings.

11. Cultural anthropologists in general—but particularly applied anthropologists—face a number of

ethical problems when conducting their research. One very important ethical issue to which applied anthropologists must be sensitive is whether the people being studied will benefit from the proposed changes. Both the American Anthropological Association and the Society for Applied Anthropology have identified areas of ethical responsibility for practicing anthropologists, including responsibilities to the people under study, the local communities, the host governments and their own government, other members of the scholarly community, organizations that sponsor research, and their own students.

Key Terms

analyzing data	dependent variable	independent variable	research clearance
AnthroSource	document analysis	informant	research design
attitudinal data	ethnographic mapping	interpreting data	research proposal
behavioral data	event analysis	narrative ethnography	sociometric tracking
bicultural perspective	fieldwork	photography	structured interview
census taking	genealogical method	Project Camelot	survey methods
collecting data	Human Relations Area Files (HRAF)	proxemic analysis	unstructured interview
culture shock		reflexive ethnography	

Suggested Readings

Agar, Michael H. *The Professional Stranger,* 2d ed. San Diego: Academic, 1996. An up-to-date consideration of a wide range of methodological issues facing anthropologists. Drawing from his own extensive fieldwork experiences, Agar integrates traditional notions of science with more recent developments in narrative and interpretation.

Bernard, H. Russell. *Research Methods in Anthropology,* 4th ed. Lanham, MD: AltaMira Press, 2005. Now in its fourth edition, this is the best single textbook on both qualitative and quantitative methods in cultural anthropology.

DeVita, Philip R., ed. *Stumbling Toward Truth: Anthropologists at Work.* Prospect Heights, IL: Waveland Press, 2000. A collection of twenty-nine essays by cultural anthropologists who share some informative and amusing insights learned from doing fieldwork.

Fetterman, David M. *Ethnography: Step by Step,* 2d ed. Thousand Oaks, CA: Sage, 1997. A practical guide for doing ethnographic field research, this volume deals with topics such as participant-observation, sampling, interviewing, the use of technical equipment, analyzing data, and writing an ethnography.

Fife, Wayne. *Doing Fieldwork: Ethnographic Methods for Research in Developing Countries and Beyond.* New York:

Palgrave Macmillan, 2005. Drawing upon his own research in Papua New Guinea and parts of Canada, Fife shows beginning students of anthropology how to prepare for fieldwork, navigate through the fieldwork experience, collect data, analyze findings, and write up the final reports.

Jackson, Bruce, and Edward Ives. *The World Observed: Reflections on the Fieldwork Process.* Urbana: University of Illinois Press, 1996. A collection of sixteen essays by anthropologists, folklorists, and sociologists describing how the chaos of fieldwork comes into focus and how things eventually tend to make sense.

Jorgensen, Danny L. *Participant Observation: A Methodology for Human Studies.* Thousand Oaks, CA: Sage, 1989. A practical handbook for the collection of anthropological data through the technique of participant-observation.

Kutsche, Paul. *Field Ethnography: A Manual for Doing Cultural Anthropology.* Upper Saddle River, NJ: Prentice-Hall, 1997. This small volume aims to teach ethnography by doing ethnography. It contains college-level field assignments on topics such as ethnographic mapping and observing body language—as well as a number of exemplary student ethnographies.

Language and Communication

This woman and man are communicating nonverbally through sign language.

6

PERHAPS THE MOST DISTINCTIVE feature of being human is the capacity to create and use language and other symbolic forms of communication. It is hard to imagine how culture could even exist without language. Fundamental aspects of any culture such as religion, family relationships, and the management of technology would be virtually impossible without a symbolic form of communication. Our very capacity to adapt to the physical environment—which involves identifying usable resources, developing ways of acquiring them, and finally forming groups to exploit them—is made possible by language. It is generally held that language is the major vehicle for human thought because our linguistic categories provide the basis for perception and concept formation. Moreover, it is largely through language that we pass on our cultural heritage from one generation to the next. By translating our experiences into linguistic symbols, we are able to store them, manipulate them, and pass them on to future generations. Without the capacity to symbolize, we would not be able to practice religion, create and maintain systems of law, engage in science, or compose a symphony. Language, then, is such an integral part of the human condition that it permeates everything we do. In other words, humans are humans because, among other things, we can symbolize through the use of language.

THE NATURE OF LANGUAGE

Like so many other words we think we understand, the term *language* is far more complex than we might imagine. Language, which is found in all cultures of the world, is a symbolic system of sounds that, when put together according to a certain set of rules, conveys meanings to its speakers. The meanings attached to any given word in all languages are totally *arbitrary*. That is, the word *cow* has no particular connection to the large bovine animal that the English language refers to as a cow. The word *cow* is no more or less reasonable a word for that animal than would be *kaflumpha*, *sporge*, or *four-pronged squirter*. The word *cow* does not look

arbitrary nature of language The meanings attached to words in any language are not based on a logical or rational system but rather are arbitrary.

What We Will Learn

- How does human language differ from forms of communication in other animals?

- How do languages change?

- Are some languages superior to others?

- Do people from different cultures have different styles of linguistic discourse?

- What is the relationship between language and culture?

- How do people communicate without using words?

 Click!

For interactive exercises and study aids, Go to **www.ichapters.com**; enter the author name and select your text, then click the Study Help tab to purchase the following online resources:

- **ThomsonNOW** for chapter-specific online tutorials, quizzes, and a personalized study plan

- **Anthropology Resource Center** for interactive maps, modules, videos, and the Applied Anthropology site

- **Thomson Audio Study Products** for a brief overview of the major chapter themes and to test your knowledge with quiz questions

© AP/Wide World Photos

In an attempt to revive a moribund language, this young man on the left is learning the Walla Walla language of his ancestors from one of the few remaining speakers on the Umatilla Indian reservation in Oregon.

like a cow, sound like a cow, or have any particular physical connection to a cow. The only explanation for the use of the word is that somewhere during the evolution of the English language the word *cow* came to be used to refer to a large, milk-giving, domesticated animal. Other languages use different, and equally arbitrary, words to describe the very same animal.

Human communication differs from other animal communication systems in at least two other important respects. One feature of human language is its capacity to convey information about a thing or an event that is not present. This characteristic, known as *displacement*, enables humans to speak of purely hypothetical things, events that have happened in the past, and events that might happen in the future. In contrast to other animals, which communicate only about particular things that are in the present and in the immediate environment, language enables humans to think abstractly. Another feature of human communication that distinguishes it from nonhuman forms of communication is that it is transmitted largely through tradition rather than through experience alone. Although our propensity (and our physical equipment) for language is biologically based, the specific language that any given person speaks is passed from one generation to another through the process of learning. Adults in a linguistic community who already know the language teach the language to the children.

displacement   The ability to talk about things that are remote in time and space.

Diversity of Language

Given the very arbitrary nature of languages, it should come as no surprise that there is enormous linguistic diversity among human populations. Even though linguists do not agree on precisely how many discrete languages exist, a reasonable estimate would be six thousand (Diamond 2001). The criterion used to establish such estimates is mutual unintelligibility. That is, linguists assume that if people can understand one another, they speak the same language; if they are unable to understand one another, they speak different languages. The application of this criterion is not as straightforward as it might appear, however, because there are differing degrees of intelligibility. Nevertheless, despite our inability to establish the precise number of discrete languages found in the world today, the amount of linguistic diversity is vast. (For a comprehensive map of the major language families of the world, see page 117.)

Not only is there considerable variation in the number of languages of the world, but the size of the different language communities varies widely as well. It has been estimated (Katzner 1975) that 95 percent of the world's people speak fewer than one hundred of the approximately six thousand different languages. (See Table 6.1.) Mandarin alone accounts for about one in every five people on earth. When we add English, Hindi, Spanish, and Russian, the figure jumps to about 45 percent. Thus, the last 5 percent of the world's people speak thousands of discrete languages that have relatively few speakers.

Linguists today are particularly concerned about this last 5 percent of the world's languages, which are in danger of disappearing. The larger languages, which have both the power of the state and large numbers on their side, are in no danger of sliding into oblivion. Some linguists, such as Michael Krauss of the University of Alaska, estimate that as many as 90 percent of all languages will be extinct within a hundred years. If they do not die out altogether, they will become moribund—spoken only by a few older people and unknown to children (Dreifus 2001).

Traditional North American languages serve as tragic examples of how languages become moribund and eventually extinct. Of the many hundreds of languages that existed in North America when Europeans arrived, only about two hundred have survived into the twenty-first century, and most of these face a dubious future. How this loss of linguistic diversity has come about is not hard to understand. From the sixteenth century onward, Native Americans have been conquered, subdued, pacified, resettled, and moved onto reservations. After relegating them to the marginal areas of society, the Bureau of Indian Affairs, in a heavy-handed attempt to civilize the "savage beasts," took Native American children from their families, put them into boarding schools, and forced them to speak English. More recently, Native American children were punished or expelled from publicly supported schools if caught speaking their tradi-

tional languages. Clearly this is not an ideal environment for children to learn their traditional languages.

While many Native American languages have become moribund or extinct, there have been attempts recently to revive some of these languages. In 2004 the Linguistics Department at the University of California at Berkeley helped about fifty Native Americans learn to read, write, and speak their languages. Drawing on the ethnographic notes and recordings of anthropologists found in the university's archives, these Native Americans are becoming the first people to speak their language since the early part of the twentieth century. In some cases these Native Americans are learning directly from recordings made of their own grandparents and other family members. These Native American speakers of their lost tongues participated in a university-sponsored "Breath of Life" conference in June 2004 to demonstrate their new linguistic skills. The university sponsored a companion conference ("Stabilizing Indigenous Languages") attended by several hundred linguists and indigenous peoples from around the world to share strategies and success stories on how to rescue their own dying languages (*Seattle Times* 2004: 6).

Although such efforts to revive dying languages are admirable, the challenges facing those who would re-

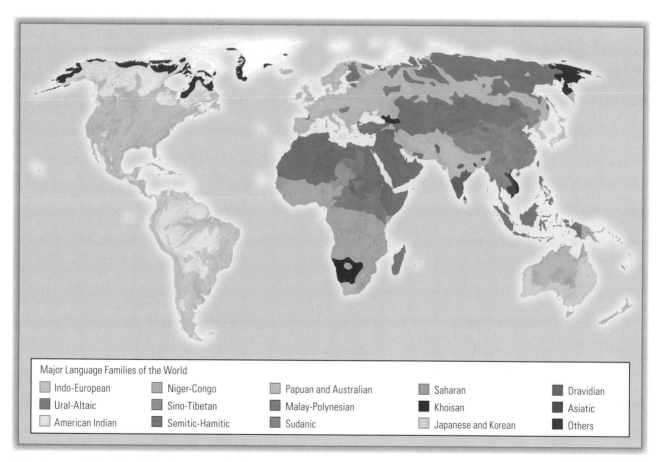

Major Language Families of the World

Indo-European   Niger-Congo   Papuan and Australian   Saharan   Dravidian
Ural-Altaic   Sino-Tibetan   Malay-Polynesian   Khoisan   Asiatic
American Indian   Semitic-Hamitic   Sudanic   Japanese and Korean   Others

Major Language Families of the World

Table 6.1 Major Languages of the World		
Language	**Primary Country**	**Number of Speakers**
Mandarin	China	873,000,000
Spanish	Spain/South America	322,000,000
English	United Kingdom/ United States	309,000,000
Hindi	India	180,000,000
Portuguese	Portugal/Brazil	177,000,000
Bengali	Bangladesh	171,000,000
Russian	Russia	145,000,000
Japanese	Japan	122,000,000
German (standard)	Germany	95,000,000
Wu	China	77,000,000
Korean	Korea	67,000,000

SOURCE: *The World Almanac and Book of Facts.* New York: World Almanac Education Group, 2006, p. 731.

verse the process are daunting. Not all of the extinctions are the direct result of hostility and repression from a dominant government, as was the case with Native Americans throughout most of U.S. history. The revolutionary changes in high-speed transportation and communication in recent decades have turned many young people throughout the world to the languages found on television and the Internet. Whatever the reason, the world is losing a significant number of languages every year. The tragedy is that because every language has its own way of encoding and expressing human experience, an entire way of thinking is lost each time a language becomes extinct.

But just as national governments can lead to languages becoming extinct, they can also add to the linguistic diversity of their people through national language policy. Some countries today—for example Mongolia, a large land-locked country located between Russia and China—has recently adopted a policy that English will be the major foreign language taught in the nation's schools. Using Singapore as a model, Mongolian officials see English as the best single world language for economic development and for opening windows on the wider world. Similarly, on the other side of the world, the Chilean government has embarked on a plan to teach the English language in all elementary and high schools, with the goal of English proficiency by the next generation. And in South Korea, six privately developed English-speaking villages are being established where residents will be able to take total immersion English language courses, live in buildings designed by Western architects, and live alongside English-speaking permanent residents (Brooke 2005; Rohter 2004).

Communication: Human Versus Nonhuman

Communication is certainly not unique to humans, for most animals have ways of sending and receiving messages. Various bird species use specific calls to communicate a desire to mate; honeybees communicate the distance and direction of sources of food very accurately through a series of body movements; certain antelope species give off a cry that warns of impending danger; even amoebae seem to send and receive crude messages chemically by discharging small amounts of carbon dioxide.

Communication among primates is considerably more complex. Some nonhuman primate species, such as gorillas and chimpanzees, draw on a large number of modes of communication, including various calls as well as nonverbal forms of communication such as facial expressions, body movement, and gestures. Yet despite the relative complexity of communication patterns among nonhuman primates, these patterns differ from human patterns of communication in some significant ways. For example, because animal call systems are to a large extent genetically based, they are rigidly inflexible to the extent that each call always has the same form and conveys the same meaning.

Open and Closed Communication Systems

Chimpanzees make one sound when they have found a plentiful source of food, another when threatened, and a third when announcing their presence. Each of these three sounds is unique in both form and message. And each sound (call) is mutually exclusive. That is, the chimpanzee cannot combine elements of two or more calls in order to develop a new call. To this extent we speak of nonhuman forms of communication as being *closed systems of communication*. Humans, on the other hand, operate with languages that are *open systems of communication* because they are capable of sending messages that have never been sent before.

Unlike nonhuman primates, language enables humans to send an infinite array of messages, including abstract ideas, highly technical information, and subtle shades of meaning. Starting with a limited number of sounds, human languages are capable of producing an infinite number of meanings by combining sounds and words into meanings that may have never been sent before. To illustrate, by combining a series of words in a certain order, we can convey a unique message that

closed system of communication Communication system in which the user cannot create new sounds or words by combining two or more existing sounds or words.
open system of communication System of communication in which the user can create new sounds or words by combining two or more existing sounds or words.

Joyce Butler of Columbia University shows famous chimpanzee Nim Chimpsky the sign configuration for "drink" and Nim imitates her. Even though Nim has been trained to use sign language, the differences between his form of communication and human language are vast.

Susan Kuklin/Photo Researchers, Inc.

has, in all likelihood, never been previously uttered: "I think that the woman named Clela with the bright orange hair left her leather handbag in the 1951 Studebaker that was involved in a hit-and-run accident later in the day." This productive capacity of human language illustrates how efficient and flexible human communication can be.

To suggest that the communication system of non-human primates such as chimps and gorillas is closed in contrast to the open system used by humans is an oversimplification. Some linguistic scholars, such as Noam Chomsky (1972), have posited that because human language is so radically different from other forms of animal communication, humans must be endowed with certain genetically based mental capacities found in no other species. As we have learned more about the communication systems of nonhuman primates, however, a growing number of scholars have questioned this theory by claiming that certain species, such as chimpanzees and gorillas, have a latent capacity to learn language.

A major limitation to the development of language among gorillas and chimps is physical, for they do not possess the vocal equipment for speech. In an effort to circumvent this physical limitation, recent researchers have taught some aspects of American Sign Language to chimpanzees and gorillas with some startling results. In four years, Allen and Beatrice Gardner (1969) taught a chimp named Washoe to use 130 different signs. Of even greater significance is the fact that Washoe was able to manipulate the signs in ways that previously had been thought possible only by humans. For example, Washoe was able to combine several signs to create a new word (having no sign for the word *duck*, she called it *waterbird*), thereby "opening up" her system of commu-

nication. In another important research effort in nonhuman communication, a gorilla named Koko by age four was able to use more than 250 different signs within a single hour and, like Washoe, was able to name new objects by combining several different signs.

These recent developments suggest that chimps and gorillas have more-complex powers of reasoning than had been believed earlier. Some have used this evidence to support the notion that chimpanzee and gorilla linguistic abilities differ from those of humans only in degree, not in kind. We must keep in mind, however, that nonhuman primates, despite their capacity to master several aspects of American Sign Language, do not have a language in the human sense of the term. There remain many features of human language that nonhuman primates, left to their own devices, do not possess and never will. Nonhuman primate systems of communication are complex and functional. They deserve to be studied on their own terms, rather than giving us the false impression that chimps and gorillas are really incipient humans (linguistically speaking) who simply need a little more time and assistance before being able to debate the sociopolitical complexities of globalization.

THE STRUCTURE OF LANGUAGE

Every language has a logical structure. When people encounter an unfamiliar language for the first time, they are confused and disoriented, but after becoming familiar with the language, they eventually discover its rules and how the various parts are interrelated. All languages have rules and principles governing what sounds are to be used and how those sounds are to be combined to convey meanings. Human languages have two aspects of structure: a sound (or phonological) structure and a grammatical structure. *Phonology* involves the study of the basic building blocks of a language, units of sound called phonemes, and how these phonemes are combined. The study of grammar involves identifying recurring sequences of phonemes, called morphemes, the smallest units of speech that convey a meaning. The *descriptive linguist*, whose job is to make explicit the structure of any given language, studies both the sound system and the grammatical system of as many different human languages as possible.

Phonology

The initial step in describing any language is to determine the sounds that are used. Humans have the vocal apparatus to make an extraordinarily large number of sounds, but no single language uses all possible sounds. Instead, each language uses a finite number of sounds, called *phonemes*, which are the minimal units of sound that signal a difference in meaning. The English language contains sounds for twenty-four consonants, nine vowels, three semivowels, and some other sound features—for a total of forty-six phonemes. The number of phonemes in other languages varies from a low of about fifteen to a high of about one hundred.

Clearly, the twenty-six letters of the English alphabet do not correspond to the total inventory of phonemes in the English language. This is largely because English has a number of inconsistent features. For example, we pronounce the same word differently (as in the present and past tense of the verb *read*) and we have different spellings for some words that sound identical, such as *meet* and *meat*. To address this difficulty, linguists have developed the International Phonetic Alphabet, which takes into account all of the possible sound units (phonemes) found in all languages of the world.

The manner in which sounds are grouped into phonemes varies from one language to another. In English, for example, the sounds represented by *b* and *v* comprise two separate phonemes. Such a distinction is absolutely necessary if an English speaker is to differentiate between such words as *ban* and *van* or *bent* and *vent*. The Spanish language, however, does not distinguish between these two sounds. When the Spanish word *ver* ("to see") is pronounced, it would be impossible for the English speaker to determine with absolute precision whether the word begins with a *v* or a *b*. Thus, whereas *v* and *b* are two distinct phonemes in English, they belong to the same sound class (or phoneme) in the Spanish language.

> *phonology*   The study of a language's sound system.
> *descriptive linguistics*   The branch of anthropological linguistics that studies how languages are structured.
> *phonemes*   The smallest sound contrasts in a language that distinguish meaning.

CROSS-CULTURAL MISCUE

Difficulties in communication can arise even between two people who ostensibly speak the same language. Although both New Yorkers and Londoners speak English, there are enough differences between American English and British English to cause communication miscues. Speakers of English on opposite sides of the Atlantic often use different words to refer to the same thing. To illustrate, Londoners put their trash in a dustbin, not a garbage can; they take a lift, not an elevator; and they live in flats, not apartments. To further complicate matters, the same word used in England and the United States can convey very different meanings. For example, in England the word *homely* (as in the statement "I think your wife is very homely") means warm and friendly, not plain or ugly as it means in the United States; for the British, the phrase "to table a motion" means to give an item a prominent place on the agenda rather than to postpone taking action on an item, as it means in the United States; and a rubber in British English is an eraser, not a condom. These are just a few of the linguistic pitfalls that North Americans and Brits may encounter when they attempt to communicate using their own versions of the "same" language.

Morphemes

Sounds and phonemes, though linguistically significant, usually do not convey meaning in themselves. The phonemes *r, a,* and *t* taken by themselves convey no meaning whatsoever. But when combined, they can form the words *rat, tar,* and *art,* each of which conveys meaning. Thus, two or more phonemes can be combined to form a *morpheme*.

Even though some words are made up of a single morpheme, we should not equate morphemes with words. In our example, the words *rat, tar,* and *art,* each made up of a single morpheme, cannot be subdivided into smaller units of meaning. In these cases, the words are made up of a single morpheme. However, the majority of words in any language are made up of two or more morphemes. The word *rats,* for example, contains two morphemes, the root word *rat* and the plural suffix *-s,* which conveys the meaning of more than one. Similarly, the word *artists* contains three morphemes: the root word *art;* the suffix *-ist,* meaning one who engages in the process of doing art; and the plural suffix *-s.* Some of these morphemes, like *art, tar,* and *rat,* can occur in a language unattached. Because they can stand alone,

> *morphemes*   The minimal linguistic forms (usually words) that convey meaning.

they are called *free morphemes*. Other morphemes, such as the suffix *-ist*, cannot stand alone, for they have no meaning except when attached to other morphemes. These are called *bound morphemes* (Figure 6.1).

Grammar

When people send linguistic messages by combining sounds into phonemes, phonemes into morphemes, and morphemes into words, they do so according to a highly complex set of rules. These rules, which are unique for each language, make up the *grammar* of the language and are well understood and followed by the speakers of that language. These grammatical systems, which constitute the formal structure of the language, consist of two parts: the rules governing how morphemes are formed into words (*morphology*) and the principles guiding how words are arranged into phrases and sentences (*syntax*). In some languages, meanings are determined primarily by the way morphemes are combined to form words (morphological features), whereas in other languages meanings are determined primarily by the order of words in a sentence (syntactical features).

The distinction between morphology and syntax can be illustrated by looking at an example from the English language. From a grammatical point of view, the statement "Mary fix Tom phone" does not make much sense. The order of the words in the statement (the syntax) is correct, but clearly some revision in the way that the words themselves are formed (morphology) is required for the statement to make grammatical sense. For example, because the English language requires information about verb tense, we must specify whether Mary fixed, is fixing, or will fix the phone. The English grammar system also requires information about the number of phones and the nature of the relationship between the phone and Tom. To make this statement grammatical, we can add an *-ed* to *fix*, an *-s* to *phone*, and an *-'s* to *Tom*. The revised statement ("Mary fixed Tom's phones"), which is now grammatically correct, tells us that Mary has already fixed two or more phones that belong to Tom.

Whereas the English grammar system requires that tense, number, and relationship be specified, other lan-

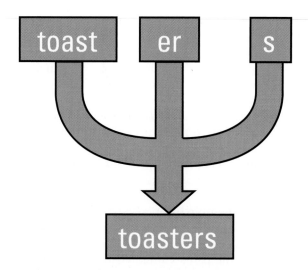

FIGURE 6.1 Morphemes Make Up Words. The word *toasters* is made up of the morphemes *toast, er*, and *s*. Which morphemes are free and which are bound?

guage systems require other types of information. For example, in Latin or Czech, a noun must have the proper case ending to indicate its role (such as subject or direct object) in the sentence. In some languages, such as Spanish, the ending on a noun determines the noun's gender (masculine or feminine). In the Navajo language, certain verbs such as "to handle" take different forms depending on the size and shape of the object being handled. Thus, every language has its own systematic way of ordering morphemes within a word to give linguistic meaning.

Syntax, on the other hand, is the aspect of grammar that governs the arrangement of words and phrases into sentences. In our original example ("Mary fix Tom phone"), the syntax is correct because the words are in the proper sequence. The statement would be totally meaningless if the words were ordered "fix Tom phone Mary," because the parts of speech are not in proper relationship to one another. Moreover, in English, adjectives generally precede the nouns they describe (such as "white horse"), whereas in Spanish adjectives generally follow the nouns they describe (such as "caballo blanco"). The order of the words, then, determines—at least in part—the meaning conveyed in any given language.

LANGUAGE CHANGE

When linguists look at the sound system or the structure of a language, they are engaging in *synchronic analysis* (that is, analysis at a single point in time). However, like

free morpheme A morpheme that appears in a language without being attached to other morphemes.
bound morpheme A morpheme that can convey meaning only when combined with another morpheme.
grammar The systematic ways sounds are combined in a language to allow users to send and receive meaningful utterances.
morphology The study of the rules governing how morphemes are turned into words.
syntax The linguistic rules, found in all languages, that determine how phrases and sentences are constructed.

synchronic analysis The analysis of cultural data at a single point in time, rather than through time.

all other aspects of culture, language is not static but rather is constantly changing. When linguists study how languages change over time, they are engaged in *diachronic analysis* (that is, analysis over a period of time). Languages can be studied diachronically or historically in various ways. For example, *historical linguists* may study changes in a single language, such as changes from Old English to modern English. Or linguists can look at changes that have occurred in related languages (comparative linguistics). Thus, historical linguists are interested in studying both the changes that have occurred in a single language over time as well as the historical relationship of languages to one another.

To better understand how a single language changes over time, we can look at certain versions of English over the past six hundred years. Following are three different versions of the Lord's Prayer, one written in Middle English (about 1400), one in early modern English (1611), and a contemporary version:

Middle English (about 1400)
Oure fadir that art in heuene halowid be thi name, thi kyngdom come to, be thi wille don in erthe es in heuene, yeue to us this day oure bread ouir other substance, & foryeue to us oure dettis, as we forgeuen to oure dettouris, & lede us not in temptacion: but belyuer us from yuel, amen.

Early Modern English (1611)
Our father which art in heaven, hallowed be thy Name. Thy kingdome come. Thy will be done, in earth, as it is in heaven. Giue vs this day our dayly bread. And forgiue vs our debts, as we forgiue our debters. And leade vs not into temptation, but deliuer vs from euill: For thine is the kingdome, and the power, and the glory, for euer, Amen.

Contemporary English
Our Father, who is in heaven, may your name be kept holy. May your kingdom come into being. May your will be followed on earth, just as it is in heaven. Give us this day our food for the day. And forgive us our offenses, just as we forgive those who have offended us. And do not bring us to the test. But free us from evil. For the kingdom, the power, and the glory are yours forever. Amen.

As we can see from this example, the English language has changed in a number of aspects, including phonology, morphology, and syntax. Clearly spelling has changed, as in the cases of *erthe* to *earth* and *fadir* to *father*. Moreover, even the meanings of words change over time. In the early modern version the prayer speaks of forgiving our "debts" whereas in the contemporary version the meaning changes to "offenses" (Campbell 1999: 6).

diachronic analysis   The analysis of sociocultural data through time, rather than at a single point in time.
historical linguistics   The study of how languages change over time.

Changes in the meaning of words reflect changing cultural values. The value placed on being old in the United States, for example, changed dramatically between the eighteenth and nineteenth centuries. To illustrate, the English word *fogy* was a term of respect for a veteran in the 1700s. By the mid-1800s, however, the word took on a derisive meaning, largely because our values and attitudes toward the elderly were changing from deference and respect to contempt and neglect. Later in the century (as we became more of a youth culture), the term *fogy* was joined with new disparaging terms for the elderly, including *codger, coot, fuddy-duddy,* and *geezer*. And the derogatory terms used for the elderly continue into the present with such words as *fossil, blue hair, senior, gray panther, golden ager, cottontop,* and *gerry* (short for geriatric).

Just as languages change for internal reasons, they also are changed by external forces, or linguistic borrowing. It is generally thought that languages borrow from one another for two primary reasons: need and prestige. When a language community acquires a new cultural item such as a concept or a material object, it needs a word to describe it. This explains why different cultures have similar words referring to the same item such as automobiles, computers, and coffee. The other reason that words are borrowed from other languages is that they convey some measure of prestige to the speakers of the recipient language. To illustrate, the French word *cuisine* (from *kitchen*) was adopted into English because French food was considered more prestigious than English food during the period of French dominance (700 to 950 years ago).

Interestingly, the introduction of new words into a language parallels the events that shape that language community's history. In fact, knowing the history of a group of people, and particularly its relationships with other linguistic groups, is an excellent way to study historical linguistics. Again, we can illustrate the history of changes in the English language by knowing something about early English history. For example, approximately 2,800 years ago the British Isles were settled by the Celts, which accounts for the original Celtic language. An initial introduction of Latin words was caused by Roman military forays 2,100 years ago. In the mid-fifth century, the German language was introduced when the Germans from mainland Europe defeated the Celts. More Latin words (for example, *altar, school, chalice,* and *relic*) were introduced when England converted to Christianity around the sixth century. Scandinavian words such as *sky, trust,* and *skirt* came into the English language as a direct result of the Scandinavian invasions between the ninth and eleventh centuries. A major period of word borrowing from the French language occurred after the Norman invasion (1066). More Latin and some Greek words were diffused into English during the times of Shakespeare and the European Renaissance. The era of British imperialism from the sixteenth to the nineteenth centuries—when the British

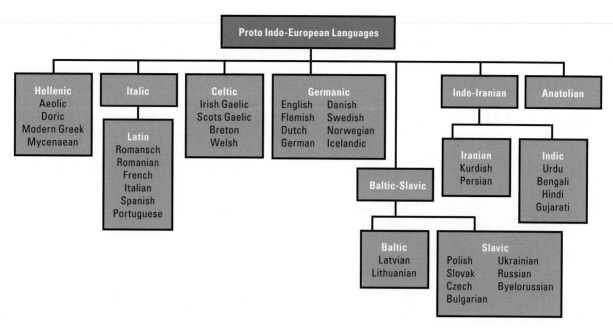

FIGURE 6.2   Proto Indo-European Languages.

acquired spheres of influence outside of Europe—resulted in a number of new words (such as *safari, mogul,* and *pajama*) borrowed from Africa, Asia, and India. And the industrial revolution of the nineteenth century and the postindustrial information age of the late twentieth century brought a large number of words into the English language, primarily of a technological nature.

Only slightly more than 60 percent of all English words used today are derived from Old English (Cipollone, Keiser, and Vasishth 1998). In a survey of widely used English words, 38.3 percent of the words had their origins in other languages. The French language, by far, has had the greatest lexical influence on English, with more than 30 percent of all English words being derived from French. Approximately 3 percent of English words came from Latin, 1.7 percent from Scandinavian languages, and less than 1 percent from German and Dutch.

Language Families

The study of historical linguistics dates back to the 1880s, when Sir William Jones, a British scholar living in India, noticed the remarkable similarities between Sanskrit, an ancient Indian language, and classical Greek and Latin. Jones accounted for these similarities by suggesting that all three languages were descended from a common ancestral language. Because Jones was writing at the time that Darwin's notion of evolution was popular, it is not surprising that Jones assumed that languages evolve in much the same way as do biological organisms. Thus, Jones and the first generation of historical linguists suggested that languages had family trees. By comparing similar languages, linguists are able to identify their common features, which probably derive from an ancestral language or protolanguage.

Thus, a *language family* comprises all of the languages that derive from its common protolanguage. And in keeping with the family analogy, historical linguists use terms such as *mother, parent, sister,* and *daughter* languages. To illustrate, the English language is part of the family known as the Indo-European language family (see Figure 6.2). Within this family structure, Germanic is the mother of English; French and Spanish (whose mother is Latin) are sister languages, whereas Russian, Bulgarian, and Polish share a common Slavic mother. Linguists generally agree that there are more than 250 different language families in the world today and about six thousand distinct, mutually unintelligible languages. Of these 250 language families, 150 are found in the Americas, 60 in New Guinea, 26 in Australia, 20 in Africa, and 37 in Europe and Asia.

Such diagrams of language families show the direction of linguistic change and how the various languages of a region are interconnected. They read very much like kinship diagrams (see Chapter 10) indicating the genealogical relationships between relatives. However, they can be misleading in their simplicity. Even though Figure 6.2 presents each language as a distinct, discrete entity, the boundaries are not quite so well defined in real life. Every language has internal variations as well as ongoing relationships with nearby language communities. That is, all languages have internal dialects while at the same time sharing linguistic features with other languages. It is also misleading to assume that the splitting of a parent language into daughter languages occurs suddenly or abruptly. In reality, languages split apart very slowly, starting as dialects and then gradually

language family   A grouping of related languages.

establishing their own identity as separate languages. This gradual fission makes it very difficult to tell exactly when it is that a language becomes a separate entity.

ARE SOME LANGUAGES SUPERIOR TO OTHERS?

Until the start of the twentieth century, European linguists were convinced that Western languages were superior to all others in terms of elegance, efficiency, and beauty. It was generally assumed that small-scale, non-Western cultures characterized by simple technologies had equally simple languages. In short, preliterate people were thought to have primitive languages with a diminished capacity for expressing abstract ideas. Today, however, anthropological linguists, following the lead of Franz Boas, consider such views untenable.

Table 6.2 English Is No Easy Language to Learn

The medic *wound* the bandage around the *wound*.

The dump was so full that it had to *refuse* more *refuse*.

The *Polish* woman decided to *polish* her dining room table.

He could not *lead* the way because his pants were full of *lead*.

The soldier decided to *desert* his *dessert* in the *desert*.

When Mr. Cheney fired his gun, the *dove dove* into the bushes.

I did not *object* to the *object*.

The *invalid* had an *invalid* driver's license.

Two members of the Harvard crew team had a *row* about how to *row*.

They were too *close* to the door to *close* it.

The buck *does* funny things when the *does* are around

After the dentist gave me a *number* of injections, my jaw finally got *number*.

I shed a *tear* when I noticed a *tear* in my new suit jacket.

I had to *subject* the *subject* to a series of tests.

How can I *intimate* this to my most *intimate* friend.

Or have you ever asked yourself these questions?

- If the plural of *tooth* is *teeth*, then why isn't the plural of *moose, meese?*

- Why are boxing rings square?

- Why do I push the *start* button when I want to *shut down* my computer?

- Why do we say that the alarm *went off* when in fact it *turned on?*

- How do we explain that eggplant contains no *eggs*, hamburgers contain no *ham*, and pineapple contains neither *pine* nor *apples?*

- Do you know the difference between *groundhog meat* (the flesh of an animal called a groundhog) and *ground hog meat* (ground pork)?

Based on studies of American Indian languages, linguists have demonstrated time and again that people from technologically simple societies are no less capable of expressing a wide variety of abstract ideas than are people living in high-technology societies.

To illustrate this point, we can compare the English language with that of a traditionally technologically simple society: the Navajo people of the American Southwest. It is true that Navajo speakers are unable to make certain grammatical distinctions commonly made in English. For example, Navajo does not have separate noun forms for singular and plural (such as are found in English with the *-s* in *dogs* or the *-ren* in *children*); the third person pronoun is both singular and plural and gender nonspecific (it can be translated *he, she, it*, or *they*, depending on the context); and there are no adjectives, because the role of the adjective to describe nouns in English is played by the verb.

Although the Navajo language does not make the same grammatical distinctions as does the English language, in other areas it can express certain information with considerably more precision and efficiency than English. According to Peter Farb (1968: 56), making a vague statement such as "I am going" is impossible in the Navajo language. Because of the structure of this language, the verb stem would include additional information on whether the person is going on foot, by horseback, in a wagon, by boat, or in an airplane. If the selected verb form indicates that the person is going on horseback, it is necessary to further differentiate by verb form whether the horse is walking, trotting, galloping, or running. Thus, in the Navajo language a great deal of information is conveyed in the single verb form that is selected to express the concept of going. To be certain, the grammatical systems of the English and Navajo languages are very different. The English language can convey all of the same information, but it requires many more words. Nevertheless, it is hardly reasonable to conclude that one language is more efficient at expressing abstract ideas than the other.

LANGUAGE AND CULTURE

For the cultural anthropologist, the study of language is important not only for the practical purpose of communicating while doing fieldwork but also because a close relationship exists between language and culture. It would be difficult, if not impossible, to understand a culture without first understanding its language, and it would be equally impossible to understand a language outside its cultural context. For this reason, any effective language teacher will go beyond vocabulary and grammar by teaching students something about such topics as eating habits, values, and behavior patterns of native speakers. This important relationship between language and culture—which is the subject matter of **cultural linguistics**—was recognized in the early twentieth century by the father of modern American cultural anthropology, Franz Boas:

> The study of language must be considered as one of the most important branches of ethnological study, because, on the one hand, a thorough insight into ethnology cannot be gained without a practical knowledge of the language, and, on the other hand, the fundamental concepts illustrated by human languages are not distinct in kind from ethnological phenomena; and because, furthermore, the peculiar characteristics of language are clearly reflected in the views and customs of the peoples of the world.
> (1911b: 73)

How Culture Influences Language

Although little research has been conducted to explore how culture influences the grammatical system of a language, there is considerable evidence to demonstrate how culture affects vocabulary. As a general rule, the vocabulary found in any language tends to emphasize the words that are considered to be adaptively important in that culture. This concept, known as *cultural emphasis*, is reflected in the size and specialization of vocabulary.

In standard American English, we find large numbers of words that refer to technological gadgetry (such as *tractor, microchip,* and *intake valve*) and occupational specialties (such as *teacher, plumber, CPA,* and *pediatrician*) for the simple reason that technology and occupation are points of cultural emphasis in our culture. Thus, the English language helps North Americans adapt effectively to their culture by providing a vocabulary well suited for that culture. Other cultures have other areas of emphasis.

The Nuer

A particularly good example of how culture influences language through the elaboration of vocabularies is provided by the Nuer, a pastoral people of the Sudan, whose daily preoccupation with cattle is reflected in their language (Evans-Pritchard 1940). The Nuer have a vast vocabulary used to describe and identify their cattle according to certain physical features such as color, markings, and horn configuration. The Nuer have ten major color terms for describing cattle: *white (bor), black (car), brown (lual), chestnut (dol), tawny (yan), mouse-gray (lou), bay (thiang), sandygray (lith), blue and strawberry roan (yil),* and *chocolate (gwir).* When these color possibilities are merged with the many possible marking patterns, there are several hundred combinations. And when these several hundred possibilities are combined with

terminology based on horn configuration, there are potentially thousands of ways of describing cattle with considerable precision in the Nuer language.

U.S. Example of Cultural Emphasis

In small-scale cultures such as the Nuer, where most people's lives revolve around herding, areas of cultural emphasis are fairly obvious. In middle-class American culture, which tends to be more complex occupationally, it is not always easy to identify a single area of cultural emphasis. Nevertheless, sports is one area of U.S. culture that can be shared by people from a wide variety of occupational or class backgrounds. As Nancy Hickerson (1980: 118) points out, we have many colloquialisms in American English that stem from the game of baseball, our national pastime:

- He made a grandstand play.
- She threw me a curve.
- She fielded my questions well.
- You're way off base.
- You're batting a thousand (five hundred, zero) so far.
- What are the ground rules?
- I want to touch all the bases.
- He went to bat for me.
- He has two strikes against him.
- That's way out in left field.
- He drives me up the wall.
- He's a team player (a clutch player).
- She's an oddball (screwball, foul ball).
- It's just a ballpark estimate.

cultural emphasis of a language The idea that the vocabulary in any language tends to emphasize words that are adaptively important in that culture.

Technology—one aspect of culture—is also influencing language, and even the authenticity of our communication, in twenty-first-century America. With the dramatic growth of cell phone use over the past decade (more than a billion are in use worldwide), a new phenomenon has emerged, at least in many Western cultures—faking cell phone conversations. Some people in public spaces pretend to be talking on their cell phones to avoid social contact with panhandlers or unwanted approaches by men. Others, frequently men, conduct phony conversations to give themselves an air of importance while "checking out" women. Still others may engage in cell phone subterfuge just to communicate to others around them that they are sufficiently socially connected to at least have someone to call, even if they don't. And, who could forget about the brazen woman who robbed four banks in northern Virginia in October 2005 while chatting on her cell phone the entire time?

Cell phone technology now makes it possible to send deceptive or false messages. For example, Sounder Cover, a new application for Nokia Series 60 cell phones, allows users to add various background sounds to phone calls to make it seem as if they are somewhere else, such as caught in traffic or near heavy machinery rather than in a singles' bar. For those with video phones, it is now possible for users to select a background of their choice before answering the phone, thus allowing a cheating husband or wife to answer a call with a photo of the office in the background. Cell phone users who want to get out of work or an unwanted social engagement now have a convenient excuse. According to Matt Richtel (2004), a group of several thousand cell phone users have formed an "alibi and excuse club" in which one member lies on behalf of another. Along the same lines, Cingular Wireless now offers a new technological mechanism (at $4.95 per month) for sending false messages called "Escape-A-Date." If you are going on a date with someone for the first time, you can arrange to have your cell phone ring at a prearranged time. A prerecorded message then guides you through a script that makes it sound to the unsuspecting first-time date as though you must rush off. If the date is going well, however, you simply turn off your cell phone. All of these recently developed cell phone "functionalities" have affected the way Westerners send and receive messages (or, to use a contemporary euphemism, provide "disinformation").

How Language Influences Culture

A major concern of linguistic anthropology since the 1930s has been the question of whether language influences or perhaps even determines culture. There is no consensus on this topic among ethnolinguists, but some have suggested that language is more than a symbolic inventory of experience and the physical world and that it actually shapes our thoughts and perceptions—the very way in which we see the world. Edward Sapir stated this notion in its most explicit form:

> The real world is to a large extent unconsciously built up on the language habits of the group. No two languages are ever sufficiently similar to be considered as representing the same social reality. The worlds in which different societies live are distinct worlds, not merely the same world with different labels attached. (1929: 214)

The Sapir–Whorf Hypothesis

Drawing on Sapir's original formulation, Benjamin Lee Whorf, a student of Sapir, conducted ethnolinguistic research among the Hopi Indians to determine whether

Would this skier have a more robust vocabulary focusing on different words for snow than would a non-skiing Floridian?

Although the Navajo and English languages have vastly different structures, these Navajo speakers can express abstract ideas every bit as effectively as native English speakers.

different linguistic structures produced different ways of viewing the world. Whorf's observations convinced him that linguistic structure was in fact the causal variable for different views of the world. This notion has come to be known as the *Sapir–Whorf hypothesis*.

Both Sapir and Whorf were suggesting that language is more than a vehicle for communication; it actually establishes mental categories that predispose people to see things in a certain way. For example, if my language has a single word—*aunt*—that refers to my mother's sister, my father's sister, my mother's brother's wife, and my father's brother's wife, it is likely that I will perceive all of these family members as genealogically equivalent and consequently will behave toward them in essentially the same way. Thus, Sapir and Whorf would suggest that both perception and the resulting behavior are determined by the linguistic categories we use to group some things under one heading and other things under another heading.

Testing the Hypothesis Since Sapir and Whorf's original formulation, a number of ethnolinguists have attempted to test the hypothesis. One very creative attempt at testing the Sapir–Whorf hypothesis was conducted by Joseph Casagrande (1960), using a matched sample of Navajo-speaking children. Half of the sample, who spoke only

Navajo, were matched on all significant sociocultural variables (such as religion, parental education, family income) with the other half, who spoke both Navajo and English. Because the groups were identical on all important variables except language, it would be logical to conclude that whatever perceptual differences emerged between the two groups could be attributed to language.

Having a thorough knowledge of the Navajo language, Casagrande understood that Navajo people, when speaking about an object, are required to choose among a number of different verb forms depending on the shape of the object. When asking a Navajo speaker to hand you an object, you use one verb form if the object is long and rigid like a stick and another verb form if it is long and flexible like a rope. Based on this linguistic feature, Casagrande hypothesized that children speaking only Navajo would be more likely to discriminate according to shape than the English-speaking children. English-speaking children would be more likely to discriminate according to other features such as size or color. This hypothesis was tested by having both groups of children participate in a number of tasks. The children were shown two objects (a yellow stick and a blue rope) and then asked to tell which of these two objects was most like a third object (a yellow rope). In other words, both groups of children were asked to categorize the yellow rope according to likeness with either the yellow stick or the blue rope. Casagrande found that the children who spoke only Navajo had a significantly greater tendency to categorize according to shape (yellow rope and blue rope) than the bilingual children, who were more likely to categorize according to color.

Sapir and Whorf were primarily concerned with the effects of language on perception. Whatever the exact nature of that relationship is, there is little disagreement among cultural linguists that people from different cultural groups do not see the world in exactly the same way. According to their hypothesis, languages establish in our minds categories that force us to distinguish between the things we consider different and the things we consider similar. For example, if Spaniards and Japanese are shown instantaneously projected images of bull fighters and sumo wrestlers, the Spaniards are likely to identify only the images of bull fighting while the Japanese will see only the images of sumo wrestling. The explanation of this phenomenon is that perception is selective. Because we are constantly being bombarded with far more stimuli than we can effectively process, our brains filter out the less familiar pieces of information so that we can concentrate on the more familiar. And, of course, what is familiar to any given person will be based on his or her learned experiences occurring within a cultural context.

The power of language can also be seen in the way people use language to alter other people's perceptions of various things. For example, language can be used to mislead by making things appear better than they ac-

Sapir–Whorf hypothesis The notion that a person's language shapes her or his perceptions and view of the world.

APPLIED PERSPECTIVE

Applied Anthropology and Ebonics

AP/Wide World Photos

When language may have an outcome in a court case, anthropologists (or more precisely, sociocultural linguists) may be brought in to give expert testimony. In 1979, a federal court in Ann Arbor, Michigan, concluded that Black students from a public elementary school were being denied their civil rights because they were not being taught to read, write, and speak standard English as an alternative to their dialect of Black English Vernacular (BEV). The presiding judge ruled that because the school system failed to recognize and use BEV as the basis for teaching standard English, the Black children were put at a disadvantage for succeeding in school and, consequently, in life (Chambers 1983).

This precedent-setting court decision rested on establishing the basic premise that BEV (now known as Ebonics) is a bona fide language. It was popularly held that the language of Black students was nothing more than slang, street talk, or a pathological form of standard English. But, as William Labov, a sociolinguist from the University of Pennsylvania, was able to establish to the satisfaction of the court, BEV is a full-fledged linguistic system with its own grammatical rules, phonology, and semantics. In other words, Labov's testimony demonstrated that BEV is governed by linguistic rules rather than being the result of errors in Standard English; BEV is as capable of expressing a wide range of abstract and complex ideas as is standard English; and the BEV spoken by children in Ann Arbor is the same as the BEV spoken in New York, Washington, Chicago, and Los Angeles.

On the basis of Labov's testimony, the federal court concluded that language is a vital link between a child and the education the child receives. Children who speak the same language as the language of instruction learn more effectively than those who speak a nonstandard version of the language of

---

tually are. Large organizations, such as corporations and branches of the federal government, are particularly adept at using euphemisms—forms of language used to conceal something unpleasant, bad, or inadequate. Companies no longer *fire* employees; rather, employees are *outplaced, released, dehired,* or *nonrenewed.* Corporate structures are *downsized, reengineered,* or *restructured.*

Terms like *reducing redundancy* and *enhancing efficiency* are designed to conceal the fact that the company is having problems. Military organizations use such euphemisms as *tactical redeployment* to refer to a retreat of troops, *preemptive strike* to disguise the fact that they attacked first, or *regime change* to gloss over the fact that a country's sovereignty has been violated. And when the

© Olivier Coret/In Visu/Corbis

This Iraqi man became totally distraught when an American missile attack reduced his house to rubble. A "preemptive war," designed to create "shock and awe," can lead to "collateral damage."

instruction. It should be pointed out that the court did not rule that children had to be taught in BEV. Rather the court ordered that the local schools were to acknowledge the fact that language used at home and in the community can pose a barrier to student learning when teachers fail to recognize it, understand it, and incorporate it into their instructional methods.

Even though this court case is now a quarter of a century old, the controversy is hardly over. In 1996 the school board of Oakland, California, approved a resolution recognizing Ebonics as the primary language of the district's African-American students. The public response, not only in Oakland but throughout the country, was instantaneous and almost universally negative. Everyone from the Reverend Jesse Jackson to White conservatives condemned the resolution as absolutely ridiculous. They argued that Black children need to learn Standard English if they are to succeed in school and in the job market. Unfortunately, most of the public outcry missed the point. By recognizing Ebonics, the school board certainly wasn't saying that African-American students should not be taught Standard English. On the contrary, the board was drawing on the very

principles for which Labov had fought years earlier. Their point was that the mastery of Standard English would be facilitated if the differences in Ebonics and Standard English were recognized and built into the educational program. The linguistic research conducted since Labov appeared in court in the late 1970s strongly suggests that Ebonic speakers learn Standard English more efficiently by using an approach that contrasts and compares the two languages.

Questions for Further Thought

1. Why did the judge in this court case rule that Black children were being placed at a disadvantage?
2. How was Labov able to argue that BEV was a bona fide language in its own right?
3. Why did the public outcry against Ebonics miss the point?
4. Of the various roles played by applied anthropologists discussed in Chapter 3, which one best describes Labov's role in this case study?

---

occupation of Iraq by the "coalition of the willing" failed to keep control of certain Iraqi cities, the world witnessed the "re-Bathicization of Falluja," a clever euphemism for handing the city back to the very people they went to war to replace. This type of language, designed to alter our perception of what is real, is called *doublespeak* by linguist William Lutz (1995: 54):

> Doublespeak, such as that which calls cab drivers *urban transportation specialists*, elevator operators *members of the vertical transportation corps*, and automobile mechanics *automotive internists*, can be considered humorous and relatively harmless. However, doublespeak that calls a fire in a nuclear reactor building *rapid oxidation*, an explosion in a nuclear power plant an *energetic disassembly*, the illegal overthrow of a legitimate administration *destabilizing a government*, and lies *inoperative statements* is language that attempts to avoid responsibility, that attempts to make the bad seem good, the negative appear positive, something unpleasant appear attractive, and that which seems to communicate but does not.

Drawbacks to the Hypothesis The problem with the Sapir–Whorf hypothesis—and the reason that it remains a hypothesis rather than a widely accepted fact—is one of causation. Sapir and Whorf were linguistic determinists who posited that language *determines* culture. In fact, Sapir

suggested that people are virtual prisoners of their language when he stated that "human beings ... are very much at the mercy of the particular language which has become the medium of expression for their society" (1929: 209). Others have suggested that language simply reflects, rather than determines, culture. To be certain, language and culture influence each other in a number of important ways. Yet problems arise when attempting to demonstrate that language determines culture, or vice versa, in any definitive way. What does seem obvious, however, is that all people, being constantly bombarded with sensory stimuli, have developed filtering systems to bring order to all of these incoming sensations. Sapir and Whorf have suggested that the filtering system is language, which provides a set of lenses that highlight some perceptions and de-emphasize others. Whatever may be the precise effect of language on culture, the Sapir–Whorf hypothesis has served to focus attention on this important relationship. For an interesting discussion of the Sapir–Whorf hypothesis and how it applies to language use in the United States, see David Thomson (1994).

Language Mirrors Values

In addition to reflecting its worldview, a language also reveals a culture's basic value structure. For example, the extent to which a culture values the individual, as compared to the group, is often reflected in its linguistic style. The value placed on the individual is deeply rooted in the North American psyche. Most North Americans start from the cultural assumption that the individual is

doublespeak The use of euphemisms to make things appear better than they actually are.

supreme and not only can, but should, shape his or her own destiny. That individualism is highly valued in the United States and Canada can be seen throughout their cultures, from the love of the automobile as the preferred mode of transportation to a judicial system that goes as far as any in the world to protect the individual rights of the accused. Even when dealing with children, North Americans try to provide them with a bedroom of their own, respect their individual right to privacy, and attempt to instill in them a sense of self-reliance and independence by encouraging them to solve their own problems.

Because of the close connection between language and culture, values (such as individualism in mainstream North America) are reflected in Standard American English. One such indicator of how our language reflects individualism is the number of words found in any American English dictionary that are compounded with the word *self*. To illustrate, one is likely to find in any standard English dictionary no fewer than 150 such words, including *self-absorbed*, *self-appointed*, *self-centered*, and *self-confidence*. This considerable list of English terms related to the individual is significantly larger than are found in a culture that places greater emphasis on corporate or group relationships.

Another indicator is that the first person (singular) pronoun *I* plays a prominent role in Standard American English. The words *I*, *me*, or *mine* are among the first words learned by an English-speaking child. Teachers encourage youngsters to use the pronoun *I* in order to be both assertive and become good autobiographers. Therapists and counselors encourage their patients to preface their statements with "I believe that . . ." or "It is my understanding that . . ." as a way of seeking both self-knowledge and good mental health. English-speaking North Americans even use the word *I* as a mechanism

to hold the floor when they can't think of anything else to say. Outside of the U.S. mainstream, however, the assertion of self through the frequent use of *I* is considered boorish, insensitive, self-promoting, impertinent, and even hostile.

In group-oriented cultures such as Japanese, people strive for the good of the larger group—such as the family or the community. Rather than stressing the pursuit of individual happiness, the Japanese are more concerned with justice (for group members) and righteousness (of group members). Group members in Japan don't want to stand out or assert their individuality because, according to a Japanese proverb, "The nail that sticks up gets hammered down." John Condon (1984: 9) reminds us that the group in Japan is always more prominent than the individual: "If Descartes had been Japanese, he would have said, 'We think, therefore we are.'"

LINGUISTIC STYLE

When we state that there are approximately six thousand mutually unintelligible languages spoken in the world today, we are implying that they all have unique vocabularies, grammar systems, and syntax. But each language group also varies in terms of linguistic style. For example, some linguistic groups send explicit messages directly, while other groups communicate indirectly by sending more implicit messages. In Canada and the United States, where words and eloquence are highly valued, people strive to communicate in a way that is precise, straightforward, and unambiguous. We are expected to "tell it like it is" and avoid "beating around the bush." Communication in some Asian cultures, by way of contrast, is noticeably more ambiguous, implicit, and inexact. With much less emphasis placed on words, many Asian cultures rely heavily on nonverbal cues and social context to derive meaning.

These differing linguistic styles can lead to cross-cultural misunderstandings. The very indirect style of the Japanese has been known to test the patience of Westerners, who mistakenly interpret it as sneaky and devious. In fact, Japanese indirectness stems from a predominating concern to allow others to "save face" and avoid shame. Direct communicators, such an Americans, Canadians, and Germans, choose their words carefully because they want to be as clear and unambiguous as possible. Japanese, on the other hand, also choose their words carefully, but for different reasons. Their meticulous choice of words stems from their desire to avoid blunt, offensive language, which would cause others to "lose face."

This stylistic difference between directness and indirectness can be illustrated by looking at TV commercials in the United States and Japan. Advertising in the United States clearly uses a hard-sell approach. Products are prominently displayed while viewers are bombarded with words aimed at convincing them to buy the product. How could we not buy a particular product if "nine

CROSS-CULTURAL MISCUE

An imperfect understanding of other languages has had some embarrassing consequences for North Americans engaging in international marketing. U.S. chicken entrepreneur Frank Perdue decided to translate one of his very successful advertising slogans into Spanish. Unfortunately, the new slogan didn't produce the desired results. The slogan "It takes a tough man to make a tender chicken" was translated into Spanish as "It takes a virile man to make a chicken affectionate."

The Pepsi-Cola Company, when attempting to use its catchy advertising slogan "Come alive with Pepsi" in Asia, learned that it was translated "Pepsi brings your dead ancestors back from the grave." And the Dairy Association's wildly successful U.S. ad campaign of "Got milk?" had the unfortunate translation "Are you lactating?" when used in Mexico. Although all of these cross-cultural advertising blunders cause us to snicker, they can result in a loss of revenue and diminished product credibility.

out of ten doctors agree …" or if "studies at a leading university confirm …"? North Americans are likely to see the fast- and loud-talking announcer telling us why we must not miss this weekend's "48-hour Sale-A-Thon" at the local car dealership. Television commercials in Japan, with their more subdued and indirect approach, are very different from those seen on U.S. or Canadian television. They do not preach or try to coerce you into buying the product. They do not use strong, persuasive language. In fact, sometimes it is not altogether clear what product is being advertised. One such Japanese commercial was described by Robert Collins (1992: 130–31), in which a man is sitting in a folding chair on a beautiful sunny day at the beach, with a dog at his side. He is wearing jeans, drinking an amber liquid from a glass, while his head bobs back and forth, apparently in time to music from his earphones. Classical music is playing on the soundtrack. Toward the end of the commercial, the man holds up his glass to toast the camera, while a voice announces the name of the product. End of commercial. This was not an advertisement for beer or for designer jeans, but rather for stomach medicine. Clearly, this is a very subtle and indirect message. The intended message was that the man would not be having such a wonderful time at the beach if he was at home with stomach distress. While there was much left unsaid in this commercial, the typical Japanese viewer would have no difficulty understanding the indirect, implicit, and subtle message.

Another aspect of indirect versus direct linguistic style is the role of silence in communication. People from indirect societies see silence as useful; they tolerate intermittent periods of silence so as to gain a better understanding of their communication partners. Direct communicators, such as the majority of North Ameri-

cans, avoid silence at all costs. Many Native American groups use silence as an integral part of their normal mode of discourse. Keith Basso (1970) has described the role of silence among the Apache of Arizona, who define silence as the proper way of dealing with certain categories of people. For example, Basso found that silence was used with strangers, during the initial stages of courtship, with children coming home after a long absence, with people who "cuss them out," with people who are sad, and with those involved in curing ceremonies. Interestingly, what was common to each of these six categories of people was that they all involved relationships that were ambiguous and unpredictable. Thus, in some cultures silence (that is, whether or not a person actually uses words) is determined by the nature of the social relationship between people and the social context in which they find themselves.

SOCIOLINGUISTICS

Anthropological linguistics has devoted much of its time and energy to the study of languages as logical systems of knowledge and communication. Recently, however, linguists have taken a keen interest in how people actually speak to one another in any given society. Whereas earlier linguists tended to focus on uniform structures (morphology, phonology, and syntax), sociolinguists concentrate on variations in language use depending on the social situation or context in which the speaker is operating.

In much the same way that entire speech communities adapt their language to changing situations, so do the individuals in those speech communities. Bilingualism and multilingualism are obvious examples of the situational use of language. A Hispanic junior high school student in Miami, for example, may speak English in the classroom and Spanish at home. But often people who are monolingual speak different forms of the same language depending on the social situation. To illustrate, the language that a college sophomore might use with a roommate would be appreciably different from that used when talking to his grandparents; or the choice of expressions heard in a football locker room would hardly be appropriate in a job interview. In short, what is said and how it is said are often influenced by variables such as the age, sex, and relative social status of the people involved. Whether we are talking about selectively using either totally different language or variations on the same language, the process is known as *code switching*.

The major focus of sociolinguistics is the relationship between language and social structure. What can we tell about the social relationships between two people from the language they use with each other? The analysis

This type of "in-your-face" advertising would not be well received in Japan.

code switching   The practice of using different languages or forms of a language depending on the social situation.

The form of the English language these teenagers from the United States use with their minister is quite different from the form used with their close friends.

of terms of address can be particularly useful in this regard. Professor Green, for example, could be addressed as Dr. Green, Ma'am, Professor, Ms. Green, Elizabeth, Darling, Doc, Prof, or Beth, depending on who is doing the addressing. One would not expect that her mother or husband would refer to her as Ma'am or that her students would call her Beth. Instead we would expect that the term of address chosen would reflect appropriately the relative social status of the two parties. That is, in middle-class American society, the reciprocal use of first names indicates a friendly, informal relationship between equals; the reciprocal use of titles followed by last names indicates a more formal relationship between people of roughly the same status; and the nonreciprocal use of first names and titles is found among people of unequal social status. We would also expect that the same person might use different terms of address for Professor Green in different social situations. Her husband might call her Beth at a cocktail party, Darling when they are making love, and Elizabeth when engaged in an argument.

Information technology, and particularly the cell phone, has altered the way people are communicating in the twenty-first century. Because it is less expensive to "text message" than to actually speak on one's cell phone, many messages today lack both intimacy and specific details. Because the typical cell phone screen accommodates only about 160 characters, this new craze of text messaging encourages blandness, brevity, superficiality (even though it does encourage creativity in devising such shorthand symbols as "gr8" and "2moro"). Because of the need to be brief, text messaging frees us of having to communicate with any type of intimacy or emotional content. One can flirt, make a date, or even break up with your "significant other" without having to divulge your emotions. While text messaging has become very widespread in the United States, it is even more widely used in Asia. According to data reported in the *New York Times* (McGrath 2006), during the third quarter of 2005, there were 19.4 billion text messages sent in the United States and 76.4 billion sent in China. This greater popularity in China is due, at least in part, to the nature of the Chinese language. Because in Mandarin Chinese the names of numbers sound very similar to certain words, it is possible to send the message "I love you" by simply typing in the number 520 or "Drop dead" by using 748.

Diglossia

The situational use of language in complex speech communities has been studied by Charles Ferguson (1964), who coined the term *diglossia*. With this term, Ferguson was referring to a linguistic situation in which two varieties of the same language (such as standard form, dialect, or pidgin) are spoken by the same person at different times and under different social circumstances.

diglossia   The situation in which two forms of the same language are spoken by people in the same language community depending on the social situation.

Ferguson illustrates the concept of diglossia by citing examples from a number of linguistic communities throughout the world, including the use of classical or Koranic Arabic and local forms of Arabic in North Africa and the Middle East, the coexistence of standard German and Swiss German in Switzerland, and the use of both French and Haitian Creole in Haiti. In speech communities where diglossia is found, there is a long-standing connection between appreciably different linguistic varieties. Which form is used carries with it important cultural meanings. For example, in all cases of diglossia, one form of the language is considered to be high and the other low (Table 6.3). High forms of the language are associated with literacy, education, and, to some degree, religion. The high forms are usually found as part of religious services, political speeches in legislative bodies, university lectures, news broadcasts, and newspapers. Low forms are likely to be found in the marketplace, when giving instructions to subordinates, in conversations with friends and relatives, and in various forms of pop culture, such as folk literature, television and radio programs, cartoons, and graffiti.

It is generally agreed that high forms of the language are superior to low forms, and often the use of the high form is associated with the elite and the upwardly mobile. This general superiority of the high form is at least partially the result of its association with religion and the fact that much of the literature of the language is written in the high form.

A variation on code switching between two distinct languages involves *blending* of the two languages simultaneously. So-called Spanglish (the blending of Spanish and English) is becoming a popular vernacular today in places like Los Angeles and Miami. To illustrate, words from both languages are combined into a single sentence such as: "Vamos a la store para comprar milk." (Translation: "Let's go to the store to buy milk.") While once disparaged by language purists, Spanglish is gaining considerable respectability among academics such as Amherst College professor Ilan Stavans, who recently published a Spanglish dictionary with 4,500 entries (Stavans 2003). As we proceed in the new millennium, Spanglish is becoming more mainstream, showing up in television and film scripts, in McDonald's advertising spots, and even on a line of Hallmark greeting cards. As the use of Spanglish becomes increasingly more widespread, a debate is emerging as to whether Spanglish is a fleeting form of slang or an emerging new language. It may be too early to answer that question at the present time, largely because it is still highly spontaneous and fluid (Hernandez 2003). Interestingly, a similar composite language called Denglish (a combination of Deutsch and English) is becoming commonplace in Germany, and is finding its way into advertising commercials for such German companies as Lufthansa and Douglas Perfumes.

Table 6.3 Diglossia	
High Form	**Low Form**
Religious service	Marketplace
Political speeches	Instructions to subordinates
Legislative proceedings	Friendly conversations
University lectures	Folk literature
News broadcasts	Radio/TV programs
Newspapers	Cartoons
Poetry	Graffiti

SOURCE: Charles A. Ferguson, "Diglossia," in *Language in Culture and Society: A Reader in Linguistics,* ed. Dell Hynes (New York: Harper & Row, 1964), pp. 429–39.

Specialized Vocabularies

The issue of code switching is seen quite dramatically in complex societies comprising a number of special-interest groups, each with its own specialized vocabulary. Lave and Wenger (1991) introduce the concept of "community of practice," a group of people within a large society who interact regularly around specialized activities. They may involve skateboarders or stockbrokers, prostitutes or politicians, or truck drivers or computer geeks. They may spend much time together or they may have only limited contact with one another. Similarly, members of a community of practice may have contact for decades with one another or their membership may be much more short lived. From a linguistic perspective, however, these "communities" develop unique ways of communicating, complete with their own signature expressions.

One highly visible community in twenty-first-century America is that of chic, young, single, urban women, who find their most obvious expression on HBO's *Sex and the City*. Members of this group are single, upwardly mobile, independent, and feel comfortable talking about themselves, their relationships, and their sex lives. And, of course, this group has spawned an entire glossary of terminology, which one social commentator (Levy 2004: 18) has called "chickspeak." In this lexicon we are likely to find words such as *gaydar* (an intuitive sense for determining whether a man is gay), *fatkin* (an adherent to the Atkins Diet, who takes the "all the fat you can eat" to its illogical extreme), *phone zit* (a blemish on the chin resulting from excess use of the telephone), and *teenile* (an adjective used to describe a middle-aged person who tries to act younger, such as a forty-two-year-old woman wearing low-rider jeans). Some of these words may be short lived, but some eventually may become part of mainstream American English. What is important, however, is that there are many "communities of practice" in complex societies that have established their own specialized vocabularies and ways of speaking.

Much of the specialized vocabulary used by single, urban women in the United States had its origin in the HBO show *Sex in the City*.

Dialects

The study of dialects is also the concern of sociolinguistics. *Dialects* are defined as regional or class variations of a language that are sufficiently similar to be mutually understood. It is not uncommon for certain dialects in complex speech communities to be considered substandard or inferior to others. Such claims are based on social or political rather than linguistic grounds. That is, minority dialects are often assigned an inferior status by the majority for the purpose of maintaining the political, economic, and social subordination of the minority. People who are not from the South regard certain Southernisms such as "y'all" (as in the statement, "Y'all come by and see us now") as quaint and colorful regional expressions (at best) or inferior and inappropriate incursions into standard American English (at worst). A more obvious example would be majority attitudes toward the nonStandard English dialect used by Black Americans in northern cities. Clearly, such usages as "You be goin' home" or "Don't nobody go nowhere" will never be used by major network newscasters. Although such expressions are considered to be inferior by the speakers of Standard English, these forms demon-

strate logically consistent grammatical patterns and in no way prevent the expression of complex or abstract ideas. NonStandard English should not be viewed as simply a series of haphazard mistakes in Standard English. Rather, it is a fully efficient language with its own unique set of grammatical rules that are applied consistently. Thus, in linguistic terms, the grammar and phonology of Black urban English are no less efficient than the language of the rich and powerful (Hecht, Collier, and Ribeau 1993; Rickford 1999).

Some linguists have suggested that during the last several decades of the twentieth century, regional dialects in the United States became less noticeable because of mass media, increased geographic mobility, and differing immigration patterns. Another possible explanation is that because regional dialects or accents are associated with certain socioeconomic classes, they are often dropped as people move up the social ladder. This seems to be the case with New Yorkese, the accent that the rest of the nation loves to hate. No matter where you are from, you will probably recognize some of these classic New Yorkese expressions:

- Didja (did you) or dincha (didn't you) go to the park?
- I need to go to the terlet (toilet).
- I understand you had a baby goil (girl).
- You wanna cuppa (cup of) kawfee (coffee)?
- Hey, alla (all of) youze (you) guys, get ovuh heee (over here).

This last example of dropping the *r* sound in the word *here* is characteristic of New Yorkese. Several linguists have shown, however, that "*r*-lessness" is more common among lower-class than upper-class New Yorkers. William Labov (1972) conducted a series of spontaneous interviews with salespeople in three New York department stores: S. Klein's (a low-prestige store), Macy's (moderate prestige), and Saks Fifth Avenue (high prestige). Labov found that clerks in the high-prestige store were significantly more likely to pronounce their *r*'s than were clerks in the low-prestige store. The Labov study reminds us, first, that dialects can vary according to social class, and second, that these linguistic patterns are constantly changing. During the 1940s, for example, *r*-lessness was found widely in the speech of all New Yorkers. But over the course of the last half century, wealthy, fashionable, and upwardly mobile New Yorkers have modified their twang for social reasons. It is no coincidence that there are twenty-eight listings for diction coaches in the Manhattan Yellow Pages.

Perhaps the accent that carries the highest status in the United States in not from the United States at all, but from the United Kingdom. The so-called British accent is associated—often erroneously—with high levels of charm, sophistication, wealth, and education.

---

dialects   Regional or class variations of a language that are sufficiently similar to be mutually intelligible.

Considerable differences in dialects are found between these upperclass people and sanitation workers.

In other words, it is considered classier than Standard American English, and even a bit regal. Consequently, people with British accents often are sought out for jobs as receptionists, voices on radio commercials, and as employees of telephone message production companies.

Language, Nationalism, and Ethnic Identity

It should be recognized that language plays an important symbolic role in the development of national and ethnic identities. In some situations powerful political leaders or factions attempt to suppress local languages for the sake of standardization across a nation-state. The country of Tanzania is a case in point. When Tanzania became independent in the 1960s, its leaders were faced with the task of running a country that contained 120 mutually unintelligible languages. Faced with the challenge of administering a country with such linguistic diversity, the government adopted Swahili as the official national language. This entailed Swahili becoming the language of instruction in schools, government bureaucracies, and parliament. Although Swahili (an Arabicized Bantu language) is no one's first language, it has served as a unifying *lingua franca* (common language) for the many linguistic communities that reside in Tanzania. To be certain, each linguistic group would have preferred to have had its own language declared the official language, but that decision early in its history as a sovereign nation enabled the country to standardize its national language and get on with the business of nation building.

In many other situations, the establishment of official languages has not gone so smoothly. In an attempt to strengthen the power of the Spanish nation, the Franco government made a number of unsuccessful attempts to suppress the minority Basque and Catalan languages by forbidding people from speaking them in public or using them on signs or billboards. But people take their languages seriously, and they often become a rallying point for expressing one's cultural identity. Each time a strong national government tries to suppress a minority language or establish the majority language as the official one, it is likely that minority populations will strongly resist. The government of India, for example, has had to abort its several attempts to establish Hindi as the official language of India because of riots erupting in non-Hindi-speaking areas of the country. And closer to home, the French-speaking province of Quebec, which for decades has had laws restricting the use of the English language in schools and on signs, nearly won its independence from Canada largely over the issue of language policy.

The issue of official languages is again a hot topic in the news with the recent expansion of the European Union from fifteen nations to twenty-five nations in 2004. The inclusion of these ten new member nations has increased the number of official languages from eleven to twenty and the number of translations needed from 110 to 380. Unlike the United Nations with its 191 members, which conducts its business in six official languages, the European Union has decided to adopt the democratic principle of allowing business to be conducted in *all* of the twenty official languages. The problems involved with 380 translations and interpretations are thought to be less objectionable than silencing any particular language, such as Maltese or Czech. While cumbersome, the actual cost of salaries for all of these translators is estimated to be less than $2.50 per citizen. So, unlike many nations that have excluded certain languages from the conduct of business, the European Union has affirmed the democratic ideal of cooperation and linguistic parity (Riding 2004: 3).

In some parts of the world, the influence of culture on language is a very deliberate, and indeed, political process. In France, the Académie Francaise, an official branch of the French government created by Cardinal Richelieu in 1635, has served as a form of "language police," protecting the French people from having to accept foreign words into their language. The Internet revolution of the 1990s has spawned a number of "e-words" from English that have been incorporated directly into many world languages. For example, nouns such as *web, spam,* and *virus* and verbs such as *surf, chat,* and *boot* have been adopted in their original English form by many language communities. But not so with the French. The recommended term for the World Wide Web is not *le web,* but rather *la toile* (the spider's web); moreover, the French "language police" prefer to use the term *les fouineurs* (nosy people) rather than the English word *hacker* for someone who breaks into computer systems illegally.

Thus, the French for more than 350 years have supported an official branch of the government whose mission is to keep non-French words out of its language. And where has this pride in the superiority of the French language gotten them? Not very far in terms of winning friends and influencing people. It is conceivable that if all linguistic communities could be less arrogant, and more willing to learn someone else's language, the world might be a more peaceful place in which to live. A recent study by Donitsa-Schmidt, Inbar, and Schohamy (2004) on the effects of teaching spoken Arabic to Israeli students tends to support such a statement. Based on a study of 692 elementary school students and 362 parents, the findings revealed that those students studying Arabic, as compared to those who did not, had more positive attitudes toward the Arabic language, its culture, and its native speakers. While running the risk of appearing to be an idealist, liberal, secular humanist vegan, it just might be that all people will be less likely to go to war with people whose language they understand.

NONVERBAL COMMUNICATION

To comprehend fully how people in any particular culture communicate, we must become familiar with their nonverbal forms of communication in addition to their language. *Nonverbal communication* is important because it helps us to interpret linguistic messages and often carries messages of its own. In fact, it has been suggested that up to 70 percent of all messages sent and received by humans are nonverbal in nature.

Like language, nonverbal forms of communication are learned and, as such, vary from one culture to another. Even though some nonverbal cues have the same meaning in different cultures, an enormous range of variation in nonverbal communication exists among cultures. In some cases, a certain message can be sent in a number of different ways by different cultures. For example, whereas in the United States we signify affirmation by nodding, the very same message is sent by throwing the head back in Ethiopia, by sharply thrusting the head forward among the Semang of Malaya, and by raising the eyebrows among the Dyaks of Borneo.

Humans communicate without words in a number of important ways, including hand gestures, facial expressions, eye contact, touching, space usage, scents, gait, and stance. A thorough discussion of these and other aspects of nonverbal communication, based on the recent literature, is beyond the scope of this textbook. A brief examination of three of the more salient types of nonverbal communication—hand gestures, posture, and touching—will help convey the importance of this form of human communication.

Hand Gestures

Consider how many hand gestures we use every day. We cup our hand behind the ear as a nonverbal way of communicating that we cannot hear. We thumb our noses at those we don't like. We can thumb a ride on the side of the highway. We can wave hello or good-bye. We tell people to be quiet by holding our forefinger vertically against our lips. We give the peace sign by

---

nonverbal communication   The various means by which humans send and receive messages without using words (for example, gestures, facial expressions, and touching).

CONTEMPORARY ISSUES

What You Don't Know Can Hurt You

The United States has been called, only half-jokingly, the "land of the free, and the home of the monolingual." One is hard-pressed to name another country in which a higher percentage of its native-born population speaks only one language. According to a recent study (European Union 2005), 50 percent of the total population of the European Union and 80 percent of students between the ages of fifteen and twenty-four have functional proficiency in a second language, as compared to only 9 percent of U.S. citizens. The United States is the only country in the world where it is possible to earn a university education without attaining functional literacy in a second language. Not only can it be done, but in actual fact, most university graduates in the United States never do master a second language. In 1998 only 6 percent of all undergraduates in the United States were enrolled in foreign language courses. Moreover, the existing instructional programs in foreign languages, from elementary school through the university, are largely voluntary, short term, superficial, and often the first to be cut when budgets are trimmed. In the current era of globalization, the need to understand other languages has become more critical than ever before, because what we don't know can hurt us.

The level of global ignorance in the United States, which is a national problem reaching epidemic proportions, is embarrassing and an unpleasant joke in the global community. To be certain, it can be debilitating to the extent that it prevents North Americans from meeting their professional objectives in the highly competitive world marketplace. At present, the United States has approximately ten thousand of its citizens attempting to conduct business in Japan, and fewer than 5 percent of them speak any Japanese whatsoever. And then we wonder why those "inscrutable" Japanese are reluctant to buy our products. If we are serious about being leaders in the global economy, we will have to do much better in terms of foreign language proficiency.

Getty Images

In addition to putting us at a marked disadvantage in the global marketplace, our ignorance of other languages and cultures is downright dangerous to our national security. To illustrate, in the late 1970s, Adolph Dubs, the U.S. ambassador to Afghanistan, was kidnapped and taken to the Kabul Hotel. The *Washington Star* reported that before the ambassador was slain, U.S. Embassy officials had a brief chance to seize the initiative because they reached the hotel before the Afghan police. Unfortunately, none of the American officials could speak either Dari or Pushtu, the two most widely spoken languages in Afghanistan. Had the embassy officials been able to communicate directly with the kidnappers, it is possible that the ambassador's life could have been spared.

Unfortunately, things have not changed since Ambassador Dubs was kidnapped and murdered a quarter of a century ago. The FBI has acknowledged that prior to the 1993 bombing of the World Trade Center they were in possession of notebooks, tapes, and phone taps that might have provided some warning signs, but the FBI could not decipher them because they were all in Arabic. And even now after the tragic events of September 11, 2001, the major U.S. government agencies leading the war on terrorism—namely, the CIA, the FBI, the Pentagon, and the State Department—are scrambling to find Americans who can speak Arabic (the fifth most widely spoken language in the world) as well as Dari and Pushtu. If we hope to be successful in the war on terrorism, the people of the United States need to become more linguistically savvy.

Despite these negative examples, we should remember that there are some North Americans—even some in the government—who are not hopelessly monolingual. For example, former U.S. president Jimmy Carter in 2002 gave a major address to the Cuban people in Havana completely in Spanish.

holding up our forefinger and middle finger, but send a very different message when we flash half of the peace sign. Or, by making a circle with our thumb and forefinger we can communicate that everything is "A-OK." However, problems arise with these gestures when we cross national boundaries. Although the "A-OK" sign carries a positive, upbeat message in North America, it refers to money in Japan, zero (worthless) in France, male homosexuality in Malta, and is an obscene gesture in parts of South America. Thus, a single hand gesture

carries with it many different meanings throughout the world. There are also many examples of the opposite phenomenon—namely, the use of different gestures to send the same message. For example, the nonverbal ways of communicating admiration for an attractive woman vary widely throughout the world. The Frenchman kisses his fingertips, the Italian twists an imaginary moustache, and the Brazilian curls one hand in front of another as if he is looking through an imaginary telescope.

The same gesture often carries different meanings in different languages. Beware! Don't do this in parts of South America. It doesn't mean "okay."

Posture (Body Stance)

The way that people hold their bodies often communicates information about their social status, religious practices, feelings of submissiveness, desires to maintain social distance, and sexual intentions—to mention several areas. When communicating, people tend to orient their bodies toward others by assuming a certain stance or posture. A person can stand over another person, can kneel, or can "turn a cold shoulder," and in each case something different would be communicated by the body posture. The meaning attached to different body postures varies from one culture to another and is learned in the same way that other aspects of a culture are internalized. To illustrate this point, we can look at differences in body posture that people assume when relaxing. People in the United States, for example, are sitters, whereas people in some rural parts of Mexico are squatters. This basic cultural difference has actually been used by the U.S. Border Patrol to identify illegal immigrants. According to Larry Samovar and Richard Porter (1991), by flying surveillance planes at low altitudes over migrant worker camps in southern California, the border patrol can tell which groups of campers are squatting and which are sitting, the implication being that the squatters are the illegal aliens.

Perhaps one of the most visible and dramatic nonverbal messages sent by posture is that of submissiveness. Generally, submissiveness is conveyed by making oneself appear smaller by lowering the body (crouching, cowering, or groveling). As part of their religious practices, some Christians kneel, Catholics genuflect, and Muslims kowtow, an extreme form of body lowering in which the forehead is brought to the ground. Nowhere is bowing more important to the process of communication today than in Japanese society. Bowing initiates interaction between two Japanese, it enhances and embellishes many parts of the ensuing conversation, and it is used to signal the end of a conversation. As an indication of

how pervasive bowing is in contemporary Japan, some Japanese department stores employ people whose sole function is to bow to customers as they enter the store. In fact, bowing is so ingrained into the Japanese psyche that some Japanese actually bow to invisible partners at the other end of a telephone line.

Touching

Touching is perhaps the most personal and intimate form of nonverbal communication. Humans communicate through touch in a variety of ways or for a variety of purposes, including patting a person on the head or back, slapping, kissing, punching, stroking, embracing, tickling, shaking hands, and laying-on of hands. Every culture has a well-defined set of meanings connected with touching. That is, each culture defines who can touch whom, on what parts of the body, and under what circumstances. Some cultures have been described as high-touch cultures and others as low-touch. Some studies (Montagu 1972; Sheflen 1972; Mehrabian 1981) have suggested that eastern European, Jewish, and Arab cultures tend to be high-touch cultures, whereas northern European cultures such as German and Scandinavian cultures tend to be low-touch. The difference between high- and low-touch cultures can be observed in public places, such as subways or elevators. For example, Londoners (from a low-touch culture) traveling in a crowded subway are likely to assume a rigid posture, studiously avoid eye contact, and refuse to even acknowledge the presence of other passengers. The French (from a high-touch culture), on the other hand, have no difficulty leaning and pressing against one another in a crowded Parisian subway. It is surprising that there can be such significant differences in touching behavior between the English and the French, two groups separated by a narrow channel of water.

If we need a reminder that touching is indeed a form of communication, we need only to observe hand touching behavior in urban African-American communities in Chicago or New York City. African-American males use a vast number of stylized touches to convey different types of meanings. As early as 1972 Benjamin Cooke analyzed a variety of ways of "giving skin" in the African-American community to convey greetings, agreement, farewell, emphasis, and compliments. Since then, handshakes have evolved in both style and meaning. When neighbors in Harlem meet one another today, they are likely to use the 1-4-5, a three-part greeting consisting of a single finger on the nose, four fingers placed over the heart, and a light five-finger slap. Another variation of greeting through touch involves three consecutive hand slaps followed by a half embrace, or the Tiger Claw, whereby interlocking fingers held at eye level push against each other. To be certain, there are many varieties and styles of handshakes in urban African-American communities that reflect creativity and individual expression. What they all have in common is that they send very intelligible messages (Moynihan 2004: 13). ∎

Summary

1. Language—and the capacity to use symbols—is perhaps the most distinctive hallmark of our humanity.

2. While there are approximately six thousand discrete languages in the world today, many languages from small-scale societies are becoming moribund or extinct at an alarming rate.

3. Although nonhumans also engage in communication, human communication systems are unique in several important respects. First, human communication systems are open; that is, they are capable of sending an infinite number of messages. Second, humans are the only animals that can communicate about events that happened in the past or might happen in the future. Third, human communication is transmitted largely through tradition rather than experience alone.

4. All human languages are structured in two ways. First, each language has a phonological structure comprising rules governing how sounds are combined to convey meanings. Second, each language has its own grammatical structure comprising the principles governing how morphemes are formed into words (morphology) and how words are arranged into phrases and sentences (syntax).

5. Like other aspects of culture, languages change over time in response to internal and external factors. Historical linguists want to know not only how languages change but also why they change.

6. Despite considerable structural variations in the many languages of the world, there is no evidence to support the claim that some languages are less efficient than others at expressing abstract ideas.

7. Cultures can influence language to the extent that the vocabulary in any language tends to emphasize words that are adaptively important in that culture. Thus, the highly specialized vocabulary in American English involving the automobile is directly related to the cultural emphasis that North Americans give to that particular part of their technology.

8. According to the Sapir–Whorf hypothesis, language is thought to influence perception. Language, according to Sapir and Whorf, not only is a system of communicating but also establishes mental categories that affect the way in which people conceptualize the real world.

9. Just as languages vary widely in terms of vocabulary, grammar systems, and syntax, they also vary in terms of features of linguistic style such as directness or tolerance for silence.

10. Sociolinguists are interested in studying how people use language depending on the social situation or context in which they are operating.

11. As important as language is in human communication, the majority of human messages are sent and received without using words. Human nonverbal communication—which, like language, is learned and culturally variable—can be transmitted through facial expressions, gestures, eye contact, touching, and posture.

Key Terms

arbitrary nature of language
bound morpheme
closed system of communication
code switching
cultural emphasis

cultural linguistics
descriptive linguistics
diachronic analysis
dialects
diglossia
displacement
doublespeak

free morpheme
grammar
historical linguistics
language family
morphemes
morphology
nonverbal communication

open system of communication
phonemes
phonology
Sapir–Whorf hypothesis
synchronic analysis
syntax

Suggested Readings

Bonvillain, Nancy. *Language, Culture and Communication: The Meaning of Messages,* 4th ed. Upper Saddle River, NJ: Prentice-Hall, 2002. This is a solid introduction to the field of anthropological linguistics that explores the connections among language, culture, and meaning.

Fromkin, Victoria, Robert Rodman, and Nina Hyams. *An Introduction to Language,* 7th ed. Boston: Heinle, 2002. A classic introduction to anthropological linguistics.

Ottenheimer, Harriet. *The Anthropology of Language: An Introduction to Linguistic Anthropology.* Belmont, CA: Wadsworth, 2005. A readable introduction to the field of linguistic anthropology, which includes lively discussions of language and culture, language structure, nonverbal communication, and linguistic change.

Rickford, J.R. and R.J. Rickford. *Spoken Soul: The Story of Black English.* New York: Wiley, 2000. A scholarly, yet readable, account of the history, structure, and meaning of BEV, which includes a section on the Oakland Ebonics controversy.

Salzmann, Zdenek. *Language, Culture, and Society: An Introduction to Linguistic Anthropology,* 3d ed. Boulder, CO: Westview, 2003. A comprehensive, up-to-date introduction to anthropological linguistics, this textbook looks at phonology, the origins of language, the social context of language, nonverbal communication, and the ethnography of communication.

Samovar, Larry A., Richard E. Porter, and Edwin R. McDaniel, eds. *Intercultural Communication: A Reader,* 11th ed. Belmont, CA: Wadsworth, 2005. A wide-ranging reader that introduces students to both the theory and practical implications of the field of intercultural communications.

Wardhaugh, Ronald. *An Introduction to Sociolinguistics,* 4th ed. Oxford: Blackwell, 2001. Designed as a beginning text in sociolinguistics, this volume deals with topics such as dialects and regional variations, speech communities, language change, gender differences, the relationship between language and culture, and language policy.

Making a Living

David Edwards/National Geographic Image Collection

In Mongolia, trained birds of prey are used for hunting small animals.

CHAPTER 7

TO SURVIVE, ANY CULTURE needs to solve certain societal problems. As we pointed out in our discussion of cultural universals in Chapter 2, all societies must develop systematic ways to control people's behavior, defend the group from outside forces, pass on cultural traditions from generation to generation, mate, rear children, and procure food from the environment. Of these basic societal needs, the need to secure food from one's surroundings is the most critical. The human body can survive for as long as a week or so without water and perhaps up to a month without food. Unless a society can develop a systematic and regular way of getting food for its members, the population will die off.

Like other aspects of culture, food-getting strategies vary widely from one society to another. Nevertheless, it is possible to identify five major food-procurement categories found among the world's populations:

- *Food collection:* The systematic collection of wild vegetation, the hunting of animals, and fishing

- *Horticulture:* A basic form of plant cultivation using simple tools and small plots of land and relying solely on human power

- *Pastoralism:* Keeping of domesticated animals (such as cows, goats, and sheep) and using their products (such as milk, meat, and blood) as a major food source

- *Agriculture:* A more productive form of cultivation than horticulture because of the use of animal power (such as horses or oxen) or mechanical power (tractors, reapers) and usually some form of irrigation

- *Industrialization:* Food production of food by means of complex machinery.

In this chapter we examine a number of different ways by which societies get their food, how food-getting strategies are influenced by technology and environment, and how humans adapt to a wide variety of environments. Traditional means of livelihood such as food collecting or nomadic pastoralism are often seen in the West as being backward, irrational, inefficient, and an obstacle to the development of modern economies. Before concluding, however, that one particular means of livelihood is superior to all others, it is important to first look at the

What We Will Learn

- What are the different ways by which societies get their food?

- How do technology and environment influence food-getting strategies?

- How have humans adapted to their environments over the ages?

 Click!

For interactive exercises and study aids, Go to **www.ichapters.com**; enter the author name and select your text, then click the Study Help tab to purchase the following online resources:

- **ThomsonNOW** for chapter-specific online tutorials, quizzes, and a personalized study plan

- **Anthropology Resource Center** for interactive maps, modules, videos, and the Applied Anthropology site

- **Thomson Audio Study Products** for a brief overview of the major chapter themes and to test your knowledge with quiz questions

inherent logic in each food procurement system. When we do that, we are likely to see how that particular food-getting strategy is the most rational for that particular environment.

HUMAN ADAPTATION

Anthropologists, particularly those specializing in environmental anthropology, have always had an interest in how humans adjust to their natural environments. They want to know how a particular environment influences people and their culture, and conversely, how the culture (and people's activities) influences the physical environment. When we speak of human adaptation to a particular environment, we are referring to two types of adaptation, *cultural* and *biological*. Cultural responses to cold climates include "technological" solutions such as building fires, using animal skins as clothing and blankets, and seeking refuge from the elements in caves or constructed dwellings. Humans living in cold climates also engage in certain behaviors that are adaptive: they tend to eat more food, particularly fats and carbohydrates; they engage in greater amounts of activity, which increases internal body temperature; and they curl up when sleeping to reduce the surface area of exposure and subsequent heat loss.

Adaptations to cold climates have also resulted in changes in body stature over time. Being short and stocky, and having short extremities, is the ideal body type for conserving energy because it reduces surface area of the body for dissipation of heat. Darwin's theory of natural selection is certainly well demonstrated by examining body types found in different climatic zones. To illustrate, Arctic people, such as the Inuit, are gener-ally short and stocky with short extremities. People living in hot equatorial zones, by way of contrast, tend to be taller and less stocky, with longer arms and legs. Although there are always exceptions to these general trends, human body weight (relative to height) tends to be higher in colder climates and lower in warmer climates.

It is commonly believed that the more sophisticated the technology, the better adapted a group will be to its environment. After all, in today's Western world, technology enables us to produce nearly infinite amounts of food, protect ourselves from the heat and cold with air conditioners and furnaces, and even replace human organs in order to prolong life. Yet many small-scale societies have made very satisfactory adaptations to their natural environment without the benefit of modern science and technology. Many groups living in remote parts of the world are so well tuned to their surroundings that they are able to manage their essential resources in highly efficient ways. They often have enormous knowledge of plant life that can be useful for eating, building houses, or curing illnesses. They cultivate crops by managing the soil, controlling proper moisture, preventing erosion, attracting certain organisms to reduce pests, and pacing their horticultural activities to correspond to seasonal cycles. In short, they use their accumulated knowledge to maximize the land's productivity and their own long-term benefits.

The Moken people of South Surin Island (off the coast of Thailand) are a living example of how adapting to one's physical environment can literally save your life. On December 26, 2004, when a massive tsunami killed more than one hundred and seventy thousand people from Indonesia to East Africa, all but one person in the total population of approximately two hundred coastal dwelling Moken people survived the tidal wave.

Most anthropologists agree that the environment sets broad limits on the possible form that food-getting patterns may take. Cultures help people adapt to a number of generally inhospitable environments.

This Moken woman—along with others in her coastal village—survived the deadly tsunami of 2004 because the local people had adapted sufficiently well to know how to predict tidal waves before they arrived.

Jean Chung/The New York Times/Redux

Because they have lived for centuries as fishermen and divers on an isolated island in the Andaman Sea, the Moken are closely attuned to the water. Moken elders, for generations, have passed down (orally) the knowledge that a tsunami (referred to as a "people eating wave") can be expected when the tide recedes rapidly and far. As soon as the elders witnessed this environmental phenomenon, they warned the entire village to seek higher ground in the nearby hills. No one in the Moken village could read or write, their technology was modest indeed, and they could not give a scientific explanation of the tsunami's cause. Nevertheless, traditional knowledge of the sea and their environment had been culturally transmitted so successfully that it led to the ultimate environmental adaptation—that is, avoiding a major catastrophe, while many other peoples in South Asia, who had higher levels of technology, never saw the tsunami coming (Goodnough 2005: 8).

We should not overly romanticize small-scale societies, however, by thinking that they always live in total harmony with their environments. Some cultures overfarm their soil, overgraze their pastures, and severely jeopardize both their livelihoods and their environments. This has become particularly true in recent years as many small-scale societies enter modern market economies. However, when not dealing with colonial governments or strong world market forces, many small-scale societies develop and maintain means of livelihood that are highly adaptive, productive, sustainable, and environmentally friendly.

There are a number of studies by environmental anthropologists documenting highly successful adaptations to the environment among contemporary societies, and we now have archaeological evidence to demonstrate successful land management in prehistoric socie-

ties. According to Kevin Krajick (1998), archaeological research in southern Peru indicates that Incas used conservation practices such as irrigation canals, terracing, and tree planting to build a highly efficient agricultural system in the Peruvian highlands. Archaeologists and geologists have found that between 2000 B.C. and 100 A.D., pre-Incan people had overfarmed the land, causing severe soil erosion and degradation. Core soil samples indicate that by the time the Incas took over the area, alder trees were beginning to proliferate, while soil erosion lessened and seeds from maize began to appear. Terraces were built by people who hauled soil to the hillsides from the valley and riverbeds below. And the Incas built a 31.2-mile canal system that provided water to hillside cultivators from streams and lakes located at higher altitudes. Researchers have suggested (based on both archaeological evidence and written accounts after the Spanish conquest in the early 1500s) that the Incas actually practiced agro-forestry by purposefully planting trees and managing them as part of the agricultural system.

As yet one more example of the usefulness of anthropological data, some of the ancient Incan farming practices are being revived for contemporary residents of the area. Since 1995 local Peruvian farmers have rebuilt the terraces by using traditional methods, reconstructed the canal system, and put 160 hectares under cultivation. Preliminary reports suggest that the crops are growing well and using less fertilizer than is required in other areas. Clearly the Incas had hundreds of years to develop an agricultural system that maximized the utility of the land without degrading it. Modern development specialists might learn something by paying attention to how local people traditionally related to their environments.

Examining the often disastrous effects of Western influences has given anthropologists heightened respect for the ways in which traditional peoples have adapted to their natural environments. Worldwide consumer appetites for cash crops such as coffee, tea, cocoa, sugar, pineapples, tobacco, and heroin (among many others) have led to the demise of traditional ecosystems all over the globe. Consumer demand for hardwood furniture has resulted in deforestation of tropical areas. Drilling for precious metals and fossil fuels (coal and oil) has also led to environmental degradation and the demise of traditional ecosystems. Even when Western governments have administered their "foreign aid" programs for economic development, inattention to how local people relate to their natural environments has produced unfortunate consequences.

The relationship between environment and culture is presently being tested in the Arctic region of the world. Despite the denials of some government officials that there is any such thing as "global warming," the Inuit populations residing in the Arctic regions of Alaska, Canada, Greenland, and northern Russia are the first to experience some of the rapid and dramatic changes that are occurring to their environment. Inuit residents in Pangnirtung on Canada's Baffin Island were shocked when temperatures in February 2006 were recorded at 68 degrees above normal; fish and wildlife are migrating still farther north of permanent Inuit settlements; Inuit hunters are having their expensive snowmobiles fall through the rapidly melting ice; and the shrinking of ice floes, used by polar bears for acquiring food, are causing more hungry polar bears to show up in Inuit villages. The effects of environmental change on Inuit culture are captured by one Inuit elder: "These are things that all of our old oral history has never mentioned. We cannot pass on our traditional knowledge, because it is no longer reliable. Before, I could look at cloud patterns or the wind, or even what stars are twinkling, and predict the weather. Now everything is changed" (Struck, 2006: 17A). With environmental changes occurring so rapidly, the effects of climate change on cultures such as the Inuit (most of which, unfortunately, is negative) can be studied over the course of years or decades rather than centuries.

ENVIRONMENT AND TECHNOLOGY

Which food-getting strategy is actually developed by any given culture depends, in large measure, on the culture's environment and technology. The relationship between physical environment and food-getting methods is not tidy; that is, the earth cannot easily be divided into neat ecological zones, each with its own unique and mutually exclusive climate, soil composition, vegetation, and animal life. Nevertheless, geographers often divide the world's land surface into a number of categories, including grasslands, deserts, tropical forests, temperate forests, polar regions, and mountain habitats. Some of these environments are particularly hospitable to the extent that they support a number of modes of food acquisition. Others are more limiting in the types of adaptations they permit. Anthropologists generally agree that the environment does not determine food-getting patterns but rather sets broad limits on the possible alternatives. For example, subsisting on horticulture in the polar region is not an ecological possibility, but other alternatives are possible.

It is technology—a part of culture—that helps people adapt to their specific environment. In fact, the human species enjoys a tremendous adaptive advantage over all other species precisely because it has developed technological solutions to the problems of survival. In many cases, cultures with complex technologies have gained greater control over their environments and their food supplies.

However, to suggest that such variations in technological adaptations exist is not to imply that societies with simple technologies are less intelligent or less able to cope with their environment. On the contrary, many societies with simple technologies adapt very ingeniously to their natural surroundings, and they do it without negative consequences to their environments. As John Collins reminds us:

> Among some Eskimo groups, wolves are a menace— a dangerous environmental feature that must be dealt with. They could perhaps be hunted down and killed, but this involves danger as well as considerable expenditure of time and energy. So a simple yet ingenious device is employed. A sharp sliver of bone is curled into a spring-like shape, and seal blubber is molded around it and permitted to freeze. This is then placed where it can be discovered by a hungry wolf, which, living up to its reputation, "wolfs it down." Later, as this "time bomb" is digested and the blubber disappears, the bone uncurls and its sharp ends pierce the stomach of the wolf, causing internal bleeding and death. The job gets done! It is a simple yet fairly secure technique that involves an appreciation of the environment as well as wolf psychology and habits. (1975: 235)

The specific mode of food getting is influenced by the interaction of a people's environment with its technology. To illustrate, the extent to which a foraging society is able to procure food successfully depends on not only the sophistication of the society's tools but also the abundance of plant and animal life the environment provides. Similarly, the productivity of a society based on irrigation agriculture varies according to the society's technology as well as environmental factors such as the availability of water and the natural nutrients in the water. These environmental factors set an upper limit on the ultimate productivity of any given food-getting system and the size of the population it can

Given Inuit ingenuity in keeping down the wolf population, this wolf would have a better chance of survival if only his mother had taught him to chew his food more carefully.

support. Cultural ecologists call this limit the environment's *carrying capacity* (Glossow 1978).

A natural consequence of exceeding the carrying capacity is damage to the environment, such as killing off too much game or depleting the soil. Because of this carrying capacity, societies cannot easily increase their food-getting productivity. Thus, if a society is to survive, it must meet the fundamental need of producing or procuring enough food and water to keep its population alive. But beyond satisfying this basic minimal requirement for survival, societies also satisfy their idiosyncratic and quite arbitrary desires for certain types of food. To a certain degree, people regularly consume the foods that are found naturally (or can be produced) in their immediate environment. Often, however, people go out of their way to acquire some special foods

while avoiding other foods that may be both plentiful and nutritious.

Although early anthropologists wrote off such behavior as irrational and arbitrary, cultural ecologists in recent years have examined these peculiar behaviors more carefully and have found that they often make sense in terms of the energy expended versus the caloric value of the foods consumed. This theory—known as the *optimal foraging theory*—suggests that foragers will choose the animal and plant species that tend to maximize their caloric return for the time they spend searching, killing, collecting, and preparing (Smith 1983). In other words, when specific foraging strategies are examined in ethnographic detail, decisions to seek out one food source and not others turn out to be quite rational, because they are based on a generally accurate assessment of whether the search will be worth the effort. To illustrate, the Ache, a foraging group from Paraguay, prefer to hunt peccaries (wild pigs) rather than armadillos, even though armadillos are easier to find and easier to kill. This is, however, a rational decision because the peccaries produce considerably more calories of food per hour of hunting: 4,600 calories per hour for the peccaries as compared to only 1,800 calories for the armadillos (Hill et al. 1987).

MAJOR FOOD-GETTING STRATEGIES

The five forms of food procurement (food collection, horticulture, pastoralism, agriculture, and industrialization) are not mutually exclusive, for in most human societies we find more than one strategy being used. Where this is the case, however, one form usually predominates. Moreover, in each category we can expect to find considerable variation largely because of differences in environment, technology, and historical experiences. These five categories of food getting are explored in more detail in the following sections.

Food-Collecting Societies

Food collecting (also known as *foraging* and *hunting and gathering*)—as compared to food producing—involves the exploitation of wild plants and animals that already exist in the natural environment. People have been food collectors for the overwhelming majority of time that they have been on earth. It was not until the

---

carrying capacity The maximum number of people a given society can support, given the available resources.

optimal foraging theory A theory that foragers look for those species of plants and animals that will maximize their caloric intake for the time spent hunting and gathering foods.
food collecting A form of subsistence that relies on the procurement of animal and plant resources found in the natural environment (aka *foraging* and *hunting and gathering*).

APPLIED PERSPECTIVE

Community-Based Water Management in Mexico

It is well known that waterborne diseases account for a significant number of deaths throughout the world, particularly in developing countries. Less well known perhaps is that many people struggle simply to gain access to enough water for daily needs—regardless of whether the water is suitable for drinking. In excess of 1 billion of the world's people lack access to sufficient water for drinking, bathing, preparing food, doing laundry, and disposing of human waste. Many have access to less than the thirteen gallons of water recommended as the minimum daily need. Water scarcity can burden poor rural people who often spend considerable time, money, and labor ensuring that their households have adequate water supplies. Limited water also means people cannot follow preventative hygiene measures, a situation that puts people at risk for cholera, skin and eye infections, and other health problems.

Attempts to improve household water supplies in developing countries have met with limited long-term success. Up to half of newly installed community drinking water and sanitation systems become inoperable within five years. Michael C. Ennis-McMillan (2001, 2002, 2005), an anthropologist who studies environmental health issues in Mexico, argues that part of the problem may be that international health and development programs have focused largely on technical and administrative

© Macduff Everton/The Image Works

aspects of installing piped water systems. By studying a successful community-based water project, Ennis-McMillan demonstrates that cultural factors play an important role in the long-term success of such programs.

Ennis-McMillan carried out ethnographic research in La Purificación Tepetitla, a peasant community of about six thousand people living in the foothills of the Valley of Mexico just outside of Mexico City. His case study examines the thirty-year history of a community-based structure for managing a piped water system. By living in the community for more than a year and a half, Ennis-McMillan observed and participated in a wide range of activities related to the use of drinking water in daily life. He also collected data from interviews with more than one hundred local authorities who participated in managing the piped water system. He attended committee meetings, policy discussions, and water shutoffs, and he provided labor for drinking water projects.

La Purificación Tepetitla's form of water management emphasizes a long-standing tradition of distributing water resources in an equitable fashion, ensuring that each household receives about two hours of water every other day. Each household gains a right to the water by paying water fees and fulfilling community obligations. All households must provide a certain amount of unpaid labor to help dig ditches, lay water

neolithic revolution—approximately ten thousand years ago—that humans for the first time produced their food by means of horticulture or animal husbandry. If we view the period of human prehistory as representing an hour in duration, then humans have been food collectors for all but the last ten seconds! With the rise of food production, the incidence of food collecting has steadily declined, as George Murdock reminds us:

> Ten thousand years ago the entire population of the earth subsisted by hunting and gathering, as their ancestors had done since the dawn of culture. By the time of Christ, eight thousand years later, tillers and herders had replaced them over at least half of the earth. At the time of the discovery of the New World, only perhaps 15 percent of the earth's surface was

still occupied by hunters and gatherers, and this area has continued to decline at a progressive rate until the present day, when only a few isolated pockets survive. (1968: 13)

Even though most societies have become food producers, a handful of societies in the world today (with a combined population of less than a half million people) are still food collectors. These few food-collecting societies vary widely in other cultural features and are found in a wide variety of environments (semideserts, tropical forests, and polar regions, among others). For example, some hunting and gathering societies such as the Ju/'hoansi of the Kalahari Desert (formerly called the !Kung) live in temporary encampments, have small-scale populations, do not store food, and are essentially egalitarian. At the other end of the spectrum are groups such as the Kwakiutl of the Canadian Pacific coast, who live in permanent settlements, have relatively dense populations, live on food reserves, and recognize marked distinctions in rank. Despite these considerable variations among contemporary food collectors, how-

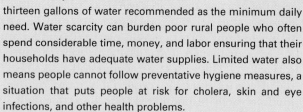

neolithic revolution   A stage in human cultural evolution (beginning around ten thousand years ago) characterized by the transition from hunting and gathering to the domestication of plants and animals.

pipes, build water tanks, and complete other construction tasks. The community also expects every resident to help oversee the water system and provide other community service when called upon. Failure to fulfill obligations results in the imposition of sanctions, including the withholding of piped water.

Ennis-McMillan also collected information on how people perceived and talked about suffering from water scarcity. People expressed less concern about waterborne diseases than about ongoing water shortages as well as attempts by outsiders to channel water away from rural communities to supply Mexico City's growing population. Residents linked their physical and emotional hardships with inadequate amounts of water and ongoing struggles to maintain a low-cost, equitable, and participatory piped water system.

La Purificación Tepetitla's case illustrates how traditional institutions allow communities to maintain *equitable* water management practices. The community maintains local control to set and collect water fees, resolve conflicts, and coordinate labor requirements for repair, maintenance, and operation of the system. In this way, residents avoid less desirable alternatives for obtaining water, such as carrying water from streams, using polluted irrigation water, buying water in urban centers and carrying it home, requesting water from trucks, and allowing Mexico City to take irrigation water in exchange for treated and untreated urban wastewater.

This sort of research demonstrates the importance of incorporating a broader cultural perspective in water development programs. An anthropological approach takes into account how people link concerns about water *quality* with equally pressing concerns about *quantity* and *distribution*. This work shows how the collective concern regarding water scarcity reinforces local interest in traditional nonmarket principles of natural resource management. The community maintains direct authority over water management and impresses upon all residents the need to participate in running the water system by paying fees, providing unpaid labor for projects, and supporting local policies.

Ennis-McMillan's research serves as a strong reminder to policy makers of how water development projects risk failure if they do not adequately provide a fair distribution of household water to all residents. People living in poor communities throughout the world view water as part of a social contract between citizen and community rather than simply as a service for which one pays money. When water is a scarce and costly resource, community-based water management is more likely to succeed if it takes into account cultural principles of equity and fairness.

Questions for Further Thought

1. What are some of the consequences of inadequate water supplies for rural populations?

2. Do you think that water in any society should be treated as a *community resource* to be distributed equitably or as a *commodity* to be purchased by those who can afford it?

3. How would you summarize the significance of Ennis-McMillan's research on water management in Mexico?

---

ever, it is possible to make the following generalizations about most of them:

1. *Food-collecting societies have low population densities.* The reason for this is that food collection has built-in checks that prevent it from becoming a particularly efficient method for procuring large amounts of food. In other words, increased efficiency in the collection methods of these societies ultimately destroys their source of food.

2. *Food-collecting societies are usually nomadic or seminomadic rather than sedentary.* As a direct result of this continual geographic mobility, food-collecting peoples usually do not recognize individual land rights. By and large, food collectors move periodically from place to place in search of wild animals and vegetation. Because game often migrate during the yearly cycle, hunters need to be sufficiently mobile to follow the game. Conversely, food producers such as cultivators tend to be more sedentary because of the large investment farmers usually have in their land. There are notable exceptions to both of these generalizations, however. Some food collectors, such as certain groups from the Canadian Pacific coast, live in particularly abundant environments that permit permanent settlements; some horticultural societies (such as the Bemba of Zambia) practice shifting cultivation and, for all practical purposes, are seminomadic.

3. *The basic social unit among food collectors is the family or band, a loose federation of families.* The typical form of social organization found among foragers is small groups of kinsmen coming together at certain times of the year. These bands tend to be highly flexible in membership, with various family members coming and going with considerable regularity. Social control revolves around family institutions rather than more formal political institutions, and, in fact, disputes can be avoided by group fission rather than fighting.

4. *Contemporary food-collecting peoples occupy the remote and marginally useful areas of the earth.* These areas include such places as the Alaskan tundra, the

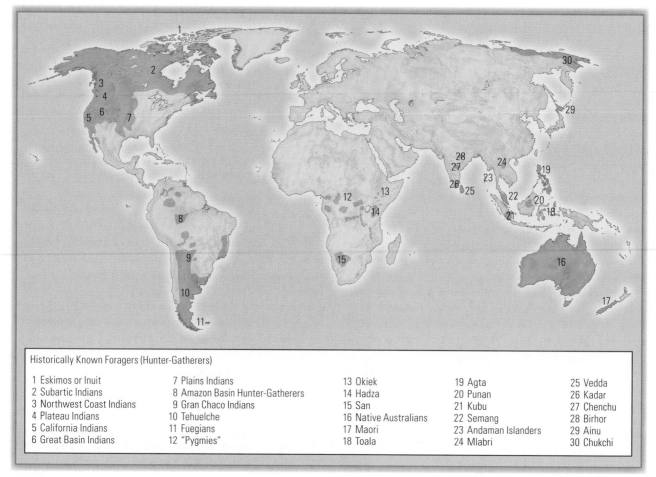

Historically Known Foragers

Historically Known Foragers (Hunter-Gatherers)

1 Eskimos or Inuit	13 Okiek	19 Agta	25 Vedda
2 Subartic Indians	14 Hadza	20 Punan	26 Kadar
3 Northwest Coast Indians	15 San	21 Kubu	27 Chenchu
4 Plateau Indians	16 Native Australians	22 Semang	28 Birhor
5 California Indians	17 Maori	23 Andaman Islanders	29 Ainu
6 Great Basin Indians	18 Toala	24 Mlabri	30 Chukchi
7 Plains Indians			
8 Amazon Basin Hunter-Gatherers			
9 Gran Chaco Indians			
10 Tehuelche			
11 Fuegians			
12 "Pygmies"			

Kalahari desert, the Australian outback, and the Ituru forest of central Africa. It is reasonable to suggest that these food-gathering societies, with their simple levels of technology, have been forced into these marginal habitats by food producers, with their more dominating technologies.

The association of food collecting with an absence of social, political, and economic complexity is an accurate portrayal of contemporary foraging societies. With several notable exceptions (such as the Ainu of northern Japan and certain northwest coast Indian groups), most contemporary foraging societies are small-scale, unspecialized, egalitarian, and decentralized. In recent years, however, archaeologists have pointed out that foraging societies in prehistoric times in all likelihood had considerably greater social complexity (Price and Brown 1985).

In many societies that rely on both hunting game and collecting wild vegetable matter, the latter activity provides the greatest amount of food. Although hunting wild animals is both spectacular and highly prized, it has been suggested that the bulk of the diets of most food collectors consists of foods other than meat. For example, Richard Lee (1968) estimates that the Ju/'hoansi of the Kalahari desert derive between 60 and 80 percent of their diet (by weight) from vegetable sources. The near-total absence of vegetable matter from the diet of the Arctic Inuit is the notable exception to this generalization.

Early anthropological accounts tended to portray food collectors as living precariously in a life-or-death struggle with the environment. In the 1960s, however, some anthropologists (Sahlins, Lee) suggested that certain food-gathering groups are well off despite inhabiting some very unproductive parts of the earth. The question of abundance within food-collecting societies became a topic of heated debate at a major conference of seventy-five scholars on "Man the Hunter" held in Chicago in 1966. In fact, Marshall Sahlins (1968) described foragers as representing the "original affluent society." Foragers, he argued, spent little time working, had all the food they needed, and enjoyed considerable leisure time. Although many scholars today would take issue with such a formulation, considerable evidence suggests that food collectors are capable of adapting to harsh environments with creativity and resourcefulness. Perhaps we can get a better idea of how foragers procure their food by examining two very different contemporary groups—the Ju/'hoansi of present-day Namibia and the Inuit of the Arctic region—in greater detail.

Despite popular misconceptions, foragers such as the Ju/'hoansi do not live on the brink of starvation.

The Ju/'hoansi of the Kalahari Region

One of the best-studied food-collecting societies, the Ju/'hoansi, inhabit the northwestern part of the Kalahari desert, one of the least hospitable environments in the world. Inhabiting an area that is too dry to support either agriculture or the keeping of livestock, the Ju/'hoansi have been until recently totally dependent on foraging for their food. Food-procuring activities were fairly rigidly divided between men and women. Women collected roots, nuts, fruits, and other edible vegetables, and men hunted medium and large animals. Although men and women spent roughly equivalent amounts of time on their food-procuring activities, women provided two to three times as much food by weight as men.

Even though the terms *affluence* and *abundance* tend to be relative, Lee (1968) presents convincing evidence to suggest that the Ju/'hoansi were not teetering on the brink of starvation. In fact, their food-gathering techniques were both productive and reliable. For example, the Ju/'hoansi's most important single food item was the mongongo nut, which accounted for about half of their diet. Nutritionally, the mongongo, which is found in abundance all year long, contains five times more calories and ten times more protein per cooked unit than cereal crops. Thus, quite apart from hunting, the Ju/'hoansi had a highly nutritious food supply that was more reliable than cultivated foods. It is little wonder that they had no strong urge to take up cultivation when there were so many mongongo nuts available.

Another measure of Ju/'hoansi affluence was their selectivity in taking foods from the environment. If they had indeed been on the brink of starvation, we would have expected them to exploit every conceivable source of food. But in actual fact, only about one-third of the edible plant foods were eaten, and only 17 of the 223 local species of animals known to the Ju/'hoansi were hunted regularly (Lee 1968).

Moreover, if the Ju/'hoansi had been in a life-or-death struggle with the natural environment, their survival rate and life expectancy would have been low, infant mortality would have been high, malnutrition would have been rampant, and the elderly and infirm would have been abandoned. This is hardly the demographic picture for the Ju/'hoansi. Based on fieldwork conducted in the 1960s, Lee (1968) found that approximately 10 percent of his sample population was sixty years of age or older, a percentage that was not substantially different from that in industrialized societies.

And finally, the abundance of resources of the Ju/'hoansi could be judged from the amount of time they devoted to procuring food. Although food getting was the most important activity among the Ju/'hoansi, the same is true for cultivators and pastoralists. Although the number of work hours varies from one food-collecting society to another, it appeared that the Ju/'hoansi, despite what might appear to be their harsh environment, were hardly overworked. Lee (1968) estimated that the average Ju/'hoansi adult spent twelve to nineteen hours per week in the pursuit of food. Usually, women could gather enough food in one day to feed their families for three days, leaving a good deal of time for such leisure activities as resting, visiting, entertaining visitors, and embroidering. Even though men tended to work more hours per week than women, they still had considerable leisure time for visiting, entertaining, and dancing.

The ethnographic accounts of traditional Ju/'hoansi society were written mostly in the 1960s or before. Since then, the Ju/'hoansi people have experienced enormous cultural changes. In the early years of the twenty-first century, their foraging, seminomadic way of life has, for all practical purposes, disappeared. In less than half a century, the land occupied by the Ju/'hoansi has been invaded by trading stores, boreholes, schools, health clinics, airstrips, and government bureaucrats. Now, rather than relying predominantly on hunting and gathering for their subsistence, the majority of Ju/'hoansi get most of their food by raising small domestic livestock, tending small gardens, participating in government food programs, and purchasing items from food stores. And, of course, changes in their means of livelihood result in other, often far-reaching, changes in their way of life (Yellen 1990; and Lee 2003).

During the 1960s, when the first ethnographic studies were conducted, the Ju/'hoansi were general foragers, with men hunting with bows and poisoned arrows and the women gathering edible plants. The band, the basic unit of social organization, was fluid in its membership to the extent that families could readily join other bands that were having greater success at procuring food. With the major group values of sharing and reciprocity, security for the Ju/'hoansi was ensured by giving rather than hoarding, because during hard times people could cash in on their accumulated obligations.

By the mid-1970s, however, the Ju/'hoansi were adopting many of the lifeways of the neighboring Bantu peoples. Many families had begun to plant fields and keep goats, two agricultural pursuits that had been unheard of just a decade earlier. Traditional grass huts were beginning to be replaced by more substantial (and permanent) mud structures. The Ju/'hoansi began to substitute manufactured clothing for their traditional skin garments, and even though bows and arrows were still made, they were primarily sold to the tourist market rather than used in hunting. All of these changes were accompanied by a major infusion of cash and consumer goods into Ju/'hoansi society.

Along with these changes in material culture, Yellen (1990) found that the Ju/'hoansi began to place less emphasis on personal intimacy, sharing, and interdependence. The spatial layout of the Ju/'hoansi camps changed from a circular arrangement with the doors facing one another to a linear layout that gave families greater privacy; the distance between huts increased; and the hearth, which traditionally had been a focal point of socializing, was moved inside each hut rather than located outside. Yellen also found increasing hoarding of material goods purchased with the newfound

cash. As the Ju/'hoansi accumulated more and more possessions, they became less mobile and less willing to continue their seminomadic foraging lifestyle. These changes indicated that the Ju/'hoansi were retreating from their traditional behavior of sharing and interdependence. The major impetus for the relatively sudden changes in culture was not a disenchantment with the foraging lifestyle but rather the introduction of money and commodities into Ju/'hoansi culture. With the globalization of world markets and the free flow of information via the Internet, the likelihood of far-reaching cultural changes occurring among similar small-scale societies has greatly increased.

The Inuit

Like the Ju/'hoansi, the traditional Inuit of the Arctic region inhabit one of the least hospitable regions of the world. Living in a very delicate balance with their environment, the Inuit rely almost entirely on fishing and hunting of sea and land mammals. Plant life is so scarce that it plays a very minor role in their diet. Living in the barren Arctic and sub-Arctic regions stretching from Greenland in the east to Alaska in the west, the Inuit have had to adapt to a climate of bitterly cold temperatures, short summers, and a terrain almost devoid of vegetation. To adapt to this harsh environment, the Inuit have developed a number of creative survival strategies. (For much of the twentieth century, the term *Eskimo* has been used by Westerners, both scholars and nonscholars alike, to refer to the aboriginal peoples of Canada and Alaska. Because the term is not found in any of the indigenous languages, the people themselves prefer to be called *Inuit*.)

During the harsh winter months, when the sea is completely frozen over, the Inuit rely very heavily on seal hunting. The most efficient way of hunting seals under these winter conditions is in large hunting parties. To maximize their chances for successful seal hunting, the

Inuit often organize themselves into large communities of up to sixty people from several distantly related extended families. During this time, social life is most intense, and various ceremonies are most likely to occur.

Under these frozen conditions, seals maintain breathing holes in the ice. Inuit hunters station themselves at these breathing holes and wait patiently, sometimes for hours, for a seal to surface. When a seal appears, the Inuit hunter thrusts his harpoon through the breathing hole in the head or neck of the seal. The head of the harpoon (which is attached to a line) separates from the shaft. As the seal attempts to swim away, the hunter pulls on the line until the animal can be brought to the surface, where it is then killed.

During the summer months when seals bask in the sun on top of the ice, the seal-hunting techniques change to include stalking. In order to use a throwing harpoon, the hunter needs to get very close to the animal. Sometimes the stalking involves wearing light-colored clothing to blend into the snow and cloudy background. At other times, the hunter wears dark clothing and imitates the behavior of his prey. According to Norman Chance (1990: 93), "By mimicking the animal's movements and timing his advance with the seal's short 'naps,' a capable hunter could approach within a few feet."

The most dramatic form of hunting, at least among the western Inuit, involves whaling, an activity that demands both courage and daring. Hunting whales using modern technology is dangerous enough, but doing it with harpoons from small boats is even more so. Chance (1990: 90) describes the hunt for bowhead whales among the peoples of northern Alaska:

> When a whale was sighted the boat crew launched the umiaq [skin-covered boats] and approached the animal in such a way that the bow of the boat could be placed on its back, or at least close enough for the harpooner to sink one or more of his toggle-headed harpoons into the thick skin. Attached to each harpoon were floats that other crew members quickly cast over the side. The purpose of these floats was not only to indicate the location of the whale, but also to slow it down during its attempts to sound or swim away. Once the whale had become exhausted, the crew could safely approach and the lancer begin his work. The aboriginal lance was ten to twelve feet long and tipped with a razor-sharp flint blade. To prevent the whale from sounding, the lancer severed the tendons controlling the whale's flukes and then probed deeply into its vital organs. As the wounded animal went into its death flurry, the crew retreated to a safe distance. The dead whale was then hauled onto the sea ice and butchered by the local village members.

Following the whaling season in April and May, the Inuit turn their attention to other forms of food collection. As the ice begins to break up, game becomes more plentiful, and the traditional Inuit hunt caribou with bows and arrows and fish for salmon and trout with pronged spears. During these summer months, people tend to live in smaller groups, and their social interaction is less intense. Thus, the Inuit adapt to a difficult environment by organizing their economic and social lives around the availability of different types of game and the strategies required for hunting them. That is, large social and hunting groups that are more efficient for winter seal hunting split up during the summer into smaller groups that are more functional for fishing and hunting caribou.

Much of what we have described about traditional Inuit food-collection practices has changed over the last several decades. Today, most Inuit live in villages, hunt with guns rather than spears and harpoons, and use

To survive in their harsh environment, the Inuit from Nunavut, Canada, have had to develop a number of creative hunting strategies, including the recent adoption of snowmobiles.

snowmobiles rather than dogsleds. Some live in houses with modern conveniences such as telephones and TVs, and a growing number of Inuit are engaged in wage employment. Also, since the turn of the new millennium Inuit hunters have used regularly updated ice flow maps, provided by the European Space Agency, for tracking the rapidly changing ice edge conditions (which determine where wildlife is most likely to be found). These maps, generated by satellite imaging, are posted by Canadian park officials or obtained from a dedicated website by the more Internet-savvy Inuit.

Even though they may eat some imported foods, most Inuit still engage in traditional hunting and fishing. Moreover, they have not abandoned their traditional system of food distribution, which ensures that no one goes hungry. Today, when someone bags a caribou, the local radio station is likely to broadcast the news so no one goes without.

The Inuit people became masters over their own land when the Canadian government created a new territory called Nunavut ("our land" in the Inuit language), as of April 1, 1999. The new territory is 1.2 million square miles, twice the size of Alaska, larger than all of western Europe, and comprises one-fifth of the entire Canadian landmass. Yet the total population for the vast territory is about twenty-seven thousand, roughly the size of a small suburban commuter town on the outskirts of Toronto. The creation of this new territory gives the Inuit a measure of control over their own lives and an opportunity to preserve their traditional culture. Inuit culture over the years has been influenced by contact with the whaling industry, fur trappers, and even official government attempts to convert young Inuit by placing them in schools where only English was spoken. Nevertheless, much of Inuit culture has remained intact, possibly because for much of the twentieth century the European-dominant Canadian government regarded the Inuit as so remote and dispersed over such a wide area that it seemed pointless to subdue them. Interestingly, unlike most other places in the world seeking self-determination, the Inuit were able to achieve theirs peacefully, without civil unrest or even lawsuits.

While the creation of the autonomous region of Nunavut occurred peacefully in 1999, the creation of an efficient, self governing territory will take considerably more time and effort. Several Canadian Government reports indicate that Nunavut is struggling to establish itself as a fully functioning administrative unit. Urgent social problems abound. For example, only 25 percent of high school students actually graduate, unemployment is running as high as 30 percent, and the exceptionally young population (nearly 4 of 10 Inuit are under 14) is plagued by alcoholism, drug abuse, family abuse, and suicide. Moreover, even though the official language of the government is English, 75 percent of Nunavut's citizens speak only their native language of Inuktitut. This has resulted in fewer than half of all government jobs in Nunavut being filled by Inuit. Given the fact that Inuits have never had formal government organizations, it is unreasonable to expect them to become fully functioning bureaucrats in a matter of several years (Krauss, 2006: 4).

Because the new territory of Nunavut is both self-governing and relatively "off the beaten path," twenty-first-century Inuits are in a good position to preserve at least some elements of their traditional society. In the summer of 2005, an ecotourist company by the name of Cruise North Expeditions, owned by Inuits, began a series of one-week cruises to the northern regions of their new self-governing territory. Based on the fundamental Inuit belief that everything in nature is infused with the spirit of life, these tours allow ecotourists to visit Inuit communities and see, first hand, how local residents continue to live with, and be supported by, a wide variety of birds and animals—seals, whales, walruses, caribou, thick-billed murres, and polar bears. Such locally owned and controlled initiatives into ecotourism not only result in added sources of revenue for the Inuit people, but can also serve as incentives to preserve their traditional culture, which is, after all, what the tourists want to see (Connelly 2005).

These two ethnic groups—the Ju/'hoansi and the Inuit—have been used consistently for the past several decades as classic examples of hunting-and-gathering societies. In fact, the Ju/'hoansi have come to be regarded as the quintessential food collectors. Research since the 1980s, however, questions how well these two groups represent the world's food collectors. Today, we are beginning to revise our view of food collectors as being clever "lay ecologists" who live in an affluent society. To illustrate, studies (Hawkes and O'Connell 1981; Hill et al. 1985) indicate that some foraging groups spend as much as seven or eight hours per day working in subsistence pursuits, not the twelve to nineteen hours per week that Lee found to be typical for the Ju/'hoansi. It also appears that a number of food-collecting groups experience seasonal fluctuations in their dietary intake; in fact, some are chronically undernourished (see, for example, Howell 1986; Isaac 1990). Moreover, the idyllic, nonviolent existence attributed to foragers has in all likelihood been overstated, for they have been found fighting and raiding one another for food, revenge, or to defend territory (Ferguson 1984; Knauft 1987).

It is also important to keep in mind that although foragers occupy remote habitats, they have always had contact with nonforaging peoples. Today, food collectors do not live in a pristine, isolated world nor is there evidence to suggest that they did in the past. Instead, they are experiencing increased contact with a world of computers, civil wars, and World Bank–sponsored development projects. Many people from food-collecting societies have interacted for years with neighboring groups through trade, employment, and, in some cases, marriage. As Robert Kelly (1995: 24–25) reminds us: "Virtually no hunter-gatherer in the tropical forest today lives without trading heavily with horticulturalists for carbohydrates, or eating government or missionary rations.... Long before anthropologists arrived on the scene, hunter-gatherers had already been contacted, given diseases, shot at, traded with, employed and exploited by colonial powers, agriculturalists, and/or pastoralists."

Although hunting and gathering has been largely replaced by food production, there remains one very important form of hunting that many world economies depend upon—that is, commercial fishing. Today's fishermen are equipped with global positioning satellite (GPS) technology to locate large schools of fish, high-tech equipment and strong synthetic nets that are invisible to fish. Despite their enormous technological advantages, modern fishermen may very well become victims of their own success. The rivers, lakes, and oceans of the world, which not too long ago seemed inexhaustible, have limits in terms of the number of fish they can produce. The northwest Atlantic Ocean is a case in point. After World War II, a number of commercial fishing boats from Europe and Asia began fishing the waters off the coast of the United States and Canada. By the 1960s, the cod stock had declined so dramatically from overfishing that the governments of the United States and Canada extended their exclusive fishing rights to two hundred nautical miles from shore. Although this prevented foreign fishing vessels in the area, it encouraged the proliferation of domestic fishermen. Fishing became excessive, fish stock shrank, and even future stocks were in jeopardy because fish could not sustain themselves. The problem remains today, with too many boats fishing for a dwindling number of fish. Commercial fishing—the last form of big-time "hunting"—illustrates the traditional dilemma of foraging people. As people become more efficient hunters, they run the risk of destroying their food supply and, in the process, eliminating biodiversity and ruining the health of their ecosystem.

As with so many aspects of the global economy, the overfishing of our oceans has had more negative consequences for some segments of the world's population than for others. Since fish populations in the northern hemisphere have been drastically reduced by commercial fishing interests in the United States, Canada, Japan, Russia, and northern Europe, many fishing companies from the developed world have moved south of the equator to the oceans around Africa and South America. Fleets of modern trawlers are now fishing within the two-hundred-mile limits of independent countries. Most are there legally because they pay cash-poor governments for fishing rights. A growing number of commercial fishing companies, however, are harvesting these waters illegally. While scientists and government officials refer to this euphemistically as "illicit biomass extraction," the local fishermen, whose livelihoods are threatened, call it piracy. The consequence is that people in New York and Atlanta (for the present) can find all of their favorite fish at the supermarket, while local fishermen in Angola are going out of business and their countrymen are being deprived of a sorely needed source of protein (Salopek 2004).

Food-Producing Societies

Approximately ten thousand years ago, humans made a revolutionary transition from food collecting to food production (the domestication of plants and animals). For hundreds of thousands of years before this time, humans had subsisted exclusively on foraging. Then, for reasons that are still not altogether clear, humans began to cultivate crops and keep herds of animals as sources of food. For the first time, humans gained a measure of control over their food supply. That is, through tilling of the soil and animal husbandry, humans were able to *produce* food rather than having to rely solely on what nature produced in the environment. This shift from collecting to producing food, known as the neolithic revolution, occurred in several different areas of the world independently of one another. The earliest known plant and animal domestication occurred around ten thousand years ago in the so-called Fertile Crescent, including parts of Jordan, Israel, Syria, southern Turkey, northern Iraq, and western Iran. Other early centers of food production had emerged in China by around eight thousand years ago, Thailand around 8,800 years ago, and sub-Saharan Africa around five thousand years ago.

A number of theories have been suggested to explain why the neolithic revolution occurred. Although no definitive explanation has emerged, most archaeologists agree that the shift to food production was a response to certain environmental or demographic conditions, such as variations in rainfall or population pressures. It is reasonable to suggest that most of the early foragers did not rush to adopt agriculture because of its inherent superiority. Farming requires a greater expenditure of labor than does foraging, it involves more monotonous work, it provides less security, and it usually involves a less varied (and less interesting) diet. Rather than foragers purposefully choosing agriculture as a way of life, it is likely that food production came about because of the need to feed an increasing number of people who could not be sustained by foraging alone. As Jared Diamond (1987: 66) has suggested, "Farming could support many more people than hunting, albeit with a poorer quality of life."

Whatever the cause or causes may have been, there is little doubt of the monumental consequences of the neolithic revolution. What made the neolithic revolution so revolutionary was that it produced the world's first population explosion. Even though the early neolithic communities were small, they were far larger than any others in human prehistory had been. Throughout the Near East, Egypt, and Europe, thousands of skeletal remains have been unearthed from the neolithic period (10,000 to 5,500 years ago) compared to only a few hundred for the entire paleolithic period, even though the paleolithic lasted hundreds of times longer than the neolithic.

Changes Resulting from Food Production

That food producing, as compared to food collecting, should result in a dramatic increase in population is not difficult to understand. As pointed out earlier, food collectors are subject to natural dietary limitations, for increased efficiency can ultimately destroy their source of food. Cultivators, however, can increase the food supply (and thus support larger populations) simply by sowing more seeds. Moreover, children are more useful economically for farmers and herders than they are for food collectors. Whereas children tend to be a burden for the hunter, for food producers they can be taught to perform useful tasks such as weeding fields, scaring off birds or other small animals, and tending flocks. Population studies (Kasarda 1971; White 1973) have suggested that fertility rates tend to be higher in societies where children make an economic contribution.

Not only did populations become larger as a result of the neolithic revolution, they also became more sedentary. Whereas most food collectors must be mobile enough to follow migrating game, cultivators are more likely to invest their time and energy in a piece of land, develop the notion of property rights, and establish permanent settlements. In other words, a gradual settling-in process occurred as a result of the neolithic revolution. This is not meant to imply that all, or even most, people became tied to the land after the neolithic revolution. Many remained food collectors; some became nomadic or seminomadic pastoralists, and still others became shifting cultivators. Nevertheless, the neolithic (or food-producing) revolution initiated the gradual trend toward a more settled way of life.

The cultivation of crops also brought about other important, even revolutionary, cultural changes. For example, because farming is more efficient than food collecting, a single farmer can produce enough food to feed ten people. This frees up nine people to engage in some activity other than food procurement. Thus, the neolithic revolution stimulated a greater division of labor. That is, people could for the first time become specialists, inventing and manufacturing the tools and machinery needed for a more complex social structure. Once some people were liberated from the food quest, they were able to develop new farm implements such as the plow, pottery storage containers, metallurgy, improved hunting and fishing technology, the wheel, and stone masonry. Without these and other inventions that resulted from an increase in labor specialization,

CROSS-CULTURAL MISCUE

A British fertilizer company from Manchester, England, decided to venture into the potentially lucrative markets of sub-Saharan Africa. After conducting research on locally appropriate fertilizers, the company developed a marketing plan that involved giving, free of charge, one hundred pound bags of fertilizer to selected farmers in certain areas of Kenya. It was thought that those using the free fertilizer would be so impressed with the dramatic increases in crop output that they would spread the word to their friends, family, and neighbors.

Teams of marketers went from hut to hut offering each male head of household a free bag of fertilizer along with an explanation of how to use it. While very polite, every farm contacted turn down the offer of free fertilizer. The marketing staff concluded that these Kenyan farmers were either not interested in growing more crops or were too stupid to understand the benefits of the new product. But both of these conclusions failed to take into account the cultural realities of the small-scale farmers in Kenya. First, company officials tried to convince the village *men* to accept an agricultural innovation when, in fact, it was the women who were responsible for farming. Failure to understand this basic ethnographic fact did little for their overall credibility. Second, many East Africans have two important beliefs that can help explain their reaction: (a) the theory of limited good, which assumes that there is a finite amount of good in the world (such as fertility), and (b) witchcraft, the notion that evil forces embodied in people can be harmful. Given these two beliefs, the typical East African farmer would never participate in a scheme that promises to produce more crops than any of one's neighbors, because to do so would open you up to charges of having bewitched the fertility out of other peoples' soil. In short, to continue to grow the same amount as one had in the past is a far more preferable alternative to being killed for witchcraft.

it is unlikely that we would have ever reached the second revolution: the rise of civilization.

The multitude of changes brought about by the neolithic revolution cannot be overestimated. The introduction of agriculture and animal husbandry ten thousand years ago set humankind on a radically different evolutionary path. Although it enabled humans to move toward civilization (urban societies), the industrial revolution, and eventually the global information age, these transformations had their downside. Recent discoveries by paleopathologists (physical anthropologists who study disease among ancient peoples) suggest that early agriculture actually led to a decline in overall health as compared to foraging. To illustrate, skeletal remains of foragers from Greece and Turkey at the end of the ice age (approximately twelve thousand years ago) indicate that the average height was five feet nine inches for men and five feet five inches for women; but by five thousand years ago, the predominantly agricultural people from the same region were appreciably smaller (averaging five feet three inches for men and five feet zero inches for women), indicating a nutritional decline. Moreover, the excavation of burial mounds in the Illinois and Ohio River valleys indicates a number of negative health consequences of a population that changed from foraging to maize cultivation in the twelfth century. For example, when compared with the foragers who preceded them, the maize farmers had a 50-percent increase in tooth enamel defects caused by malnutrition, four times the incidence of iron-deficiency anemia, and a 300-percent increase in bone lesions, indicative of infectious disease (Cohen and Armelagos 1984). With the onslaught of agriculture in the area, the average life expectancy dropped from twenty-six to nineteen years.

There are several reasons why early farmers paid a high price for their newfound food-getting strategy. First, foragers generally had a better balanced diet (composed of both plants and animal proteins) than did early farmers, who were often limited to one or several starchy crops. Second, if early farmers were dependent on a small number of crops, they ran the risk of serious malnutrition or even starvation if the crops should fail. And finally, the increased population densities caused by the neolithic revolution brought people into greater contact with one another and consequently made everyone more susceptible to both parasitic and infectious diseases.

Not only did food production have negative health consequences, it also had some dramatic social effects as well. The egalitarianism of foraging societies was rapidly replaced by increasing social inequality and other deleterious trappings such as poverty, crime, war, aggression, and environmental degradation. Thus, even though we often glorify the introduction of agriculture as a defining moment in human evolution, it certainly had some negative consequences.

Horticulture

Horticulture is the simplest type of farming, which involves the use of basic hand tools such as the hoe or digging stick rather than plows or other machinery driven by animals or engines. Because horticulturalists produce low yields, they generally do not have sufficient surpluses to allow them to develop extensive market systems. The land, which is usually cleared by hand, is neither irrigated nor enriched by the use of fertilizers. A major

technique of horticulturalists is *shifting cultivation*, sometimes called *swidden cultivation* or the *slash-and-burn method*. This technique involves clearing the land by manually cutting down the growth, burning it, and planting in the burned area. Even though the ash residue serves as a fertilizer, the land is usually depleted within a year or two. The land is then allowed to lie fallow to restore its fertility, or it may be abandoned altogether. This technique of slash-and-burn cultivating can eventually destroy the environment, for if fields are not given sufficient time to lie fallow, the forests will be permanently replaced by grasslands.

The crops grown by horticulturalists can be divided into three categories: tree crops, seed crops, and root crops. Tree crops include bananas and plantains, figs, dates, and coconuts; major seed crops (which tend to be high in protein) are wheat, barley, corn, oats, sorghum, rice, and millet; main root crops (which tend to be high in starch and carbohydrates) include yams, arrowroots, taro, manioc, and potatoes. Because seed crops require a greater quantity of nutrients than root crops, seed cultivators need to allow longer periods of time between plantings. In some cases, these delays can have consequences for settlement patterns. That is, if seed cultivators do need a longer time to rejuvenate their fields, they may be less likely to live in permanent settlements than are root cultivators. However, even though swidden cultivation involves the shifting of fields, it does not necessarily follow that the cultivators also periodically shift their homes.

Many horticulturalists supplement their simple cultivation with other food-getting strategies. For example, some, such as the Yanomamo (Chagnon 1983), may engage in hunting and gathering; others, such as the Swazi (Kuper 1986), keep a variety of domesticated animals, including cows, goats, sheep, horses, donkeys, and pigs; still others (such as the Samoans) supplement their crops with protein derived from fishing.

At first glance it appears that slash-and-burn cultivation makes very poor use of the land. Because most land must be left fallow at any given time, the system of slash and burn cannot support the high densities of population that can be sustained by intensive agriculture. Although there are inherent limitations to the technique, slash-and-burn horticulturalists are often extremely adept at maximizing their resources. A number of slash-and-burn farmers produce quite abundant harvests of tropical forest products and do so without destroying the land. To illustrate, R. Jon McGee (1990)

---

horticulture   A form of small-scale crop cultivation characterized by the use of simple technology and the absence of irrigation.

---

shifting cultivation (swidden, slash and burn)   A form of plant cultivation in which seeds are planted in the fertile soil prepared by cutting and burning the natural growth; relatively short periods of cultivation are followed by longer periods of fallow.

An Indian boy from Venezuela practices slash-and-burn agriculture by setting fire to an old garden in order to cultivate it again.

© Jacques Jangoux/Alamy

has shown that the Lacandon Maya of Chiapas, Mexico, disperse more than forty different crops throughout their cleared fields (milpas). By spreading many crops over a milpa, the Lacandon are imitating both the diversity and the dispersal patterns found in the natural primary forest. According to McGee:

> In contrast to monocrop agriculture as practiced in the United States, the milpa attempts to maintain rather than replace the structure of the tropical rainforest ecosystem. In effect, the milpa is a portion of jungle where a greater than normal population of food-producing crops has been concentrated. This concentration of food is aided by the fact that Lacandon farmers plant their milpas with crops that take advantage of different environmental niches within the same cleared area. For example, at ground level, hills of corn, beans, squash, and tomatoes are sown. A few meters above the surface grow tree crops such as bananas and oranges, and finally, subsurface root crops such as manioc and sweet potatoes are cultivated below the ground's surface. Thus, a Lacandon farmer achieves at least three levels of production from the same piece of land. (1990: 36)

McGee points out that this form of slash-and-burn horticulture is quite efficient, for the typical Lacandon Mayan family can feed itself while working fewer than half the days in a year. In regions with vast areas of unused land, slash-and-burn horticulture can be a reasonably efficient form of food production.

The governments of many developing countries are interested in transforming traditional economies (such as those based on slash-and-burn agriculture) into world market economies, thereby attracting foreign capital, providing jobs for local people, and raising GNP. These government officials in parts of Africa, Asia, and South America argue that by restricting (or prohibiting altogether) slash-and-burn horticulture, overall productivity will be increased, people will eat better and be healthier, and the export economy will be expanded. However, a major problem in these efforts to transform traditional horticulture has been that government officials often have different value assumptions from the local farmers whose culture they are trying to change. To illustrate, Brewer's (1988) study of small-scale horticulturalists in Indonesia demonstrated that government programs started with the assumption that wet rice agriculture would be far preferable to slash-and-burn cultivation because of its high return *per unit of land*. The local Indonesian horticulturalists, however, preferred their traditional slash-and-burn technique because of its relatively high return *per unit of labor*. Local farmers, in other words, preferred their traditional methods because they did not require much intensive labor and made fewer demands on their time. They valued their leisure time more than the possibility of producing larger crops. This is extremely important ethnographic information for government planners to have, for it will enable them to either (a) scale down their costly (and frequently unsuccessful) efforts to eliminate slash-and-burn horticulture or (b) design alternative programs that will, to a great extent, take the local values into account.

The Bemba

A specific example will help illustrate the practice of horticulture. Audrey Richards (1960) provides a particularly good case study with her writings on the Bemba of Zambia (formerly northern Rhodesia). The Bemba, like a number of other peoples in south central Africa,

practice a type of shifting cultivation that involves clearing the land, burning the branches, and planting directly on the ash-fertilized soil without additional hoeing. Using the simplest technology (hoes and axes), the Bemba plant a fairly wide range of crops—including finger millet, bulrush millet, beans, cassava, and yams—but they rely most heavily on finger millet as their basic staple. Although predominantly horticultural, the Bemba supplement their diet with some hunting, gathering, and fishing. The largest and most highly organized group (politically) in Zambia, the Bemba live in small, widely scattered, low-density communities comprising thirty to fifty huts.

Traditionally, Bemba society had a highly complex political system based on a set of chiefs whose authority rested on their alleged supernatural control over the land and the prosperity of the people. These supernatural powers were reinforced by the physical force that chiefs could exert over their subjects, whom they could kill, enslave, or sell. The power, status, and authority of the chiefs were based not on the accumulation of material wealth but rather on the amount of service they could extract from their subjects in terms of agricultural labor or military service. Interestingly, the marked status differences between chiefs (with their unchallenged authority) and commoners are not reflected in these people's diets. Although chiefs and their families may have a somewhat more regular supply of food, both rich and poor eat essentially the same types and quantities of food throughout the yearly cycle. Similarly, there are no significant differences in diet between Bemba men and Bemba women.

Because sparse rainfall at certain times of the year permits only one crop, a common feature of the Bemba diet is the alternation between scarcity and plenty. The harvest of finger millet, the mainstay of the Bemba diet, lasts only nine months (roughly from April through December). During the lean months of January through March, dramatic changes take place in village life.

Because of the low energy levels of underfed people, most activity—both leisure and work related—is reduced to a minimum. Given these alternating periods of feast and famine, it is not surprising that food and diet occupy a prominent place in Bemba culture. In much the same way that pastoralists often appear obsessed with their cattle, the Bemba tend to fixate on food. In fact, according to Richards, food and beer are the central topics of conversation among the Bemba:

> Anyone who can follow the ordinary gossip of a Bemba village will be struck at once by the endless talk shouted from hut to hut as to what is about to be eaten, what has already been eaten, and what lies in store for the future, and this with an animation and a wealth of detail which would be thought quite unusual in this country.... The giving or receipt of food is a part of most economic transactions, and many come to represent a number of human relationships whether between different kinsmen or between subject and chief.... To speak of a chief is to mention before the end of the conversation his reputation for generosity or meanness in the giving of porridge and beer. To describe an attitude of any particular kinsman leads almost invariably to a comment, for instance, on the food in his granary, the numbers of relatives he supports, the share of meat he has asked for, or the amount of beer he contributed at the marriage of his daughter or the visit of an elder. In daily life the women, whether at work in the kitchen or sitting gossiping on their verandas at night, exchange interminable criticisms as to the way in which some particular dish of food has been divided, or the distribution of the four or five gourds of beer made at a brew. (1960: 106)

Pastoralism

Like horticulture, *pastoralism* first appeared in the neolithic period. This form of food production involves the keeping of domesticated herd animals and is found in areas of the world that cannot support agriculture because of inadequate terrain, soils, or rainfall. However, these environments do provide sufficient vegetation to support livestock, provided the animals are able to graze over a large enough area. Thus, pastoralism is associated with geographic mobility, because herds must be moved periodically to exploit seasonal pastures (Barfield 1993).

Some anthropologists have differentiated between two types of movement patterns: transhumance and nomadism. With *transhumance*, some of the men in a

pastoralism   A food-getting strategy based on animal husbandry—found in regions of the world that are generally unsuited for agriculture.
transhumance   Movement pattern of pastoralists in which some of the men move livestock seasonally while the other members of their group, including women and children, stay in permanent settlements.

Tibetan yak herders must move their animals periodically to ensure adequate pasturage.

© Bennett Dean; Eye Ubiquitous/CORBIS

pastoral society move their livestock seasonally to different pastures while the women, children, and other men remain in permanent settlements. With *nomadism*, on the other hand, there are no permanent villages, and the whole social unit of men, women, and children moves the livestock to new pastures. But as Rada and Neville Dyson-Hudson have pointed out (1980), the enormous variations even within societies render such a distinction somewhat sterile. For example, following seven Karamojong herds over a two-year period, the Dyson-Hudsons found that "each herd owner moved in a totally different orbit, with one remaining sedentary for a full year and one grazing his herd over 500 square miles" (1980: 18).

Even though anthropologists tend to lump pastoralists into a single food-getting category, pastoralism is not a unified phenomenon. For example, there are wide variations in the ways animals are herded. The principal herd animals are cattle in eastern and southern Africa, camels in North Africa and the Arabian Peninsula, reindeer in the sub-Arctic areas of eastern Europe and Siberia, yaks in the Himalayan region, and various forms of mixed herding (including goats, sheep, and cattle) in a number of places in Europe and Asia. In addition to variations in the type of animals, a number of other social and environmental factors can influence the cultural patterns of pastoral people, including the availability of water and pasturage, the presence of diseases, the location and timing of markets, government restrictions, and the demands of other food-

getting strategies (such as cultivation) that the pastoralists may practice.

A general characteristic of nomadic pastoralists is that they take advantage of seasonal variations in pasturage so as to maximize the food supply of their herds. The Kazaks of Eurasia, for example, keep their livestock at lower elevations during the winter, move to the foothills in the spring, and migrate to the high mountain pastures during the summer. Such seasonal movement provides optimal pasturage and avoids climatic extremes that could negatively affect the livestock. This willingness to move their animals at different times of the year avoids overgrazing and enables them to raise considerably more livestock than they could if they chose not to migrate.

The consensus among anthropologists is that pure pastoralists—that is, those who get all of their food from livestock—are either extremely rare or nonexistent. Because livestock alone cannot meet all of the nutritional needs of a population, most pastoralists need some grains to supplement their diets. Many pastoralists, therefore, either combine the keeping of livestock with some form of cultivation or maintain regular trade relations with neighboring agriculturalists. Moreover, the literature is filled with examples of nomadic pastoralists who produce crafts for sale or trade, occasionally work for the government, or drive trucks. Thus, many pastoralists have long engaged in nonpastoral activities, but they have always considered animal husbandry to be their normal, or certainly ideal, means of livelihood.

It is clear that in pastoral societies livestock play a vital economic role not only as a food source but in other ways as well. In addition to the obvious economic importance of meat, milk, and blood as food sources, cattle provide dung (used for fertilizer, house building, fuel),

nomadism   A lifestyle involving the periodic movement of human populations in search of food or pasture for livestock.

bone (used for tools and artifacts), skins (used for clothing), and urine (used as an antiseptic). But in addition to these important economic uses, there are a number of important non-economic or *social functions of cattle*. Livestock often influence the social relationships among people in pastoral societies. For example, an exchange of livestock between the families of the bride and the groom is required in many pastoral societies before a marriage can be legitimized. In the event of an assault or a homicide, in some societies livestock is used to compensate the victim's family as a way of restoring normal social relations. The sacrifice of livestock at the grave site of ancestor gods is a way in which people keep in touch with their deities. These and other social uses of livestock should remind us that domesticated animals in pastoral societies not only serve as the major food source but also are intimately connected to other parts of the culture, such as the systems of marriage, social control, and religion.

The Maasai of East Africa   The Maasai culture of Kenya and Tanzania is an excellent example of a pastoral society. As one of a number of cultures within the East African cattle complex (e.g., the Turkana, Jie, Samburu, among others), the Maasai have experienced enormous sociocultural changes in the last forty years. Occupying an area of about 160,000 square kilometers of savanna in southern Kenya and northern Tanzania, the Maasai, numbering approximately four hundred thousand people, traditionally lived mainly on their abundant herds of cattle, goats, and sheep. Like many other pastoralists in the region, the Maasai got most of their sustenance in the form of milk and blood from their cows, consuming meat only on rare ritual occasions. This high-protein diet was occasionally supplemented with grains and honey obtained through trade with neighboring peoples.

Over the past century and a half, the Maasai have gained the reputation, among Africans and Europeans alike, of being quintessential cattle keepers. According to their creation myth, Ngai (God) gave all cattle on earth to the Maasai, and they have used this myth to justify raiding cattle from other neighboring people. If Ngai did indeed give all cattle to the Maasai, then it logically follows that any non-Maasai in possession of cattle obtained their livestock unlawfully. Maasai have long felt that cattle raids were not theft, but rather reclaiming their God-given property. It is little wonder that cattle are the major source of wealth among the Maasai, in much the same way that cash is a major concern of Westerners. Cattle serve both economic purposes (milk and blood for food, dung for building houses, and bone for tools) and non-economic purposes

(*stock friendship*, marriage payments, and ceremonial sacrifices).

British colonial administrators have often claimed that the Maasai, with their unending quest to expand the size of their herds, were being ecologically destructive. While it is true that no pastoral societies live in complete harmony with their environments, the Maasai over the centuries have developed a functional system for managing their resources. Because the Maasai have never engaged in hunting as a means of livelihood, they did not manage their environment for the benefit of wildlife, but rather for the benefit of their domesticated herds. However, traditional Maasai transhumance patterns followed those of the wildlife (i.e., wildebeest, zebras), with whom their herds competed for grass and water. During the dry season (June through October), the Maasai, and the abundant wildlife of East Africa, would congregate at permanent water sources such as rivers and lakes; during the wet season (November through May), both would disperse in search of temporary pastures and water.

The Maasai have traditionally combined their detailed knowledge of the environment (climatic cycles, vegetation, permanent water sources, and the presence of mosquitoes and tsetse flies) with a willingness to remain mobile, flexible, and cooperative. During the dry season when both wildlife and the Maasai pastoralists congregate at the permanent sources of water, a queuing schedule is created by a council of elders to ensure that all of the animals have access to the water in an orderly fashion. The Maasai reserve a pasture very close to the permanent watering areas for young, sick, and

social functions of cattle   The use of livestock by pastoralists not only for food and its byproducts but also for purposes such as marriage, religion, and social relationships.

stock friendship   A gift of livestock from one man to another to strengthen their friendship.

lactating animals that cannot travel to more distant pastures. Moreover, because "rainy seasons" sometimes fail to produce adequate water, the Maasai have established a system of "drought insurance," whereby water sources and pastures that never dry up are not used during normal times. When a drought occurs, which happens typically once every decade, these reserves will be opened up as emergency sources of food and water for their cattle.

The Maasai, however, have not only managed, but actually transformed, their environment for the benefit of their livestock in several important ways. First, owing to their military prowess, they were able to prevent permanent settlement of farmers on the grasslands, thereby preserving the savanna for open grazing. And second, they engaged in the controversial practice of controlled burning of the grasslands for two reasons: first, to destroy the breeding grounds of the tsetse fly, which causes trypanosomiasis ("sleeping sickness", affecting both people and cattle) and second, the burning stimulates the growth of new, more nutritious grasses. In other words, burning is believed to provide Maasai cattle with better pasturage as well as protect them from disease.

For centuries the Maasai system of cattle keeping has worked effectively for all parties concerned: the Maasai, the abundant wildlife, and the environment itself. The key to this success lies in the fact that it is based on an open-access land system, whereby land is not privately owned, but rather managed (according to well-understood procedures) by cooperating groups of Maasai. For centuries the Maasai have had access to vast areas of savanna in southern Kenya and northern Tanzania. Permanent water sources and nearby pasturage have traditionally been controlled by local communities.

If Maasai from outside these areas want to use these watering places, they need to seek the permission of the local Maasai clan elders. We should keep in mind, however, that these requests are not made by complete strangers, but rather by an extensive network of distant relatives, in-laws, age mates, or trading partners.

We have been describing the Maasai pastoral adaptation to the East African savanna that has existed for centuries. With the arrival of colonial governments in the late nineteenth century, however, the Maasai began to experience increasing difficulty in practicing their traditional patterns of pastoralism. Early in the twentieth century, the Maasai lost some of their best dry-season pastures and water supplies to colonial settlers. Since the 1950s, large portions of the Maasai traditional grazing lands have been appropriated as official game reserves (for encouraging tourism), from which the Maasai and their herds have been excluded. Today, the Maasai are being forced into marginal areas or onto smaller and smaller parcels of land, which resemble cattle ranches. Sandwiched between the fenced fields of cultivators, the Maasai are being confined to small land holdings. Gone are the days of moving their herds over vast areas of land. Today, they are becoming permanently settled, investing money into the land (drilling wells), sending their children to school, and engaging in the previously unthinkable practice of selling their livestock for cash. Of course, the governments of Kenya and Tanzania (which have been independent since the 1960s) are delighted to be able to convert the Maasai into Texas-style ranchers for a number of reasons: (a) a permanently settled Maasai population will be much easier to control and tax; (b) they will raise cattle for sale, which will contribute to the national economy; and, perhaps

The use of draft animals, as practiced by this farmer from Hoi An, Vietnam, involves a more complex form of crop production than swidden farming.

most importantly, (c) Maasai herds will not compete for water and grass with the most valuable natural resource, wildlife, which tourists spend considerable money to photograph.

The contrasts in Maasai life between 1970 (when this author conducted research on the contiguous Kikuyu) and 2003 (when he revisited Maasailand) are startling. Today, Maasai herders, while still dressing in their traditional red togas, drive pick-up trucks, talk on cell phones, and belong to NGOs. Many of their traditional houses are now permanent, some women are growing crops, and in some cases, the Maasai are keeping chickens, not a traditional herding animal. Today, the Maasai are becoming integrated into the modern global economy. Some Maasai who live near game reserves are tapping into the tourist dollar by selling beaded leather goods, opening up their compounds for "home tours," and performing traditional Maasai dances for Europeans in zebra-striped minivans.

For much of the twentieth century, the Maasai were viewed as charming relics from the past. They were the proud, independent (even arrogant), noble herdsmen who were convinced that the West had nothing to offer them. Westerners thought it quaint that Maasai Moran (warriors) would come into Nairobi and hold up traffic at spear-point. But Westernization can push only so far before a proud people begin to push back. Believing that they have been pushed off their ancestral land, large groups of Maasai are protesting by driving their herds onto nearby farmland. Despite their hand-carried placards proclaiming "We want our land back," Maasai are being told by the Kenya government to return to their ranches and accept the fact that their free-roaming life as pastoralists is rapidly coming to an end (Lacey 2004).

Agriculture

Agriculture (intensive cultivation) differs from horticulture in that agriculture relies on animal power and technology rather than on human power alone. Agriculture, a more recent phenomenon than horticulture, is characterized by the use of the plow, draft animals to pull the plow, fertilizers, irrigation, and other technological innovations that make intensive cultivation much more productive than horticulture. A single cultivator using a horse-drawn plow, for example, not only can put a larger area of land under cultivation but also, because the plow digs deeper than the hoe or digging stick, unleashes more nutrients from the soil, thereby increasing the yield per acre. Animal fertilizers (from the excrement of the draft animals) permit land to be used year after year rather than having to remain fallow to restore

its fertility naturally. Irrigation of fields that do not receive sufficient or consistent rainfall is another innovation contributing to the increased efficiency of intensive agriculture. Moreover, the invention of the wheel has been a boon to the intensive farmer in the form of transportation, the water-raising wheel, and pottery making (storage vessels for surplus crops). Thus, through the application of technology, the intensive cultivator has access to a much greater supply of energy than is available to the horticulturalist.

This greater use of technology enables the agriculturalist to support many times more people per unit of land than the horticulturalist. There is a price for this greater productivity, however, because intensive agriculture requires a greater investment of both labor and capital. First, in terms of labor, agriculturalists must devote vast numbers of hours of hard work to prepare the land. In hilly areas, the land must be terraced and maintained, and irrigation systems may involve drilling wells, digging trenches, and building dikes. All of these activities increase the land's productivity enormously but are extremely labor intensive. Second, intensive agriculture, as compared to horticulture, requires a much higher investment of capital in terms of plows (which must be maintained), mechanical pumps (which can break down), and draft animals (which can become sick and die).

Agriculture is closely associated with both higher levels of productivity and more settled communities. In fact, not until early horticultural societies had developed into more intensive forms of agriculture could humankind develop civilizations (that is, urban societies). In other words, a fully efficient system of food production, brought about by intensive agriculture, is a necessary, if not sufficient, condition for the rise of civilization.

This terraced form of farming, as found in Indonesia, involves a long-term commitment to the land and a considerable expenditure of labor.

agriculture A form of food production that requires intensive working of the land with plows and draft animals and the use of techniques of soil and water control.

As farming became more intensive, the specialization of labor became more complex. Under a system of intensive agriculture, people were freed up to engage in activities other than food production, such as manufacturing, education, and public administration. Thus, the intensification of agriculture did not cause, but rather enabled, the development of a more complex division of labor. Societies became more stratified (that is, marked by greater class differences), political and religious hierarchies were established to manage the economic surpluses and mediate among the different socioeconomic classes, and eventually, state systems of government (complete with bureaucracies, written records, taxation, a military, and public works projects) were established. Although the relationship is not necessarily a causal one, these structural changes would not have occurred without the development of an efficient system of food production that agriculture provided.

Peasantry

With the intensification of agriculture and the rise of civilization came the development of the *peasantry*. Peasant farmers differ from Native American horticulturalists, Polynesian fishing people, or East African herders in that they are not isolated or self-sufficient societies. Instead, peasants are tied to the larger unit (the city or state)—politically, religiously, and economically. More specifically, peasants are subject to the laws and controls of the state, are influenced by the urban-based religious hierarchies, and exchange their farm surpluses for goods produced in other parts of the state. Peasants usually make up a large percentage of the total population and provide most of the dietary needs of the city dwellers.

The intimate relationship peasants have with the cities and the state is succinctly stated by George Foster, who calls peasants "a peripheral but essential part of civilizations, producing the food that makes possible urban life, supporting the specialized classes of political and religious rulers and educated elite" (1967: 7). Foster's statement is important because it reminds us that the relationship between the peasants and the state is hardly egalitarian. The peasants almost always occupy the lowest strata of society. Although they supply the rest of the society with its food, peasants have low social status, little political power, and meager material wealth. The more powerful urbanites, through the use of force or military power, often extract both labor and products from the peasants in the form of taxation, rent, or tribute.

CROSS-CULTURAL MISCUE

The Maasai herders of East Africa have so many cows that their environment cannot support them very well. As a result, the land is overgrazed, and the cows are rather scrawny and give little milk. With this in mind, the British colonial officials tried to get the Maasai to reduce the size of their herds so that they would have healthier, fatter, and better milking cows. The British officials reasoned (correctly) that by reducing the number of cows, the Maasai would actually have more milk and more beef in the long run. But the Maasai strongly refused to reduce the size of their herds. The British concluded (this time incorrectly) that the Maasai were simply too stupid to know any better.

The British officials failed to understand the basic value system of the Maasai, a value system that is very different from their own. Unlike dairy farmers in Wisconsin, the Maasai are not interested in maximizing the total quantity of milk given by their cows—because they already have far more milk than they can drink, and they are not in the business of selling milk. For the Maasai, cows are far more than simply sources of milk. Rather, cows are significant for social reasons. For example, cows are used to legalize marriages, to bond friends together, and to increase one's prestige. In short, the more cows the Maasai have, the better off they are. They are not interested in having fat cows that give large quantities of milk. Instead, they are interested in having a great number of cows, even if they are scrawny and poor milkers. Given such a value system, it would be as unreasonable for the Maasai to voluntarily thin out their herds as it would be for us to exchange five old, wrinkled dollar bills for two new, crisp dollar bills. From a Maasai perspective, it is the quantity, not the quality, of the cows that counts.

Industrialized Food Getting

As we have seen, the domestication of plants and animals around ten thousand years ago expanded people's food-getting capacity exponentially from what it had been when they relied on hunting and gathering alone. Similarly, the intensification of agriculture brought about by the invention of the plow, irrigation, and fertilizing techniques had revolutionary consequences for food production. A third major revolution in our capacity to feed ourselves occurred several hundred years ago with the coming of the industrial revolution. *Industrialization* in food production relies on technological sources of energy rather than human or animal energy. Water and wind

---

peasantry Rural peoples, usually on the lowest rung of society's ladder, who provide urban inhabitants with farm products but have little access to wealth or political power.

industrialization A process resulting in the economic change from home production of goods to large-scale mechanized factory production.

power (harnessed by waterwheels and windmills) were used in the early stages of the industrial period, but today industrialized agriculture uses motorized equipment such as tractors and combines. The science of chemistry has been applied to modern agriculture to produce fertilizers, pesticides, and herbicides, all of which increase agricultural productivity.

In addition to the quantum leaps in agricultural productivity in the past two hundred years, technology has been applied with equally dramatic results to other areas of food production. For example, ocean-going fishing vessels harvest enormous quantities of fish from the seas, scientific breakthroughs in genetics and animal husbandry now produce increasingly larger supplies of meat and poultry, and a certain amount of food in the modern person's diet is actually manufactured or reconstituted.

Farmers operating in industrialized societies today have a wealth of new technology at their disposal to increase productivity. Like most other professionals, industrialized farmers are now using the Internet for acquiring a wide range of agricultural information—from equipment sales to pesticide use to marketing opportunities. Moreover, new systems of gathering weather information are also helping farmers with crop management. Rather than individual farmers having to take weather measurements in their own orchards, fields, and vineyards, precise local information is now available on rainfall, temperature, humidity, and soil water content that comes directly to the farmer's own desktop computer. With such information at their fingertips, farmers are able to assess their risk and react quickly to protect their crops.

With industrialized farming becoming increasingly competitive, a small but growing number of farmers in North America are attempting to gain a competitive edge by using the very latest information technology. For example, some farmers are equipping their grain-harvesting combines with transmitters that allow a global positioning satellite (GPS) to track their exact position in their fields at any given point in time (Friedman 1999). This technology provides information on precisely how much grain is being harvested from each acre of land. Armed with such exact data on crop outputs, farmers can determine the precise crop variety, water level, and fertilizer that will produce the highest possible yield for each parcel of land. This high-tech solution to farm management is good for the environment because it uses fertilizer more economically, and it is good for the farmer because it increases the overall yield per unit of land. Thus, the information age is not just something that is transforming urban areas. Rather, it is having—and will continue to have—an important impact on rural, agricultural populations as well.

Food getting—and agriculture in particular—in contemporary industrialized societies has experienced some very noticeable changes since the late eighteenth century. Before the industrial revolution, agriculture was carried out primarily for subsistence; farmers produced crops for their own consumption rather than for sale. Today, however, agriculture is largely commercialized in that the overwhelming majority of food today is sold by food producers to nonproducers for some form of currency. Moreover, industrialized agriculture requires complex systems of market exchange because of its highly specialized nature.

Within the past several decades in the Western world, the trend toward commercialization of agriculture has seen its most dramatic expression in the rise of agribusiness—large-scale agricultural enterprises involving the latest technology and a sizable salaried workforce. The rise of agribusiness in recent years has been accompanied by the decline of mom-and-pop farms that drew mainly on family labor. As the number of family farms has declined and agriculture has become more highly mechanized, the developed world has witnessed a dramatic decrease in the percentage of the world's population that is engaged in food production.

Even though the industrialization of agriculture has produced farms of enormous size and productivity, these changes have come at a very high cost. The machinery and technology needed to run modern-day agribusiness are expensive. Fuel costs to run the machinery are high. With the vast diversification of foods found in modern North American diets (oranges from Florida, cheese from Wisconsin, corn from Iowa, avocados from California, and coffee from Colombia), additional expenses are incurred for processing, transporting, and marketing food products. In addition, large-scale agriculture has been responsible for considerable environmental destruction. For example, large-scale agriculture in various parts of the world has led to lowering of water tables, changes in the ecology of nearby bodies of surface water, the destruction of water fauna by pesticides, the pollution of aquifers by pesticides, salinization of soil from over-irrigation, and air pollution from crop spraying. Moreover, large-scale commercial fishing has decimated fish stock throughout the world, and commercial animal operations such as hog farms in North Carolina have given us what are euphemistically called "swine lagoons" (manmade reservoirs filled with hog feces and urine), which have a nasty habit of breaking and dumping their contents into local rivers. And, as if this were not enough, the twenty-first century is witnessing a proliferation of genetically modified seeds (such as corn), the long-term use of which has potentially harmful effects on both human health and traditional varieties of corn seeds (Dellios 2004). The litany of the negative effects of agriculture is almost endless. In fact, one anthropologist (Diamond 1987) has described agriculture as "the worst mistake in the history of the human race."

APPLIED PERSPECTIVE

World's Drug Companies Rely on "Primitive Medicine"

Over the centuries indigenous peoples have accumulated vast amounts of scientific data that could contribute to the solution of contemporary societal problems. They have learned to use their knowledge of ocean currents to navigate long distances in the Pacific; they have cultivated numerous strains of crops useful to Western botanists; and they have exploited a wide variety of food sources without damaging their delicate ecosystems. However, much of this scientific knowledge is being lost as these indigenous peoples lose their land, their languages, and their cultures.

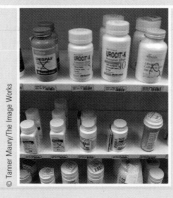
© Tanner Maury/The Image Works

The South American tropical rain forest is the home of about one-quarter (sixty thousand) of all plant species on the planet. Of those, only a small fraction have been studied to determine their chemical properties or their therapeutic potential. In other words, there are tens of thousands of plant species in the Amazon jungle that could hold a key to solving a number of pressing medical problems, including AIDS and various forms of cancer. Western medical science is just beginning to realize that local tribal people know more about these plants and their healing properties than we do. Cultural anthropologists specializing in ethnobotany (the study of how tribal societies use local plant life) are now studying tribal pharmacology so that Western medicine can use this knowledge.

About one-quarter of all prescription drugs sold in the United States are derived from plants, and half of these come from the tropical rain forest of South America. Mark Plotkin (1995) estimates that people in the United States alone spend more than $6 billion per year on drugs derived from tropical plants. Among the many tropical plants used in Western medicine (which have been used to treat precisely the same maladies among indigenous rain forest cultures) are the following (Maybury-Lewis 1992: 50):

Horse chestnuts	Anti-inflammatory
Lily of the valley	Heart stimulant
Common foxglove	Heart stimulant
Turmeric	Heart stimulant
May apple	Anticancer agent
Goldenseal	Astringent
Toothpick plant	Aid for breathing
Rattlebox	Antitumor agent
False hellebore	Tranquilizer
Yellow azalea	Tranquilizer
Quinine	Antimalarial
Cocoa	Diuretic
Kuntze	Diuretic

The pink-flowered periwinkle plant is an example of the impact of tribal pharmacology on Western medicine. Although native to Madagascar, the pink-flowered periwinkle was transported throughout the tropical world by European explorers who valued it for its beautiful flowers. They did not realize that the plant had been used by native cultures of Asia, Africa, and the New World for its therapeutic properties. When researchers noticed that healers in Jamaica were using the plant to treat diabetes, they decided to test the chemical properties of periwinkle on rats. Due to the plant's ability to lower white blood cell counts, it is now used to treat leukemia.

Ethnobotanists such as Plotkin are collecting specimens of plant life that indigenous peoples of the rain forest have used for medicinal purposes. There are thousands of such species awaiting discovery by Western scientists. The important contribution that these cultural anthropologists are making is in the collection of the folk knowledge from the local medicinal practitioners as to how (and for what purposes) these medicines are used. The challenge is to collect this information before the rain forest, the traditional cultures, and their systems of drug use are lost forever. The rain forest is being destroyed at such an alarming rate that as of 2000, 10 percent of the rain forest's plant species became extinct (Plotkin 1995). As David Maybury-Lewis (1992: 49) has warned, "What we are witnessing makes the burning of the library of Ancient Alexandria look insignificant by comparison. It is as if the greatest medical library in the world is burning faster than we can read its contents, which we have just begun to catalogue."

Questions for Further Thought

1. In addition to the medicinal properties of certain plants, what other things might the industrialized world learn from inhabitants of the rain forest?
2. Why are the Amazon rain forests disappearing so rapidly? What suggestions can you offer that would prevent the destruction of the rain forest and the cultures that inhabit it?
3. If anthropologists collect plants and knowledge regarding their use from rain forest medical experts, and then have the plants produced commercially by Western drug companies, should the local tribes benefit from the profits of the sale of these drugs?

FOOD-COLLECTING STRATEGIES AND SCIENCE

When most Westerners think about foragers, pastoralists, or horticulturalists, we tend to think of societies with minimal technology, inefficient means of survival, and little or no scientific rationality. But all of these so-called "primitive" means of livelihood require processing large amounts of information about the environment over long periods of time. Only through systematic observations over the long haul is it possible to see patterns and regularities. It is the generalizations made on the basis of these observations, resulting in scientific understanding, that enable indigenous peoples to adapt successfully to their environments. To illustrate, Inupiaq hunters of Alaska possess knowledge based on generations of systematic observations that are no less scientific than what we would expect from a trained zoologist. Ringed seals, they have found, can reliably forecast the weather by accurately predicting unexpected gales. Stable weather

This Kayapo woman from Brazil knows not to kill the foraging ants in her garden because they actually weed and fertilize her crops.

is in the forecast when the seals rise chest-high in the water with their noses pointing to the sky. But beware of a sudden storm when the seals surface briefly, with their heads low and their noses parallel to the water. Such scientific weather forecasting can be a matter of life or death for the Inupiaq hunter (Nelson 1993).

Systematic observations by horticulturalists have also led to important scientific discoveries that have enhanced adaptation to their ecosystems. For example, Kayapo women of the Brazilian rain forest have discovered that foraging ants are positive influences in their gardens. Rather than wanting to destroy the pests, Kayapo women have found that the foraging ants actually protect their manioc and maize crops. Attracted by the manioc nectar, the ants eat the wild vines that would choke the crops. Thus, the ants not only weed the garden, they also fertilize it, for the decaying vines enrich the soil (Maybury-Lewis 1992).

Pastoralists, too, have developed certain canons of ecological wisdom by studying their environment with the same meticulousness found in the modern laboratory. Although government officials and development agencies have long criticized Gabra pastoralists of East Africa for overgrazing the landscape, they are beginning to realize that traditional Gabra scientific wisdom must be incorporated into development planning. For example, short-term overgrazing by Gabra cattle actually enhances the grass that eventually grows back. Western scientists (with the help of Gabra pastoral scientists) have now realized that the hoof pressure of the grazing animals activates nitrogen regeneration by crushing the grass (Maybury-Lewis 1992).

The three examples from the Inupiaq, the Kayapo, and the Gabra illustrate successful adaptations to the environment. There are, of course, cases of adaptive failure, in which societies have become extinct by mismanaging their environment and squandering their natural resources. One case in point is Easter Island civilization, which flourished between 400 and 1500 A.D. Easter Island, best known for its huge stone statues of heads (some of which were thirty-three feet high and weighed eighty-two tons) is one of the most remote islands in the Pacific Ocean. When the island was first inhabited in approximately 400 A.D., the land was lushly vegetated with trees, woody bushes, ferns, and grasses. The natural fauna (comprising fish, porpoises, sea birds, land birds, and seals) were also abundant. By 1722, when the island was "discovered" by a Dutch explorer, Easter Island was an ecological wasteland, having lost much of its abundant plant and animal life.

For the last several centuries, scholars have wrestled with the question of how a civilization that made magnificent monumental sculptures could exist in such an impoverished environment. Owing to the recent work of archaeologists and paleontologists, it is now clear that at its height Easter Island civilization inhabited an environment much different from what the Dutch explorer

	Foragers	Horticulturalist	Pastoralist	Intensive agriculture
Also known as:	Hunters and Gatherers	Slash and burn, shifting cultivation, swidden	Herders	Industrial agriculture
Population size	Small	Small/Moderate	Small	Large
Permanency of settlement	Nomadic (or semi-)	Generally sedentary	Nomadic (or semi-)	Permanent
Surpluses	Minimal	Minimal	Moderate	Usual
Trade	Minimal	Minimal	Moderate	Very important
Labor specialization	None	Minimal	Minimal	Highest degree
Class differences	None	Minimal	Moderate	Highest degree

FIGURE 7.1 Features of Four Major Food Procurement Categories

found in the early eighteenth century. Trees, used for boat building, rope making, and firewood, were over-exploited to the point of species extinction. The widespread deforestation led to soil erosion, which further decimated other plant life and animal habitats. With dwindling food supplies, the bureaucrats and priests, so essential to running a complex society, could no longer be supported. In the end, Easter Island civilization gradually disintegrated because it could not manage its rapidly growing population and shrinking environmental resources. As Jared Diamond (1995) so poignantly points out, this failure of Easter Island civilization to adapt to its environment has important implications for today's world, which is also faced with rapidly growing populations and shrinking supplies of renewable resources. ■

Summary

1. If any culture is to survive, it must develop strategies and technologies for procuring or producing food from its environment. Although they are not mutually exclusive, five major food-procurement categories are recognized by cultural anthropologists: food collecting (foraging), horticulture, pastoralism, agriculture, and industrialization.

2. Humans adapt to cold climates both culturally (dietary patterns, activity levels, and so on) and biologically (over time, developing short, stocky body types).

3. Despite their lack of high levels of technology, many small-scale societies have made very good adaptations to their natural environments.

4. The success of various food-getting strategies depends on the interaction between a society's technology and its environment. Although different environments present different limitations and possibilities, it is generally recognized that environments influence rather than determine food-getting practices. The level of technology that any society has at its disposal is a critical factor in adapting to and using the environment.

5. Carrying capacity is the limiting effect an environment has on a culture's productivity. If a culture exceeds its carrying capacity, permanent damage to the environment usually results.

6. Food collecting, the oldest form of food getting, relies on procuring foods that are naturally available in the environment. Approximately ten thousand years ago, people for the first time began to domesticate plants and animals. Since then the percentage of the world's population engaged in foraging has declined from 100 percent to a small fraction of 1 percent.

7. Compared to societies with other food-getting practices, foraging societies tend to have low-density populations, are nomadic or seminomadic, live in small social groups, and occupy remote, marginally useful areas of the world.

8. Foraging societies tend to be selective in terms of the plant and animal species they exploit in their habitats. Which species are actually exploited for food can be explained by the optimal foraging theory, a theory developed by cultural ecologists that suggests that foragers do not select arbitrarily but rather on the basis of maximizing their caloric intake for the amount of time and energy expended.

9. Horticulture, a form of small-scale plant cultivation relying on simple technology, produces low yields with little or no surpluses. Horticulture most often uses the slash-and-burn technique, a form of cultivation that involves clearing the land by burning it and then planting seeds in the fertile ash residue.

10. Pastoralism, the keeping of domesticated livestock as a source of food, is usually practiced in areas of the world that are unable to support any type of cultivation. Pastoralism most often involves a nomadic or seminomadic way of life, small family-based communities, scarcity of food and other resources, and regular contact with cultivators as a way of supplementing the diet.

11. Agriculture, a more recent phenomenon than horticulture, uses technology such as irrigation, fertilizers, and mechanized equipment to produce high crop yields capable of supporting large populations. Unlike horticulture, agriculture is usually associated with permanent settlements, cities, and high levels of labor specialization.

12. Industrialized food getting, which began several centuries ago, uses vastly more powerful sources of energy than had ever been used previously. It relies on high levels of technology (such as tractors and combines), a mobile labor force, and a complex system of markets.

13. While many societies have made ingenious adaptations to their environments, examples do exist of societies that have died out because of mismanaging the environment and squandering their natural resources.

Key Terms

agriculture	hunting and gathering	pastoralism	stock friendship
carrying capacity	industrialization	peasantry	swidden cultivation
food collecting	neolithic revolution	shifting cultivation	transhumance
foraging	nomadism	slash-and-burn method	
horticulture	optimal foraging theory	social functions of cattle	

Suggested Readings

Barfield, Thomas J. *The Nomadic Alternative.* Englewood Cliffs, NJ: Prentice-Hall, 1997. A historical and ethnographic discussion of pastoral societies in East Africa, the Middle East, and Central Eurasia focusing on topics such as comparative social organization, relations with non-pastoral peoples, and the ecology of nomadic pastoralism.

Bates, Daniel. *Human Adaptive Strategies: Ecology, Culture, and Politics,* 3d ed. Boston: Allyn & Bacon, 2005. By drawing upon a number of case studies, the author discusses different adaptive strategies and their implications for political organization.

Bishop, Naomi H. *Himalayan Herders.* Belmont, CA: Wadsworth, 2002. This ethnographic case study describes life in a high-altitude Himalayan village centered on transhumant herding of zomo, a hybrid cross between a cow and a yak. Bishop examines traditional life as well as the numerous changes that are occurring as a result of the globalizing economy.

Harris, M., and E. B. Ross, eds. *Food and Evolution: Toward a Theory of Human Food Habits.* Philadelphia: Temple University Press, 1987. This compendium of twenty-four essays by scholars from a number of disciplines explores why people in different parts of the world and at different periods of history eat the things they do. Perspectives from a wide range of academic disciplines are represented, including physical anthropology, psychology, archaeology, nutrition, and primatology.

Igoe, Jim. *Conservation and Globalization: A Study of National Parks and Indigenous Communities from East Africa* *and South Dakota.* Belmont, CA: Wadsworth, 2004. As a case study in the Wadsworth series on Contemporary Social Issues, Igoe examines the processes and consequences of displacing the pastoral Maasai from their traditional lands in the interest of enforcing national park boundaries.

Kent, Susan. *Cultural Diversity Among Twentieth-Century Foragers: An African Perspective.* Cambridge: Cambridge University Press, 1996. While much of the literature on foraging societies in Africa has stressed their similarities, this volume explores the considerable variations in African societies that rely on hunting and gathering as a major food-getting strategy.

Khazanov, Anatoly M. *Nomads and the Outside World,* 2d ed. Madison: University of Wisconsin Press, 1994. A comprehensive study of nomadic pastoralism from a comparative perspective. Discussing the major areas of the world where pastoralism is found, Khazanov looks at the nature of pastoralism from its earliest origins to modern times.

Lee, Richard B. *The Dobe Ju/'hoansi,* 3d ed. Belmont, CA: Wadsworth, 2003. This basic ethnographic case study of the Ju/'hoansi, foragers living in Botswana and Namibia, was written by one of the leading contemporary authorities on food-collecting societies.

Lee, Richard B., and Richard Daly, eds. *The Cambridge Encyclopedia of Hunters and Gatherers.* Cambridge: Cambridge University Press, 1999. More of a handbook than an encyclopedia, this collection of eighty-three articles by leading authorities on foraging societies provides well-structured and readable answers to questions concerning hunting and gathering societies.

O'Meara, J. Tim. *Samoan Planters: Tradition and Economic Development in Polynesia.* Belmont, CA: Wadsworth, 2002. O'Meara presents evidence contradicting the common belief among development experts that small-scale village farmers remain undeveloped because of their incurable economic irrationality.

Economics

Sellers hawk their goods at a busy street market in Grenada, West Indies.

8

WHEN WE HEAR THE WORD *economics,* many images come to mind. We usually think of such things as money, supply and demand curves, lending and borrowing money at some agreed-upon interest rate, factories with production schedules, labor negotiations, buying stocks and bonds, foreign exchange, and gross domestic product. Although all of these are found in an economics textbook, they are not integral parts of all economic systems. Many small-scale cultures have no standardized currencies, stock markets, or factories. Nevertheless, all societies (whether small-scale or highly complex) face a common challenge: they all have at their disposal a limited amount of vital resources, such as land, livestock, machines, food, and labor. This simple fact of life requires all societies to plan carefully how to allocate scarce resources, produce needed commodities, distribute their products to all people, and develop efficient consumption patterns for their products so people can better adapt to their environment. In other words, every society, if it is to survive, must develop systems of production, distribution, and consumption.

ECONOMICS AND ECONOMIC ANTHROPOLOGY

The science of *economics* focuses on how production, distribution, and consumption occur within the industrialized world. The sub-discipline of *economic anthropology,* on the other hand, studies production, distribution, and consumption comparatively in *all* societies of the world, industrialized and non-industrialized alike. The relationship between the formal science of economics and the sub-specialty of economic anthropology has not always been a harmonious one. Formal economics has its philosophical roots in the study of Western, industrialized economies. As a result, much of *formal economic theory* is based on assumptions

economics   The academic discipline that studies systems of production, distribution, and consumption, most typically in the industrialized world.
economic anthropology   A branch of the discipline of anthropology that looks at systems of production, distribution, and consumption, most often in the nonindustrialized world.
formal economic theorists   Those economic anthropologists who suggest that the ideas of Western economics can be applied to any economic situation.

What We Will Learn

- How do anthropologists study economic systems cross-culturally?

- How do people use culture to help them adapt to their environment?

- How are resources such as land and property allocated in different cultures?

- What principles of distribution are used in various parts of the world?

▶ **Click!**

For interactive exercises and study aids, Go to **www.ichapters.com**; enter the author name and select your text, then click the Study Help tab to purchase the following online resources:

- **ThomsonNOW** for chapter-specific online tutorials, quizzes, and a personalized study plan

- **Anthropology Resource Center** for interactive maps, modules, videos, and the Applied Anthropology site

- **Thomson Audio Study Products** for a brief overview of the major chapter themes and to test your knowledge with quiz questions

derived from observing Western, industrialized societies. For example, economic theory is predicated on the assumption that the value of a particular commodity will increase as it becomes scarcer (the notion of supply and demand) or on the assumption that when people are exchanging goods and services, they naturally strive to maximize their material well-being and their profits. As we will see in this chapter, these basic assumptions are not found in all the cultures of the world.

Economists use their theories (based on these assumptions) to predict how people will make certain types of choices when producing or consuming commodities. Owners of a manufacturing plant, for example, are constantly faced with choices. Do they continue to manufacture only men's underwear, or do they expand their product line to include underwear for women? Do they move some or all of their manufacturing facilities to Mexico, or do they keep them in North Carolina? Should they give their workers more benefits? Should they spend more of their profits on advertising? Should they invest more capital on machinery or on additional labor? Western economists assume that all of these questions will be answered in a rational way so as to maximize the company's profits. Similarly, Western economists assume that individuals as well as corporations are motivated by the desire to maximize their material well-being.

A long-standing debate among schools of economics and anthropology has centered on the question of whether these and other assumptions that Western economists make about human behavior are indeed universal. How applicable are these economic theories to small-scale, non-industrialized societies? Are the differences between industrial and non-industrial economies a matter of degree or a matter of kind? Some anthropologists contend that classic economic theories cannot be applied to the study of non-industrialized societies. They argue that tribal or peasant societies, based as they are on subsistence, are different in kind from market economies found in the industrialized societies.

Whereas in Western societies production and consumption choices are usually made on the basis of maximization of profits, in non-industrialized societies they often are based on quite different principles, such as reciprocity or redistribution. The principle of reciprocity (as in the biblical injunction to "Do unto others as you would have them do unto you") emphasizes the fair exchange of equivalent values and as such is in direct contrast to the principle of maximizing one's profits. Likewise, the principle of chiefly redistribution, found in some subsistence economies, discourages the accumulation of personal wealth by moving or redistributing goods from those who have wealth to those who do not. Principles such as reciprocity and redistribution, with their emphasis on cooperation and generosity, are in stark contrast to the principle of maximization, which encourages individual accumulation and competition and consequently can lead to jealousy, hostility, and antagonism.

We do not, however, have to travel to remote parts of rural Africa or Micronesia to witness people who do not always maximize their economic well-being. For the past several decades in the United States, a growing number of Americans have voted consistently against their own economic interests. They are largely working-class people from rural and small town America—reverent, practical, hard-working producers who work as truck drivers, laborers, farmers, shopkeepers, electricians, meat packers, and factory workers all across the heartland of the United States. These are the people who several generations ago would have held union cards and advocated for Roosevelt's New Deal. Today, many of them have put on the back burner "pocketbook" issues such as wages, working conditions, social security, unemployment, minimum wages, job outsourcing abroad, affordable health care, and pension plans. Now, cultural values seem to be much more important issues than economics. In other words, many working-class people today are voting for candidates who promise to support their strongly held cultural (i.e., non-economic) values, such as opposing abortion, gay marriage, big government, arrogant liberal elites, affirmative action, embryonic stem cell research, pornography, politically correct college professors, and Darwinian evolution. They seem to spend their emotional and political capital on fighting to keep monuments of the Ten Commandments in public spaces while failing to notice that (a) they are working longer hours for less money, (b) their jobs are being exported abroad, (c) health insurance is becoming less affordable, (d) their pension funds are being laid waste by corporate malfeasance, (e) the environment is being degraded, (f) their children's future is being mortgaged, (g) energy costs are rising rapidly, and (h) the rich are getting richer while they are struggling to pay the rent. For an excellent discussion of this phenomenon, see Thomas Frank (2004).

Cross-Cultural Examination of Economic Systems

A good deal of debate has taken place during the last several decades over the extent to which the principles of classic economics can be useful for the study of all societies. Despite the substantial differences of economic systems found throughout the world—as well as the different theories used to analyze them—it is possible to examine economic systems cross-culturally along certain key dimensions:

1. *The regulation of resources:* How land, water, and natural resources are controlled and allocated

2. *Production:* How material resources are converted into usable commodities

3. *Exchange:* How the commodities, once produced, are distributed among the people of the society

THE ALLOCATION OF NATURAL RESOURCES

Every society has access to certain natural resources in its territorial environment, including land, animals, water, minerals, and plants. Even though the nature and amount of these resources vary widely from one group to another, every society has developed a set of rules governing the *allocation of resources* and how they can be used. For example, all groups have determined systematic ways for allocating land among their members. Hunters and gatherers must determine who can hunt animals and collect plants from which areas. Pastoralists need to have some orderly pattern for deciding access to pasturage and watering places. Agriculturalists must work out ways of acquiring, maintaining, and passing on rights to their farmland.

In our own society, where things are bought and sold in markets, most of the natural resources are privately owned. Pieces of land are surveyed, precise maps are drawn, and title deeds are granted to those who purchase a piece of property. Individual property rights are so highly valued in the United States that under certain circumstances, a property owner is justified in killing someone who is attempting to violate those property rights. Small pieces of land are usually held by individuals, and larger pieces of property are held collectively, either by governments (as in the case of roads, public buildings, and parks) or by private corporations on behalf of their shareholders.

To be certain, there are limitations on private property ownership in the United States. To illustrate, certain vital resources such as public utilities are either strongly regulated or owned outright by some agency of government; rights of eminent domain enable the government to force owners to sell their land for essential public projects, and zoning laws set certain limits on how property owners may use their land. Nevertheless, the system of resource allocation found in the United States is based on the general principle of private ownership, whereby an individual or a group of individuals has total or near total rights to a piece of property and consequently can do with it as they see fit.

Property rights are so strongly held in the United States (and other parts of the Western world) that some observers have suggested that humans have a genetically based territorial instinct that compels them to stake out and defend their turf (Ardrey 1968). However, the degree to which humans are territorial varies widely throughout the world. By and large, the notion of personal land ownership is absent in many societies that

allocation of resources   Rules adopted by all societies that govern the regulation and control of such resources as land, water, and their by-products.

Individual property rights are strongly valued and protected in the United States, but in some parts of the world they are more loosely defined.

base their livelihood on food collecting, pastoralism, or horticulture. Let's examine how each of these types of societies deals with the question of access to land.

Food Collectors

In most food-collecting societies, land is not owned, in the Western sense of the term, either individually or collectively. Food collectors have a number of compelling reasons to maintain flexible or open borders. First, because food collectors in most cases must follow the migratory patterns of animals, it makes little sense for people to tie themselves exclusively to a single piece of land. Second, claiming and defending a particular territory requires time, energy, and technology that many foraging peoples either do not have or choose not to expend. Third, territoriality can lead to conflict and warfare between those claiming property rights and those who would violate those claims. Thus, for food-collecting societies, having flexible territorial boundaries (or none at all) is the most adaptive strategy.

Even though food collectors rarely engage in private ownership of land, there is some variation in the amount of communal control. At one extreme are the Inuit of Canada and the Hadza of Tanzania, two groups that have no real concept of trespassing whatsoever. They could go where they wanted, when they wanted, and were generally welcomed by other members of the society. The Ju/'hoansi of the Kalahari region do recognize, to some degree, the association of certain territories with particular tribal bands, but territoriality is not rigorously maintained. For example, members of one Ju/'hoansi band are allowed to track a wounded animal into a neighbor's territory. Moreover, anyone can use the watering holes of any neighboring territory provided she or he seeks permission, which is always granted. This type of reciprocity, cooperation, and permissive use rights is adaptive in that it increases the chances of survival of all Ju/'hoansi peoples. In a smaller number of societies, however, territorial boundaries between individual bands or extended families were maintained quite rigorously. Robert Kelly (1995) cites a number of examples from the ethnographic literature. To illustrate, certain Native American groups living on the coast of southwestern Canada maintained exclusive rights to particular stretches of beaches. The food-collecting Maidu regularly patrolled their borders to guard against poachers and would claim as their own any animal that died within their territory after being shot by an outsider. The Vedda of India marked their hunting territory with small archers carved into tree trunks along the borders.

As a general rule, a food-collecting society will have open or flexible boundaries if animals are mobile and food and water supplies are unpredictable. Conversely, food collectors are more likely to live in permanent settlements and maintain greater control over land in the areas where food and water supplies are plentiful and predictable (Dyson-Hudson and Smith 1978).

Pastoralists

Like food collectors, nomadic or seminomadic pastoralists require extensive territory. For pastoralists to maintain their way of life, it is imperative that they have access to two vital resources for their livestock: water and pasturage. Depending on the local environment, the availability of these two resources may vary widely. In marginal environments where grass and water are at a premium, pastoralists need to range over wide territories and consequently require free access to land. In more environmentally friendly regions of the world where grass and water are more abundant, one is likely to find greater control over land and its resources. In any event, pastoral groups must work out arrangements among themselves and with nonpastoralists to gain access to certain pasturage.

Variations can be found, but corporate (that is, non-individual) control of pastures is the general rule among pastoral peoples. At one extreme, there are pastoral societies whose entire territory is considered to belong to the society as a whole. In such societies (best represented by East African groups such as the Turkana, Jie, and Samburu), there are no fixed divisions of land that are used by different segments of the society. At the other extreme, we find societies in which the rights to use certain pastures are divided among certain segments of the society. These pastoral societies are most often found in the Eurasian steppes and in the Middle East. And in some pastoral societies, the use of wells or natural watering sources is controlled, to some degree, by individuals or groups to the exclusion of others. However, as Anatoly Khazanov (1994) reminds us, the variations found in how pastoral societies allocate land

Because this group of East African pastoralists treats land as belonging to everyone in the society, you are not likely to find any "No Trespassing" signs here.

© Sue Cunningham Photographic/Alamy

During the colonial period in Kenya, the British failed to understand that land among the Kikuyu was allocated according to lineage membership and had much more than mere economic importance.

© Carl & Ann Purcell/Corbis

and resources depend on a number of factors, including ecological variables (such as climate and rainfall), types of animals herded, the size of the population relative to the land, and the relationship of the pastoralists to the wider society.

To avoid overgrazing and conflict, pastoralists may have to enter into agreements with other pastoralist families to share certain areas, or they may have to form contractual arrangements with sedentary cultivators to graze their animals on recently harvested fields. The pastoral Fulani of northern Nigeria, for example, although remaining removed from village life on an everyday basis, nevertheless have had to maintain special contacts with sedentary horticulturalists for rights of access to water and pastures. According to Derrick Stenning, "This has brought them into the orbit of the Muslim states of the western Sudan, in whose politics and wars they became involved principally to maintain or extend their pastoral opportunities" (1965: 365).

Horticulturalists

In contrast to hunters and gatherers and most pastoralists, horticulturalists tend to live on land that is communally controlled, usually by an extended kinship group. Individual nuclear or polygynous families may be granted the use of land by the extended family for growing crops, but the rights are limited. For example, the small family units usually retain their rights for as long as they work the land and are in good standing with the larger family. Because they do not own the land, however, they cannot dispose of it by selling it. They simply use it at the will of the larger group. Such a method of land allocation makes sense, given their farming technology. Because horticulturalists often are shifting cultivators, there would be no advantage to having claims of ownership over land that cannot be used permanently.

This communal type of land tenure is well exemplified by the Samoans of Polynesia. Under their traditional system, any piece of land belongs to the extended family that clears and plants it. Individual members of the extended family work the land under the authority of a *matai*, an elected family member who holds the title to the land on behalf of the entire group. The *matai*'s authority over the land depends on his meeting his responsibility to care for his extended family. If he does not fulfill his obligations, the family can remove his title. Any individual of the extended family group has undisputed rights to use the land provided he or she lives on the family land and serves and pays allegiance to the *matai* (O'Meara 1990).

Intensive Agriculturalists

In North America, and in most other parts of the industrialized world, resources such as land are allocated according to the principle of private individual ownership. Most English-speaking people have no difficulty understanding the concept of private ownership. When we say we "own" a piece of land, the term means that we have absolute and exclusive rights to it. We are able to sell it, give it away, rent it, or trade it for another piece of property, if we so choose. In other words, we have 100-percent rights to that piece of land. This association between private individual land ownership and intensive agriculture is at least partially due to the possibility of using the land year after year, thereby giving the land a permanent and continual value.

This concept of individual *property rights* is so entrenched in our thinking and our culture that we sometimes fail to realize that many other cultures do not share that principle with us. This cultural myopia led

property rights Western concept of individual ownership (an idea unknown to some non-Western cultures) in which a large kinship group, instead of the individual, determines limited rights to property.

APPLIED PERSPECTIVE

Is Nepotism Always Bad?

Social scientists often make distinctions between societies that are large, industrialized, complex, bureaucratic, and stratified, and those that are small, non-industrialized, egalitarian, and kinship oriented. People who operate in complex, bureaucratic organizations are expected to behave toward one another in an objective and straightforward manner, without regard to personal considerations. Social relations in these organizations should be based on **universalism**—

© Gilbert Liz/Corbis Sygma

that is, determined by a universally applicable set of rules rather than personal statuses. Strong kinship ties and obligations have no place within a bureaucracy. Decisions such as who gets hired are to be determined by objective, universally applied criteria (examination results, previous job experience, educational background) rather than by such particularistic considerations as how the applicant is related to the research director.

In many traditional societies, people relate to one another in particularistic, not universalistic, terms. With **particularism**, people emphasize personal status relationships with one another, such as kinship connections or common ethnic affilia-

tion. A person is expected to show particular loyalty to a kinsman *because* that person is a relative. Thus, in particularistic societies, a person is likely to hire someone for a job because she or he has a special relationship (such as being cousins) rather than because of any universally applicable set of criteria (such as a high score on a standardized test).

In the developing world, this basic value contrast between particularism and universalism can be seen most dramatically in urban areas. Rural migrants, with their particularistic values, come to cities seeking jobs in large corporations with bureaucratic norms of universalism. Western bureaucrats assume that new workers must shed their particularistic values, which they see as incompatible with bureaucratic structures. This notion was the starting point of an applied cultural research project conducted by Peter Blunt (1980) on workers in Nairobi, Kenya. Blunt wanted to examine hiring practices and organizational efficiency in several large companies to see whether workers with a particularistic orientation were incompatible with the more universalistic orientation of bureaucratic organizations.

some early anthropologists to ask the wrong types of questions when they first encountered certain non-Western peoples. To illustrate, when studying a small group of East African horticulturalists who also kept cattle, some early anthropologists, using their own set of linguistic categories, asked what to them seemed like a perfectly logical question: "Who owns that brown cow over there?" In actual fact, no one "owned" the cow in our sense of the term because no single individual had 100-percent rights to the beast. Instead, a number of people may have had limited rights and obligations to the brown cow. The man we see with the cow at the moment may have rights to milk the cow on Tuesdays and Thursdays, but someone else has rights to milk it on Mondays and Wednesdays. The cows are actually controlled by the larger kinship group (the lineage or extended family); the individual merely has limited rights to use the cow. This fundamental difference in

property allocation is reflected in the local East African language of Swahili, which contains no word that would be comparable to the English word *own*. The closest Swahili speakers can come linguistically to conveying the notion of ownership is to use the word *nina*, which means literally "I am with."

This fundamentally different way of allocating property was at the heart of the sixty-year dispute between the Kikuyu of Kenya and the British colonialists. The feud began with the alienation of Kikuyu land in the early 1900s and ended with the Mau Mau uprising of the 1950s. In a misguided attempt at economic development, the British colonial office encouraged British citizens to resettle in the Kikuyu highlands and start planting marketable crops such as tea and coffee. The colonial government thought it was respecting Kikuyu land rights by allocating only unused parcels of land to the European settlers. It was convenient for the government—pressured by a small but vocal settler population—to assume that all land not under cultivation was unoccupied and thus could be given to the European settlers. But in terms of Kikuyu perception, this land, although temporarily unoccupied, was hardly ownerless. Because Kikuyu lineages (large extended families) controlled land and its inheritance, the land reverted to the surviving family

universalism   The notion of rewarding people on the basis of some universally applied set of standards.
particularism   The propensity to deal with other people based on one's particular relationship to them rather than according to a universally applied set of standards.

Blunt conducted his research on two companies in Kenya that actually recruited new workers on the basis of their kinship or ethnic relations with the present workers. In both situations most employees were from the same ethnic group, and many of them were related to one another. In one of the two companies the homogenization of the workforce took place rapidly over the course of a single year. At the beginning of the twelve-month period, only one-third of the employees were from the same ethnic group; a year later the proportion had risen to 95 percent.

Blunt was interested in measuring the organizational efficiency both before and after the homogenization of this particular workforce. Contrary to conventional wisdom about bureaucracies, Blunt found that ethnic/kinship homogenization, rather than damaging the organization, actually improved organizational efficiency. For example, turnover rates fell to less than half, customer complaints declined while the number of written commendations of workers by customers more than doubled, damage to company property was reduced 27 percent, and the number of poor performance warnings fell by 63 percent. Working with friends, relatives, or "people from home" enabled workers to cope more effectively with the alienation and loneliness so prevalent in cities. The new recruit developed a stronger allegiance to the company because it employed a kinsman. Moreover, the employee-recruiter felt a measure of satisfaction because he was now able to fulfill his kinship obligations.

Blunt's findings are significant because they remind us that theories that might be applicable in Detroit are not necessarily relevant for other parts of the world. Multinational companies working in non-Western countries should take notice of the implications. Our Western idea of nepotism (allowing supervisors to hire kinfolk or fellow tribesmen) may actually maximize organizational efficiency in some situations even though the new recruit may have weaker skills than other candidates for the job.

Questions for Further Thought

1. In your own words, how would you distinguish between particularism and universalism?
2. Do you think that hiring on the basis of family connections would ever work at a company in your country? Why or why not?
3. What does this case study tell us about the wisdom of importing Western thinking into other parts of the world?

members. Kikuyu lineages were more than just groups of kin; rather, they were corporate landowning groups. Without land, the lineage lost its sense of unity. The land, which was the material symbol of lineage solidarity, was associated with an elaborate network of rights and obligations among kin. When a lineage lost control over its land, much more was at stake than the loss of a piece of property; it involved the suspension or drastic alteration of an entire set of social relationships. Had the British colonial government understood how the Kikuyu traditionally allocate land (their most valuable resource), much of the hostility between the British and the Kikuyu might have been avoided.

There has been an ongoing debate in recent years among economists and economic anthropologists as to whether communal ownership of land eventually leads to disaster. Garrett Hardin (1968) put forth the idea ("the tragedy of the commons") that, because people are natural maximizers, they will tend to destroy common property (e.g., common pastures or farmland) because no one individual has a stake in preserving it. Individual herders will graze as many animals as possible, thereby degrading the common pasturage through overgrazing. By way of contrast, if land is privately controlled, Hardin argues, herders will be more likely to avoid environmental degradation by conserving their resources (land and water). Although this argument would probably hold true for Western farmers (who want to maximize their yields of crops or livestock), there is ample ethnographic evidence to conclude that pastoralists in many parts of the world have adopted strategies that prevent overgrazing and the degradation of common land. One such strategy is seasonal movement of livestock in search of new sources of water and grass, thereby allowing certain resources to replenish themselves instead of becoming totally depleted. And as we have seen in the previous chapter, the pastoral Maasai use a system of "drought insurance," involving setting aside during normal times certain pastures and watering places that never dry up. These vital resources, commonly held, are used only as emergency resources during times of drought. Thus, the "tragedy of the commons" argument does not hold up when viewing traditional pastoral societies.

According to Jim Igoe (2004: 55–56), the notion of the "tragedy of the commons" appeals to Westerners "because it resonates with how they were socialized to look at the world, and it also appears to be scientific. It was appealing to policy makers at the time it was written, because its conclusion is that a global system of private property protects the environment, and that communism will lead to the ecological ruin of the planet."

PRODUCTION

The initial step in meeting the material needs of any society is to establish a system of allocating the right to use resources to certain people. In very few situations, however, can resources be used by people in exactly the form they are found in nature. Animals must be butchered; grains must be ground and cooked; metal ores must be mined, smelted, combined with other chemical elements, and crafted before becoming tools; stones must be shaped before they can be put into the wall of a house. This process of obtaining goods from the natural environment and transforming them into usable objects is what economists call *production*.

All humans must meet certain fundamental material needs (such as food, water, and shelter), but how these needs are satisfied varies enormously from society to society. Some groups, such as the Siriono of eastern Bolivia, meet most of their material needs with goods procured from hunting and gathering. Others, such as the Maasai and Samburu of East Africa, live essentially from the products of their livestock. Still others, such as people of the United States and certain western European nations, go well beyond meeting their basic physical needs through a complex system of technology and industrialization. How do we explain such diverse systems of production? Why do two cultures inhabiting apparently similar environments develop substantially different systems of production?

The answers to these questions can be partially expressed in economic terms. For example, why any society produces the things it does is determined, to some extent, by economic factors such as the accessibility of certain resources, the technology available for processing the resources, and the abundance of energy supplies. This is only part of the explanation, however, because cultural values also play a role in determining production. To illustrate, the Hadza of Tanzania are aware of the horticultural practices of their neighbors but choose not to engage in horticulture themselves for the simple reason that it involves too much effort for the anticipated yield. Also, most societies fail to exploit all of the resources at their disposal. Some societies living alongside bodies of water have strong prohibitions against eating fish. The Hindus in India, despite an abundance of cows, refuse to eat beef on religious grounds. The Inuit, even though they often experience food shortages, maintain a number of taboos against eating certain types of food. And, of course, people in the United States would never dream of routinely eating the flesh of dogs, cats, or rats, although these animals are a rich source of protein.

The apparent failure by some societies to exploit all available resources may not stem from irrationality or arbitrariness. As some cultural ecologists have shown convincingly, often there are good reasons for certain types of economic behavior that at first glance might appear irrational. The sacred cow in Hindu India is a case in point. Even though the Indian population needs more protein in its diet, the Hindu religion prohibits the slaughter of cows and the eating of beef. This taboo has resulted in large numbers of half-starved cows cluttering the Indian landscape, disrupting traffic, and stealing food from marketplaces. But as Marvin Harris has demonstrated (1977, 1979a), the taboo makes good economic sense because it prevents the use of cows for less cost-effective purposes. To raise cows as a source of food would be an expensive proposition, given the economic and ecological conditions found in India. Instead, cows are used as draft animals and for the products they provide, such as milk, fertilizer, and fuel (dung). The religious taboo, according to Harris, rather than being irrational, serves to regulate the system of production in a very effective way by having a positive effect on the carrying capacity of the land.

Units of Production

Like other parts of culture, the way people go about producing is not haphazard or random but rather is systematic, organized, and patterned. Every society breaks up its members into some type of productive unit comprising people with specific tasks to perform. In industrialized societies such as our own, the productive unit is the private company that exists for the purpose of producing goods or services. These private firms range from small, individually owned operations to gigantic multinational corporations. Whatever the size and complexity, however, these private companies are made up of employees performing specific roles, all of which are needed to produce the goods and services that are then sold for a profit. The employees do not consume the products of the firm, but instead receive salaries, which they use to purchase the goods and services they need.

Production in the Household

In most non-industrialized societies, the basic unit of production is the household. In these small-scale societies, most if not all of the goods and services consumed are produced by the members of the household. The household may be made up of a nuclear family (husband, wife, and children) or a more elaborate family structure containing married siblings, multiple wives, and more than two generations. While household members are most often kin, they can also include nonrelatives as well. Moreover, some members may not actually

production   A process whereby goods are obtained from the natural environment and altered to become consumable goods for society.

In Hindu India the cow is sacred and never killed for food. This is an excellent example of how a religiously based food prohibition can be economically rational as well.

© DPA/The Image Works

live in the household but contribute to its economic well-being while living and working elsewhere. In a typical horticultural society, household members produce most of what they consume; their work includes planting, tending, and harvesting the crops; building houses; preparing and consuming food; procuring firewood and other fuels from the environment; making their own tools; keeping some livestock; making their own clothes; and producing various containers for storing and cooking foods. When a particular task is too complex to be carried out by a single household, larger groups of family members or neighbors usually join together to complete the task.

Even though both the business firm and the household are units of production, there are significant structural differences between them. Whereas the business firm is primarily—if not exclusively—just a unit of production, the household performs a number of overlapping functions. When two male kinsmen who are part of the same household work side by side threshing wheat, it is very likely that they play a number of other roles together. For example, one man, because of his advanced age, may be a religious specialist; the other man, because of his leadership skills, may play an important political role in the extended family; and both men may enjoy spending their leisure time together drinking beer and telling stories. Thus, this productive unit of the household is the very same group that shares certain religious, political, and social activities.

A second structural difference between the business firm and the household is that the household is far more self-sufficient. In most cases, the members of the household in small-scale societies can satisfy their own material needs without having to go outside the group. People employed in a business firm, on the other hand, rely on a large number of people for their material well-being, including the butcher, the television repairperson, the barber, the schoolteacher, the

auto mechanic, and all of the thousands of people who make all of the things with which people surround themselves.

A third difference is that a business firm concentrates exclusively on its economic function and is therefore a more productive unit than the household. Because the family household is more than just a productive unit and must also be concerned with the emotional, social, psychological, and spiritual needs of its members, it is likely to use some of its resources in nonproductive ways. Consequently, the family-based household is less likely to use highly productive, progressive, or innovative methods than the business firm.

In much the same way that family businesses today are blurring the line between households and corporate enterprises, we should not assume that the highly productive methods of technology used in modern businesses are without limitations. For example, computer technology and the Internet enable us to communicate and process information infinitely faster than we could twenty years ago. Nevertheless, this same office technology is contributing to making workers less productive. According to a study reported in *Advertising Age,* 25 percent of U.S. workers regularly read blogs during business hours, losing roughly 9 percent of their workweek (Johnson 2005). This represents 551,000 years of labor lost in 2005. Moreover, according to a survey conducted by Information Mapping, Inc. (www.infomap .com), a majority of U.S. office workers, who routinely spend between one and three hours a day reading and writing e-mails, had difficulty understanding the messages because they were disorganized, missing critical information, or unclear as to how to act on the message. Thus, despite significant gains in efficiency provided in recent years by information technology, there are limits of information technology to productivity as well.

We should not take these structural differences between traditional households and business too literally.

Are there any physical reasons the job of umpiring a baseball game could not be done by a woman?

In today's volatile global economies—with changing workforces and unexpected periods of unemployment—we are beginning to see a number of examples of households transitioning into family businesses. For example, economist Gonzalo Hernandez Licona (2000) found that during the economic downturn of 1995 in Mexico (in which the country lost 7.5 percent of its GDP in a single year), there was a significant increase in the formation of household businesses. Fortunately, the economic crisis lasted only about a year. However, Hernandez Licona studied economic patterns for the two years prior to 1995 as well as the following two years of recovery. With many household members having lost their jobs in 1995, families used their underutilized family members as employees in new family businesses. The larger the household, the more likely it was to evolve into a family business; and the lower the level of education, the more likely it was to transition from household to family business. The significance of this study is that it demonstrates that for many households starting a family business was a rational survival strategy during those periods of high unemployment.

This same proliferation of family businesses can be seen during times of economic transition away from industrialized cash crops. The demise of the henequen (sisal) agro-industry in Yucatan during the 1980s resulted in a dramatic rise in household businesses as a way of coping with the loss of salaried employment. Cindy Hull (2007: 184), who has conducted six separate field studies of a Yucatan village between 1976 and 1998, found a dramatic increase in the number of small house-front stores managed by various members of their immediate and extended families. Whereas men, formerly employed in the henequen industry, frequently do the purchasing of goods sold in the house-front stories, most of the actual labor in the stores is provided by the women and children.

Division of Labor

One very important aspect of the process of production is the allocation of tasks to be performed—that is, deciding which types of people will perform which categories of work. Every society, whether large or small, distinguishes, to some degree, between the work appropriate for men and women and for adults and children. Even though many societies have considerably more complex *divisions of labor*, all societies make distinctions on the basis of gender and age.

Gender Specialization

Although some roles (jobs) found in the world are played by both women and men, many others are associated with one gender or the other. For example, women generally tend crops, gather wild foods, care for children, prepare food, clean house, fetch water, and collect cooking fuel. Men, on the other hand, hunt, build houses, clear land for cultivation, herd large animals, fish, trap small animals, and serve as political functionaries. There are exceptions to these broad generalizations about what constitutes men's and women's work. In some parts of traditional Africa, for example, women are known to carry much heavier

division of labor   The set of rules found in all societies dictating how the day-to-day tasks are assigned to the various members of a society.

loads than men, work long hours in the fields, and even serve as warriors.

Several theories have been set forth to explain the very common, if not universal, division of labor by gender. One explanation is that because men have greater body mass and strength, they are better equipped physically to engage in hunting, warfare, and land clearing. A second argument is that women do the things they do because those tasks are compatible with child care. That is, unlike certain male tasks, such as hunting and warfare, women's tasks are more easily interrupted and can be accomplished without jeopardizing the child's safety and without having to leave home. A third explanation is that, in terms of reproduction, men tend to be more expendable than women. In other words, because women have more limited (and therefore more valuable) reproductive capacities, they are less likely to be required to engage in dangerous activities. For example, if men risk their lives hunting buffalo or whales, reproduction in the group will not suffer, provided that women continue to have access to men. All three theories, when taken together, go a long way toward helping us understand this very common gender division of labor.

Yet along with these apparently rational theories, we must also note that men and women are often assigned roles for various social, political, or historical reasons. When these factors are inadequately understood, they can appear to be quite arbitrary. For example, although sewing clothes for the family is thought of as women's work in North America (most men have neither operated a sewing machine nor made a purchase in a fabric store), among the traditional Hopi of Arizona, it is the men who are the spinners, weavers, and tailors. Moreover, in our own society, women have been virtually excluded from a number of occupations (such as jockey, U.S. senator, and Major League Baseball umpire), even though men have no particular biological advantage over women in performing these jobs.

Sometimes the division of labor by gender is so rigid that both men and women remain ignorant of the occupational skills of the opposite sex. This point is well illustrated by the Mixe Indians of Mexico, where men traditionally grew corn while women processed it for eating. According to Ralph Beals, Harry Hoijer, and Alan Beals,

> Men received no training in the processing of maize and were incapable of surviving unless a woman was available to process the maize that the man produced. Although man's work involving the planting and raising of maize constituted a complicated technological process, it only represented one half of the food-producing revolution. The other half, the processing of the crop, was equally complicated and time consuming. The processing involved removing the maize from the cob; boiling it with the proper amount of lime for a sufficient time to remove the hard outer shell and soften the kernel; grinding it on a flat stone slab until it reached the proper texture; working water into the dough; and shaping it between the palms until a flat cake of uniform thickness was formed. The cake was then cooked at the correct heat on a flat griddle, properly treated to prevent sticking. A Mixe woman with a family of five would spend about six hours a day manufacturing tortillas. Under such circumstances it would be impossible for her to engage in the raising of the maize, just as it would be impossible for her husband to engage in the processing of the maize. (1977: 348–50)

Age Specialization

In much the same way that societies divide labor on the basis of sex, they also allocate tasks according to age. Because of their lack of knowledge and physical strength, children are often excluded from certain tasks. In our own society, where formal education routinely lasts through the late teens (and often beyond), young people generally do not engage in much productive work. By way of contrast, children in less industrialized societies usually become involved in work activities at a considerably earlier age. In traditional times children were expected to do household chores, help with subsistence farming, and tend to flocks of animals. Today, however, an increasing number of children fourteen and under are engaged in wage employment or commercial activity. According to a study by the U.S. Department of Labor, approximately 250 million children between the ages of five and fourteen work throughout Asia, Africa, and Latin America, and of these, nearly half work full-time. It was found that 41.7 percent of children

These Pakistani children are working full time in an embroidery shop for pennies a day rather than going to school. According to the International Labor Organization (ILO), there were an estimated 246 million children between the ages of five and seventeen in the workforce worldwide in 2002.

CROSS-CULTURAL MISCUE

While managing a project in Mexico City, you notice that one of your employees is particularly intelligent, successful, and diligent. Thinking he would make a great addition to the home office in Chicago, you offer him a job. Although your employee would receive a promotion, a large salary increase, and a company car if he moves to Chicago, he declines your offer. You simply can't understand why he refuses the offer when it would be so beneficial to his career.

Many highly successful people in Mexico (and parts of Central and South America) do not make career decisions based primarily on their own self-interest, as is often the case north of the Rio Grande. In Mexico people tend to first consider the needs of their family or company before considering their own self-interest. Receiving a promotion and higher salary would not be the most compelling reason for taking a new position. Rather, your employee would think primarily about the interests of extended family members, many of whom probably would not want him to move. Then the employee would consider the interests of the local company, which probably needs him to continue working in Mexico City. What is best for the individual is not always the prime factor in deciding to take a new job.

in this age range worked in Nepal, while Kenya and Tanzania had only slightly smaller percentages of 41.3 percent and 39.5 percent, respectively. Although India had only 5.4 percent of its children younger than fourteen years of age in the workforce, it constituted the largest number of children by far, owing to India's population of nearly 1 billion people. Children in Kenya are working in light industry, in mines (salt and soapstone), plantation agriculture (tea, sugar cane, pineapple, and coffee), and in the service areas as street vendors, domestic servants, scavengers, and bus conductors.

Unlike child labor in traditional societies, which is conducted as part of the family subsistence pattern, child labor in the twenty-first century has some serious negative consequences. Young children today are exposed to dangerous substances (pesticides, asbestos, and mercury), work under dangerous conditions (mines or factories), and are often expected to exert enormous effort over long hours. The extent to which child labor exists in any society depends largely on its level of affluence and the availability of educational opportunities for children.

At the other end of the age continuum, the elderly, because of their waning physical strength, are often prohibited from engaging in certain tasks or are expected to engage in different activities from those they performed when they were younger. For example,

according to C. W. M. Hart and Arnold Pilling (1960), old men among the Tiwi of north Australia give up the strenuous work of hunting in favor of staying at home to make hunting tools, such as spears and throwing sticks, for the younger men. Among the Abkhasians in the nation of Georgia, who are known for their longevity, the elderly do not retire, but the nature of their work becomes less strenuous. Men in their eighties and nineties no longer are expected to plow fields but to continue doing light work like weeding; women of similar age stop working in fields and confine their chores to light housework, knitting, and feeding chickens (Benet 1976).

Although normal adult work generally ceases during old age in these societies, the elderly do assume new roles dealing with spiritual matters. Moreover, because of their advanced years, they take on the role of societal historians and advisors because they are the repositories of traditional wisdom. By way of contrast, the transition from being employed to being retired in the United States is considerably more abrupt. When most workers reach the age of sixty-five, they receive a plaque or a certificate and cease their productive activity. Unlike the situation among the Tiwi and Abkhasians, when workers in the United States retire, they usually suffer a noticeable loss of prestige and self-esteem.

Labor Specialization

Labor specialization—another term for *division of labor*—is an important descriptive characteristic of any society. At one extreme, subsistence societies with low population densities and simple technologies are likely to have a division of labor based on little more than gender and age. Most men in these societies engage in essentially the same activities, and the same holds true for most women. If specialists do exist, they are usually part-timers engaged in political leadership, ceremonial activities, or specialized tool-making. At the other extreme are industrialized societies, where most people are engaged in very specialized occupations, such as computer programmer, TV repairperson, kindergarten teacher, janitor, CPA, or thoracic surgeon. One need only consult the Yellow Pages of the phone directory to get an idea of the vast diversity of specialized occupations in our own society. These two extremes should be viewed as opposite poles on a continuum of division of labor, between which all of the societies of the world could be placed.

One of the major consequences of the transition from hunting and gathering to plant and animal domestication (the neolithic revolution) has been the increasing amount of labor specialization in the world.

labor specialization   See division of labor, page 182.

Because agriculture is a far more efficient way of producing food than hunting and gathering, some people were freed up from the tasks of food production. Simple horticulture evolved into more complex forms of cultivation, which eventually led to the rise of civilizations (urban society).

With each advance in food-producing capacity came an increase in the complexity of labor specialization. This more complex division of labor is significant because the increase in specialized tasks provided a new basis for social solidarity. According to French sociologist Emile Durkheim (1933), in highly specialized societies in which people engage in complementary roles, social solidarity arises from their mutual dependence on one another. That is, teachers need to be on good terms with a butcher, a carpenter, and an auto mechanic because teachers are so highly specialized that they cannot procure meat on their own, build a wood deck, or fix a faulty carburetor. Durkheim calls the social solidarity resulting from this labor specialization and mutual interdependence *organic solidarity*. In contrast, societies with minimal division of labor also possess a form of solidarity, but of a different type. This type of solidarity, which Durkheim calls *mechanical solidarity*, is based on commonality of interests, social homogeneity, strict conformity, kinship, mutual affection, and tradition.

DISTRIBUTION OF GOODS AND SERVICES

Once goods have been produced or procured from the environment, they need to get into people's hands. Although people often consume some of the commodities they produce, surpluses sometimes remain. Systems of exchange are essential for every economy, for they allow people to dispose of their surpluses and, at the same time, maximize the diversity of the goods and services consumed. As Karl Polanyi (1957) reminds us, goods and services are allocated in all societies according to three different modes of distribution: reciprocity, redistribution, and market exchange.

In the United States, most commodities are distributed according to a free-market exchange system based on the principle of "capacity to pay." People receive money for their labor, and then use that money to purchase the goods and services they need or want. In theory, at least, if people have the money, they can

In hunting and gathering societies such as the Ju'/hoansi of the Kalahari region, food is routinely distributed along kinship lines.

purchase a loaf of bread; if they don't, they can't. While this is the prevailing type, we can see examples of the other two modes operating in the United States as well. The principle of reciprocity operates, for example, when friends and relatives exchange gifts for birthdays, holidays, and other special occasions. We can see the principle of redistribution at work when people hand over a certain portion of their personal income to the government for taxes. Even though more than one mode of distribution can operate in any given society at the same time, usually only one mode predominates. Let's examine each of these three modes of distribution in greater detail.

Reciprocity

Reciprocity is the exchange of goods and services of roughly equal value between two parties without the use of money. Economic anthropologists generally recognize three types of reciprocity, depending on the degree of closeness of the parties involved in the exchange: generalized reciprocity, balanced reciprocity, and negative reciprocity (Sahlins 1972).

Generalized Reciprocity
Generalized reciprocity, which is usually played out among family members or close friends, carries with it the highest level of moral obligation. It involves a form of gift giving without any expectation of immediate return. Generalized reciprocity is perhaps best illustrated by the type of giving that takes place between parents and children in our own society. Parents usually

organic solidarity   A type of social integration based on mutual interdependence; found in societies with a relatively elaborate division of labor.
mechanical solidarity   A type of social integration based on mutuality of interests found in societies with little division of labor.

reciprocity   A mode of distribution characterized by the exchange of goods and services of approximately equal value between parties.
generalized reciprocity   The practice of giving a gift without an expected return.

give their children as much as they can while their children are growing up: food, toys, educational advantages, a room of their own, and the like. In fact, providing goods and services for children often continues after the children become adults. For example, parents may provide babysitting services, a down payment on a first home, or a subsidized vacation for their adult children.

In most cases, parents provide for their children materially without expecting that their children will repay them at any time in the future. Because of the intimate bonds between parents and children, parents usually provide for their children out of a sense of love, obligation, and social responsibility. In reality, this sense of love and obligation typically becomes a two-way street, for children usually come to the assistance of their elderly parents when the parents become too old to care for themselves. Thus, even in this most generalized form of reciprocity, the exchange of goods and services often balances out over the long run.

Even though generalized reciprocity is found in our own society, it is not the predominant form of exchange, as it is in smaller-scale societies, where the primary unit of economic organization is the family and where material resources may be uncertain. An exchange system based primarily on generalized reciprocity is common among food collectors and indeed contributes to their very survival.

In most foraging societies, when a large animal such as a bushbuck is killed, the hunter keeps enough for his own immediate family and distributes the rest to his more distant relatives. With no refrigeration or other way of preserving meat, it would make little sense for the hunter to hoard all of the meat himself, for it would spoil before it could be eaten. Instead, sharing with others becomes the expected norm. And, of course, given the uncertainty of hunting, sharing your kill today would entitle you to share someone else's kill tomorrow. Such an economic strategy helps all family members sustain themselves by providing a fairly steady supply of meat despite the inconsistent success of most individual hunters. In such societies generosity is perhaps the highest ideal, and hoarding and stinginess are seen as being extremely antisocial.

We should not think of generalized reciprocity as being motivated totally by altruism. For all people who live at a subsistence level, maintaining reciprocal exchange relationships is vital to their economic self-interest. At subsistence levels, a person is more dependent on others for her or his material security. In the absence of worker's compensation, unemployment insurance, and bank loans, people must rely on others when their crops fail or they become too sick to hunt. Subsistence farmers, for example, might not survive without occasional help from their relatives, friends, and neighbors. A farmer may need extra seeds for planting, help with fixing a roof, or extra cash to pay for a child's school fees. The best way of ensuring that these needs

CROSS-CULTURAL MISCUE

One form of economic distribution—the giving of gifts—can be confusing when gifts are exchanged between culturally different peoples. Kai Hendrickson, a software developer from San Jose, California, was working on a joint venture project with an information technology firm based in Bogota, Colombia. To demonstrate his goodwill, Kai gave each of his three immediate colleagues from Colombia an expensive, beautifully wrapped, box of chocolates. The three Colombians, however, merely nodded in appreciation and put their gifts aside without ever opening them. In fact, Kai is particularly miffed because after a week had gone by, the three Colombians still had not thanked him for the gifts. He couldn't stop wondering if he had done something wrong, or if his colleagues were just ungrateful bores.

Kai could have spared himself considerable anxiety had he understood the cultural practices of gift giving in Colombia. Typically, Colombians do not immediately open gifts in front of the giver, as is expected in the United States or Canada, because they do not want to appear greedy. Moreover, Colombians do not usually acknowledge a gift with a formal thank-you note or heart-felt words at the time of receiving the gift. But, the lack of an explicit written or verbal expression of thanks does not mean that Kai's Colombian colleagues did not appreciate or treasure the gift.

will be met is to respond quickly and unselfishly to the requests of others for similar types of assistance.

Although we don't always recognize it, reciprocal gift giving in our own society takes a number of different forms. Either consciously or unconsciously, we often give gifts with the expectation of getting something in return. We may expect gratitude, acceptance, friendship, or obligation rather than a material item. For example, why do we send wedding invitations to our friends? Is it solely for the sake of sharing with them the joy of the ceremony? When we give our brother a birthday present, would we not be hurt or disappointed if he did not reciprocate on our birthday? And do Western industrialized nations give millions of dollars in foreign aid to less industrialized nations totally out of a sense of altruism and generosity? Or are the donor nations looking for something in return, such as access to natural resources, political cooperation, or prestige? Thus, it appears that in all societies, including our own, gifts almost always come with strings attached.

After having lived in Kandoka village in Papua New Guinea on several different occasions, anthropologist David Counts (1995: 95–98) learned several important lessons about life in a society that practices reciprocity:

First, in a society where food is shared or gifted as part of social life, you may not buy it with money.... [Second,] never refuse a gift, and never fail to return a gift. If you cannot use it, you can always give it to someone else.... [Third,] where reciprocity is the rule and gifts are the idiom, you cannot demand a gift, just as you cannot refuse a request.

Balanced Reciprocity

Balanced reciprocity is a form of exchange involving the expectation that goods and services of equivalent value will be returned within a specified period of time. In contrast to generalized reciprocity, balanced reciprocity involves more formal relationships, greater social distance, and a strong obligation to repay the original gift. The repayment in balanced reciprocity does not have to be immediate, for, as Marcel Mauss (1954) has suggested, any attempt to repay the debt too quickly can be seen as an unwillingness to be obligated to one's trading partner.

A major economic motivation of balanced reciprocity is to exchange surplus goods and services for those that are in short supply. Shortfalls and surpluses can result from different levels of technology, environmental variations, or different production capacities. But whatever the cause, balanced reciprocity enables both parties in the exchange to maximize their consumption. The Indians of Oaxaca, Mexico, exemplify balanced reciprocity in the exchange of both goods and services. According to social custom, a man is expected to sponsor at least one fiesta celebrating a major saint's day. Such events, involving an elaborate amount of food, beverages, and entertainment, almost always are beyond the capacity of a man to provide by himself. Consequently, the man solicits the help of his relatives, friends, and neighbors, thereby mortgaging his future surpluses. Those who help out expect to be repaid in equivalent amounts when sponsoring a similar fiesta.

The Semang   In some cases of balanced reciprocity, people go to considerable lengths to maintain the relationship. For example, the Semang of the Malay Peninsula engage in a form of *silent trade*, whereby they studiously avoid any face-to-face contact with their trading partners. The Semang leave their products collected from the forest at an agreed-upon location near the village of their trading partners. They return at a later time to receive the commodities (usually salt, beads, and tools) left in exchange. By avoiding social contact, both the Semang and their exchange partners eliminate the

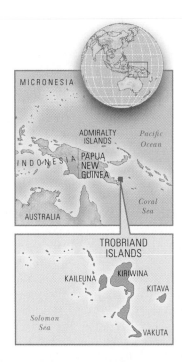

risk of jeopardizing the relationship by haggling or arguing over equivalencies (Service 1966).

The Kula Ring   Perhaps the most widely analyzed case of balanced reciprocity is the *kula ring* found among the Trobriand Islanders off the coast of New Guinea. First described by Bronislaw Malinowski (1922), the kula involves an elaborate and highly ritualized exchange of shell bracelets and shell necklaces that pass (in opposite directions) among a ring of islands. The necklaces move in a clockwise direction and the bracelets move counterclockwise. Many of these shell objects have become well known for their beauty, the noble deeds of their former owners, and the great distances they have traveled. Their main significance is as symbols of the reciprocal relationships among trading partners. These partnerships are often maintained for long periods of time.

The Trobriand Islanders and their neighbors have fairly diversified systems of production with considerable labor specialization. They produce garden crops such as yams and taro, are skilled at fishing, build ocean-worthy boats, raise pigs, and produce a wide range of crafts—including dishes, pots, baskets, and jewelry. When trading partners meet, they exchange shell necklaces for shell bracelets according to a set of ceremonial rituals. Then, for the next several days, they also exchange many of their everyday commodities, such as yams, boats, pigs, fish, and craft items.

balanced reciprocity   The practice of giving with the expectation that a similar gift will be given in the opposite direction either immediately or after a limited period of time.

silent trade   A form of trading found in some small-scale societies in which the trading partners avoid face-to-face contact.

kula ring   A form of reciprocal trading found among the Trobriand Islanders involving the use of white shell necklaces and red shell bracelets.

These shell necklaces and bracelets have been used for generations to facilitate trade among the Trobriand Islands.

The shell necklaces and bracelets have no particular monetary value, yet they are indispensable, for they symbolize each partner's good faith and willingness to maintain the longevity of the trading relationship. Trading partners must avoid at all costs any attempt to gain an advantage in the exchange. Generosity and honor are the order of the day. Whoever receives a generous gift is expected to reciprocate.

This very complex system of trade found among the Trobriand Islanders has been surrounded with ritual and ceremony. Individuals are under a strong obligation to pass on the shell objects they receive to other partners in the chain. After a number of years, these bracelets and necklaces will eventually return to their island of origin and from there continue on the cycle once again. Thus, the continual exchange of bracelets and necklaces ties together a number of islands, some of which are great distances from one another.

Because the ceremonial exchange of shell objects has always been accompanied by the exchange of everyday, practical commodities, the kula ring has clearly functioned as an effective, albeit complicated, system of exchange of goods. Yet, the kula ring is more than just an economic institution. Because there are no all-encompassing political institutions to maintain peace among all of these islands, the maintenance of cordial relationships between trading partners no doubt serves as a peacekeeping mechanism. Moreover, the kula ring also plays an important sociocultural role by creating and maintaining long-term social relationships and by fostering the traditional myths, folklore, and history associated with the circulating shell bracelets and necklaces.

Negative Reciprocity

Negative reciprocity is a form of exchange between equals in which the parties attempt to take advantage of one another. It is based on the principle of trying to get something for nothing or to get the better end of the deal. Involving the most impersonal (possibly even hostile) social relations, negative reciprocity can take the form of hard bargaining, cheating, or out-and-out theft. In this form of reciprocity, the sense of altruism and social obligation is at its lowest, and the desire for personal gain is the greatest. Because negative reciprocity is incompatible with close, harmonious relations, it is most often practiced against strangers and enemies.

Redistribution

Another principle of exchange is *redistribution*, whereby goods are given to a central authority and then given back to the people in a new pattern. The process of redistribution involves two distinct stages: an inward flow of goods and services to a social center, followed by an outward dispersal of these goods and services back to society. Although redistribution is found in some form in all societies, it is most common in societies that have political hierarchies.

Redistribution can take a number of different forms. In its simplest form, we can see redistribution operating within large families, where family members give their agricultural surpluses to a family head, who in turn stores them and reallocates them back to the individual family members as needed. In complex societies with state systems of government, such as our own, taxation is a form of redistribution. That is, we give a certain percentage of our earnings to the government in exchange for certain goods and services, such as roads, education, and public health projects. The giving of gifts to charitable institutions (such as the Salvation Army or Goodwill) can also involve a form of redistribution because the gifts are usually given to the poor or homeless.

negative reciprocity A form of economic exchange between individuals who try to take advantage of each other.
redistribution A form of economic exchange in which goods (and services) are given by members of a group to a central authority (such as a chief) and then distributed back to the donors, usually in the form of a feast.

Big men, such as this one from Papua New Guinea, play a major role in the redistribution of goods within their societies.

Chiefly Redistribution (Tribute)

In some societies without standardized currency, tribal chiefs are given a portion of food and other material goods by their constituents. Most of these food items are then given back to the people in the form of a feast. Such a system of *chiefly redistribution*—also known as *tribute*—serves several important social functions at once. In addition to serving as a mechanism for dispensing goods within a society, it is a way of affirming both the political power of the chief and the value of solidarity among the people.

A good illustration of chiefly redistribution can be seen in traditional Nyoro of Uganda (Taylor 1962). Even though most goods and services were dispersed within the family or local village, some chiefly redistribution followed feudal lines. The rank and file often gave gifts of beer, grain, labor, and livestock to the king and to various levels of chiefs. The king and chiefs in return

gave gifts to their trusted followers and servants. These gifts might have included livestock, slaves, or pieces of land. Among the Nyoro, the major criterion for redistribution was, by and large, loyalty to the political hierarchy. Consequently, the king and the chiefs had no particular incentive to make an equitable redistribution or to see that the commoners received in return something roughly equivalent to what they donated.

Equitable distribution is rarely found in most situations where tribute is given. Instead, the chiefs, headmen, and other high-status people invariably come out ahead. For example, among the Fijian Islanders of Moala, somewhat larger quantities and higher quality goods usually went to the chiefs and people of high status; leaders among the Hottentots in southern Africa often took the best portions of meat at the communal feasts; and according to Jesuit accounts, important Huron chiefs in North America always took the large share of furs at ritual redistributions. As Laura Betzig (1988: 49) describes it, the redistributor "seems inclined to skim the fat off the top."

Big Men/Feast-Givers

In less centralized societies that do not have formal chiefs, redistribution is carried out by economic entrepreneurs whom anthropologists call *big men*. Unlike chiefs, who usually inherit their leadership roles, big men are self-made leaders who are able to convince their relatives and neighbors to contribute surplus goods for the sake of communitywide feasting. Big men are found widely throughout Melanesia and New Guinea. By using verbal coercion and setting an example of diligence, they persuade their followers to contribute excess food to provide lavish feasts for the followers of other big men. The status of a local big man—and of his followers—increases in direct proportion to the size of the feast, his generosity, and hospitality. Big men of the South Pacific distinguish themselves from ordinary men by their verbal persuasiveness, generosity, eloquence, diligence, and physical fitness. Unlike chiefs, who are usually not producers themselves, big men work hard to produce surpluses and encourage their followers to do so as well, all for the sake of giving it away. In fact, because generosity is the essence of being a big man, many big men often consume less food than ordinary people in order to save it for the feasts.

The many studies on big men during the first half of the twentieth century described exclusively males playing these roles. However, there is a growing body of evidence to suggest that there are also *big women*

chiefly redistribution See redistribution.
tribute The giving of goods (usually food) to a chief as a visible symbol of the people's allegiance.

big men/big women Self-made leaders, found widely in Melanesia and New Guinea, who gain prominence by convincing their followers to contribute excess food to provide lavish feasts for the followers of other big men or big women.

© Irven DeVore/Anthro-Photo

in Melanesia. Anthropologist Maria Lepowsky (1990) found that on the island of Vanatinai (located in the southeastern part of Papua New Guinea) there are *giagia* (singular *gia*), a gender-neutral term that simply means "giver." These *giagia*, who are both men and women, are successful in accumulating and then redistributing ceremonial goods and in hosting mortuary feasts for their kin and neighbors. In some parts of the Pacific such as the Trobriand Islands, women have their own sphere of exchange of goods and products (yams and skirts) that they have produced by their own labor. But on Vanatinai, Lepowsky (1990: 37) found that "women and men exchange valuables with exchange partners of both sexes and compete with each other to obtain the same types of valuables.... He or she accumulates ceremonial valuables and other goods in order to give them away in acts of public generosity." Under this system it is possible for a woman to be more prominent and influential than her husband, owing to her greater ability to acquire and redistribute valuables. Although there are, in fact, more big men than big women in Vanatinai, there are some women who are far more active and successful at exchanging goods than most men.

Bridewealth

In addition to chiefly redistribution and big-manship, several other social institutions also function to allocate material goods according to the principles of redistribution and reciprocity. Because some of these social institutions perform functions other than economic ones, we often overlook their economic or distributive functions. One such social institution (discussed in detail in Chapter 9) is *bridewealth*, which involves the transfer of valuable commodities (often livestock) from the groom's extended family to the bride's extended family as a precondition for marriage.

Even though bridewealth performs a number of non-economic or social functions—such as legalizing marriages, legitimizing children, creating bonds between two groups of relatives, and reducing divorce—it also serves as a mechanism for maintaining the roughly equitable distribution of goods within a society. Because extended families are the giving and receiving groups and are made up of a relatively equal number of men and women, the practice of bridewealth ensures that all people will have access to the valued commodities. That is, no extended family is likely to get a monopoly on the goods because each group must pay out a certain number of cows when marrying off a son while receiving a roughly equivalent number of cows when marrying off a daughter. Even though the amounts paid may differ depending on the social status of the bride's family, all

families have access to some of the material goods of the society.

Potlatch

Still another customary practice that serves as a mechanism of redistribution is the *potlatch* found among certain Native Americans of the Northwest Coast (Jonaitis 1991). Perhaps the best-known example of the potlatch was found among the Kwakiutl Indians of British Columbia, for whom social ranking was of great importance (Rohner and Rohner 1970). Potlatches were ceremonies in which chiefs or prominent men publicly announced certain hereditary rights, privileges, and high social status within their communities. Such claims were always accompanied by elaborate feasting and gift giving provided by the person giving the potlatch. In fact, at a potlatch, the host would either give away or destroy all of his personal possessions, which could include such articles as food, boats, blankets, pots, fish oil, elaborately engraved copper shields, and various manufactured goods.

Marvin Harris (1990: 89) provides a glimpse into how a Kwakiutl potlatch worked:

> The host chief and his followers arranged in neat piles the wealth that was to be given away. The visitors stared at their host sullenly as he pranced up and down, boasting about how much he was about to give them. As he counted out the boxes of fish oil, baskets full of berries, and piles of blankets, he commented derisively on the poverty of his rivals.
>
> Laden with gifts, the guests finally were free to paddle back to their own village. Stung to the quick, the

---

bridewealth   The transfer of goods from the groom's lineage to the bride's lineage to legitimize marriage.

---

potlatch   A form of competitive giveaway found among Native Americans from the Northwest Coast that serves as a mechanism for both achieving social status and distributing goods.

© Historical Society of Seattle & King County dba MOHAI/Corbis

Tlingit dancers in Alaska pose in traditional ceremonial attire (circa 1895) during a potlatch ceremony, which serves as a mechanism for both allocating social status and distributing goods.

guest chief and his followers vowed to get even. This could only be achieved by inviting their rivals to a return potlatch and obliging them to accept even greater amounts of valuables than they had given away.

The number of guests present and the magnitude of the personal property given away were a measure of the prestige of the host. The more the host could give away, the stronger would be his claim to high social status. In a sense the gifts given at a potlatch served as payment to the guests for serving as witnesses to the host's generosity. In addition to providing a way of allocating social status, the potlatch was an important mechanism for the dispersal of material goods, for each time a person was a guest at a potlatch, she or he would return home with material goods. In addition to serving as a mechanism of distribution, the potlatch is a multifaceted ceremonial activity that also serves a number of important sociopolitical functions. According to Kenneth Tollefson (1995), potlatches, as practiced by the Northwest Coast Tlingit, were occasions for clans to gather for the purpose of (a) installing new clan leaders, (b) verifying clan titles to certain resources, (c) bestowing clan titles, (d) resolving interclan disputes, (e) establishing and reaffirming alliances, and (f) maintaining regional stability.

Potlatches, widely practiced during the nineteenth century, fell into disfavor with the Canadian government, which saw them as shamefully wasteful. Despite potlatches being declared illegal by the Canadian government they have not ceased to exist as we begin the new millennium. Owing to their illegal status, they went underground for a number of decades, but the laws have since elapsed, and the potlatch is today making somewhat of a comeback. In May 1999, the *Christian Science Monitor* reported a potlatch held by the Makah people (who live in the northwestern part of Washington State) in honor of the revival of their centuries-old

whale-hunting tradition (Porterfield 1999). People from a number of neighboring Native American groups—including the Tulalip, Hoh, Quinault, and Yakima—attended the week-long celebration, which included traditional costumes, food, dancing, and, of course, gift giving.

In this section we have looked at several redistribution systems found in the non-Western world, including the kula ring, the phenomenon of big men and big women, and the potlatch. All of these economic institutions do, in fact, serve as mechanisms for the redistribution of goods and services throughout the societies in which they are practiced. But they also serve as ways of allocating social status and prestige. To illustrate, Trobrianders used the exchanges of kula necklaces and bracelets to create prestige, reputations, and a place in history for themselves. Both the potlatch found among Northwest Coast Indians and the big men in New Guinea illustrate the notion of *prestige economies*, whereby people gain fame and prestige by the extent to which they can give away wealth. In all of these cases, prestige is as much a commodity as are the everyday goods being traded or given away. Moreover, many of these systems of redistribution also play important ceremonial, political, and integrative roles within the society. That these so-called economic institutions play important societal roles other than economic distribution should serve as a reminder that various domains of culture are interrelated, not separate and isolated.

prestige economies A category of economic institutions, such as the potlatch or big men/big women, which serves to distribute goods and to allocate prestige and status.

Market Exchange

The third major form of distribution is based on the principle of *market exchange*, whereby goods and services are bought and sold, often through the use of a standardized currency. In market exchange systems, the value of any particular good or service is determined by the market principle of supply and demand. Market exchange tends to be less personal than exchanges based on reciprocity or redistribution, which often involve ties of kinship, friendship, or political relationships. In this respect, market exchanges are predominantly economic in nature because people are more interested in maximizing their profits than in maintaining a long-term relationship or demonstrating their political allegiance to a chief or leader.

Market exchange systems are most likely to be found in sedentary societies that produce appreciable surpluses and have a complex division of labor. Societies with very simple technologies, such as food collectors, are likely to have no surpluses or such small ones that they can be disposed of quite simply by reciprocity or redistribution. The amount of labor specialization in a society also contributes to a market exchange system, for an increase in the division of labor brings with it a proliferation of specialized commodities and an increased dependency on market exchange.

Standardized Currency

A commonly found trait of market economies is the use of *standardized currency (money)* for the exchange of goods and services. *Money* can be defined as a generally accepted medium of exchange that also measures the value of a particular item. Money is significant for a number of reasons. First, the use of money to purchase items is a more flexible system than direct exchange of one item for another, and as the range of goods increases, it becomes more difficult to find another person who has exactly what you want and wants something that you have to give. Second, money is divisible to the extent that its various forms and values are multiples of each other. Third, money comes in conveniently small sizes, which allows it to be transported from one transaction to another; in other words, a bag of coins is easier to deal with than a herd of camels. And fourth, money serves as a form of deferred payment in that it represents a promise to pay in the future with similar value. The anthropological literature suggests that money is most often found in those societies with high levels of economic development.

> **market exchange**   A form of distribution in which goods and services are bought and sold and their value is determined by the principle of supply and demand.
> **standardized currency (money)**   A medium of exchange that has well-defined and understood value.

Market economies do not always involve money, however. In some small-scale societies, for example, market exchanges may be based on *barter*: the exchange of one good or service for another without using a standardized form of currency. In a bartering situation, a metal smith may exchange a plow blade for several bushels of wheat, or an artist and a migrant laborer may swap a piece of sculpture for three days of labor. Even in the highly complex market economy found in the United States, we find bartering institutions that facilitate the wholesale bartering of goods and services between large corporations. By turning over part of its surplus to a bartering corporation, a company that manufactures office furniture can exchange its surplus furniture for items it may need (such as air conditioners, automobile tires, or computers). In the United States and Canada, an increasing number of people (such as artists, therapists, and other freelance suppliers) are creating an underground economy by using bartering as a way of avoiding paying taxes on goods and services.

The major prerequisite of a market exchange is not whether the exchange is based on currency or barter but rather that the value (or price) of any good or service is determined by the market principle of supply and demand. That is, we can consider an exchange to be based on the market principle when a pig can be exchanged for ten bushels of corn when pigs are scarce but bring only four bushels of corn when pigs are plentiful.

Variety of Markets

The extent to which markets are responsible for the distribution of goods and services in any given society varies widely throughout the world. The market economy of the United States, with its vast network of commercial interests and consumer products, represents one extreme. There is virtually nothing that cannot be bought or sold in our highly complex markets. In some of our markets (such as supermarkets, shops, and retail stores), buyers and sellers interact with one another in close proximity to the goods. But other types of markets in the United States are highly impersonal because the buyers and sellers have no personal interaction. For example, stock, bond, and commodities markets are all conducted electronically (through brokers), with buyers and sellers having no face-to-face contact with one another. Beginning in the late 1990s an increasing number of goods and services (everything from books, CDs, and household items from Amazon.com to personal banking with Bank of America) have been marketed over the Internet. Such markets, which exist for the sole purpose of buying and selling, serve an exclusively economic function and fulfill no social functions.

> **barter**   The direct exchange of commodities between people that does not involve a standardized currency.

© Reuters/Mike Segar/CORBIS

At some markets in the western world, such as the Stock Exchange of New York, buyers and sellers have no face-to-face interaction.

At the opposite extreme are certain small-scale economies that have little labor specialization, small surpluses, and a limited range of goods and services exchanged in markets. Most of the material needs of a household are met by the productive activities of its members. Whatever surpluses exist are brought to market for sale or exchange; the profits are used to purchase other goods or to pay taxes. In such societies, the actual location of the market is important because many social functions are performed in addition to the economic exchange of goods and services. In traditional West Africa, for example, the market is the place where buyers and sellers meet to exchange their surplus goods. But it may also be the place where a man will go to meet his friend, settle a dispute, watch dancing, hear music, pay respects to an important chief, have a marriage negotiated, catch up on the latest news, or see distant relatives.

Many societies today find themselves in a transition between these two fundamentally different types of market economies. Some cultural anthropologists (Chambers and Chambers 2001) are examining this transition by asking a number of important questions such as How will societies change when individualistic market rationality replaces the values of sharing, personal relationships, and community well-being? Is it possible to hang on to one's traditional core of community values in the face of global satellites, cell phones, and the World Wide Web? And to what extent do people in small-scale societies choose to participate in the global economy? These and other questions concerning the impact of global markets on local communities are being posed with increased frequency by anthropologists all over the world.

This worldwide transition from small-scale to global markets raises the distinction between formal and informal sectors of market economies. Informal economies involve legal but unregulated producers of goods and services that, for a variety of reasons, escape government control/regulation (taxation, public monitoring, and auditing). The informal economy should not be confused with the underground economy, which includes illegal activities such as prostitution, selling drugs, and racketeering. Informal economies include some self-employed individuals as well as those employed at factories operating "under the radar." Workers do not claim income on personal tax forms, nor do employers file employment records. Working conditions, earnings, and safety standards in the informal economic sector are almost always far inferior to those in the formal sector. The variety of informal economic activities is wide, including house cleaning, construction work, gardening, begging, child care, petty retailing, making of crafts, and hair cutting.

These informal economic activities have been recognized by economists for years, but because they are difficult to track, they have not been widely studied. In some parts of the developing world, the informal economy has generated more economic activity than the formal economy. The presence of informal activity has been obvious for decades in many of the megacities of Africa, south Asia, and South America—where millions of people struggle to survive by hawking single pieces of fruit on the street. But even in the developed world, economists are beginning to find that informal economic activity is significant. For example, one recent study of the informal economy in the United States (Edgecomb and Thetford 2004: 12) has estimated that

APPLIED PERSPECTIVE

Anthropology and Market Research

As we have pointed out, all economies, wherever they may be found, involve systematic ways of producing goods, distributing them, and then using those goods to satisfy basic human and societal needs. Anthropologists traditionally have studied consumption patterns as part of their analyses of economies. Recently, the business world has discovered that anthropologists' insights can be helpful, particularly in the area of new product development.

© Jannie Woodcock: Reflections Photolibrary/Corbis

In recent years, anthropologists have become increasingly important players in the market research industry. Market research is aimed at learning how and why people use certain products or fail to do so. Manufacturers need this information so they can modify their products in ways that will make them more attractive to consumers. During the 1980s, anthropologist Steve Barnett served as senior vice president of Planmetrics Cultural Analysis Group, a market research firm in New York that studied consumer behavior through direct observations (Baba 1986). Many market researchers gather data by interviewing people randomly in shopping malls, but

Barnett and his associates used a number of innovative techniques designed to learn what people actually do rather than what they say they do. To illustrate, in order to learn more about dishwashing practices in the United States, Barnett put video cameras in people's kitchens for a period of three weeks. The information gathered by this direct observational research enabled Procter and Gamble to alter its television commercials to bring them more into line with actual dishwashing behavior.

More recently, studying consumer habits at close range has become popular in the high-tech arena, where the time pressures, stakes, and failure rates for new products are high. Anthropologist John Sherry, who years ago studied communications technology among the Navajo, is now a member of an interdisciplinary team of design ethnographers with Intel Corporation. Their purpose is to learn as much as possible (by using anthropological methods) about how people work and use high-tech tools so that Intel can design more efficient tools in the future. Sherry and his teammates venture out to homes,

© Laura Dwight/PhotoEdit

This man selling goods on the streets of New York City illustrates the informal economy operating in the United States.

approximately 10 percent of the $10 trillion GNP in the United States is generated by the informal sector. This informal economy in the United States includes the Dominican "houseguest" who swaps housekeeping

chores and child care for room, board, and a small wage; the highly mobile street vendor selling "knock-off" watches out of a briefcase on Madison Avenue in New York City; the urban street mechanic who will tune your engine, adjust your brakes, or change your oil while you park your car on a city street; and the handyman who shows up at your house with an extension ladder to clean your gutters.

Societies with well-developed market economies have always struggled with the question of how much to rely on the forces of the market or on the government to regulate the economy. Free markets and governments represent different modes that can be used to determine what goods and services will be available and, consequently, what the population will consume. Historically, the United States, perhaps as much as any country in the world, has relied on the free enterprise system for economic decision making. By and large, the U.S. economy is based on the principle that prices are set by market forces as buyers and sellers vie with one another in a changing balance of supply and demand. Motivated by what Western economists call enlightened self-interest, decisions to produce goods and services are made on the basis of the public's desire or willingness to purchase them. A number of other countries during the twentieth century opted for state-controlled economies in which the government (not impersonal market

businesses, public spaces, and any other places where they can observe people interacting with technology.

Anthropologists are trained to patiently observe human behavior for hours on end while recording those behaviors in minute detail. Intel (along with other high-tech firms such as IBM, Hewlett-Packard, Motorola, and Xerox) is betting that useful insights will emerge from those minute details. Because technology design always carries with it a number of assumptions about the people who eventually use it, Sherry and his band of high-tech ethnographers frequently must determine the degree to which those design assumptions actually jibe with those of real end-users.

As one example of this application of anthropology, Sherry and his fellow design ethnographers spent large amounts of time hanging out in teenagers' bedrooms (Takahashi 1998). They talked to more than one hundred teenagers, analyzed still photos, and studied hours of videotapes that catalogued how teenagers' bedrooms were used. The team concluded that teenagers would like to be able to send photos to one another by transmitting images over telephone lines that would enter a friend's computer, and then be displayed in a bedside electronic picture frame. Such a product is now available for mass consumption.

This type of market research, which draws on traditional anthropological techniques and concerns, provides us with an excellent example of how cultural anthropology is making useful contributions to the private sector. With traditional academic positions in anthropology becoming more scarce, some anthropologists will need to look to alternative professional venues. Sherry provides an excellent role model of someone interested in applying the methods, theories, and insights of cultural anthropology to the growing field of technology design and development.

Questions for Further Thought

1. Why have anthropologists become so important to the market research industry in recent years?
2. What major data-gathering techniques could be used by anthropologists to assist in market research?
3. How many different subcultural groups in your society can you identify that should be researched before marketing a product such as a light beer? What do you know about these groups that might affect how an advertising campaign might be structured?

---

forces) determined what goods and services would be produced and what they would cost. The collapse of the former Soviet Union in the 1980s exposed many of the liabilities of relying too heavily on government bureaucracies for making basic economic decisions. Nevertheless, every economy is a blend of both government control and free markets. Even in its heyday, the Soviet economy relied heavily on free markets, particularly with domestic farm products; and at different times, the U.S. economy has experimented with varying levels of governmental control. The controversy arises when attempting to determine just what that blend should be.

Supporters of the free-market economy during the 1990s point to the collapse of the Soviet Union as a vindication of the free market system. Those enamored with a free-market economy point to a number of inefficient government enterprises such as the U.S. Postal Service and Amtrak. Calling for a minimum of government regulation, they claim that the forces of the free market are most likely to produce the highest quality of goods and services. But supporters of more government regulation argue that an uncontrolled free-market economy is not in the public interest for several reasons. First, they claim that markets are not likely to produce low-profit products that are needed by the poor.

Because building low-income housing is not likely to generate large profits, for example, builders operating in a free-market economy will choose to build middle- and upper-class housing instead. If governments had not intervened to either build or subsidize low-income housing, the poor would have even fewer places to live. Second, capitalistic, free-market economies lead to increased social stratification—where the rich get richer and the poor get poorer. And third, critics argue that unregulated market economies can lead to a number of negative tendencies, including price gouging by monopolistic companies, misrepresentation of corporate profits to shareholders (now known as Enronization), disregard for dangerous working conditions, inflation, and harm to consumers because of faulty products. Although most people prefer some economic regulation, what the balance should be continues to be debated throughout North America and the rest of the world.

GLOBALIZATION OF WORLD ECONOMIES

Since the end of the Cold War in the late 1980s, world markets have experienced dramatic changes. This process, known as *globalization*, essentially involves the spread of free-market economies to all parts of the world. The basic idea behind globalization is that economies will be healthier and growth will occur more rapidly if we allow market forces to rule and if we open up all economies to free trade and competition. This involves lowering tariff barriers (or eliminating them altogether), deregulating the economy, and privatizing services formerly provided by governments.

Globalization also involves making substantial capital investments in other countries. For example, direct foreign investments in the U.S. economy increased from $141 billion in 1990 to $895 billion in 2001, an increase of 630 percent. And, in the opposite direction, U.S. investment abroad grew from $81 billion in 1990 to $439 billion in 2001, an increase of 540 percent (U.S. Census Bureau 2002). The world's economies are becoming so intricately interconnected that with BMWs being made in South Carolina and Nike running shoes being made in Taiwan, it is often difficult to determine the nationality of certain brands.

With the disintegration of the former Soviet Union in the late 1980s, the world has witnessed a stunning proliferation of free trade, opening up of markets, and heightened competition. The European Union (EU), NAFTA (North American Free Trade Agreement), and CAFTA (Central American Free Trade Agreement) are good examples of this process of globalization. And with the advent of e-commerce, anyone with a good product, a computer, a telephone, access to the Internet, a website, and a UPS account has the potential to become a successful entrepreneur. The global revolution has encouraged the participation of large numbers of new players in the markets. It is now possible to enter the world marketplace one day, with very little capital outlay, and become a global competitor by the next afternoon.

Not only has trade become globalized, but so has the process of manufacturing. For much of the twentieth century, most countries, including the United States and Canada, had relatively self-contained systems of production. Goods were manufactured domestically (in-country) by local laborers and then sold either at home or abroad. But since the 1970s, wages and the general prosperity of workers in the industrialized world have increased significantly. As a way of reducing production costs, many multinational corporations have moved their production operations to less developed countries where labor costs a fraction of what it does at home. In many cases, a worker in Chile or Honduras receives a weekly salary comparable to several hours' pay

for a worker doing the same job in Toronto or Atlanta. Moreover, the overwhelming majority of offshore laborers, particularly in the area of light assembly, are women—because they are more docile and are willing to work for less than their male counterparts. Although a growing number of multinational corporations regard this "labor outsourcing" as a good business decision, many workers at home (and their unions) complain that the domestic workforce is losing its livelihood.

Since the turn of the new millennium, the world has witnessed the outsourcing of not just light manufacturing jobs, but white-collar jobs as well. Accounting firms in the United States, for example, have been sending electronically the tax information of their clients to CPA firms in Bangalore, India, who, for a fraction of the cost, are filling out the IRS tax forms. The Internet revolution now makes it possible to send large amounts of information all over the world for almost no cost at all. Moreover, the development of a number of software applications such as TurboTax, e-mail, Microsoft Office, and so on provide workforce platforms that can be used anywhere in the world. This means that a wide variety of white-collar service jobs in addition to accounting—such as radiology, film animation, and software engineering—will continue to be outsourced to skilled workers around the world.

For many Western policy makers, globalization, involving the intensification of the flow of money and information throughout the world, is seen as a new planetary reality linking Wall Street with the streets of the poorest sections of Manila, Nairobi, and Buenos Aires. Some pundits see globalization as the savior of humankind, while others see it as a boon to the rich and a curse for the poor. Proponents of globalization are quick to point out how the revolutions in technology, open markets, and information flow have stimulated production, consumerism, and rapid communication. They see McDonald's, Citicorp, and Microsoft creating a dynamic new world in which the boats of the poor (as well as the wealthy) are being lifted by the rising tide of global economics. Yet, many other people, particularly those in poorer countries, blame these same forces for joblessness, the economic collapse in Southeast Asia in the late 1990s, political corruption, environmental degradation, public services reduction, poor enforcement of international labor standards, and a growing gap between the rich and the poor. They believe that large global businesses, in their relentless quest for maximizing profits, are benefiting most from this unregulated (or minimally regulated) free trade, while at the same time are demonstrating little concern about the human and environmental costs of globalization.

Globalization is perceived in different ways depending on whose perspective is being considered. The perspective most widely disseminated in the United States is that of Thomas Friedman, initially spelled out in *The Lexus and the Olive Tree* (1999). Friedman's view is

globalization The worldwide process, dating back to the fall of the Berlin Wall, that involves a revolution in information technology, a dramatic opening of markets, and the privatization of social services.

unquestionably pro-corporation, showing deference toward big business while glossing over the negative consequences of globalization on labor, the poor, and the environment. He conducts his research by traveling widely throughout the world, staying at world-class hotels, and talking to high-level government officials, journalists, hedge fund administrators, heads of multinational corporations, and researchers (economists and other social scientists) at universities and think tanks—all of whom are primarily concerned with what is best for business. While admitting that globalization impoverishes as well as enriches, Friedman nevertheless concludes that it is the best hope for the future for the world's poor.

The ideological clash between these two radically different views of globalization came into stark relief at the Seattle meetings of the World Trade Organization in December 1999. In his *New York Times* column entitled "Senseless in Seattle," Thomas Friedman criticized the hundreds of anti-WTO protestors for being nothing more than protectionist union organizers, hippies in search of some cheap weed, and traditionalists from the olive grove. But Friedman was so enamored with his facile description of the new world order that he misunderstood the protestor's agenda. These were not people who were anti-modern, anti-globalization traditionalists who simply wanted to be left alone in peace to tend to their backyard gardens. They did not seek to put the genie of free trade back into its bottle. Instead, these street demonstrations were about global social justice and the expansion of democratic participation in setting the global rules of world trade—rules that would allow the poorer nations to compete with the wealthier nations with fewer unfair obstacles. Thus, one of the

major groups of protestors in Seattle (as well as in subsequent anti-WTO demonstrations since 1999) was composed of farmers and workers from poor countries who criticized the WTO for imposing rules favoring the rich and harming the poor.

What were the injustices these farmers and workers were hoping to rectify? What rules did these protestors want the WTO to change? Were there really systemic inequities in the system of free trade? In actual fact these protestors in Seattle were not just the embittered poor expressing their resentment because they couldn't win on a level playing field. Rather they were protesting some very specific and purposeful decisions made by the U.S. government that had the consequences of not only making them less competitive, but in some cases actually putting them out of business. Perhaps the most damaging *specific government action* against the farmers of the developing world is the continuing practice of paying subsidies to U.S. farmers. From 1995 to 2002 U.S. taxpayers gave $114 billion to U.S. farmers, and in 2002 President Bush signed legislation that will provide an additional $190 billion over a ten-year period. For the sake of perspective, the amount of subsidies paid to U.S. farmers in the single year of 2002 was greater than the combined GNP (gross national product) of the seventy poorest countries in the world.

How, then, do these subsidies to U.S. farmers hurt poor farmers? Let us look at a single crop of cotton, grown in both the United States and in a number of poor African countries. Cotton is produced in the United States at a cost of roughly $.68 per pound as compared to only $.35 per pound in the west African country of Benin. In a totally open world market system, the farmer from Benin would be able to sell his cotton at

Protestors demonstrate against the abuses of globalization at the 1999 meetings of the World Trade Organization in Seattle.

the world market price of $.50 per pound, while the U.S. farmer would have to sell his crop at a loss. But if Congress subsidizes U.S. farmers by giving them (from tax revenues) $.40 for each pound of cotton grown, then the wealthy U.S. farmer sells his cotton on the world market at a loss, while still making a profit through government subsidies. These subsidies encourage farmers to grow as much cotton as possible so as to receive the largest possible subsidies. But, as the subsidized U.S. cotton finds its way into the world marketplace, the increased supplies force the world price of cotton down. Subsidized U.S. farmers can tolerate these lower prices for cotton, but the unsubsidized African farmer (who probably works for less than a dollar a day and whose government depends on cotton exports to fund public services such as health and education) has no such cushion. Thus, if the African farmer is forced to sell his crops at below his production costs, he loses his means of livelihood. Thus, U.S. subsidies mean that the world's highest priced producers of cotton increase their share of the world's cotton market (more than 40 percent), and in the process, drive the low-priced producers of cotton out of business. According to World Bank estimates, the end of U.S. farm subsidies would bring in approximately $250 million to the cotton-producing countries of west and central Africa (Prestowitz 2003). This is the type of unlevel playing field that protestors had in mind when demonstrating in Seattle in 1999.

For the past several decades, Western policy makers have claimed that greater global economic integration would reduce poverty and economic inequality throughout the world. Because deregulated economies tend to grow faster, they argued, all countries would benefit, rich and poor alike. Yet, the facts paint a very different picture. The World Bank reports that (in-country) inequality in developed countries has seriously increased since 1980. In the developing world, nations from all regions except sub-Saharan Africa have shown greater income inequality for the past several decades. Moreover, the inequality gap among countries has widened, not narrowed. According to Christian Weller and colleagues (2002), median income in the richest 10 percent of the countries in 1980 was 77 times greater than in the poorest 10 percent. Nineteen years later that gap grew to 122 times greater. If we look at absolute numbers of income, we see that global deregulation has failed to reduce poverty around the world. To illustrate, in 1980 the poorest 10 percent of the world's population (about 400 million people) lived on $.72 cents per day. Whereas that figure did, in fact, rise to $.78 cents per day in 1999, the income of the world's poorest people did not even keep up with inflation, thereby worsening their economic burden over the two-decade period. Thus, after several decades of global economic deregulation, the gap between the haves and the have-nots is wider than ever.

The process of globalization over the past several decades has indeed produced a mixed bag of benefits

© Brian Lee/Corbis

Not only are U.S. factory jobs being outsourced abroad, but so are white-collar jobs.

and drawbacks. While some people have benefited from global deregulation, many others have not fared so well. Some have argued that globalization is at a turning point, and world leaders need to address the many social inequities in the world economy. Even the wealthy countries, threatened by global terrorism, are beginning to rethink the future of open markets. Among the issues that need to be considered are (a) improving international governance, (b) providing a level playing field for poorer countries, and (c) better enforcement of international labor standards.

It is important to realize that the globalization of markets is not an uncontrollable force of nature. Indeed, there are limits to cross-national economic integration. Sometimes countries refuse, for a number of reasons, to trade or become economically involved with other countries. For example, for more than four decades the U.S. government has legally prohibited U.S. companies from doing business with Cuba, in an attempt to bring Mr. Castro to his knees. In March 2002 President George W. Bush, normally a strong advocate of free trade, imposed an 8-percent to 30-percent tariff on foreign steel, largely as a way of gaining voter support in the steel-producing states of Pennsylvania and West Virginia for the 2002 mid-term elections. The bid of a Chinese oil company to buy the U.S. oil company Unocal was rejected because Americans objected to helping the Chinese in its struggle to obtain oil reserves. And the most recent example of "selective globalization" occurred in 2006 when an outcry of U.S. legislators and policy makers nixed the takeover of port security operations by a company based in Dubai, United Arab Emirates. In this case, the issue of national security (i.e., not entrusting the security of our shipping industry to an Arab-owned company) trumped the notion of open markets and cross-national economic integration.

If national economic systems are becoming more interconnected, then in the future we can expect to travel to other parts of the world with increased frequency. Whether we work in the private sector, public sector, or are self-employed, we will find ourselves managing overseas employees, marketing our products to foreign markets, dealing with overseas suppliers, and engaging in international/cross-cultural negotiations.

Thus, understanding other cultures is now more important than ever before. The formula is pretty straightforward: the more we know about the cultures of our overseas employees, partners, clients, customers, suppliers, and colleagues, the more likely we will be to meet our professional objectives. And, of course, the opposite is also true: if we fail to understand cultural differences in the global economy, we are likely to shoot ourselves in the foot, as illustrated in many of the cross-cultural miscues described throughout this book. ■

Summary

1. The study of economic anthropology involves a theoretical debate between those who believe the concepts of Western economics are appropriate for the study of all economic systems and those who do not.

2. Economic anthropology involves examining how resources are allocated, converted into usable commodities, and distributed.

3. Whereas property rights to land are tightly held in the United States, in most food-collecting societies land is not owned either individually or collectively. The extent to which people have free access to land in pastoral societies depends on local environmental conditions, with free access to land found in environments where water and pasturage are scarce. Land rights are more rigidly controlled among horticulturalists and agriculturalists than among foragers and pastoralists.

4. People in some parts of the world do not share most North Americans' notion of property ownership. Instead of owning something in our sense of the word, people have limited rights and obligations to a particular object.

5. Every society, to one degree or another, allocates tasks according to gender. Because the same type of activity (such as weaving) may be associated with the opposite gender in different cultures, the division of labor by gender is sometimes seen as arbitrary.

6. The amount of specialization (division of labor) varies from society to society. Based on the extent of division of labor, French sociologist Durkheim distinguished between two different types of societies: those based on mechanical solidarity and those based on organic solidarity. According to Durkheim, societies with a minimum of labor specialization are held together by mechanical solidarity, which is based on a commonality of interests, whereas highly specialized societies are held together by organic solidarity, which is based on mutual interdependence.

7. Goods and services are distributed according to three different modes: reciprocity, redistribution, and market exchange. Reciprocity is the exchange of goods and services of roughly equal value between two trading partners; redistribution, found most commonly in societies with political bureaucracies, is a form of exchange whereby goods and services are given to a central authority and then reallocated to the people according to a new pattern; and market exchange systems involve the use of standardized currencies to buy and sell goods and services.

8. Economic anthropologists generally recognize three types of reciprocity depending upon the degree of closeness of the parties: generalized reciprocity involves giving a gift without any expectation of immediate return; balanced reciprocity involves the exchange of goods and services with the expectation that equivalent value will be returned within a specific period of time; and negative reciprocity involves the exchange of goods and services between equals in which one or both parties try to gain an advantage over the other.

9. Whereas reciprocity is essentially the exchange of goods and services between two partners, redistribution involves a social center from which goods are distributed. The material tribute paid to an African chief, bridewealth, and the potlatch ceremony among the Native Americans of the Northwest Coast are all examples of redistribution.

10. Market exchange, based on standardized currencies, tends to be less personal than either reciprocity or redistribution because people in such an exchange are interested primarily in maximizing their profits. As a general rule, the higher the degree of labor specialization in a society, the more complex the system of market exchange.

11. Since the 1980s the economies of the world have become globalized, whereby tariffs are lowered and trading is deregulated. Although globalization has stimulated world trade, it has also increased the gap between the haves and the have-nots. Societies with market economies have to decide to what extent they will allow free markets or the government to control the economy.

Key Terms

allocation of resources

balanced reciprocity

barter

big men

big women

bridewealth

chiefly redistribution

division of labor

economic anthropology

economics

formal economic theory

generalized reciprocity

globalization

kula ring

labor specialization

market exchange

mechanical solidarity

negative reciprocity

organic solidarity

particularism

potlatch

prestige economics

production

property rights

reciprocity

redistribution

silent trade

standardized currency (money)

tribute

universalism

Suggested Readings

Edgecomb, Elaine L., and Tamra Thetford. *The Informal Economy: Making It in Rural America.* FIELD (The Microenterprise Fund for Innovation, Effectiveness, Learning, and Dissemination), a Program of the Aspen Institute, February 2004. By examining low-income workers in the informal economy of rural Nebraska, this study sheds light on the broader investigation of the nature and size of the informal sector of the economy in the United States.

Ensminger, Jean, ed. *Theory in Economic Anthropology.* Lanham, MD: Rowman and Littlefield, 2002. By examining the contributions anthropologists have made to the study of economics, this excellent book looks at a number of issues—including debates about wealth, systems of exchange, informal economies, and the relationships between small producers and the wider world.

Gudeman, Stephen, ed. *Economic Anthropology.* Northampton, MA: Edward Elgar, 1999. An impressive collection of essays highlighting the differences and convergences between economists and anthropologists from 1922 until the turn of the century.

Haugerud, Angelique. "Globalization and Thomas L. Friedman," in Catherine Besteman and Hugh Gusterson, eds., *Why America's Top Pundits are Wrong.* Berkeley, CA: University of California Press, 2005. Shows the one-sidedness (and consequently, the limited utility) of the conceptualization of globalization put forth by *New York Times* columnist Thomas Friedman.

Levitt, Steven D. and Stephen J. Dubner. *Freakonomics: A Rogue Economist Explores the Hidden Side of Everything.* New York: William Morrow, 2005. Starting with the basic premise that economics is the study of incentives, the authors use the traditionally dry science of economics to analyze a wide variety of social issues, including the motivations of real estate agents, cheating among public school teachers and Sumo wrestlers, and what makes a perfect parent.

Ortiz, Sutti, and Susan Lees, eds. *Understanding Economic Process.* Lanham, MD: University Press of America, 1992. The essays in this volume, presented at the tenth annual meeting of the Society for Economic Anthropology, represent a ten-year review of the central issues in economic studies of market and nonmarket societies.

Plattner, Stuart, ed. *Economic Anthropology.* Stanford, CA: Stanford University Press, 1989. This compilation of articles in the field of economic anthropology covers the traditional topics of economic behavior in all of the different types of economic systems from foraging societies, through horticultural and agricultural societies, to industrialized societies. It also deals with contemporary issues such as the informal economy, sex roles, and urban economic systems.

Pryor, F. L. *The Origins of the Economy: A Comparative Study of Distribution in Primitive and Peasant Economies.* New York: Academic Press, 1977. An empirical approach to the cross-cultural study of distribution systems in primitive and peasant economies.

Wilk, Richard. *Economies and Culture: Foundations of Economic Anthropology.* Boulder, CO: Westview, 1996. Examines a number of questions such as whether people are inherently greedy or generous and whether markets should be viewed as promoting equality and prosperity or poverty and mean-spiritedness. Wilk makes the point that an anthropological perspective is most useful for arriving at answers to these universal questions.

Marriage and the Family

A bride and groom pose for their wedding photo at a traditional Islamic ceremony in Malaysia.

9

IN ALL KNOWN SOCIETIES, people recognize a certain number of relatives who make up the basic social group generally called the family. This is not to imply, however, that all societies view the family in the same way. In fact, humans have developed a wide variety of family types. To most middle-class North Americans, the family includes a husband and a wife and their children. To an East African herdsman, the family might include hundreds of kin related through both blood and marriage. Among the Hopi, the family would be made up of a woman and her husband and their unmarried sons and married daughters, along with the daughters' husbands and children. This chapter examines the variety of family types found throughout the world and the process of marriage that leads to the formation of families.

MARRIAGE AND THE FAMILY

Even though we use the terms *family* and *marriage* routinely, their meanings are ambiguous. Because social scientists and laypeople alike use these terms indiscriminately, it will be helpful to define them in more detail. A *family* is a social unit characterized by economic cooperation, the management of reproduction and child-rearing, and common residence. It includes both male and female adults who maintain a socially approved sexual relationship. Family members, both adults and children, recognize certain rights and obligations toward one another. *Marriage* can be defined as a series of customs formalizing the relationship between adult partners within the family. Marriage is a socially approved union between two or more adult partners that regulates the sexual and economic rights and obligations between them. Marriage usually involves an explicit contract or understanding and is entered into with the assumption that it will be permanent.

It is critical to point out that our definition of marriage uses the term *partners* rather than *wives* and *husbands*. Although most Westerners assume that marriage takes place only between men and women, some cultures recognize marriages of men to men and women to women as being legitimate. In parts of West Africa, a successful woman merchant, who may already be married to a man, will take a wife to help with the domestic duties while she is at work (Amadiume 1987). Moreover, among the Nandi of Kenya, a woman can marry a woman (female husband)

What We Will Learn

- Is the family found in all cultures?

- What functions do family and marriage systems perform?

- Why do all societies have incest taboos?

- What economic considerations are associated with marriage in the world's contemporary societies?

▶ Click!

For interactive exercises and study aids, Go to **www.ichapters.com**; enter the author name and select your text, then click the Study Help tab to purchase the following online resources:

- **ThomsonNOW** for chapter-specific online tutorials, quizzes, and a personalized study plan

- **Anthropology Resource Center** for interactive maps, modules, videos, and the Applied Anthropology site

- **Thomson Audio Study Products** for a brief overview of the major chapter themes and to test your knowledge with quiz questions

The legality of same sex marriage remains a contentious issue in the United States.

when the female bride's father has only daughters and no male heirs. Under such conditions, the female husband arranges for a male consort to father children biologically for her bride. Among the Cheyennes of the Great Plains, warriors were permitted to take male transvestites as second wives (Hoebel 1960).

Until very recently, same sex couples could not legally marry anywhere in the world. In a limited number of Western countries, however, same sex marriage has been legalized and thus protected under the law in the same way as heterosexual unions. The Netherlands was the first country to legalize same sex marriage in April 2001, followed in 2003 by neighboring Belgium. By 2004, three Canadian provinces (British Columbia, Ontario, and Quebec) had legalized same sex marriage. In the United States, only residents of Massachusetts can be legally married in same sex unions, while most other states have banned same sex marriage either through legislation ("defense of marriage" acts) or amendments to state constitutions. Clearly, the meaning and legality of same sex marriage will be fought out in courts and legislatures in the years to come.

In 2004, the president of the United States, George W. Bush, called for a constitutional amendment ban-

ning gay marriage as a threat to civilization. The American Anthropological Association (AAA), the world's largest organization of anthropologists, has weighed in on this controversial issue by releasing the following statement:

> The results of more than a century of anthropological research on households, kinship relationships, and families, across cultures and through time, provide no support whatsoever for the view that either civilization or viable social orders depend upon marriage as an exclusively heterosexual institution. Rather, anthropological research supports the conclusion that a vast array of family types, including families built upon same-sex partnerships, can contribute to stable and humane societies. (posted on the AAA website: www.aaanet.org)

Sexual Union

As with any term, the definition of *marriage* often must be qualified. *Marriage*, according to our definition, is a socially legitimate sexual union. When a man and a woman are married, it is implied that they are having a sexual relationship or that the society permits them to have one if they desire it. Although this is generally true, we should bear in mind that this social legitimacy is not absolute, for there may be specified periods during which sexual relations with one's spouse may be taboo. To illustrate, in many societies, sexual relations between spouses must be suspended during periods of menstruation and pregnancy. After a child is born, women in many societies are expected to observe a *postpartum sex taboo*, lasting in some cases until the child is weaned, which can be as long as several years. As William Stephens has suggested, "There may be other sex taboos in honor of special occasions: before a hunting trip, before and after a war expedition, when the crops are harvested, or during various times of religious significance" (1963: 10). Given this wide range of occasions when sex with one's spouse is prohibited, it is possible that in some societies, husbands and wives will be prevented from having sexual relations for a significant segment of their married lives.

Permanence

A second qualification to our definition involves the permanence of the marital union. Often, as part of the marriage vows recited in Western weddings, spouses pledge to live together in matrimony "until death do us part." Even though it is difficult to ascertain a person's precise intentions or expectations when entering a marriage, an abundance of data suggests that the per-

postpartum sex taboo A husband and wife abstaining from any sexual activity for a period of time after the birth of a child.

manance of marriage varies widely, and in no societies do all marriages last until death. For example, recent statistics indicate that more than one of every two marriages in the United States ends in divorce. Impermanent marriages can also be found in smaller-scale societies. Dorothea Leighton and Clyde Kluckhohn report that they often encountered Navajo men who had "six or seven different wives in succession" (1948: 83). In short, when it comes to the permanence of marriage, there is always a discrepancy between ideal expectations and actual behavior.

Common Residence

A qualifying statement must also be added about the notion that family members share a common residence. Although family members usually do live together, there are some obvious definitional problems. If we define "sharing a common residence" as living under the same roof, a long list of exceptions can be cited. In Western society, dependent children sometimes live away from home at boarding schools and colleges. Additionally, in this age of high-speed transportation and communication, it is possible for a husband and wife to live and work in two different cities and see each other only on weekends. On a more global scale, 94 of the 240 African societies listed in George Murdock's "Ethnographic Atlas: A Summary" (1967) are characterized by wives and their children living in separate houses from the husbands. In some non-Western societies, adolescent boys live with their peers apart from their families; and in some cases, such as the Nyakyusa, adolescent boys have not only their own houses but their own villages. In each of these examples, family membership and participation are not dependent on living under the same roof (Wilson 1960).

Thus, as we are beginning to see, the terms *marriage* and *family* are not easy to define. For years, anthropologists have attempted to arrive at definitions of these terms that will cover all known societies. Anthropologists have often debated whether families and the institution of marriage are universals. The Nayar of southern India are an interesting case. According to Kathleen Gough (1959), they do not have marriage in the conventional sense of the term. Although pubescent Nayar girls take a ritual husband in a public ceremony, the husband takes no responsibility for the woman after the ceremony, and often he never sees her again. Instead of cohabitating with her "husband," the Nayar bride continues to live with her mother, mother's sister, and mother's brother while being visited over the years by other "husbands." The bride's family retains full responsibility for the woman and whatever children she bears during her lifetime. Thus, it appears that the Nayar do not have marriage according to our definition in that there is no economic cooperation, regulation of sexual activity, cohabitation, or expectation of permanency.

The family, such as this one in Japan, provides a structured environment that supports and meets the needs of children.

MARRIAGE AND THE FAMILY: FUNCTIONS

The formation of families through marriage serves several important functions for the societies in which the families operate. One such benefit is the creation of fairly stable relationships between men and women that regulate sexual mating and reproduction. Because humans are continually sexually receptive and (in the absence of contraceptives) heterosexual intercourse often leads to reproduction, it is imperative that societies create and maintain unions that will regulate mating, reproduction, and child-rearing in a socially approved manner.

A second social function of marriage is that it provides a mechanism for regulating the sexual division of labor that exists to some extent in all societies. For reasons that are both biological and cultural, men in all societies perform some tasks, and women perform others. To maximize the chances of survival, it is important for a society to arrange the exchange of goods and services between men and women. Marriage usually brings about domestic relationships that facilitate the exchange of these goods and services.

Third, marriage creates a set of family relationships that can provide for the material, educational, and emotional needs of children. Unlike most other animal species, human children depend on adults for the first decade or more of their lives for their nourishment, shelter, and protection. Moreover, human children require adults to provide the many years of cultural learning needed to develop into fully functioning members of the society. Even though it is possible for children to be reared largely outside a family unit (as is done on the kibbutzim of Israel), in most societies marriage creates a set of family relationships that provide the material, educational, and emotional support children need for their maturation.

Mate Selection: Who Is Out of Bounds?

Every society known to anthropology has established for itself rules regulating mating (sexual intercourse). The most common form of prohibition is mating with certain types of kin who are defined by the society as being inappropriate sexual partners. The prohibition on mating with certain categories of relatives is known as the *incest taboo*. Following the lead of Robin Fox (1967), it is important to distinguish between sexual relations and marriage. Incest taboos are prohibitions against having sexual relations with certain categories of kin. This is not exactly the same thing as rules prohibiting marrying certain kin. Although incest taboos and rules prohibiting marrying certain kin often coincide with each other (that is, those who are forbidden to have sex are also forbidden to marry), it cannot be assumed that they always coincide.

The most universal form of incest taboo involves mating between members of the immediate (nuclear) family—that is, mothers and sons, fathers and daughters, and brothers and sisters—although there are several notable yet limited exceptions. For political, religious, or economic reasons, members of the royal families among the ancient Egyptians, Incas, and Hawaiians were permitted to mate with and marry their siblings, although this practice did not extend to the ordinary members of those societies. The incest taboo invariably extends beyond the scope of the immediate or nuclear family, however. In a number of states in the United States, people are forbidden by law from mating with their first cousins. In some non-Western societies, the incest taboo may extend to large numbers of people on one side of the family but not on the other. And in still other societies, a man is permitted (even encouraged) to mate with and marry the daughter of his mother's brother (a first cousin) but is strictly prohibited from doing so with the daughter of his mother's sister (also a first cousin). Thus, although it seems clear that every society has incest taboos, the relatives that make up the incestuous group vary from one society to another. Given that incest taboos are universally found throughout the world, anthropologists have long been interested in explaining their origins and persistence. A number of possible explanations have been suggested.

Natural Aversion Theory

One such theory, which was popular about a hundred years ago, rests on the somewhat unsatisfying concept that there is a natural aversion to sexual intercourse among those who have grown up together. Although the existence of any natural (or genetically produced) aversion to having sexual relations within the nuclear family is rejected today, there is some evidence to suggest that such an aversion may be developed. For example, according to Yohina Talmon (1964), sexual attraction between Israelis reared on the same *kibbutz* is extremely rare, a phenomenon attributed by the kibbutz members themselves to the fact that they had grown up together. Another study (Wolf 1968) of an unusual marital practice in Taiwan, whereby infant girls are given to families with sons to be their future brides, found that these marriages were characterized by higher rates of infidelity, sexual difficulties, and fewer children. Thus, it appears that in at least some situations, people who have grown up together have little sexual interest in each other. Nevertheless, this familiarity theory does not appear to be a particularly convincing explanation for the existence of the incest taboo.

If familiarity does lead to sexual aversion and avoidance, how do we explain why incest does occur with considerable regularity throughout the world? Indeed, in our own society, it has been estimated that 10 to 14 percent of children younger than eighteen years of age have been involved in incestuous relationships (Whelehan 1985). The familiarity theory does not explain why we need a strongly sanctioned incest taboo if people already have a natural aversion to incest.

Inbreeding Theory

A popular theory that attempts to explain the existence of the incest taboo focuses on the potentially harmful effects of inbreeding on the family. This inbreeding theory, proposed well before the introduction of the science of genetics, holds that mating between close kin, who are likely to carry the same harmful recessive genes, tends to produce a higher incidence of genetic defects (which results in an increased susceptibility to disease and higher mortality rates). There is, however, little solid genetic evidence to support this view. What we do know is that outbreeding, which occurs in human populations with strong incest taboos, has a number of positive genetic consequences. According to Bernard Campbell (1979), benefits of outbreeding include increases in genetic variation, a reduction in lethal recessive traits, improved health, and lower rates of mortality. This inbreeding theory has, no doubt, led to numerous state laws prohibiting cousin marriage in the United States. It should be noted, however, that there is hardly consensus on this issue among state legislatures, for thirty states have laws against cousin marriage whereas twenty do not. Moreover, there are no European nations that prohibit cousin marriage. Martin Ottenheimer

---

incest taboo The prohibition of sexual intimacy between people defined as close relatives.

kibbutz A communal farm or settlement in Israel.

In addition to causing disruption among nuclear family members through sexual competition, incest creates the further problem of *role ambiguity*. For example, if a child is born from the union of a mother and her son, the child's father will also be the child's half brother, the child's mother will also be the child's grandmother, and the child's half sister will also be the child's aunt. These are just some of the bizarre role combinations created by such an incestuous union. Because different family roles, such as brother and father, carry with them vastly different rights, obligations, and behavioral expectations, the child will have great difficulty deciding how to behave toward his or her immediate family members. Does the child treat the male who biologically fathered him or her as a father or as a brother? How does the child deal with the woman from whose womb he or she sprung—as a mother or a grandmother? Thus, the incest taboo can be viewed as a mechanism that prevents this type of role ambiguity or confusion.

Theory of Expanding Social Alliances

Incest avoidance can also be explained in terms of positive social advantages for societies that practice it. By forcing people to marry out of their immediate family, the incest taboo functions to create a wider network of interfamily alliances, thereby enhancing cooperation, social cohesion, and survival. Each time one of your close relatives mates with a person from another family, it creates a new set of relationships with people toward whom your family is less likely to become hostile. This theory, first set forth by Edward Tylor (1889) and later developed by Claude Lévi-Strauss (1969), holds that it makes little sense to mate with someone from one's own group with whom one already has good relations. Instead, there is more to be gained, both biologically and socially, by expanding one's networks outward. Not only does mating outside one's own group create a more peaceful society by increasing one's allies, but it also creates a larger gene pool, which has a greater survival advantage than a smaller gene pool.

The extent to which wider social alliances are created by requiring people to mate and marry outside the family is illustrated by a study of Rani Khera, a village in northern India. In a survey of the village population (Lewis 1955), it was found that the 226 married women residing in the village had come from approximately two hundred separate villages and that roughly the same number of village daughters married out. Thus, the village of Rani Khera was linked through marriage to hundreds of other northern Indian villages. In fact, this pattern of mating and marrying outside one's own

Charles Darwin (1809–1882), the author of *Origin of Species*, had ten children with his wife, who was also his first cousin.

Mary Evans/Photo Researchers, Inc.

(1996) argues that this confusion is the result of a long-standing nineteenth-century myth that cousin marriage would threaten the civilized world. Ottenheimer notes that there is no compelling scientific evidence to support legislation forbidding cousin marriage.

Family Disruption Theory

Whereas the inbreeding theory focuses on the biological consequences of incest, a third theory centers on its negative social consequences. This theory, which is most closely linked with Bronislaw Malinowski (1927), holds that mating between a mother and son, father and daughter, or brother and sister would create such intense jealousies within the nuclear family that the family would not be able to function as a unit of economic cooperation and socialization. For example, if adolescents were permitted to satisfy their sexual urges within the nuclear family unit, fathers and sons and mothers and daughters would be competing with one another, and consequently normal family role relationships would be seriously disrupted. The incest taboo, according to this theory, originated as a mechanism to repress the desire to satisfy one's sexual urges within the nuclear family.

role ambiguity   Confusion as to how one is expected to behave.

group (created out of a desire to avoid incest) is an important factor integrating Indian society.

MATE SELECTION: WHO SHOULD YOU MARRY?

As we have seen, every society defines a set of kin with whom a person is to avoid marriage and sexual intimacy. In no society is it permissible to mate with one's parents or siblings (that is, within the nuclear family), and in most cases the restricted group of kin is considerably wider. Beyond this notion of incest, people in all societies are faced with rules either restricting their choice of marriage partners or strongly encouraging the selection of certain people as highly desirable mates. These are known as rules of *exogamy* (marrying outside of a certain group) and *endogamy* (marrying within a certain group).

Rules of Exogamy

Because of the universality of the incest taboo, all societies have rules for marrying outside a certain group of kin. These are known as rules of exogamy. In societies such as the United States and Canada, the exogamous group extends only slightly beyond the nuclear family. It is considered either illegal or inadvisable to marry one's first cousin and, in some cases, one's second cousin, but beyond that one can marry other more distant relatives and encounter only mild disapproval. In societies that are based on unilineal descent groups, however, the exogamous group is usually the lineage, which can include hundreds of people, or even the clan, which can include thousands of people who are unmarriageable. Thus, when viewed cross-culturally, rules of exogamy based on kinship do not appear to be based on genealogical proximity.

Rules of Endogamy

In contrast to exogamy, which requires marriage outside one's own group, the rule of endogamy requires a person to select a mate from within one's own group. Hindu castes found in traditional India are strongly endogamous, believing that to marry below one's caste would result in serious ritual pollution. Caste endogamy is also found in a somewhat less rigid form among the Rwanda and Banyankole of eastern central Africa. In addition to being applied to caste, endogamy can be applied to other social units, such as the village or local community, as was the case among the Incas of Peru, or to racial

© David Young-Wolff/PhotoEdit

At one time in the United States, interracial marriage was against the law. Although these laws no longer exist, the overwhelming majority of Blacks and Whites in the United States continue to practice racial endogamy.

groups, as was practiced in the Republic of South Africa for much of the twentieth century.

Even though there are no strongly sanctioned legal rules of endogamy in the United States, there is a certain amount of marrying within one's own group based on class, ethnicity, religion, and race. This general de facto endogamy found in the United States results from the fact that people do not have frequent social contacts with people from different backgrounds. Upper-middle-class children, for example, tend to grow up in the suburbs, take golf and tennis lessons at the country club, and attend schools designed to prepare students for college. By contrast, many lower-class children grow up in urban housing projects, play basketball in public playgrounds, and attend schools with low expectations for college attendance. This general social segregation by class, coupled with parental and peer pressure to "marry your own kind," results in a high level of endogamy in complex Western societies such as the United States.

Arranged Marriages

In Western societies, with their strong emphasis on individualism, mate selection is largely a decision made jointly by the prospective bride and groom. Aimed at satisfying the emotional and sexual needs of the individual, the choice of mates in Western society is based on such factors as physical attractiveness, emotional compatibility, and romantic love. Even though absolute freedom of choice is constrained by such factors as social class, ethnicity, religion, and race, individuals in most contemporary Western societies are free to marry whomever they please.

In many societies, however, the interests of the families are so strong that marriages are arranged. Nego-

exogamy   A rule requiring marriage outside of one's own social or kinship group.

endogamy   A rule requiring marriage within a specified social or kinship group.

Mr. He Xin, a 25-year-old lawyer in Shanghai, arranges marriages for his billionaire clients looking for brides.

tiations are handled by family members of the prospective bride and groom, and for all practical purposes, the decision of who one will marry is made primarily by one's parents or other influential relatives. In certain cultures, such as parts of traditional Japan, India, and China, future marriage partners are betrothed while they are still children. In one extreme example—the Tiwi of North Australia—females are betrothed or promised as future wives before they are born (Hart and Pilling 1960). Because the Tiwi believe that females are liable to become impregnated by spirits at any time, the only sensible precaution against unmarried mothers is to betroth female babies before birth or as soon as they are born.

All such cases of *arranged marriage*, wherever they may be found, are based on the cultural assumption that because marriage is a union of two kin groups rather than merely two individuals, it is far too significant an institution to be based on something as frivolous as physical attractiveness or romantic love.

Arranged marriages are often found in societies with elaborate social hierarchies, perhaps the best example of which is Hindu India. Indeed, the maintenance of the caste system in India depends largely on a system of arranged marriages. Indian arranged marriages are further reinforced by other traditional Indian values and beliefs. Fathers, it was traditionally held, sinned if they failed to marry off their daughters before puberty. Indeed, both parents in India shared the common belief that they were responsible for any sin the daughter might commit because of a late marriage. For centuries, Hindu society has viewed females as lustful beings who tempt males with their sexual favors. Thus, a girl had to

arranged marriage Any marriage in which the selection of the spouse is outside the control of the bride and groom.

be married at an early age to protect both herself and the men who might become sinners. And, if girls were to become brides before reaching adolescence, they could hardly be trusted to select their own husbands. Prompted by this belief, in certain parts of India, girls marry at a very young age. According to a government survey of five thousand women in Rajastan in northern India, more than half were married before they were fifteen years old, and of these, 14 percent married before they were ten and 3 percent before they were five. Even though the Indian government passed a law in 1978 setting a minimum age of marriage for females at eighteen, the law has been largely unenforced.

Anthropologist Serena Nanda reminds us that arranging marriages in India is serious business and should not be taken frivolously. In addition to making certain that a mate is selected from one's own caste, parents must be careful to arrange marriages for their children that take into consideration such factors as level of education, physical attractiveness, compatibility with future in-laws, and level of maturity. Requiring seriousness, hard work, and patience, an arranged marriage may take years to bring about, as one of Nanda's Indian informants explains: "This is too serious a business. If a mistake is made we have not only ruined the life of our son or daughter, but we have spoiled the reputation of our family as well. And, that will make it much harder for their brothers and sisters to get married" (1992: 142).

Indian couples were once introduced by family members who spent months, even years, researching potential partners. Today, these matchmaking kinsmen are being rendered obsolete by an explosion of matrimonial websites. Would-be brides and grooms from India (as well as Indians living abroad) can go to websites with URLs such as Asianmatches.com, Suitablematch .com, and Matrimonials.com, where they can search

APPLIED PERSPECTIVE

Hawaiian Children at School and at Home

A basic premise of educational anthropology is that the cultural patterns students bring with them into the classroom must be taken into account if these students are to be successfully integrated into the culture of the school. This is precisely the objective that educational anthropologist Cathie Jordan brought to her work with the Kamehameha Elementary Education Program (KEEP), a privately funded educational research effort designed to develop more effective methods for teaching Hawaiian children in the public schools.

© Michael S. Yamashita/Corbis

For decades, children of Hawaiian ancestry, particularly those from low-income families, have been chronic underachievers in the public school system. Classroom teachers often describe these children as lazy, uncooperative, uninvolved, and disinterested in school. Differences do exist between their dialect, known as Hawaiian Creole English, and the Standard English used by teachers, but the linguistic differences are minimal. Thus, Cathie Jordan and her colleagues at KEEP needed to look beyond linguistic differences to find an explanation for why Hawaiian children were not succeed-

ing in school. Accordingly, KEEP focuses on the wider Hawaiian culture—particularly interaction patterns within the family—in order to discover learning skills the children had developed at home that could be used and built upon in the classroom.

When dealing with parents and siblings at home, Hawaiian children behave very differently than when interacting with teachers and classmates. From a very early age, Hawaiian children contribute significantly to the everyday work of the household. Tasks that all children are expected to perform regularly include cleaning, cooking, laundry, yard work, caring for younger siblings, and (for male children) earning cash from outside employment. Working together in cooperative sibling groups, brothers and sisters organize their own household work routines with only minimal supervision from parents. Young children learn to perform their household tasks by observing their older siblings and adults. And, according to Jordan and her colleagues (1992: 6), these chores are performed willingly

---

for the ideal partner according to language, religion, caste, level of education, occupation, and even height, complexion, or astrological sign. By participating in these electronic matchmaking services, Indian young people are essentially agreeing with the traditional notion of arranged marriages, but asking for (and getting) more input into the process. These new high-speed matrimonial websites greatly expand the pool of potential candidates, increase the amount of information that is available for prescreening, and allow the bride and groom more time to make up their minds. Traditional parents and elders are adapting to these modern ways, largely because they are more efficient and are likely to lead to what both parents and children want: strong, long-lasting marriages between compatible partners and compatible families. In fact, many parents today are searching these matrimonial websites themselves on behalf of their unmarried sons and daughters.

Even though mate selection in North America generally is a matter of individual choice, many singles are not opposed to seeking help. Whereas Indians use the Internet to find potential marriage partners, the matchmaking services used by North Americans focus on dating, romance, and finding the right relationship, with possible marriage as a more distant goal. The number of websites devoted to matchmaking has exploded in the last five years. For example, a simple search for the term

matchmakers in April 2006 resulted in 597,000 "hits" on Yahoo! and nearly 1.2 million on Google. Online dating services, which have millions of subscribers and generate hundreds of millions of dollars in revenue each year, are no longer for the socially inept. Rather, they have become a normal part of the singles scene for people of all ages. Many services specialize in a variety of demographics, such as nationality (Russia, China, Colombia), ethnicity (Latino, African-American), religion (Catholic, Jewish, Hindu), sexual orientation (gay, lesbian, straight), or lifestyle preferences (vegetarians, Harley-Davidson enthusiasts, or yoga practitioners). There are even matchmaking services today that specialize in helping subscribers find their political soul mates. For example, Conservativematch.com and Singlerepublican.com are custom made for those "red state" types looking for love; while Democraticsingles.com is where "blue state" singles can go to find a politically compatible partner for a relationship.

Matchmaking services in the twenty-first century are not just for the common folks. Singles who are trying to manage their fast-track careers often have special needs that require special services. To illustrate, Wall Street has its own "romantic headhunter," Janis Spindel, who for a finder's fee of $20,000 offers financial high rollers a dozen dates over the course of a year. While client confidentiality makes it impossible to verify the statistics,

within a "context of strong values of helping, cooperation, and contributing to the family."

The paradox facing KEEP was, how could children be so cooperative and responsible at home and yet so disengaged and lazy in school? A comparison of the home and school cultures revealed some major structural differences. When a mother wants her children to do a job around the house, she makes that known and then allows the children to organize how it will be done. In other words, she gives responsibility for the job to the children. In contrast, the classroom is almost totally teacher dominated. The teacher makes the assignments, sets the rules, and manages the resources of the classroom. Children are controlled by the classroom rather than being responsible for it. Once these cultural differences between home and school were revealed by anthropological fieldwork, the educational anthropologist was able to suggest some changes for improving student involvement in their own education. The solution was fairly straightforward: Have teachers run their classrooms in much the same way as Hawaiian mothers run their households. Specifically, teachers should minimize verbal instructions, withdraw from direct supervision, and allow students to take responsibility for organizing and assigning specific tasks. When these changes were made, Hawaiian students became more actively involved in their own education, and consequently their achievement levels improved.

Here, then, is an example of how educational anthropologists can apply their findings to improve the learning environment for Hawaiian children. Interestingly, this case of applied anthropology did not follow the traditional solution to problems of minority education, which involves trying to change the child's family culture to make it conform to the culture of the classroom. Rather, Jordan and her colleagues at KEEP solved the problem by modifying the culture of the classroom to conform to the skills, abilities, and behaviors that Hawaiian students brought with them from their family culture.

Questions for Further Thought

1. What is educational anthropology?
2. Can you think of any subcultural groups living in your town or region whose family patterns should be studied by the local school system?
3. What other types of educational problems might applied anthropologists be able to solve?

Ms. Spindel claims to have brokered more than seven hundred marriages among her upper-class clients (Thernstrom 2005: 36). Even the formerly socialistic country of China now has its own version of a "love broker" for the rich and famous. Mr. He Xin, a twenty-five-year-old lawyer in Shanghai, has been approached by more than fifty *billionaires* in China looking for brides. As of January 2006, Mr. He had found suitable marriage partners for three of his well-heeled clients and appears to be headed toward a lucrative career as a marriage broker for his wealthy clients (French 2006).

All of these recent matchmaking services—both electronic and the more personal services—are noticeably different from the traditional forms of matchmaking, which were largely in the hands of family members. Nevertheless, these new mechanisms for arranging marriages fit in nicely with the pressures of the modern world. Young people, particularly those trying to manage their careers, simply do not have the time to cruise single bars in hopes of finding Ms. or Mr. Right.

Preferential Cousin Marriage

A somewhat less coercive influence on mate selection than arranged marriages is found in societies that specify a preference for choosing certain categories of relatives as marriage partners. A common form of preferred marriage is *preferential cousin marriage*, which is practiced in one form or another in most of the major regions of the world. Some kinship systems distinguish between two different types of first cousins: cross cousins and parallel cousins. This distinction rests on the gender of the parents of the cousin. *Cross cousins* are children of siblings of the opposite sex—that is, one's mother's brothers' children and one's father's sisters' children. *Parallel cousins*, on the other hand, are children of siblings of the same sex (the children of one's mother's sisters and one's father's brothers). In societies that make such a distinction, parallel cousins, who are considered family members, are called "brother" and "sister" and thus are excluded as potential marriage partners. However, because one's cross cousins are not thought of as family members, they are considered by some societies as not just permissible marriage partners but actually preferred ones.

> *preferential cousin marriage*   A preferred form of marriage between either parallel or cross cousins.
> *cross cousins*   Children of one's mother's brother or father's sister.
> *parallel cousins*   Children of one's mother's sister or father's brother.

CONTEMPORARY ISSUES

Is Marriage a Crime?

Most Americans take considerable pride in the fact that theirs is a nation of immigrants. Since our earliest days as a nation, immigrants have come to our shores in search of a better life. They settled in urban neighborhoods, learned to speak English, worked hard, and eventually (after several generations) moved to the suburbs, where they joined the country club and became registered Republicans. However, when immigrants first arrive, sometimes they are surprised to discover that practicing their traditional cultural customs can put them on the wrong side of the laws of their new country.

In 1996, a recent Iraqi refugee was the proud father of two brides in a traditional double wedding ceremony for his two eldest daughters at their home in Lincoln, Nebraska (Terry 1996). An Islamic cleric was flown in from Ohio to perform the ceremony in front of more than a hundred friends and relatives. For all attending, it was a festive social event celebrating the sacred event of matrimony. But for local authorities, it was the scene of a crime.

The problem stemmed from the fact that the two Iraqi brides, who were thirteen and fourteen years old, were marrying men who were twenty-eight and thirty-four. According to marital law in the state of Nebraska, seventeen is the minimum legal age for marriage. Authorities charged the father with two counts of child abuse, while the mother was charged with contributing to the delinquency of a minor. Moreover, it is illegal for anyone older than the age of eighteen to have sexual relations with anyone younger than eighteen years of age. Because the two grooms consummated their marriages on the night of the wedding, both men were charged with statutory rape, which carries a maximum sentence of fifty years in prison. Both the parents and their two sons-in-law were shocked when police came to arrest them.

© Michael S. Yamashita/Corbis

The issue in this tragic case revolves around two very different definitions of *marriage*. According to both law and custom in the United States, marriage represents a voluntary union between two consenting individuals. The criteria for selecting a spouse in the United States include personal compatibility, physical attractiveness, and romantic love. And a major objective of marriage in the United States is happiness and personal fulfillment on the part of the two principal players, the wife and the husband. By way of contrast, marriage in traditional Iraqi society is based on an entirely different set of cultural assumptions. Marriages are arranged by the parents, with little or no input on the part of the prospective brides. Traditional Iraqi marriage is viewed more as a union between two large families than as a way of providing happiness and individual fulfillment for the husband and wife. In addition, traditional Iraqi parents fear that their daughters will engage in premarital sexual relations and thereby dishonor the entire family. To their way of thinking, the best way to protect their daughters and their families from such disgrace is to marry them off at an early age.

Clearly, this case presented a real dilemma for Nebraska law enforcement officials. The Iraqis, who were ignorant of marital law in Nebraska, had no intention of violating the law. Nevertheless, their traditional marriage practices did violate some strongly held American values and some strongly sanctioned laws. Many Americans want to be sensitive to the cultural pluralism that has made our country unique. At the same time, Americans need to be true to their core values of protecting the rights of women and children. Should culture be taken into consideration when dealing with civil and criminal cases, and if so, to what extent? How would you resolve this case if you were serving on the jury?

The most common form of preferential cousin marriage is between cross cousins because it functions to strengthen and maintain ties between kin groups established by the marriages that took place in the preceding generation. That is, under such a system of cross cousin marriage, a man originally would marry a woman from an unrelated family, and then their son would marry his mother's brother's daughter (cross cousin) in the next generation. Thus, because a man's wife and his son's wife come from the same family, the ties between the two families tend to be solidified. In this respect, cross cousin marriage functions to maintain ties between groups in much the same way that exogamy does. The major difference is that exogamy encourages the formation of ties with a large number of kinship groups, whereas preferential cross cousin marriage solidifies the relationship between a more limited number of kin groups over a number of generations.

A much less common form of cousin marriage is between parallel cousins, the children of one's mother's sister or father's brother (Murphy and Kasdan 1959). Found among some Arabic-speaking societies of the Middle East and North Africa, it involves the marriage of a man to his father's brother's daughter. Because parallel cousins belong to the same group, such a practice can prevent the fragmentation of family property.

The Levirate and Sororate

Individual choice also tends to be limited by another form of mate selection that requires a person to marry the husband or wife of deceased kin. The *levirate* is the custom whereby a widow is expected to marry the brother (or some close male relative) of her dead husband. Usually, any children fathered by the woman's new husband are considered to belong legally to the dead brother rather than to the actual father. Such a custom serves as a form of social security for the widow and her children and preserves the rights of the husband's family to her future children. The levirate, practiced in a wide variety of societies found in Oceania, Asia, Africa, and India, is closely associated with placing high value on having male heirs. African men and ancient Hebrews, for example, prized sons so that a man's lineage would not die out. In such cases, men were under great pressure to marry their dead brothers' widows.

The levirate is found in patrilineal societies in which the bride marries into her husband's family while essentially severing her ties with her original family. Under such an arrangement, the levirate functions to look after the interests of the woman in the event that she becomes a widow. The solution is for her to become the bride of one of the male relatives of her brother. But, in more recent times, particularly in India, widows are not always supported by their dead husband's families. It has been estimated (Burns 1998) that there are approximately 33 million widows in India living in abject poverty because their husband's families have chosen not to support them. These widows cannot return to their natal families because they severed those ties when they married. Thus facing a type of "social death," these Indian widows are at the mercy of inadequate support provided by either the government or local Hindu temples.

The *sororate*, which comes into play when a wife dies, is the practice of a widower's marrying the sister (or some close female relative) of his deceased wife. If the deceased spouse has no sibling, the family of the deceased is under a general obligation to supply some equivalent relative as a substitute. For example, in societies that practice the sororate, a widower may receive as a substitute wife the daughter of his deceased wife's brother.

levirate   The practice of a man marrying the widow of a deceased brother.
sororate   The practice of a woman marrying the husband of her deceased sister.

NUMBER OF SPOUSES

In much the same way that societies have rules regulating who one may or may not marry, they have rules specifying how many mates a person may or should have. Cultural anthropologists have identified three major types of marriage based on the number of spouses permitted: *monogamy* (the marriage of one man to one woman at a time), *polygyny* (the marriage of a man to two or more women at a time), and *polyandry* (the marriage of a woman to two or more men at a time).

Monogamy

The practice of having only one spouse at a time is so widespread and rigidly adhered to in the United States and Canada that most people would have great difficulty imagining any other marital alternative. We are so accustomed to thinking of marriage as an exclusive relationship between husband and wife that, for most North Americans, the notion of sharing a spouse is unthinkable. Any person who chooses to take more than one marriage partner at a time is in direct violation of conventional norms, most religious standards, and the law.

So ingrained is this concept of monogamy in Western society that we often associate it with the highest standards of civilization, while associating plural marriage with social backwardness and depravity. Interestingly, many societies that practice monogamy circumvent the notion of lifelong partnerships by either permitting extramarital affairs (provided they are conducted discreetly) or practicing *serial monogamy* (taking a number of different spouses one after another rather than at the same time). In fact, serial monogamy is very common in the United States, Canada, and much of western Europe.

Polygyny

Even though monogamy is widely practiced in the Western world, the overwhelming majority of world cultures do not share our values about the inherent virtue of monogamy. According to Murdock's *World Ethnographic Sample*, approximately seven out of every ten cultures of the world both permit and prefer the practice of polygyny. It was practiced widely in traditional India and China and remains a preferred form of marriage throughout Asia, Africa, and the Middle East. There is

monogamy   The marital practice of having only one spouse at a time.
polygyny   The marriage of a man to two or more women at the same time.
polyandry   The marriage of a woman to two or more men at the same time.
serial monogamy   The practice of having a succession of marriage partners—but only one at a time.

also evidence to support the idea that polygyny played a significant role in our own Western background by virtue of the numerous references to polygyny in the Old Testament of the Bible. Many Westerners, steeped in a tradition of monogamy, interpret the very existence of polygyny as having its basis in the male sex drive. Because they presume that men have a stronger sex drive than women, polygyny is seen as a mechanism for men to satisfy themselves at the expense of women. This interpretation is flawed on a number of counts. First, there is little hard evidence to suggest that the sex drive is innately stronger for men than for women. Moreover, if men were interested in increasing their sexual options, it is not likely that they would choose multiple wives as a way of solving the problem. Instead, they would resort to multiple extramarital liaisons, which would be far less complicated than taking on the responsibilities of multiple wives.

To suggest that approximately 70 percent of the world's *cultures* practice polygyny is not to say that 70 percent of the world's *population* practices polygyny. Many cultures that practice polygyny are small-scale societies with small populations. Moreover, even in polygynous societies, the majority of men at any given time still have only one wife. Even in societies where polygyny is most intensively practiced, we would not expect to find more than 35 to 40 percent of the men actually having two or more wives. Polygyny in these societies is the *preferred*, not the usual, form of marriage. It is something for which men strive but only some attain. Just as the ideal of becoming a multi-millionaire is usually not realized in the United States, so too in polygynous societies, only a minority of men actually have more than one wife at a time.

There are a number of reasons why most men in polygynous societies never acquire more than one wife. First, marriage in many polygynous societies requires the approval (and financial support) of large numbers of kinsmen, and this support is not always easy to obtain. Second, in some polygynous societies it is considered inappropriate for men of low rank to seek additional wives, thereby restricting a certain segment of the males in the society to monogamy. And third, being the head of a polygynous household, which invariably carries with it high prestige, is hard work. The management of two or more wives and their children within a household requires strong administrative skills, particularly if relations between the wives are not congenial. A study of polygyny among the present-day Zulu of South Africa (Moller and Welch 1990) indicates that Zulu men tend to opt for monogamy over polygyny for the additional reasons that they are under increasing pressure to accept the socially dominant values of South African Whites, and the dominant White Christian churches have opposed polygyny militantly. In short, most men in polygynous societies, for a variety of reasons, have neither the inclination, family power base, nor social skills needed to achieve the high status of being a polygynist.

Polygyny is practiced in many parts of the world. At left, a man from the Rashaida Tribe in Eritrea travels by camel while his three wives walk. At right is Tom Green, a 21st century polygynist from Utah, posing with his five wives and some of his twenty-nine children.

Economic Status of Women in Polygynous Societies

The rate of polygyny varies widely from one part of the world to another. A critical factor influencing the incidence of polygyny is the extent to which women are seen as economic assets (where they do the majority of labor) or liabilities (where men do the majority of work). To illustrate, in areas of the world such as sub-Saharan Africa where women are assets, it has been estimated (Dorjahn 1959) that the mean rate of polygyny is approximately 35 percent, ranging from a low of 25 percent (Ju/'hoansi) to a high of 43 percent (Guinea Coast). Conversely, in societies where women are an economic liability (such as among the Inuit, where only about 5 percent of the men practice polygyny), few men can afford the luxury of additional wives (Linton 1936).

Sex Ratio in Polygynous Societies

For polygyny to work, a society must solve the very practical problem of the sex ratio. In most human populations, the number of men and women is roughly equal. The question therefore arises: Where do the excess women who are needed to support a system of polygyny come from? It is theoretically possible that the sex ratio could swing in favor of females if males were killed off in warfare, if women were captured from other societies, or if the society practiced male infanticide. All of these quite radical solutions may account for a small part of the excess of women needed for a polygynous marriage system in some societies. More commonly, this numerical discrepancy is alleviated simply by postponing the age at which men can marry. That is, if females can marry from age fourteen on and males are prohibited from marrying until age twenty-six, a surplus of marriageable women always exists in the marriage pool.

Advantages of Polygyny

Having two or more wives in a polygynous society is usually seen as a mark of prestige or high status. In highly stratified kingdoms, polygyny is one of the privileges of royalty and aristocrats, as was the case with the late King Sobhuza of Swaziland, who, it was estimated, had well over a hundred wives. In societies that are stratified more on age than on political structure, such as the Azande of the Sudan and the Kikuyu of Kenya, polygyny is a symbol of prestige for older men. Whether a man is an aristocrat or commoner, however, having multiple wives means wealth, power, and high status for both the polygynous husband and the wives and children. That is, a man's status increases when he takes additional wives, and a woman's status increases when her husband takes additional wives. For this reason, women in some African societies actually urge their husbands to take more wives. Clearly, these African women do not want to be married to a nobody.

Sometimes multiple wives are taken because they are viewed by the society as economic and political assets. Each wife not only contributes to the household's goods and services but also produces more children, who are valuable economic and political resources. The Siuai of the Solomon Islands provide an excellent example of how having multiple wives can be an economic advantage for the polygynous husband. Pigs are perhaps the most prized possession of Siuai adults. According to Douglas Oliver, "To shout at a person 'you have no pigs' is to offer him an insult" (1955: 348). Women are particularly valuable in the raising of pigs, for the more wives a man has, the more hands are available to work in the garden, the more pig food can be produced, and, consequently, the more pigs can be raised. Because polygynous households average more pigs than monogamous ones, it is not unusual for some men to take additional wives for the sake of enlarging their gardens and pig herds.

The old anthropological literature (written before the 1970s) gave the impression that women in polygynous societies generally favored polygyny over monogamy. However, such a conclusion was to some extent the result of male bias because the majority of ethnographers for the first half of the twentieth century were men. Nevertheless, there is evidence to suggest that polygyny remains popular among women in many parts of the world (Ware 1979; Mulder 1992; Kilbride 1997). It is also true that men in polygynous societies view the practice even more positively than women. Opposition to polygyny usually comes from younger, better-educated women, who prefer monogamy (or remaining single) to polygyny.

Competition Among Wives

Despite the advantages just discussed, living in a polygynous household has drawbacks. Even though men desire multiple wives, they recognize the potential pitfalls. The major problem is jealousy among the wives, who often compete for the husband's attention, sexual favors, and household resources. In fact, in some African societies, the word for *co-wife* is derived from the root word for *jealousy*. As related here, jealousy and dissension among wives are common among the Gusii of western Kenya:

> Each wife tends to be the husband's darling when she is the latest, and to maintain that position until he marries again.... This tendency in itself causes jealousy among the wives. In addition, any inequality in the distribution of gifts or money, or in the number of children born and died, or the amount of education received by the children, adds to the jealousy and hatred. A woman who becomes barren or whose children die almost always believes that her co-wife has achieved this through witchcraft or poisoning. She may then attempt retaliation. (LeVine quoted in Stephens 1963: 57)

Even though competition among wives in polygynous societies can threaten domestic tranquility, there are several ways to minimize the friction. First, wives will feel less jealousy if they have a hand in selecting subsequent wives. Some societies practice a form of polygyny called *sororal polygyny*, where a man marries sisters or other female relatives. It is possible that sisters may be less likely to feel jealous of one another when they become wives. Second, wives in many polygynous societies are given their own separate living quarters. As Paul Bohannan and Philip Curtin (1988) remind us, because women may have more difficulty sharing their kitchens than their husbands, jealousy can be minimized by giving each wife her own personal space. Third, dissension is lessened if the rights and obligations among the wives are clearly understood. Fourth, potential conflict among wives can be reduced by establishing a hierarchy among the wives. Because the senior wife often exerts considerable authority over more junior wives, she can run a fairly smooth household by adjudicating the various complaints of the other wives.

Not only can the jealousies among wives be regulated, but some ethnographic reports from polygynous societies reveal considerable harmony and cooperation among the wives. Sometimes co-wives become companions and allies, because they are all "outsiders" to the husband's kin group. Elenore Smith Bowen (1964: 127–28) relates the story of Ava, a Tiv woman who was the senior of five wives:

> The women were fast friends. Indeed it was Ava who had picked out all the others. She saved up forty or fifty shillings every few years, searched out an industrious girl of congenial character, then brought her home and presented her to her husband: "Here is your new wife." Ava's husband always welcomed her additions to his household and he always set to work to pay the rest of the bridewealth, for he knew perfectly well that Ava always picked hard-working, healthy, handsome, steady women who wouldn't run away.

Although North America is adamantly monogamous, the practice of having more than one wife at a time does exist, particularly in the state of Utah. Although members of the Church of Jesus Christ of Latter Day Saints outlawed polygyny in 1890, the practice persists on a small scale, and, in fact, has experienced a resurgence over the last thirty years. Officially, polygyny is prohibited by both the church and the state of Utah, but because it is considered relatively benign, it is generally not prosecuted. Although accurate statistics are unavailable, it is estimated that as many as thirty thousand people practice polygyny in the United States. Some practice polygyny today because of its deep-seated religious significance. Others practice it because it provides a desirable lifestyle choice. Some of the polygynist homesteads in this subculture are quite elaborate. The *Charlotte Observer* (Williams 1998) ran a picture of one such home: a thirty-five-thousand-square-foot structure with thirty-seven bathrooms and thirty-one bedrooms, which housed a wealthy Mormon fundamentalist, his ten wives, and twenty-eight children!

Viewed from a global perspective, polygyny is one of a number of legitimate forms of marriage. There is nothing inherently immoral or exploitive about the practice of having more than one wife at a time. However, polygyny, as practiced in the United States, has come under fire recently because of certain *abuses* to the practice. As long as consenting adults choose to live in a polygynous relationship, authorities tended to look the other way. But in some communities—such as Hildale, Utah, and Colorado City, Arizona—young girls barely in their teens are being coerced to marry men more than twice their age. Moreover, since the beginning of the new millennium more than four hundred teenage boys have been cast out of their families and their communities, largely as a way of reducing competition for wives. These "lost boys," some of whom are as young as thirteen, are experiencing severe emotional and psychological trauma because they are relegated by their elders to homelessness without any education or the support of their families. Rather than targeting polygyny per se as a marriage practice, law enforcement officials in Utah and Arizona are going after the adults of these communities, focusing on sexual abuse, child neglect, child endangerment, welfare fraud, and tax evasion (Kelly 2005; Madigan 2005).

Polyandry

Polyandry involves the marriage of a woman to two or more men at a time. A much rarer form of plural marriage than polygyny, polyandry is found in less than 1 percent of the societies of the world, most notably in Tibet, Nepal, and India. Polyandry can be fraternal (where the husbands are brothers) or nonfraternal.

Perhaps the best-known case of polyandry is found among the Toda of southern India, who practice the fraternal variety. When a woman marries a man, she also becomes the wife of all of his brothers, including even those who have not yet been born. Marriage privileges rotate among the brothers. Even though all of the brothers live together with the wife in a single household, there is little competition or sexual jealousy. Whenever a brother is with the wife, he places his cloak and staff at the door as a sign not to disturb him. When the wife becomes pregnant, paternity is not necessarily ascribed to the biological father (genitor) but is determined by a ceremony that establishes a social father (pater), usually the oldest brother. After the birth of two or three children, however, another brother is chosen as the social father for all children born to the woman thereafter.

Toda society is characterized by a shortage of females brought about by the traditional practice of female infanticide, and this shortage of women may be one of the reasons for the existence of polyandry among the Toda. Because of the influence of both the Indian government and Christian missionaries, however, female infanticide has largely disappeared today, the male–female sex ratio has become essentially balanced, and polyandry among the Toda is, for all practical purposes, a thing of the past.

In addition to explaining the existence of polyandry by the shortage of women, there are certain economic factors to consider. According to William Stephens (1963), senior husbands among the wealthier families on the Marquesas Islands recruited junior husbands as a way of augmenting the manpower of the household. It has also been suggested (Goldstein 1987) that Tibetan serfs practice polyandry as a solution to the problem of land shortage. To prevent the division of small plots of land among their sons, brothers could keep the family land intact by marrying one woman. By marrying one woman, two or more brothers are able to preserve the family resources; that is, if all of the sons split up to form their own monogamous households, the family would multiply and the family land would rapidly fragment. In such a monogamous situation, the only way to prevent this fragmentation of family land is to practice primogeniture (all land is inherited by the oldest son only). Such a system, though keeping the land intact, does so at the expense of creating many landless male offspring. In contrast, the practice of fraternal polyandry does not split up the family land but rather maintains a steady ratio of land to people.

ECONOMIC CONSIDERATIONS OF MARRIAGE

Most societies view marriage as a binding contract between at least the principal partners, and in many cases, between their respective families. Such a contract includes the transfer of certain rights between the parties involved—rights of sexual access, legal rights to children, and rights of the spouses to each other's economic goods and services. Often the transfer of rights is accompanied by the transfer of some type of economic consideration. These transactions, which may take place either before or after the marriage, can be divided into four categories: bridewealth, bride service, dowry, and reciprocal exchange.

Bridewealth

Bridewealth is the compensation given upon marriage by the family of the groom to the family of the bride. According to Murdock's *World Ethnographic Sample* (reported in Stephens 1963: 211), approximately 46 percent of all societies give substantial bridewealth payment as a normal part of the marriage process. Although bridewealth is practiced in most regions of the world, it is perhaps most widely found in Africa, where it is estimated (Murdock 1967) that 82 percent of the societies require the payment of bridewealth; most of the remaining 18 percent practice either token bridewealth or *bride service* (providing labor, rather than goods, to the bride's family).

Bridewealth is paid in a wide variety of currencies, but in almost all cases, the commodity used for payment is highly valued in the society. For example, reindeer are given as bridewealth by the reindeer-herding Chukchee, horses by the equestrian Cheyenne of the Central Plains, sheep by the Navajo, and cattle by the pastoral Maasai, Samburu, and Nuer of eastern Africa. In other societies, marriage payments take the form of blankets (Kwakiutl), pigs (Alor), mats (Fiji), shell money (Kurtachi), spears (Somali), loincloths (Toda), and even the plumes of the bird of paradise (Siane).

Just as the commodities used in bridewealth transactions vary considerably, so does the amount of the transaction. To illustrate, an indigent Nandi of Kenya can obtain a bride with no more than a promise to transfer one animal to the bride's father. A suitor from the Jie tribe of Uganda, on the other hand, normally transfers fifty head of cattle and one hundred head of small stock (sheep and goats) to the bride's family before the marriage becomes official. Large amounts of bridewealth, as found among the Jie, are significant for several reasons. First, the economic stakes are so high that the bride and groom are under enormous pressure to make the marriage work. Second, large bridewealth payments tend to make the system of negotiations between the two families more flexible and, consequently, more cordial. When the bridewealth is low, the addition or subtraction of one item becomes highly critical and is likely to create hard feelings between the two families.

Not only do bridewealth payments vary among different cultures, but variations also exist within a single cultural group. In a study of bridewealth payments among the Kipsigis of western Kenya, Monique Mulder (1988) found that intragroup variations depended on several key factors. First, high bridewealth is given for brides who mature early and are plump because such women are thought to have greater reproductive success. Second, lower bridewealth is given for women who have given birth previously. And third, women whose natal homes are far away from their marital homes command higher bridewealth because they spend less time in their own mother's household and therefore are more available for domestic chores in their husband's household.

---

bridewealth The transfer of goods from the groom's lineage to the bride's lineage to legitimize marriage.

bride service Work or service performed for the bride's family by the groom for a specified period of time either before or after the marriage.

Among the Maasai of Kenya and Tanzania, cows are used as the medium of exchange in marriage transactions.

© Peter Horree/Alamy

The meaning of *bridewealth* has been widely debated by scholars and nonscholars for much of the twentieth century. Early Christian missionaries, viewing bridewealth as a form of wife purchase, argued that it was denigrating to women and repugnant to the Christian ideal of marriage. Many colonial administrators, taking a more legalistic perspective, saw bridewealth as a symbol of the inferior legal status of women in traditional societies. Both of these negative interpretations of bridewealth led to a number of vigorous yet unsuccessful attempts to stamp out the practice.

Less concerned with moral or legal issues, cultural anthropologists saw the institution of bridewealth as a rational and comprehensible part of traditional systems of marriage. Rejecting the interpretation that bridewealth was equivalent to wife purchase, anthropologists tended to examine how the institution operated within the total cultural context of which it was a part. Given such a perspective, cultural anthropologists identified a number of important functions that the institution of bridewealth performed for the well-being of the society. For example, bridewealth was seen as security or insurance for the good treatment of the wife, as a mechanism to stabilize marriage by reducing the possibility of divorce, as a form of compensation to the bride's lineage for the loss of her economic potential and her childbearing capacity, as a symbol of the union between two large groups of kin, as a mechanism to legitimize traditional marriages in much the same way that a marriage license legitimizes Western marriages, and as the transference of rights over children from the mother's family to the father's family.

Although a much-needed corrective to the earlier interpretations of bridewealth as wife purchase, the anthropological interpretation overlooked the very real economic significance of bridewealth. It was not until the end of the colonial period that Robert Gray (1960) reminded social scientists that it also was legitimate to view bridewealth as an integral part of the local exchange system. It is now generally held that a comprehensive understanding of the practice of bridewealth is impossible without recognizing its economic as well as its noneconomic functions. (see Chapter 8 for a discussion of how bridewealth functions as a mechanism for distributing economic goods.)

Since the mid-1980s bridewealth has become "monetized" (that is, money is becoming the typical medium of exchange). The transition from subsistence-based to cash-based economies has profoundly affected traditional bridewealth practices. Traditionally, bridewealth was an exchange of (often valuable) commodities from the groom's lineage to the bride's lineage. Because traditional bridewealth solidifies long-term ties between two entire lineages, the bride and groom did not benefit directly from the exchange. However, when bridewealth becomes tied to money that can be earned by the individual prospective groom, the close interdependence of family members (and their sanctioning of the marriage) becomes much less important. Today, a growing number of wage earners in societies that practiced traditional bridewealth are becoming independent of their kinship group when it comes time to get married.

The monetization of bridewealth in Oceania is particularly well described in a volume called *The Business of Marriage* (Marksbury 1993). Contributing authors show how people from the Fiji Islands and Papua New Guinea are viewing marriage increasingly as a financial transaction. This commercialization of bridewealth is having a number of important consequences on the entire marital process. According to Richard Marksbury

CROSS-CULTURAL MISCUE

Geraldine Brooks (1990) relates an incident of intercultural misunderstanding that occurred in Saudi Arabia between a North American woman and her local Saudi landlord. The woman, the wife of a U.S. Marine chaplain stationed in Saudi Arabia, was at home when the landlord arrived with several workmen to make repairs. Upon entering, the landlord passed the American woman but never spoke to her or even acknowledged her presence. The chaplain's wife thought that the landlord's behavior was extremely rude. Actually, according to Saudi culture, the landlord was treating her with the utmost respect and politeness. He did not want to invade her privacy by speaking to her without her husband being present. As Brooks explains, "He was honoring her the best way he knew how."

(1993), people are postponing getting married until a later age, marriage payments are being used for personal fulfillment rather than being redistributed among a wide range of kin, men are incurring serious debts in their attempts to meet their payments, marriages are becoming less stable, and traditional husband–wife roles are changing.

The monetization of bridewealth, coupled with general inflation, is making marriage a financial burden on many prospective grooms throughout the world. To illustrate, in the country of Kuwait, it costs the average groom (and his family) about $66,000 for the bridewealth, wedding party, honeymoon, and furnishings for the home. As a way of defraying some of these expenses, voluntary religious organizations in Kuwait are beginning to raise money for group weddings. In one such group wedding in December 1999, twenty-eight couples tied the knot in a single ceremony. Local merchants contributed flowers, gowns, makeovers for the brides, and small electrical appliances for the newly-weds. Hotels provided a hall for the collective reception, dinners for the guests, and a wedding night suite for the newlyweds. Even the cost of pilgrimages to Mecca (in lieu of a honeymoon) was covered by several charitable travel agencies. Thus, through cost-sharing and donations, some Kuwaiti families are doing something about the high cost of getting married (Associated Press 1999).

Whatever the medium of exchange may be, bride-wealth is still widely practiced today in certain parts of the world. Studies conducted by this author in Kenya in 1976 and in Swaziland (1983) found that the traditional practice of bridewealth had survived amazingly well in the face of significant forces of change. A decade later, Bert Adams and Edward Mburugu (1994), studying a sample of 297 Kikuyu interviewees, reported that more than 90 percent claimed that bridewealth was still being paid. Interestingly, neither educational level nor long-standing urban residence seemed to reduce the likelihood or amount of bridewealth. African social scientists

T. S. Mwamwenda and L. A. Monyooe (1997) found that 88 percent of South African university students interviewed (84 percent of the men and 90 percent of the women) supported the continuation of bridewealth payments. Rather than thinking, as many Westerners do, that bridewealth is demeaning to women, these highly educated young adults believed that bridewealth functioned to heighten the woman's dignity, increase the husband's gratitude, and decrease the divorce rate.

Bride Service

In societies with considerable material wealth, marriage considerations take the form of bridewealth paid in various forms of commodities. But because many small-scale societies cannot accumulate capital goods, men often give their labor to the bride's family instead of material goods in exchange for wives. This practice, known as bride service, is found in approximately 14 percent of the societies listed in Murdock's *World Ethnographic Sample.*

Bride service is likely to be found in nomadic foraging societies such as the traditional Ju/'hoansi of southwestern Africa. According to Janice Stockard (2002: 28–29), Ju/'hoansi men select husbands for their daughters based largely, but not exclusively, on the hunting skills of the prospective groom. Suitors must demonstrate considerable hunting expertise before they are eligible to marry, because the father-in-law will depend on the daughter's husband to provide him with adequate supplies of meat through a prolonged period of bride service.

In some cases, bride service is practiced to the exclusion of property transfer; in other cases, it is a temporary condition, and the transfer of some property is expected at a later date. When a man marries under a system of bride service, he often moves in with his bride's family, works or hunts for them, and serves a probationary period of several weeks to several years.

This custom is similar to that practiced by Jacob of the Old Testament (Genesis, Chapter 29), who served his mother's brother (Laban) for his two wives, Leah and her sister, Rachel. In some cases where bride service is found, other members of the groom's family, in addition to the groom himself, may be expected to give service, and this work may be done not only for the bride's parents but also for her other close relatives, as is the case with the Taita of Kenya (Harris 1972).

Dowry

In contrast to bridewealth, a *dowry* involves a transfer of goods or money in the opposite direction, from the bride's family to the groom or to the groom's family.

dowry The transfer of goods or money from the bride's family to the groom or groom's family in order to legalize or legitimize a marriage.

Family members of a Kazakh bride-to-be carry her dowry on camels in Xinjiang, China.

© Reza: Webistan/Corbis

The dowry is always provided by the bride or the bride's family, but the recipient of the goods varies from one culture to another. In some societies, the dowry was given to the groom, who then had varying rights to dispose of it. In rural Ireland, it was given to the father of the groom in compensation for land, which the groom's father subsequently bequeathed to the bride and groom. The dowry was then used, wholly or in part, by the groom's father to pay the dowry of the groom's sister. Practiced in less than 3 percent of the societies in Murdock's sample, the dowry is confined to Eurasia, most notably in medieval and renaissance Europe and in north India.

More often than not, the dowry was not given to the husband but was something that the bride brought with her into the marriage. In traditional society in Cyprus, the dowry often consisted of a house or other valuable property. If the husband mistreated his wife or if the marriage ended in divorce, the woman was entitled to take the dowry with her. The dowry in this sense, very much like bridewealth, functioned to stabilize the marriage by providing a strong economic incentive not to break up.

In certain European countries, where it is still practiced to some extent today, substantial dowry payments have been used as a means of upward mobility, that is, as a way to marry a daughter into a higher-status family. Around the beginning of the twentieth century, a number of daughters of wealthy U.S. industrialists entered into mutually beneficial marriage alliances with European nobles who had fallen upon hard economic times. The U.S. heiresses brought a substantial dowry to the marriage in exchange for a title.

Even though bridewealth is the usual form of marriage payment in Africa, there are several instances in which payment takes a different direction. One such case is found among the Nilo-Hamitic Barabaig of Tanzania. Although a small number of goods are given to the bride's kin group, her family confers on her a dowry of two to forty head of large stock, depending on their means. These dowry cattle, which often outnumber the cattle held originally by the groom, are kept in trust as inheritance cattle for the bride's sons and as dowry cattle for the bride's daughters. Because the Barabaig are patrilocal, the wife and her dowry cattle reside at the husband's homestead. Even though the husband has nominal control over the herd, he still must ask his wife's permission to dispose of any of the cattle, for technically the herd belongs to his wife's father. Until the herd is finally redistributed among their own children, it will remain a source of friction between the husband and wife because the very existence of such a dowry gives the wife considerable economic leverage in her marital relations.

Reciprocal Exchange

Reciprocal exchange is found in approximately 6 percent of the societies listed in Murdock's *Ethnographic Atlas*, most prominently in the Pacific region and among traditional Native Americans. It involves the roughly equal exchange of gifts between the families of both the bride and the groom. Such a custom was practiced by the traditional Vugusu people of western Kenya, who exchanged a large variety of items between a sizable number of people from both families. According to Gunter Wagner, the gifts made and the expenses incurred were basically reciprocal, with only "a slight preponderance on the bride's side" (1949: 423). The variety of the reciprocal gift giving and the number of people involved in Vugusu society tend to emphasize the generally valid tenet that marriages in many parts of the world are conceived not simply as a union between a man and a woman but rather as an alliance between two families.

---

reciprocal exchange The equal exchange of gifts between the families of both the bride and groom to legitimize a marriage.

DIVORCE

Just as all cultures have established a variety of ways of legitimizing marriages, they also have many ways of dealing with separation and *divorce*. Divorce arrangements found in the many cultures of the world vary widely according to reasons for divorce and how easy or difficult it may be to get divorced. Although marriages break down in all societies, some societies are reluctant to officially sanction divorce, and some may even forbid it. Some societies have no official mechanism for legally dissolving a marriage, while some organizations, such as the Roman Catholic Church, prohibit divorce outright. By way of contrast, a Hopi woman from Arizona could divorce her husband quite easily by simply putting his belongings outside the door.

As a general rule, divorce rates are lower in societies that have strong (corporate) kinship groups that control offspring through large bridewealth payments, which represent compensation for a woman's limited procreative power. The larger the bridewealth payment, the more complete the transfer of rights over children from the bride's lineage to the groom's lineage. If a marriage is subsequently dissolved, the bridewealth payment would have to be returned to the groom's lineage, which could be a problem if it has already been allocated to a wide range of the bride's kin. Thus, relatively large bridewealth payments, coupled with strong lineage involvement, promote greater marriage stability. By way of contrast, in foraging societies, such as the Ju/'hoansi or the Inuit, divorce is quite easily accomplished. In such nomadic or seminomadic societies, because material wealth is limited, marriage payments are either very limited or nonexistent. Moreover, foraging societies generally lack large, formal social groups beyond the nuclear family that could complicate divorce proceedings.

In the industrialized world, divorce has increased dramatically over the last hundred years, and most industrialized nations have legal procedures for dissolving marriages. To illustrate, the United States, which has one of the highest divorce rates in the world, experienced a tenfold increase in the rate of divorce between 1890 and 1990. Divorce rates rose precipitously from 1950 to 1980, but the rate has been receding somewhat since 1980 (see Table 9.1). A number of factors have been cited for the dramatic rise of divorce in the United States. First, industrialization and urbanization have undermined the traditional functions of the family. When the basic unit of production changed from family to factory, the economic ties holding the family together were weakened. The expanding role of public education usurped the traditional educational function of the family. And, as people had more disposable income, the notion of recreation and leisure time changed from family-based activities to attendance at paid events, such as movies and concerts. Thus, this erosion of family functions has resulted in an increase in divorce. Second, the rise of individualism and the pursuit of personal happiness has led some to spend less time with family members and made some less willing to make sacrifices for the good of the family. Third, the emphasis Western

Table 9.1 Divorce Rates in the United States, 1950 to 2000	
Year	Divorce Rate/1000 Population
1950	2.6
1960	2.2
1970	3.5
1980	5.2
1990	4.7
2000	4.2

SOURCE: National Center for Health Statistics (Centers for Disease Control) (www.cdc.gov/nchs/hus.htm).

© Hubert Boesl/dpa/Corbis

Like approximately half of all marriages in the United States, the marriage of Brad Pitt and Jennifer Aniston ended in divorce.

---

divorce   The legal and formal dissolution of a marriage.

culture puts on romantic love as the basis for marriage makes marriages vulnerable when sexual passion subsides. Fourth, there is much less of a stigma attached to divorce today than there was a century ago. As recently as the 1950s, a divorced couple was looked at with pity, if not contempt, for not being able to "save their marriage," whereas in contemporary U.S. society, roughly half of all marriages end in divorce. And fifth, divorce in the United States today is a relatively easy thing to obtain. No longer must a spouse prove infidelity or physical abuse. Rather, today in most states a wife or husband seeking to end a marriage needs to claim only that the marriage has "failed" or that there are "irreconcilable differences." As one law professor has commented, "It is easier to walk away from a marriage than from a commitment to purchase a new car" (quoted in Etzioni 1993).

RESIDENCE PATTERNS: WHERE DO WIVES AND HUSBANDS LIVE?

In addition to mate selection, the number of spouses one can have, and the types of economic considerations that must be transferred, societies set guidelines regarding where married couples will live. When two people marry in North American society, it is customary for the couple to take up residence in a place of their own, apart from the relatives of either spouse. This residence pattern is known as *neolocal residence* (that is, a new place). As natural as this may appear to us, by global standards it is an atypical residence pattern, practiced in only about 5 percent of the societies of the world. The remaining societies prescribe that newlyweds will live in the same household with or close to relatives of the wife or the husband.

One question facing these societies is, which children stay at home when they marry, and which ones leave? Also, of those who leave, with which relative are they expected to reside? Most residence patterns fall into one of five patterns (percentages based on tabulations from Murdock's "Ethnographic Atlas" [1967]):

Patrilocal residence: The married couple lives with or near the relatives of the husband's father (69 percent of the societies).

Matrilocal residence: The married couple lives with or near the relatives of the wife (13 percent of the societies).

Avunculocal residence: The married couple lives with or near the husband's mother's brother (4 percent of the societies).

Ambilocal (bilocal) residence: The married couple has a choice of living with either the relatives of the wife or the relatives of the husband (9 percent of the societies).

Neolocal residence: The married couple forms an independent place of residence away from the relatives of either spouse (5 percent of the societies).

To a significant degree, residence patterns are linked to the types of kinship systems (discussed in Chapter 10) found in any society. For example, there is a reasonably close correlation between patrilocal residence and patrilineal descent (tracing one's important relatives through the father's side) and between matrilocal residence and matrilineal descent (tracing one's important relatives through the mother's side). To be certain, residence patterns do not determine kinship ideology, but social interaction between certain categories of kin can be facilitated if those kin reside in close proximity to one another.

It should be kept in mind that these five residence patterns, like most other aspects of culture, are ideal types. Consequently, how people actually behave—in this case, where they reside—does not always conform precisely to these ideals. Sometimes normative patterns of residence are altered or interrupted by events such as famines or epidemics that force newlyweds to reside in areas that will maximize their chances for survival or their economic security. To illustrate, during the Depression years of the 1930s, the normal neolocal pattern of residence in the United States was disrupted when many young married adults moved in with one set of parents to save money.

MARRIAGE: CONTINUITY AND CHANGE

As with any aspect of culture, marriage practices and customs change over time. In some cultures, and at certain times in their histories, changes are rapid and far reaching, while at other times these customary practices remain fairly stable. In the United States, for example, marital practices (at least in the Christian tradition) have not undergone widespread changes. In the 1940s men were expected to propose matrimony, the father of the bride usually "gave her away," the ceremony was officiated by a religious functionary or someone licensed by the state, the bride's family was responsible for the major expenses of a wedding, brides wore white dresses, and the newlyweds typically took time after the ceremony for a honeymoon. These practices are still adhered to today.

In contemporary Japanese society, however, changes in wedding practice have occurred both dramatically and rapidly. Until just several decades ago, the overwhelming majority of Japanese were married according to the traditional Shinto wedding ceremony conducted at a religious shrine by a Shinto priest and attended by only the close family members of the bride and groom. The wedding couple were purified, drank rice wine (*sake*), and only the groom read the words of commitment. The couple, dressed in the traditional *kimono*, gave symbolic offerings to the *kami* (Shinto spirit gods who took the form of wind, trees, rivers, and fertility). Most Japanese weddings today, however, are conducted in Western-style hotels, the bride wears a white wedding gown while the groom is clad in a tuxedo, and the ceremony is officiated by an English-speaking American or European wearing white vestments and a gold cross. The so-called "ministers" or "pastors" are not required to have any seminary education whatsoever, and in fact most are teachers, disc jockeys, or part-time actors looking to make some extra money. Even though fewer than 2 percent of all Japanese are practicing Christians, it has been estimated that these Christian/Western-style ceremonies account for three of every four Japanese marriages conducted today (Brooke 2005).

Immediately to the west of Japan, the country of South Korea illustrates just the opposite trend—that is, a deliberate attempt, by means of education, to preserve certain aspects of traditional weddings and marriage. For nearly a quarter of a century the Institute of Decorum and Wisdom, located in the capital city of Seoul, has provided bridal courses for young upper-class women in Korean society. Women learn everything from how to bow properly, to proper table manners, to how a "proper" woman should rebuff the amorous advances of a suitor. The curriculum includes etiquette, cooking, how to walk, and the use of proper techniques of nonverbal communication. While Korea has certainly experienced a good deal of change in its marriage customs and practices in recent decades, the bridal courses offered by the Institute of Decorum and Wisdom illustrate a very deliberate effort to preserve and maintain certain parts of marital customs (Onishi 2004).

FAMILY STRUCTURE

Cultural anthropologists have identified two fundamentally different types of family structure: the nuclear family and the extended family. The *nuclear family* is based on marital ties, and the *extended family*, a much larger social unit, is based on blood ties among three or more generations of kin.

The Nuclear Family

Consisting of husband and wife and their children, the nuclear family is a two-generation family formed around the conjugal or marital union. Even though the nuclear family to some degree is part of a larger family structure, it remains an autonomous and independent unit. That is, the everyday needs of economic support, child care, and social interaction are met within the nuclear family itself rather than by a wider set of relatives. In societies based on the nuclear family, it is customary for married

nuclear family The most basic family unit—composed of wife, husband, and children.
extended family The family that includes in one household near relatives in addition to a nuclear family.

couples to live apart from both sets of parents (neolocal residence). The married couple is also not particularly obliged or expected to care for their aging parents in their own home. Generally, parents are not actively involved in mate selection for their children, in no way legitimize the marriages of their children, and have no control over whether their children remain married.

The nuclear family is most likely to be found in societies with the greatest amount of geographic mobility. This certainly is the case in the United States and Canada, which currently have both considerable geographic mobility and the ideal of the nuclear family.

During much of our early history, the extended family—tied to the land and working on the family farm—was the rule rather than the exception. Today, however, the family farm—housing parents, grandparents, aunts, uncles, cousins, and siblings—is a thing of the past. Now, in response to the forces of industrialization, most adults move to locations where they can find suitable employment. Because one's profession largely determines where one will live, adults in the United States and Canada often live considerable distances from their parents or other extended family members.

In addition to being found in such highly industrialized societies as our own, the nuclear family is found in certain societies located at the other end of the technological spectrum. In certain foraging societies residing in environments where resources are meager (such as the Inuit of northern Canada and the Shoshone of Utah and Nevada), the nuclear family is the basic food-collecting unit. These nuclear families remain highly independent

Courtesy of Gary Ferraro

What type of residence pattern is followed by this North American nuclear family?

foraging groups that fend for themselves. Even though they cannot expect help from the outside in an emergency, they have developed a family structure that is well adapted to a highly mobile life. Thus, both U.S. society and some small-scale food-collecting societies have adopted the nuclear family pattern because of their need to maintain a high degree of geographic mobility.

Although the independent nuclear family was the ideal in the United States for much of the twentieth century, significant changes have occurred in recent years. According to recent census data, only one in four households consists of the nuclear family (two parents and one or more children), a sharp decline from earlier decades. The remaining U.S. households comprise married couples without children, single adults, single parents, unmarried couples, roommates, extended family members, or adult siblings. There are several explanations for the decline of the nuclear family in the United States as we begin the twenty-first century. First, as more and more women complete higher education and enter the job market, they are more likely to delay marrying and having children. Second, the increasing cost of maintaining a middle-class household that includes the parents, children, a three- or four-bedroom house, a golden retriever, and an SUV or two has caused some couples to opt for remaining childless altogether. Third, the ever-increasing divorce rate in the United States has contributed to the increase in non-nuclear families in recent decades.

The Extended Family

Extended families consist of two or more nuclear families that are linked by blood ties. Most commonly, this takes the form of a married couple living with one or more of their married children in a single household or homestead and under the authority of a family head. Such extended families, which are based on parent–child linkages, can be either patrilineal (comprising a man, his sons, and the sons' wives and children) or matrilineal (comprising a woman, her daughters, and her daughters' husbands and children). It is also possible for extended families to be linked through sibling ties consisting of two or more married brothers and their wives and children. According to Murdock's "Ethnographic Atlas" (1967), approximately 46 percent of the 862 societies listed have some type of extended family organization.

When a couple marries in a society with extended families, the newlyweds are not expected to establish a separate and distinct family unit. Instead, for example, the young couple may take up residence in the homestead of the husband's father, and the husband continues to work for his father, who also runs the household. Moreover, most of the personal property in the household is not owned by the newlyweds but is controlled by the husband's father. In the event that the extended family is large, it may be headed by two or more powerful male elders who run the family in much the same way that a board of directors runs a corporation. Eventually, the father (or other male elders) will die or retire, allowing younger men to assume positions of leadership and power within the extended family. Unlike the nuclear family, which lasts only one generation, the extended family is a continuous unit that can last an indefinite number of generations. As old people die off, they are replaced through the birth of new members.

In extended family systems, marriage is viewed more as bringing a daughter into the family than acquiring a wife. In other words, a man's obligations of obedience to his father and loyalty to his male kin are far more impor-

An extended family gathering in Henan Province, China.

Tony Manza, a high-level sales executive with a Canadian office furniture company, was in Kuwait trying to land a large contract with the Kuwaiti government. Having received an introduction from a mutual friend, Manza made an appointment with Mr. Mansour, the chief purchasing agent for the government. In his preparation for the trip, Manza had been told to expect to engage in a good deal of small talk before actually getting down to business. So Manza and Mansour chatted about the weather, golf, and Tony's flight from Toronto. Then, quite surprisingly, Mansour inquired about Manza's seventy-year-old father. Without giving it much thought, Manza responded by saying that his father was doing fine, but that the last time he had seen him four months ago in the nursing home, he had lost some weight. From that point onward, Mansour's attitude changed abruptly from warm and gracious to cool and aloof. Manza never did get the contract he was after.

Although Manza thought he was giving Mansour a straightforward answer, his response from Mansour's perspective made Manza an undesirable business partner. Coming from a society that places very high value on family relationships, Mansour considered putting one's own father into a nursing home (to be cared for by total strangers) to be inhumane. If Manza could not be relied upon to take care of his own father, he surely could not be trusted to fulfill his obligations in a business relationship.

tant than his relationship to his wife. When a woman marries into an extended family, she most often comes under the control of her mother-in-law, who allocates chores and supervises her domestic activities.

In some extended family systems, the conjugal relationship is suppressed to such an extent that contact between husband and wife is kept to a minimum. Among the Rajputs of northern India, for example, spouses are not allowed to talk to each other in the presence of family elders. Public displays of affection between spouses are considered reprehensible; in fact, a husband is not permitted to show open concern for his wife's welfare. Some societies take such severe measures to subordinate the husband–wife relationship because it is feared that a man's feelings for his wife could interfere with his obligations to his own blood relatives.

Extended families are more likely to be found in certain types of economies than others. As previously mentioned, economies based on either foraging or wage employment (which require considerable geographic mobility) are more likely to be associated with nuclear than with extended families. In addition, a rough correlation exists between extended family systems and an agricultural way of life. Several logical explanations have been suggested for this correlation. First, extended families provide large numbers of workers, who are necessary for success in both farm production and the marketing of surpluses. Second, in farm economies, where cultivated land is valuable, an extended family system prevents the land from being continually subdivided into smaller and less productive plots.

Modern-Day Family Structure

Most Western social thinkers over the past century have been in general agreement concerning the long-term effects of urbanization and modernization on the family. In general, they see a progressive nuclearization of the family in the face of modernization. This position is perhaps most eloquently presented by William Goode, who has stated that industrialization and urbanization have brought about "fewer kinship ties with distant relatives and a greater emphasis on the 'nuclear' family unit of couple and children" (1963: 1). Although in many parts of the world we can observe the association between modernization and fewer extended kinship ties, there are a number of exceptions, most notably in certain developing countries. To illustrate, in the Kenya Kinship Study (KKS) discussed in Chapter 5, no significant differences were found in the extended family interaction between rural Kikuyu and Kikuyu living in Nairobi.

Interestingly, we do not need to focus on developing countries to find the retention of extended kin ties in urban, industrialized areas. For example, Carol Stack (1975) and Jagna Sharff (1981) have shown how urban Blacks in the United States use extended kinship ties as a strategy for coping with poverty. Moreover, there is evidence to suggest that the number of multigenerational households is on the rise in the United States. Although still relatively small (only 4 percent of all types), the multigenerational family grew by 38 percent between 1990 and 2000. Increases in these modern extended households were particularly noticeable in states with high real estate costs (such as California) or areas with high levels of out-of-wedlock births. But there are more positive explanations as well. According to Navarro (2006: 1): "Multigenerational living, especially those in which grandparents care for their grandchildren, have long been common in Asian and Hispanic countries, and the arrangement is popular among immigrants from those nations. Also driving the trend are . . . active baby boomers who want to be involved in the lives of their offspring and who see little appeal in flying off to a Sun Belt retirement in isolation."

For at least the first half of the twentieth century, popular opinion (buttressed by the Judeo-Christian tradition) upheld a fairly uniform notion of what form the typical U.S. family should take. The "natural" family, according to this view, was a nuclear family consisting of two monogamous heterosexual parents (the breadwinning male and the female homemaker) with their children. In the past three decades, however, this so-called typical family has become harder to find. In fact, there is no longer a "typical family" in the United States.

Families headed by same sex partners are becoming increasingly more common than in decades past. Here two male partners are holding their adopted twin daughters as they take their wedding vows at City Hall in San Francisco in 2004.

© Kim Kulish/Corbis

Table 9.2	Marital Status of U.S. Population, 1980 to 1999 (as percentage of total population)			
	1980	**1990**	**1995**	**1999**
Never Married	20.3	22.2	22.9	23.9
Married	65.5	61.9	60.9	59.5
Widowed	8.0	7.6	7.0	6.7
Divorced	6.2	8.3	9.2	9.9

SOURCE: U.S. Census Bureau, *Statistical Abstract of the United States*, 2002, Table 53.

According to U.S. census figures, only 24 percent of all families in the United States in 2000 were made up of married couples with children younger than eighteen years of age, down from 40 percent thirty years earlier. During this same period nonfamily households (people not living with kin) increased from 1.7 to 5.7 percent; single-mother households from 12 to 26 percent; single-father households from 1 to 5 percent; and households containing only one person from 17 to 26 percent. Table 9.2 provides additional data on the changing nature of family life in the United States over the past several decades.

Moreover, even fewer of all U.S. families fit the typical model with the breadwinning husband, home-making wife, and their children. In twenty-first-century America, three out of every four families are atypical in that they are headed by either female or male single parents, unmarried partners, childless or post-child-rearing couples, or grandparents raising their grandchildren. There are also stepfamilies, extended families, families headed by same sex couples, and communal families, all of which are generally accepted alternative family forms. As Conrad Kottak (2004: 260) has observed, these changing patterns of family life have been reflected in a number of television sitcoms. For example, during the 1950s the family was depicted by Ozzie and Harriet Nelson and their sons, David and Ricky, and by Ward and June Cleaver and their sons, Wally and Beaver. Within the last several years, however, an increasing number of TV shows have featured alternative living arrangements such as roommates, single adults, working mothers, and single parents. In fact, some of the most popular TV sitcoms in the last several decades feature characters who are neither related to nor living with one another (examples include *Seinfeld, Friends, Ally McBeal, Will and Grace,* and *Sex and the City*). When nuclear families are portrayed on television today, they tend to be dysfunctional ones, such as the Osbournes, the Sopranos, and the Simpsons. If we assume that television is a reasonably accurate reflection of popular culture, the nuclear family in the United States has changed dramatically from Ozzie and Harriet in the 1950s to wives being swapped on the Fox reality show *Trading Spouses* in 2004.

It is interesting to note in twenty-first-century America, at a time of rapid immigration into the United States, a recent increase in extended family living. Despite the overall decline of extended families throughout the past

150 years, many people in the United States admire (in a general sense) the values and philosophy behind the extended family, a humane family type, which tends to shelter non-nuclear relatives from such difficulties as illness, old age, and unemployment. However, many mainstream Americans are less than enthusiastic about the extended family's twenty-first-century reincarnation as practiced by recent immigrant families. Rather than viewing these new extended family living arrangements in the United States as examples of good old family values, all we see are eighteen extended family members living in a single family house designed for a family of four, crowded on-street parking, and enormous numbers of garbage cans on the sidewalk. These recent examples of extended family living among newly arrived immigrants do not signify a general return to the extended families of the early nineteenth century. Rather they represent a short-term economic solution to unemployment, low wages, and a scarcity of affordable housing. ■

Summary

1. Because of the vast ethnographic variations found in the world, the terms *family* and *marriage* are not easy to define. Recognizing the difficulties inherent in such definitions, the family is a social unit, the members of which cooperate economically, manage reproduction and child-rearing, and most often live together. Marriage, the process by which families are formed, is a socially approved union between adult partners.

2. The formation of families through the process of marriage serves several important social functions by reducing competition for spouses, regulating the sexual division of labor, and meeting the material, educational, and emotional needs of children.

3. Every culture has a set of rules (incest taboos) regulating which categories of kin are inappropriate partners for sexual intercourse. A number of explanations have been suggested for this universal incest taboo, including the natural aversion theory, the inbreeding theory, the family disruption theory, and the theory of expanding social alliances.

4. Cultures restrict the choice of marriage partners by such practices as exogamy, endogamy, arranged marriages, preferential cousin marriage, the levirate, and the sororate.

5. All societies have rules governing the number of spouses a person can have. Societies tend to emphasize either monogamy (one spouse at a time), polygyny (a man marrying more than one wife at a time), or polyandry (a woman marrying more than one husband at a time).

6. In many societies, marriages involve the transfer of some type of economic consideration in exchange for rights of sexual access, legal rights over children, and rights to each other's property. These economic considerations involve such practices as bridewealth, bride service, dowry, and reciprocal exchange.

7. Just as all societies have customary ways of establishing marriages, they also have ways of dissolving them. As a rule, divorce rates are lower in societies that have strong kinship groups and systems of bridewealth.

8. All societies have guidelines regarding where a married couple should live after they marry. Residence patterns fall into five different categories. The couple can live with or near the relatives of the husband's father (patrilocal), the wife's relatives (matrilocal), the husband's mother's brother (avunculocal), the relatives of either the wife or the husband (ambilocal), or the husband and wife can form a completely new residence of their own (neolocal).

9. Cultural anthropologists distinguish between two types of family structures: the nuclear family, comprising the wife, husband, and children; and the extended family, a much larger social unit, comprising relatives from three or more generations.

Key Terms

ambilocal (bilocal) residence	dowry	monogamy	preferential cousin marriage
arranged marriage	endogamy	neolocal residence	reciprocal exchange
avunculocal residence	exogamy	nuclear family	role ambiguity
bride service	extended family	parallel cousins	serial monogamy
bridewealth	incest taboo	patrilocal residence	sororate
cross cousins	kibbutz	polyandry	
divorce	levirate	polygyny	
	matrilocal residence	postpartum sex taboo	

Suggested Readings

Coontz, Stephanie, Maya Parson, and Gabrielle Raley, eds. *American Families: A Multicultural Reader.* New York: Routledge, 1999. This collection of essays shows the considerable diversity in family forms, gender roles, values, and parenting practices found in the United States.

Fox, Robin. *Kinship and Marriage: An Anthropological Perspective.* Baltimore: Penguin Books, 1967. An excellent introduction to the cross-cultural study of marriage, particularly exogamous systems.

Hart, C. W. M., Arnold Pilling, and Jane C. Goodale. *The Tiwi of North Australia,* 3d ed. New York: Holt, Rinehart & Winston, 1988. A fascinating ethnographic account of the Tiwi of Melville Island (off the northern coast of Australia), who practice an extreme form of polygyny, whereby all females are always married and males spend much of their lives competing for the society's major status symbol: wives.

Kendall, Laurel. *Getting Married in Korea: Of Gender, Morality, and Modernity.* Berkeley: University of California Press, 1996. An in-depth ethnographic examination of what it takes to get married in contemporary Korea, including topics such as courtship, the exchange of goods between families, and the ceremony itself.

Krause, Elizabeth. *A Crisis of Births: Population Politics and Family-Making in Italy.* Belmont, CA: Wadsworth, 2005. This case study in contemporary social issues examines how Italy has attained the lowest birthrate in the world by its silent revolution against patriarchy and the traditional notion that motherhood is defined by large families.

Stockard, Janice E. *Marriage in Culture.* Belmont, CA: Wadsworth, 2002. This excellent study shows how marriage practices play an integral role in four different cultures, the !Kung San (Ju/'hoansi), Chinese, Iroquois, and Nyinba.

Weston, Kath. *Families We Choose: Lesbians, Gays, Kinship,* 2d ed. New York: Columbia University Press, 1997. This award-winning book, based on participant-observation and in-depth interviews in the San Francisco area, examines gay and lesbian families from a historical perspective.

Kinship and Descent

A Tuareg family gathers for a meal near the outskirts of Timbuktu, Mali.

CHAPTER 10

I T HAS BEEN SAID many times that humans are social animals. Even though other species display certain social features (such as baboons living in permanent troops), what sets humans apart from the rest of the animal world is the complexity of their social organization. People live in groups to a much greater degree than any other species. Individuals play specific social roles, have different statuses, and form patterned relationships with other group members. Human social groups are formed on the basis of a number of factors including occupation, kinship, social class, gender, ethnic affiliation, education, and religion.

Since cultural anthropologists began conducting fieldwork, they appear to have spent a disproportionate amount of time and energy describing kinship systems. Not only have they devoted more time to studying kinship systems than any other single topic, but they have spent more time on kinship systems than have other social scientists. The reason cultural anthropologists spend so much time on what Malinowski called "kinship algebra" is related to the type of societies they have traditionally studied.

Cultural anthropologists, though interested in all societies of the world, have in actual practice concentrated on studying small-scale societies where kinship relations tend to be all-encompassing. In highly urbanized, technological societies, such as those studied most often by sociologists, fewer social relationships are based on kinship. In the United States, for example, social relationships that are essentially political, economic, recreational, or religious are usually not played out with kin. But even in the United States, where kinship ties are sometimes overshadowed by nonkinship ties, kin relations are usually more long term, intense, and emotionally laden than are relations with nonkin. By way of contrast, in small-scale, non-Western, preliterate, and technologically simple societies, kinship is at the heart of the social structure. Who a person marries, where he or she lives, and from whom a person inherits property and status all depend on the person's place within the kinship system. In such societies, it might not be an exaggeration to say that kinship relations are tantamount to social relations.

Whether we are considering small- or large-scale societies, kinship systems are important because they help people adapt to interpersonal and environmental challenges. Kinship systems are adaptive because they

What We Will Learn

- Why have cultural anthropologists spent so much time studying kinship?

- What are the various functions of descent groups?

- What are the different ways in which cultures categorize kin?

- Why is it important to know something about the kinship systems in other cultures?

 Click!

For interactive exercises and study aids, Go to **www.ichapters.com**; enter the author name and select your text, then click the Study Help tab to purchase the following online resources:

- **ThomsonNOW** for chapter-specific online tutorials, quizzes, and a personalized study plan

- **Anthropology Resource Center** for interactive maps, modules, videos, and the Applied Anthropology site

- **Thomson Audio Study Products** for a brief overview of the major chapter themes and to test your knowledge with quiz questions

Cultural anthropologists generally have studied societies in which kinship activities play an important role. This Tibetan family includes three generations.

provide a plan for aligning people and resources in strategic ways. They set limits on sexual activity and on who can marry whom; they establish the parameters of economic cooperation between men and women; and they provide a basis for proper child-rearing. Moreover, kinship systems often provide a mechanism for sharing certain pieces of property (such as land or cattle) that cannot be divided without being destroyed. But, beyond the limits of the immediate family unit, kinship systems extend one's relationship to a much wider group of people. To illustrate, membership in a small, local group of kin enables an individual to draw on more distant kinsmen for protection or economic support during difficult times. Also, when small family groups are confronted with large-scale projects, they often recruit cooperative labor from among already existing groups of extended kinsmen.

KINSHIP DEFINED

Kinship refers to the relationships—found in all societies—that are based on blood or marriage. Those people to whom we are related through birth or blood are our *consanguineal relatives*; those to whom we are related through marriage are our *affinal relatives*. Each society has a well-understood system of defining relationships between these different types of relatives. Every society, in other words, defines the nature of kinship interaction by determining which kin are more socially important than others, the terms used to classify various types of

Parenthood as defined by this Western family is very different from the Zumbaguan definition of *parenthood*.

kin, and the expected forms of behavior between them. Although the systems vary significantly from one society to another, one thing is certain: relationships based on blood and marriage are culturally recognized by all societies.

Sometimes kinship terms are used with people who are not related by either blood or marriage. This usage, known as *fictive kinship*, can take a number of different forms. For example, the process of adoption creates a set of relationships between the adoptive parents and child that have all of the expectations of relationships based on descent or marriage. Often, close friends of the family are referred to as aunt or uncle, even though they have no biological or marital relationship. College fraternities and sororities and some churches use kinship terminology (such as brothers and sisters) to refer to their members. Members of the Black community in the United States often refer to one another as brother and sister. And, of course, the godparent–godchild relationship,

consanguineal relatives One's biological or blood relatives.
affinal relatives Kinship ties formed through marriage (that is, in-laws).

fictive kinship Relationships among individuals who recognize kinship obligations although the relationships are not based on either consanguineal or affinal ties.

The Bari of Venezuela believe in partible paternity, the idea that a child can have more than one biological father.

which carries with it all sorts of kinship obligations, often involves people who do not share blood or marriage connections. These examples should remind us that it is possible to have kinship-like relationships (complete with well-understood rights and obligations) without having an actual biological or marital connection.

In the United States, the *biological* meaning of kinship is very powerful. This is particularly true when determining legal parenthood. For example, surrogate mothers who have borne children for wealthy women have had some success in the courts in reclaiming those children purely on the basis of being the biological mother. And biological fathers who have abandoned their families have returned to claim custody of their children solely on the basis of biological paternity. In some parts of the world, however, the *social* component of kinship is given far more weight than in the United States. For the Zumbagua of highland Ecuador, parenthood is not established solely and automatically on the basis of either giving birth or impregnating a woman. Rather, it involves a relationship that must be achieved over a relatively long period of time. According to Mary Weismantel (1995: 697):

> Among the Zumbagua, if the biological father's role ends after conception, or if the mother's role ends

shortly after birth, these biological parents have a very weak claim to parenthood should they re-enter the child's life at a later time. Thus, the Zumbagua notion of parenthood involves *working* at nurturing the child over a number of years; mere conception or childbirth alone does not, in and of itself, give a man or a woman the right to claim parenthood of a child.

Thus, the Zumbagua of Ecuador place a higher priority on *social* parenthood that is earned than would be found in mainstream U.S. society, which places a higher value on genetically based parenthood. This, of course, has very important implications for the process of adoption in these two cultures. Rather than automatically designating parenthood on the basic of biological connections, Zumbaguan culture insists that claims to parenthood are created by the adult nurturing and caring for the child over a long period of time. In fact, the Zumbaguan notion of nurturing is taken quite literally, defined as actually *feeding or sharing food with* the child. In a sense, food is what binds parents to children, for according to Weismantel (1995: 695), "Those who eat together in the same household share the same flesh."

In Zumbaguan society, social parenthood is given higher priority than biological parenthood. There are additional ethnographic examples in which kinship is socially constructed rather than universally defined. For example, some aboriginal cultures in South America believe in "partible paternity"—the notion that a child can have more than one biological father. In other words, it is believed that all men who have sex with a woman during her pregnancy actually contribute to the formation of the fetus. When the baby is born, the mother names the men whom she identifies as fathers, who then are expected to assume social responsibility for the child. Even though this concept of partible paternity flies in the face of our scientific understanding of conception, recent studies have shown that defining fatherhood as a multiple phenomenon actually is beneficial for children. For example, among the Bari people of Venezuela, children with two or more official fathers had an 80-percent chance of reaching adulthood as compared to only 64 percent for those with one father (Beckerman and Valentine 2002). In societies such as the Bari, a strong case can be made for a pregnant woman taking lovers so that her child will have more than one male provider. The Bari notion of multiple fatherhood is significant because it illustrates how, as in the Zumbaguan case, kinship categories such as father or parent are defined differently in various cultures.

CULTURAL RULES REGARDING KINSHIP

All kinship systems are founded on biological connections. Family and kinship groups would not exist if men and women did not mate and have children. However, kinship systems involve more than biological relationships. Rather, each society classifies its kin according to a set of cultural rules that may or may not account for biological factors. For example, according to our own kinship system, we refer to both our father's brother and our father's sister's husband as uncles even though the former is a blood relative and the latter is not. In many societies, a man refers to his father's brother and his mother's brother (both blood relatives) by different terms and is expected to behave very differently toward the two. This distinction between the biological and cultural dimensions of kinship can be seen in U.S. society when we refer to our adopted children as sons and daughters (with all of the rights and obligations that biological children have), even though they have no genetic connection. Thus, as we can see, the way that different societies sort and categorize kinship relationships is as much a matter of culture as it is a matter of biology.

FUNCTIONS OF KINSHIP SYSTEMS

All kinship systems, wherever they may be found, serve two important functions for the well-being of the total society. First, by its *vertical function*, a kinship system provides social continuity by binding together a number of successive generations. Kinship systems are most directly involved with the passing of education, tradition, property, and political office from one generation to the next. Second, kinship systems tend to solidify or tie together a society horizontally (that is, across a single generation) through the process of marriage. Because kinship systems define the local kin groups outside of which people must take a spouse, it forces groups to enter into alliances with other kinship groups, thereby creating solidarity within a much larger society. This

horizontal function of kinship was perhaps best illustrated by the case of the late King Sobhuza II of Swaziland, who solidified his entire kingdom (composed of approximately a half million people) by taking a wife from virtually every nonroyal lineage in the country.

USING KINSHIP DIAGRAMS

Although kinship systems are found in every society, how any particular society defines the relationships between kin varies widely from one group to another. In different societies, people with the same biological connection may be defined differently, labeled differently, and expected to behave differently toward one another. And, as we shall see, societies can choose from a vast array of possibilities. Before trying to sort out the complexities of different kinship systems, it would be helpful to introduce a form of shorthand used by cultural anthropologists in analyzing kinship systems.

As a way of simplifying kinship systems, anthropologists use kinship diagrams rather than relying on verbal explanations alone. In this standardized notational system, all kinship diagrams are viewed from a central point of reference (called *EGO*), the person from whose point of view we are tracing the relationship. All kinship diagrams use the symbols found in Figure 10.1.

Starting with our point of reference (EGO) and using the various symbols, it is possible to construct a hypothetical family diagram, as in Figure 10.2. If we start with EGO as our point of reference, we can refer to all of the people in the diagram in the following way:

1. Father's sister (FZ)
2. Father's sister's husband (FZH)
3. Father's brother's wife (FBW)
4. Father's brother (FB)
5. Father (F)
6. Mother (M)
7. Mother's sister's husband (MZH)
8. Mother's sister (MZ)
9. Mother's brother (MB)
10. Mother's brother's wife (MBW)
11. Father's sister's son (FZS)
12. Father's sister's daughter (FZD)
13. Father's brother's son (FBS)

---

vertical function of kinship   The way in which all kinship systems tend to provide social continuity by binding together different generations.

horizontal function of kinship   The ways in which all kinship systems, by requiring people to marry outside their own small kinship group, function to integrate the total society through marriage bonds between otherwise unrelated kin groups.

EGO   The person in kinship diagrams from whose point of view we trace the relationship.

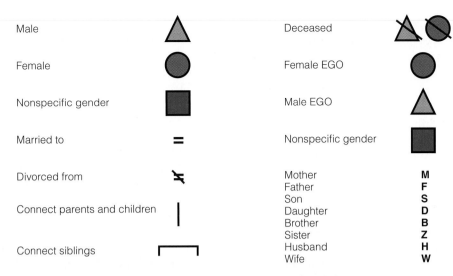

FIGURE 10.1 Kinship Diagram Symbol. Note: Symbols with the same numbers below them are referred to in the same way by EGO.

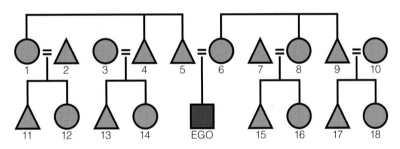

FIGURE 10.2 Generic Kinship Diagram

14. Father's brother's daughter (FBD)
15. Mother's sister's son (MZS)
16. Mother's sister's daughter (MZD)
17. Mother's brother's son (MBS)
18. Mother's brother's daughter (MBD)

PRINCIPLES OF KINSHIP CLASSIFICATION

No kinship system in the world uses a different term of reference for every single relative. Instead, all kinship systems group relatives into certain categories, refer to them by the same term, and expect people to behave toward them in a similar fashion. How a particular society categorizes relatives depends on which principles of classification are used. Various kinship systems use a number of principles to group certain relatives together while separating others, as discussed in the following subsections.

Generation

In some kinship systems—our own being a good example—distinctions between kin depend on generation. Mothers, fathers, and their siblings are always found in the first ascending generation, immediately above EGO;

sons, daughters, nieces, and nephews are always one generation below EGO in the first descending generation; grandmothers and grandfathers are always two generations above EGO, and so forth. Although this seems like the natural thing to do, some societies have kinship systems that do not confine a kin category to a single generation. It is possible, for example, to find the same kin category in three or four different generations. The Haida of British Columbia use the same kinship term to refer to one's father's sister, father's sister's daughter, and the daughter of the father's sister's daughter.

Sex or Gender

Some kinship systems group certain kin together because of common gender (Collier and Yanagisako 1987). In our English system, kin categories such as brother, father, father's brother, son, and grandfather are always males; sister, mother, mother's sister, daughter, and grandmother are always females. The one area where we do not distinguish on the basis of gender is at the cousin level (but, then, the consistent application of a particular principle is not required). Even though this principle of gender operates at most levels of our own system, it is hardly universally applicable. In other words, some societies allow for the possibility of both males and females occupying a single kin category.

Lineality Versus Collaterality

Lineality refers to kin related in a single line, such as son, father, grandfather. *Collaterality*, on the other hand, refers to kin related through a linking relative, such as the relationship between EGO and his or her parents' siblings. Whereas the principle of lineality distinguishes between father and father's brother, the principle of collaterality does not. That is, in some societies, EGO uses the term *father* to refer to both his or her father and his or her father's brother; similarly, EGO's mother and her sisters may be referred to by the single term *mother*.

Consanguineal Versus Affinal Kin

Some societies make distinctions in kinship categories based on whether people are related by blood (consanguineal kin) or through marriage (affinal kin). Our own kinship system uses this principle of classification at some levels but not at others. To illustrate, we distinguish between sons and sons-in-law and between sisters and sisters-in-law. But in EGO's parents' generation, we fail to distinguish between mother's brother (a blood relative) and mother's sister's husband (an affinal relative), both of whom we call uncle.

Relative Age

In certain kinship systems, relative age serves as a criterion for separating different types of relatives. In such societies, a man will have one kinship term for younger brother and another term for older brother. These different terms based on relative age carry with them different behavioral expectations, for often a man is expected to act toward his older brother with deference and respect while behaving much more informally toward his younger brother.

Sex of the Connecting Relative

Some societies distinguish between different categories of kin based on the sex of the connecting (or intervening) relative. To illustrate (see Figure 10.2), a mother's brother's daughter (18) and a mother's sister's daughter (16), who are both called cousins in our system, are given two different kinship terms. Similarly, a father's brother's daughter (14) and a father's sister's daughter (12) are given different kinship terms. One category of cousins (12 and 18) is called cross cousins and the other (14 and 16) is called parallel cousins. According to this principle, these first cousins are considered to be different by virtue of the sex of their parents.

Social Condition

Distinctions among kin categories can also be made based on a person's general life condition. According to this criterion, different kinship terms would be used

for a married brother and a bachelor brother or for a living aunt and one who is deceased.

Side of the Family

A final principle has to do with using different kin terms for EGO's mother's side of the family and EGO's father's side of the family. The kinship system used in the United States makes no such distinction, for we have aunts, uncles, cousins, and grandparents on both sides of our family. In societies that use this principle of classification, different terms would be used to refer to a mother's brother and a father's brother.

CROSS-CULTURAL MISCUE

Medical anthropologist Geri-Ann Galanti (1991) tells of a tragic incident that resulted from a U.S. physician working in Saudi Arabia failing to understand the culture of one of his patients. An eighteen-year-old Bedouin girl from a remote village was brought in to the hospital with a gunshot wound in the pelvis. When the doctors took X-rays to determine the extent of the girl's injury, they discovered, much to their surprise, that she was pregnant. Because Bedouin girls receive no sex education, the girl was unaware that she was pregnant.

Three doctors were involved in the case: an American neurosurgeon who had worked in the region for several years, a European gynecologist who had worked in the Middle East for a decade, and a young internist from the United States who had just arrived in the area. They all realized that the girl's pregnancy presented a real problem because tribal custom punishes out-of-wedlock pregnancies with death.

In order to save the girl's life, the physicians decided to send the girl to Europe for a secret abortion, telling her parents that her gunshot wound needed special treatment available only in Europe. The young American physician was very hesitant to make such a recommendation, but the other two doctors, more experienced in Middle Eastern cultures, convinced him of the seriousness of the situation. They explained that a pregnant unmarried girl was a terrible slur on the reputation of the men of the family, who were responsible for her protection. Her pregnancy was a sure sign that they had not done their job. The only way that the family could restore its honor would be to put the girl to death.

The young American reluctantly agreed not to tell the parents, but at the last minute changed his mind because he could not be deceitful. He decided to tell the girl's father as she was being wheeled to the airplane. The father immediately grabbed the girl off the stretcher, rushed her to his car, and drove away. Several weeks later the hospital staff learned that the girl had been killed by her family. The family's honor had been restored. But the ethnocentric internist had a nervous breakdown and returned to the United States.

---

lineality   Kin related in a single line such as son, father, and grandfather.
collaterality   Kin relations traced through a linking relative.

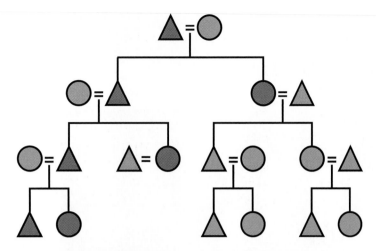

FIGURE 10.3   Patrilineal Descent. In a patrilineal descent system, a person is connected to relatives of both sexes related through males only. Sons and daughters belong to their father's descent group, as do the father's sons' children but not the father's daughters' children.

THE FORMATION OF DESCENT GROUPS

As we have seen, kinship systems play an important role in helping people sort out how they should behave toward various relatives. In anthropological terms, *kinship systems* encompass all of the blood and marriage relationships that help people distinguish among different categories of kin, create rights and obligations among kin, and serve as the basis for the formation of certain types of kin groups.

Anthropologists also use the narrower term *descent* to refer to the rules a culture uses to establish affiliations with one's parents. These rules of descent often provide the basis for the formation of social groups. These social groups, or descent groups, are collections of relatives (usually lineal descendants of a common ancestor) who live out their lives in close proximity to one another.

In societies that have descent groups, the group plays a central role in the lives of its members. Descent group members have a strong sense of identity, often share communally held property, provide economic assistance to one another, and engage in mutual civic and religious ceremonies. In addition, descent groups function in other ways by serving as a mechanism for inheriting property and political office, controlling behavior, regulating marriages, and structuring primary political units.

Rules of descent can be divided into two distinct types. The first is unilineal descent, whereby people trace their ancestry through either the mother's line or the father's line, but not both. Unilineal groups that trace their descent through the mother's line are called matrilineal descent groups; those tracing their descent through the father's line are called patrilineal descent groups. The second type of descent is known as cognatic (or nonunilineal) descent, which includes double descent, ambilineal descent, and bilateral descent. Because descent is traced in mainstream North America according to the bilateral principle, many Westerners have difficulty understanding unilineal kinship systems.

Unilineal Descent Groups

Approximately 60 percent of all kinship systems found in the world are based on the unilineal principle. *Unilineal descent* groups are particularly adaptive because they are clear-cut, unambiguous social units. Because a person becomes a member of a unilineal descent group by birth, there is no confusion as to who is a group member and who is not. For societies that rely on kinship groups to perform most of their social functions (such as marriage, dispute settlement, or religious ceremonies), unilineal descent groups, with their clear-cut membership, provide a social organization with unambiguous roles and statuses. Because it is clear to which group one belongs, a person has no questions about her or his rights of inheritance, prestige, and social roles.

Patrilineal Descent Groups
Of the two types of unilineal descent groups, *patrilineal descent* is by far the most common. Patrilineal descent

kinship system   Those relationships found in all societies that are based on blood or marriage.
descent   Tracing one's kinship connections back through a number of generations.

unilineal descent   Tracing descent through a single line (such as matrilineal or patrilineal) as compared to both sides (bilateral descent).
patrilineal descent   A form of descent whereby people trace their primary kin relationships through their fathers.

This Kikuyu family of Kenya has a patrilineal descent system.

Courtesy of Gary Ferraro

groups are found on all of the major continents and in a wide range of societies, including certain food collecting Native American groups, some East African farmers and pastoralists, the Nagas of India, the Kapauku Papuans of the New Guinea Highlands, and the traditional Chinese. In societies with patrilineal descent groups, a person is related through the father, father's father, and so forth. In other words, a man, his own children, his brother's children (but not his sister's children), and his son's children (but not his daughter's children) are all members of the same descent group. Females must marry outside their own patrilineages, and the children a woman bears belong to the husband's lineage rather than to her own. The principle of patrilineal descent is illustrated in Figure 10.3.

Although there are hundreds of well-documented studies from which to choose, we will use traditional China to illustrate patrilineages, as China is by far the largest patrilineal society in the world. It is important to emphasize here that we are talking about *traditional* China for approximately a hundred years prior to the communist takeover in 1949. During this period, the Chinese family, at least ideally, was made up of the patrilineage, comprising a man, his wife or wives, his sons, daughters-in-law, grandchildren, and great-grandchildren. When a son reached marriageable age, a wife was provided for him by the extended family. In most cases the wives came from other unrelated families, but sometimes Chinese couples adopted unrelated infant girls for the express purpose of providing a future bride for one of the sons, a practice known as *simpua*. A family with many sons became large by producing many children. Residence pattern was patrilocal (see Chapter 9), whereby the wives became part of the husband's lineage and produced children for it. The extended family typically

occupied a set of buildings forming a single estate. As with any patrilineal society, inheritance passed from the father to his son(s) and grandson(s).

In the United States and much of western Europe, parents are expected to give priority to the needs of their children. But in the traditional Chinese family, the reverse is true, for it is the children who have the major obligation to the family. Children must show deference, respect, and obedience to their parents for as long as the parents are alive. Children are obligated to provide for the comfort of their aging parents, and even after their death, must attend to the parents' spiritual needs through various ceremonies of ancestor worship. And, of course, sons are under constant pressure to perpetuate their father's lineage by producing sons of their own. The male members of the families are responsible for maintaining the ancestral tablets, kept in the family shrine and upon which all of the names of the family are carefully recorded. A man takes very seriously the place of his name in the family tablets as a way of connecting himself to his ancestors and his descendants. As Margery Wolf (1972: 15) has suggested, "Few men would wish to be responsible for bringing such a history to a close."

What has been described here is an ideal patrilineal family in traditional China. Such a patrilineal arrangement, composed of three or four generations living together as an economic and social unit, lasted for as long as the head of the family lived. Upon the death of the father, however, the family estate would usually be partitioned, and sons would form their own families. In fact, it was possible for sons to break away from their father's household before his death. In less affluent families, in which the subordination of the son(s) to the father was relatively weak, a son would be less likely to remain part of his father's extended family. Another scenario is that a married son with sons of his own would feel a stronger allegiance to his wife and children than to his father and brothers. Moreover, longevity of the extended family may be jeopardized when adult brothers become rivals over the issue of who will replace their father as the head of the extended family. Thus, the crucial relationships that influence when the extended family divides are the father–son, husband–wife, and brother–brother relationships. Even when a son breaks away to form his own family, however, he maintains his family name and close attention to his heritage (Freedman 1979).

To be certain, the traditional Chinese patrilineal family was male focused. Men are born into a patrilineage and remain in that group for the rest of their lives. A man's sisters leave his patrilineage to take up residence with their husbands, while his own wife has left her father's homestead to take up residence with his family. When young women marry, they sever their ties with their father's family, literally, with a ritual slamming of the door. The bride can return for visits to her natal lineage for as long as her mother is alive, but the frequency of such visits varies with geographic proximity. Women in traditional China are raised in one family and then, upon marriage, are expected to transfer both their residence and their allegiance to the families of their husbands. By way of contrast, men's lives in patrilineal societies have continuity, security, and predictability.

Owing to the predominance of male ethnographers during much of the twentieth century, early ethnographic accounts of Chinese patrilineages have almost exclusively looked at the family from the male perspective, and by default, have assumed that both men and women view the "family" in essentially equivalent terms. But, according to Margery Wolf (1972), the most meaningful family for a Chinese woman is neither her father's patrilineage, which she will eventually leave, nor her husband's patrilineage, into which she will marry. Instead, it is what Wolf refers to as the "uterine family," composed of her mother and her mother's children. After the woman marries and takes up residence with her husband's lineage, her allegiances slowly transfer from the uterine family headed by her mother to a uterine family of her own, which includes her own children. The uterine family lacks the continuity of a patrilineage, for it lasts only as long as the mother is alive. Although the uterine family has no official ideology, formal structure, or public recognition, it is nevertheless a real family in terms of feelings and behaviors.

The uterine family does not exist solely within the context of the husband's larger patrilineage. Women, who are strangers and outsiders in their husbands' lineages, also form strong alliances in the village with other women, who, by definition, are also outsiders. Much of women's work is conducted outside of the family compound. Thus, while washing clothes at the river, a woman is able to make alliances with other women (both within and outside her husband's patrilineage), which she can draw upon to advance the interests of her own uterine family. A woman who has exercised good judgment and has nurtured productive allegiances over the years is able to exert considerable influence over her husband and his patrilineage.

Margery Wolf's work on women and the family in rural Taiwan serves as a useful corrective to our understanding of the Chinese patrilineal family. It also is a reminder to anthropologists, as well as to other social scientists, that the gender and perspective of the investigator very well may contribute to a skewed picture of reality. Moreover, it justifies Franz Boas's insistence (see Chapter 4) many decades ago that anthropology needs both men and women ethnographers in order to construct the most complete description of another culture.

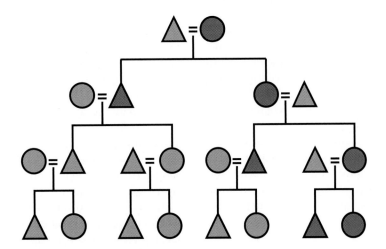

FIGURE 10.4 Matrilineal Descent. In a matrilineal descent system, a person is connected to kin of both sexes related through females only. Sons and daughters belong to their mother's descent group, as do the mother's daughters' children but not the mother's sons' children.

APPLIED PERSPECTIVE

Redesigning an Agricultural Development Program in West Africa

In much the same way that salvage archaeologists excavate sites threatened by the construction of dams, roads, or buildings, cultural anthropologists have been called upon to help reformulate international development projects that are not working. When development programs are foundering due to an inadequate understanding of the sociocultural features of the target populations, cultural anthropologists have helped to analyze the program and recommend changes that will enable the program to meet its objectives more effectively.

One such case of "salvage anthropology" was the redesign of an agricultural development program in the West African country of Guinea by Robert Hecht (1986). Sponsored by USAID, the original project was a five-year, nearly $5 million project aimed at improving farm production by training agricultural researchers, extension workers, and administrators. As originally conceived in the late 1970s, the project involved building an agricultural laboratory, teaching facilities at an agricultural college, and running a research demonstration farm. The project was aimed at the physical construction of these three facilities and equipping them with U.S. technology. The original program designers assumed that national agricultural productivity would be increased by improving

the quality of research and the training of extension personnel. Because the initial emphasis was on technology and training, the original designers paid little attention to the sociocultural realities of the local farmers.

By 1981, it was apparent that the project had some serious problems. First, the construction of the three facilities was running nearly two years behind and the projected costs had escalated to $15 million. Second, it became clear that the plans for using these facilities were inadequate. To address this inadequacy, USAID appointed a team composed of an anthropologist (Hecht), an economist, and an agronomist to study the programs and make recommendations for change.

The "salvage team" concluded that the project's most glaring weakness was that it totally ignored the cultural realities of most of the small farmers in Guinea. The original planners neither consulted the farmers nor provided for their participation in the program. There were no mechanisms for obtaining feedback from the farmers or for enabling them to become auxiliary extension agents. In short, the original project did not include the local farmers in designing, implementing, or evaluating the project.

Matrilineal Descent Groups

In a matrilineal kinship system, a person belongs to the mother's group. A *matrilineal descent* group comprises a woman, her siblings, her own children, her sisters' children, and her daughters' children. Matrilineal descent groups make up about 15 percent of the unilineal descent groups found among contemporary societies. They are found in a number of areas of the world, including some Native Americans (such as Navajo, Cherokee, and Iroquois), the Truk and Trobriand Islanders of the Pacific, and the Bemba, Ashanti, and Yao of Africa.

It is important not to confuse matrilineal descent with *matriarchy*, a situation known only in myth, in which the women in a society have greater authority and decision-making prerogatives than the men. In most cases where matrilineal descent is practiced, men retain

the lion's share of power and authority. Political offices are held by men, and it is men, not women, who control property. In matrilineal societies, both property and political office pass from one man to another, but through a woman. To illustrate, whereas in a patrilineal society a man passes his property and hereditary political office to his own son, in a matrilineal society property and office pass from a man to his sister's son. In fact, in a matrilineal society, the most important male relationship a man has is with his sister's son (or mother's brother). The principle of matrilineal descent is illustrated in Figure 10.4.

A good example of a matrilineal society is the Zuni people of New Mexico, one of the best-described and most typical groups among the western Pueblos. The Zuni are divided into thirteen matrilineal clans, each of which comprises several lineages. The clan, not the lineage, is the exogamous group. The household, which is the essential economic unit, is occupied by a woman or group of women (made up of the grandmother, her sisters, and their daughters) who are descended through females. Because the Zuni practice matrilocal residence, husbands

matrilineal descent A form of descent whereby people trace their primary kin connections through their mothers.

matriarchy The rule of domination of women over men.

To gain a better understanding of the problems facing the original project design, Hecht gathered data on the economic and sociocultural features of the Malinke farmers who comprised the majority of the local population. On the basis of participant-observation and interview data, Hecht (1986: 21–22) made some significant findings about the Malinke family and kinship system:

1. The average household is relatively large (approximately nine people), in part because of the high incidence of polygyny and in part because of the complex patrilineal structure. These large kin-based households have important implications for the project because of the potential for economic cooperation among corporate lineage members (e.g., forming producer groups or building communal storage facilities for fertilizer).

2. Because land in Malinke society is controlled by corporate lineages, a household had rights to land only by virtue of its membership in a particular lineage. Rank among lineages in the village determined the allocation of land, with chiefly and higher status lineages controlling more land than commoner lineages. Even within lineages, elders have more and better land than heads of more junior households. Given this hierarchy within the land tenure system, Hecht (1986: 22) recommended that the revised project should "be sensitive to the needs of those at the bottom of the distribution hierarchy, who possessed the smallest plots and least fertile land."

3. Most (nonwage) farm labor among the Malinke was supplied largely by household members and supplemented by other kin outside the household.

The basic picture that emerged from Hecht's research was one of a kin-based farming system, conducted on lineage con-trolled land, and carried out by a kinship-based labor force. Only after this strong connection between kinship and farming had emerged through anthropological research could adequate changes be made to this multimillion-dollar agricultural project.

The traditional data-gathering techniques of household sur-veys, interviews, and participant-observation yielded the type of sociocultural data necessary for redesigning a successful program. As Hecht reminds us, "The multidisciplinary or holis-tic approach usually associated with anthropology, and the emphasis placed by anthropologists on learning from the local population, may even make the anthropologist an appro-priate person to serve as a team leader" (1986: 25).

Questions for Further Thought

1. What erroneous assumptions had the original planners made that contributed to the near collapse of the program?

2. What data-gathering techniques did Hecht use in his applied anthropological research? Were these methods appropriate for the problem under investigation?

3. What is meant by the term *corporate lineage*? How was an understanding of this term instrumental in contributing to the success of the development project?

---

live with their wives and their wives' matrilineal kin. The women, however, are the permanent residents of the house and are bound together by their joint care of all the sacred objects in the house. Just as wives are viewed as strangers or outsiders in the traditional Chinese extended family, so too are the husbands in the Zuni family.

Wives have no practical connection to their hus-bands' families. Husbands, however, need to divide their energy and allegiances between their wife's matri-lineage and that of their mothers and sisters. When important ceremonial activities need to be conducted, it is the married brothers (presently married and living with the matrilineages of their wives) who return to perform them at their mother's house. Even though husbands contribute to the economic well-being of their wives' matrilineal household, they play no role in the ritual or ceremonial activities of the household, because this role is performed by the brothers and uncles of the wife's matrilineage. Thus, men perform economic roles for their wives but ritual roles for their own matrilineages. And, in fact, the ritual roles in every-day Zuni life are more important than how many mate-

rial possessions a man can accumulate. The important Zuni man of high prestige is not the wealthiest in a material sense but rather the one who performs many ceremonial roles with his family's religious fetishes.

These Zuni of New Mexico practice matrilineal descent.

© Ernesto Burciaga/Alamy

Because Zuni men are divided between serving the economic interests of their wives and the ceremonial needs of their sisters and mothers, it is not surprising that marriages are fairly fragile. According to the ethnographic accounts, Zuni men tend to desire marriage more than women, for if a man should divorce or never marry at all, he would be forced to live at home with his female kin, a living arrangement that most Zuni men would consider undignified at best. In Zuni society, men are more willing to become husbands than women are to become wives. Women in Zuni society always have a desirable home, while men do not (Benedict 1934; Eggan 1950).

Types of Unilineal Descent Groups

Anthropologists recognize different types of kinship groups that are based on the unilineal principle. Categorized according to increasing levels of inclusiveness, the four major types of descent groups are lineages, clans, phratries, and moieties. These four types of unilineal descent groups can form an organizational hierarchy, with moieties comprising two or more phratries, phratries comprising two or more clans, and clans comprising two or more lineages. Not every society has all four types of groups, but some do.

Lineages A *lineage* is a unilineal descent group up to approximately ten generations in depth; its members can trace their ancestry back (step-by-step) to a common founder. When descent is traced through the male line, the groups are known as patrilineages; when it is traced through the female line, they are known as matrilineages.

Sometimes lineages undergo a process known as *segmentation*, a subdivision into smaller units depending on the social situation. This process can occur when antagonisms arise among lineage members. For example, a lineage can be divided into two secondary lineages, divided again into tertiary lineages, and further subdivided into minimal lineages. These minimal lineages may be only three or four generations in depth. Such a segmentation process is diagrammed in Figure 10.5.

At certain times and under certain social situations, different segments compete with one another, but at other times they are allied. In Figure 10.5, because all of the minimal lineages are autonomous, normally (a) and (b) do not have a lot to do with each other. But if (d) becomes involved in a dispute with (b), then (a) is likely to ally itself with (b) because of their common ancestry within (1). However, if (d) has a conflict with (f), it is likely that (a), (b), and (c) would all come to the defense of (d) because of their common genealogical connection to (A). It is also likely that (a) through (h) will all come together on certain ritual occasions to acknowledge their common relationship to (I). Thus, sublineages are allied with one another at some times and in conflict with one another at other times.

Clans Another type of unilineal descent group is the *clan*. A clan is a group of kin usually comprising ten or

segmentation The process that takes place within a lineage whereby small subdivisions of a lineage will oppose one another in some social situations but will coalesce and become allies in other social situations.

clans Unilineal descent groups, usually comprising more than ten generations, consisting of members who claim a common ancestry even though they cannot trace step-by-step their exact connection to a common ancestor.

lineage Unilineal descent group whose members can trace their line of descent to a common ancestor.

Table 10.1 Differences Between Patrilineal and Matrilineal Descent Groups

	Patrilineal Groups	**Matrilineal Groups**
Role of Women	Give birth to their husband's descendants; play minimal role in their own group	Play a central role in their own group by bearing their own descendants
Authority of Husband/father	Strong authority	Weak in marital household; strong in the household of his sister
Status of husband/father	High status	Relatively low status
Father/child relationship	Characterized by deference, strong authority and formality	Relatively weak authority and general informality
Strength of marital bonds	Strong	Relatively weak
Residence pattern	Typically patrilocal	Typically matrilocal

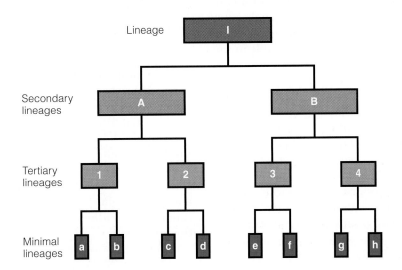

FIGURE 10.5 Lineage Segmentation

more generations whose members believe they are all related to a common ancestor but are unable to trace that genealogical connection step-by-step.

When clans and lineages are found together, the clan is usually made up of a number of different lineages. Depending on which line is emphasized, the clan can be either a matriclan or a patriclan.

In some societies, clans are close-knit groups, very much like lineages, whose members have a high degree of interaction with one another. More commonly, however, clan members are widely dispersed geographically and rarely get together for clan-wide activities. Unlike lineages, which serve as corporate, functioning groups, clans tend to be larger and more loosely structured categories with which people identify. Often, clans are associated with animals or plants (that is, totems) that provide a focal point for group identity.

Phratries At the next order of magnitude are *phratries*, unilineal descent groups composed of two or more clans.

In societies in which phratries are found, the actual connections among the various clans usually are not recognized. Generally, phratries are rare, and, when they are found, they do not serve important social functions. Although phratries have been significant social, political, and religious groups in some cases, such as traditional Aztec society, this is the exception rather than the rule.

Moieties In some cases, societies are divided into two unilineal descent groups called *moieties* (a term derived from the French word for *half*). In societies that have only two clans, the clans and the moieties are identical to each other. But when moieties are made up of more than two clans (as is usually the case), the moiety is the larger unit.

Moieties are an excellent example of social reciprocity. For example, if a society is made up of two large exogamous moieties, each moiety provides the other group

phratries Unilineal descent groups composed of a number of related clans.

moieties Complementary descent groups that result from the division of a society into two halves.

with its marriage partners. Moreover, moiety affiliation has been used for seating arrangements at ceremonial occasions or for sports competitions. Among the Seneca Indians, one moiety performs mourning rituals for the other. Thus, although moieties can play important roles in the society, they are not a part of the political structure in the same way as are lineages and clans.

The Corporate Nature of Unilineal Descent Groups

One feature of all unilineal descent groups—whether we are talking about lineages, clans, phratries, or moieties—is that they clearly define who is a member and who is not. These collective kinship groups also endure over time. Even though individual members are born into the group and leave it by dying, the unilineal descent group continues on. Because of their unambiguous membership and continuity, unilineal descent groups are good examples of corporate entities that play a powerful role in the lives of the individual members.

We can cite a number of indicators of the corporate nature of unilineal descent groups. First, unilineal groups such as lineages often shape a person's identity in significant ways. When a stranger asks the simple question, "Who are you?" lineage members are likely to respond, "I am a member of such and such a lineage," rather than "I am John Smith." Lineage members, in other words, see themselves first and foremost as members of the kinship group rather than as individuals. Second, unilineal descent groups regulate marriage to the extent that large numbers of kin on both the bride's and the groom's side of the family must give their approval before the marriage can take place. Third, property (such as land and livestock) is usually regulated by the descent group, rather than being controlled by the individual. The group allocates specific pieces of property to individual members for their use but only because they are kin members in good standing. Fourth, even the criminal justice system in unilineal societies has a strong corporate focus. For example, if a member of lineage (a) assaults a member of lineage (q), the entire lineage (q) will seek compensation from or revenge on lineage (a). The assaulter would not be held solely accountable for her or his individual actions, but rather the group (the lineage or clan) would be culpable.

The corporate nature of unilineal descent groups is no better illustrated than in the strong bonds of obligations that exist among members. The kinship group provides a firm base of security and protection for its individual members. If crops fail, an individual can always turn to her or his unilineal descent group members for assistance; in the event of any threat from outsiders, a person should expect support and protection from members of her or his own descent group. The strength of these bonds of obligation depends on the closeness of the ties. Mutual assistance is likely to be taken very seriously among lineage members, less so among clan members, and not very seriously at the phratry or moiety level.

Cognatic (Nonunilineal) Descent Groups

Approximately 40 percent of the world's societies have kinship systems that are not based on the unilineal principle. Anthropologists call these *cognatic descent* or nonunilineal descent groups and classify them into three basic types: double descent, ambilineal descent, and bilateral descent.

Double Descent

Some societies practice a form of *double descent* (or double unilineal descent), whereby kinship is traced both matrilineally and patrilineally. In such societies, an individual belongs to both the mother's and the father's lineage. Descent under such a system is matrilineal for some purposes and patrilineal for others. For example, movable property such as small livestock or agricultural produce may be inherited from the mother's side of the family, whereas nonmovable property such as land may be inherited from the father's side.

Double descent is rare; only about 5 percent of the world's cultures practice it. One such culture, the Yako of Nigeria, has been particularly well described by Daryll Forde (1967). For the Yako, both matrilineality and patrilineality are important principles of kinship. Among the traditional Yako, cooperation in everyday domestic life is strongest among members of the patriclan for the obvious reason that they live with or near one another. Resources such as land, forest products, and trees as well as membership in men's associations are inherited by patrilineal descent.

The mother's line is also important, even though matriclan members are not likely to live in close proximity to one another. Because the Yako believe strongly that all life stems from the mother, a mother's children are honor-bound to help one another and maintain peaceful and harmonious relations among themselves. Certain movable property, such as livestock and currency, passes from one matriclan member to another. Moreover, matriclans supervise funeral ceremonies and are responsible for providing part of the bridewealth payment. Thus, as the Yako well illustrate, in a double descent system the patrilineal groups and the matrilineal groups are active in different spheres of the culture.

> **cognatic descent**   A form of descent traced through both females and males.
>
> **double descent**   A system of descent in which individuals receive some rights and obligations from the father's side of the family and others from the mother's side.

Ambilineal Descent

In societies that practice *ambilineal descent*, parents have a choice of affiliating their children with either kinship group. Compared with unilineal systems, which restrict one's membership to either the mother's or the father's group, ambilineal systems are more flexible because they allow for individual choice concerning group affiliation. The range of choice varies from one ambilineal system to another. In some cases, the parents are expected to choose the group with which their children eventually affiliate. Other systems allow the individual to move continuously through life from one group to another, provided he or she affiliates with one descent group at a time. Still other systems permit the overlapping of membership with a number of groups at the same time. This flexibility does not come without a price, however. As a general rule, the greater the flexibility concerning membership, the weaker the group's loyalties, cohesiveness, and impact on the lives of its members.

Bilateral Descent

In societies (such as mainstream U.S. society) that practice *bilateral descent*, a person is related equally to both the mother's and the father's sides of the family. A bilateral system tends to be symmetrical to the extent that what happens on one side of the kinship diagram also happens on the other side. In other words, the grandparents, aunts, uncles, and cousins are treated equally on both sides of the family. In unilineal systems, a person is affiliated with a large number of kin over many generations but only on one side of the family. By way of contrast, bilateral systems create links from both sides of the family but usually include only close kin from a small number of generations.

The kinship group recognized in a bilateral system is known as the *kindred*: a group of closely related relatives connected through both parents to one living relative (or to EGO). Unlike unilineal descent, which forms discrete, mutually exclusive groups, bilateral systems give rise to a situation in which no two individuals (except siblings) have the same kindred. The kindred is not a group at all but rather a network of relatives.

Unlike the lineage or the clan, the kindred has no founding ancestor, precise boundaries, or continuity over time. In short, because kindreds are not corporate groups, they cannot perform the same types of functions—such as joint ownership of property, common economic activities, regulation of marriage, or mutual assistance—as unilineal groups. To be certain, an individual can mobilize some members of his or her kindred to perform some of these tasks, but the kindred does not function as a corporate entity. This type of loosely structured network of relatives works particularly well in a society like our own, which highly values personal independence and geographic mobility.

DIFFERENT SYSTEMS OF CLASSIFICATION

Every society has a coherent system of labeling various types of kin. In any given system, certain categories of kin are grouped together under a single category, whereas others are separated into distinct categories. In our own society, we group together under the general heading of "aunt" our mother's sisters, father's sisters, mother's brothers' wives, and father's brothers' wives. Similarly, we lump together under the heading of "uncle" our father's brothers, mother's brothers, father's sisters' husbands and mother's sisters' husbands. In contrast, other societies might have separate terms for all eight of these categories of kin. Whatever system of classification is used, however, cultural anthropologists have found them to be both internally logical and consistently applied. Even though individual societies may have their own variations, six basic classification systems have been identified: Eskimo, Hawaiian, Iroquois, Omaha, Crow, and Sudanese (distribution shown in Figure 10.6). Four such classification systems, the Eskimo, Hawaiian, Iroquois, and Crow will be described in greater detail following.

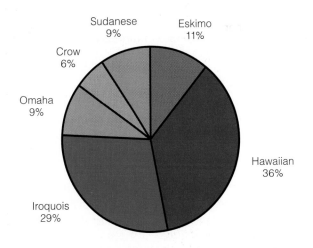

FIGURE 10.6 World Distribution of Kinship Systems

SOURCE: George P. Murdock, "Ethnographic Atlas: A Summary." *Ethnology* 6(2) (April 1967): 109–236.

---

ambilineal descent   A form of descent that affiliates a person to a kin group through either the male or the female line.

bilateral descent   A type of kinship system whereby individuals emphasize both their mother's kin and their father's kin relatively equally.

kindred   All of the relatives a person recognizes in a bilateral kinship system.

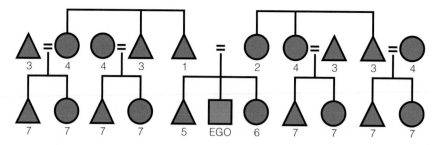

FIGURE 10.7 Eskimo Kinship System. Note: Symbols with the same numbers below are referred to in the same way by EGO.

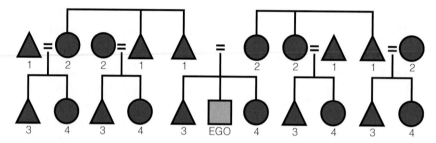

FIGURE 10.8 Hawaiian Kinship System. Note: Symbols with the same numbers below are referred to in the same way by EGO.

Eskimo System

Found in approximately one-tenth of the world's societies, the *Eskimo (Inuit) system* of kinship classification (Figure 10.7) is associated with bilateral descent. The major feature of this system is that it emphasizes the nuclear family by using separate terms (such as *mother, father, sister, brother*) that are not used outside the nuclear family. Beyond the nuclear family, many other relatives (such as aunts, uncles, and cousins) are lumped together. This emphasis on the nuclear family is related to the fact that societies using the Eskimo system lack large descent groups such as lineages and clans. Moreover, the Eskimo system is most likely to be found in societies (such as U.S. society and certain food-collecting societies) where economic conditions favor an independent nuclear family.

Hawaiian System

Found in approximately one-third of the societies in the world, the *Hawaiian system* (Figure 10.8) uses a single term for all relatives of the same sex and generation. To illustrate, a person's father, father's brother, and

Eskimo (Inuit) system The kinship system most commonly found in the United States; it is associated with bilateral descent. Usually, a mother, father, and their children live together.
Hawaiian system Associated with ambilineal descent, this kinship system uses a single term for all relatives of the same sex and generation.

mother's brother are all referred to by the single term *father*. In EGO's own generation, the only distinction is one based on sex, so that male cousins are equated with brothers and female cousins are equated with sisters. The Hawaiian system, which uses the least number of terms, is often associated with ambilineal descent, which permits a person to affiliate with either the mother's or the father's kin. The Hawaiian system is found in societies that submerge the nuclear family into a larger kin group to the extent that nuclear family members are roughly equivalent in importance to more distant kin.

Iroquois System

In the *Iroquois system* (Figure 10.9), EGO's father and father's brother are called by the same term, and EGO's mother's brother is called by a different term. Likewise, EGO's mother and mother's sister are lumped together under one term, and a different term is used for EGO's father's sister. Thus, a basic distinction of classification is made between the sex of one's parents' siblings (that is, mother's brothers and sisters and father's brothers and sisters). Within EGO's own generation, EGO's own siblings are given the same term as the parallel cousins (children of one's mother's sister or father's brother), and different terms are used for cross cousins (children of one's mother's brother or father's sister). Thus, the terminological distinction made between cross and par-

Iroquois system A system associated with unilineal descent in which the father and father's brother are called by the same term, as are the mother and mother's sister.

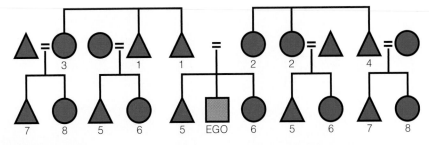

FIGURE 10.9 Iroquois Kinship System. Note: Symbols with the same numbers below are referred to in the same way by EGO.

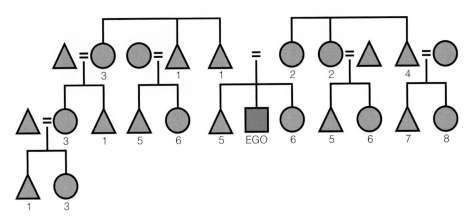

FIGURE 10.10 Crow Kinship System. Note: Symbols with the same numbers below are referred to in the same way by EGO.

allel cousins is logical, given the distinction made between the siblings of EGO's parents. The Iroquois system emphasizes the importance of unilineal descent groups by distinguishing between members of one's own lineage and those belonging to other lineages.

Crow System

By concentrating on matrilineal rather than patrilineal descent, the *Crow system* of kinship classification (Figure 10.10) is the mirror image of the Omaha system. The Crow and Omaha systems are similar in that both use similar terms for EGO's father and father's brother, EGO's mother and mother's sister, and EGO's siblings and parallel cousins. But because of its less important nature, the father's side of the family merges generations. That is, all males in the father's line, regardless of generation, are combined under a single term (1), as are all women in that line (3). However, on EGO's mother's side of the family, which is the important descent group, generational distinctions are recognized.

Crow system A kinship system, associated with matrilineal descent, in which similar terms are used for (1) one's father and father's brother, (2) one's mother and mother's sister, and (3) one's siblings and parallel cousins.

We have shown how four of the six kinship systems (Eskimo, Hawaiian, Iroquois, and Crow) divide kinsmen into different categories. It is not necessary to specify in similar detail how all of the common types of kinship systems are structured. What is important, however, is to grasp the notion that different societies divide up the kinship pie in different ways. As a general rule, those kinsmen in any system that are given similar labels are expected to be treated in equivalent ways, while those having different labels are not. The particular form any given system takes is neither better nor worse than any other; they are simply different. However different they are, every kinship system tends to be internally logical and consistently adhered to.

KINSHIP AND THE MODERN WORLD

Unless they are born into a family that has kept careful records of its history, most people have little knowledge of their ancestors beyond three or four generations. However, within the last decade the revolution in information technology has made it possible for people to reconstruct their genealogies many generations into the past. The Internet now hosts a number of online sites that enable people to find information about long-forgotten family members. The site with the largest fam-

Newly arrived immigrants are processed at Ellis Island in New York City, the initial point of entry into the United States during the first half of the 20th century. Recent developments in information technology now enable us to search immigration records to learn more about our family histories.

Anthropologist Nancy Scheper-Hughes has studied the effects of poverty on the mother-infant bond in northern Brazil.

ily database in the world is Ancestry.com, which for a fee of approximately $200 provides access to digitized records on immigration, births, marriages, and deaths. Moreover, the database includes more than four hundred historical newspapers as well as twenty thousand family histories and biographies from the United States, Canada, and Great Britain dating back to the mid-1500s. All of these documents have been scanned into this company's database, allowing subscribers to find information on a particular relative by using "optimal name recognition" technology. So, if you are interested in reconstructing your family connections or would like to learn more about your bizarre great-great-great Uncle Harry, the technology now exists to enable you to do so with relative ease.

In this chapter we have examined the basic features of kinship systems in all of their various forms. By necessity our discussion has been simplified. Kinship systems and relationships are never as neat and tidy in real life as they are in theory. Exceptions to the rules and aberrant forms of individual behavior can be found in any system. Moreover, kinship systems are constantly experiencing changes through contact with external forces such as industrializing economies, colonization and decolonization, missionary intrusions, and cultural diffusion in general.

Of all aspects of human societies, kinship systems represent the most intimate, intense, and long-lasting set of social relationships a person will experience. Based as they are on birth and marriage, they create social ties that are often close and emotional. Kinship groups often involve strong bonds of obligation, security for their members, and moral coercion to adhere to

social norms. We cannot assume, however, that these well-integrated kinship groups remain unchanged in the face of external pressures such as urban migration, poverty, unemployment, and a host of other hardships.

Anthropologist Nancy Scheper-Hughes (1989) has documented how one essential feature of all kinship systems, the mother–infant bond, has been altered among poor women living in a shantytown in Brazil. Conducting fieldwork in the sugar plantation area of northeast Brazil, Scheper-Hughes described this area's vast array of social problems. Life expectancy is only about forty years, largely because of the high incidence of infant mortality. Children are at high risk of death due to inadequate child care, poor diet, and lack of access to breastfeeding. Single mothers are the norm in this shantytown. Wages for these single mothers are extremely low, sometimes less than a dollar a day. Mother–infant contact is minimal because babies cannot be taken to work, nor can mothers carry them to the river where they wash clothes because of the danger of parasitic infections. Consequently, infants spend a good deal of their early lives in the care of older siblings who are reluctant babysitters, or they are simply left alone at home.

Following an outbreak of infant deaths in the shantytown in 1965, Scheper-Hughes observed an apparent indifference on the part of the mothers toward the death of their infants. After nearly a quarter of a century of conducting research in this shantytown, Scheper-Hughes has come to see what appears to be maternal indifference to be the result of their living with continuously high infant mortality rates in conditions of hunger,

CROSS-CULTURAL MISCUE

Understanding kinship systems in other cultures can have very practical repercussions on how effectively we do our jobs. Anthropologist Clyde Kluckhohn, who spent much of his career studying the Navajo of the American Southwest, tells of an intelligent and successful Chicago public school teacher who had just started teaching in a Navajo reservation school. When he asked how her Navajo students compared to her Chicago students, she responded that she was puzzled by the apparently bizarre behavior of several of her Navajo students. She told Kluckhohn, "The other night we had a dance in the high school. I saw a boy who is one of the best students in my English class standing off by himself. So I took him over to a pretty girl and told them to dance. But they just stood there with their heads down. They wouldn't even say anything" (1949: 19–20).

What appeared to the teacher to be strange behavior can make sense only if we first understand several features of Navajo culture—features that are radically different from the culture of a White middle-class schoolteacher from Chicago. First, the type of dancing that the teacher expected of these two Navajo teenagers is considered quite promiscuous by Navajo standards. Whereas middle-class North Americans attach little, if any, sexual meaning to the type of bodily contact involved in ballroom dancing, the Navajo think it highly inappropriate for adults of opposite sexes to move around the dance floor in a semi-embrace with the fronts of their bodies touching.

And second, according to the Navajo kinship system, which is made up of exogamous clans, the incest taboo applies as strictly to all clan members as it does to members of one's own nuclear family. Unfortunately, the Navajo boy and girl the teacher had chosen were members of the same clan and, as such, were strictly forbidden from engaging in the public display of intimacy implied in Western-style dancing. As Kluckhohn suggested, the humiliation these two Navajo youngsters must have experienced would have been roughly equivalent to the embarrassment the teacher would have felt had the manager of a crowded hotel asked her to share a bed with her adult brother. Here, then, was a poignant and needless miscommunication that was the direct result of the teacher not understanding the nature of the kinship system of her students.

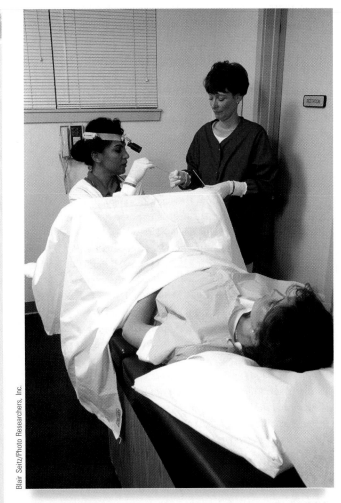

(vertical credit) Blair Seitz/Photo Researchers, Inc.

New reproductive technologies are changing the way we think about kinship.

poverty, powerlessness, and economic exploitation. Under such conditions, infant deaths have come to be expected. As a psychological coping strategy, mothers do not allow themselves to become emotionally attached to their infants until they are reasonably certain their children will survive. Thus, Scheper-Hughes provides a poignant case study of what can happen to kinship systems—and the mother–infant bond that is at the heart of such systems—in the face of radical change, abject poverty, and powerlessness.

The study of kinship, because of the numerous ways by which different cultures reckon kinship, has always presented a challenge to students of anthropology. Even the study of a single system requires an ease with working at different levels of abstraction. The task of understanding our own kinship system in recent years has been made all the more difficult by such complex phenomena as transnational adoptions, gay and lesbian families, and new *reproductive technologies* at our disposal, such as sperm banks, in vitro fertilization, and surrogate motherhood. For example, we now have the technology to create an embryo in a laboratory by

reproductive technologies Recent developments, such as in vitro fertilization, surrogate motherhood, and sperm banks, that are making the reckoning of kinship relationships more complex.

APPLIED PERSPECTIVE

The Ethnography of Homeless Youth in the United States

It has been estimated that between 500,000 and 1.5 million youth in the United States either run away from home or are kicked out of their homes every year. Although most runaways eventually return home, a sizeable percentage of young people never return home. Instead, they separate themselves permanently from their parents and families and adopt a risky lifestyle of homelessness, vagrancy, and delinquency. This world of homeless youth often operates below the radar of societal institutions that might provide them with needed social services.

Courtesy of Marni Finkelstein

In an effort to learn more about their hardships and adventures, anthropologist Marni Finkelstein (2005) conducted ethnographic research among a group of these nomadic street youth in East Village of New York City. The researcher defined her subject group as young people under the age of twenty-one who have separated themselves (either voluntarily or not) from their families and who do not live in homeless shelters. Previous studies of homeless youth have used their family backgrounds as the major explanatory variable of their behavior. By way of contrast, Finkelstein's more emic approach (see Chapter 1) describes the world of these homeless youth by observing and interviewing them about their own experiences on the streets. Allowing her informants to use their own words, Finkelstein describes the process of leaving home, developing functional social networks, finding sources of food and cash, and coping with the often violent and hostile world of the street.

Finkelstein uncovered a number of useful features of the culture of street kids. First, contrary to popular stereotypes, the homeless youth who congregated in East Village did not come from wealthy homes in suburban New York and were not playing the role of street kids for the summer because it was a cool thing to do; rather, these were kids from the South and the West Coast who had been on the streets for, in many cases, a number of years. Second, the lifestyle of these homeless youth was nomadic. They tended to glorify mobility, while rejecting the notions of boundaries, territories, and conventional definitions of sedentary communities. Not unlike European Roma (gypsies), the street kids romanticized their nomadism as a natural part of their life journey, in which they were free from the constraints of established society. Third, street kids have an extensive network of friends and companions, many of whom take on the character of fictive kin. These

family-like relationships—which take the place of the real family relationships they have left behind—are important mechanisms for socializing the newly homeless to life on the street and enhancing access to resources, opportunities, and psychological support.

Finkelstein's unique study of traveling street youth has important implications for improving social services and health care resources. For example, an important finding from this study was that these homeless youth did not take advantage of conventional social service agencies because they were too restrictive and invasive of their privacy. These young migrants were less likely to sleep at youth shelters, preferring instead to sleep on the street and use "drop-in" centers that provide some basic services without asking many questions. Given this lifestyle preference, Finkelstein suggests that social service providers must become more proactive by going to where street kids congregate (such as known parks) to provide information and basic services. Another suggestion derived from the study is that social service providers must "find a balance between not coming on too strong because of street kids' mistrust of adults, and not being too relaxed because of perceptions that adults don't care about them" (Finkelstein, 2005: 134). And finally, Finkelstein learned that service providers tried to entice the street kids to use their services by offering food and condoms, commodities that were fairly easy to come by. What the homeless youth wanted most was to have their hygiene needs met, such as access to hot showers, clean socks, toothpaste, and tampons. If social service providers can follow the recommendation that emerged from this ethnographic study, perhaps these highly mobile street youth will more readily utilize the available services.

Questions for Further Thought

1. In what way(s) was Finkelstein's study of homeless youth in the East Village of New York City different from other studies?
2. How would some of the findings from this study be useful for law enforcement officials in New York City?
3. What do these homeless youth have in common with European Roma (gypsies)?

combining a husband's sperm with an egg from a woman other than his wife and then implanting it into the uterus of a surrogate mother who will carry the baby for nine months. When the baby is born, the original sperm-donating husband and his wife will then raise the child as their own. The question arises: Who is the mother? Is it the woman who donated the egg (the genetic mother)? Is it the woman who carried the child and gave birth to it (the gestational mother)? Or is it the woman who will raise the child (nurturing/social mother)? A number of difficult court cases have arisen over disputes involving children conceived through various reproductive technologies. These new technologies have created challenges for our legal system, our ethical and moral standards, and our basic vocabulary of kinship. ■

Summary

1. Although kinship relations are more important in some societies than others, kinship is the single most important aspect of social structure for all societies. Kinship is based on both consanguineal (blood) relationships and affinal (marriage) relationships. Most societies recognize some type of fictive kinship, whereby kinship terms and obligations are applied to people with no biological connection.

2. Kinship has both a biological and a cultural dimension. This is the reason some categories of relatives include some people who have biological connections and others who do not.

3. A fundamental feature of all kinship systems is that they group relatives into certain categories, call them by the same name, and expect people to behave toward these relatives in similar ways. How a particular culture categorizes its relatives varies according to different principles of classification. These principles are based on criteria such as generation, gender, lineality, consanguineality, relative age, sex of the connecting relative, social condition, and side of the family.

4. Many societies have sets of rules, called rules of descent, that affiliate people with different sets of kin. Patrilineal descent affiliates a person with the kin group of the father, matrilineal descent affiliates a person with the kin group of the mother, and ambilineal descent permits an individual to affiliate with either the mother's or the father's kin group.

5. Patrilineal descent groups, which are more common than matrilineal, are found in most areas of the world. In a patrilineal system, a man's children belong to his lineage, as do the children of his son, but not the children of his daughter. Women marry outside their own lineage.

6. In matrilineal systems, a woman's children are affiliated with her lineage, not her husband's. Because the mother's brother is the social father of the woman's children, the relations between husband and wife in a matrilineal system tend to be more fragile than in patrilineal societies.

7. In societies that trace their descent unilineally (through a single line), people identify themselves with a particular unilineal descent group or series of groups. These different levels of kinship organization include lineages (a set of kin who can trace their ancestry back through known links), clans (a unilineal group claiming descent but unable to trace all of the genealogical links), phratries (groups of related clans), and moieties (two halves of a society related by descent).

8. Bilateral descent, which is found predominantly among foraging and industrialized societies, traces one's important relatives on both the mother's and the father's sides of the family. Bilateral systems, which are symmetrical, result in the formation of kindreds, which are more like loose kinship networks than permanent corporate functioning groups.

9. There are six primary types of kinship systems based on how the society distinguishes different categories of relatives: Eskimo, Hawaiian, Iroquois, Omaha, Crow, and Sudanese.

10. Reproductive technologies (such as in vitro fertilization and surrogate motherhood), which have become available in recent decades, have raised many legal and ethical questions about the nature of kinship.

Key Terms

affinal relatives	clans	consanguineal relatives	double descent
ambilineal relatives	cognatic descent	Crow system	EGO
bilateral descent	collaterality	descent	Eskimo (Inuit) system

fictive kinship

Hawaiian system

horizontal function of
   kinship

Iroquois system

kindred

kinship system

lineage

lineality

matriarchy

matrilineal descent

moieties

patrilineal descent

phratries

reproductive technologies

segmentation

unilineal descent

vertical function of kinship

Suggested Readings

Carsten, Janet. *After Kinship: New Departures in Anthropology.* Cambridge: Cambridge University Press, 2004. Explores how the areas of gender, reproductive technologies, and the social construction of science have influenced the anthropological study of kinship.

Feinberg, Richard and Martin Ottenheimer, eds. *The Cultural Analysis of Kinship: The Legacy of David M. Schneider.* Champaign-Urbana: University of Illinois Press, 2002. A collection of essays appraising the writings on kinship of David M. Schneider and the implication of his work for cultural relativity, gender, and feminist anthropology.

Fox, Robin. *Kinship and Marriage: An Anthropological Perspective.* Baltimore: Penguin, 1967. An excellent introduction to the broad and complex field of cultural anthropology written for serious students and laypeople alike. Fox not only brings together a number of different theories to explain the workings of different types of systems but also suggests some interesting theories of his own on the question of incest.

Parkin, Robert. *Kinship: An Introduction to Basic Concepts.* Malden, MA: Blackwell, 1997. A comprehensive introduction to the anthropology of kinship that deals with both theoretical and fieldwork issues.

Parkin, Robert, and Linda Stone, eds. *Kinship and Family: An Anthropological Reader.* Malden, MA: Blackwell, 2004. A comprehensive collection of articles on how anthropologists have analyzed kinship from the early twentieth century (Evans-Pritchard, Leach, and Schneider) to more contemporary debates on surrogate motherhood and gay/lesbian kinship.

Schusky, Ernest. *Manual for Kinship Analysis,* 2d ed. Lanham, MD: Rowman and Littlefield, 2002. A short text designed to give beginning anthropology students a clear statement of some of the essential features of kinship systems. By including a number of student activities, Schusky introduces the student to concepts of kinship logically and sequentially.

Stone, Linda. *Kinship and Gender: An Introduction.* Boulder, CO: Westview, 2000. This useful book provides an up-to-date introductory-level discussion of kinship as a framework for the study of gender. The author discusses the implications of the new reproductive technologies on concepts of kinship and gender.

Sex and Gender

Pictured here is Tula, a man impersonating a woman. Although it is possible to find men dressing and behaving like women in the United States, this practice is not considered a legitimate lifestyle alternative by the wider society.

11

O NE NEED NOT be a particularly keen observer of humanity to recognize that men and women differ physically in a number of important ways. Men on average are taller and have considerably greater body mass than women. There are noticeable differences between men and women in their sex organs, breast size, hormonal levels, body hair, and muscle/fat ratios. With their larger hearts and lungs and greater muscle mass, men have greater physical strength. Moreover, men and women differ genetically, with women having two X chromosomes and men having an X and a Y chromosome. Unlike humans, some animals (such as mice and pigeons) manifest no obvious sexual differences between males and females. Because of these significant physiological differences, we say that humans are *sexually dimorphic.*

Most researchers can agree on the physiological (genetically based) differences between men and women, but there is considerably less agreement on the extent to which these differences actually cause differences in behavior or in the way men and women are treated in society. As is the case with so many other aspects of behavior, the nature–nurture debate is operating in the area of behavioral differences between men and women. In other words, do men and women behave differently because of their genetic predisposition or because of their culture? During the twentieth century, ethnographers showed that the definition of femaleness and maleness varies widely from society to society. Because of this considerable cultural variability regarding differences in behaviors and attitudes between the sexes, most anthropologists now prefer to speak of gender differences rather than sex differences. For our purposes in this chapter, we can use Alice Schlegel's (1990: 23) definition of *gender*: "the way members of the two sexes are perceived, evaluated, and expected to behave."

Although the use of the term *gender* acknowledges the role that culture plays, it is not always possible to determine the extent to which culture or biology determines behavioral or attitudinal differences

---

sexual dimorphism   Refers to the physiological differences between men and women.
gender   The way members of the two sexes are perceived, evaluated, and expected to behave.

What We Will Learn

- To what extent does biology influence maleness and femaleness?

- Are males dominant over females in all societies?

- How similar are gender roles throughout the world?

- Do women and men in the same culture communicate differently?

- How can extreme gender ideology lead to the exploitation of women?

▶ Click!

For interactive exercises and study aids, Go to **www.ichapters.com**; enter the author name and select your text, then click the Study Help tab to purchase the following online resources:

- **ThomsonNOW** for chapter-specific online tutorials, quizzes, and a personalized study plan

- **Anthropology Resource Center** for interactive maps, modules, videos, and the Applied Anthropology site

- **Thomson Audio Study Products** for a brief overview of the major chapter themes and to test your knowledge with quiz questions

255

A nine year old girl from Vermont in camouflage is being taught to hunt black bear with her own 20-gauge shotgun. This is certainly an atypical definition of femininity in the United States.

Jodi Hilton/The New York Times/Redux

between the sexes. What we can say, however, is that biological differences influence (or set broad limits on) social definitions of maleness and femaleness to varying degrees. To illustrate, the fact that only women can give birth provides a basis for developing a set of attitudes and behaviors for women that are maternal, supportive, and nurturing. Likewise, because of their greater body mass, men may be defined as inherently strong, courageous, aggressive, and warlike. Nevertheless, as we will see, many different social definitions of *masculinity* and *femininity* can be found throughout the world.

Margaret Mead's (1935) classic study of sex and temperament in three New Guinea cultures illustrates the range of gender variation found among the Arapesh, Mundugumor, and Tchambuli. Mead found that among the Arapesh, both men and women were cooperative, nonaggressive, and responsive to the needs of others—all traits that most Westerners would consider to be feminine. In contrast, both genders among the Mundugumor were expected to be fierce, ruthless, and aggressive.

Among the Tchambuli, there was a complete reversal of the male–female temperaments found in our own society; that is, females were the dominant, impersonal partners who were aggressive food providers, whereas males were less responsible, more emotionally dependent, more preoccupied with art, and spent more time

masculinity   The social definition of maleness, which varies from society to society.
femininity   The social definition of femaleness, which varies from culture to culture.

on their hairdos and gossiping about the opposite sex. Mead argued that if those temperaments that we regard as feminine (that is, nurturing, maternal, and passive) can be held as a masculine ideal in one group and can be banned for both sexes in another, then we no longer have a basis for saying that masculinity and femininity are biologically based. Although Mead's work has been criticized in recent years for its subjectivity, it nevertheless demonstrates the enormous variability in gender roles across cultures.

More recently, we saw radically different views of masculinity and femininity during the 1999 Women's World Cup Soccer Championships. Throughout the championship matches, the U.S. Women's Soccer Team attracted spectacular crowds in the stadium and an enormous amount of media attention. The U.S. women were talented, quick, disciplined, and tough, both mentally and physically. Players such as Mia Hamm and Brandi Chastain were the idols of tens of thousands of young girls and women who aspired to become world-class athletes. And throughout all of the hype and excitement of winning the World Cup, there were few, if any, comments about how these women were compromising their femininity. Their success on the soccer field, in other words, in no way diminished them as women in the eyes of the nation. By way of contrast, the women on Brazil's soccer team (where men's soccer is revered) were viewed by their own countrymen more with suspicion than with adoration. In Brazil, soccer, defined as a masculine sport, is associated with physical confrontation, dominance, conflict, and control. Women, on the other hand, are viewed as delicate objects and consequently are seen as inappropriate participants in high-contact sports. The general Brazilian public assumes that any woman who plays a highly competitive sport such as soccer has compromised her femininity. How these two female soccer teams are seen in their own countries illustrates the very significant role that culture plays in defining masculinity and femininity.

Cross-cultural studies further complicate our understanding of gender. In mainstream U.S. culture, only two genders, male and female, are recognized, leaving no room for other gender alternatives such as transgender or androgynous individuals. Westerners, uncomfortable with these ambiguous gender identities, tend to explain them away by categorizing them as pathological, illegitimate, and perhaps even criminal. However, some cultures not only accommodate the ambiguities of these gender alternatives but see them as legitimate or, in some cases, as powerful. Third gender individuals, or transgenders, are well established in the Native American literature, particularly in the Plains area between the Great Lakes and California. According to Callender and Kochems (1983), at least 113 Native American groups provided a third gender as a legitimate social alternative. Also known as Two-Spirits, this phenomenon refers to both females and males who adopt some of the roles and traits of the opposite gender. To illustrate, the Lakota of the northern plains region had transgendered men called *winkte,* who possessed both masculine and feminine spirits; the Zuni of the southwestern part of the United States recognized as fully legitimate members of society a third gender that they called *We'wha;* and the Cheyenne have a similar transgender category called *hemanah* (literally meaning "half-woman, half-man"), who often accompanied war expeditions in ceremonial roles as noncombatants. In all of these cases, people became transgendered either through spiritual calling, parental selection, or individual inclination.

This Hijra man, who presents himself as being "like a woman," is an excellent example of the socially constructed basis for sexuality.

One stunning example is the male/female Hijra role found in Hindu India. The notion of a combined male/female role is a major theme in Hindu art, religion, and mythology. For example, androgynous people and impersonators of the opposite sex are found widely in Hindu mythology among both humans and their deities. These same themes are played out in parts of contemporary India. For example, according to Serena Nanda (1990: 20–21):

> In Tamil Nadu, in South India, an important festival takes place in which hijras, identifying with Krishna, become wives, and then widows, of the male deity Koothandavar.... For this festival, men who have made vows to Koothandavar dress as women and go through a marriage ceremony with him. The priest performs the marriage, tying on the traditional wedding necklace. After one day, the deity is carried to a burial ground. There, all of those who have "married" him remove their wedding necklaces, cry and beat their breasts, and remove the flowers from their hair, as a widow does in mourning for her husband. Hijras participate by the thousands in this festival, coming from all over India. They dress in their best clothes and jewelry and ritually reaffirm their identification with Krishna, who changes his form from male to female.

The Hijra of Hindu India are significant because they provide an example of a society that tolerates a wider definition of gender than is found in our own society. The Hijra, who undergo an emasculation rite, present themselves as being "like women," or female impersonators. In fact, this "emasculation rite," involving voluntary castration, indicates the high level of commitment to this special gender category. They do not function sexually as men, claim to have no sexual feelings for women, dress in women's clothing, adopt women's hairstyles, and even walk and carry themselves as women do. Clearly, Hijra are neither male nor female in the conventional sense of the term. But rather than being viewed as social deviants who should be discouraged, the Hijra are seen as a special, even sacred, gender group.

HUMAN SEXUALITY

Even though cultural anthropology has the reputation of concerning itself with documenting the exotic sexual practices of non-Western people, in actual fact the discipline of anthropology has not been interested in *human sexuality* until quite recently. Indeed, the subject of human sexuality was not formally recognized until 1961, when the AAA held a plenary session on the topic at its national meetings. To be certain, a number of anthropologists had documented exotic sexual practices, usually as part of general ethnographies, but before the 1960s there had been relatively little research on comparative human sexuality. There are several important reasons for the lack of solid anthropological data on human sexuality. First, because sexual activity in all societies is a private matter, it remains off-limits to anthropological observation. Second, when anthropologists in recent decades have interviewed people about sexuality, they have routinely confined their questions to matters of legitimate sexual partners, frequency of sexual intercourse, or acceptance of premarital sexual activity. Conspicuously absent from anthropological inquiries have been questions about the feelings or emotions attached to sexual activity. Thus, because individual cultures influence the way people define, experience, and express their sexuality, anthropologists since the 1960s have produced only a partial view of human sexuality cross-culturally. And, third, until fairly recently, there has been a strong male bias in the study of human sexuality, with mostly male anthropologists asking questions of male informants.

Within the last four decades, however, anthropologists have become more interested in the theoretical aspects of human sexuality. Perhaps the most fundamental generalization that has emerged in recent decades is that human sexuality varies widely from culture to culture. In other words, we find enormous variations throughout the world in terms of sexual behaviors permitted or encouraged before marriage, outside marriage, and within marriage.

Although no society fails to regulate sexual conduct, some societies are permissive and others are more restrictive. Some cultures have very serious sanctions against premarital sex and others treat it much more casually. Among the more sexually restricted cultures were the traditional Cheyenne Indians of the American Plains, whose women were legendary for their chastity. When adolescent Cheyenne girls began to attract the attention of suitors, they were constantly chaperoned by aunts to ensure total abstinence from sexual behavior. The courting process was long and not particularly intense, often lasting five years before the couple could marry. Adolescent boys and girls had little or no contact, and young men were taught to suppress their sexual impulses, a Cheyenne value that they took with them into marriage. Premarital and extramarital sex were extremely rare among the Cheyenne, and when they occurred, they were met with powerful social sanctions (Hoebel 1960).

Another example of a society with limited sexual expression is the Dani of New Guinea. Whereas the Cheyenne were socialized to avoid intimate sexual displays from early childhood and deviants were punished, the Dani appear to be uninterested in sexual behavior. According to Karl Heider (1979), the Dani adhere to a five-year period of postpartum sexual abstinence. That is, husband and wife abstain from any sexual activity for five years after the birth of a child. Although all societies practice some form of abstinence after the birth of a child, usually it lasts for several weeks or several months; in some societies, however, it lasts until the child is weaned, which may take several years. Not only do the Dani practice these long periods of abstinence, but they appear to have no other sexual outlets such as *extramarital activity* or homosexuality. Nor do Dani adults seem to be bothered by these five-year abstinences. Although Dani sexual restraint does not derive from awesome sanctions designed to punish the deviant, Dani people seem to learn in subtle ways that low sexual expressiveness is normal. As hard as it may be for Westerners to believe, the Dani simply have a low *sex drive*.

At the other extreme from such groups as the Cheyenne and the Dani are societies in which people are expected to have a great deal of sexual experience before marriage. Among such Oceanian societies as the Trobriand Islanders, the Tikopia, and the Mangaians of Polynesia, premarital sex is not only permitted but encouraged; indeed, it is viewed as a necessary

---

human sexuality The sexual practices of humans, usually varying from culture to culture.

extramarital activity Sexual activity outside marriage.
sex drive Desire for sexual activity.

preparatory step for marriage. Young boys and girls in these societies receive sex education at an early age and are given permission to experiment during their adolescent years. Premarital lovers are encouraged, and in some societies in the Pacific, trial marriages are actually permitted.

The Mangaians of central Polynesia provide an interesting case of a society that draws a dichotomy between the public and private domains. This society is characterized by near total segregation of men and women in their public lives. Around the age of four or five, boys and girls separate into gender-defined groups that will identify them for the rest of their lives. Brothers and sisters, husbands and wives, old men and old women, and female and male lovers have very little social contact in their everyday lives. Nevertheless, in their private lives, away from the public eye, men and women engage in sexual behavior that is both frequent and intense. Sexual intercourse is a principal concern for both Mangaian men and women, a concern that is backed up by a detailed knowledge of the technical/biological aspects of sex. According to ethnographer Donald Marshall (1971: 110), "The average Mangaian youth has fully as detailed a knowledge—perhaps more—of the gross anatomy of the penis and the vagina as does a European physician."

Like the Mangaians, the Ju/'hoansi of southwestern Africa believe that sexual activity is a natural, and indeed essential, part of life. Ju/'hoansi adolescents are permitted to engage in both *heterosexual* and *homosexual* play, and discreet extramarital sexual activity is condoned. Conversations between women about their sexual exploits are commonplace, as is sexually explicit joking between men and women. According to Marjorie Shostak (1983: 31), sexual activity is considered essential for good mental and physical health, for as one female informant put it, "If a girl grows up without learning to enjoy sex, her mind doesn't develop normally . . . and if a woman doesn't have sex her thoughts get ruined and she is always angry."

Sexual behavior in the United States and Canada tends toward the more permissive end of the continuum. Although accurate documentation of sexual activity in North America has been difficult to obtain, the most recent wide-scale studies (Laumann et al. 1994; Michael et al. 1994) reveal some interesting trends over recent decades. For example, young people are becoming sexually active at an earlier age; the percentage of sexually active young people is increasing; and among those who are sexually active, sex is becoming more frequent.

heterosexual A person who is sexually attracted to people of the opposite sex.
homosexual A person who is sexually attracted to people of the same sex.

Just as men and women in all societies learn their socially constructed gender roles, they also learn about male and female sexual expectations. We are socialized by our families, our peers, the schools we attend, the religious institutions to which we belong, the games we play, and the media to which we are exposed. In all of these ways, children learn scripts that either explicitly or implicitly teach them appropriate sexual behavior. Generally, men in North America are socialized to be more competitive, dominant, and physically aggressive than women. In sexual terms, this means that men are expected to be the initiators and high performers, while women are conditioned to be more passive and reticent. While this dichotomy may appear to be stereotyping male and female sexual expectations, it is generally valid. Men in the twenty-first century now have a technological aid to help them meet their societal performance expectations: erectile dysfunction drugs with names like Viagra, Cialis, and Levitra. Originally designed as a cure for impotence in middle-aged and elderly men, these performance-enhancing drugs are now being used recreationally by men of all ages, under the erroneous assumption that the pills will somehow transform good performance into superb performance (Kirby 2004).

The range of permissiveness and restrictiveness among societies in terms of heterosexual relationships also holds true for same sex relationships. Because there is very little cross-cultural data on female homosexuality this discussion of same sex relationships will be limited to male homosexuality. Because the existence of homosexuality (same sex relationships) is both denied and viewed with disgust in restrictive societies, our knowledge of homosexual orientation or sexual activity in such societies is minimal at best. In societies that are more permissive of same sex activity, the range of socially acceptable behavior is wide. But this very vari-

© Sherri Barber/NewSport/Corbis

Gentlemen, start your engines. Such performance enhancing drugs as Viagra—designed to treat impotence in older men—are being used today recreationally by men of all ages.

ability makes it difficult to determine how prevalent the actual practice of homosexuality is in different societies. In permissive societies, which are generally tolerant of same sex relationships, homosexuals tend to be fairly open about their behavior. In more restrictive societies, where homosexual activity is stigmatized and/or punished, most homosexuals do not manifest their sexual orientation openly. Yet, the incidence of homosexual activities in both restrictive and permissive societies could be the same; the only difference is in the extent to which it is openly discussed and practiced.

When examining variations in male homosexuality, it is useful to distinguish between *sexual preference* and *sexual activity*. It is possible to engage in homosexual activity while maintaining a heterosexual preference; and conversely, it is possible to live in a heterosexual marriage and have homosexual preferences. Patrick Gray and Linda Wolfe (1988) provide three culturally distinct patterns of male homosexuality: mainstream United States, the Azande of the Sudan, and the Sambia of New Guinea.

In the United States, the cultural definition of male homosexuality does not distinguish between preference and activity. Rather, it is assumed that a man who engages voluntarily in homosexual activity does so because of a dominant homosexual preference. At the same time, many North Americans define male homosexuals as less masculine than heterosexual men and as either sick or morally depraved. Data on homosexuality in the United States vary widely, depending on how the term is defined. According to Edward Laumann and colleagues (1994), 9.1 percent of males surveyed reported having participated in homosexual activity, but only 2.8 percent claimed a homosexual preference and identity. The normative view of homosexuality in the United States today remains generally negative.

Male homosexuality carries less of a stigma than previously because of two main factors. First, sexologists such as Alfred Kinsey and his colleagues have concluded that homosexuality is so widespread that it can hardly be considered an illness affecting only a small segment of the society. And, second, homosexual minorities themselves, by building strong communities with political influence, have legitimized their lifestyle preferences among an ever-increasing section of the public. In national opinion surveys conducted over the last three decades, the percentage of Americans saying that sexual relations between people of the same sex is "always or almost always wrong" dropped from a high of 75 percent in 1973 to 60 percent in 1998 (Macionis 2001: 230). That gays and straights are beginning to find common ground is perhaps best illustrated by the success of contemporary TV shows such as *Will and Grace* and *Queer Eye for the Straight Guy*, and by such Oscar-winning movies as *Boys Don't Cry* and *Brokeback Mountain*.

By contrast with the United States, the cultural definition of male homosexuality among the precolonial Azande of the Sudan made an explicit distinction between sexual preference and sexual activity. Owing to a shortage of marriageable women, young Azande men sought sexual satisfaction, for a limited time period, through homosexual activity. Unmarried men serving in organized military units often married boys between the ages of twelve and twenty. The husband paid bridewealth to the boy's father and was expected to have the same relationship with his in-laws that he would have had if he had married their daughter. These younger "male wives" performed domestic household chores for their husbands and also served as sexual partners. However, when the husband was old enough to take a female wife of his own, the marriage to the "boy-wife" ended, and he too was free to marry a woman.

Thus, here was an accepted institutional arrangement for men (albeit a minority of men) to engage in limited homosexual activity while retaining their basic heterosexual preferences. Men who took temporary boy-wives were not defined by the wider Azande society as feminine or morally despicable, because, after all, they were military men performing very definite masculine roles. Instead, in the words of Gray and Wolfe (1988), such male homosexual behavior "was a poor substitute for heterosexual behavior, an unfortunate necessity due to the shortage of women."

A third variation, practiced among the Sambia of New Guinea, defines male homosexuality as a necessary requirement before men can assume their masculine roles and heterosexual relationships. While Sambian women are viewed as sexually desirable, they are also seen as dangerous in that they can be polluting and can sap a man of his semen. Before a boy can develop into a fully functioning male adult, the Sambia believe, he must receive numerous ingestions of semen from older men, perhaps as often as every day for six to eight years during adolescence. This frequent ingestion of another man's semen is not done for the sake of satisfying an erotic homosexual preference. Rather, it is designed to protect Sambian adult men from sexual pollution and weakening at the hands of their future wives. If we were to view this form of Sambian homosexuality from the perspective of North American culture, we might conclude that years of homosexual behavior during adolescence would be likely to produce many lifelong homosexuals. Yet Gilbert Herdt (1981), who conducted the original research on the Sambia, argues that the overwhelming majority of Sambian adult males have a strong heterosexual preference, with perhaps fewer than 5 percent preferring homosexuality in later life.

GENDER ROLES

As mentioned in Chapter 8, all societies make some distinctions between what men are expected to do and what women are expected to do. In some societies

This baseball player engaged in child care in the locker room is just one example of changing gender roles in the United States.

Sometimes our culture can get us into trouble despite our best intentions. While conducting ethnographic fieldwork among the Kikuyu of Kenya in the 1970s, this author became involved in an embarrassing incident that he could not seem to prevent (Ferraro 2006: 93):

> Even before going to Kenya I had known through ethnographic readings that Kikuyu men routinely held hands with their close personal friends. After several months of living and working with Kikuyu, I was walking through a village in Kiambu District with a local headman who had become a key informant and a close personal acquaintance. As we walked side by side, my friend took my hand in his. Within less than thirty seconds my palm was perspiring all over his. Despite the fact that I knew cognitively that this was a perfectly legitimate Kikuyu gesture of friendship, my own cultural values (that is, that "real men" don't hold hands) were so ingrained that it was impossible for me not to communicate to my friend that I was very uncomfortable.

gender roles are rigidly defined, but in others the roles of men and women overlap considerably. Yet despite the universality (and some variation) of division of labor by gender, the cultures of the world are noticeably uniform in the way they divide tasks between women and men. To illustrate, in most cases men engage in warfare, trap small animals, work with hard substances such as wood and stone, clear land, build houses, and fish. Women, on the other hand, are more likely to tend crops, gather wild fruits and plants, prepare food, care for children, collect firewood, clean house, launder clothing, and carry water. In addition, a number of tasks are performed by both men and women. These include tending small domesticated animals, making crafts (pottery, baskets, and the like), milking animals, planting and harvesting crops, and collecting shellfish. (See Table 11.1)

Some of these gender-specific roles (such as hunting for men and child care for women) are very closely associated with one gender or the other. For example, Murdock's "Ethnographic Atlas" (1967) classifies hunting as an exclusively male activity in more than 99 percent of the societies listed; the remaining 1 percent are described as societies in which both males and females hunt, but "males do appreciably more than females." On the other side of the equation, child care is an overwhelmingly female activity, although in some cases men do make minor contributions. The fact that

activities such as hunting and child care are so thoroughly gender-specific requires some explanation.

A number of theories have been put forth to explain this very common division of labor by gender. One explanation is that because men have greater body mass and strength, they are better equipped to engage in physical activities such as hunting, warfare, and land clearing. To be certain, this explanation has a certain underlying logic, for men tend to be better equipped physically than women to lift heavy loads, run fast, and fight ferociously. Proponents of this theory would argue that men are more likely than women to have the traits needed to be an efficient hunter (strength, speed, and endurance). Like any theory, however, this biological theory does not provide a complete explanation.

There are some notable exceptions to the general rule that men engage in roles demanding maximum physical strength. To illustrate, in certain parts of East Africa, women routinely carry enormous loads of firewood on their backs for long distances. Not only is this a normative practice, but among some groups a woman's femininity is directly related to the size of the load she is able to carry. Also, among the foraging Agta of the Philippines, hunting is not exclusively a male activity; women hunt regularly. According to Frances Dahlberg (1981: 12):

> Hunting is not confined to the oldest daughters in families without sons, young widows, deserted wives, or unusually vigorous personalities.... Agta women do not hunt only in cooperation with men (as do Mbuti women in net hunting) nor do they hunt only in the absence of men (as do Chipewyan women)....

gender roles   Expected ways of behaving based on a society's definition of masculinity and femininity.

Table 11.1 Division of Labor by Gender (Worldwide Trends)

Generally Male Tasks

- Hunting large animals
- Fishing as a primary task
- Tending large animal herds
- Mining, smelting, and metalworking
- Conducting warfare
- Boat building
- Working wood and stone
- Clearing/preparing the land for crops
- Making musical instruments
- Making nets and ropes

Generally Male and Female Tasks

- Hunting small animals
- Fishing as a secondary task
- Tending small animals
- Planting and harvesting crops
- House building
- Making certain craft items
- Local market trading

Generally Female Tasks

- Childcare
- Collecting fuel and water
- Food preparation
- Gathering wild plants, fruits, and nuts
- Making clothes
- Household maintenance

The Agta do not restrict any type of food collecting to one sex. Hunters, both female and male, begin hunting when their stamina and ability make it worthwhile and cease when they lose strength.... Each hunter uses techniques that work for her or for him; hunting techniques are not sex typed.

Although these exceptions do not invalidate the general rule, some have argued (Burton, Brudner, and White 1977) that the division of labor by gender is more the result of constraints stemming from childbirth and infant care than it is from differences in strength.

This brings us to a second argument often used to explain this nearly universal type of gender division of labor: women do the things they do because those tasks are compatible with pregnancy, breastfeeding, and child care. Unlike certain male tasks, such as hunting and warfare, women's tasks can be accomplished without jeopardizing their own and their children's safety and

without having to stray too far from home. This theory suggests that pregnant women would be at a marked disadvantage in running after game; lactating mothers would need to interrupt their tracking/hunting activities several times a day to nurse their children; and, given the danger involved in hunting, small children accompanying their mothers would not be safe. Judith Brown (1970) was the first to hypothesize that women tend to concentrate on tasks that are compatible with child care (that is, nursing and looking after children). Such tasks tend to be monotonous and require little concentration, can be interrupted without reducing efficient performance, pose no threat to the safety of small children, and can be performed in or near the home.

Although this theory is sensible and no doubt can account for some of the division of labor by gender, it also doesn't tell the whole story. A number of ethnographic studies from around the world since the late 1970s have seriously questioned this connection between female reproductive/child care roles and the division of labor. To illustrate, some researchers (Burton, Brudner, and White 1977) have argued that although pregnancy and breastfeeding do limit work roles for women, a woman's economic (work) obligations sometimes take precedence over child care considerations. In other words, a woman may make alternative child care arrangements in order to engage in some type of work outside the home. This can be seen in parts of the preindustrial world, where women leave their small children in the care of older siblings or other adults, and in the United States, where working mothers leave their infants at professional day care centers. In addition, others (Raphael and Davis 1985) have shown how women purposefully choose supplemental feeding rather than breastfeeding for their children because of work considerations.

As was mentioned in Chapter 9, the traditional American family of the breadwinning father and the stay-at-home mother has long since disappeared. Today, the stay-at-home father is becoming a less unusual phenomenon. It is difficult to determine with any degree of precision how many fathers are stay-at-home dads because some fathers work from home, have part-time jobs, or are between jobs. Nevertheless, it has been estimated that in 2000 there were more than 2 million stay-at-home dads in the United States, a 400-percent increase in the previous twenty years. According to the 2000 census, 20 percent of preschool children from married-couple households were cared for by their fathers, up from 17 percent just three years earlier. A leading indicator of this growing trend is the proliferation of websites devoted to stay-at-home fathers. Sites such as Dadstayshome.com, Fatherville.com, and Slowlane.com provide chat room opportunities and supportive information on topics such as time management, how to talk with children to facilitate learning, part-time work that can be performed from home, and effective parenting strategies for stay-at-home dads.

Traditional gender roles are sometimes reversed in 21st century America, as with this female fire fighter above and the stay at home dad below.

In the United States, it is estimated that approximately 20 percent of all preschool children are cared for primarily by their fathers.

GENDER AND LANGUAGE

A degree of *sexual asymmetry* is often evident in the forms of language spoken by men and women. Sometimes the linguistic distinctions between men and women are reflected in vocabulary. Some languages have pairs of words (called doublets) that carry the same meaning, but men use one word and women the other. To illustrate, among the Island Carib of the West Indies, men use the word *kunobu* to mean "rain" and women use the word *kuyu* (Hickerson 1980). Among the Merina in Madagascar (Keenan 1974), for example, speech patterns associated with men, which are indirect, allusive, and formal, are considered respectable and sophisticated. Merina women, on the other hand, are thought to be ignorant of the subtleties of sophisticated speech and, consequently, are considered to be inferior. Moreover, submissiveness and lack of social power can be observed in female speech patterns in the United States in terms of intonation, loudness, and assertiveness. For example, women in the United States tend to have a less forceful style of speaking than men in that they use a greater number of qualifiers (such as "It may be just my opinion, but . . ."). Also, many U.S. women soften the impact of a declarative statement by ending it with a question, such as "Wouldn't you agree?" (Kramer 1974).

These linguistic gender differences in the United States (called *genderlects*) have been the subject of a best-selling book by Deborah Tannen (1990), who claims that women and men in the United States have different linguistic styles and communication goals. Women engage in "rapport-talk" and men use "report-talk." Rapport-talk, characteristic of women, seeks to establish connections, negotiate relationships, and reach agreement. Women's speech tends to be cooperative, with women acknowledging one another's contributions and engaging in more active listening. Report-talk, in contrast, is a male mode of discourse that is more competitive. Men's conversations are less social, more individualistic, and aimed at controlling the flow of talk. In cross-sex conversations, men tend to dominate women by talking more, interrupting women more often, and focusing the conversation on topics of their own choice.

Julia Wood (1994) has suggested that these basic speech differences between men and women in the United States result, at least in part, from the childhood games that girls and boys play. Girls tend to play games that are cooperative, collaborative, and inclusive. There is little incentive to outdo others, and there is a strong inclination to be sensitive to others' feelings. Boys, on the other hand, are expected to assert themselves,

sexual asymmetry   The universal tendency of women to be in a subordinate position in their social relationships with men.
genderlects   Linguistic gender differences.

In what ways do the communication styles of men and women differ in the United States?

establish their leadership, and win. By focusing on outcomes, boys' games encourage participants to solve problems, achieve goals (such as scoring a touchdown), and generally "make things happen." Because of these differences in childhood games and socialization, Wood finds that women talk for the purpose of building and supplementing rapport with others, but men use talk to assert themselves; women use self-disclosure as a way of learning about others, but men tend to avoid self-disclosure; women's discourse strives for equality in social relationships, but men's discourse attempts to establish status and power; women often match experiences with others for the sake of showing understanding and empathy ("I know how you feel"), but men match experiences for the sake of gaining attention ("I can top that"); and finally, women show their support by expressing their understanding, but men show their support by giving advice or wanting to solve a problem.

These differences in linguistic style between men and women have important implications for everyday interactions in the workplace. As Deborah Tannen points out (1994: 136), a woman manager, relying on her cooperative/collaborative communication style, does not want to appear heavy-handed in her dealings with her co-workers. She, therefore, solicits feedback by asking her subordinates many questions before making decisions. But, her boss views this management style as tentative, indecisive, and ineffectual. As a result, the female manager, when being considered for a promotion, is likely to be passed over in favor of a more assertive, authoritarian, competitive male.

Whereas Deborah Tannen and Julia Wood have focused on the spoken word, Shlomo Argamon, a computer scientist at the Illinois Institute of Technology, has developed WINNOW, a computer program designed to determine the gender of the authors of written works. He found that women writers have a more interactive style than men, wanting to create a relationship between themselves and the reader. As a result, women tend to use such relationship-oriented words as "for" and "with" more frequently than men. Men, by way of contrast, tend to use more numbers, adjectives, and determiners (words like *this* or *that*). Using his computer program to analyze 566 books and articles to determine the gender of the authors, Argamon claims to have predicted the gender of the author correctly 80 percent of the time (Boyd 2003).

GENDER STRATIFICATION

It is generally recognized that the status of women varies from one society to another. In some societies, women are in a clearly subordinate position in their social relationships with men. In other societies, the relationships between the genders are more egalitarian. Social scientists would generally agree that *gender stratification* exists to some degree in all societies, but there is considerably less agreement as to how one measures the status of men and women because gender stratification involves a number of different components that may vary independently of one another. It is now recognized that there are a number of important indicators of women's status, including economic, power, prestige, autonomy, and ideological dimensions. To illustrate, when considering the relative status of women in any society, one needs to look at the roles played by women, the value society places on their contributions, their legal rights, whether and to what degree they are expected to be deferential to men, their economic independence, and the degree to which they decide on the major events of their lives such as marriage, profession, and childbearing.

The multidimensional nature of women's status was illustrated by Martin Whyte's (1978) comparative study of ninety-three societies, which identified fifty-two status dimensions found in the anthropological literature. Interestingly, all of these status dimensions varied independently of one another. In other words, no single cluster or complex of variables of women's status varied consistently from culture to culture. To illustrate, women in certain western African societies, because of their influence in the marketplace, may have an appreciable amount of economic independence, but they nevertheless remain subordinate to their husbands in most other respects. Thus, determining the status of women is difficult because it is not a unidimensional phenomenon.

Another difficulty in ascertaining the status of women is that it is not static. In some societies, the relative status of men and women fluctuates along with political changes. For example, during the reign of the shah of Iran, women's roles kept pace with moderni-

gender stratification A division in society where all members are hierarchically ranked according to gender.

Cary Wolinsky/Stock Boston

In some societies women are excluded from certain areas that are "for men only," such as this all-men's bar in Perth, Australia.

zation. During the 1960s and 1970s, increasingly large numbers of Iranian women abandoned the rules of *purdah* (domestic seclusion and veiling), obtained higher education, and gained entry to traditionally male professional roles. With the return of religious and cultural fundamentalism under the Ayatollah Khomeini, however, women returned to the veil and resumed more traditional female roles. Moreover, in a less dramatic fashion, the relative status of women in the United States has undergone some significant changes over the last several generations in terms of job opportunities and legal rights.

Yet another complicating factor in determining the status of women is the relative age of women in any given society. The Tiwi of northern Australia are an interesting case in point. In this polygynous society, the accumulation of wives was a man's single most important measure of power and prestige. As C. Hart, Arnold Pilling, and Jane Goodale (1988: 58) describe it, daughters, sisters, and mothers were for men "the main currency of the influence struggle, the main 'trumps' in the endless bridge game." Men would give their own daughters to other men in exchange for their daughters as future brides. An influential man could gain control of his sisters and his widowed mother as "chips" in his never-ending quest for additional wives for himself. Some observers have seen women in Tiwi society as nothing more than chattel—pieces of property with few rights of their own. This was generally the case with younger women because daughters were subordinate to the wishes of their fathers, and wives were controlled

by their husbands. But as widowed mothers or sisters, they could not be manipulated, or even coerced, by their sons or brothers. A son who wished to give his widowed mother or sister to a political ally needed her full consent and collaboration. Hart, Pilling, and Goodale (1988: 59) go on to say:

> Young girls thus had no bargaining power but young widows had a good deal.... Thus, for women, as for men, age and political skill were the crucial factors in determining their position.... Not as independent operators, but as behind-the-scenes allies of their sons and brothers, Tiwi mothers and sisters enjoyed much more essential freedom in their own careers as often remarried widows than would appear at first sight in a culture that ostensibly treated all women as currency in the political careers of the men.

purdah   Rules involving domestic seclusion and veiling for women in small towns in Iraq, Iran, and Syria.

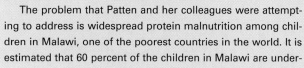

APPLIED PERSPECTIVE

Improving Child Nutrition in Malawi

The United States Agency for International Development (USAID) is that branch of the U.S. federal government responsible for administering nonmilitary foreign assistance for developing countries. Rather than giving cash to other countries to do with as they please, U.S. foreign aid programs provide technical expertise geared toward programs of sustainable development in areas such as education, agriculture, family planning, and health services. In recent decades, USAID has relied on applied anthropologists to provide insights into the cultures of the people to whom these programs are directed. Sonia Patten (2003) provides an excellent example in the role she played as a medical anthropologist on a USAID-funded team involved in a nutritional program for children in Malawi.

nourished and that one out of every four children will die before age five. The most vulnerable group is the toddlers, who go from breast milk to a nutritionally inadequate substitute of gruel made of water and corn flour. Even if children survive on such a protein-deficient diet, they are susceptible to a number of diseases and often do not develop into robust adults. The challenge for Patten's group was to craft a pilot program that would address this problem of child malnutrition. They decided upon a goat project that would give milk-producing goats to mothers with children under the age of five.

Although many families keep goats, they are non-milk-producing goats that are eaten for meat or sold as a source of needed cash. After developing a hearty breed of milk-producing goat, Patten and

The problem that Patten and her colleagues were attempting to address is widespread protein malnutrition among children in Malawi, one of the poorest countries in the world. It is estimated that 60 percent of the children in Malawi are under-

her colleagues were ready to introduce the program to local women. Patten's contribution to the group (composed of nutritionists, health specialists, and animal husbandry experts) was to provide the cultural baseline information needed to ensure

---

Hindu society in northern India is among the most highly stratified along gender lines of any society in the world. India as a whole, and particularly northern India, has enormously skewed sex ratios, which are due to widespread neglect of girls in terms of health care and nutrition. In this part of the world, sons are more highly valued than daughters. Sex ratios have become even more unbalanced in recent years with the widespread use of ultrasound equipment to determine sex prenatally. The termination of female fetuses has increased so rapidly in the last several decades that the female population of some rural villages has been reduced by nearly 25 percent. And even for those who make it to adulthood, many females face impoverished widowhood or dowry death.

In contrast to the marked status distinctions between the genders found in traditional India, the relationship between men and women in some foraging societies tends to be more egalitarian. For example, Colin Turnbull (1981) reports a good deal of mutual respect between the sexes among the Mbuti Pygmies of Central Africa, particularly among elders of the group. Adult Mbuti call their parents "tata" (elders) without distinguishing by gender. Mbuti men and women see themselves as equals in all respects but one: women have

the enormously important power of giving birth. This equation of womanhood with motherhood, which affords Mbuti women high status, is played out through a number of rituals in their everyday lives. Even their natural habitat (the forest), which is considered to be both sacred and supreme, is often called "mother." Moreover, Mbuti women choose their own mates, determine their own daily activities, and exercise considerable power as social critics.

In such food-collecting societies, the roles performed by men and women are very different, but their relative statuses are not. Such sexual equality is not surprising, however, for marked status differences of any type are rare in foraging societies. Because constant migration inhibits the accumulation of property, foraging societies tend to have very little private property, and sharp status distinctions are minimized for both men and women.

Although it is possible to identify societies where gender distinctions are kept to a minimum, the overwhelming evidence suggests that in many critical areas of life women are subordinate to men. From time to time women in various cultures have wielded considerable power, but there is no ethnographic or archaeological evidence to support the notion that matriarchy—

that local people participated in the project. She collected information on their daily activities, the traditional patterns of controlling livestock, dietary patterns, and gender roles, among other topics. Most of the local people were from the Chewa ethnic group, a matrilineal group that practiced matrilocal residence. As we saw in Chapter 10, it is men, not women, who are the chiefs and control property in matrilineal societies. Thus, among the Chewa, men routinely decided whether a goat would be slaughtered or sold. When it was proposed that women would be given control over the new milk goats, the Chewa men initially objected on the grounds that men had always controlled the use of livestock. Because she had studied gender relations between Chewa men and women, medical anthropologist Patten was able to predict the male objections and deal with them directly *before* the goats were distributed to families. Team members were able to convince the men that this project was designed to help their children eat better and live longer, not to increase the number of goats men were free to sell or slaughter. Eventually, the men agreed to support the project, goats were distributed to mothers of small children, and the project began.

Once under way, the team took periodic height and weight measurements of the children participating in the milk-goat project. The results showed that even small amounts of milk resulted in normal growth for children. The program has been so successful that it has been expanded to other parts of the country. Although anthropologist Patten was not an expert in either children's health or animal husbandry, she nevertheless played an important role in the success of this project. By understanding the everyday cultural patterns of the Chewa, and particularly the roles played by men and women, she was able to help the multidisciplinary team overcome potential problems and ensure that the program would reach those it was intended to help.

Questions for Further Thought

1. How would you describe the role Sonia Patten played in this interdisciplinary health team?
2. Why were Patten and her team so insistent on ensuring that the milk-goats remained in the hands of the mothers of small children?
3. What other types of projects might USAID fund in the country of Malawi?

rule or domination of women over men—exists anywhere in the world or, for that matter, has ever existed (Bamberger 1974).

Nevertheless, it is possible to find societies that the people themselves describe as matriarchies—where women exert considerable power without dominating males (or ruling them in a political sense) to the same degree that men dominate women in many patriarchal societies. For example, among the Minangkabau of West Sumatra, Indonesia, females and males interact more like partners than competitors. The foundation of gender relationships among the Minangkabau is based on their central philosophical notion of *adat:* people, animals, and wildlife should be nurtured so that society will be strong. This emphasis on nurturing tends to favor cooperation and the maternal in everyday life rather than competition and male dominance. According to Peggy Sanday (2004), women in Minangkabau society on ceremonial occasions are addressed by the term reserved for the mythical queen; and symbolically, the maternal is viewed as the spiritual center and the original foundation of the society. Moreover, women exert considerable power in everyday social life. Women control land inheritance, husbands reside in their wives' residences, and in the event of divorce, the husband gathers his belongings and leaves. Yet, despite the central role of women within society, this is hardly an example of matriarchy. Rather, neither men nor women rule in Minangkabau society because decision making is based on consensus and cooperation.

Despite such examples as the Minangkabau, what we find is that women, to one degree or another, tend to be excluded from the major centers of economic and

Among the Minangkabau of west Sumatra, decision making among wives and husbands is relatively equal and cooperative.

political power and control in most societies. Moreover, the roles women play as mothers and wives invariably carry with them fewer prerogatives and lower prestige than male roles. Although to speak of *universal male dominance* would be an oversimplification, the evidence does suggest a general gender asymmetry among most cultures of the world in the allocation of power and influence.

This gender asymmetry is so pervasive that some anthropologists have attributed it to biological differences between men and women, such as greater size, strength, and physical aggressiveness. Ernestine Friedl (1978), however, has argued that men tend to dominate not because of biological traits, but rather because they control the distribution of scarce resources. Irrespective of who may produce the goods, Friedl contends that the person *controlling* the allocation of resources (which men do most of the time) possesses the currency needed

> *universal male dominance*   The notion that men are dominant over women in all societies.

to create and maintain powerful political alliances and obligations. By using examples from a number of societies, Friedl demonstrates how men dominate in those societies in which women have little or no control over the allocation of scarce resources and, conversely, how women with some control of resources have achieved greater equality.

Even a cursory examination of statistics on the status of women reveals what one social scientist (Smith 1995: 237) has called the "apartheid of gender." This gender inequality, however, is not a unified phenomenon, for it takes many different forms in different societies. We will discuss some of the varieties of these gender disparities in the following pages.

Education

Women throughout the world have made progress toward equal educational enrollment, but huge gaps remain. Two-thirds of all the illiterate people in the world today are women. More than 70 percent of women age twenty-five and older in sub-Saharan Africa, southern Asia, and western Asia are illiterate. There are more illiterate women than men in every major region of the world. Even though world literacy has been on the rise in recent decades, it has risen faster for men than for women, thereby widening the gender gap.

Sometimes gender bias in the field of education can be very subtle. Several recent studies (Mincer 1994; Smith 2000) have suggested that girls in the United States are shortchanged in the classroom because they are given less attention by their teachers than boys receive. This gender bias undermines the girls' confidence and self-esteem and often discourages them from taking additional math and science courses. Because of its subtle nature, this form of gender bias does not receive a lot of attention. Nevertheless, it is important to note that girls on average are ahead of boys academically when they enter elementary school, but they have fallen behind boys in nearly every subject area by the time they graduate from high school. These studies concluded that this slippage is due primarily to the loss of female self-esteem caused by systematic gender bias in the schools.

Employment

The percentage of women in the world's workforce has increased in the last several decades, due largely to economic necessity. However, the world's women, particularly in developing countries, are concentrated in the lowest-paid occupations and receive lower pay and fewer benefits than men. Women are also more likely to work part-time, have less seniority, and occupy positions with little or no upward mobility. Moreover, an increasing number of women in Asia, Africa, and South America are being pushed into the informal economy: small-scale, self-employed trading of goods and services. Some of the activities associated with the informal econ-

This boy from Gambia (west Africa) is much more likely to attend school than his younger sister.

omy—such as street vending, beer brewing, and prostitution—are outside the law. All of this has led to the impoverishment of women worldwide, a phenomenon known as the *feminization of poverty*. It is now estimated that between 60 and 70 percent of all people living in poverty throughout the world are women, and the inequities are increasing. To illustrate, the number of women living in poverty increased disproportionately to the number of men during the previous decade. Moreover, the increasing trends in the feminization of poverty were particularly acute in poorer, developing countries and for minority women living in wealthier, more industrialized nations.

Reproductive Health

A third area in which the world's women have not fared well is reproductive health. Although most women in the developed world control the number of children they have, in some parts of the world there is pressure to have large numbers of children, and these women on average have four to five children. In certain countries with particularly high birthrates (such as Malawi,

feminization of poverty   Refers to the high proportion of female-headed families below the poverty line, which may result from the high proportion of women found in occupations with low prestige and income.

Yemen, Ethiopia, and the Ivory Coast), the average woman has more than seven children in her lifetime (MacFarquhar 1994). Pregnant women in developing countries face a number of risks, including malnutrition and a lack of trained medical personnel to deal with high-risk pregnancies. In fact, it has been estimated that pregnant women in developing countries are eighty to six hundred times more likely to die of complications of pregnancy and birthing than are women in the industrialized world.

A related health issue for women is the extent to which gender inequalities make them more vulnerable to HIV/AIDS. Women's economic dependence upon men, as well as the threat of violence against wives and girlfriends, makes them less able to protect themselves. In many parts of the world, it is unacceptable for a woman to say no to unwanted or unprotected sex. A study conducted in Zambia (Urdang 2001) revealed how vulnerable wives can be to HIV/AIDS and other diseases sexually transmitted by their husbands. Fewer than one in every four women, according to the study, believed that they could refuse to have sex with their husbands, even if the husband had been unfaithful and was infected. Similarly, anthropologist Richard Lee (2007: 159) attributed the low incidence of HIV/AIDS among the Ju/'hoansi of Namibia and Botswana to, among other factors, the traditional high status of women and their relative gender equality. Because the typical Ju/'hoansi wife tends to be relatively empowered, she is more likely to insist that her husband wear a condom, and should he refuse, to not have sex with him. In addition, social customs are so restrictive in some countries that often young women are denied access to information about the dangers of HIV/AIDS and how best to protect themselves. It is little wonder that, in societies where women have relatively little control over their own sexual behavior, the incidence of this deadly disease is much higher for young women than it is for their male counterparts.

Finance

The women of the world are also at a disadvantage in terms of obtaining credit from financial institutions. According to World Bank estimates, 90 percent of the more than half billion women living in poverty around the world do not have access to credit. Small loans of $100 would go a long way in helping women to start their own small businesses, which could substantially improve their economic conditions. But both private lenders and aid organizations, by and large, have not made even this level of credit available to women. A notable exception has been the Grameen Bank in Bangladesh, the world's best-known microlender, which for three decades has made small business loans to the poorest segments of Bangladesh society. By 1995 the Grameen Bank had made more than 2 million loans, many of them to women in subsistence farming and craft occupations,

APPLIED PERSPECTIVE

Using Family Planning Clinics in Ecuador

For the past several decades, many development experts have identified high birthrates as the major obstacle to economic development. No matter how successful programs in health, education, and agriculture may be, any gains will be offset if the society is experiencing high annual population growth. Consequently, many international development organizations have given top priority to programs designed to slow population growth through family planning.

A common method of evaluating the success of family planning programs is to measure the extent to which people actually use them. A number of significant factors may affect whether women initially attend (or return to) family planning clinics, including the women's attitudes toward contraception, the quality of the interaction with staff members, and the length of time they must wait to see a doctor. Susan Scrimshaw (1976), an applied anthropologist studying family planning clinics in Ecuador, identified another significant factor—women's modesty—that had important implications for how women felt about using family planning clinics.

Using traditional anthropological methods, Scrimshaw collected data on sixty-five families living in Guayaquil, Ecuador, a tropical port city of approximately 1 million people. Scrimshaw found that small girls in Guayaquil—as in South America generally—are taught the virtues of modesty at a very early age.

Even though boys are often seen without pants until the age of four or five, little girls always have their genitals covered. Because girls usually reach puberty without any prior knowledge of menstruation, their first menstruation is both frightening and embarrassing. In general, Scrimshaw found that girls and women in Guayaquil do not have very positive attitudes about their bodies, their sexuality, or natural bodily processes such as menstruation, all of which are associated with the word *verguenza* (shame or embarrassment). Given this strong sense of modesty about their bodies, their sexuality, and reproduction, it is not surprising that these Ecuadorian women would feel uncomfortable even talking about contraceptives, let alone submitting to gynecological examinations.

Scrimshaw also conducted a survey on the use of family planning clinics among 2,936 women. She found that although 74 percent of the respondents wanted more information on birth control methods, only 20 percent of them had actually taken the initiative to obtain the information, and less than 5 percent had ever been to a family planning clinic. When the women who had been to a clinic were asked why they had never returned, nearly half (48 percent) said they had been influenced by *verguenza*.

Information gained through participant-observation at a number of these family planning clinics helped explain why

who used the modest loans to turn their operations into viable businesses. Extending this type of credit to impoverished women has proved to be an excellent investment for several reasons. First, World Bank data show that women repay their loans in 98 percent of the cases, as compared with 60 to 70 percent for men. And second, the World Bank has found that credit given to women has a greater impact on the welfare of the family because women tend to spend their money on better nutrition and education for their children—areas given lower priority by male borrowers (Kaslow 1995).

Thus, it is clear that women throughout the world continue to carry a heavy burden of inequality. Although they make up half of the world's population, women do approximately two-thirds of the work, earn one-tenth of the world's income, and own less than 1 percent of the world's property. Even in the wake of some political and economic advances, women in many parts of the world are falling further behind their male counter-

parts Moreover, gender inequality does not necessarily depend on how wealthy a country is. Vicki Bakhshi (1999) notes that some developing countries are doing much better at narrowing the gender gap than are some wealthy, industrialized nations. In terms of women's participation in politics and jobs, for example, Costa Rica is doing considerably better than Italy or France, Poland outranks Japan, and Zimbabwe is ahead of Greece.

The United Nations has generated an indicator of progress toward equality for women called the Gender Empowerment Measure (GEM), which captures gender inequality in three main areas: (1) political participation and decision-making power (i.e., parliamentary seats); (2) economic participation and decision-making power; and (3) power over economic resources (i.e., income). A score of 1.0 indicates equality between men and women. As is apparent from from Table 11.2, the Scandinavian countries of Norway, Iceland, Sweden, and Denmark

women were so reluctant to return to the clinics. Screening questions were asked by an intake worker, usually within earshot of other patients. Doctors gave patients very little explanatory information while requesting a large amount of information from them, much of which was never used. The clinics provided no private place for women to undress and did not supply the women with gowns, nor were the women properly draped during their physical exams. Even for women in the United States, who are usually afforded these courtesies, gynecological exams are often uncomfortable and embarrassing. Submitting to a physical exam under conditions of minimal privacy, however, was even more difficult for these Ecuadorian women because of their strong cultural emphasis on feminine modesty.

On the basis of these findings on women's modesty, Scrimshaw (1976: 177–78) made the following practical recommendations for maximizing the utility of family planning clinics in Guayaquil:

1. *Discreetness:* Women in clinics should not be interviewed within the hearing of anyone but the parties directly involved. Questions should be kept to a minimum.
2. *Privacy:* Wherever possible, a woman should be given privacy to undress. The examining room should ensure security and privacy.
3. *Awareness of modesty:* A drape should be provided for a woman's legs.
4. *Talk during the examination:* Talking during the examination both between the doctor and other staff and between the

doctor and the patient should be confined to the examination. Trivial talk should be avoided.
5. *Frequency of visits to the clinic and examination:* Many clinics require monthly visits for examinations and supplies. In most cases, such frequent examinations are unnecessary, and supplies can be picked up every three months.
6. *Male versus female physicians:* All women questioned said they preferred female physicians. Thus, women doctors need to be actively recruited.

These types of recommendations can be useful to those in charge of administering family planning clinics in Ecuador. None of the proposed changes alone will make or break a family planning program, but this case study does point to the need for the clinical staff to understand and acknowledge the modesty of Ecuadorian women and the role that cultural anthropologists can play in bringing this important social value to the attention of the clinical staff.

Questions for Further Thought

1. In what ways can applied anthropologists contribute to family planning programs in developing nations?
2. How does female modesty in Guayaquil shape attitudes about family planning clinics and gynecological examinations?
3. Do you think that the gender of the researcher studying family planning clinics affects the type of information that can be gathered?

score the highest on the GEM, while such countries as Bangladesh, Egypt, and Sri Lanka have the lowest scores.

GENDER IDEOLOGY

This generalized male dominance is buttressed by a *gender ideology*, which we can define as a system of thoughts and values that legitimizes gender roles, statuses, and customary behavior. In religion, women are often excluded categorically by gender ideology from holding major leadership roles or participating in certain types of ceremonies. In some African societies, men's physical well-being is thought to be jeopardized by contact with a woman's menstrual discharge. In

> **gender ideology** A system of thoughts and values that legitimizes sex roles, statuses, and customary behavior.

Bangladesh and in some African cultures, men are associated with the right side and women are associated with the left side, a dichotomy that also denotes purity–pollution, good–bad, and authority–submission. Even in the area of food production, foods procured by men (such as meat from the hunt) are often more highly valued than those procured by women (such as roots or berries), even though the latter foods are the major source of nutrition. In many parts of the world, women are treated legally as minors in that they are unable to obtain a driver's license, bank account, passport, or even a birth control device without the consent of their husbands or fathers. One particularly effective ideological mechanism for keeping women in a subordinate position is found among the Luo of western Kenya, whose creation myth (no doubt originated and perpetuated by men) blames women for committing the original sins that resulted in the curse of work for men.

Table 11.2	Countries with the Highest and Lowest Scores on the Gender Empowerment Measure	
	Norway	0.84
	Iceland	0.83
	Sweden	0.82
	Denmark	0.82
	Finland	0.80
	Netherlands	0.78
	Canada	0.78
	United States	0.76
	Sri Lanka	0.27
	Egypt	0.26
	Bangladesh	0.22

SOURCE: United Nations, 2002.

Although they assume a subordinate position in their family lives, some African women are able to maintain considerable powers, authority, and autonomy by virtue of their economic activities, as with this vegetable vendor in Ethiopia.

In many parts of the world, the devaluation of women starts early in life. The birth of a son is often cause for rejoicing, but the birth of a daughter is met with silence. In a number of patrilineal societies, boys are more highly valued because they will contribute to the longevity of the lineage, whereas their sisters will produce children for their husband's lineage. Because parents often assume that sons will provide for them in their old age, they are much more likely to give sons preferential treatment for education and careers. Because girls are not likely to support their parents financially later in life, they are more often denied access to schooling, medical facilities, and nutritious diets. There are some rare societies that prefer female children (found in East Africa, Pakistan, and New Guinea), but the dominant trend is toward a preference for male children.

These are just some of the values that legitimize the subordination of women, as reported in the ethnographic literature. Nevertheless, we need to ask whether women in societies with such powerful gender ideologies actually buy into the ideologies. In other words, do they accept these ideological justifications for their subjugation? Because so many ethnographic reports were based on male testimony given to male ethnographers, it is likely that women, if their opinions were solicited, would describe themselves quite differently from the way they are portrayed in the ethnographic literature. Within the last several decades, a number of studies (Strathern 1984; Kirsch 1985; Errington and Gewertz 1987) have been written from the perspective of female informants; they demonstrate how distorted our interpretations of gender ideology have been.

An example of this distortion is provided by Thomas Buckley (1993), who has shown how our own Western view of menstruation and pollution has led to a very one-sided view of the culture of the Yurok Indians of California. Early ethnographic accounts of the Yurok suggested that menstruating women were required to seclude themselves as a way of protecting men from the pollution of menstrual blood. Buckley's study of Yurok women, however, gives a very different interpretation of female seclusion during menstruation. Yurok women went into seclusion for a ten-day period not because they saw themselves as unclean or polluting, but because they were at the height of their power. Because this was a time of meditation, introspection, and personal growth, they did not want to be distracted by mundane tasks or concerns of the opposite sex. Rather, women were taught to be proud of their menstrual cycle and were expected to accumulate spiritual energy by meditating about the mysteries of life. Thus, for Yurok women menstruation was a highly positive part of their lives. As Buckley (1993: 135) describes it, "The blood that flows serves to 'purify' the woman, preparing her for spiritual accomplishment."

Another study that illustrates the complexity of gender ideology was conducted by Sandra Barnes (1990) among Yoruba women in Lagos, Nigeria. Female subordination among the Yoruba can best be described as contextual or situational. That is, women subordinate themselves in some contexts by showing great deference to their husbands, male family elders, employers, and public officials, but in other situations (such as market activity) they are independent, assertive, and powerful. Thus, we see a basic paradox in Yoruba society: Although female subordination is clearly the norm, particularly in family affairs, it is widely held that women can, and even should, strive for powerful positions in the world of economics and politics. Barnes explains the apparent paradox in terms of home ownership. Because of their success in the markets, women are able to attain high status through home ownership, and once they become homeowners, they are able to cross over into the realm of politics and public affairs.

These and many other studies in recent years have suggested that because traditional ethnographies have tended to be conducted by male anthropologists focusing on male informants, the perspective of women has often been overlooked or misinterpreted. Nowhere is this more evident than in the Middle East, where women are secluded and protected from the wider society. To most Westerners, the veil is a symbol of repression, representing extreme restrictions, coercion, immobility, and degradation. However, in a number of Islamic countries, well-educated computer experts and business professionals wear the veil. Many of these women look at the veil not in terms of what it denies them but rather in terms of the demands that it makes on the men in the society. For many Islamic women, educated and uneducated alike, the veil is a symbol of safety, security, protection, and privacy that they would not readily choose to abandon.

Studies written from a woman's perspective provide a long-overdue corrective to the male gender bias found in many of our ethnographies. They also remind us that gender issues are far more complex than one might perceive by looking at a society only from a male perspective. Nevertheless, these new studies, although providing a richer and more accurate description of reality, should not obscure the fact that in most societies men still enjoy the majority of power, prestige, and influence.

EXPLOITATION CAUSED BY GENDER IDEOLOGY

In some parts of the world, gender ideology is so extremely male biased that females can suffer dire consequences. In certain parts of the world, there are large numbers of females who are missing in census counts. It has been estimated (Sen 2001) that the countries of China and India together have more than 80 million fewer females than would be expected. In most countries, including the United States and Canada, women slightly outnumber the men (approximately 105 women for every 100 men). But in India and China, where there is a strong gender bias against females, the sex ratio strongly favors males. In China, for example, the government reported (Yardley 2005: 3) that the nationwide sex ratio had reached 119 boys for every 100 girls. This imbalance in the sex ratio is caused by females receiving less adequate nutrition and medical care, selective sex abortions, or the underreporting or hiding of female births. Demographers predict that in twenty years China could have 40 million bachelors unable to find a wife. However, despite government efforts to provide incentives to have girl babies (such as free tuition for girls and annual pensions for elderly people who have only daughters), there remains a strong cultural preference, particularly in rural areas, for male children.

A particularly malignant manifestation of *male gender bias* in North India is *female infanticide*, which involves the outright killing of female children. Sons are much more desirable than daughters because they are considered economic assets. They are needed for farming, are more likely to be wage employed, are the recipients of marriage dowry, and because they don't leave home when they marry, they can support the parents in their later years.

Yet, there are also more subtle forms of female child abuse, such as sustained *nutritional deprivation*, which, although not fatal, can retard learning, physical development, or social adjustment. Amartya Sen (2001) reports that in his home country of India gender biases against girls lead to significant differences in weight-for-age statistics for boys and girls younger than five years of age. Barbara Miller (1993) found considerable evidence of this less direct form of gender exploitation. For example, the sex ratio of children being admitted to hospitals is at least two to one in favor of boys, an imbalance caused by the sex-selective child care practices of the parents. Betty Cowan and Jasbir Dhanoa (1983) examined a large sample of *infant mortality* cases in Ludhiana District in North India and found that 85 percent of all deaths of children between seven and thirty-six months of age were female. They also found that the incidence of malnutrition for children between the ages of one and three was more than three times as high for females as it was for males. Moreover, there is evidence

---

male gender bias   A preference found in some societies for sons rather than daughters.
female infanticide   The killing of female children.
nutritional deprivation   A form of child abuse involving withholding food; can retard learning, physical development, or social adjustment.
infant mortality   Infant death rate.

(Ramanamma and Bambawale 1980) of sex-selective abortion. For seven hundred pregnant women applying for prenatal sex determination in a North Indian hospital, 250 fetuses were determined to be male and 450 fetuses were female; all of the male fetuses were kept to term but 430 of the 450 female fetuses were aborted. All of these studies indicate how an extreme gender ideology can lead to a lethal form of gender exploitation.

Not all situations of male gender bias lead to high mortality among girls. In parts of China, where the preference for sons is stronger than most other parental impulses, trafficking in female infants has become a major problem. Because daughters marry into their husbands' family, having a son is a couple's only security in old age. Because strict family planning laws in China limit how many children a couple has, many couples who have not produced a son will put up their daughters for sale or adoption in hopes of producing a son with their next pregnancy. Eighty percent of the babies traded in China are female, while the remaining 20 percent are boys with birth defects or health problems (Rosenthal 2003). The two major markets for female babies in China are childless urbanites or rural couples who already have a son and want a daughter to help with housework. While this trafficking in female babies is more humane than female infanticide, it nevertheless illustrates the type of exploitation resulting from extreme gender ideology.

Another form of extreme gender bias involves *honor killings* of women practiced in a number of countries of the Middle East as well as in India and Pakistan. As illustrated in the Cross-Cultural Miscue in Chapter 10, the men of a traditional family believe that a woman's purity is the most important part of the family's reputation. If it is even rumored that a daughter has lost her virginity, the family as a group will experience shame. An unchaste woman is considered worse than a murderer because she doesn't merely affect a single victim but her entire family. The only way for the family to restore its honor and avoid public humiliation, it is thought, is to kill the daughter. Despite laws against it, the practice remains widespread because an unchaste woman is seen as a threat. Because honor killings are often disguised to look like accidents, and because of the general reluctance in traditional societies to blow the whistle on the killer, it is very difficult to determine the number of honor killings that occur each year. According to one source (Jehl 1999), there were more than four hundred such killings in 1997 in the country of Yemen (population of 16 million). Whatever the number, however, this particular practice of honor killings places the entire burden of maintaining the family's honor on the woman, rather than punishing the man who also played a part in the loss of the girl's virginity.

Another example of inequality-related crimes against women is that of *dowry deaths* in rural India, Pakistan, and Bangladesh. Following marriage and the required giving of a dowry, the family of the groom often makes additional demands on the bride's family for more money or goods. Because the bride is living with her husband's family, she is subject to harassment, humiliation, abuse, and even death from beatings, burnings, and suicide for failing to meet the dowry demands of her in-laws. A commonly reported form of dowry death involves a wife being drenched in kerosene and set on fire. It is difficult to determine precisely how many dowry deaths occur every year in countries such as India, because they are often disguised as kitchen accidents. Nevertheless, one international news source (Xinhua News Agency) cited that as of June 11, 2001, there were more than sixteen thousand unresolved dowry death cases pending in the Indian court system.

Although not as lethal as honor killings or dowry death, the people of Kyrgyzstan have practiced a form of bride abduction for generations that is its own unique form of gender exploitation. In a custom known as *ala kachuu* (literally, "grab and run"), a would-be groom literally snatches off the streets, with some help from his friends or family, the woman he would like to be his bride. In its most benevolent form, a man whisks away his willing girlfriend, but often the practice is tantamount to an abduction of a stranger. The woman is taken to the home of the groom where her future in-laws try to calm her and convince her to submit to the wedding. If the groom's relatives can keep the woman in the house overnight, the woman has little choice but to agree to the marriage. Even if she were to escape, her reputation would be so damaged that few other men would ever want to marry her. Although many women fight mightily, it is estimated (Smith 2005: 1) that four of every five women kidnapped eventually submit to the marriage, often at the urging of their own parents. The incidence of this form of bride abduction has actually increased over the past several decades, and in fact, one-third of all Kyrgyz women married today are forced to marry against their will. This is gender exploitation for the simple reason that woman do not have the equivalent right to abduct their future husbands and marry them, with society's approval, against their will.

Widespread female abuse in other cultures is deeply disturbing and shocking, but we should not assume that equally appalling gender-based violence

---

honor killings   A euphemism referring to a practice found in various Middle Eastern cultures whereby women are put to death at the hands of their own family members because they are thought to have dishonored the family.

dowry death   The killing of a wife by her in-laws if the wife's parents fail to pay additional dowry.

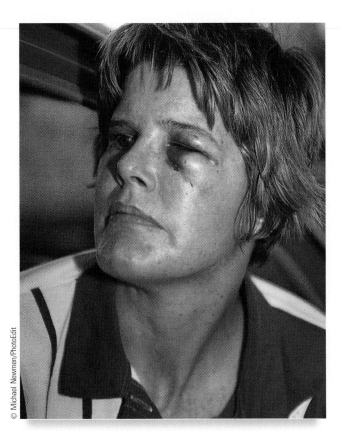

Physical violence against women, the result of gender ideology, continues to be a problem in the United States.

does not occur in our own culture. Both physical violence, in the form of wife-battering and homicide, and sexual assault against women are pervasive and direct consequences of extreme gender ideology. Sexual and physical violence against women has been, and continues to be, a serious problem in the United States. Most violence against women in the United States occurs not in a dark alley but within the home. According to the American Medical Association (2002), nearly one-quarter of all women in the United States (more than 12 million) will be abused by a former or current partner during their lifetime. FBI statistics indicate that 30 percent of female murder victims are killed by their husbands or boyfriends, and 52 percent are killed by current or former intimate partners. And, according to Diana Russell (1990), who interviewed more than nine hundred women, 3 percent of the sample had experienced completed rape by a stranger, while 14 percent of married women had experienced completed rape by a husband.

Because many women still do not define a sexual assault by their husband as a rape, it is likely that many such assaults go unreported, and consequently these findings must be considered low estimates. With data like these, it is little wonder that Richard Gelles (quoted in Roesch 1984) has suggested that, with the exception of the police and the military, the family is the most violent institution in the United States.

From a cross-cultural perspective, it is clear that domestic violence against women exists in all parts of the world. For example, the United Nations (1995) cites studies from around the world on the most pervasive form of gender-based violence: abuse by a husband or intimate partner. Survey results indicate that the percentage of women who have been physically assaulted by an intimate partner ranged from a low of 17 percent in New Zealand, to 28 percent in the United States, to as high as 60 percent in Sri Lanka, Ecuador, and Tanzania. We need not cite any additional statistics to illustrate that male-biased gender ideologies can have powerfully negative, and often lethal, consequences for the subordinate gender.

GENDER IN THE UNITED STATES

When we think of traditional gender roles in the United States, two words usually come to mind: *breadwinner* and *housewife*. According to this traditional view, males, who are often characterized as logical, competitive, goal oriented, and unemotional, were responsible for the economic support and protection of the family. Females, on the other hand, with their warm, caring, and sensitive natures, were expected to restrict themselves to child-rearing and domestic activities. However, this traditional view of gender roles in the United States was valid only for a relatively brief period in our nation's history, from roughly 1860 through the 1950s. Kingsley Davis and Wilbert Moore (1988: 73) have called the period between 1860 and 1920 the "heyday of the breadwinner system"; they identify 1890 as its peak because less than 3 percent of native-born married women in the United States worked outside the home at that time. Before industrialization, pioneer women were fully productive members of the rural homestead.

With the rise of industrialization in the late nineteenth century, the nation's economy shifted from agriculture to manufacturing. This rapid industrialization was revolutionary because it tended to separate work life from family life. Unlike work on the family farm, factory work could not be easily combined with child-rearing and domestic tasks. As women became more confined to the home, their direct contribution to economic production decreased. As men's and women's spheres were separated, the terms *breadwinner* and *housewife* became entrenched in our vocabulary. Interestingly, we maintained this view of separate spheres for men and

breadwinner A traditional gender role found in the United States that views males as being responsible for the economic support and protection of the family.
housewife A traditional gender role found in the United States that views females as responsible for child-rearing and domestic activities.

women well into the twentieth century even though forces for change that eroded those separate spheres were under way by the early 1900s.

It is true that men entered the workforce in greater numbers than women during the twentieth century, but we must not assume that women did not also make significant contributions to factory production. This is particularly true of poor and working-class women, minority women, immigrant women, and single mothers. The entry of women into the workforce was facilitated by a number of factors. First, as industrialization became more complex, more clerical workers were needed, and most of them were women. Second, as infant mortality rates fell, women bore fewer children, thereby increasing the number of years they could work outside the home. Third, many women gravitated toward the textile industry because they were thought to possess greater manual dexterity than men and therefore to be more adept at sewing clothes. Fourth, the rising rate of divorce forced many women to support themselves and their children without the financial aid of a spouse. Fifth, the development of infant formula enabled many women to work outside the home without jeopardizing the nutritional needs of their infants. And, finally, periodic economic downturns drove an increasing number of women to join the workforce because two salaries are often needed to make ends meet.

Today, both men and women are in the paid labor force, with approximately 74 percent of men and 60 percent of women participating. The percentage of women working outside the home has changed dramatically over the past several decades. Specifically, the percentage of working women between the ages of twenty-five and fifty-four has increased from 50 percent in 1970 to 74 percent in 2001. It is important to point out that employed married women, particularly those with children, often carry a *double workload* by being both wage employed and primarily responsible for housework and child care.

Another characteristic of the wage sector of the U.S. economy is its high rate of *occupational segregation* along gender lines. Despite decades of legislation aimed at reducing gender discrimination in the workplace, the majority of both men and women continue to work in gender-segregated occupations. The majority of women in the United States work as clerk/secretaries, hairdressers, sales clerks, food service workers, health care personnel, and child care workers, all relatively low-

double workload Situation in which employed married women, particularly those with children, are both wage employed and primarily responsible for housework and child care.
occupational segregation The predominance of one gender in certain occupations.

CROSS-CULTURAL MISCUE

While working in Milan, Ted Oppenheim decided to spend part of a Saturday at a local art museum. Not knowing the exact location of the museum, he asked a man on the street for directions. While the Italian was explaining how to get to the museum, Ted had an uncontrollable itch on his left earlobe. He tried to satisfy the itch by tugging on his earlobe. However, the Italian man immediately became upset and started to yell at him. Ted couldn't understand what he might have done to caused such a negative reaction.

Had you been present, you, as a student of cultural anthropology, could have explained to Ted that his seemingly innocuous gesture of tugging on his earlobe is the Italian way of questioning a person's manhood. Such a gesture implies, according to Italian nonverbal communication, that the individual is so effeminate that he should be wearing an earring. Little wonder that the man became so insulted.

paying jobs. More than 90 percent of nurses, 80 percent of librarians, and 70 percent of teachers are women. At the other end of the spectrum, women make up only 1 percent of corporate CEOs, 6 percent of partners in private law firms, and 8 percent of state and federal judges. In addition, men tend to dominate the supervisory positions, even in areas where a majority of workers are women. Moreover, this occupational segregation is even more pronounced for women of color because gender segregation is aggravated by race.

Despite these data illustrating occupational segregation, in the last several decades women have made considerable inroads into high-status professions. According to Richard Morin and Megan Rosenfeld (1998), between 1983 and 1996 the percentage of female judges and lawyers doubled to 29 percent while the percentage of female physicians increased from 16 to 26 percent. Moreover, approximately three out of every ten professional athletes are female, nearly a 100-percent increase since the mid-1980s.

Not only are jobs segregated by gender in the United States, but men are better paid for their efforts. Wages for full-time female employees are only 74 percent of wages for full-time male employees. And although this is up from 61 percent during the 1960s, the gap between male and female earnings remains wide. To illustrate, the median income for full-time female employees was $26,855 in 2000 as compared with $36,252 for men. Many of the jobs that are predominantly female are low-paying jobs with low upward mobility. But even in professions that require high levels of training and education—such as teaching, library science, and nursing—women earn less than their male counterparts.

Men tend to have a shorter life span than women, in part because they engage in more high-risk occupations.

Although an increasing number of women are entering professions that require advanced education, such as law, medicine, and engineering, occupations associated with low prestige and low income still have higher proportions of women. Poverty in the United States has become "feminized" just as it has in other parts of the world. For example, more than half of all female-headed families with children are living below the poverty line—a poverty rate that is approximately four times higher than the poverty rate for two-parent families. The feminization of poverty is particularly acute when we look at minorities. Whereas 45 percent of White female-headed families live in poverty, approximately 70 percent of families headed by African-American or Hispanic women are officially living in poverty. A number of factors have contributed to the feminization of poverty in the United States in recent decades. These include the continued involvement of women in low-paying jobs; the additional responsibilities for child-rearing, which many men do not have; the relative dearth of women in political or policy-making positions; and limited access to education, skills training, financial credit, and health care.

Looking back on our discussion of gender stratification in the United States, it would seem fairly obvious that, given a choice, most sane people would opt to be males. But the costs of gender stratification for men are also high. Without implying that men are more victimized than women, the culturally constructed male and female roles and statuses in the United States do have negative consequences for men. For example, adult men of all ages die more frequently in the United States than do women. Men have higher mortality rates than women for most of the fifteen leading causes of death. They abuse their bodies with drugs, alcohol, and tobacco more than women. And men engage in certain professions that carry higher risks, such as mining, construction, and NASCAR racing. In addition, in order to live up to culturally defined notions of masculinity, many men engage in high-risk (health-reducing) behaviors. The pressure to be a tough, competitive winner can lead *homo Americanus* to take on more than he can handle, thereby resulting in excessive stress. And when things do not go well, a growing sense of failure can lead to what Terrence Real (2001) calls "covert depression," a form of the sickness that often goes undiagnosed because it is largely repressed. Adult males in the United States infrequently seek help for stress, depression, or other emotional problems because to do so would be to admit weakness. The disadvantages of being male in the United States have led some men to support gender equality. ■

Summary

1. The word *gender* refers to the way members of the two sexes are perceived, evaluated, and expected to behave. Although biology sets broad limits on gender definitions, there is a wide range of ideas about what it means to be feminine or masculine, as Margaret Mead demonstrated in her classic study of sex and temperament in New Guinea.

2. There are considerable differences in degrees of permissiveness, but all societies regulate the sexual conduct of their members. Some societies, such as the Cheyenne Indians of the American Plains, are sexually restrictive, whereas others, such as the Mangaians of Polynesia, not only permit but actually encourage frequent and intense sexual activity between men and women.

3. In very general terms, there is considerable uniformity in sex roles throughout the world. Men engage in warfare, clear land, hunt animals, build houses, fish, and work with hard substances; women tend crops, prepare food, collect firewood, clean house, launder clothes, care for children, and carry water.

4. The status of women is multidimensional, involving such aspects as the division of labor, the value placed on women's contributions, economic autonomy, social and political power, legal rights, levels of deference, and the extent to which women control the everyday events of their lives.

5. Hindu society in northern India is among the most highly stratified along gender lines. At the other extreme, certain foraging societies, such as the

Mbuti Pygmies of Central Africa, take the most egalitarian (or least stratified) approach to men and women. Although these represent the two extremes of the status of women in the world, it is clear that in most critical areas women tend to be subordinate to men in nearly all societies of the world.

6. Gender ideology is used in most societies to justify this universal male dominance. Deeply rooted values about the superiority of men, the ritual impurity of women, and the preeminence of men's work are often used to justify the subjugation of women. However, it has been demonstrated in recent years that women do not perceive themselves in the same ways that they are portrayed in these (largely male) gender ideologies.

7. In some societies, gender ideologies become so extreme that females suffer serious negative conse-quences such as female infanticide, female nutri-tional deprivation, dowry death, honor killings, rape, and spouse abuse.

8. Although the words *breadwinner* and *housewife* accurately described the middle-class American household around the beginning of the twentieth century, the separate spheres implied by these two terms have become more myth than reality. In fact, over the past four decades the number of women in the United States working outside the home has increased dramatically.

9. The economy of the United States is characterized by a high rate of occupational segregation along gender lines. Not only are occupations gender segregated, but women tend to earn considerably less than men. Moreover, there has been a trend in recent decades toward the feminization of poverty.

Key Terms

breadwinner	gender	honor killings	occupational segregation
double workload	gender ideology	housewife	purdah
dowry death	genderlects	human sexuality	sex drive
extramarital activity	gender roles	infant mortality	sexual asymmetry
female infanticide	gender stratification	male gender bias	sexual dimorphism
femininity	heterosexual	masculinity	universal male dominance
feminization of poverty	homosexual	nutritional deprivation	

Suggested Readings

Bonvillain, Nancy. *Women and Men: Cultural Constructs of Gender*, 3d ed. Upper Saddle River, NJ: Prentice-Hall, 2001. The author examines gender roles cross-culturally in societies ranging from foraging cultures to industrialized states.

Brettell, Caroline B., and Carolyn Sargent. *Gender in Cross-Cultural Perspective*, 4th ed. Upper Saddle River, NJ: Prentice-Hall, 2005. A collection of articles written by anthropologists on gender inequity, sexuality, division of labor, and related topics. Each major section of the volume is prefaced by a substantive essay written by the editors.

Cohen, Theodore F. *Men and Masculinity: A Text Reader.* Belmont, CA: Wadsworth, 2001. This collection of forty-two readings on the male gender illustrates the many ways in which male experiences are shaped by the culture's definition of masculinity.

Mencher, Joan P., and Anne Okongwu, eds., *Where Did All the Men Go? Female-Headed/Female-Supported Households in Cross-Cultural Perspective.* Boulder, CO: Westview, 1993. This collection of essays looks at the rising number of female-headed households and the increasing economic hardships of mothers and their children in different parts of the world. Specifically, the volume examines factors contributing to this worldwide phenomenon, coping strategies that women have developed, and policy recommendations for addressing the issue.

Spain, Daphne, and Suzanne Bianchi. *Balancing Act: Motherhood, Marriage, and Employment Among American Women.* New York: Russell Sage Foundation, 1996. By using a wide range of census and survey data, this study examines how American women balance their careers with their roles as wives and mothers.

Strum, Philippa. *Women in the Barracks: The VMI Case and Equal Rights.* Lawrence, KS: University Press of Kansas, 2002. A fascinating account, combining both legal and cultural history, of the integration of women into the Virginia Military Institute. This is a highly readable story of the legal battle for gender equality in the United States.

Suggs, David N., and Andrew Miracle, eds., *Culture and Human Sexuality: A Reader.* Pacific Grove, CA: Brooks/Cole, 1993. A collection of articles on human sexuality, this volume contains case studies and theoretical essays from cultures in various parts of the world.

Topics include sex and the nature of humanity, sexual practices, sexual orientations, and the relationships between culture and sexually transmitted diseases.

Tannen, Deborah. *Talking From 9 to 5.* New York: Morrow, 1994. Building on her best-selling work (*You Just Don't Understand: Women and Men in Conversation.* 1990), Tannen shows how gender differences in

communicating influences what takes place in the U.S. workplace, everything from simple exchanges to such complex issues as sexual harassment.

Ward, Martha C. *A World Full of Women*, 3d ed. Boston: Allyn & Bacon, 2002. A cross-cultural examination of gender issues in societies around the world, focusing on topics such as work, love, and partnering.

Social Stratification

The rich and poor living in Hong Kong.

12

AN IMPORTANT DISTINGUISHING characteristic of various societies is the degree to which individuals have equal access to wealth, power, and prestige. In every society, people are socially differentiated on the basis of such criteria as physical appearance, ethnicity, profession, family background, gender, ideology, age, or skill in performing certain kinds of economic or political roles. Societies confer a larger share of the rewards (that is, wealth, power, and prestige) on those possessing the most admired characteristics. Scholars generally agree that all complex societies are *stratified*—that is, these societies make distinctions among certain groups or categories of people that are hierarchically ranked relative to one another. Anthropologists do not find clear-cut social strata in many of the simpler societies of the world, yet even these societies have role and status differences.

DIMENSIONS OF SOCIAL INEQUALITY

Max Weber (1946) has delineated three basic criteria for measuring levels of social inequality: wealth, power, and prestige. First, people are distinguished from one another by the extent to which they have accumulated economic resources, or their *wealth*. The forms that wealth may take vary from one society to the next. For the Mexican farmer, wealth resides in the land; for the Samburu of East Africa, a man's wealth is measured by the number of cows he has; and in the United Kingdom, most people equate their wealth with income earned in wages, property, stocks, bonds, equity in a home, or other resources that have a cash value.

The extent of economic inequality varies from society to society. In some societies, such as that of the Pygmies, there are virtually no differences in wealth. In terms of their material possessions and well-being, all people in egalitarian societies are virtually indistinguishable from one another. By way of contrast, enormous differences in wealth exist in certain capitalistic societies such as the United States. The range of wealth in the United States runs at one end of the spectrum from the unemployed father who sells his blood several times a month to feed his children to Bill Gates, chairman of Microsoft, whose total net worth in 2006 (according

---

What We Will Learn

- To what extent do the societies of the world vary in terms of the equitable distribution of power, prestige, and wealth?

- How do class systems differ from caste systems?

- What are the different ways of interpreting systems of social stratification?

  Click!

For interactive exercises and study aids, Go to **www.ichapters.com**; enter the author name and select your text, then click the Study Help tab to purchase the following online resources:

- **ThomsonNOW** for chapter-specific online tutorials, quizzes, and a personalized study plan

- **Anthropology Resource Center** for interactive maps, modules, videos, and the Applied Anthropology site

- **Thomson Audio Study Products** for a brief overview of the major chapter themes and to test your knowledge with quiz questions

---

wealth   The accumulation of material objects that have value within a society.

With a net worth of over $50 billion in October 2006, Microsoft's Bill Gates represents the upper level of wealth in the United States and the world.

to the Forbes list of wealthiest people in the world) was approximately $50 billion (that's billion, not million!) at the other. Over the last decade, Gates's net worth has fluctuated between $80 and $27 billion depending on the per share value of his stock holdings. Interestingly, in the top twenty on the Forbes list are the widow and four children of Sam Walton (founder of Wal-Mart), each of whom has a net worth of $20 billion. Thus, if Sam Walton had not died in 1992, he would be nearly twice as wealthy as Bill Gates is today. Economists Paul Samuelson and William Nordhaus (1989: 644) capture the magnitude of the economic inequities in the United States: "If we made an income pyramid out of a child's blocks, with each layer portraying $500 of income, the peak would be far higher than Mount Everest, but most people would be within a few feet of the ground."

A second dimension of social inequality, according to Weber, is *power*, which he defined as the ability to achieve one's goals and objectives even against the will of others. Power, to be certain, is often closely correlated with wealth, for economic success, particularly in Western societies, increases one's chances of gaining power. Nevertheless, wealth and power do not always overlap. In certain parts of the world, power can be based on factors other than wealth, such as the possession of specialized knowledge or eloquence as a speaker. In such cases, the wealth or material possessions of the powerful and the not-so-powerful may not differ significantly.

Where does power reside in the United States? According to our democratic ideology, power is in the hands of the people. We all exercise our power by voting for our political representatives, who see to it that our will is carried out. Although this is how it works in

theory, in real life the picture is quite different. Some social scientists (Hellinger and Judd 1991) have suggested that this ideology is no more than a democratic façade that conceals the fact that the real power resides with an unofficial power elite. As early as the 1950s, C. Wright Mills (1956) insisted that power was concentrated in the hands of a power elite comprising corporate, government, and military leaders.

Since then William Domhoff (1990) has arrived at a similar conclusion. The power elite share many of the same values, belong to the same clubs, sit on the same boards of directors, are graduates of the same schools, and even vacation at the same resorts. They are the owners and managers of major corporations, advisors to governments, and members of commissions and agencies. They give large sums of money to the fine arts, contribute heavily to their favorite political candidates, and are often on a first-name basis with the political establishment. According to Mills and Domhoff, the concentration of real power in the hands of an elite in the United States has been a constant for the past fifty years.

The third dimension of social stratification, according to Weber's formulation, is *prestige*: the social esteem, respect, or admiration that a society confers on people. Because favorable social evaluation is based on the norms and values of a particular group, sources of prestige vary from one culture to another. For example, among certain traditional Native American groups, warriors on horseback held high prestige; in certain age-graded societies, such as the Samburu of Kenya, old men were accorded the highest prestige; and in the United States, high prestige is closely associated with certain professions.

Research indicates that occupations in the United States carry different levels of prestige and that those rankings have remained remarkably stable since the early twentieth century (Hodge, Treiman, and Rossi, 1966; Coleman and Rainwater 1978; Nakao and Treas 1990; and National Opinion Research Center, 1996). That is, the occupations that ranked high in the 1950s still rank high in the twenty-first century. Not surprisingly, physicians, corporate presidents, scientists, and top-ranking government officials enjoy high levels of occupational prestige, whereas garbage collectors, day laborers, and janitors are at the low end of the prestige scale. Essentially, there are four factors that separate the occupations at the top from those at the bottom. The occupations at the top end are higher paying, require more education, offer greater autonomy (less supervision), and require more abstract thinking and less physical labor.

It is interesting to note that occupational rankings in the United States are surprisingly consistent with rankings from other parts of the world. To illustrate, in

power   The capacity to produce intended effects on oneself, other people, social situations, or the environment.

prestige   Social honor or respect within a society.

all countries where ranking has been conducted, college professors are ranked higher than nurses, nurses higher than electricians, and electricians higher than janitors (Treiman 1977).

It should be kept in mind that although wealth, power, and prestige are often interrelated, they can also operate independently of one another. Consider that it is possible to possess both power and wealth while having little prestige, as is the case with leaders of organized crime. Some people, such as classical pianists, may be highly esteemed for their musical virtuosity yet have modest wealth and little power or influence over people. And, odd as it may seem to Westerners, people in some societies (such as the Kwakiutl of British Columbia) acquire high prestige by actually destroying or giving away all of their personal possessions (refer to the discussion of the potlatch in Chapter 8).

TYPES OF SOCIETIES

Following the lead of Morton Fried (1967), most anthropologists distinguish three types of societies based on levels of social inequality: egalitarian, rank, and stratified societies. Egalitarian societies have few or no groups that have greater access to wealth, power, or prestige; they are usually found among food collectors, have economies based on reciprocity, and have little or no political role specialization. In rank societies, certain groups enjoy higher prestige, even though power and wealth are equally distributed; they are usually found among chiefdoms, have economies based on redistribution, and exhibit limited political role specialization. Stratified societies manifest the greatest degree of social inequality in terms of all three forms of social rewards (wealth, power, and prestige). They are found in industrialized societies, have market economies, and are associated with state systems of government. Rather than thinking of these three types of societies as discrete and mutually exclusive, it is more accurate to view them as points on a continuum, ranging from egalitarian societies (the least amount of social inequality) to stratified societies (the greatest degree of social inequality).

Egalitarian Societies

In *egalitarian societies*, which are located at the low end of the inequality continuum, no individual or group has appreciably more wealth, power, or prestige than any other. Of course, even in the most egalitarian societies, personal differences in certain skills are acknowledged. Some people are more skilled than others at hunting, others may be recognized as particularly adept at crafts, and still others may be well known and respected for

egalitarian societies Societies that recognize few differences in status, wealth, or power.

their skills at settling disputes. Even though certain individuals in an egalitarian society may be highly esteemed, they are not able to transform their special skills into wealth or power. No matter how much or how little respect an individual in an egalitarian society may have, he or she is neither denied the right to practice a certain profession nor subject to the control of others. Moreover, whatever esteem an individual manages to accrue is not transferable to his or her heirs.

In an egalitarian society, the number of high-status positions for which people must compete is not fixed. According to Fried, "There are as many positions of prestige in any given age–sex grade as there are persons capable of filling them" (1967: 33). The esteem gained by being a highly skilled dancer is given to as many individuals in the society as there are good dancers. If fifteen people are highly skilled dancers this year, all fifteen will receive high status. If next year there are twenty-four skilled dancers, all twenty-four will be so recognized. Thus, the number of high-status positions in an egalitarian society is constantly changing to reflect the number of qualified candidates. In other words, everyone, depending on her or his personal skill level, has equal access to positions of esteem and respect.

Egalitarian societies are found most readily among geographically mobile food collectors such as the Ju/'hoansi of the Kalahari region, the Inuit, and the Hadza of Tanzania. There are a number of logical reasons why unequal access to wealth, power, and prestige would be discouraged among nomadic foragers. First, the very nature of a nomadic existence inhibits the accumulation of large quantities of personal possessions. Second, because foragers do not hold claims to territory, individuals can forage in whatever areas they please. If one person wants to exercise control over others, the others can choose to live in some other territory. Finally, food collectors tend to be egalitarian because sharing tends to maximize their chances for adaptation. When a hunter kills a large animal, he is unlikely to try to keep the entire carcass for himself, given the lack of refrigeration. Rather, it makes much more sense for the hunter to share the meat with the expectation that others will share their kills with him. In fact, foraging societies, with economies based on the principle of generalized reciprocity, place a high value on sharing. Generosity in such societies is expected, and attempts to accumulate possessions, power, or prestige are ridiculed.

Often, egalitarian societies are transformed considerably when they come into contact with highly stratified (statelike) societies. Sometimes this transformation from egalitarian to nonegalitarian society is the result of normal cultural diffusion. Often it occurs because such a change meets the needs of colonial governments. For example, during the early part of the twentieth century, the British colonial government in Kenya created, for its own administrative convenience, local chiefs among the Kikuyu, a traditionally egalitarian people with no history

Small-scale foraging societies, such as the Hadza of Tanzania, tend to be egalitarian.

of any type of chief. Although the colonial government thought it was creating new high-status positions, the Kikuyu people themselves adhered to their egalitarian ideals and refused to recognize the legitimacy of these new government-appointed chiefs.

Rank Societies

Rank societies have unequal access to prestige or status but not unequal access to wealth or power. In rank societies, there is usually a fixed number of high-status positions, which only certain individuals are able to occupy. Other candidates for these positions are systematically excluded regardless of their personal skills, wisdom, industriousness, or other personal traits. High-prestige positions such as chief—which are largely hereditary in nature—establish a ranking system that distinguishes among various levels of prestige and esteem. In fact, kinship plays an important role in rank societies. Because some clans or lineages may be considered aristocratic, their members qualify for certain titles or high-status positions. Other kin groups are rank ordered according to their genealogical proximity to the aristocratic kin groups. Thus, the number of high-status positions in ranked societies is limited, and the major criterion for allocating such positions is genealogical.

Even though the chiefs in a rank society possess great prestige and privilege, they generally do not accumulate great wealth, for their basic standard of living is not noticeably different from that of an ordinary person. Chiefs usually receive gifts of tribute from members of other kin groups, but they never keep them for their

personal use. Instead, they give them all away through the process of redistribution (refer to Chapter 8). In many rank societies, chiefs are considered to own the land but not in the Western sense of the term. The chief certainly has no power to keep anyone from using the land. The chief may control land to the extent that he encourages people not to neglect either the land or their obligation to contribute to the chief's tribute. But the chief has no real power or control over the land. He maintains his privileged position as chief not by virtue of his capacity to impose his will on others but because of his generosity.

Examples of rank societies are found in most areas of the world, but most prominently in Oceania and among Native Americans of the Northwest Coast. In fact, for reasons that are not fully understood, some strikingly similar cultural traits are found in parts of Polynesia and among Native Americans residing in a narrow coastal region between northern California and southern Alaska. These cultural similarities are particularly noticeable in the area of status ranking. One such group that exemplifies a rank society is the Nootka of British Columbia (Service 1978). Like a number of ethnic groups in the American Northwest, the Nootka, a hunting-and-fishing society, live in an area so abundant in food resources (such as big game, wild edible plants, waterfowl, and fish) that their standard of living is comparable to societies that practice horticulture and animal husbandry.

Social ranking among the Nootka is closely related to the principle of kinship proximity. People are ranked within families according to *primogeniture*: position, privileges, and titles pass from a man to his eldest son. Younger sons are of little social importance because they are not in direct line to inherit anything from the father. Furthermore, in much the same way that individuals are ranked within the family, lineages are graded according to the birth order (or genealogical proximity) of the founding ancestors of each lineage. Nootka society does not comprise clearly marked social strata but rather a large number of individual status positions ranked relative to one another. Thus, no two individuals have exactly the same status.

Differential status takes a number of forms in Nootka society. First, the most visible symbol separating people of different rank is clothing. As a general rule, the higher the social position, the more ornate a person's dress. More specifically, wearing ornaments of teeth and shells or robes trimmed with the fur of sea otters is the exclusive privilege of chiefs. Second, an individual's status is directly linked to the bestowal of certain hereditary titles that are the names of important

rank societies   Societies in which people have unequal access to prestige and status but not unequal access to wealth and power.

primogeniture   The exclusive right of the eldest child (usually the son) to inherit his father's estate.

ancestors. Third, social position is expressed economically in terms of the amount of tribute (in surplus goods) a chief receives from the lower-ranked individuals who acknowledge his higher status. The receipt of tribute in no way enhances the personal wealth of the chief, for he redistributes the surplus goods back to the society in the form of elaborate feasts and ceremonies. Finally, social rank is determined by one's success in potlatch ceremonies, wherein prominent men compete with one another to see who can give away the largest quantities of material goods, such as food, blankets, and oil. Unlike Western societies, which equate high status with the accumulation of material wealth, the Nootka confer high status on those who can give away the greatest quantities of material goods. Even though potlatch ceremonies function to distribute needed material goods throughout the society, they also serve as a mechanism for validating rank.

Stratified Societies

Unlike rank societies, which are unequal only in terms of prestige, *stratified societies* are characterized by considerable inequality in all forms of social rewards (power, wealth, and prestige). The political, economic, and social inequality in stratified societies is both permanent and formally recognized by the members of the society. Some people—and entire groups of people—have little or no access to the basic resources of the society. Various groups in stratified societies, then, are noticeably different in social position, wealth, lifestyle, access to power, and standard of living. The unequal access to rewards found in stratified societies is generally inheritable from one generation to the next.

Although distinctions in wealth, power, and prestige began to appear in the early neolithic period (approximately ten thousand years ago), the emergence of truly stratified societies is closely associated with the rise of civilization approximately 5,500 years ago. A basic prerequisite for civilization is a population with a high degree of role specialization. As societies become more specialized, the system of social stratification also becomes more complex. Different occupations or economic interest groups do not have the same access to wealth, power, and prestige but rather are ranked relative to one another. As a general rule, the greater the role specialization, the more complex the system of stratification.

Class Versus Caste

Social scientists generally recognize two different types of stratified societies: those based on class and those based on caste. The key to understanding this funda-

mental distinction is *social mobility*. In *class* systems, a certain amount of upward and downward social mobility exists. In other words, an individual can change his or her social position dramatically within a lifetime. An individual, through diligence, intelligence, and good luck, could go from rags to riches; conversely, a person born to millionaire parents could wind up as a homeless street person (Newman 1988). *Caste* societies, on the other hand, have no social mobility. Membership in a caste is determined by birth and lasts throughout one's lifetime. Whereas members of a class society are able to elevate their social position by marrying into a higher class, caste systems are strictly endogamous (allowing marriages only within one's own caste).

Another important distinction is how statuses (positions) within each type of society are allocated. Class systems are associated with an *achieved status* whereas caste systems are associated with an *ascribed status*. Achieved statuses are those that the individual chooses or at least has some control over. An achieved status is one that a person has attained as a result of her or his personal effort, such as graduating from college, marrying someone, or taking a particular job. In contrast, a person is born into an ascribed status and has no control over it. Statuses based on such criteria as sex, race, or age are examples of ascribed statuses, which are found mainly in caste societies.

It is important to bear in mind that stratified societies cannot all be divided neatly into either class or caste systems. In general, class systems are open to the extent that they are based on achieved statuses and permit considerable social mobility, and caste systems tend to be closed to the extent that they are based on ascribed statuses and allow little or no social mobility, either up or down. Having made these conceptual distinctions, however, we must also realize that in the real world, class and caste systems overlap. In other words, most stratified societies contain elements of both class and caste. Rather than think in either–or terms, we should think in terms of polarities on the ends of a continuum.

There are no societies that have either absolute mobility (perfect class systems) or a total lack of mobility (perfect caste systems). Rather, all societies found in the world fall somewhere between these two ideal polarities,

stratified societies Societies characterized by considerable inequality in all forms of social rewards—that is, power, wealth, and prestige.

social mobility The ability of people to change their social position within the society.

class A ranked group within a stratified society characterized by achieved status and considerable social mobility.

caste A rigid form of social stratification in which membership is determined by birth, and social mobility is nonexistent.

achieved status The status an individual acquires during the course of her or his lifetime.

ascribed status The status a person has by virtue of birth.

In stratified societies, different groups, ranging from the homeless to the upper class, have different levels of power, prestige, and wealth. In the United States over the past three decades, the gap between those at the bottom and those at the top has widened.

depending on the amount of social mobility permitted in each.

Class Societies

Even though the boundaries between social strata in a class society are not rigidly drawn, social inequalities nevertheless exist. A social class is a segment of a population whose members share similar lifestyles and levels of wealth, power, and prestige. The United States is a good example of a class society (Table 12.1). In some areas of the United States, such as coal-mining towns in Appalachia, there may be only two classes: the haves and the have-nots. More often, however, social scientists have identified a number of social classes: capitalist (upper), upper middle, middle, working, working poor, and underclass (Bensman and Vidich 1987; Vanneman and Cannon 1987; Sullivan and Thompson 1990; Gilbert 2003).

The *capitalist class* in the United States, comprising approximately 1 percent of the population, consists of old wealth (Carnegies, Rockefellers), corporate CEOs, and owners of lucrative businesses, whose income derives largely from returns on assets such as stocks, bonds, securities, and real estate. The ownership of the means of production by the capitalist class affords them the power over jobs for the rest of society. Moreover, their control of the media largely shapes the nation's consciousness. Because they are the main source of *soft money* contributions to political campaigns, they exert enormous influence over national politics. Primarily because of the rapid development of the postindustrial economy, the number of people in this class has increased in recent decades, as have their power and influence.

soft money A form of political contribution not covered by federal regulation, which works to the advantage of wealthy candidates and their benefactors.

The *upper middle class*, comprising about 14 percent of the U.S. population, is made up of business and professional people with high incomes and considerable amounts of overall wealth. This is the class that is most shaped by education. Nearly all members of the upper middle class are college educated, and many have postgraduate degrees. These people are professionals (such as doctors and lawyers), own their own businesses, or manage the corporations owned by members of the capitalist class. This class consists of the working rich, whose incomes are generated by executive salaries or fees rather than from income-producing assets. They have secure economic positions, almost always send their children to college, drive new automobiles, and are likely to be active in civic organizations and local politics.

The *middle class*, constituting approximately 30 percent of the population, is made up of hardworking people of modest income, such as small entrepreneurs, teachers, nurses, civil servants, and lower-level managers. People in this class make a modest income, enjoy relative security (threatened occasionally by rising taxes and inflation), and have the potential for upward social mobility. Though sometimes indistinguishable from the working class, the lower middle class generally has slightly higher income and more prestige.

Comprising approximately 30 percent of the population, members of the *working class* hold occupations that tend to be fairly routine, closely supervised, and usually require no more than a high school education (blue-collar and some white-collar jobs). Included in this category are factory workers, sales clerks, construction workers, office workers, and appliance repairpersons. Because of their lack of higher education, members of this group tend to have little social mobility. Vulnerable to downturns in the economy, working-class people are

Table 12.1 U.S. Class Structure

Class	Annual Income	Education	Occupation	Percent
Privileged Classes				
Capitalist	$1,000,000+	Prestige universities	CEOs, investors, heirs	1
Upper middle	$100,000+	Top colleges/postgraduate	Upper managers, professionals	14
Majority Classes				
Middle	$55,000	High school/some college	Lower managers, teachers, civil servants	30
Working class	$35,000	High school	Clerical, sales, factory	30
Lower Classes				
Working poor	$22,000	Some high school	Service jobs, laborers	13
Underclass	$10,000 or less	Some high school	Unemployed	12

NOTE: Based on the Gilbert-Kahl Model in Gilbert 2003.

subject to layoffs during recessions and justifiably feel threatened by our increasingly globalized economy, in which many jobs are going to workers abroad. The working class, which has a low rate of political participation, is also most vulnerable to the shift to a postindustrial economy with fewer manufacturing jobs and more high-tech positions requiring higher levels of education.

The *working poor*, about 13 percent of the population, barely earn a living at unskilled, low-paying, unpleasant, and often temporary jobs with little security and frequently no benefits. They tend to be undereducated, and even though some may have completed high school, others are functionally illiterate. They live from paycheck to paycheck, often depend on food stamps, and have little or no savings as a safety net. Members of the working poor are often just a layoff away from living on the streets or in a homeless shelter. Nevertheless, the working poor in the United States, despite their lack of rewards, maintain a strong work ethic (Newman 1999).

The *underclass* occupies the lowest sector of U.S. society. Some have suggested that the underclass actually represents the people who are beneath the class structure, a type of castelike group that has little or no chance of ever making it to the first rung of the social ladder. The underclass are unemployed (or severely underemployed), are homeless, and often suffer from substance abuse and in some cases mental illness. They are almost always confined to blighted urban areas plagued by violence, gangs, and drugs.

Is the class system in the United States changing? If we examine the years since World War II, the relationship among the different classes has gone through two distinct periods. According to Dennis Gilbert (2003), the period from 1945 until 1975 was a period of "shared prosperity" in which class differences were shrinking. Since 1975, however, there has been a marked expansion of class disparities. For example, the official poverty rate plunged during the 1960s, but since 1970 the pov-

erty level has remained fairly constant even as the size of the overall economy has doubled. Since 1975 incomes have grown very slowly or not at all at the lower and middle-class levels and soared at the top. Inequalities of wealth (measured by the concentration of wealth held by the top 1 percent of the population) shrank between 1960 and 1975 from 32 percent to 20 percent. Since the mid-1970s, however, the inequalities have grown steadily to more than 38 percent by the turn of the century. In 1970, the average income for the top 5 percent of the population was six times what it was for the bottom 40 percent; by 2000 it was twelve times as high.

Class in the United States has also changed its appearance in recent decades. During the 1960s and 1970s the outward appearances of class were fairly unambiguous. The upper class drove Cadillacs, played golf, and vacationed abroad; the middle class sent their children to public schools, drove Fords and Chevys, and spent a quarter of a century paying off their home mortgages; the working classes carried a union card and voted Democratic. Today, however, our consumer economy makes it difficult to determine with any clarity who belongs to which social class because cell phones, iPods, designer jeans, and classy cars cut across all class levels. In other words, it has become harder to read a person's social status in the United States by the clothes he wears, the church he attends, the political party he supports, or even the color of his skin. Nevertheless, while the contours of class in recent decades may have blurred somewhat, the class system in America has taken on greater, not lesser, significance.

Nowhere was the U.S. class structure more dramatically demonstrated than in the aftermath of Hurricane Katrina in New Orleans in September 2005. Almost all the people stranded for days without food and water in the Superdome and the Convention Center were the city's poor; clearly everyone else had driven their Volvos to higher ground. Those images that horrified the rest

AP Images/Bill Haber

Many Katrina victims waited for days at the New Orleans Superdome for government help because they didn't have a Saab to drive to a Marriott Hotel further inland.

of the nation, and indeed the world, drove home a long forgotten truth about life in the United States—that is, substantial pockets of poverty persist in spite of the nation's unsurpassed affluence. According to the U.S. Bureau of Census, the number of people living below the poverty line in 2004 increased by 1.1 million people, for a total of 37 million Americans (or 12.7 percent). And, in fact that same report stated that the poverty rate had risen for the fourth year in row.

The growing inequity in earnings is most dramatic at the highest levels. The compensation of CEOs in the United States grew 600 percent between 1980 and 2000, while earnings at the middle were rising slowly, and those at the bottom were actually shrinking. According to a survey conducted by Pearl Meyer and Partners (an executive compensation consulting firm), chief executives' median pay (the point at which half are above and half are below) was $8.4 million in 2005, an increase of more than 10 percent from 2004 (Dash 2006: 5). That is more than $23,000 per day. When compared to CEOs in other parts of the world, heads of U.S. corporations earn twenty-three times as much as their counterparts in China, ten times as much as Indian CEOs, and five times as much as corporate chiefs in Japan.

The high-flying fortunes of corporate CEOs are well illustrated by the case of Jack Welch, former head of General Electric Corporation. When he retired in 2000, Mr. Welch received annual compensation of $16.7 million, had a retirement plan that would pay him $9 million per year for the rest of his life, and was worth more than $900 million. But the corporate benefits did not end with retirement, for GE continued to pay for the following: use of the corporate jet, use of a corporate

apartment in Manhattan (complete with cook and wait staff, housekeepers, food, flowers, and wine); box seats at the Metropolitan Opera; courtside seats at Wimbledon, the U.S. Open, and the French Open; season tickets for the New York Knicks, the New York Yankees, and the Boston Red Sox; annual fees for four country clubs; security services for his four homes; limousine services while traveling; and personal security guards while traveling abroad (Fabrikant 2002).

Does the general U.S. population resent this enormous concentration of wealth in the hands of a small elite? Probably not, if the wildly popular television show, *The Apprentice* (starring Donald Trump), is any indication. In this reality show, nominated for four Emmy awards, Mr. Trump plays the role of the affable tyrant who mercilessly weeds out the less desirable candidates competing for a high-level position in his real estate dynasty. On this show, the boss is king and there is no room for sentimentality. If a participant fails to demonstrate the personal traits of a successful entrepreneur, he or she is dismissed from the competition with a wave of the hand and the fateful words, "You're fired!" In this game, where theater imitates life, Mr. Trump holds all the cards, he decides the fate of others with surgical precision, and the viewing audience seems to love it.

Not only has money been concentrated increasingly in the hands of the capitalist class in recent decades, but so has political power. In fact, money is intimately interconnected with political power and influence. The largest contributors to political campaigns in the United States are, not surprisingly, the wealthiest. Even though the post-Watergate reforms of the 1970s capped individual donations at $1,000 per candidate and total giv-

"You're fired!" The capitalist class has considerable power over jobs held by the rest of society.

ing to federal candidates at $25,000, the so-called soft money, which escapes federal regulation, allows almost unlimited giving to party organizations and political action committees. In the 2000 federal election, corporations (headed by members of the capitalist class) gave $842 million to campaigns, while all other interest groups gave a total of $267 million. And, of course, there are no limitations on the amount of their own money candidates can spend on their campaigns. Members of the Senate and House have spent millions of their own fortunes to buy their way into political office. Senator Jay Rockefeller of West Virginia and Mayor Michael Bloomberg of New York City immediately come to mind. In 2000, Wall Street multimillionaire Jon Corzine spent $67 million on getting elected to the Senate from the state of New Jersey.

The capitalist class has played an increasingly prominent role in the political decision-making process because of their direct contributions (either individually or as representatives of corporations) to political campaigns. But they also exert vast influence (well beyond their numbers) through other means as well. For example, members of the capitalist class are recruited for a number of top-level positions in the federal government such as cabinet posts or ambassadorships. Second, the capitalist class exerts untold pressure on all levels of government decision making through their corporate

lobbying efforts. Third, many policy planning groups (such as the Council for Economic Development and the Business Council) and private foundations (Rockefeller and Ford) are funded and represented by members of the capitalist class. And finally, virtually all mass media (television, newspapers), which have enormous influence on public opinion and public policy, are owned and controlled by the capitalist class.

CROSS-CULTURAL MISCUE

Tom Holmes, a high-ranking official in an American-based company, had been his company's chief architect of a joint venture with a Japanese company. After months of meetings, Holmes and his Japanese counterpart, Mr. Hayashi, were sitting down with their two teams to review the details of the joint venture. Both teams had worked hard to bring about a relationship that Holmes believed to be satisfactory to both companies. Over the months Holmes and Hayashi had developed a good working relationship, and both men were optimistic about the upcoming joint venture. In fact, Holmes was so pleased with the draft proposal that he had invited his boss, Vice President Frank Mistretta, to be present at this final review meeting.

Once the meeting started, however, Holmes's optimism began to wane. He found himself doing all of the talking, while Hayashi and his team remained silent. Holmes wondered what had gone wrong. Now that everything had been worked out, were the Japanese changing their minds? After about forty-five minutes, Holmes called for a recess. Looking very frustrated, Holmes took Hayashi aside and asked him, "What's wrong? I thought we agreed on all of the details of our proposal. This meeting was simply to review the details to make certain everything was in place. But you are not saying anything. Are there parts of the proposal you are having difficulty with? I just don't understand!"

In actual fact, the Japanese team had not changed its position on the proposal. Hayashi was still in agreement with all of the details that the two sides had agreed upon. The problem for the Japanese was the presence of Holmes's boss, Mistretta. During the months of negotiations Holmes and Hayashi, and their respective teams, were of equal status. Thus, they could speak with one another openly as equals. But the introduction of Mistretta into the equation changed things dramatically for the Japanese. Because Mistretta was of obviously higher status than any of the Japanese, Hayashi and his team were reluctant to speak. Tom had invited his boss as a way of showing commitment to the proposed partnership with the Japanese. Unfortunately, for the very status-conscious Japanese, Mistretta's presence at the meeting was seen as intimidating.

Not only is life at the top of the U.S. social hierarchy more opulent, prestigious, and influential, but it is also healthier and lasts longer. Even though medical advances over the past half century have increased longevity throughout the entire society, the benefits have disproportionately gone to the upper echelons—namely, those with the greatest income, education, and connections. In other words, class very definitely influences people's diet, the understanding of their illnesses, the support they receive from their families, their relationship with medical providers, and even their capacity to afford health insurance.

What accounts for this increasing inequality over the last several decades? The growing disparity has been the result of a combination of factors. First, the change from an industrial to a postindustrial society created a high demand for people with advanced training and education, most of whom are from the upper classes. At the same time, many manufacturing jobs, on which the lower classes depend, have been moving abroad. Second, the influence of labor unions, which traditionally have fought for higher wages for U.S. workers, has declined in recent decades. Third, current trends in family life (such as increasing divorce rates and people choosing to remain single) have led to more female-headed households, which tend to have lower family incomes. Fourth, the tendency for U.S. corporations to become leaner and meaner through "downsizing" has had its most negative effects on the lower income groups. And finally, the gap between the haves and the have-nots widened due to the substantial tax cuts during the Reagan years and again under President George W. Bush, which had the effect of helping the wealthy far more than the rest of the population.

Our national mythology includes the belief that a good deal of social mobility exists in the United States. After all, there are no formal or legal barriers to equality, and we all grow up believing that it is possible for anyone (or at least, any White male) to become president of the United States. Although it is possible to cite a number of contemporary Americans who have attained great wealth, power, and prestige from modest beginnings, studies of social class in the United States have shown that most people remain in the class into which they are born and marry within that class as well.

In many cases, a child's physical and social environment greatly influences her or his career opportunities and identification with a particular class. To illustrate, the son of a school janitor in Philadelphia living in a lower-class neighborhood will spend his formative years playing in crowded public playgrounds, working at the grocery store after school, and generally hanging out with kids from the neighborhood. The son of a bank president, on the other hand, also living in Philadelphia, will attend a fashionable prep school, take tennis lessons at the country club, and drive his own car. When the two youths finish high school, the janitor's son will probably

not continue his education, whereas the banker's son will go off to a good college, perhaps go on to law school, and then land a high-paying job. Even though it is possible that the janitor's son could go to Harvard Law School and become upwardly mobile (or that one of the overly privileged class could become downwardly mobile), such scenarios are not very likely.

Members of the same social class share not only similar economic levels but also similar experiences, educational backgrounds, political views, memberships in organizations, occupations, and values. In addition, studies of social class have shown, not surprisingly, that members of a social class tend to associate more often with one another than with people in other classes. In other words, a person's life chances, though not determined, are very much influenced by social class.

Caste Societies

In contrast to class societies, those that are based on caste rank their members according to birth. Membership in castes is unchangeable, people in different castes are segregated from one another, social mobility is virtually nonexistent, and marriage between members of different castes is strictly prohibited. Castes, which are usually associated with specific occupations, are ranked hierarchically.

Caste societies, wherever they may be found, have a number of characteristics in common. First, caste membership is directly related to economic issues such as occupation, workloads, and control of valuable resources. The higher castes have a monopoly on high-status occupations, control the allocation of resources to favor themselves, and avoid engaging in difficult or low-status work. In short, the higher castes have more resources and do less. Second, members of the same caste share the same social status, largely because of their strong sense of caste identity, residential and social segregation from other castes, and uniformity of lifestyles. Third, caste exclusiveness is further enhanced because each caste has its own set of secret rituals, which tend to intensify group awareness. Fourth, the higher castes are generally most interested in maintaining the caste system for the obvious reason that they benefit from it the most.

Hindu Caste System   Caste societies can be found in a number of regions of the world, such as among the Rwandans in Central Africa, but the best-known—and certainly the best-described—example of the caste system is in Hindu India. Hinduism's sacred Sanskrit texts rank all people into four categories, called **varnas**, which are associated with certain occupations. Even though local villagers may not always agree as to who belongs

---

varnas   Caste groups in Hindu India that are associated with certain occupations.

AP/Wide World Photos

The Dalits in India engage in only the lowest-status jobs.

to which varna, most people accept the varna categories as fundamentally essential elements of their society.

According to a Hindu myth of origin (see Mandelbaum 1970), the four major varnas originated from the body of primeval man. The highest caste, the Brahmins (priests and scholars), came from his mouth, the Kshatriyas (warriors) emanated from his arms, the Vaishyas (tradesmen) came from his thighs, and the Shudras (cultivators and servants) sprang from his feet. Each of these four castes is hierarchically ranked according to its ritual purity. Below these four castes—and technically outside the caste system—is still another category, called the Untouchables or, literally, outcasts. The Untouchables, who are confined to the lowest and most menial types of work, such as cleaning latrines or leather-working, are considered so impure that members of the four legitimate castes must avoid all contact with them. Today this lowest caste prefers the term *Dalit*, which means literally the "crushed" or "oppressed" people.

Ideally, all of Hindu India is hierarchically ranked according to these four basic castes. In practice, however, each of these four categories is further subdivided

and stratified. To add to the complexity of the Indian caste system, the order in which these subcastes are ranked varies from one region to another. These local subgroups, known as *jati*, are local family groups that are strictly endogamous. All members of a jati, who share a common social status, are expected to behave in ways appropriate for that jati. A person's jati commands his or her strongest loyalties, serves as a source of social support, and provides the primary basis for personal identity. Thus, the jati serves as the important social entity in traditional Hindu society. The members of each jati maintain its corporateness in two ways: first, through egalitarian socializing with members of their own jati; and second, by scrupulously avoiding any type of egalitarian socializing (such as marriage or sharing of food) with members of other jati. Although the jati were originally linked to traditional occupations, that is no longer the case. For instance, today most members of the traditional leather-worker caste are landless laborers.

While the prohibitions against social intercourse among castes are rigidly defined, the amount of interdependence among local castes should not be overlooked. This interdependence is largely economic in nature rather than social. Like any society with a complex economy, India has an elaborate division of labor. In fact, one of the basic features of caste in traditional India is that each jati is associated with its own occupation that provides goods or services for the rest of the society. Certain lower-caste jati (such as barbers, potters, and leather-workers) provide vital services for the upper castes from which they receive food and animal products. For the economy to work, lower castes sell their services to the upper castes in exchange for goods. Thus, despite the very high level of social segregation among the castes in India, there is considerable economic interrelatedness, particularly at the village level.

Even though intercaste mobility has always been very limited in India, there are increasing instances in recent years of people moving up the caste ladder. The process, known as *Sanskritization*, involves taking on the behaviors, practices, and values associated with the Brahmin caste, such as vegetarianism, giving large dowries for their daughters, and wearing sacred clothing associated with Brahmins. According to Pauline Kolenda (1978), people accomplish this type of upward mobility by acquiring considerable wealth and education, migrating to other parts of the country, or becoming political activists.

An important tenet of Hindu religious teachings is *reincarnation*—the notion that at death a person's soul is

Dalits   The politically correct term for those formerly called the Untouchables in India.

jati   Local subcastes found in Hindu India.
Sanskritization   A form of upward social mobility found in contemporary India whereby people born into lower castes can achieve higher status by taking on some of the behaviors and practices of the highest (Brahmin) caste.

APPLIED PERSPECTIVE

Anthropology and Architecture

© Ariel Skelley/Corbis

A basic premise of this chapter is that, to one degree or another, all societies are segmented into groups that have different access to wealth, power, and prestige. In class societies such as the United States, various groups differ appreciably in terms of their access to power, social position, lifestyles, and standards of living. These segments of U.S. society often display marked differences in life experiences, educational backgrounds, and values.

Anthropologist Setha Low (1981), while a professor of landscape architecture at the University of Pennsylvania, took this basic principle into consideration when planning the restoration of Farnham Park in Camden, New Jersey. A derelict park located along the Cooper River, Farnham Park was the subject of a rehabilitation project by a class of University of Pennsylvania architecture students during the 1980s. Located on a once ecologically rich tidal estuary, the park was drastically altered by decades of industrialization and was eventually abandoned because the surrounding area suffered from social and economic decline. When the rehabilitation study was initiated, the site was surrounded by a highway, some schools, and several ethnic neighborhoods, all of which were suffering from urban decay. Trash (including tires, mat-

tresses, appliances, and various forms of debris) was strewn throughout the park, and it was used for little more than dumping, breaking bottles, or drinking.

Once the city expressed an interest in restoring the park, important design questions emerged. What did the city, and particularly this neighborhood, need in the way of a park? The design team attempted to answer this question by conducting a comprehensive research project using anthropological data-gathering strategies, including participant-observation, ethnographic interviewing, and social mapping. Data were gathered on the values and behavior patterns of local residents, their current use of the space, their perception of problems, their past memories of the area, and their preferences for a park for the future.

Much of the data collection for this project involved identifying the dominant values and cultural features of the major social constituencies. In other words, who were the major players who had an interest in the rehabilitation of the park? The research team identified six interest groups:

1. The parkside residents, who wanted a nice, quiet park for families to picnic

reborn in an endless sequence of new forms. The caste into which a person is born is considered to be her or his duty and responsibility for that lifetime. Hindu scripture teaches that the good life involves living according to the prescriptions of the person's caste. Members of higher castes must do everything possible to retain their ritual purity by avoiding any type of intimate interaction with members of lower castes. Correspondingly, members of lower castes must refrain from polluting higher castes. It is taught that those who violate their caste prescription will come back in a lower caste or, if the transgression is sufficiently serious, in a nonhuman form. Hindu scripture is very explicit about the consequences of violating prescribed caste behaviors. For example, the Brahmin who steals the gold of another Brahmin will be reincarnated in the next thousand lives as a snake, a spider, or a lizard. That's a powerful sanction! In other words, people believe that their caste status is determined by how they behaved in former lives and that their present behavior determines their caste status in future lives.

The caste system in India, which has persisted for two thousand years, has subjected millions of people to degrading poverty and human rights abuses. From its inception, the caste system created an ideology allowing upper castes to create and maintain their monopoly over knowledge, education, status, power, and material wealth. The

Dalits (or Untouchables) are taught from their earliest years to avoid the upper castes at all costs. In the words of a nineteen-year-old from a village in western India:

> At the tea stalls, we have separate cups to drink from, chipped and caked with dirt, and we're expected to clean them ourselves. We have to walk for 15 minutes to carry water to our homes, because we're not allowed to use taps in the village that the upper castes use. We're not allowed into temples, and when I attended school, my friends and I were forced to sit just outside the classroom ... the upper caste children would not allow us even to touch the football they played with ... we played with stones instead. (Guru and Sidhva 2001: 27)

The early codes establishing the rigidly stratified caste system were written to benefit the upper castes at the expense of the lower castes. For example, in parts of southern India, Brahmins ordered Dalits to get no closer than twenty-two meters from them in order to maintain their ritual purity. And yet, this discrimination carries no logical consistency when the upper castes stand to benefit. To illustrate, even though Dalits are defined as being polluting, even when accidentally touched on the street, they are permitted to massage the bodies of upperclasswomen whom they serve, and upper-caste men think nothing of raping Dalit women.

2. The unemployed youth and teenagers, who hung out on the basketball courts

3. The teachers and administrators from nearby schools, who wanted the park to be restored as a nature center for educational purposes

4. The young children, who wanted to use the gym equipment but were reluctant to do so because they were afraid of the older children

5. Members of the city government, who would finance improvements to the park

6. County government officials, who would finance the ongoing maintenance of the park

Each group was asked to prepare a plan for the proposed park that reflected their own values, interests, and needs. These plans were then analyzed by the research team, which tried to identify points of commonality among the constituencies. Agreement was found on the following elements: restoration of the dike that would stabilize the size of the pond; creation of a large grassy area; maintenance of a wildlife area; provision of picnic tables; creation of sports fields; encouragement of fishing and other passive water sports; provision of special skills equipment; creation of a cultural activities center; and inclusion of biking, walking, and jogging trails. Once the team was able to identify elements that appealed to all constituencies, they were able to start the design phase of the park rehabilitation project.

This is another example of the utility of cultural knowledge. In this case, research into the norms, values, and behavior patterns of different subcultures in a community assisted landscape architects to design a public park. The use of anthropological methods such as social mapping, participant-observation, and ethnographic interviewing provided essential data that was then wedded to the aesthetic principles of architectural design. This anthropological approach to designing public places serves to remind architects that the perceptions, values, and interests of the user groups must be taken into account if the end product is to be functional.

Questions for Further Thought

1. In what ways can anthropologists be valuable employees of an architectural firm?

2. How can cultural knowledge contribute to the style and function of architectural design?

3. Would the restoration of the park have been successful (or even possible) without the input of the major neighborhood groups? Why?

While the Indian government has attempted to discourage it, the caste system still plays an important role in the lives of most contemporary Indians. The author of the Indian constitution in 1950, B. R. Ambedkar, himself a Dalit, tried to eliminate some of the worst features of the caste system by making it a criminal offense to discriminate against Dalits. He also established the world's first affirmative action program by establishing quotas for Dalits (and other underprivileged groups) for proportional representation in the parliament, government jobs, and education. And in 1997, India elected its first president, K. R. Narayanan, from among the ranks of the Dalit caste.

Nevertheless, even though caste inequities have been explicitly prohibited by the constitution, India has a long way to go before the injustices of the past are eliminated. Despite government efforts to legislate change, attitudes in Hindu India die hard. Politics in contemporary India are becoming increasingly caste oriented. Lower-caste politicians promise to protect the lower castes; middle-caste politicians promise to look after their own; and the upper-caste Brahmins in recent years have become increasingly defensive because they can no longer count on those lower castes whose servitude they had always taken for granted. As the demands of the Dalits and other lower castes have increased recently, there has

been a rise in caste-related violence. Disputes over jobs, wages, land ownership, and water rights often flare up into open conflict. Caste violence over the issue of affirmative action in higher education has broken out at a leading medical school in India, where students claim to have been beaten by upper-caste students who oppose the admission of those from lower castes (Lloyd 1999). And as recently as 2001, United Press International reported a case from the state of Uttar Pradesh in which a twenty-year-old Brahmin man and his eighteen-year-old non-Brahmin lover were hanged by their parents and families for carrying on an intercaste relationship.

European Gypsies (Roma)   Numbering between 7 and 9 million people, the Roma or Gypsies of present-day Europe represent a migratory version of Indian untouchables. Linguistic and genetic evidence indicates that the Roma originated on the Indian subcontinent about a thousand years ago as low-caste Hindus and subsequently migrated westward, through Persia, into the Balkans, and eventually throughout all of Europe. Wherever they arrived in Europe, they were met with hostility and discrimination. In Romania they were enslaved for nearly five hundred years, while elsewhere in Europe they were either expelled or subjected to forced labor. It is estimated that during WWII the Nazis

A Gypsy (Roma) woman and children beg outside a church in Bratislava, Slovakia.

© Paul Glendell/Alamy

murdered at least several hundred thousand Roma as part of their deliberate program of genocide. Under the Communist regimes of eastern Europe, Roma experienced serious restrictions of cultural freedom. For example, the Romany language and Romany music were banned from public performance in Bulgaria, while in Czechoslovakia Romani women were sterilized as part of a state policy of ethnic cleansing.

Up to the present time, Roma remain an oppressed underclass, often living in squatter settlements, experiencing high levels of unemployment, and being denied adequate educational facilities for their children. However, in an unusual multinational initiative, eight central and southeastern European countries in 2005 with significant Roma populations (Bulgaria, Croatia, the Czech Republic, Hungary, Macedonia, Romania, Serbia/Montenegro, and Slovakia) have committed to closing the gap in welfare and living conditions between the Roma and non-Roma populations. Started in 2005, the initiative called "Decade of Roma Inclusion," will provide state funds to improve housing, employment, health, and education among the various Roma populations. It will be interesting to see if a multinational (or regional) approach to eliminating a longstanding underclass of people will be successful. Some skeptics have suggested that it may be easier to eliminate poverty among the Roma than to eliminate the centuries of social exclusion they have had to endure.

RACIAL AND ETHNIC STRATIFICATION

The discipline of anthropology has as its primary goal to study the extraordinary physical and cultural diversity found among the world's population. This vast physical and cultural diversity is also of great interest to the people themselves, because human relationships are often shaped by the differences, either real or imagined, between groups of people. To one degree or another, all societies differentiate among their members, and these differences can become the basis for social inequalities. People are often characterized on the basis of their distinctive physical characteristics or their learned cultural traits. Those sharing similar physical traits are often defined as belonging to the same *race*. Those sharing similar cultural characteristics are said to belong to the same *ethnic group*.

Throughout history, and in many parts of the world, racial and ethnic differences have led to inequality, discrimination, antagonism, and, in some cases, violence. Each day we read in the newspaper about racial or ethnic conflict in various parts of the world: Irish Republican Army bombings in England, ethnic cleansing in Bosnia, and terrorist attacks on Palestinians and Jews in Israel. Much closer to home, we have racial rioting in Los Angeles, ethnic gang wars in our cities, and racial and ethnic profiling in the aftermath of September 11. So even in the United States—a country constitutionally and legally committed to social equality—racial and ethnic differences still greatly affect relations between groups and their relative positions in the social hierarchy.

The terms *race* and *ethnicity* are sometimes used synonymously in everyday speech, but to anthropologists

race A subgroup of the human population whose members share a greater number of physical traits with one another than they do with members of other subgroups.
ethnic group A group of people sharing many of the same cultural features.

they have very different meanings. Technically, a *race* is an interbreeding population whose members share a greater number of traits with one another than they do with people outside the group. During the first half of the twentieth century, physical anthropologists devoted considerable effort to dividing the world's populations into racial categories based on shared physical traits. They carefully measured such traits as hair color and texture, eye color and shape, thickness of lips, breadth of the nose, body stature, and skin color, among others. But when the measuring frenzy was over, what did we really have? Depending on who was doing the categorizing, some racial typologies had hundreds of categories (that is, "races") and others had as few as three (Mongoloid, Caucasoid, and Negroid).

Race, then, is no more than a statistical statement about the occurrence of physical traits. When people who share a large number of biological traits intermarry, it is likely (but by no means certain) that they will have offspring who share those traits. When two blond-haired, blue-eyed Norwegians mate and have children, those children are statistically more likely to look like other Norwegians than like Nigerians. Similarly, when we cross two Chihuahuas, the offspring are more likely to look like Chihuahuas than Great Danes. Based on our knowledge of genetics, we know that there are no pure races because recessive traits are not lost but can reappear in future generations. Because different populations have been interbreeding for thousands of years, a continuum of human physical types has resulted.

The widespread use of DNA evidence has been a major reason for the success of such TV shows as *CSI, CSI Miami, CSI New York, Bones,* and *Injustice.* Today, however, DNA testing is also being used as a very effective mechanism for teaching university students a central concept about race; that is, racial groups or categories, as we normally define them, are not pure, mutually exclusive biological entities, but rather are arbitrary and socially constructed. In a sociology class on "race and ethnic relations" at Penn State University, students are learning, in a very personal way, that they are not quite who they thought they were (Daly 2005). As part of this course taught by Dr. Samuel Richard, students are able to have their DNA analyzed. Most students want to have their DNA tested for a variety of reasons. Some want to be able to prove to themselves that they are 100 percent racially pure; others think it might be cool to find traces of some other racial or biological groups; still others hope to find some unexpected racial footprints so they will be able to shock their parents. One black student from Philadelphia was startled to learn that 52 percent of his DNA was associated with Africans and 48 percent with Europeans. Even though this Black student is genetically 48-percent white, he was brought up in a Black family and neighborhood, has always identified himself as Black, and has no intention of altering that identity. This example is significant because it reminded

him, as well as others in the class, that race is not a neat and tidy way of compartmentalizing people into one biological category or another.

A major problem with racial classifications is that the schemes differ depending on the traits on which they are based. That is, it would be possible to put all of the world's people into a number of different categories based on skin color. But if those same people were categorized according to body stature, many people would be assigned to different categories. Each physical trait is biologically determined by distinct genes that vary independently of one another. Therefore, having a particular color of hair in no way determines what your eye color will be. All physical anthropologists who have attempted to classify people according to race have arbitrarily selected the traits they have used. For example, instead of using skin color or hair texture, we could classify people according to their earlobe structure (attached or detached earlobes), which is also a genetically determined physical trait. Although no one ever has, we could divide the world's population into two major races: those with attached earlobes and those with detached earlobes. Then, also quite arbitrarily, we could assert that people with attached earlobes (like your author) are clearly more intelligent than those with detached earlobes. Furthermore, we could claim that they are of better character and are more likely to practice good personal hygiene. Moreover, we could then insist that we don't want people with detached earlobes living in our neighborhoods, going to our schools, or marrying our daughters. Taking such a position, however, would make as much scientific sense as basing it on any other physical characteristic, such as skin color.

As a scientific concept, then, race is not terribly significant, for it gives us very little insight into human behavior. Nevertheless, because of the way people interpret physical differences, race is important *socially.* Race relations and stratification based on race are affected by people's beliefs, not necessarily by scientific facts. Because race is socially constructed, racial definitions vary from group to group. For example, North Americans classify people into discrete racial categories such as Caucasoid (White), Negroid (Black), and Mongoloid (Yellow). In some states in the United States (Tennessee and North Carolina), a person is defined as Black if one of his or her great-grandparents is Black. Brazilians, on the other hand, have at least seven categories of race, all based on gradations of skin color, hair texture, and facial features (Fish 1995). Because a husband and wife are able to have children who differ considerably on all of these traits, Brazilians acknowledge that two children having the same biological parents can be classified as racially different. Using the Brazilian criteria for determining race, many U.S. Blacks would not be considered Black in Brazil. Nevertheless, no matter how racial categories are defined, the accompanying beliefs about race are socially constructed and can have very real social consequences. All too often in human history, groups have separated themselves according to physical differences. They soon decide that physically different people are inferior and then use that belief to exclude, exploit, or brutalize them.

Whereas *race* refers to physical traits, *ethnicity* refers to cultural traits that are passed on from generation to generation. These cultural traits may include religion, dietary practices, language, humor, clothing, cultural heritage, folklore, national origins, and a shared ancestry and social experience. Members of an ethnic group perceive themselves as sharing these (and perhaps other) cultural characteristics. Moreover, ethnic group members have a sense of ethnic identity whereby they define themselves and members of their group as "us" and everyone else as "them."

The European Union, an economic, political, and cultural alliance between most western European nations, provides an interesting microcosm of modern ethnicity. Initially formed as a union to promote economic growth for its members, the EU is composed of autonomous nation-states with their own unique cultures, histories, languages, and traditions. People identify with their own ethnicity (for example, French, Spanish, Italian) rather than seeing themselves as generalized Europeans. To be certain, if an Italian woman was blindfolded and dropped off in any other city in western Europe, she would (a) know she was in Europe and (b) have little difficulty finding a meal or a toilet. But, in response to a question about developing a European ethnic identity, one Italian scholar responded, "The people here in Italy know and care nothing about Europe. They hate the people in the next village. Europe is nothing" (Byatt 2002: 48). This opinion speaks volumes about the continued influence of ethnicity and ethnic identity, even in a world that is experiencing rapid globalization.

Ethnic groups are more than mere social entities based on shared cultural origins. Rather, ethnic groups exist because of their shared social experiences over time. To illustrate, during the first several decades of the twentieth century, hundreds of thousands of Italians immigrated to New York City through Ellis Island. Coming, as they did, from all over Italy, they had identified themselves before leaving Italy with their town, village, or city, and with their extended family networks. Upon arrival in the new world, however, they shared a number of common experiences, including living in the lower east side of Manhattan, reading Italian-language newspapers, competing with other groups for jobs and resources, and buying ricotta cheese by the pound rather than in little eight-ounce plastic containers. These shared experiences over time forged a new ethnic identity as Italian-Americans, an identity which to some degree still exists today.

In some cases, certain groups are both racially and ethnically distinct from their neighbors. For example, some Native Americans, such as the Zuni, have distinctive physical features and identify themselves strongly using their native language, political organizations, family networks, and cultural practices. Other groups, such as Italian-Americans and Greek-Americans, may be physically indistinguishable from the majority but form their own distinctive (and usually exclusive) social clubs and social networks.

RACE AND ETHNICITY IN THE UNITED STATES

Because individual states in the United States define *race* differently, attempting to compare the sizes of different racial groups is an exercise in futility. The task is further complicated by the existence of people of mixed race, such as professional golfer Tiger Woods, whose mother is Asian-American and father was African-American. The current practice of U.S. Census takers is to allow people like Tiger Woods to check more than a single racial box. Moreover, the categories used in various census enumerations have changed over time. For examples, according to Lee (1993), Native Americans have explicitly included Eskimos (that is, Inuits) in some years, but not others; Hindus (a religious category) have been included under the heading of Asians in some years but not others; and not since the 1920 census has the U.S. Census included the term *Mulatto* under the general heading of Black or African-American. Although each ten-year census attempts to measure racial representation in the country, the results should (at best) be taken with a grain of salt because of the myriad problems of both definition and categorization.

For much of the twentieth century, the United States was described as a large melting pot in which people from many cultural backgrounds merged into a homogeneous American nationality. However, this image of mass cultural amalgamation does not match reality. Although significant numbers of individuals have broken out of their ethnic patterns, ethnic groups remain. To illustrate, large numbers of Asian-Americans (Chinese, Japanese, Vietnamese) live in California; Latinos in Miami, Los Angeles, Chicago, and New York; Arabic-speaking peoples in Detroit; Amish in Pennsylvania and Indiana; and hundreds of different Native American groups throughout North America. In fact, the United States has experienced a revival of ethnic consciousness in recent decades, particularly in urban areas. We often hear about ethnic neighborhoods, ethnic foods, and various ethnic studies programs at universities. Thus, the notion of the melting pot appears to be more of a metaphor than a reality. Perhaps we should think of contemporary American society less as a melting pot and more as a salad bowl, in which the individual ethnic groups are mixed together but retain their distinctiveness and identity.

If Tony Manero, played by John Travolta in the 1977 film *Saturday Night Fever*, was living in Brooklyn today, he would be sharing his Italian-American neighborhood with large numbers of Chinese, Russians, and Ukrainians.

Tiger Woods, one of the greatest golfers of all time, is the son of an Asian-American mother and an African-American father. What race is he?

Not only do ethnic groups maintain their identity within a pluralistic society, but the ethnic landscape is constantly rearranging itself. New York City, over the past century, reflects this changing ethnic mosaic. The unified ethnic communities of Chinatown, Little Italy, and Germantown (East 80s) that gave New York City much of its character in the early 1900s, while still in existence, are much less monolithic today. According to a report entitled "The Newest New Yorker 2000," there are today seventeen distinct neighborhoods in the city with a majority of foreign residents. In fact between the 1990 and 2000 census reports, the number of foreign-born residents in the five boroughs of NYC increased from 2.1 to 2.9 million, or 38 percent. Unlike the ethnic neighborhoods of the previous century, those of the twenty-first century are much more multicultural. To illustrate, in the Elmhurst section of Queens it is possible to see a Korean woman having her hair styled by either a Mexican or Jewish Russian hair stylist in the Bollywood Beauty Salon, which is owned by an Indian Muslim. Even the Bensonhurst section of Brooklyn (an Italian-American neighborhood, which was both this author's birthplace and the home of Tony Manero, aka John Travolta, who starred in the 1977 film *Saturday Night Fever*) is now composed of more than seventy-eight thousand Chinese

immigrants as well as sizeable Russian and Ukrainian populations (Berger 2005).

At the start of the twenty-first century, the fastest growing ethnic category in the United States is really not an ethnic group at all. Referred to by the catch-all term *Hispanics* by the U.S. Census Bureau, this rapidly growing segment of the U.S. population is composed of a number of different subcultural groups that share a common language. Linda Robinson (1998) describes seventeen different Hispanic subcultures within the continental United States. Some have lived in the United States for generations, but the majority have immigrated from Central and South America more recently.

Coming from more than twenty different countries, many prefer to be identified by their former nationality (for example, Cubans, Mexicans, Guatemalans) rather than as *Hispanics*. Others prefer the term *Latino*, which we will use to refer to this large and complex group.

However we may choose to classify them, collectively they are changing the face of the country and having an enormous impact on the nation's economy, politics, entertainment, and educational systems. The Latino population during the 1990s grew approximately 58 percent (from 22.3 million to 35.3 million) as compared to 13 percent for the overall population. According to the Statistical Abstract of the United States (2006), Latinos have replaced African-Americans as the largest minority group. It is estimated that by 2050 Latinos will represent one-quarter of the total U.S. population (Chambers 1999).

Not only do they have numbers, but many Latinos are making their mark on all aspects of U.S. culture. Young Americans of all types are dancing to salsa music, buying CDs recorded by Jennifer Lopez, Enrique Iglesias, and Christina Aguilera, and cheering for their favorite Major League Baseball players with names such as Sosa, Ramirez, and Rodriguez. Yet, not everyone in

CROSS-CULTURAL MISCUE

Several years ago while walking to class with an armload of books, I (your textbook author) met a group of five of my students who were also on their way to my class. Four of the students were local students, born and raised in North Carolina, while the fifth was a foreign student from Nigeria. Upon meeting, we all greeted one another, and proceeded to walk together to class. Almost immediately, the Nigerian student turned to me and asked if he could carry my load of books. I refused, but because the Nigerian young man insisted, I relented. As soon as I handed over the books, I noticed that the Nigerian student was receiving some "funny looks" from the North Carolina students. It became immediately apparent to me that we were witnessing a classic example of a cross-cultural misunderstanding.

When we arrived in class, I decided to see if this incident could provide us with some insight into the nature of cross-cultural *mis*communication. After describing the incident to the class, I asked the four students from North Carolina to share with us what was behind those negative "nonverbal" looks they were giving their classmate from Nigeria when he took my load of books. As predicted, all four of the students thought that the Nigerian had offered to carry my books in an effort to curry favor with the professor and perhaps get a higher grade in the course than he might deserve. The four U.S. students were clearly put off by what they considered to be a blatant attempt to "suck up" to the professor.

Hearing this explanation, the Nigerian student was shocked that his gesture was so thoroughly misunderstood. He then explained that he offered to carry my books out of a deep sense of respect for my high status as a college professor. Professors in Nigeria enjoy much higher social status than do their counterparts in the United States. It would be considered demeaning for a Nigerian professor to engage in any form of manual labor, including carrying a heavy load of books. The somewhat startled Nigerian student went on to say that he offered to carry my books so I would not "lose face" by engaging in physical labor. Clearly, the status system in Nigeria is appreciably different from that found in the United States.

the United States has been willing to embrace this rapidly growing Latino presence. In California, which has the largest number of Latinos of any state, voters supported several initiatives to deny schooling and social services to undocumented immigrants and to eliminate bilingual education programs in the schools.

This backlash is based on a number of myths about the Hispanic population. First, because of the widespread use of Spanish on signs in cities such as Los Angeles and Miami, many people assume that Latinos do not speak English or have no desire to learn it. But the rate of learning English for Latinos is approximately the same as for other immigrant groups, and, in fact, one-third of Latinos living in Los Angeles speak only English. Second, Latinos are sometimes viewed (erroneously) as not fully participating in the economy. However, Mexicans and Central Americans have a labor force participation rate of 62 percent, which exceeds the Anglo rate and far exceeds that of African-Americans. Latinos generally are found doing the jobs that other Americans refuse to do: harvesting crops, making beds, landscaping, and doing construction-related work such as house framing, roofing, and masonry. They have the diligence and enterprise, coupled with strong family ties, that characterized the Irish, Italians, and Poles during the early 1900s. And third, many mainstream Americans view recent migrants as "short-timers" who are interested only in making enough money to return home. But when asked in a national survey if they planned to stay permanently in the United States, more than 90 percent of the legal immigrants said yes (Pachon 1998). To be certain, some immigrants do return home, and others continue to send sizable portions of their income to relatives back home. But, like their European counterparts a century earlier, most Latinos plant their roots and commit to becoming citizens.

FORMS OF INTERGROUP RELATIONS

Some racial and ethnic groups live together in peace and with a large degree of social equality. In most situations, however, racial and ethnic groups tend to experience varying levels of conflict and inequality. How racial and ethnic groups relate to one another can be viewed as a continuum ranging from cooperation to outright hostility. George Simpson and J. Milton Yinger (1985) have identified six major forms of interracial and interethnic relations, arranged from most humane to least humane.

1. *Pluralism.* In this situation, two or more groups live in harmony with one another while each retains its own ethnic heritage, pride, and identity. Swiss society—composed of Germans, Swiss Germans, French, and Italians living together peacefully, if not always amicably—is a good example of pluralism. However, not all situations are as harmonious as the multicultural country of Switzerland. Present-day Canada is an excellent example of a multicultural society that is experiencing a number of challenges to its national cohesion by French separatists who want to assert their cultural uniqueness. A truly multicultural society has been realized when there is no longer a single dominant ethnic or racial group.

2. *Assimilation.* Assimilation occurs when a racial or ethnic minority is absorbed into the wider society.

assimilation   The process of absorbing a racial or ethnic group into the wider society.

Photofest

Don Cheadle stars in the true-life story of Paul Rusesabagina, a hotel manager who housed over a thousand Tutsis refugees during their struggle against genocide by Hutu militia in Rwanda.

The many Asian and Pacific ethnic groups that have peacefully and voluntarily assimilated themselves into Hawaiian society over the past several centuries are an example. Assimilation involves several different forms, which usually progress in sequential stages. The first stage of assimilation is cultural, whereby minority group members gradually surrender their own cultural features (such as language, values, and behaviors) while accepting those of the dominant group. The second form is social assimilation, in which minority group members join into secondary and eventually primary group relationships (such as churches, unions, and neighborhood associations) with members of the mainstream. The final stage of assimilation involves physical integration through intermarriage, whereby the biological distinctions between the minority and the majority groups gradually decline or disappear.

3. *Legal protection of minorities.* In societies where racial and ethnic groups are hostile toward one another, the government may step in to legally protect the minority group. In Great Britain, the Race Relations Act makes it a criminal offense for anyone to express publicly any sentiments that might lead to racial or ethnic hostility. In the United States, three constitutional amendments (the thirteenth, fourteenth, and fifteenth), several civil rights laws, and a number of executive directives have provided legislative and administrative protection to minorities over the past decades. The recent passage of the Native Title Bill in Australia guarantees a number of territorial rights to the country's indigenous population (a mere two centuries after European settlers drove them off their ancestral land!). None of these pieces of legislation has given equal citizenship to minority groups, but they have provided a measure of security against some of the more blatant forms of prejudice and discrimination.

4. *Population transfer.* One solution to intergroup conflict is **population transfer**, which involves the physical removal of a minority group to another location. The forced relocation of sixteen thousand Cherokee Indians from North Carolina to Oklahoma in 1838 is a case in point. A more recent example from the United States, although a temporary situation, was the forced relocation of thousands of Japanese-Americans into internment camps during World War II. Unfortunately, this particular form of intergroup relationship has been played out in a number of different places in the world in recent years. For example, tens of thousands of Vietnamese people have fled from Cambodia to Vietnam to avoid being killed by the Cambodian government. Large numbers of ethnic Tutsi from Rwanda have fled to Zaire, Tanzania, and Uganda to avoid persecution by the majority Hutu government. Often these population transfers cause enormous hardships both for those being moved and for the local people into whose territories they are arriving.

5. *Long-term subjugation.* In some parts of the world, racial and ethnic minorities have been politically, economically, and socially repressed for indefinite periods of time. Until the changes in the mid-1990s, the repression of Blacks under the apartheid system in the Republic of South Africa was an example of the long-term institutionalized (legal) repression of one ethnic and racial group by another. Separate and unequal facilities (schools, restrooms, housing) and strict legalized segregation were government policy in South Africa for much of the twentieth century. The White population (13 percent) controlled the best 87 percent of the land, whereas the non-Whites (87 percent) lived on the worst 13 percent of the land. The situation that until recently existed in South Africa was just slightly better than slavery for the non-White population.

6. *Genocide.* Sometimes the symbols of race and ethnicity can be so powerful that they can cause people to engage in **genocide**: mass annihilation of groups of people. The most notorious example, of course, is Adolph Hitler, who during World War II sent more than 6 million people (Jews, Gypsies, Slavs, homosexuals, and others he considered to be subhuman) to be killed in death camps. Unfortunately, there are many other examples of genocide from around the world that, although involving fewer deaths, are just as inhumane. To illustrate, in what used to be Yugoslavia, Serbian forces under the leadership of

population transfer   The practice of physically relocating a minority group from one area to another.

genocide   The systematic attempt to eliminate entire cultures or racial groups.

Diabetes Among Mexican-Americans

It has been found that non-insulin-dependent diabetes mellitus (NIDDM), a serious health problem in the United States, is now verging on epidemic proportions. According to projections by the Center for Disease Control and Prevention, one-third of all children born in 2000 are expected to become diabetic in their lifetime. The prediction for Latino children of the same age is even bleaker: one in two. Medical researchers have found that Mexican-Americans living in the southwestern part of the United States are two to three times more likely to suffer from diabetes than are non-Hispanic Whites. Factors accounting for this higher incidence among Mexican-Americans include a genetic predisposition, culture, geography, and a number of variables associated with low socioeconomic status (such as income, access to health facilities, and literacy).

Diabetes is not curable. Rather, it must be managed over the course of the patient's lifetime. To manage diabetes, patients need to take medication in the proper doses, exercise regularly, and adhere to a healthy diet. A major problem in the treatment of NIDDM is that patients often fail to follow through on recommended treatment behaviors. Noncompliance with prescribed treatment is particularly high among Mexican-Americans.

Medical anthropologist Linda Hunt, along with her colleagues Jacqueline Pugh and Miguel Valenzuela, wanted to know more about the factors influencing self-care among Mexican-American patients with NIDDM so they could develop recommendations to improve intervention strategies (1995). Hunt and her colleagues conducted open-ended interviews with fifty-one Mexican-American patients with NIDDM in San Antonio and Laredo, Texas. Their findings showed that none of the patients in the sample followed the recommended treatment exactly. However, it wasn't because of disinterest or ignorance. Rather, they were adapting their self-care behavior to the social realities of their everyday lives, making choices based on two important sociocultural factors: (1) their limited financial resources and (2) their desire to conduct "normal" social relationships. Let us look at each of these factors.

Because all interviewees were low-income patients, their diabetes imposed several hardships on them. Many felt too sick to work, thereby reducing their income; the cost of treatment, despite the clinics' sliding fee scales, was still a major financial burden; and the cost of changing their diets usually involved substituting more expensive foods (such as fresh fruits and vegetables) for the things that they normally ate. Because of their limited finances, patients would conserve resources not by discontinuing a certain treatment (such as taking medication or testing for blood sugar level) but rather by doing it less often than prescribed.

President Slobodan Milosevic engaged in what has been euphemistically called "ethnic cleansing," in which Muslims and Croats were murdered by the thousands, and many more were raped and brutalized. And in 1994, in a very purposeful attempt at genocide, the Hutu extremists in Rwanda massacred an estimated million Tutsi. Although widely condemned by most people in the world, genocide is still used by some groups as a way to gain political advantage.

It is important to note that these ways of classifying racial and ethnic relations are not mutually exclusive. More than one classification can exist in a society at the same time.

THEORIES OF STRATIFICATION

The unequal distribution of wealth, power, and prestige appears to be a fundamental characteristic of most societies, particularly those with complex, highly differentiated economies. Some modern societies—such as the former Soviet Union, the People's Republic of China,

and Albania—have attempted to become classless by eliminating all vestiges of inequality. But even in these societies, high-ranking government officials have been far more generously rewarded than the workers. The basic question is, Why is inequality a nearly universal trait of social life? The debate among social scientists, which at times has been heated, revolves around two conflicting positions that are based on different philosophical assumptions and have distinct political implications. The more conservative position, the *functional theory*, holds that social inequality exists because it is necessary for the maintenance of society. The more liberal *conflict theory* explains social inequality as the

functionalism/functional theory   A theory of social stratification holding that social stratification exists because it contributes to the overall well-being of a society.
conflict theory   A theory of social stratification that argues that society is always changing and in conflict because individuals in the upper stratum use their wealth, power, and prestige to exploit those below them.

The second factor that influenced decisions about self-care was a desire on the part of both men and women to "feel normal" by continuing in the same roles as they had before they developed diabetes. Because many women play the role of family caregiver, those who have sick relatives at home find it impossible to get out of the house to get the proper exercise. Moreover, female patients with diabetes find it very difficult to cook food for their families that they themselves are not allowed to eat. Men find it particularly difficult to change their eating habits because they want to maintain their masculine image, to be able to make their own decisions about what to eat and drink, and to participate in social events such as parties or watching football, which often involve drinking alcohol. Thus, for both men and women, having to alter one's usual roles and behavior was seen as interfering with having a normal social life.

Understanding the social and cultural realities of Mexican-Americans, the researchers could recommend improved intervention strategies. Rather than blaming the patients for failed treatments, the researchers appreciated the patients' limited finances and were able to come up with some creative solutions. It was possible to cut the cost of self-treatment without sacrificing quality. For example, Hunt and her colleagues suggested cost cutting strategies such as establishing safe procedures for reusing syringes, using phone follow-up to replace some of the clinic visits, and formulating ways of reducing the cost of the foods needed for a healthy diet. There were also recommendations that took into account the need of patients to maintain normal social relationships. To illustrate, people who feel pressure to eat and drink inappropriate things at social events need culturally acceptable strategies for turning down food or decreasing the amount they eat. In some cases, the solution may be as simple as getting people to use different language when describing food. As Hunt and her colleagues have suggested, "the concept of a 'diabetic diet' could be replaced by pointing out that it is really just a 'healthy diet' for everyone."

Hunt's research suggests that clinicians, particularly when working with culturally different patients, need to understand why people make certain choices concerning their self-care treatment. Rather than assuming that ignorance or indifference is the cause of poor outcomes, clinicians need to explore what patients are doing and why they are doing it. Only by entering into a continuing dialogue with culturally different patients can clinicians help them make the most medically appropriate choices for managing their illness.

Questions for Further Thought

1. Why did none of the Mexican-American patients in Hunt's study strictly follow the prescribed self-care behaviors?
2. Can you think of additional reasons why it might be more difficult for low-income Mexican-Americans to get regular exercise than it would be for upper-middle-class people living in the suburbs?
3. From what you know about proper self-care behavior for diabetes, can you identify other ethnic groups in your area of the country that would have similar difficulties adhering to prescribed forms of self-care?

---

result of benefits derived by the upper classes that use their power and privilege to exploit those below them.

The Functionalist Interpretation

By stressing the integrative nature of social systems, functional anthropologists argue that stratification exists because it contributes to the overall well-being of the society. According to Kingsley Davis and Wilbert Moore (1945), complex societies, if they are to survive, depend on the performance of a wide variety of jobs, some of which are more important than others because they require specialized education, talent, and hard work. If people are to make the sacrifices necessary to perform these vital jobs, they must be adequately rewarded. For example, because the skills of a physician are in greater demand by our society than are those of a fast food employee, the rewards (money and prestige) are much greater for the physician. Functionalists argue that these differential rewards are necessary if societies are to recruit the best-trained and most highly skilled people for these highly valued positions. If physicians and fast-food workers received the same pay and social status, few people would opt to become physicians. Thus, according to the functionalist interpretation, social stratification is necessary or *functional* for the society because it serves as a mechanism for allocating rewards and motivating the best people to fill the key jobs in the society.

Although the functionalist view seems plausible, it has weaknesses. First, some critics of the functionalist position point out that stratified societies do not always give the greatest rewards to those filling the most vital positions. Rock singers, baseball players, and movie stars often make many times more money than teachers, pediatricians, or U.S. Supreme Court justices. Second, the functionalists do not recognize the barriers that stratification systems put in the way of certain segments of the society, such as members of low-prestige and low-power groups. Ethnic and racial minorities, women, and the poor do not always have equal opportunities to compete because they are too poor or have the wrong accent, skin color, or gender. Third, the functionalist position can be called into question because it tends to make a fundamentally ethnocentric assumption. That is, the functionalists assume that people in all societies are motivated by the desire to maximize their wealth, power, and prestige. In actual fact, however, a number of societies emphasize the equitable distribution of social rewards rather than rewarding individuals for amassing as much as possible for themselves.

The Conflict Theory Interpretation

Whereas the functionalist view starts with the assumption of social order, stability, and integration, conflict theorists assume that the natural tendency of all societies is toward change and conflict. According to this theory, stratification exists because the people occupying the upper levels of the hierarchy are willing and able to use their wealth, power, and prestige to exploit those below them. The upper strata maintain their dominance through the use of force or the threat of force and by convincing the oppressed of the value of continuing the system. Thus, those at the top use their wealth, power, and prestige to maintain—perhaps even strengthen—their privileged position.

This conflict theory of social stratification is derived largely from the late-nineteenth-century writings of Karl Marx, who, unlike the functionalists, did not view stratification systems as either desirable or inevitable. Believing that economic forces are the main factors shaping a society, Marx (1909) viewed history as a constant class struggle between the haves and the have-nots. Writing during the latter stages of the industrial revolution in Europe, Marx saw the classic struggle occurring between the *bourgeoisie* (those who owned the means of production) and the *proletariat* (the working class who exchanged their labor for wages).

Because of their control of the means of production, the small capitalist class exerts significant influence over the larger working class. By controlling such institutions as schools, factories, government, and the media, the bourgeoisie can convince the workers that the existing distribution of power and wealth (that is, the status quo) is preferable and that anyone can be successful if only he or she works hard enough. Thus, according to the classic Marxist view, the capitalists create a false consciousness among the workers by leading them to believe that if they are not successful, it is because they have not worked hard enough rather than because their opportunities for advancement were blocked by the powerful upper class.

As long as the workers accept this ideology legitimizing the status quo, the inequities of the stratification

---

bourgeoisie Karl Marx's term referring to the middle class (those who own the means of production).
proletariat The term used in conflict theories of social stratification to describe the working class who exchange their labor for wages.

---

system will continue to exist. Believing that class conflict is inevitable, Marx predicted that eventually the proletariat would recognize both the extent of its own exploitation and its collective power to change it. When the workers develop a class consciousness, he asserted, they will revolt against the existing social order, replace capitalism with communism, and eliminate scarcity, social classes, and inequality.

Functionalists Versus Conflict Theorists

Functionalists and conflict theorists—with their radically different interpretations of social inequality—have been locking horns for years. Functionalists hold that systems of stratification exist and are necessary because they benefit the societies of which they are a part. Conflict theorists, on the other hand, claim that systems of stratification exist because they help the people at the top (that is, the wealthy and powerful) maintain their privileged position. The functionalist position emphasizes the positive benefits of social stratification for the total society. Conflict theorists draw our attention to negative aspects such as the unjust nature of stratification systems and how that inherent unfairness can lead to rebellions, revolts, and high crime rates.

Although there is truth in both of these interpretations, neither theory can be used exclusively to explain the existence of all types of stratification systems. Functionalists are correct to point out that open class systems, for example, are integrative to the extent that they promote constructive endeavor that is beneficial to the society as a whole. Yet, once established, these class systems often become self-perpetuating, with those at the top striving to maintain their superior positions at the expense of the lower classes. At the same time, the underclasses—through political mobilization, revitalization movements, and even violent revolutions—seek to free themselves from deprivation and exploitation. In short, functional integration is real, but so is conflict.

Not only do the functionalist and conflict theories represent two contrasting interpretations of social inequality, but they also have radically different policy implications for modern society. The functionalist view implies that social stratification systems should be maintained because the best-qualified people, through the competitive process, will be motivated to fill the top positions. In contrast, conflict theory implies that social inequality should be minimized or eliminated because many people in the lower strata never have a chance to develop their full potential. Thus, the functionalist position would want the government to take no action (such as welfare programs or a progressive income tax) that would redistribute wealth, power, or prestige. Conflict theorists would call for exactly the opposite course of action, arguing that eliminating barriers to social mobility would unleash the hidden brilliance of those currently living in the underclasses.

The average income of people in the United States is roughly 376 times as much as this Ethiopian farmer.

Global Stratification

This chapter has looked at social stratification—that is, how societies comprise different groups that are ranked relative to one another in terms of wealth, power, and prestige. Not only are people stratified relative to one another within a society, but societies (nation-states) are also stratified relative to one another. In much the same way that we can identify upper-, middle-, and lower-class people within a society, it is also possible today to speak of wealthy/powerful countries and poor/weak countries within the global system. If the world was not so intimately interconnected (and becoming more so with each passing year), we would be living in a world comprising many countries with simply different levels of wealth and power. But as we have shown in previous chapters, the nations of the world, however different they may be, are not isolated and insulated from one another. Rather, the decisions being made in New York or Chicago today are having real effects on the status and personal wealth of people in Bangladesh.

Perhaps the most concrete measure of global stratification is based on differential levels of wealth. One of the more common ways of measuring national wealth is by using the *per capita gross national income* index (GNI). This measure is calculated by adding the output of goods and services in a country to the income of residents and dividing by the total population. Of the

per capita gross national income   A commonly used index of relative wealth among nations calculated by adding the output of goods and services in a country to the income of residents and dividing by the total population.

Table 12.2 Per Capital GNI (2004)

Ten Richest Nations	Per Capita GNI
Luxembourg	$56,380
Norway	$51,810
Switzerland	$49,600
Bermuda	estimated
United States	$41,400
Denmark	$40,750
Liechtenstein	estimated
Iceland	$37,920
Japan	$37,050
Sweden	$35,840
Ten Poorest Nations	**Per Capita GNI**
Niger	$210
Rwanda	$210
Sierra Leone	$210
Eritrea	$190
Guinea Bissau	$160
Malawi	$160
Liberia	$120
Congo Democratic Republic	$110
Ethiopia	$110
Burundi	$90

SOURCE: World Bank Atlas (www.web.worldbank.org/wbsite/external/datastatistics)

more than two hundred nation-states in the world today, half have per capita GNI of less than $2500. The United States has a per capita GNI of more than $41,000 while countries such as Ethiopia and Burundi have per capita GNI of less than $120. This means that the average U.S. citizen earns roughly 460 times more than the average citizen of Burundi. Looked at somewhat differently, the average U.S. worker in a regulated textile factory earns more than $9.00 per hour as compared to $.31 in Bangladesh, $.34 in Indonesia, and $.76 in Nicaragua. Consequently, factory (sweatshop) workers in poor countries (who may be eleven years old and earning less than $2.00 per day) are working so that people in North America can jog in Nike running shoes and wear the latest fashions from the Gap, the Banana Republic, or Nordstrom.

These enormous inequities in wealth found throughout the world have a number of important social consequences. First, poor countries have the highest birth rates and the lowest life expectancies. Women in poor countries on average have five children during their lifetime as compared to only two children for women in wealthy nations. With high rates of fertility, the populations of poor countries are growing more rapidly than those of wealthy countries, have higher proportions of young children, and have relatively fewer adults to provide for them. Second, in terms of health, poorer countries have higher infant mortality, more children born underweight, and a lower life expectancy. Whereas virtually 100 percent of people living in Switzerland and Luxembourg have access to safe drinking water and functioning sewage systems, only about one in ten Afghans do. And third, wealthy countries have near universal education and most adults are functionally literate, while this is not the case in the poorer countries. Thus, we can see the profound differences (in terms of mortality, health, sanitation, education, and population size) between the rich countries and the poor countries within the global system of the twenty-first century. ■

Summary

1. Social ranking is an important feature found to one degree or another in all societies. The degree to which societies distribute wealth, power, and prestige on an equitable basis can be used to distinguish among three different types of societies. Egalitarian societies are unstratified in that they allocate wealth, power, and prestige fairly equally. In rank societies, which are partially stratified, people have equal access to power and wealth but not to prestige. The most completely stratified societies are those based on classes or castes and that have unequal access to wealth, power, and prestige.

2. Stratified societies, which are associated with the rise of civilization, range from open class societies, which permit high social mobility, to more rigid caste societies, which allow for little or no social mobility. Class societies are associated with achieved status—positions that the individual can choose or at least have some control over. Caste societies, on the other hand, are based on ascribed statuses into which one is born and cannot change.

3. The United States is often cited as a prime example of a class society with maximum mobility. Although our national credo includes a belief in the possibility of going from rags to riches, most people in the United States remain in the class into which they are born because social environment has an appreciable effect on a person's life chances.

4. For the past several decades, class inequality in the United States has increased, not decreased. The income gap between the upper and lower classes has widened, and there has been an increasing concentration of political power in the hands of the capitalist class.

5. Hindu India is often cited as the most extreme form of caste society found in the world. Social boundaries among castes are strictly maintained by caste endogamy and strongly held notions of ritual purity and pollution. The Indian caste system, which has persisted for two thousand years, has created an ideology enabling the upper castes to maintain a monopoly on wealth, status, and power.

6. Race is a classification of people based on physical traits, whereas ethnicity is a scheme based on cultural characteristics. Although the concept of race is not particularly meaningful from a scientific standpoint, it is important because people's ideas of racial differences have led to very powerful systems of stratification and discrimination. Despite globalization of world economies, ethnic group identity remains strong throughout the world.

7. There are two conflicting interpretations of social stratification. The functionalist theory emphasizes the integrative nature of stratification systems, pointing out how class systems contribute to the overall well-being of a society by encouraging constructive endeavor. Conflict theorists believe that stratification systems exist because the upper classes strive to maintain their superior position at the expense of the lower classes.

8. Just as individuals are stratified within a society, so too are nation-states stratified within the world system. Wealthy countries, which can have hundreds of times more wealth than poor countries, have better systems of education and health care and much longer life expectancies.

Key Terms

achieved status	Dalit	population transfer	Sanskritization
ascribed status	egalitarian societies	power	social mobility
assimilation	ethnic group	prestige	soft money
bourgeoisie	functional theory	primogeniture	stratified societies
caste	genocide	proletariat	varnas
class	jati	race	wealth
conflict theory	per capita gross national income	rank societies	

Suggested Readings

Berreman, Gerald D., and Kathleen M. Zaretsky, eds. *Social Inequality: Comparative and Development Approaches.* New York: Academic Press, 1981. A collection of fifteen essays on the topic of social inequality that attempts to treat the subject comparatively across a wide range of cultures, comparatively over time, and within the appropriate sociocultural context.

Domhoff, G. William. *Who Rules America?* Mountain View, CA: Mayfield, 1998. Using a power elite model, Domhoff argues that power in the United States is in the hands of an elite composed of corporate CEOs, political leaders, and military leaders, all of whom are intimately interconnected.

Ehrenreich, Barbara. *Nickel and Dimed: On (Not) Getting By in America.* New York: Metropolitan Books, 2001. A participant-observation study by a journalist who spent months working at a number of low-paying jobs in the United States. This firsthand account demonstrates how millions of people in the United States fail to make ends meet while working in dead-end and socially demeaning jobs.

Fluehr-Lobban, Carolyn. *Race and Racism: An Introduction.* Lanham, MD: AltaMira Press, 2006. This engaging new book offers an explanation for both the persistence of racism and why it is not openly discussed or confronted in American society.

Gilbert, Dennis. *American Class Structure in an Age of Growing Inequality,* 6th ed. Belmont, CA: Wadsworth, 2003. Drawing on census data, Gilbert documents the growing inequalities (in terms of power, wealth, and prestige) in the United States over the past three decades. Now in its sixth edition, this book is the most comprehensive study of class in the contemporary United States.

Goldberg, David T. *The Racial State.* Malden, MA: Blackwell, 2001. This title argues that the concept of race has played an integral role in the emergence of the state as a political form.

Lenski, Gerhard E. *Power and Privilege: A Theory of Social Stratification.* New York: McGraw-Hill, 1966. A wide-ranging analysis of human inequality that takes the reader through centuries and to all parts of the world. Lenski asks the fundamental question of stratification studies: Who gets what and why? He then answers the question by using anthropological, historical, and sociological data.

Newman, Katherine S. *No Shame in My Game: The Working Poor in the Inner City.* New York: Knopf, 1999. A firsthand anthropological study of three hundred low-wage fast-food service workers in Harlem, New York. Challenging many of our assumptions about the inner-city working poor, Newman shows that despite the available alternatives of welfare or crime, most of the working poor persevere with a strong work ethic.

Parrenas, Rhacel Salazar. *Servants of Globalization: Women, Migration, and Domestic Work.* Stanford, CA: Stanford University Press, 2001. A moving analysis of the immigration of Filipina domestic workers in Rome, Italy, and Los Angeles, California. The study demonstrates how this domestic labor provides menial services for the global economy while at the same time having very negative effects on the family relations of the migrant Filipinas.

Romanucci-Ross, Lola. *Ethnic Identity: Creation, Conflict, and Accommodation,* 3d ed. Walnut Creek, CA: AltaMira, 1995. This reader includes a number of articles showing how ethnic identity is related to language, nationalism, religion, and localism in locations such as the former Yugoslavia, Sri Lanka, Southeast Asia, and Latino communities in the United States.

Political Organization and Social Control

A chief in Kaduna, Nigeria.

13

AS MENTIONED IN the discussion of cultural universals in Chapter 2, all societies, if they are to remain viable over time, must maintain social order. Every society must develop a set of customs and procedures for making and enforcing decisions, resolving disputes, and regulating the behavior of its members. Every society must make collective decisions about its environment and its relations with other societies and about how to deal with disruptive or destructive behavior on the part of its members. These topics generally are discussed under headings such as political organization, law, power, authority, social control, and conflict resolution. In addition to exploring all of these subjects, this chapter deals with the cultural arrangements by which societies maintain social order, minimize the chances of disruption, and cope with whatever disruptions do occur (Vincent 1990; McGlynn and Tuden 1991).

When most North Americans think of politics or political structure, a number of familiar images come to mind, such as the following:

- Political leaders such as presidents, governors, mayors, or commissioners
- Complex bureaucracies employing thousands of civil servants
- Legislative bodies ranging from the smallest town council to the U.S. Congress
- Formal judicial institutions that comprise municipal, state, and federal courts
- Law enforcement bodies such as police departments, national guard units, and the armed forces
- Political parties, nominating conventions, and secret ballot voting

All of these are mechanisms that our own society uses for making and enforcing political decisions as well as coordinating and regulating people's behavior. Many societies in the world have none of these things—no elected officials, legislatures, formal elections, armies, or bureaucracies. We should not conclude from this, however, that such societies do not have some form of political organization, if by political organization we mean a set of customary procedures that accomplish decision making, conflict resolution, and social control.

What We Will Learn

- What are the different types of political organization?

- What are the various theories concerning the origins of the state?

- In the absence of kings, presidents, legislatures, and bureaucracies, how is social order maintained in stateless societies?

- What are the causes of war?

 Click!

For interactive exercises and study aids, Go to **www.ichapters.com**; enter the author name and select your text, then click the Study Help tab to purchase the following online resources:

- **ThomsonNOW** for chapter-specific online tutorials, quizzes, and a personalized study plan

- **Anthropology Resource Center** for interactive maps, modules, videos, and the Applied Anthropology site

- **Thomson Audio Study Products** for a brief overview of the major chapter themes and to test your knowledge with quiz questions

TYPES OF POLITICAL ORGANIZATION

The term *political organization* refers to the way in which power is distributed within a society so as to control people's behavior and maintain social order. All societies are organized politically, but the degree of specialized and formal mechanisms varies considerably from one society to another. Societies differ in their political organization based on three important dimensions:

- The extent to which political institutions are distinct from other aspects of the social structure; that is, for example, in some societies, political structures are barely distinguishable from economic, kinship, or religious structures.
- The extent to which legitimate *authority* is concentrated into specific political roles.
- The level of *political integration* (that is, the size of the territorial group that comes under the control of the political structure).

These three dimensions are the basis for classifying societies (Service 1978) into four fundamentally different types of political structure: band societies, tribal societies, chiefdoms, and state societies. Although some societies do not fit neatly into a single category, this fourfold scheme can help us understand how different societies administer themselves and maintain social order.

Although our discussions of all four types of political organization are written using the "ethnographic present," we need to remember that there are no pure bands, tribes, or chiefdoms in the world today. Rather, these nonstate forms of political organization have had more complex state political systems superimposed over them.

Band Societies

The least complex form of political arrangement is the band, characterized by small and usually nomadic populations of food collectors. Although the size of a band can range anywhere from twenty to several hundred individuals, most bands number between thirty and fifty people. The actual size of particular bands is directly related to food-gathering methods; that is, the more food a band has at its disposal, the larger the number of people it can support. Although bands may be loosely associated with a specific territory, they have little or no concept of individual property ownership and place a high value on sharing, cooperation, and reciprocity. *Band societies* have very little role specialization and are highly egalitarian in that few differences in status and wealth can be observed. Because this form of political organization is so closely associated with a foraging technology, it is generally thought to be the oldest form of political organization.

Band societies share a number of traits. First, because bands are composed of a relatively small number of people who are related by blood or marriage, a high value is placed on "getting along" with one another. Whatever conflicts arise within the band are often settled informally by direct negotiation. In the unlikely event that a just resolution of a conflict cannot be reached, the dissatisfied party has the option of leaving the band and joining another one in which he has relatives.

Second, band societies have the least amount of political integration; that is, the various bands (each comprising fifty or so people) are independent of one another and are not part of a larger political structure. The integration that does exist is based largely on ties of kinship and marriage. All of the bands found in any particular culture are bound by a common language and general cultural features. However, members of band societies do not all pay political allegiance to any overall authority.

Third, in band societies political decisions are often embedded in the wider social structure. Because bands are composed of kin, it is difficult to distinguish between purely political decisions and those that we would recognize as family, economic, or religious decisions. Political life, in other words, is simply one part of social life.

Fourth, leadership roles in band societies tend to be very informal. In band societies, there are no specialized political roles or leaders with designated authority. Instead, leaders in foraging societies are often, but not always, older men respected for their experience, wisdom, good judgment, and knowledge of hunting. Most decisions are made through discussions by the adult men. The headman can persuade and give advice but has no power to impose his will on the group. The headman often gives advice on such matters as migratory movements, but he has no permanent authority. If his advice proves to be wrong or unpopular, the group members will look to another person to be headman. Band leadership, then, stems not so much from power as from personal traits admired by the others in the group.

The Ju/'hoansi of the Kalahari exemplify a band society with a headman. Although the position of head-

---

authority   The power or right to give commands, take action, and make binding decisions.

political integration   The process that brings disparate people under the control of a single political system.

band societies   Bands are the basic social unit found in many hunting-and-gathering societies; these societies are characterized by being kinship based and having no permanent political structure.

Tribal societies, such as the Samburu of Kenya, have certain pan-tribal mechanisms, such as clans and age organizations, which serve to integrate the tribe as a whole.

man is hereditary, the actual authority of the headman is quite limited. The headman coordinates the movement of his people and usually walks at the head of the group. He chooses the sites of new encampments and has first pick of location for his own house site. But beyond these limited perks of office, the Ju/'hoansi headman receives no other rewards. He is not responsible for organizing hunting parties, making artifacts, or negotiating marriage arrangements. These activities fall to the individual members of the band. The headman is not expected to be a judge of his people. Moreover, his material possessions are no greater than any other person's. As Lorna Marshall so aptly put it when referring to the Ju/'hoansi headman: "He carries his own load and is as thin as the rest" (1965: 267).

Tribal Societies

Whereas band societies are usually associated with food collecting, *tribal societies* are found most often among food producers (horticulturalists and pastoralists). Because plant and animal domestication is far more productive than foraging, tribal societies tend to have populations that are larger, denser, and somewhat more sedentary in nature. Tribal societies are similar to band societies in several important respects. Both are egalitarian to the extent that there are no marked differences in status, rank, power, and wealth. In addition, tribal societies, like bands, have local leaders but do not have centralized leadership. Leadership in tribal societies is informal and not vested in a centralized authority. A man is recognized as a leader by virtue of certain personality traits such as wisdom, integrity, in-

telligence, and concern for the welfare of others. While tribal leaders often play a central role in formulating decisions, they cannot force their will upon a group. In the final analysis, decisions are arrived at through group consensus.

The major difference between tribes and bands is that tribal societies have certain *pan-tribal mechanisms* that cut across and integrate all of the local segments of the tribe into a larger whole. These mechanisms include tribal associations such as clans, age grades, or secret societies. Pan-tribal associations unite the tribe against external threats. These integrating forces are not permanent political fixtures, however. Most often the local units of a tribe operate autonomously. The integrating mechanisms come into play only when an external threat arises. When the threat is eliminated, the local units return to their autonomous state. Even though these pan-tribal mechanisms may be transitory, they nevertheless provide wider political integration in certain situations than would never be possible in band societies.

In many tribal societies, the kinship unit known as the clan serves as a pan-tribal mechanism of political integration. The *clan* is defined as a group of kin who consider themselves to be descended from a common ancestor, even though individual clan members cannot trace, step-by-step, their connection to the clan founder. Clan elders, though not holding formal political offices, usually manage the affairs of their clans (settling disputes between clan members, for example) and represent their clans in dealings with other clans.

tribal societies   Small-scale societies composed of a number of autonomous political units sharing common linguistic and cultural features.

pan-tribal mechanisms   Mechanisms such as clans, age grades, and secret societies found in tribal societies that cut across kinship lines and serve to integrate all of the local segments of the tribe into a larger whole.

Another form of pan-tribal association based on kinship that is found in tribal societies is lineage segmentation (discussed in Chapter 10). Though less common than tribal societies based on clans, those based on lineage segmentation are instructive because they demonstrate the shifting or ephemeral nature of the political structure in tribal societies. In a segmentary system, individuals belong to a series of different descent units (corresponding to different genealogical levels) that function in different social contexts.

The most basic or local unit is the minimal lineage, comprising three to five generations. Members of a minimal lineage usually live together, consider themselves to be the closest of kin, and generally engage in everyday activities together. Minimal lineages, which tend to be politically independent, form a hierarchy of genealogical units. For example, minimal lineages make up minor lineages, minor lineages coalesce into major lineages, and major lineages form maximal lineages. When a dispute occurs between individuals of different segments, people are expected to side with the disputant to whom they are most closely related. Thus, people who act as a unit in one context merge into larger aggregates in other social situations. This process of lineage segmentation means that segments will unite when confronted by a wider group. In the words of John Middleton and David Tait:

> A segment that in one situation is independent finds that it and its former competitors are merged together as subordinate segments in the internal administrative organization of a wider overall segment that includes them both. This wider segment is in turn in external competitive relations with other similar segments, and there may be an entire series of such segments. (1958: 6–7)

It is important to keep in mind that these various segments—minimal, minor, major, and maximal lineages—are not groups but rather alliance networks that are activated only under certain circumstances. This process tends to deflect hostilities away from competing kin and toward an outside or more distant enemy. Such a level of political organization is effective for the mobilization of a military force either to defend the entire tribe from outside forces or to expand into the territories of weaker societies.

The pastoral Nuer of the southern Sudan are a good example of a tribal form of political organization (Evans-Pritchard 1940). The Nuer, who number approximately three hundred thousand people, have no centralized government and no government functionaries with coercive authority. Of course, there are influential men, but their influence stems more from their personal traits than from the force of elected or inherited office. The Nuer, who are highly egalitarian, do not readily accept authority beyond the elders of the family. Social control among the Nuer is maintained by seg-

mentary lineages in that close kin are expected to come to the assistance of one another against more distantly related people.

The term *tribe* has carried with it a generally negative connotation in the Western world for the past several centuries. During the colonial period of the nineteenth century, the term *tribal*, often equated with "uncivilized," was used to disparage any group without centralized hierarchical authority. To a large degree, this negative view of tribal societies was based on the observation that in the early stages of colonialism, tribal groups were involved in brutal warfare with one another. However, studies of the early years of initial contact between tribal societies and European colonial governments suggest that this brutal warfare, mostly absent during precolonial times, was actually *caused* by the colonial presence. Moreover, the colonial powers, believing that nation-states are more economically viable entities than tribal societies, were determined to create nation-states such as Tanganyika (later to be called Tanzania), containing 120 different ethnic or tribal entities. In fact, during the last two decades of the nineteenth century, all of Africa, and parts of other regions as well, were formed into European-style nation-states. The rationale was based on the very dubious assumption that small-scale units based on tribe or ethnicity are inherently weaker and less economically viable than are large-scale nation-states. This logic is seriously flawed, because we can cite some small (homogeneous) groups such as Switzerland, Bahrain, and Singapore that are highly viable economically, and some large-scale nation-states, such as Bangladesh and Ethiopia, that are economically dysfunctional.

Anthropologists do not associate the term *tribal society* with anything negative. Rather, the term is used to describe a group of ethnically homogeneous people capable of coordinating political action, yet lacking a centralized bureaucracy. Awareness of negative stereotyping of tribal societies is important because Westerners often speak of "ancient tribal hatreds" (caused by inherent cultural differences) when, in fact, present day intertribal hostilities often result from the intervention of other cultures. Negative stereotyping can lead us to misunderstand the nature of contemporary ethnic/tribal conflicts in places such as Somalia, the former Yugoslavia, and Iraq (see Whitehead and Ferguson 1993).

Chiefdoms

As we have seen, in band and tribal societies, local groups are economically and politically autonomous, authority is decentralized, and populations tend to be generally egalitarian. Moreover, roles are unspecialized, populations are small, and economies are largely subsistent in nature. But as societies become more complex—with larger and more specialized populations, more sophisticated technology, and growing surpluses—their need for more formal and permanent political structures increases. In such societies, known as *chiefdoms*, political authority is likely to reside with a single individual, acting alone or in conjunction with an advisory council.

Chiefdoms differ from bands and tribes in that chiefdoms integrate a number of local communities in a more formal and permanent way. Unlike bands and tribes, chiefdoms are made up of local communities that differ from one another in rank and status. Based on their genealogical proximity to the chiefs, nobles and commoners hold different levels of prestige and power. Chiefships are often hereditary, and the chief and his or her immediate kin constitute a social and political elite. Rarely are chiefdoms totally unified politically under a single chief; more often, they are composed of several political units, each headed by its own chief.

Chiefdoms also differ from tribes and bands in that chiefs are centralized and permanent officials with higher rank, power, and authority than others in the society. Unlike band or tribal headmen or headwomen, chiefs usually have considerable power, authority, and, in some cases, wealth. Internal social disruptions are minimized in a chiefdom because the chief usually has authority to make judgments, punish wrongdoers, and settle disputes. Chiefs usually have the authority to distribute land to loyal subjects, recruit people into military service, and recruit laborers for public works projects. Chiefly authority is usually reinforced by certain alleged supernatural powers. For example, among the Nootka of Vancouver Island in British Columbia, chiefly power was derived from a spiritual power associated with whale hunting magic (Harkin 1998).

Chiefs are also intimately related to the economic activities of their subjects through the redistributive system of economics (see Chapter 8). Subjects give food surpluses to the chief (not uncommonly at the chief's insistence), which are then redistributed by the chief through communal feasts and doles. This system of redistribution through a chief serves the obvious economic function of ensuring that no people in the society go hungry. It also serves the important political function of providing the people with a mechanism for expressing their loyalty and support for the chief.

Within the past 120 years, a number of societies with no former tradition of chiefs have had chiefships imposed on them by some of the European colonial powers. As the European nations created their colonial empires during the nineteenth century, they created chiefs (or altered the nature of traditional chiefs) to facilitate administering local populations. For example, the British created chiefs for their own administrative convenience among chiefless societies in Nigeria,

Kenya, and Australia. These new chiefs—who were given salaries and high-sounding titles such as "Paramount Chief"—were selected primarily on the basis of their willingness to work with the colonial administration rather than any particular popularity among their own people. In some cases, these new chiefs were held in contempt by their own people because they were collaborators with the colonial governments, which were often viewed as repressive and coercive.

The precolonial Hawaiian political system of the eighteenth century embodied the features of a typical chiefdom. According to Elman Service (1975), Hawaiian society, covering eight islands, was layered into three basic social strata. At the apex of the social hierarchy were the *ali'i*, major chiefs believed to be direct descendants of the gods; their close relatives often served as advisors or bureaucrats under them. The second echelon, known as the *konohiki*, were less important chiefs who were often distant relatives of the *ali'i*. And finally, the great majority of people were commoners, known as *maka'ainana*. Because there was little or no intermarriage among these three strata, the society was castelike. But because the *ali'i* had certain priestly functions by virtue of their connection with the gods, Hawaiian society was a theocracy as well.

The Hawaiian economy during the precolonial period was based on intensive agriculture (taro, breadfruit, yams, and coconuts) with extensive irrigation. Because of their control over the allocation of water, the major chiefs and their subordinates wielded considerable power and authority over the general population. In addition, chiefs were in control of communal labor, artisans, and gathering people for war. Hawaiian chiefs could also bring considerable coercive power to bear on disputants to encourage them to settle their quarrels, although in actual practice most disputes were settled through collective action. In summary, the precolonial Hawaiian political system, according to Service, was a theocracy, held together by an ideology that justified and sanctified the rule of the hereditary aristocracy, buttressed by age-old custom and etiquette. Such a system is in some contrast to a primitive state, which, although it attempts to rule ideologically and customarily, has had to erect the additional support of a monopoly of force with a legal structure that administers the force (Service 1975: 154).

State Societies

The *state system of government* is the most formal and most complex form of political organization. A *state* can be defined as a hierarchical form of political organization that governs many communities within a

---

chiefdoms   An intermediate form of political organization in which integration is achieved through the office of chiefs.

state system of government   A bureaucratic, hierarchical form of government composed of various echelons of political specialists.

State systems of government are characterized by a high degree of role specialization and a hierarchical organization. Many of these specialized political roles are played out in legislative bodies, such as the German Bundestag meeting in Berlin.

© Brooks Kraft/CORBIS

large geographic area. States collect taxes, recruit labor for armies and civilian public works projects, and have a monopoly on the right to use force. They are large bureaucratic organizations made up of permanent institutions with legislative, administrative, and judicial functions. Whereas bands and tribes have political structures based on kinship, state systems of government organize their power on a supra-kinship basis. That is, a person's membership in a state is based on his or her place of residence and citizenship rather than on kinship affiliation. Over the past several thousand years, state systems of government have taken various forms, including Greek city-states; the far-reaching Roman Empire; certain traditional African states such as Bunyoro, Buganda, and the Swazi; theocratic states such as ancient Egypt; and modern nation-states such as Germany, Japan, Canada, and the United States.

The authority of the state rests on two important foundations. First, the state holds the exclusive right to use force and physical coercion. Any act of violence not expressly permitted by the state is illegal and, consequently, punishable by the state. Thus, state governments make written laws, administer them through various levels of the bureaucracy, and enforce them through mechanisms such as police forces, armies, and national guards. The state needs to be continuously vigilant against threats both from within and from without to usurp its power through rebellions and revolutions. Second, the state maintains its authority by means of ideology. For the state to maintain its power over the long run, there must be a philosophical understanding among the citizenry that the state has the legitimate right to govern. In the absence of such an ideology, it is often difficult for the state to maintain its authority by means of coercion alone.

State systems of government, which first appeared about 5,500 years ago, are associated with civilizations (see definition in Chapter 2). Thus, they are found in societies with complex socioeconomic characteristics. For example, state systems of government are supported by intensive agriculture, which is required to support a large number of bureaucrats who are not producing food. This fully efficient food-production system gives rise to cities, considerable labor specialization, and a complex system of internal distribution and foreign trade. Because the considerable surpluses produced by intensive agriculture are not distributed equally among all segments of the population, state societies are stratified. That is, forms of wealth such as land and capital tend to be concentrated in the hands of an elite, who often use their superior wealth and power to control the rest of the population. Moreover, the fairly complex laws and regulations needed to control a large and heterogeneous population give rise to the need for some type of writing, record keeping, and a system of weights and measures.

State systems of government are characterized by a large number of *specialized political roles*. Many people are required to carry out very specific tasks such as law enforcement, tax collection, dispute settlement, recruitment of labor, and protection from outside invasions. These political/administrative functionaries are highly specialized and work full-time to the extent that they do not engage in food-producing activities. These

specialized political roles   Assignment and training of people who will carry out very specific tasks such as law enforcement, tax collection, dispute settlement, recruitment of labor, and protection from outside invasions.

permanent political functionaries, like the society itself, are highly stratified or hierarchical. At the apex of the administrative pyramid are those with the greatest power—kings, presidents, prime ministers, governors, and legislators—who enact laws and establish policies. Below them are descending echelons of bureaucrats responsible for the day-to-day administration of the state. As is the case in our own form of government, each level of the bureaucracy is responsible to the level immediately above it.

The Rise of State Systems

For the overwhelming majority of their existence, humans have lived in small food-collecting bands characterized by little or no political integration and few, if any, specialized political roles. Not until the neolithic revolution (domestication of plants and animals) approximately ten thousand years ago were socioeconomic forces unleashed that permitted the formation of larger, more complex sociopolitical systems. With the new food-producing technologies arriving with the neolithic revolution, populations became larger and more heterogeneous, and as a result, political organizations became increasingly complex and centralized. Today, state systems of government predominate in the world, whereas small-scale band societies account for a very small (and decreasing) percentage of the world's societies.

Although the rise of state systems of government was clearly a significant development, there is little consensus on why these complex forms of government emerged. By examining both ancient and contemporary societies, anthropologists and social philosophers have developed a number of explanations as to why some societies have developed state systems whereas others have not. Explanations for the rise of the state hinge on the question of what induces people to surrender at least a portion of their autonomy to the power and control of the state. Some theories suggest that people purposefully and voluntarily gave up their sovereignty because of the perceived benefits. That is, these theorists reason that the limited loss of autonomy was outweighed by the benefits people derived from their integration into a wider political structure. These benefits included greater protection from hostile outside forces, more effective means of conflict resolution, and the opportunity for increased food production.

A good example of this *voluntaristic theory of state formation* was put forth by archaeologist V. Gordon Childe. According to Childe (1936), the introduction and development of intensive agriculture (stimulated by the introduction of the plow, irrigation, metallurgy, and draft animals) during the neolithic period created food surpluses. These food surpluses, in turn, freed up a certain segment of the population from tasks of food production, allowing them to engage in a wide variety of new occupational roles, such as weavers, traders, potters, and metal-workers.

This dramatic increase in occupational specialization necessitated a wider form of political integration to mediate between and protect the varied special interest groups and to provide the economic superstructure to enable them to work in an efficient and complementary fashion. Another voluntaristic explanation of the emergence of the state is the *hydraulic theory of state formation*, suggested by Karl Wittfogel. According to Wittfogel (1957), small-scale irrigation farmers in arid or semiarid areas eventually came to see certain economic advantages to surrendering their autonomy and merging their small communities into a larger political entity capable of large-scale irrigation. Even though archaeological evidence indicates that certain states (such as China, Mexico, and Mesopotamia) developed before the introduction of large-scale irrigation, centralized political governments do appear to be functional for agricultural systems dependent on irrigation.

Still another theory of state origins, set forth by Robert Carneiro (1970), suggests that the existence of the state is the direct result of warfare. Offering a *coercive theory of state formation*, Carneiro holds that "force, and not enlightened self interest, is the mechanism by which political evolution has led, step by step, from autonomous villages to the state" (1970: 217). Carneiro elaborates that although warfare is the mechanism of state formation, it operates only under certain environmental conditions—namely, in areas that have limited agricultural land for expanding populations. To illustrate his theory, Carneiro uses the case of the Inca state that developed in the narrow valleys of the Peruvian coast, which were geographically circumscribed in that the valleys faced the ocean, backed up to the mountains, and were flanked on either end by deserts. As populations grew in this region, there was no land into which to expand. Land pressure increased, resulting in intense land competition and eventually warfare. Increasingly more centralized political units developed to conduct the warfare and to administer subjugated peoples. Villages that lost wars became subjugated populations, whereas the victors headed up increasingly larger

---

voluntaristic theory of state formation The theory that suggests that stable systems of state government arose because people voluntarily surrendered some of their autonomy to the state in exchange for certain benefits.

hydraulic theory of state formation The notion that early state systems of government arose because small-scale farmers were willing to surrender a portion of their autonomy to a large government entity in exchange for the benefits of large-scale irrigation systems.

coercive theory of state formation The argument that the state came into existence as a direct result of warfare.

APPLIED PERSPECTIVE

Rebuilding Japan After World War II

Ruth Benedict

Because the U.S. government did not have a centralized intelligence agency at the start of World War II, anthropologists were recruited by the Office of War Information to conduct cultural research on our enemies—particularly the Germans and the Japanese. Ruth Benedict, for example, temporarily left her position as a professor at Columbia University in 1943 to write various cultural reports for the Office of War Information. Several months before the war ended in 1945, Benedict submitted to the U.S. government a report entitled "Japanese Behavior Patterns." Benedict's report was published the following year as *The Chrysanthemum and the Sword* and became an instant best-seller. Perhaps the greatest endorsement of Benedict's book is the fact that more than 2 million copies have been sold in Japan, and more Japanese can identify the name of Ruth Benedict today than can Americans. While the report, and subsequent book, had little effect on the outcome of the war, it was extremely important during the U.S. occupation of Japan.

The reliance on anthropological analysis to inform the rebuilding of Japan after World War II has special relevance today for postwar Iraq. Since the fall of Saddam Hussein in 2003, the U.S. government has been trying to help the Iraqi people rebuild a stable, secure, and viable society. In 1945, however, the vanquished Japanese empire was perhaps even more incomprehensible to outsiders than militant Islamic fundamentalists are today. Conventional wisdom suggested that Japan's rigidly hierarchical society and worship of the emperor as a deity made it both incapable of changing and totally unsuited to democratic institutions.

Benedict, however, was able to convince those in charge of the occupation that rather than being stubbornly rigid, Japanese society was actually quite adaptable. She argued that Japan, being a "shame" and "honor" culture, was perhaps more amenable to change than cultures such as the United States that are based on "guilt" and absolute standards of good and evil. Shame and honor cultures respond better than guilt cultures to externally imposed standards. So, she argued, if the United States wanted to change the behavior of postwar Japanese, the first step would be to change the standards. In other words, Benedict suggested that change was possible, indeed likely, if the United

and more complex warring political units. Carneiro (1970) claims that similar political evolution occurred in other parts of the world characterized by circumscribed agricultural land such as the Nile Valley, Mesopotamia, and the Indus Valley.

The Modern Nation-State

In recent times the word *state* has often been combined with the word *nation* to form the entity called a *nation-state*. Although these two words are often used interchangeably in everyday conversation, they are two quite distinct concepts. A **nation** is a group of people who share a common symbolic identity, culture, history, and often, religion. A **state**, on the other hand, is a particular type of political structure distinct from a band, tribal society, or chiefdom. When combined, the term *nation-state* refers to a group of people sharing a common cultural background and unified by a political structure that they all consider legitimate.

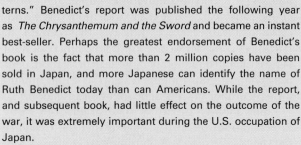

nation A group of people who share a common identity, history, and culture.

state A particular type of political structure that is hierarchical, bureaucratic, centralized, and has a monopoly on the legitimate use of force to implement its policies.

Although this is a fairly tidy definition, few of the nearly two hundred so-called nation-states in the world today actually fit the definition. This is largely because few such entities have populations with homogeneous cultural identities. For example, the country of Great Britain, which has been in existence for centuries, comprises England, Wales, Ireland, and Scotland. We sometimes refer to Great Britain as England, but the Welsh, Irish, and Scots clearly do not regard themselves as English in terms of language, tradition, or ethnicity. The collapse of the Soviet Union in recent years has given rise to a dozen new nation-states, including Belarus, Ukraine, Georgia, Azerbaijan, and Moldova. And, of course, many of the newly independent African nation-states represented in the United Nations since the 1960s have enormous ethnic heterogeneity. To illustrate, the country of Tanzania comprises approximately 120 different ethnic groups, all of which speak languages that are mutually unintelligible. Thus, even after more than four decades of living in a nation-state, the people of Tanzania tend to identify themselves more as Maasai, Wazaramo, or Wachagga than as Tanzanians.

A major challenge for some contemporary state governments is that they contain within their boundaries ethnic populations that are seeking statehood or expanded autonomy. A particularly good example is the

States were to work *within* the already existing parameters of Japanese culture rather than trying to change the culture itself.

Benedict also convinced the occupying authorities not to try to eliminate the institution of the emperor. Even though the emperor was a monarch, the continuation of the emperor would not be incompatible with building solid democratic institutions or a strong free enterprise economy. Clearly, the Japanese people venerated the emperor and gave him their unending loyalty, but for centuries the Japanese imperial system had been highly flexible. Advisors to the emperor, or the emperor himself, were replaced to reflect changing times. Given this traditional flexibility, Benedict argued that the institution of the emperor must be preserved in postwar Japan. The fact that the emperor had been defeated by the Allies could be explained away by his having received bad advice from the militarists who took Japan down the road to war. So, according to Benedict, the Allies should convince the emperor to reject militarism (as shameful) and accept democracy (as honorable), and when that happened, the Japanese people (with their great loyalty to the emperor) would gladly follow. Much to their credit, the U.S. occupation authorities heeded Benedict's advice (based on her careful anthropological analysis) and the Japanese not only embraced democratic institutions, but their economy rebounded and is today the second largest in the world.

Nearly sixty years ago, Ruth Benedict showed the world that religions—even those that appear fanatical, like Japanese emperor worship—change with changing conditions. The rebuilding of postwar Japan into a democratic nation with a strong economy would very likely not have occurred if the U.S. occupying forces had followed conventional thinking by dissolving the position of the emperor and *forcing* the country to accept democratic and capitalistic institutions. Benedict's sensitive study of Japanese culture led her to conclude that conquering military powers would not be able to bring about meaningful social change by force and coercion. Is there a message here for the rebuilding of Iraq? And is the U.S. government even looking for the Ruth Benedict of the twenty-first century (Stille 2003)?

Questions for Further Thought

1. In addition to providing the U.S. government with information on various cultures, what other roles did cultural anthropologists play to assist in the war effort?
2. What advice would you offer the U.S. government regarding its efforts to rebuild the country of Iraq after the war of 2003?
3. How would you distinguish between a "shame/honor" culture and a "guilt" culture?

---

12 million Kurds living in southern Turkey, who have been struggling for an independent state since the formation of modern Turkey in 1923. Because the Kurds comprise approximately 20 percent of Turkey's population, and occupy an area that controls the headwaters of the Tigris and Euphrates rivers, the Turkish government is not the least bit interested in granting the Kurds independence. For decades the Turkish government has used political repression as the major strategy for dealing with what they call the "Kurdish problem." Not only have Kurds been oppressed and denied basic civil liberties, but so have non-Kurdish Turks who speak out in favor of Kurdish independence. And yet the Kurds of Turkey represent only one of many groups that are involved in intrastate conflicts. Others quickly come to mind, including Palestinians in Israel, Chechens in Russia, the Kayapo of Brazil, and the French in Canada.

Gender and the Modern State

Irrespective of whether we are looking at small-scale band societies or large-scale state societies, across the political spectrum women do not as a rule hold important positions of political leadership. To be certain, there are examples of women holding top leadership positions, but these exceptional cases are found in societies wherein female leadership roles are not typically extended to other women in the society. To illustrate, over the past several hundred years a number of powerful female heads of European states can be cited, including Isabella I of Spain, Elizabeth I and Victoria of England, and Catherine the Great of Russia. More recently, we have witnessed female heads of state in Israel, India, Pakistan, Great Britain, the Philippines, Norway, Sri Lanka, and the Netherlands. Within the last several decades, on average, fewer than 3 percent of the independent countries in the world have had a woman as head of state. This is an improvement over where women were a century ago, but it hardly represents a major victory for women in politics. Moreover, even this modest gain in political leadership for women must be qualified in several significant respects. First, often when women attain high office, it is because of their relationship to men. That is, queens are titular head of state by virtue of their marriage to the king, or because their father, the former monarch, had no male heirs. And second, many of the women leaders are not particularly strong advocates of women's issues, such as pay equity, access to certain professions, or protection from abuse. In other words, they tend to be "women in men's clothing," finding that they need to downplay feminist issues to garner support within a male-dominated political system.

© CHINA FEATURES/CORBIS SYGMA

The existence of millions of excess men in China, brought about by gender bias, may increase that nation's willingness to settle its disagreements through warfare.

In the previous chapter we saw how, due to extreme male gender bias, certain Asian nations have tens of millions fewer women than men. In fact, it is conservatively estimated that there are 90 million "missing" women in Asia because parents are encouraged to select sons over daughters through female infanticide, selective abortion of female fetuses, and nutritional and medical deprivation. These sizeable sexual imbalances (caused by a combination of cultural values and official population policies) can lead to serious problems of violence, both domestic and international, for the modern state. Most violent domestic crime is caused by unmarried men who lack the stable social bonds and responsibility of marriage and parenthood. With an estimated 20 million *more* unmarried men between the ages of fifteen and thirty-five than would be expected with a more balanced sex-ratio, a modern nation like China will be faced with increased crime, gangs, and even revolutions. If domestic crime within China increases too rapidly, the government may become even more authoritarian because it may need a heavier hand to combat rising crime and political instability. Moreover, these tens of millions of excess males in countries like China and India have important implications for international peace and security. Large numbers of unmarried men at home, particularly ones that are troublemakers, are expendable and can be recruited to form huge armies. In the years to come, when China wants to resolve its differences with Taiwan, or India wants to end its standoff with Pakistan over Kashmir, having armies composed of so many expendable unmarried males may be a factor in a country's willingness to go to war (Hudson and den Boer 2004).

Changing State Systems of Government

The global historical trend during the last several decades has been toward democracy and away from autocracy. *Democracy* refers to the type of political system in which power is exercised, usually through representatives, by the people as a whole. *Autocracy*, on the other hand, refers to the type of political system that denies popular participation in the process of governmental decision making. According to Freedom House (www.freedomhouse.org), an organization that tracks political trends throughout the world, by the end of 2005, 122 of the world's 192 governments were electoral democracies, up from 66 countries just eighteen years earlier. Even though some of these 122 democracies have questionable human rights records, they do allow the existence of opposition parties and meet at least the minimum standards for holding free elections. Freedom House also ranks the nations of the world in terms of three categories: free, partly free, and not free. In the three decades between 1975 and 2005, the number of free countries increased from forty to eighty-nine, the number of partially free countries increased from fifty-three to fifty-eight, and the number of countries deemed not free declined from sixty-five to forty-five. There is reason to believe that this trend toward greater

democracy   A type of political system that involves popular participation in decision making.
autocracy   A form of government that is controlled by a leader who holds absolute power and denies popular participation in decision making.

freedom and democracy will continue, if for no other reason than the advantage democracies enjoy in terms of controlling world resources. To illustrate, free societies control 86 percent of the world's economic activity, while partly free societies and not free societies each control 7 percent. These economic realities confirm the crucial association (if not causal relationship) between political democracy and economic development.

It is important to point out that the word *freedom* does not have a universally agreed upon meaning. As measured by Freedom House, freedom is equated with electoral (participatory) democracy, where the major societal issues are resolved by the will of the people through their representatives. However, when used in the United States, a number of people equate freedom with having choices, and the greater the number of choices available (whether political candidates or brands of dishwashing detergent), the more freedom one has. While this is generally true for the upper, well-educated classes, those at the lower and middle echelons of society do not necessarily equate freedom with exercising more and more choices. In a recent study at Stanford University, students whose parents were college graduates associated the word *choice* with the concepts of freedom and individual control, while those whose parents had only a high school education associated *choice* with fear, doubt, and difficulty. Thus, while upper classes tend to define freedom as choice, working-class Americans emphasize freedom from instability, insecurity, and uncertainty. That many, indeed most, Americans do not feel more free by an increased number of choices was recently illustrated by the confu-

sion and anxiety expressed by millions of seniors faced with having to select the Medicare drug plan that was best for them (Schwartz, Marcus, and Snibbe 2006).

In addition to providing greater popular participation in government, the rise of democratic governments has brought a number of other changes such as freeing of political prisoners, reduction of torture, legitimizing of dissent and opposition parties, and lifting of absolute control over information. During much of the twentieth century, governments could (and often did) control the flow of information available to the citizenry, thereby severely limiting popular participation in government. People were given only information that the government deemed necessary. As long as governments could control the content of newspapers and radio and television broadcasts, the citizenry was prevented from hearing alternative views and opinions. Since the early 1990s, widespread use of the Internet has meant that governments can no longer control the flow of information. This free flow of information is perhaps the biggest threat to despotic nation-states. To illustrate, Thomas Friedman (1999) reminds us that during the 1980s, *Pravda,* the official government newspaper of the Soviet Union, published pictures of food lines in New York City as an indicator of poverty in the capitalistic West. In actual fact these food lines turned out to be New Yorkers waiting in line to purchase their designer pastries and coffee at Zabar's—a fashionable, upscale food store on the Upper West Side of Manhattan! Such blatant campaigns of misinformation are no longer possible with the relatively free accessibility of information over the Internet. Because information is no longer provided exclusively by the government-controlled media, power is beginning to pass from potentially repressive governments to the general citizenry.

During the 1990s, as the development of information technology advanced dramatically, proponents of the Internet were claiming that it was leading to new forms of democracy. To be certain, the Internet is the most important vehicle of information technology since the printing press. Theoretically, the Internet makes it possible for everyone to have free access to information; for opposition parties to spread their agendas; and for formerly oppressed people to connect with others via e-mail in order to present a united front against those who would exploit them. In short, the World Wide Web has the *potential* to serve as a powerful tool to fight political repression, racism, and economic exploitation. Yet there is another side to this coin. As effective as the Internet can be in freeing up information and giving a voice to oppressed people, it certainly has its limitations. In reality, most oppressed people throughout the world probably do not own a personal computer, nor can they afford a monthly subscription to AOL. Although the Internet has been touted as a boon to economic development, that development tends to be very uneven. In

The worldwide trend during the last several decades has been toward greater participatory democracy. Here a South African woman casts her vote in the nation's first post-apartheid election, in 1994.

many cases, the rich are getting richer while the poor remain poor.

Thus, in order for the Internet to be a democratizing force, it must provide access to all people, not just those who can afford the technology. Moreover, as Margaret Everett has suggested (1998: 392), the Internet may permit the sending of uncensored information, but it can, at the same time, be used by oppressive governments to "create new possibilities for surveillance and sabotage."

Not only has the Internet been used by some repressive governments to quell dissent, but it appears that they have been aided and abetted by some pillars of the U.S. free enterprise system. Eager to curry favor with the government that controls access to Chinese markets, Western technology firms have been helping the Chinese government limit free expression by blocking access to political websites, snitching on users, and selling filtering equipment. For example, in December 2005, at the request of the Chinese government, Microsoft closed down the blog of a Chinese journalist who was critical of the government, and officials at Yahoo! have admitted that it had helped the Chinese government to sentence a dissident to ten years in prison by identifying him as the sender of a banned e-mail message.

In those nation-states with relatively unencumbered access to information, the Internet is significantly influencing the political and electoral processes. Within the last decade, political campaigns have become more sophisticated in taking advantage of what the Internet has to offer. Politicians of the twenty-first century have access to computer-generated mailing lists that enable them to target issue voters. They can become much more efficient in campaign fundraising by using computer programs that can identify potential donors. The Internet is a cost-effective way of disseminating information (and "disinformation") about a candidate as well as recruiting and mobilizing supporters, volunteers, and campaign funds. Moreover, a candidate's website allows for two-way communication with the voter, establishing an avenue for instant feedback on issues. In the past, an election could be (and usually was) decided by the number and effectiveness of the TV commercials a candidate could purchase. Such a system clearly worked to the advantage of those candidates with the most money. With widespread accessibility of the Internet, however, candidates can get their message across for a fraction of the cost of television ads. Thus, it is possible that the most successful candidates in the future will be those with the most creative webmasters.

There is little question that the Internet will have at least as radical an influence on politics as it has in other areas of American life, such as music, journalism, and of course, retail. According to a survey by the Pew Research Center, 29 percent of the voting population went online for their campaign news in 2004, compared to only 13 percent for the 2002 elections. It has been estimated that the number of Americans getting their daily news online nearly doubled from 27 million people in March 2002 to 50 million in March 2006. And, as might be expected, using the Internet for acquiring political information is particularly evident among younger adults. To illustrate, in the 2004 presidential campaign 80 percent of the political donors from the eighteen-to-thirty-four-year-old demographic made their contributions over the Internet (Nagourney 2006: 1).

Moreover, the development of information technology means that the nation-state of the twenty-first century sometimes plays second fiddle to the powerful forces of global economic interdependence. During the early summer of 2002, the countries of India and Pakistan, both with nuclear capabilities, were on the brink of war over the issue of Kashmir. The two countries were threatening to attack each other as the leaders of the United States and western Europe tried to bring the two parties back from the brink. In the end, the de-escalation of hostilities between India and Pakistan came from pressure exerted by the information technology industry—not the U.S. government (with more military firepower than the next fifteen most powerful nations). The global revolution in information technology (satellites, the Internet, and so on) since the early 1990s has had an enormous effect on the Indian economy, which today has an IT industry that brings in $60 billion per year. Drawing upon the large tech-savvy Indian population, many of the world's largest companies (including American Express, Nortel, Sony, Reebok, and General Electric) have located their back rooms and research facilities in India. If you lose your luggage anywhere in the world, it will likely be tracked down by an Indian techie in Bangalore (India's Silicon Valley). Accounting, inventory control, payroll, billing,

To what extent can this impoverished man from Calcutta, India, rely on the Internet to protect himself from a repressive government?

CONTEMPORARY ISSUES

Can Canadians Accommodate Islamic Law?

AP/Getty Images

For the past fifty years, the Canadian government has lived by the doctrine of multiculturalism. While preserving a strong tradition of secularism, Canada has had over the decades a very welcoming policy on immigration. Former Prime Minister Pierre Elliot Trudeau, who served from 1968 until 1984, envisioned Canada as a country with no particular dominant cultural identity, but rather a place where people from cultures around the world could live in harmony and celebrate their diversity. To illustrate, the city of Vancouver has more ethnically Chinese residents than any other city in North America; the city of Toronto is the home of more ethnic neighborhoods (and restaurants) than any other city of its size in the world; and in recent years more than a hundred mosques, serving an Islamic population of approximately six hundred thousand, have been built throughout the country.

In keeping with Canada's multicultural philosophy, the Province of Ontario passed the Arbitration Act in 1991, giving local religious authorities the right to settle civil cases as long as the parties voluntarily agreed to do so. Under this law various Christian and Jewish clerics have used the guiding principles of their religions to settle a fairly narrow range of cases (divorces, business disputes, and the violation of kosher dietary rules) outside the formal court system. Now the sizeable Islamic community in Toronto is testing this law by seeking to have Muslim clerics arbitrate a wide range of cases under the Islamic legal code called Shariah. Leaders of the Islamic community in Toronto claim this is necessary because Muslims live their everyday lives according to religious laws to a much greater extent than do practitioners of other religions.

Legal questions arise, however, from the fact that the prescribed guidelines for settling disputes under Shariah often conflict with the Charter of Rights and Freedoms, Canada's version of the Bill of Rights. For example, under Shariah sons normally receive twice the amount of inheritance allotted to their sisters, while men are entitled to divorce their wives but women cannot divorce their husbands. In addition, the prescribed sentencing guidelines under some extreme forms of Shariah include stoning of women found guilty of adultery and cutting off the right hands of thieves.

Critics of including Shariah under the Arbitration Act, while generally supporting faith-based arbitration as an alternative to litigation in the courts, argue that safeguards are necessary to ensure that vulnerable groups, particularly women, are not coerced into submitting to religious law. Many Islamic women living in Canada today are kept isolated in their own communities, speak little or no English, and do not understand their legal rights under the Canadian Charter. While some claim that it may be possible to establish safeguards for women, those on the other side of the issue argue that fifteen-year-old girls who are married off to men twice their age and then kept separate from the wider society have little choice in deciding to exercise their Canadian rights over traditional law. Whether, and in what form, Shariah will be allowed to operate alongside the Canadian legal system is still under deliberation. However, the dilemma faced by the nation-state of Canada is how to be true to two often conflicting sets of values: multiculturalism, on the one hand, and the rule of equitable law on the other (see Trichur 2004 and Krauss 2004).

and credit card approval (among other functions) for many of the world's largest corporations are electronically managed by highly skilled Indian engineers, computer scientists, and information technicians. With India so intimately involved in the IT lifeblood of so many large corporations, the possibility of India going to war threatened serious disruption of the world's economy. In the final analysis, it was the powerful international corporations that convinced the Indian government to disengage with the Pakistanis under the threat of taking their IT business elsewhere. Thus, in the words of Thomas Friedman (2002: 13), "In the crunch, it was the influence of General Electric, not General (Colin) Powell, that did the trick."

Variations in Political Structures

In the preceding sections we have looked at four fundamentally different types of political systems. Such a fourfold scheme, although recognized by some anthropologists, is not universally accepted. For example, in a classic study of political systems in Africa, Meyer Fortes and E. E. Evans-Pritchard (1940) distinguished between only two types of structures: state systems and *headless societies*. Others (Cohen and Eames 1982) recognize

headless societies   Societies without political leaders, such as a presidents, kings, or chiefs.

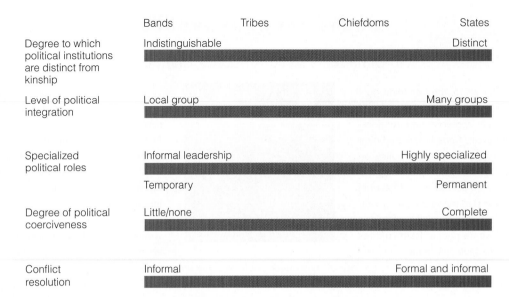

	Bands	Tribes	Chiefdoms	States
Degree to which political institutions are distinct from kinship	Indistinguishable			Distinct
Level of political integration	Local group			Many groups
Specialized political roles	Informal leadership			Highly specialized
	Temporary			Permanent
Degree of political coerciveness	Little/none			Complete
Conflict resolution	Informal			Formal and informal

FIGURE 13.1   **Variations in Political Aspects of World Cultures**

	Bands	Tribes	Chiefdoms	States
Major mode of subsistence	Foraging	Agricultural/herding		Intensive agriculture
Predominant mode of distribution	Reciprocity	Redistribution		Market
Control of land	Free access	Descent group	Chief	Public/private
Population size	Small, low density			Large, high density
Division of labor	Low role specialization			High role specialization
Level of social stratification	Egalitarian			Class/caste
Public architecture	None	Little	Some	High Level

FIGURE 13.2   **Variations in Socioeconomic Aspects of World Cultures**

three major forms of political structure: simple, intermediate, and complex. Such differences in the way various
ethnologists have conceptualized political structures
should serve as a reminder that all of these schemes
are ideal types. That is, not all of the societies in the
world will fit neatly into one box or another. Instead of
discrete categories, in reality there is a continuum with
bands (the simplest form) at one extreme and states
(the most complex form) at the other. Thus, whether

we use two, three, or four major categories of political
organization, we should bear in mind that the political
systems of the world vary along a continuum on a number of important dimensions. To illustrate, as we move
from left to right (bands through tribes and chiefdoms
to states), gradations occur, as shown in Figure 13.1.
These variations in political structures are accompanied
by corresponding variations in other aspects of world
cultures, as shown in Figure 13.2.

Societies control behavior with both positive and negative sanctions.

SOCIAL CONTROL

As the previous section explained, political structures vary from very informal structures such as bands at one extreme to highly complex state systems of government at the other extreme. Whatever form of political organization is found in a society, it must inevitably address the issue of *social control*. In other words, every society must ensure that most of the people behave themselves in appropriate ways most of the time. State-like societies, such as our own, have a wide variety of formalized mechanisms to keep people's behavior in line, including written laws, judges, bureaucracies, prisons, execution chambers, and police forces. At the other extreme, small-scale band societies, such as the Inuit or Ju/'hoansi, have no centralized political authority but nevertheless maintain social order among their members quite effectively through informal mechanisms of

social control. In fact, people deviate from acceptable behavior considerably less in most band societies than in societies with more elaborate and complex forms of political organization.

Every society has defined what it considers to be normal, proper, or expected ways of behaving. These expectations, known as *social norms*, serve as behavioral guidelines that help the society work smoothly. To be certain, social norms are not adhered to perfectly, and, in fact, there is always a certain level of deviance from them (Freilich, Raybeck, and Sayishinsky 1990). But most people in any given society abide by them most of the time. Moreover, social norms take a number of different forms, ranging from etiquette to formal laws. Some norms are taken more seriously than others. On one hand, all societies have certain social expectations of what is proper, but such behavior is not rigidly enforced. To illustrate, although it is customary in the

---

social control   Mechanisms found in all societies that function to encourage people not to violate the social norms.

social norms   Expected forms of behavior.

United States for people to shake hands when being introduced, a person's refusal to shake hands does not constitute a serious violation of social norms. The person who does not follow this rule of etiquette might be considered rude but would not be arrested or executed. At the other extreme, certain social norms (such as ours against grand larceny or murder) are taken very seriously because they are considered absolutely necessary for the survival of the society.

Social scientists use the term *deviance* to refer to the violation of social norms. However, it is important to keep in mind that deviance is relative. What people in one culture consider to be deviant is not necessarily considered deviant in other cultures. In other words, it is not the act itself but rather how people define the act that determines whether it is deviant. To illustrate, suicide among middle-class North Americans is considered to be unacceptable under any conditions. In traditional Japan, however, the practice of hara-kiri, committing ritual suicide by disembowelment, was considered in traditional times the honorable thing to do for a disgraced nobleman. Thus, whereas ritual suicide was normative for the Japanese nobleman, it is considered very deviant by the standards of a businessperson in Montreal or Miami.

All social norms, whether trivial or serious, are sanctioned. That is, societies develop patterned or institutionalized ways of encouraging people to conform to the norms. These *sanctions* are both positive and negative, as people are rewarded for behaving in socially acceptable ways and punished for violating the norms. *Positive sanctions* range from a smile of approval to being awarded the Congressional Medal of Honor. *Negative sanctions* include everything from a frown of disapproval to the death penalty.

Social sanctions may also be formal or informal, depending on whether a formal law (legal statute) has been violated. To illustrate, if a woman in a restaurant is talking in a voice that can be easily overheard by people at nearby tables, she will probably receive stares from the other diners. But if she starts yelling at the top of her lungs in the restaurant, she will probably be arrested for disturbing the peace or disorderly conduct. The difference, of course, is that in the first case the woman isn't breaking the law, but in the second case she is. Figure 13.3 illustrates a continuum of the formal–

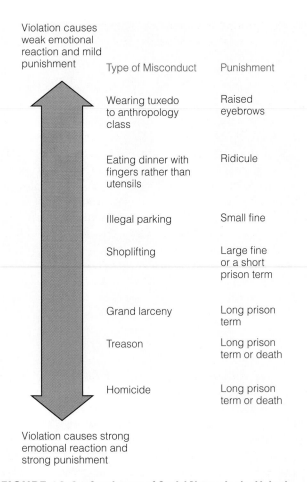

FIGURE 13.3   **Continuum of Social Norms in the United States**

---

deviance   The violation of a social norm.
sanctions   Any means used to enforce compliance with the rules and norms of a society.
positive sanctions   A mechanism of social control for enforcing a society's norms through rewards.
negative sanctions   Punishment for violating the norms of a society.

---

informal dimension of social norms and sanctions in U.S. society.

Just as the types of social norms found in any society vary, so do the mechanisms used to encourage people to adhere to those norms. For most North Americans, the most obvious forms of social control are the formal or institutionalized ones. When asked why we tend to behave ourselves, we would probably think of formal laws, police forces, courts, and prisons. We don't rob the local convenience store, in other words, because if caught, we are likely to go to prison.

Most of our "proper" behavior is probably caused by less formal, and perhaps less obvious, mechanisms of social control. In band and tribal societies that lack centralized authority, informal mechanisms of social control may be all that exist. In the remainder of this chapter, we will look at informal mechanisms of social control typical of band and tribal societies and at more formal institutions aimed primarily at social control, some of which involve laws and adjudicating bodies. It should be emphasized, however, that this distinction between formal and informal mechanisms should not imply that informal means of social control exist only in band and tribal societies. Although societies with complex political organizations (state societies in particular) are best known for written laws and courts, they also rely on an appreciable number of informal mechanisms of social control.

Informal Means of Social Control

Compared to complex state organizations, bands and tribes have little that appears to be *governmental* in the Western sense of the term. They have very low levels of political integration, few (if any) specialized political roles, and little *political coerciveness*. These small-scale political systems have been described as *headless* societies or "tribes without rulers" (Middleton and Tait 1958). In the absence of formal governmental structures, how do these headless societies maintain social order? The following subsections examine a number of informal mechanisms of social control that not only operate in headless societies but may also be found in more complex societies.

Socialization

Every society, if it is to survive, must pass on its social rules and norms from one generation to another. It seems obvious that people cannot conform to the social norms unless they learn them. Thus, all societies have some system of *socialization*, which involves teaching the young what the norms are and that they should not be violated. In other words, not only do people live in societies, but societies live in people. People learn their social norms with a certain degree of moral compulsion. We learn, for example, that in North America people wear clothes in public and that we should do so as well. Usually, we internalize our social norms so effectively that we would never consider violating them. Some social norms—such as not appearing nude in public— are so thoroughly ingrained in us through socialization that the thought of violating them is distasteful and embarrassing. Other social norms do not have the same level of moral intensity, such as driving within the speed limit or maintaining good oral hygiene. But as a general rule, when people learn the norms of their society, they are at the same time internalizing the moral necessity to obey them.

Although all societies socialize their young to learn, understand, and obey the social norms, there is considerable variation in terms of the level of coercion used by adults to get the job done. Some societies tend to be very permissive in the process of socialization, while other socities are more likely to use and condone some form of corporal punishment as a child-training technique. Even though corporal punishment of children is generally frowned upon by educators and child development experts, it has been estimated (Strauss 2001: 187) that approximately 25 percent of parents in the United States during the mid-1990s hit their children with objects other than their hands. Interestingly, in a recent study using data from the HRAF, Carol and Melvin Ember (2005: 609–19) found a positive correlation between corporal punishment and 1) the level of social inequality and 2) the use of formal currency (money). The Embers argue that in light of these two measures of social inequality, parents are likely to resort to corporal punishment, not out of a desire for conformity *per se*, but rather as a valuable life-lesson to help their children accept (and adjust to) these societal power inequities in later life.

Public Opinion

One of the most compelling reasons for not violating social norms is *public opinion* or social pressure. In general, people from all parts of the world wish to be accepted by the other members of their society. Most people fear being rejected or criticized by their friends or neighbors. This strong desire to be liked is reflected in comments such as, "Don't do that! What will the neighbors think?" Of course, it is impossible to determine how many people are deterred from violating the social norms by fear of negative public opinion. At the same time, we can cite many examples of how societies use social pressure (or what is called "strategic embarrassment") very deliberately to keep people in line. Indeed, gossip, ostracism, rumor, sarcasm, and derision are powerful corrective measures for reforming social behavior. For example, city and county governments in the United States print the names of tax delinquents in the local newspaper in an attempt to embarrass them into paying their taxes. In colonial America, the stock and pillory was an excellent example of how the society used public opinion to control people's behavior. Someone who was caught breaking the social norms (such as committing adultery or stealing) was confined to the stock and pillory, which, not coincidentally, was always located in the center of town. Even though long confinements in the stock and pillory were physically very uncomfortable, the realization that all of your friends, relatives, and neighbors would see you and know of your crime was by far the greater punishment.

In some societies, when someone strays too far from acceptable behavior, the group takes very explicit steps to indelibly brand the person as a deviant. The character Hester Prynne from Hawthorne's *The Scarlet Letter* had a large red *A* sewn to her dress to identify her as an adulteress to the rest of the community. Military officers

---

political coerciveness   The capacity of a political system to enforce its will on the general population.

socialization   Teaching the young people the norms in a society.

public opinion   What the general public thinks about some issue. When public opinion is brought to bear on an individual, it can influence his or her behavior.

found guilty in a court-martial are often ceremoniously stripped of their insignia of rank in a public display of humiliation. Harold Garfinkle (1956) has used the term *degradation ceremonies* to refer to these formal societal mechanisms to publicly humiliate a deviant.

The deliberate use of social pressure to maintain social control is particularly important and, in some cases, quite dramatic in small-scale societies. A case in point is the custom of the duel found in the Tiwi society of North Australia (Hart and Pilling 1960). Men in traditional Tiwi society achieve power and status by amassing large numbers of wives. Under such conditions of intense polygyny, all females are married or betrothed before or at birth, but men do not take their first wives until their late thirties or early forties. Thus, at any given moment in time, all women are married to older men.

If a younger Tiwi male (say, one in his twenties) is to have any intimate relations with a Tiwi woman, it must, by definition, be with an older man's wife. When this occurs, the older man challenges the young adulterer to a duel, which, like the use of the stock and pillory, is always public. All the people in the community (men, women, and children) form a circle in an open field, surrounding the older man and the accused adulterer. With the entire community watching, the older man throws spears at the younger man, along with a string of verbal insults. The younger man is expected to submit himself to this verbal harangue while sidestepping the spears. But before the event can end, the younger man must allow one of the spears to strike him, hopefully in a nonvulnerable place.

The key to understanding the Tiwi duel is its public nature. Even though the guilty party suffers some physical punishment (the superficial wound), the real punishment is the public disapproval of the younger man's behavior by all of the onlookers. The Tiwi duel, in other words, is an institutionalized form of public humiliation whereby public opinion is mobilized in an attempt to reform unacceptable behavior. The Tiwi duel is a particularly effective mechanism of social control because it not only helps to reform the behavior of the accused but also serves as a reminder to all of the other members of the community who might otherwise be tempted to violate the social norms.

Corporate Lineages

Corporate lineages play a dominant role in most small-scale (headless) societies. Members of corporate lineages (who can number in the hundreds) often live,

work, play, and pray together. Property is controlled by the lineage, people derive their primary identity from the group, and even religion (in the form of ancestor worship) is a lineage matter. Acting like a small corporation, the lineage has a powerful impact on the everyday lives of its members and can exert considerable pressure on people to conform to the social norms.

One means by which a corporate lineage exerts control over its members is economic. All important property, such as land and livestock, is controlled by the elders of the corporate lineage. Often property is allocated on the basis of conformity to societal norms. Those who behave as the society expects them to behave are likely to receive the best plots of land and use of the best livestock. Conversely, those who violate social norms are likely to be denied these valuable economic resources.

Corporate lineages, to some degree, also act as mechanisms of social control because of their scale. Corporate lineages serve as localized communities, numbering from several hundred to several thousand relatives. Because members of the lineage have frequent and intense interaction with one another on a daily basis, it is virtually impossible for anyone to maintain her or his anonymity. People's lives are played out in such close proximity to one another that everyone knows what everyone else is doing. To illustrate, a man who wants to engage in socially inappropriate behavior (such as having an extramarital affair) would think twice because it would be difficult, if not impossible, to keep it a secret. By way of contrast, it is considerably easier to have an extramarital affair and remain undetected in a large city. Thus, the small-scale nature of corporate lineage communities tends to inhibit social deviance because it is much more difficult for people to get away with breaking the rules.

The way roles are structured in corporate lineage societies also contributes to social control. In terms of role structure, corporate lineages have what Talcott Parsons and Edward Shils (1952) call "diffuse roles." People play social roles in a number of different domains, such as kinship, economic, political, ritual/religious, and recreational roles. A role is diffuse when it ranges over two or more of these domains. For example, a diffuse role structure occurs when a man's grandfather (kinship role) is also his teacher (educational role), his priest (religious role), the local chief (political role), and his hunting partner (economic role). The man has a number of overlapping roles and plays roles from a number of different domains with the same person. In contrast, roles in large-scale, complex societies such as our own tend to be segmented or narrowly defined so that single roles are played out with one person at a time. People in corporate lineage societies (with diffuse or overlapping roles) have a built-in incentive not to violate the social norms, for to do so would have very serious consequences. If the man in the preceding illustration offends his grandfather, he is not only negatively

---

degradation ceremonies Deliberate and formal societal mechanisms designed to publicly humiliate someone who has broken a social norm.

corporate lineages Kinship groups whose members engage in daily activities together.

affecting his kinship domain but is also affecting the educational, economic, political, and religious domains.

Marriage in corporate lineage societies also plays a role in social control. Marriage in such societies is regarded primarily as an alliance between two lineages—that of the bride and that of the groom—and only secondarily as a union between individuals. In many cases, the marriage is legitimized by bridewealth (the transfer of property, often livestock, from the kin group of the groom to the kin group of the bride). When a man wants to get married, he cannot pay the bridewealth himself because he does not have personal control over property. Like the rest of his relatives, he has limited rights and obligations to pieces of property such as cattle. If marriage cattle are to be transferred from one lineage to another, a group decision must be made. For example, if eight cows must be given to the prospective bride's family before the marriage can be legitimate, the prospective groom must convince a number of his kin to give up their limited use of cows. If the prospective groom has a reputation for violating the social norms, it is unlikely that the permission to transfer the cows will be given. Thus, the members of a corporate lineage, through their collective capacity to control marriage, have considerable power to coerce people into appropriate behavior.

Supernatural Belief Systems

A powerful mechanism of social control in headless societies is *supernatural belief systems*—belief in supernatural forces such as gods, witches, and sorcerers. People will refrain from antisocial behavior if they believe that some supernatural (suprahuman) force will punish them for it. Of course, it is impossible to determine how many norms are not violated because people fear supernatural retribution, but we have to assume that the belief in supernatural sanctions acts as a deterrent to some degree. Nor is it necessary to prove that the gods, for example, will punish the social deviants. If people believe that "god will get them" for doing something wrong, the belief itself is usually enough to discourage the deviant behavior. This is certainly the case in Western religions (Judeo-Christian), which teach about atonement for one's sins, Judgment Day, and heaven and hell. In small-scale societies there are other forms of supernatural belief systems (such as ancestor worship and witchcraft), which are equally effective social mechanisms for controlling people's behavior.

Ancestor Worship In some headless societies, *ancestor worship* serves as an effective means of social control. In

such societies, dead ancestors are considered to be fully functioning members of the descent group. In fact, the death of a respected elder marks that person's elevation in status to supernatural being rather than his or her departure from the group. Respect for the ancestor-gods is often demonstrated by sacrifices and proper behavior, for which the living members are believed to be rewarded or punished, depending on how well they meet these obligations.

The Lugbara society of Uganda provides a good example of ancestor worship. According to John Middleton (1965), the well-being of the entire kinship group is ensured only if people behave in socially appropriate ways. The Lugbara believe that personal and group tragedies are a direct result of the transgression of certain social norms, such as showing disrespect to living and dead elders, adultery, incest, assault, or homicide.

The Lugbara generally believe that the ancestor-gods afflict with illness the living kin who endanger the well-being of the lineage by committing any of these offenses. Sickness of any type is explained in terms of ancestral displeasure with the conduct of the living. Thus, sickness (resulting from sin) is followed by either ghost invocation or ghostly vengeance. In *ghost invocation*, a living man—typically an elder—calls forth the wrath of the ancestor-gods against the sinner. *Ghostly vengeance* is the belief that ancestor-gods inflict sickness on guilty people directly, without having to be invoked.

Whether ancestral ghosts in traditional Lugbara society were directly responsible for sickness among the living is perhaps of greater interest to the theologian than to the anthropologist. The anthropologist, however, is interested in how the belief affects the behavior of the living rather than whether it will hold up scientifically. Rites such as ghostly invocation give regular expression to fears of supernatural retribution, which in turn control, or at least influence, people's conduct.

supernatural belief systems Found in all societies, a set of beliefs that transcend the natural, observable world.
ancestor worship The worshiping of deceased relatives. These souls are considered supernatural beings and fully functioning members of a descent group.

ghost invocation The practice of a living person (typically an elder) calling forth the wrath of ancestor gods against an alleged sinner.
ghostly vengeance The belief that ancestor gods (ghosts) will punish sinners.

Many people in the world, including these Islamic worshippers in Rawalpindi, Pakistan, tend to conform to social norms out of a strong belief in supernatural forces.

Witchcraft   Belief in *witchcraft*, which is common in headless societies, also discourages people from engaging in socially deviant behavior. In many societies where witchcraft is practiced, people reject the idea that misfortunes are the result of natural causes. If crops fail or large numbers of people die, the usual explanation is that someone has been practicing witchcraft. In societies that believe in witchcraft, a deviant runs the risk of being labeled a witch, and fear of being accused of witchcraft strongly encourages conformity. For example, in colonial America, nonconformists, free-thinkers, and others who didn't conform to expected behavioral norms were driven from their communities for allegedly being witches. Jean La Fontaine notes the way witchcraft serves as a mechanism of social control among the Bantu-speaking Bagisu of East Africa:

> Witchcraft beliefs act as a form of social control in discouraging behavior that is socially unacceptable. In Bagisu the eccentric is branded a witch.... Children grow up with the realization that the stigma of nonconformity is dangerous; too great a departure from the norms of everyday conduct will attract the suspicion of others and lead to isolation and eventual destruction. (1963: 217)

Age Organization

In some headless societies, *age organizations* serve as effective means of social control. Societies with age organizations have distinct groups of people passing period-

witchcraft   An inborn, involuntary, and often unconscious capacity to cause harm to other people.

age organizations   A type of social organization, found in East Africa and among certain Native American groups, wherein people of roughly the same age pass through different levels of society together. Each ascending level, based on age, carries with it increased social status and rigidly defined roles.

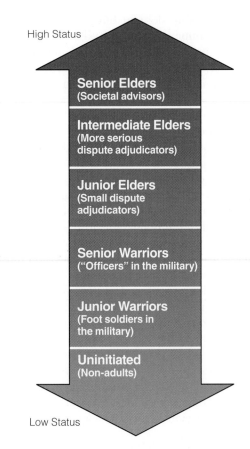

FIGURE 13.4   **Age-Graded Society**

ically through distinct age categories (Figure 13.4). This involves the basic distinction between age sets and age grades. An *age set* is a group of people (usually men) initiated during a periodic ceremony and having a strong sense of group identity with one another. An age set lasts from its inception, usually when most members are late adolescents, until its last member has died. Age sets pass (as a group) through successive categories, called *age grades*, such as those of warriors, elders, or various subdivisions within these grades. Each age grade is associated with a well-understood set of social roles (that is, they perform exclusive functions) and statuses (that is, higher prestige is associated with increasing age). To illustrate this distinction further, an age set is analogous to a group of students who go through college together. The academic grades through which they pass (freshman through senior) are comparable to the age grades. Thus, we can speak of a particular age set occupying the senior warrior grade at a particular moment.

age set   A group of people roughly the same age who pass through various age grades together.

age grades   Permanent age categories in a society through which people pass during the course of a lifetime.

The age organization into which these boys from Papua New Guinea are being initiated can serve as an effective mechanism of social control.

© David Gillison/Peter Arnold, Inc.

Age organizations control behavior in a number of significant ways. First, because age organizations establish a clear set of roles and statuses, there is little room for infringing on the authority or domain of others. There is little incentive, in other words, to try to usurp the authority of those above you for the simple reason that if you live long enough, you will eventually have that authority by virtue of your own advanced age.

Second, individuals enter the age-set system at the lowest echelon through the process of initiation. These rites of passage are almost always preceded by intense periods of training in the norms and values of the society. These periods of intense socialization teach the soon-to-become adults not only the expected behaviors but also why the behaviors should be followed and the penalties for deviation.

Third, the bonds of camaraderie that exist among members of the same age set are usually so strong that age sets tend to take on the characteristics of a corporate group. Age-set members who have experienced their initiation ceremonies together support one another throughout the remainder of their lives in much the same way as do members of the same lineage. Unlike lineages, age sets are neither self-perpetuating nor property owning, but they exert the same type of pressure toward conformity as lineages do.

Formal Means of Social Control

As previously noted, all societies use informal mechanisms of social control to some degree. Western cultures rely heavily on such mechanisms as socialization, public opinion, and supernatural sanctions to encourage people to maintain social order by behaving appropriately. Often these informal mechanisms of social control are not sufficient to maintain the desired level of conformity to the norms. The violation of social norms often results in disputes among people in the society. When such disputes become violent conflicts (such as theft, assault, or homicide), we call them crimes. Because societies face the possibility of violent conflict erupting among their members, they need to develop explicit mechanisms to address and, it is hoped, resolve the conflicts.

Although no society in the world is free from *crime*, the incidence of crime varies considerably from society to society. It appears that crime is more likely to occur in large, heterogeneous, stratified societies than in small-scale societies. For example, the crime rate in U.S. cities is approximately ten times as high as in rural areas. Several logical arguments support these findings. First, as mentioned in the discussion of corporate lineages, people in small-scale societies have little or no anonymity, which makes getting away with a crime more difficult. Second, because people in small-scale societies know most of the other people, they are more likely to be concerned with negative public opinion. Third, the heterogeneous character of populations in large-scale, complex societies means that there will be a number of groups with different, and often conflicting, interests. Finally, the fact that large-scale societies are almost always stratified into classes or castes means that the lower strata of the population may feel blocked from upward mobility and consequently may be more likely to want to violate the rights of those in the more privileged strata.

crime Harm to a person or property that is considered illegitimate by a society.

Song Duels

Just as societies differ in terms of the incidence of crime, they also differ in the way they handle disputes and crimes. One example of a formal mechanism for resolving disputes was found among the Inuit of Canada, Alaska, and Greenland. Because the Inuit had little property due to their nomadic way of life, conflicts rarely arose over violation of property rights. However, disputes often arose between men over the issue of wife stealing. A man would attempt to steal the wife of a more prominent man as a way of elevating his own standing within the community.

A common way of resolving wife stealing among the Inuit was to murder the wife stealer. In fact, Knud Rasmussen (1927) found that all of the men he studied had been a party to a murder, either as the murderer or as an accessory, and invariably these murders stemmed from allegations of wife stealing. However, there were alternative ways to resolve disputes over wife stealing. One alternative was to challenge the alleged wife stealer to a *song duel*, a derisive song contest, which was fought with song and lyrics rather than with weapons. The plaintiff and defendant, appearing in a public setting, would chide each other with abusive songs especially composed for the occasion. The contestant who received the loudest applause emerged the winner of this "curse by verse" song duel. Interestingly, the resolution of the conflict was based not on a determination of guilt or innocence but on one's verbal dexterity.

Intermediaries

Some societies use *intermediaries* to help resolve serious conflicts. The Nuer of the African Sudan are a case in point (Evans-Pritchard 1940). Even though the Nuer political system is informal and decentralized, one role in the society—the *Leopard-skin Chief*—is, to a degree, institutionalized. In the absence of any formal system of law courts to punish serious crimes such as murder, the Leopard-skin Chief serves as a mediator between the victim's family and the family of the murderer. When a homicide occurs, the murderer, fearing the vengeance of the victim's family, takes sanctuary in the home of the Leopard-skin Chief. In an attempt to prevent an all-out feud, the Leopard-skin Chief attempts to negotiate a settlement between the two families. His role is to work out an equitable settlement between the two families whereby the murderer's family will compensate the victim's family with some form of property settlement (say, forty head of cattle) for the loss of one of its members. These animals will be used as bridewealth for the lineage to obtain a wife for one of its members. It is thought that the sons from such a marriage will fill the void left by the murder victim.

If either side becomes too unyielding, the Leopard-skin Chief can threaten to curse the offending party. The Leopard-skin Chief does not decide the case, however. Rather, he is only an intermediary, with no authority to determine guilt or force a settlement between the parties. Intervening on behalf of the public interest, he uses his personal and supernatural influence to bring the disputing parties to some type of settlement of their dispute.

Moots: Informal Courts

Found in many African societies, moots serve as a highly effective mechanism for conflict resolution. *Moots* are informal airings of disputes involving kinsmen and friends of the litigants. These adjudicating bodies are ad hoc, with considerable variation in composition from case to case. Moots generally deal with the resolution of domestic disputes such as mistreating a spouse, disagreements over inheritance, or the nonpayment of debts.

Anthropologist James Gibbs (1963) describes in considerable detail the moot system as found among the Kpelle, a Mande-speaking group of rice cultivators living in Liberia and Guinea. Gibbs found that moots differ from the more formal court system that is administered by district chiefs in Kpelle society. First, unlike the more formal court system, moots are held in the homes of the complainants rather than in public places. Second, all parties concerned (*council of elders*, litigants, witnesses, and spectators) sit very close to one another in a random and mixed fashion. This seating arrangement is in marked contrast to more formalized courts, which physically separate the plaintiff, the defendant, and the judge. Third, because the range of relevance in moots is very broad, the airing of grievances is more complete than in formal courts of law. Fourth, whereas in formal courts the judge controls the conduct of the proceedings, in moots the investigation is more in the hands of the disputants themselves. Fifth, moots do not attempt to blame one party unilaterally but rather attribute fault in the dispute to both parties. Finally, the sanctions imposed by the moot are not so severe that the losing party has grounds for a new grudge against the other party. The party found to be at fault is assessed a

---

song duel   A means of settling disputes over wife stealing among the Inuit involving the use of song and lyrics to determine one's guilt or innocence.
intermediaries   Mediators of disputes among individuals or families within a society.
Leopard-skin Chief   An example of an intermediary found among the Nuer of the African Sudan.

moots   Informal hearings of disputes for the purpose of resolving conflicts, usually found in small scale societies.
council of elders   A formal control mechanism composed of a group of elders who settle disputes among individuals within a community.

small fine, is expected to give the wronged party a token gift, and is required to make a public apology.

Unlike more formal court systems—including those found in our own society—moots do not separate the guilty party from society by incarceration. Just the opposite is true. Moots attempt to reintegrate the guilty party back into the community, restore normal social relations between disputing parties, and achieve reconciliation without bitterness and acrimony. The ritualized apology given by the guilty party symbolizes the consensual nature of the resolution and its emphasis on healing the community rather than simply punishing the wrongdoer.

Oaths and Ordeals

Another way of resolving conflicts—particularly when law enforcement agencies (such as governments) are not especially strong—is through religiously sanctioned methods such as oaths and ordeals. An *oath* is a formal declaration to some supernatural force that what you are saying is truthful or that you are innocent. Although they can take many different forms, oaths almost always are accompanied by a ritual act, such as smoking a peace pipe, signing a loyalty document, or swearing upon the Bible (as in our courts of law). Because some believe that to swear a false oath could lead to supernatural retribution, oaths can be effective in determining guilt or innocence.

An *ordeal* is a means of determining guilt by submitting the accused to a dangerous test. If the person passes the test, it is believed that a higher supernatural force has determined the party's innocence; if he or she fails, the gods have signaled the party's guilt. In some African societies, an accused person is expected to plunge his hand into a pot of boiling water, lift out a hot stone, and then put his hand into a pot of cold water. The hand is then bandaged and examined the following day. If the hand is blistered, the accused is deemed guilty; if not, his innocence is proclaimed. To Westerners steeped in the principles of the physical sciences, such an approach to determining guilt or innocence would appear mystical at best. But there is often more information being gathered than meets the untrained eye. For example, those in charge of conducting the ordeal prepare the accused psychologically to take the proceedings seriously. They explain in considerable detail how the ordeal works; they may put their own hands in the water briefly to show how the innocent are protected from blistering. During these preliminaries to the actual physical ordeal, the person administering the ordeal is looking for nonverbal behaviors of the suspect that may indicate probable guilt: signs of excessive anxiety such as muscle tension, perspiration, or dilation of the pupils. Based on an assessment of these nonverbal signs of anxiety, the ordeal administrator may alter such factors as the length of time that the suspect's hand stays in the water, which, in turn, may affect the outcome of the ordeal.

It has been suggested (Roberts 1967; Meek 1972) that oaths and ordeals are most likely to be found in complex societies where the political leadership lacks the power to enforce judicial decisions; consequently, the leaders must rely on supernaturally sanctioned mechanisms such as oaths and ordeals to make certain that people will obey. Where political leaders wield greater power, oaths and ordeals are no longer needed.

Courts and Codified Law

A characteristic of state systems of government is that they possess a monopoly on the use of force. Through a system of codified laws, the state both forbids individuals from using force and determines how it will use force to require citizens to do some things and prevent them from doing others. These laws, which are usually in written form, are established by legislative bodies, interpreted by judicial bodies, and enforced by administrators. When legal prescriptions are violated, the state has the authority, through its courts and law enforcement agencies, to fine, imprison, or even execute the wrongdoer. To suggest that the state has a monopoly on the use of force does not mean that only the government uses force. State systems of government are constantly having to deal with unauthorized uses of force, such as crime (violent disputes between individuals or groups), *rebellion* (attempts to displace the people in power), and *revolution* (attempts to overthrow the entire system of government).

The system of codified laws used to resolve disputes and maintain social order in complex societies is distinct from other types of social norms. Legal anthropologist E. Adamson Hoebel (1972) has identified three basic features of *law*. Although his definition of *law* goes beyond the type of law found in Western societies, it certainly holds true for that type of law as well. First, law involves the legitimate use of physical coercion. Law without the force to punish or deprive is no law at all, although in most cases force is not necessary because the very threat of force or compulsion acts as a sufficient deterrent to antisocial behavior. But when it is needed, a true legal system can draw on the legitimate use of force.

---

oath The practice of having God bear witness to the truth of what a person says.
ordeal A painful and possibly life-threatening test inflicted on someone suspected of wrongdoing.

rebellion An attempt within a society to disrupt the status quo and redistribute the power and resources.
revolution An attempt to overthrow the existing form of political organization, the principles of economic production and distribution, and the allocation of social status.
law Cultural rules that regulate human behavior and maintain order.

Second, legal systems allocate official authority to privileged people who are able to use coercion legitimately. Third, law is based on regularity and a certain amount of predictability. That is, because laws build on precedents, new laws are based on old ones. This regularity and predictability eliminate much of the potential for whim and capriciousness from the law.

Legal systems in complex societies have different objectives from systems of conflict resolution found in other societies. The objective of the Nuer Leopard-skin Chief and the Kpelle moots, for example, was to compensate the victim and to reestablish harmony among the disputants and, consequently, peace within the community. Law enforcement and conflict resolution in complex societies, in contrast, tend to emphasize punishment of the wrongdoer, which often takes the form of incarceration or, in some cases, death. In other words, it is not aimed at either compensating the victim or reintegrating the offender back into the community. This emphasis on punishment in complex societies is understandable in that lawbreakers pose a particular threat to the authority of the government officials. Unless serious offenders are punished or separated from the rest of society, they are likely to threaten the very legitimacy of political and legal authority.

This fundamental difference in legal philosophy has played itself out in a number of conflicts around the world. In the tribal violence that has been occurring for the past two decades in northern Uganda, the International Criminal Court at The Hague is indicting rebel leaders in order to hold them responsible for killing innocent civilians. Local leaders in Uganda, however, want to use age-old rites designed to have the defendants admit publicly to their atrocities, pay a reasonable compensation to the victims, and then make amends with the total community. The traditional solution, based on a powerful capacity to forgive, emphasizes peace, healing between the parties, and reintegration of the wrongdoers back into the community. While the Ugandan government supports the efforts of the International Court, it has also adopted the traditional notion of forgiveness and healing as one of its strategies to restore peace to the country. Since 2000, an amnesty program has led thousands of rebels to lay down their arms, admit publicly to their misdeeds, and be welcomed back into the society. Using these traditional African philosophies of justice and law in Uganda is very similar to the Truth and Reconciliation Commission (headed by Bishop Desmond Tutu) used to heal racial hatred and distrust after decades of the Apartheid system in the Republic of South Africa (Lacey 2005: 1).

Warfare

Just as societies have ways of regulating the social relationships of people within their own society, they also have mechanisms for managing external relationships with other groups, be they states, tribes, bands, clans, or

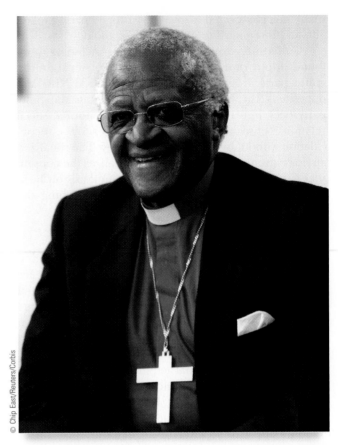

Archbishop Desmond Tutu served as Co-Chair of the Truth and Reconciliation Commission, which used traditional African philosophies of law and justice to heal racial hatreds and distrust after decades of segregation in the Republic of South Africa.

lineages. One such mechanism of social control outside one's own group or society is *warfare*, which we can define as systematic, organized, and institutionalized fighting between different groups. People will be less willing to engage in antisocial or aggressive behavior if that behavior might bring about an attack by outside forces. As with most other aspects of culture, there is enormous cultural variability in terms of the extent to which societies use warfare, or other forms of large-scale violence, as a way of resolving conflicts and controlling people's behavior. In some small-scale societies, warfare as we know it is virtually nonexistent; at the other end of the spectrum are societies like the United States, which participated in World War II at a cost of hundreds of thousands of lives and nearly $3 trillion.

It is often stated that warfare has been around as long as there have been people. Although it is probably true that violence has occurred on occasions throughout human prehistory, warfare began during the neolithic period, starting about ten thousand years ago. Most prehistorians agree that warfare, as we know it,

warfare Armed conflict between nation-states or other politically distinct groups.

By means of codified laws, state systems of government maintain a monopoly on the use of force.

© L. O'Shaughnessy/Robertstock.com

was unknown before the invention of food-production techniques. Prior to food production, foraging societies had little motivation for engaging in warfare. We can cite a number of compelling reasons why foraging societies were not warlike: First, they had no centralized governments that could finance and coordinate the relatively large numbers of people needed for military campaigns. Second, the absence of food surpluses precluded prolonged combat. Third, because foraging societies did not control land or territorial boundaries, one of the major motivations of warfare simply did not exist. And fourth, because foraging societies are small in scale (usually composed of exogamous bands), people are not likely to become hostile toward other bands into which their own relatives have married.

With the coming of food production ten thousand years ago, populations became more sedentary, people began to claim rights over specific pieces of land, and the world experienced its first population explosion. If farmers and pastoralists, by the very nature of their means of livelihood, experience significant population growth and land scarcity, they are more likely to resort to warfare as a solution to the problem of increasing resource depletion. They will, in other words, resort to warfare to procure rights to other people's land and scarce resources.

Even though small-scale warfare was a possibility ten thousand years ago, war increased in scale with the rise of civilizations (state societies) 5,500 years ago. The formation of large, hierarchically organized states allowed the creation of significant military organizations. In fact, some have argued that state systems of government could not exist without powerful armies to both protect and control their populations. Since those early states arose more than five thousand years ago, the sophistication of military organization and technology has increased steadily over the centuries. During the past century, we have witnessed an incredible escalation in the power of warfare throughout the world. Not only does humankind now possess the technological capacity to totally annihilate itself within a matter of hours, but warfare during the past century, in part due to that technology, has resulted in the killing of large segments of civilian populations. Today, in other words, modern warfare is likely to produce more civilian than military casualties.

The Causes of War

For decades anthropologists and other social scientists have been fascinated with the question, What causes war? To address this question, a number of anthropologists over the past thirty years have examined the Yanomamo peoples of the Amazon region of Brazil and Venezuela. Although these people have been in the news recently because they are threatened by the worst abuses of economic development, they have been of interest to anthropologists because of their institutionalized form of warfare and their reputation for fierceness.

Napoleon Chagnon, who has written a best-selling ethnography of the Yanomamo, has attempted to explain their system of warfare on the basis of their headless political structure and their competition over women (1983, 1992). Marvin Harris (1979c, 1984), a cultural materialist (see Chapter 4), has offered a materialist explanation, namely that Yanomamo warfare is the result of shortages of protein. The most recent entry into the debate is anthropologist Brian Ferguson (1995), who claims that the Yanomamo go to war over metal tools. Despite the popular view that the Yanomamo are isolated rainforest dwellers untouched by the outside world, Ferguson documents their relatively long-standing contact with modern society and, consequently, their exposure to and desire for metal tools. By drawing on a number of other ethnographic studies, Ferguson shows how warfare increases directly with the scarcity of metal tools. In other words, Yanomamo are more likely to go to war when their highly valued metal tools are in short supply.

Thus, we have three anthropologists attempting to explain Yanomamo warfare using three different sets of causal factors. Chagnon, taking the most emic view, ascribes Yanomamo warfare to social structure—namely their headless political structure and the competition for women. Harris and Ferguson suggest that the major reason for going to war is a shortage of either protein or metal tools. That three competent scholars can come up with three different primary causes for Yanomamo warfare illustrates the complexity of trying to understand warfare. In all likelihood, all three sets of causal factors are valid to some degree. But warfare among the Yanomamo is a multidimensional phenomenon. Any attempt to explain why Yanomamo go to war by using any single factor will be like trying to explain the motion of an airplane exclusively in terms of the power of its engine while ignoring other factors such as wind speed, altitude, the design and weight of the aircraft, and the skill of the pilot.

When trying to search for the causes of war in general, the task becomes even more daunting. When considering warfare (for all time) in both small-scale societies and modern nation-states, we can identify several general factors that contribute to warfare. These include:

- *Social problems.* When internal social problems exist, political leaders may turn the society's frustrations toward another group. The outsiders may be portrayed as having more than their share of scarce resources or even as causing the social problems. It matters little if this type of blaming is justified; what is important is that people are convinced that other groups are the cause of their problems. When that happens, one group can declare war on another. This factor is illustrated when Yanomamo go to war with neighboring villages over scarce metal tools or when Adolf Hitler moved his troops into neighboring European countries to acquire more "living room" for the German people.

- *Perceived threats.* In some cases, societies will go to war when they feel that their security or well-being is in jeopardy. The people of North Vietnam during the 1960s were willing to wage war because they felt that their security was threatened by the long-term influence of the French and Americans in the southern part of Vietnam. The Americans, on the other hand, felt, either rightly or wrongly, that Vietnam, and indeed all of Asia, was being threatened by the presence of a godless, communist regime; if South Vietnam fell to the communists, it would start a domino effect that would eventually threaten the entire free world.

- *Political motivations.* Sometimes governments will wage war for the purpose of furthering their own political objectives. The brief wars (or "military actions") that the United States initiated in Haiti, Grenada, and Somalia were motivated by the desire to show sufficient power to enforce its political will.

- *Moral objectives.* It is difficult to think of any war in human history that has been waged without a shred of moral urgency. Even when wars are waged primarily for political or economic reasons, those who commit their soldiers to battle will justify their actions on some moral grounds. Europeans waged the Crusades against the Islamic infidels because they were convinced that God was on their side. Interestingly, if we read accounts of those same wars written by Islamic historians, it is the European Christians who were the godless bad guys. Both sides justified waging wars for generations on the basis of moral correctness.

It is possible, even likely, that more than one of these factors are operating at the same time. To illustrate, the U.S. Congress authorized the use of military

© Jerry Lampen/Reuters/CORBIS

Are these Hamas "terrorists" in Gaza fighting for religious principles or secular ones?

action in Iraq in 2003 based on the perceived threat that Saddam Hussein had stockpiles of chemical and biological weapons and the intention to sell them to the terrorists who were responsible for the September 11, 2001 attacks. After the weapons of mass destruction and the links to al Qaida failed to materialize, the U.S. government then argued that its preemptive war in Iraq was justified on political grounds: that is, establishing one democratic regime in the region would cause democracy to spread throughout the Middle East. In addition, the government used the moral justification by arguing that Saddam Hussein needed to be overthrown because he was an evil dictator responsible for many atrocities perpetrated against his own people. Thus, in this example three of the four factors contributing to warfare (listed previously) have been used at one time or another to justify the war in Iraq.

The War on Terrorism

Shortly after the traumatic events of September 11, President George W. Bush announced the "war on terrorism." The prevailing impression of this new, twenty-first-century war—in large measure due to the way that the U.S. government has framed the issue—is that suicide terrorism is essentially a function of (i.e., caused by) Islamic fundamentalism. That is, Islamic "fanatics," who allegedly place no value on human life, are so inherently xenophobic that they are willing to die because they hate our freedom, our religion, and our society. One of the more vociferous Christian commentators, Jerry Falwell, has actually claimed on national television that "Mohammed was a terrorist," when compared to Jesus and Moses, who were men of peace. However, this equation of terrorism with radical Islam is misleading for two reasons. First, the Islamic religion is

no more prone to violence than any other religion, including Christianity or Judaism. A careful reading of both the Bible and the Koran reveals a sizeable number of passages advocating violence against nonbelievers. Indeed, many world religions, which distinguish all of the world's people into "us" and "them," tend to encourage violence in the name of goodness (Eller, 2005: 148–75).

There is a second reason for avoiding the "obvious" equation of terrorism with the Islamic religion. Recent research suggests that suicide attacks are more directed toward secular ends than religious ones. That is, al Qaeda and other terrorist groups strongly and publicly oppose U.S. foreign policy in the Middle East. These groups despise (and are primarily motivated by) U.S. policy regarding the Israeli-Palestinian conflict, U.S. support for repressive and undemocratic governments such as Saudi Arabia and Kuwait, and particularly the occupation of their homelands and holy lands by U.S. troops. To illustrate, according to Robert A. Pape (2005), a political scientist from the University of Chicago, more than 95 percent of all suicide attacks around the world since 1980 have been aimed at a clear strategic objective: to coerce a modern democracy to withdraw its military forces from their homeland. More specifically, when examining the nationalities of sixty-seven of the seventy-one al Qaeda suicide attackers, Pape found that two-thirds of them were from countries with a significant U.S. military presence (Saudi Arabia, Afghanistan, and the United Arab Emirates), while the remaining third were from countries whose governments were heavily backed by the United States, such as Indonesia, Pakistan, and Egypt. Pape concludes from these data that the cause of suicide terrorists is not religious fundamentalism *per se*, but rather should be seen more as a reaction to U.S. military and political policy. ■

Summary

1. All societies have political systems to manage public affairs, maintain social order, and resolve conflict. The study of political organization involves topics such as the allocation of political roles, levels of political integration, concentrations of power and authority, mechanisms of social control, and means for resolving conflict.

2. Political anthropologists generally recognize four fundamentally different levels of political organization based on levels of political integration and the degree of specialized political roles: bands, tribes, chiefdoms, and states.

3. Societies based on bands have the least amount of political integration and role specialization. They are most often found in foraging societies and are associated with low population densities, distribution systems based on reciprocity, and egalitarian social relations.

4. Tribal organizations are most commonly found among horticulturalists and pastoralists. With larger and more sedentary populations than are found in band societies, tribally based societies have certain pan-tribal mechanisms that cut across a number of local segments and integrate them into a larger whole.

5. Chiefdoms have a more formal and permanent political structure than is found in tribal societies. Political authority in chiefdoms rests with a single individual, either acting alone or with the advice of a council. Most chiefdoms, which tend to have quite distinct social ranks, rely on feasting and tribute as a major way of distributing goods.

6. State systems—with the greatest amount of political integration and role specialization—are associated with intensive agriculture, market economies, urbanization, and complex social stratification. States, which first appeared about 5,500 years ago, have a monopoly on the use of force and can make and enforce laws, collect taxes, and recruit labor for military service and public works projects.

7. Theories put forth to explain the rise of state systems of government have centered on the question of why people surrender some of their autonomy to the power and authority of the state. Some theories (such as those of Childe [1936] and Wittfogel [1957]) suggest that people voluntarily gave up their autonomy in exchange for certain perceived benefits such as protection, more effective means of conflict resolution, and greater food productivity. Other explanations, such as that offered by Carneiro, hold that states developed as a result of warfare and coercion rather than voluntary self-interest.

8. A major challenge for the many state governments today is that they contain within their boundaries distinct ethnic populations that seek independence or greater autonomy, as illustrated by the French in Canada, the Kurds in Turkey, and the Chechens in Russia.

9. As a general rule, women do not hold important positions of political leadership in state systems of government.

10. During the last several decades, there has been a general trend toward democracy and away from autocracy.

11. In the absence of formal mechanisms of government, many band and tribal societies maintain social control by means of informal mechanisms such as socialization, public opinion, corporate lineages, supernatural sanctions, and age organizations.

12. In addition to using informal means of social control, societies control behavior by more formal mechanisms with the major function of maintaining social order and resolving conflicts. These mechanisms include verbal competition, intermediaries, councils of elders, oaths, ordeals, formal court systems, and warfare.

13. A society will go to war when it (a) blames another society for its own social problems, (b) believes that it is threatened, (c) wants to further its own ends, or (d) is defending a moral position.

14. In reference to the so-called war on terrorism, the equation of terrorism with Islamic religion is misleading because (a) Islam is no more violent than other world religions (including Christianity) and (b) there is evidence to suggest that most terrorist attacks are directed toward secular ends rather than religious ones.

Key Terms

age grades	authority	coercive theory of state formation	degradation ceremonies
age organizations	autocracy	corporate lineages	democracy
age set	band societies	council of elders	deviance
ancestor worship	chiefdoms	crime	ghost invocation

ghostly vengeance	negative sanctions	rebellion	state system of government
headless societies	oath	revolution	supernatural belief systems
hydraulic theory of state formation	ordeal	sanctions	tribal societies
intermediaries	pan-tribal mechanisms	social control	voluntaristic theory of state formation
law	political coerciveness	socialization	warfare
Leopard-skin Chief	political integration	social norms	witchcraft
moots	positive sanctions	song duel	
nation	public opinion	specialized political roles	
		state	

Suggested Readings

Cohen, Ronald, and Elman R. Service, eds. *Origins of the State: The Anthropology of Political Evolution.* Philadelphia: Institute for the Study of Human Issues, 1978. A collection of essays on how and why state systems of government have evolved, written by such noted political anthropologists as Morton Fried, Elman Service, and Robert Carneiro. An excellent introductory essay is written by one of the editors, Ronald Cohen.

Ferguson, R. Brian. *The State, Identity, and Violence: Political Disintegration in the Post–Cold-War World.* New York: Routledge, 2003. This volume includes commentaries by scholars from around the world on the global forces and local beliefs that lead to civil violence, chaos, and perhaps the demise of the traditional nation-state.

Fried, M. H. *The Evolution of Political Society: An Essay in Political Anthropology.* New York: Random House, 1967. A classic work in the field of political anthropology setting forth the fourfold typology of political organization—egalitarian societies, rank societies, stratified societies, and states—that has been widely used as a model for classifying different types of sociopolitical systems.

Kurtz, Donald V. *Political Anthropology: Paradigms and Power.* Boulder, CO: Westview Press, 2001. An examination of how typical topics in political anthropology (such as power, authority, succession, leadership, and state formation) are analyzed in terms of certain theoretical orientations in anthropology (such as structural-functionalism, political evolutionism, and post-modernism).

McGlynn, Frank, and Arthur Tuden, eds. *Anthropological Approaches to Political Behavior.* Pittsburgh: University of Pittsburgh Press, 1991. A collection of sixteen essays that highlight the major theoretical concerns of political anthropology. These articles deal with such topics as conflict resolution, leadership, ideology, and authority among small-scale societies in Africa, Latin America, Europe, and Oceania.

Meggitt, Mervyn. *Blood Is Their Argument.* Palo Alto, CA: Mayfield, 1977. An ethnographic study of warfare among the Mae Enga tribesmen of New Guinea, which explores the modes of clan warfare, the reasons for fighting, the outcomes of the conflicts, and methods for establishing peace.

Vincent, Joan. *The Anthropology of Politics: A Reader in Ethnography, Theory, and Critique.* Malden, MA: Blackwell Publishers, 2002. A collection of classic and contemporary articles on topics in the field of political anthropology, including post-colonialism, political violence, political development, and identity politics.

Supernatural Beliefs

A Hindu religious pilgrim praying in Varanasi, India.

CHAPTER 14

BEGINNING IN THE nineteenth century, religion was studied from a scientific, rather than just a theological, perspective. For example, in *The Elementary Forms of Religious Life*, French sociologist Emile Durkheim (2001) argued that religion enables people to transcend their individual identities and to see themselves as part of a larger collective. Another social scientist, Max Weber, analyzed religion as it relates to economic institutions. In his classic study, *The Protestant Ethic and the Spirit of Capitalism*, Weber (1958) claimed that the Protestant faith supported the rise of capitalism in Western societies. And, of course, Karl Marx, studying religion from a nontheological perspective, linked organized religions with social inequality by suggesting that religion was a tool for oppressing the lower classes.

This rise of the scientific study of religion during the nineteenth and twentieth centuries has been interpreted by some as the beginning of the end for organized religion. Yet, the analysis of religion by social scientists has not caused people to abandon their religions in great numbers. To be certain, some religious groups in different parts of the world have lost followers, but others have gained adherents, particularly fundamentalist groups (both at home and abroad) in recent decades. For example, long before 9/11 the world witnessed a rise in Islamic fundamentalism in such places as Saudi Arabia, Iran, and Egypt; the Ariel Sharon government in Israel was elected largely by the growing number of Jewish fundamentalists; and the most dramatic growth in church affiliation in the United States in the last several decades has been among various fundamentalist (evangelical) churches such as the Assembly of God and the Church of God in Christ. Thus, the scientific study of religion has hardly inhibited these particular religious movements, and, in fact, their "anti-science" stance on most contemporary issues would suggest that a scientific view of the world may have contributed to their growth.

Cultural anthropologists have devoted considerable attention to the analysis of religion since they began to make direct field observations of peoples of the world. Although twentieth-century anthropologists have not always agreed on how to interpret different religious systems, all would agree that the many religious practices found throughout the world vary widely from one another as well as from our own. These religious systems might involve sacrificing animals to ancestor-gods, using

What We Will Learn

- What is religion?

- What functions does religion perform for the individual and the society as a whole?

- What different forms does religion take among the societies of the world?

- What role does religion play in the process of culture change?

 Click!

For interactive exercises and study aids, Go to **www.ichapters.com**; enter the author name and select your text, then click the Study Help tab to purchase the following online resources:

- **ThomsonNOW** for chapter-specific online tutorials, quizzes, and a personalized study plan

- **Anthropology Resource Center** for interactive maps, modules, videos, and the Applied Anthropology site

- **Thomson Audio Study Products** for a brief overview of the major chapter themes and to test your knowledge with quiz questions

a form of divination called ordeals to determine a person's guilt or innocence, or submitting oneself to extraordinary levels of pain as a way of communicating directly with the deities (Lehmann and Myers 1993).

DEFINING RELIGION

The forms of religion vary enormously, but they are all alike to the extent that they are founded on a belief in the supernatural. For our purposes in this chapter, we shall define *religion* as a set of beliefs in supernatural beings and forces directed at helping people make sense of the world and solve important problems. Because human beings are faced with a series of important life problems that cannot all be resolved through the application of science and technology alone, they attempt to overcome these human limitations by manipulating supernatural forces.

Anthropologists have long observed that all societies have a recognizable set of beliefs and behaviors that can be called religious. According to George Murdock's widely quoted list of cultural universals (1945), all societies have religious rituals that appease supernatural forces, sets of beliefs concerning what we would call the soul or human spirit, and notions about life after death.

To be sure, nonreligious people can be found in all societies. But when we claim that religion (or a belief in the supernatural) is universal, we are referring to a cultural phenomenon rather than an individual one. For example, we can find individuals in the Western world who do not believe personally in supernatural forces such as deities, ghosts, demons, or spirits. Nevertheless, these people are part of a society that has a set of religious beliefs and practices to which many (perhaps a majority) of the population adhere.

Because religion, in whatever form it may be found, is often taken very seriously and passionately by its adherents, there is a natural tendency for people to see their own religion as the best while viewing all others as inferior. Westerners often use science, logic, and empirical evidence (for example, through the study of biblical texts) to bolster and justify their own religious practices. Nevertheless, science and logic are not adequate to either establish the inherent validity of Western religious beliefs or to demonstrate that non-Western religions are false. In other words, no religion is able to demonstrate conclusively that its deities can work more miracles per unit of time than those of other religions, although some certainly try. The central issue for anthropologists is not to determine which religion is better or more correct but rather to identify the various reli-

religion A set of beliefs in supernatural forces that functions to provide meaning, peace of mind, and a sense of control over unexplainable phenomena.

gious beliefs in the world as well as how they function, to what extent they are held, and the degree to which they affect human behavior.

Problems of Defining Religion

Defining *religion* is difficult because anthropologists disagree on how to distinguish between religious and nonreligious phenomena. In some societies, religion is so thoroughly embedded in the total social structure that it is difficult to distinguish religious behavior from economic, political, or kinship behavior. To illustrate, when a Kikuyu elder sacrifices a goat at the grave of an ancestor-god, is he engaging in: religious behavior (he is calling for the ancestor-god to intervene in the affairs of the living), economic behavior (the meat of the sacrificed animal will be distributed to and eaten by members of the kinship group), or kinship behavior (kin will have a chance to express their group solidarity at the ceremonial event)?

Such a ritual sacrifice performs all of these functions at the same time. In highly specialized societies, such as our own, people tend to divide human behavior into what, at least for them, are logical categories: social, economic, political, religious, educational, and recreational, for example. Because many small-scale, less specialized societies do not divide human behavior into the same categories used in Western society, it is often difficult for Westerners to recognize those aspects of human behavior that we think of as religious.

Another difficulty in defining religion and the supernatural is that different societies have different ways of distinguishing between the natural world and the supernatural world. In our own society, we reserve the term *supernatural* for phenomena we cannot explain through reason or science. Other societies, however, do not dichotomize the world into either natural or supernatural arenas. For example, the Nyoro of Uganda have a word for sorcery that means "to injure another person by the secret use of harmful medicines or techniques" (Beattie 1960: 73). Sorcery in Nyoro society can take a number of different forms. Placing a person's body substances (such as pieces of hair or fingernail clippings) in an animal horn and putting the horn on the roof of the person's house with the intention of causing that person harm is an act of sorcery in Nyoro society, but so is putting poison into an enemy's food or drink.

Given our own Western dichotomy between the natural and the supernatural, we would interpret these two acts as substantially different in nature. We would interpret the first act as an attempt to harm another person by the use of magic. If the intended victim dies, our own Western law courts would never hold the perpetrator culpable, for the simple reason that it could not be proven scientifically that placing the magical substances on the roof was the cause of the death. However, Westerners would view the poisoning as premeditated murder because it could be determined scientifically (that is, through an autopsy) that the poison did cause the person to die. This illustration should remind us that not all societies share our Western definition of the supernatural. It is precisely because of this difference in viewing the natural and supernatural worlds that Westerners have so much difficulty understanding non-Western religions, which they usually label as irrational or contradictory.

Another source of confusion when trying to define religion stems from our inability to separate supernatural beliefs from other aspects of culture. People often claim to be acting in the name of their religion, but in actual fact, are using their religion to support or reject other (nonreligious) features of their culture. For example, we often think of such policy issues as the opposition to abortion, gay marriage, Darwin's theory of evolution, and stem cell research as being part of the philosophy of evangelical Christianity. Instead, these are social issues that many *rural evangelicals* in the so-called "red states" tend to support by citing their own interpretations of scripture. But, it is certainly possible—and definitely demonstrable—to believe in the central core of evangelical Christianity (e.g., personal conversion and the full authority of the Bible) without having to reject abortion, Darwinian evolution, or gay marriage. In fact, evangelical Christianity is making significant headway in various urban ministries throughout the country, from San Francisco to New York City, among well-educated members of the creative class who express just the opposite positions on these social issues. For example, Rev. Timothy J. Keller has been wildly successful at growing his Redeemer Presbyterian Church in Manhattan to 4,000 attendees over the last sixteen years. He appeals to all sorts of urban professionals—from designers to university students—because his sermons are literary and intellectual. He replaces the traditional "hell, fire, and brimstone" with well-reasoned sermons quoting such sources as C. S. Lewis and the liberal newspaper, the *Village Voice*. Reverend Keller (along with other urban evangelical ministers) has been successful because he understands the difference between the core evangelical message and a number of contemporary sociocultural issues on which Jesus and the Bible had nothing to say (Luo 2006).

Anthropologists have always been fascinated by the origins of religion, but until recently, the lack of written records and archaeological evidence has made the subject highly speculative. Within the last several decades, however, archaeological evidence has given us a more complete picture of the early origins of religion. Arthur Lehmann, James Myers, and Pamela Moro (2001) remind us that the tools, weapons, and artifacts found in Neanderthal graves (dating back about one hundred thousand years) have led anthropologists to conclude that these early people believed in an afterlife. In addition, Lewis-Williams and Dowson (1988), through the study of Paleolithic art, have made a compelling case that reli-

Evangelist Timothy J. Keller thrives in Manhattan by embracing the city and identifying with its culture.

gious symbolic representations may have appeared as early as two to three hundred thousand years ago.

Beyond these somewhat speculative pieces of archaeological evidence, scholars have developed a number of hypotheses regarding the origins of religion. In the late nineteenth century, Sir Edward Tylor (1871), one of the founding fathers of modern anthropology, suggested that the original and most primary form of religion was *animism*, the belief in the existence of spiritual beings. In Tylor's view, animists believe that humans possess souls that have a life apart from the physical bodies they inhabit. In an attempt to explain the unexplainable, our early ancestors were intrigued with dreams, altered states of consciousness, and death. When awakening from a dream or coming out of a trance, people often recall having encounters with either their own spirits or the spirits of others. Early humans devised the notion of spirits to explain the images of people they encountered in their dreams and trances. When the spirit leaves the physical, tangible body, death (as we know it) occurs, even though the soul may continue to live on. According to Tylor, animists also believed that spirits also resided in animals, plants, and even celestial bodies like the sun, moon, and stars. It is this belief in spirits (or souls) that is fundamental to the concept of animism and provides the foundation for later forms of religion.

Tylor argued that animism was the earliest form of religion and was the *sine qua non* of religion. According to Tylor, every religion, from the simplest to the most complex, shared some level of animistic belief. Because Tylor was one of the nineteenth-century evolutionist anthropologists, it is not surprising that he viewed ani-

animism   Belief that people have souls or spirits in addition to physical, visible bodies.

mism as the initial step on religion's evolutionary ladder. Tylor explained that as a way of appeasing the spirits, our early ancestors offered them sacrifices. As time passed, these spirits took on greater power and authority, until eventually they became deities. This evolutionary process eventually transformed animism into *polytheism* (the belief in the existence of many gods). The final step in the evolutionary process, according to Tylor, witnessed the transformation of polytheism into *monotheism* (the belief in only one god). As with so many of the nineteenth-century evolutionary theories, this one placed the final stage of monotheism (Christianity) at the top rung of the ladder. In other words, it assumed that the religion of the theorist was the logical end product of a long process of perfection starting with simple forms (animism) and ending with monotheism. There is no reason, however, to believe that monotheism is a more complex or superior form of religion in comparison with beliefs in spirits or multiple deities.

Not all of Tylor's contemporaries agreed with his analysis of animism as the simplest and first form of supernatural belief. British anthropologist Robert Marett (1914) was convinced that early humans were not sufficiently intellectual to envision the soul or spirit as existing outside of the body. While not arguing against the concept of animism, Marett suggested that early religion was more emotional and intuitive in origin. Rather than developing the intellectual distinction between body and soul, Marett argued that our early ancestors believed that people, animals, plants, and inanimate objects were endowed with certain powers, which were both impersonal and supernatural. Marett introduced the notion of *animatism* to refer to this supernatural force that does not derive its power from the spirit or the soul. He also used the Melanesian term *mana* to refer to a concentrated form of animatistic force. Certain objects can have mana, such as a spear that has killed many animals, a knife that has been used to carve many beautiful wood sculptures, or a rabbit's foot that brings the owner good luck. People can also have mana, such as the chief who can exert his will on large numbers of people or the musician who can make beautiful music. And conversely, the one-time powerful hunter who gets mauled by a bear is seen to have lost his mana. Thus, while not denying the existence of animism, Marett argued that animatism and mana preceded animism chronologically.

Religion and Magic

Anthropologists studying supernatural beliefs cross-culturally have long been fascinated by the relationship between religion and magic. Whereas some anthropologists have emphasized the differences between these two phenomena, others have concentrated on their similarities. It is important to examine both the similarities and the differences because even though religion and magic can be found operating separately, most often they are found in some combined form. Religion and magic share certain features. Because both are systems of supernatural belief, they are nonrational; that is, they are not susceptible to scientific verification. In other words, whether religious or magical practices actually work cannot be empirically demonstrated. Rather, such practices must be accepted as a matter of faith. Moreover, both religion and magic are practiced—at least in part—as ways of coping with the anxieties, ambiguities, and frustrations of everyday life.

On the other hand, magic and religion differ in a number of important respects. First, religion deals with the major issues of human existence, such as the meaning of life, death, and one's spiritual relationship with deities. In contrast, magic is directed toward specific, immediate problems, such as curing an illness, bringing

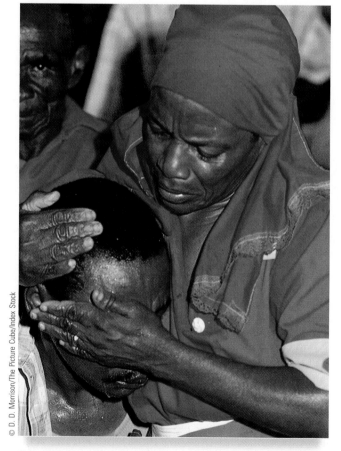

A traditional healer from Jamaica uses supernatural powers.

© D. D. Morrison/The Picture Cube/Index Stock

---

polytheism   The belief in the existence of many gods.
monotheism   The belief in only one god.
animatism   Belief in a generalized, impersonal power over which people have some measure of control.
mana   An impersonal supernatural force, inhabiting certain people or things, which is believed to confer power, strength, and success.

rain, or ensuring safety on a long journey. Second, religion uses prayer and sacrifices to appeal to or petition supernatural powers for assistance. Magicians, on the other hand, believe they can control or manipulate nature or other people by their own efforts. Third, religion by and large tends to be a group activity whereas magic is more individually oriented. Fourth, whereas religion is usually practiced at a specified time, magic is practiced irregularly in response to specific and immediate problems. Fifth, religion usually involves officially recognized functionaries such as priests, whereas magic may be performed by a wide variety of practitioners who may or may not be recognized within the community as having supernatural powers.

Despite these five differences, in actual practice elements of religion and magic are often found together. In any religion, for example, there is a fine line between praying for God's help and coercing or manipulating a situation to bring about a desired outcome. Also, it is not at all unusual for a person to use elements of both religion and magic simultaneously. To illustrate, a soldier about to enter combat may ask for divine protection through prayer while carrying a lucky rabbit's foot (a magical charm). Following the lead of nineteenth-century anthropologist Sir James Frazer, modern-day anthropologists distinguish between two types of magic: imitative magic and contagious magic. *Imitative magic* is based on the principle of "what you do is what you get." The religion of voodoo contain some elements of imitative magic. The idea behind a voodoo doll is that by doing harm to the doll (such as sticking it with pins, burning it, or throwing it into the ocean), you will be able to magically harm the person the doll represents. *Contagious magic*, by way of contrast, is the notion that an object that has been in contact with a person retains a magical connection to that person. The strongest magical connection exists between a person and something that has been a part of his or her body, such as hair, nail clippings, or teeth. Those who practice contagious magic believe that a person can be harmed by evil magicians if they can obtain any of these former body parts. In some parts of the world, economic development projects designed to build latrines to improve sanitation have been unsuccessful because people are fearful of defecating in a place where one's feces could be obtained by an evildoer.

© Carol Beckwith & Angela Fisher/HAGA/The Image Works

Vodoo, a form of imitative magic, is practiced in Togo.

Magic involves the manipulation of supernatural forces for the purpose of intervening in a wide range of human activities and natural events. The ritualistic use of magic can be found in some societies to ensure the presence of game animals, to bring rain, to cure or prevent illness, or to protect oneself from misfortune. Magic, however, can also be (and often is) directed to cause evil. In some societies it is believed that certain people called witches or sorcerers use supernatural powers to bring harm to people. Because these forms of "negative magic" hold such fascination for Westerners, it is instructive to examine them in greater detail.

Sorcery and Witchcraft

Although the terms *witchcraft* and *sorcery* are sometimes used synonymously, cultural anthropologists distinguish between them. As practiced in a wide variety of societies

---

imitative magic   A form of magic based on the idea that the procedure performed resembles the desired result, such as that sticking a doll-like image with pins will harm the person the doll represents.

contagious magic   A form of magic based on the premise that things, once in contact with a person (such as a lock of hair), continue to influence that person after separation.

magic   A system of supernatural beliefs that involves the manipulation of supernatural forces for the purpose of intervening in a wide range of human activities and natural events.

throughout the world, *witchcraft* is an inborn, involuntary, and often unconscious capacity to cause harm to other people. On the other hand, *sorcery*, which often involves the use of materials, potions, and medicines, is the deliberate use of supernatural powers to bring about harm. Some societies have specialized practitioners of sorcery, but in other societies sorcery can be practiced by anyone. Because sorcery involves the use of certain physical substances, the evidence for its existence is more easily found. Witchcraft, by contrast, is virtually impossible to prove or disprove because of the absence of any visible evidence of its existence.

Whereas sorcery involves the use of material substances to cause harm to people, witchcraft, it is thought, relies solely on psychic power (that is, thoughts and emotions). In other words, witches can turn their anger and hatred into evil deeds simply by thinking evil thoughts. How witches are conceptualized varies widely from society to society, but, in all cases, witches are viewed negatively. Witches are generally seen as being unable to control the human impulses that normal members of society are expected to keep in check. They have insatiable appetites for food, uncontrollable hatred, and perverted sexual desires. The Mandari believe that witches dance on their victims' graves. The Lugbara of Uganda speak of witches who dance naked, which for them is the ultimate social outrage. The Ganda and Nyoro of Uganda believe in witches who eat corpses. Among the Kaguru of Tanzania, witches are believed to walk upside down, devour human flesh, commit incest, and in general fail to recognize the rules and constraints of normal society. In many parts of the world, witches are associated with the night, which separates them from normal people, who go about their business during the daytime. Moreover, witches are often associated with certain animals, such as bats, rats, snakes, lizards, or leopards, which may be black in color, dangerous, and nocturnal.

Sorcerers are generally believed to direct their malevolence purposefully against those they dislike, fear, or envy rather than acting randomly or capriciously. In any given society, hostile relations can occur among people who have some relationship to one another—such as outsiders who marry into a local village, rivals for a father's inheritance, wives in a polygynous household, men who are competing for a political office, or even rivals in competitive sports. People are therefore likely to attribute their own personal misfortune to the sorcery of some rival who might gain from harming them. Thus, accusations of sorcery are patterned to the extent that

---

CROSS-CULTURAL MISCUE

While on a trip to Taipei, Matt Erskine had made plans to have dinner with his former college roommate John, who is Taiwanese. After catching up on each other's lives, Matt learned that John was about to leave his present job to start his own consulting business. However, before launching the new business, John told Matt that he must wait until the telephone company granted him the proper telephone number. Given all of the work John had done to get his new business started, Matt thought that having the proper telephone number was a minor obstacle that need not delay the opening of the business. But John insisted that he could not start his new enterprise until he had the right telephone number. Matt got the impression that John, perhaps fearful of taking risks, was using the telephone number as a lame excuse for not launching the business. But Matt misinterpreted this situation because he failed to understand some basic features of contemporary culture in Taiwan.

Despite their great economic leap into the global economy, many Taiwanese still retain many beliefs in supernatural forces. This is particularly true about certain numbers. Some primary numbers, associated with very negative things such as death or excrement, are to be avoided at all costs. Other numbers, associated with positive things such as money, growth, and wealth, should be used in house addresses, license plates, and telephone numbers. In Taiwan the telephone company receives many requests for numbers that include the lucky numbers, leaving those with unlucky numbers unused. Thus, John believed strongly that unless he got a telephone number with lucky numbers in it, his business would be doomed from the start.

---

they reflect the conflicts, rivalries, and antagonisms that already exist among the people in any given society.

Although witchcraft and sorcery are usually associated with small-scale societies in the non-Western world, they are also found in highly industrialized parts of the world such as the United States, Canada, and a number of western European countries. In the Western world, a basic distinction is made between the forms of magic used for beneficial purposes and those used for malevolent purposes. Though considerably more complex, this basic distinction is best exemplified by modern-day witches (who put their beliefs to good ends) and Satanists (who use their magic for evil purposes).

Contemporary Western witches, who use their supernatural powers for good purposes, call their belief system *Wicca*, a term meaning "witch," derived from Old

---

witchcraft An inborn, involuntary, and often unconscious capacity to cause harm to other people.

sorcery The performance of certain magical rites for the purpose of harming other people.

Wicca A modern-day movement of witches and pagans.

Led by Amy Krinner, a coven of Wiccans practices magic in Bayshore, New York.

English. Practiced largely in urban areas, witchcraft, like more orthodox religions, involves worship as a central part of its activities. Although it is possible for both men and women to practice witchcraft, in North American cities most practitioners are women, and Wicca has an unmistakably matriarchal character. Local organizations of witches, called *covens*, are often presided over by high priestesses, symbolic representations of the mother goddess. Some covens consider themselves fertility cults, and some actually involve sexual intercourse as part of their initiation, although this is relatively rare. Although this has attracted a good deal of interest in the news media, the Wiccas emphasize fertility, not sexuality.

Wicca may involve the practice of *magic*, which is defined as bringing about changes by concentrating on one's natural powers. It is important to note that Wiccans do not see their magical powers as supernatural. Wiccans use certain tools such as visualizations, spells, chants, and meditation to focus their inner powers to bring about a desired change. Practitioners of modern witchcraft claim that their early pre-Christian ancestors possessed these natural magical powers, but they were subsequently lost when they were forced to go underground by the Roman Catholic church. As a neo-pagan movement, contemporary Wiccans view themselves as rediscovering these ancient lost magical powers.

Although some have suggested that witchcraft is one of the fastest-growing religions in the United States, there are no reliable estimates on how many practitioners actually exist. The growth of the practice of Wicca has coincided with the rise of feminism, ecology movements, and movements seeking freedom from authority. Wicca tends to be nondogmatic, nonhierarchical, and nonproselytizing. It has a number of gentle rituals that appear to appeal especially to women, and is based on the principle of "do what you will, but harm no one."

In recent decades, Europe and North America have experienced a gradual decline in memberships in conventional institutionalized religions. At the same time, there has been an increase in religious pluralism, particularly among such esoteric forms of spirituality as witchcraft. In late 2006, this author, conducting a simple subject search on the Yahoo! search engine, located 4,670,000 separate Wiccan websites. The Internet bookseller Amazon.com was selling 2,164 different books on the Wiccan movement and more than thirty-five thousand books on the general topic of witchcraft near the end of 2006. The general sales of books on the practice of contemporary witchcraft have increased appreciably in the last decade. According to one publisher, although there are no blockbuster bestsellers, sales of Wiccan books had increased from three thousand copies a year in the late 1980s to as many as forty thousand copies a year by the end of the century. Moreover, the long-term success of the Wiccan movement would seem to be assured because many of the books being sold today are targeting the teenage market. Whereas many readers of witchcraft books during the 1980s were baby boomers looking for alternative forms of spirituality, today the major share of the growing market is young women in their teens (Carvajal 1998).

Contemporary witches see themselves as very different from *Satanists*, who worship the Judeo-Christian devil. Satanists view themselves as the antithesis of Christians, in league with the devil. Interestingly enough, it has been suggested that modern Satanism is a direct outgrowth of the Christian churches' strong stance against witchcraft. According to Marcello Truzzi (1993: 402), "The inquisitors so impressed some individuals with the fantastic and blasphemous picture of Satanism that they

---

covens   Local groups of witches found in major cities in the United States, which are presided over by high priestesses.

Satanists   Individuals belonging to a group of people who worship Satan.

apparently decided that they would rather reign in hell than serve in heaven."

Edward Moody presents evidence of a group of Satanists in San Francisco who use evil magic to curse their enemies. Members are taught to "hate your enemies with a whole heart, and if a man smite you on one cheek, SMASH him on the other" (Moody 1993: 236). If the group discovers that someone has harmed or hurt one of its members, the entire cult will ritually curse the perpetrator. In one case, which Moody personally witnessed, a man who allegedly slandered the name of the cult was given the most serious form of magical curse—the ritualistic casting of the death rune—the sole purpose of which is death and total destruction. When the death rune is cast, the victim's name is written in blood on a special parchment, and a lamb's-wool figurine is made to represent the victim. Then, according to Moody's account, in "an orgy of aggression … the lamb's-wool figure … was stabbed by all members of the congregation, hacked to pieces with a sword, shot with a small caliber pistol, and then burned."

The anthropologist is not particularly interested in determining whether the Satanic curse actually had its intended outcome. What is important to the anthropologist is that this is a dramatic example of how some people, even in industrialized societies, use sorcery or witchcraft to explain the unexplainable and make things happen.

MYTHS

Every society, from the smallest band society to the most complex postindustrial society, has a sacred literature called myth that states certain religious truths. *Myths*, embodying a specific worldview, contain stories of the gods, their origins, their activities, and the moral injunctions they teach. Unlike magic or witchcraft, myths serve to answer the large questions surrounding human existence—such as why we are here. Myths not only have an explanatory function, but they also validate some of the essential beliefs, values, and behavior patterns of a culture. That is, a culture's mythology is closely connected to its moral and social order. It is important to point out that myths need not have any basis in historical fact. Although there may be elements of history in myth (and vice versa), the importance of myth from an anthropological perspective is that the narrative reflects, supports, and legitimizes patterns of thought and behavior.

A common form of myth is the myth of origin, which provides answers to questions about how things began. Often, these myths tell of the origins of the gods themselves, their adventures, and how they went about creating both humans and the natural environment. Some

myths Stories that transmit culturally meaningful messages about the universe, the natural and supernatural worlds, and a person's place within them.

myths, which can be told in either sacred or profane settings, describe how various gods (or divinely inspired humans) brought about the existence of important cultural features such as government, fire, or agriculture. Another type of myth, known as a trickster myth, is less serious in tone but carries important messages. These often humorous myths serve at least two functions, as Anthony Wallace (1966: 57–58) reminds us:

> In trickster myths the successive triumphs and misadventures of an anthropomorphized animal—a raven, a rabbit, or a coyote, for instance—are told in such a way that not only the historical origins of certain features of the world are accounted for, but also a moral is conveyed: the dangers of pride, the risk of gluttony, the perils of boastfulness.

FUNCTIONS OF RELIGION

Anthropological studies of religion are no longer dominated by the search for origins. More recent studies have focused on how religious systems function for both the individual and the society as a whole. Because religious systems are so universal, it is generally held that they must fill a number of important needs at both personal and societal levels.

As anthropologists turned away from searching for the origins of religion, they became increasingly interested in a closely related question: How can we explain the universal existence of religion? This question is made all the more intriguing by the elusive nature of religion. As far as we can tell, every society has some system of supernatural belief. Yet it is impossible to prove beyond a reasonable doubt that any supernatural powers (such as gods, witches, angels, or devils) actually exist. Moreover, it should be obvious to most religious practitioners that supernatural powers don't always work as effectively as the practitioners think they should. For example, we pray to God for the recovery of a sick friend, but the friend dies nevertheless; a ritual specialist conducts a rain dance, but it still doesn't rain; or the living relatives sacrifice a goat at the grave site of the ancestor-god but still are not spared the ravages of the drought. Although supernatural beings and forces may not always perform their requested functions (that is, bring about supernatural events), they do perform less obvious functions for both the individual and the society as a whole. These latent functions, as they would be called by Robert Merton (1957), fall into two broad categories: social and psychological.

Social Functions of Religion

One of the most popular explanations for the universality of religion is that it performs a number of important functions for the overall well-being of the society of which it is a part. Let's consider three such social functions of religion: social control, conflict resolution, and reinforcement of group solidarity.

CONTEMPORARY ISSUES

Religious Freedom in Florida

Sultaana Freeman, a thirty-four-year-old Islamic resident of Winter Park, Florida, had no difficulty getting a Florida driver's license in February 2001 despite having insisted (on religious grounds) that her picture be taken behind a veil. Several months after September 11, however, officials from the Florida Department of Motor Vehicles changed their minds and informed Ms. Freeman that in order to keep her license she would have to have a new photo showing her entire face. She subsequently gave up her driver's license and then sued the state to get it reinstated (Canedy 2002; Pristin 2002). Here is a clear case of a conflict between a person's rights to be true to her religion (Islam requires that she shield her face in public) and the government's need to maintain public safety by being able to identify a person in a traffic stop.

AP/Wide World Photos

The state argued that law enforcement officials need a full-face photo in order to verify one's identity, which is, after all, why there *are* photos on driver's licenses. Admittedly, after September 11, this need for public safety and security took on greater urgency when it became painfully clear that there was a strong relationship between some religious beliefs and acts of terrorism.

On the other side of the issue, lawyers for Ms. Freeman argued that forcing her to submit to a full-face picture is unreasonable, subjective, and violates her freedom of religion. It was pointed out that Florida statutes do not prohibit a person from being veiled in photos for driver's licenses. Moreover, Florida's Religious Restoration Act explicitly states that laws that burden the exercise of religion must have a compelling government purpose. Lawyers for Ms. Freeman claimed that the state had no such compelling purpose because their client was open to providing fingerprints, DNA, or other information that could be used to verify her identity. It was patently unfair, they argued, to expect Ms. Freeman to have to choose between her religious beliefs and the convenience of having a valid driver's license.

If you were the judge in this civil case, how would you rule?

Social Control

One very important social function of religion is its use as a mechanism of social control. Through a series of both positive and negative sanctions, religion tends to maintain social order by encouraging socially acceptable behavior and discouraging socially inappropriate behavior. Every religion, regardless of the form it takes, is an ethical system that prescribes proper ways of behaving. When social sanctions (rewards and punishments) are backed with supernatural authority, they are bound to become more compelling. Biblical texts, for example, are very explicit about the consequences of violating the Ten Commandments. Because of their strong belief in ghostly vengeance, the Lugbara of Uganda scrupulously avoid engaging in any antisocial behavior that would provoke the wrath of the ancestor-gods. As mentioned in Chapter 13, Hindus in India believe that violating prescribed caste expectations will jeopardize their progress in future reincarnations.

From an anthropological perspective, it is irrelevant whether these supernatural forces really do reward good behavior and punish bad behavior. Rather than concern themselves with whether and to what extent supernatural forces work the way they are thought to, anthropologists are interested in whether and to what extent people actually believe in the power of the supernatural forces. After all, it is belief in the power of the supernatural sanctions that determines the level of conformity to socially prescribed behavior.

Conflict Resolution

Another social function of religion is the role it plays in reducing the stress and frustrations that often lead to social conflict. In some societies, for example, natural calamities such as epidemics or famines are attributed to the evil deeds of people in other villages or regions. By concentrating on certain religious rituals designed to protect themselves against outside malevolence, people avoid the potential disruptiveness to their own society that might occur if they took out their frustrations on the evildoers. Moreover, disenfranchised or powerless people in stratified societies sometimes use religion as a way of diffusing their anger and hostility that might otherwise be directed against the total social system. To illustrate, in his study of separatist Christian churches in the Republic of South Africa, Bengt Sundkler (1961) showed how small groups of Black South Africans—who until recently were systematically excluded from the power structure by apartheid—created the illusion of power by manipulating their own set of religious symbols and forming their own unique churches. By providing an alternative power structure, these breakaway Christian churches served to reduce conflict in South Africa by diverting resentment away from the wider power structure.

Sundkler's interpretation of separatist churches in South Africa is very similar to Marx's nineteenth-century interpretation of religion as the opiate of the masses. As an economic determinist, Marx claimed that religion, like other institutions, reflects the underlying modes of production in the society. The purpose of religion, according to Marx, was to preserve the economic superstructure that allowed the upper classes (bourgeoisie) to exploit the working classes (proletariat). By focusing people's attention on the eternal bliss awaiting them in heaven, religion diverts their attention from the misery of their lives in the here and now. In other words, religion blinds working people to the fact that they are being exploited by the ruling class. As long as the working class focuses on the afterlife, they are not likely to heed Marx's advice to revolt against their oppressors. Thus, religion serves as a societal mechanism to reduce conflict between differing economic subgroups.

Reinforcement of Group Solidarity

A third social function of religion is that it intensifies the group solidarity of those who practice it. Religion enables people to express their common identity in an emotionally charged environment. Powerful social bonds are often created among people who share the experiences of religious beliefs, practices, and rituals. Because every religion or supernatural belief system contains its own unique structural features, those who practice it will share in its mysteries, whereas those who do not will be excluded. In short, religion strengthens a person's sense of group identity and belonging. And, of course, as people come together for common religious experiences, they often engage in a number of other nonreligious activities as well, which further strengthens the sense of social solidarity.

The role of organized religion in creating and maintaining group solidarity is particularly important in immigrant populations. To illustrate, recent Korean immigrants to the United States, even those who are not particularly religious, often join a Korean Christian church as a way of establishing instant social networks with other Korean immigrants. According to Charles Ryu (1992: 162–63):

> In America, whatever the reason, the church has become a major and central anchoring institution for Korean immigrant society. Whereas no other institution supported the Korean immigrants, the church played the role of anything and everything—from social service, to education, to learning the Korean language: a place to gather, to meet other people, for social gratification, you name it. The way we think of church is more than in a religious connotation.... Your identity is tied so closely to the church you go to. I think almost 70 to 80 percent of Korean Americans belong to church.... Living in American society as a minority is a very difficult thing. You are nobody out there, but when you come to church, you are somebody.

Psychological Functions of Religion

In addition to promoting the well-being of the society, religion functions psychologically for the benefit of the individual. Anthropologists have identified two fundamentally different types of psychological functions of religion: a cognitive function, whereby religion provides an intellectual framework for explaining parts of our world that we do not understand, and an emotional function, whereby religion helps to reduce anxiety by prescribing some straightforward ways of coping with stress.

Cognitive Function

In terms of its cognitive/intellectual function, religion is psychologically comforting because it helps us explain the unexplainable. Every society faces a number of imponderable questions that have no definitive logical answers: When did life begin? Why do bad things happen to good people? What happens to us when we die? Even in societies like our own—where we have, or think we have, many scientific answers—many questions remain unanswered. A medical pathologist may be able to explain to the parents of a child who has died of malaria that the cause of death was a bite by an infected anopheles mosquito. But that same pathologist cannot explain to the grieving parents why the mosquito bit their child and not the child next door. Religion can provide satisfying answers to such questions because the answers are based on supernatural authority.

Unlike any other life-form, humans have a highly developed urge for understanding themselves and the world around them. But because human understanding of the universe is so imperfect, religion provides a framework for giving meaning to events and experiences that cannot be explained in any other way. Religion assures its believers that the world is meaningful, that events happen for a reason, that there is order in the universe, and that apparent injustices will eventually be rectified. Humans have difficulty whenever unexplained phenomena contradict their cultural worldview. One of the functions of religion, then, is to enable people to maintain their worldview even when events occur that seem to contradict it.

Emotional Function

The emotional function of religion is to help individuals cope with the anxieties often accompanying illness, accidents, deaths, and other misfortunes. Because people never have complete control over the circumstances of their lives, they often turn to religious ritual in an attempt to maximize control through supernatural means. In fact, the less control people feel they have over their own lives, the more they are likely to practice religion. The fear of facing a frightening situation can be at least partially overcome by believing that supernatural beings will intervene on one's behalf; shame and guilt may be reduced by becoming humble and pious in the face of the deities; and during times of bereavement, religion can provide a source of emotional strength.

People perform religious rituals as a way of invoking supernatural beings to control the forces over which they feel they have no control. This takes a number of different forms throughout the world. To illustrate, the Trobriand Islanders perform a series of magico-religious rituals for protection before a long voyage; to protect their gardens, men in parts of New Guinea put a series of leaves across their fences, believing that the leaves will paralyze the arms and legs of any thief who raids the garden; and in Nairobi, Kenya, some professional football teams reportedly hire their own ritual specialists to bewitch their opponents. In addition to providing greater peace of mind, such religious practices may actually have a positive indirect effect on the events they are intended to influence. For example, even if their witchcraft doesn't work, football players are likely to play more confidently if they believe they have a supernatural advantage. This ability to act with confidence is a major psychological function of religion.

Although most North Americans think of themselves as highly scientific, on many occasions we too use supernatural forces to ensure that our activities will have a successful outcome. For example, anthropologist George Gmelch (1994b) shows us how professional baseball players use ritual to try to influence the outcome of a game:

> To control uncertainty Chicago White Sox shortstop Ozzie Guillen doesn't wash his underclothes after a good game. The Boston Red Sox's Wade Boggs eats chicken before every game (that's 162 meals of chicken per year). Ex–San Francisco Giant pitcher Ron Bryant added a new stick of bubble gum to the collection in his bulging back pocket after each game he won. Jim Ohms, my teammate on the Daytona Beach Islanders in 1966, used to put another penny in the pouch of his supporter after each win. Clanging against the hard plastic genital cup, the pennies made an audible sound as the pitcher ran the bases toward the end of a winning season.

In some cases, Western governments will use non-Western spiritual practices when it is politically expedient to do so. In 1998 the Transit Authority of Portland, Oregon, proudly unveiled its light rail system, featuring the Washington Park Station, which, at 260 feet below ground, was the deepest subway station in the United States. However, members of local Asian communities in Portland were appalled because the tunnel ran under a cemetery, which, they claimed, disturbed the spirits of the dead and created a dangerous situation for the train riders. In fact, several above-ground traffic accidents were cited by the Asian groups as having been caused by the angry spirits of the dead. In response to these very real concerns of the Asian community, Transit Authority officials brought in a group of Lao Buddhist monks who performed rituals to appease the dead spirits. Even though transit officials were ribbed for allowing these Eastern rituals to be performed in the subway tunnel, they did ease the minds of local Asians and restored

Mark "The Bird" Fidrych, pitcher for the Detroit Tigers, practiced ritualistic magic before each game by patting and talking to the pitcher's mound.

their confidence in the local transit system (D'Antoni and Heard 1998).

TYPES OF RELIGIOUS ORGANIZATION

Like other aspects of culture, religion takes a wide variety of forms throughout the world. To bring some measure of order to this vast diversity, it is helpful to develop a typology of religious systems based on certain common features. One commonly used system of classification, suggested by Anthony Wallace, is based on the level of specialization of the religious personnel who conduct the rituals and ceremonies. Wallace (1966) identified four principal patterns of religious organization based on what he calls cults. Wallace uses the term *cult* in a general sense to refer to forms of religion that have their own set of beliefs, rituals, and goals. This analytical and nonjudgmental use of the term *cult* should not be confused with the more popular, and pejorative, definition used to refer to an antisocial religious group that brainwashes its members before leading them to mass suicide. The four forms of religious organization he has identified are individualistic cults, shamanistic cults, communal cults, and ecclesiastical cults. According to Wallace's typology, these cults form a scale. Societies with ecclesiastical cults also contain communal, shamanistic, and individualistic cults; those with a communal

---

cult Used in the early anthropological literature, in a non-judgmental way, to refer to a religious group with its own set of beliefs, practices, and rituals. In popular discourse, however, it is a pejorative term referring to an antisocial group of religious extremists whose goal is mass suicide.

Table 14.1 Characteristics of Different Religious Organizations

Role Specialization		Subsistence Pattern	Example
Individualistic	No role specialization	Food collector	Crow vision quest
Shamanistic	Part-time specialization	Food collector/pastoralism/ horticulture	Tungus shamanism
Communal	Groups perform rites for community	Horticulture/pastoralism	Totemistic rituals
Ecclesiastical	Full-time specialization in hierarchy	Industrialism	Christianity and Buddhism

SOURCE: Adapted from Anthony F. C. Wallace, *Religion: An Anthropological View*. New York: Random House, 1966.

form also contain shamanistic and individualistic cults; and those with shamanistic cults also contain individualistic cults. Although it is likely that societies with only individualistic cults could have existed in earlier times, there are no contemporary examples of such religious systems.

Wallace's four types correspond roughly to different levels of socioeconomic organization. In a very general way, individualistic and shamanistic cults are usually associated with food-collecting societies, communal cults are usually found in horticultural and pastoral societies, and ecclesiastical cults are characteristic of more complex industrialized economies. However, this association between forms of religious organization and socioeconomic types is only approximate at best, for there are some notable exceptions. For example, certain American Plains Indians and some aboriginal Australians had communal forms of religion even though they were food collectors and lived in bands. See Table 14.1 for a summary of the characteristics of the different religious organizations.

Individualistic Cults

Individualistic cults have no religious specialists and represent the most basic level of religious structure according to Wallace's typology. Each person has a relationship with one or more supernatural beings whenever he or she has a need for control or protection. Because individualistic cults do not make distinctions between specialists and laypersons, all people are their own specialists; or as Marvin Harris has put it, these cults are a type of do-it-yourself religion (Harris and Johnson 2003: 266). Even though no known societies rely exclusively on the individualistic form of religion, some small-scale band societies practice it as a predominant mode.

The *vision quest*, a ritual found among a number of traditional Plains Indian cultures, is an excellent example of the rituals practiced by an individualistic cult. During traditional times, it was expected that through visions, people would establish a special relationship with a spirit that would provide them with knowledge, power, and protection. Sometimes these visions came to people through dreams or when they were by themselves. More often, however, the individual had to purposefully seek out the visions through such means as fasting, bodily mutilation, smoking hallucinogenic substances, and spending time alone in an isolated place.

A person would go on a vision quest if he or she wanted special power (to excel as a warrior, for example) or knowledge (to gain insight into a future course of action, for example). A Crow warrior would go to a place that was thought to be frequented by supernatural spirits. There he would strip off his clothes, smoke, and abstain from drinking and eating. He might even chop off part of a finger or engage in other types of self-inflicted torture for the sake of getting the spirits' attention. In some cases, the vision seekers never did receive a vision, but Crow vision seekers often did.

Crow visions took a variety of forms but usually had several elements in common. First, the visions usually came in the form of a spirit animal, such as a bison, eagle, or snake. Second, the vision seeker gained some special knowledge or power. Third, the vision often appeared on the fourth day of the quest, four being a sacred number for the Crow. Finally, the animal spirit would adopt the quester by functioning as his or her own protector spirit.

It is important to bear in mind that for the Crow the vision quest was a normal way of dealing with the stresses and strains of everyday life. Robert Lowie reminds us of

individualistic cults The least complex form of religious organization in which each person is his or her own religious specialist.

vision quest A ritual found among a number of Plains Indian cultures wherein through visions people establish special relationships with spirits who provide them with knowledge, power, and protection.

the wide range of problems that were addressed in Crow vision quests:

> The young man who has been jilted goes off at once to fast in loneliness, praying for supernatural succor. An elk spirit may come and teach him a tune on a flute, as a means of luring the maiden back. The young man plays his tune, ensnares the haughty girl, and turns her away in disgrace, thus regaining his self-respect. Similarly, a wretched orphan who has been mocked by a young man of family hastens to the mountains to be blessed by some being, through whose favor he gains glory and loot on a raid, and can then turn the tables on his tormentor. A woman big with child fasts and in a vision sees a weed, which she subsequently harvests and through which she ensures a painless delivery.
>
> A gambler who has lost all his property retrieves his fortune through a revelation; and by the same technique a sorrowing kinsman identifies the slayers of his beloved relative and kills them. These are all typical instances, amply documented in personal recollections of informants and in traditional lore, showing the intrusion of religion into the frustrations of everyday living. (1963: 537)

Shamanistic Cults

In addition to having individualistic cults, all contemporary societies also operate at the shamanistic level. Shamanistic societies are found in the arctic and subarctic regions, Siberia, Tibet, Mongolia, parts of Southeast Asia, and widely throughout the South American rainforests. *Shamans* are part-time religious specialists who are thought to have supernatural powers by virtue of birth, training, or inspiration. These powers are used for healing, divining, and telling fortunes during times of stress, usually in exchange for gifts or fees. *Shamanistic cults* represent the simplest form of religious division of labor, for, as Wallace reminds us, "The shaman in his religious role is a specialist; and his clients in their relation to him are laymen" (1966: 86). The term *shaman*, derived from the Tungus-speaking peoples of Siberia (Service 1978), encompasses a number of different types of specialists found throughout the world, including medicine men and women, diviners, spiritualists, palm readers, and magicians.

Shamans are generally believed to have access to supernatural spirits that they contact on behalf of their clients. The reputation of a particular shaman often rests on the power of the shaman's "spirit helpers" (usually the spirits of powerful, agile, and cunning animals) and her or his ability to contact them at will. Shamans contact their spirits while in an altered state of consciousness brought on by smoking, taking drugs, rhythmic drumming, chanting, or monotonous dancing. Once in a trance, the shaman, possessed with a spirit helper, becomes a medium or spokesperson for that spirit. While possessed, the shaman may perspire, breathe heavily, take on a different voice, and generally lose control over his or her own body. Even though Westerners often view shamans as con artists, in their own societies they are seen as a combination of holy person, doctor, and social worker. In many respects, traditional shamans found in non-Western societies are not appreciably different from professional channelers in the United States, who speak on behalf of spirits for their paying clients.

In shamanistic societies, it is believed that everyday occurrences are intimately connected to events in the spirit world. The shaman's role is to enter an altered state of consciousness, allow his or her soul to travel to the spirit world, seek out the causes of earthly problems, and then coerce, beg, or do combat with the spirits to

Piaroa Indian shaman Miguel Ochoa is pictured here with medicinal plants gathered from the jungle village of Aska aja, near Puerto Ayacucho, Venezuela.

---

shaman A part-time religious specialist who is thought to have supernatural powers by virtue of birth, training, or inspiration.

shamanistic cults Forms of religion in which part-time religious specialists called shamans intervene with the deities on behalf of their clients.

intervene on behalf of the living. Inuit shamanism provides a good example of how shamans are thought to work. Most Inuit believe that water mammals are controlled by an underwater female spirit who occasionally withholds animals when Inuit hunters behave immorally. One of the most challenging tests for an Inuit shaman is to travel to the watery underworld to convince the spirit to release the seals and walruses so they can be hunted again.

How an individual actually becomes a shaman varies from society to society. In many societies shamanistic power is achieved through a series of initiations or ordeals imposed by the spirits of the underworld. Even after acquiring shamanistic power by doing battle with the spirits, it is possible for a shaman to lose those hard-won powers through subsequent unsuccessful battles with the spirits. In some societies, it is possible to become a shaman by having a particularly vivid or powerful vision in which spirits enter the body. In other societies, one can become a shaman by serving as an apprentice under a practicing shaman. Among the Tungus of Siberia, mentally unstable people who often experience bouts of hysteria are the most likely candidates for shamanism because hysterical people are thought to be the closest to the spirit world (Service 1978). In societies that regularly use hallucinogenic drugs, almost any person can achieve the altered state of consciousness needed for the practice of shamanism. For example, Michael Harner (1973) reports that among the Jivaro Indians of the Ecuadorian Amazon, who use hallucinogens widely and have a strong desire to contact the supernatural world, about one in four men is a shaman.

As practiced by the Reindeer Tungus of Siberia, shamans are people who have the power to control various spirits, can prevent those spirits from causing harm, and, on occasion, can serve as a medium for those spirits (Service 1978). Tungus shamans—who can be either men or women—use special paraphernalia, such as elaborate costumes, a brass mirror, and a tambourine. The rhythmic beating of a tambourine is used to induce a trance in a shaman and to produce a receptive state of consciousness on the part of onlookers. A shaman, possessed by rhythmic drumming, journeys into the spirit world to perform certain functions for individual clients or for the group as a whole. These functions may include determining the cause of a person's illness, finding a lost object, conferring special powers in a conflict, or predicting future events. Shamanism among the Tungus does not involve the power to cure a particular illness but rather only determines the cause of the malady. In this respect, the shaman is a medical diagnostician rather than a healer.

Interestingly, shamanism experienced a resurgence in post–Soviet Siberia during the 1990s. Due largely to the economic hard times experienced by Russians since the collapse of socialism, local peoples of Siberia began to seek comfort in shamanism and other forms of traditional worship. Cold, hungry, and jobless, many Siberians took up traditional means of livelihood (hunting and fishing) for their material needs and, at the same time, turned to the old ways of the shaman for spiritual and psychological comfort. Moreover, there is a growing literature from this same part of the world that describes a new phenomenon called "urban shamanism" (Balzer 1993; Kendall 1996a, Humphrey 1999). Urban shamans, who were mostly born and raised in urban areas, differ from their traditional counterparts in that they do not travel to other worlds to encounter the spirits, but rather the spirits come to the shamans in their urban environments. Thus, at a time when the world is increasingly embracing the Internet and cell phones, globalization seems to be passing by the descendants of the Tungus, who are turning back to their traditional ways (Matloff 1998).

Communal Cults

Communal cults—which involve a more elaborate set of beliefs and rituals—operate at a still higher level of organizational complexity. Groups of ordinary people (organized around clans, lineages, age groups, or secret societies) conduct religious rites and ceremonies for the larger community. These rites, which are performed only occasionally or periodically by nonspecialists, are considered to be absolutely vital to the well-being of both individuals and the society as a whole. Even though these ceremonies may include specialists such as shamans, orators, or magicians, the primary responsibility for the success of the ceremonies lies primarily with the nonspecialists, who at the conclusion of the ceremony return to their everyday activities. Examples of communal cults are the ancestral ceremonies among the traditional Chinese, puberty rites found in sub-Saharan African societies, and totemic rituals practiced by aboriginal peoples of Australia.

Communal rituals fall into two broad categories: rites of passage, which celebrate the transition of a person from one social status to another, and rites of solidarity, which are public rituals serving to foster group identity and group goals and having very explicit and immediate objectives, such as calling upon supernatural beings/forces to increase fertility or prevent misfortune. Let's look at these two types of communal cults in greater detail.

Rites of Passage

Rites of passage are ceremonies that mark a change in a person's social position. These ritualistic ceremonies, which have religious significance, help both individuals

communal cults Societies in which groups of ordinary people conduct religious ceremonies for the well-being of the total community.

rites of passage Any ceremony celebrating the transition of a person from one social status to another.

and the society deal with important life changes, such as birth, puberty, marriage, and death. Rites of passage are more than ways of recognizing certain transitions in a person's life, however. When a person marries, for example, he or she not only takes on a new status but also creates an entire complex of new relationships. Rites of passage, then, are important public rituals that recognize a wider set of altered social relationships.

According to Arnold Van Gennep (1960), all rites of passage, in whatever culture they may be found, tend to have three distinct ritual phases: separation, transition, and incorporation. The first phase, separation, is characterized by the stripping away of the old status. In cases of puberty rites, for example, childhood is ritually or symbolically killed by pricking the initiate's navel with a spear. In the second phase, the individual is in a transitional stage, cut off from the old status but not yet integrated into the new status. Because this transition stage is associated with danger and ambiguity, it often involves the endurance of certain unpleasant ordeals as well as the removal of the individual from normal, everyday life for a certain period of time. The third and final phase involves the ritual incorporation of the individual into the new status. Ethnographic data from all over the world have supported Van Gennep's claim that all rites of passage involve these three distinct phases.

These three ritual phases are well demonstrated in the rites of adulthood practiced by the Kikuyu of Kenya, who initiate both girls and boys (Middleton and Kershaw 1965). The Kikuyu, like other traditional East African societies, practice initiation ceremonies as a way of ensuring that children will be converted into morally and socially responsible adults. Despite some regional variations, the Kikuyu initiation rite includes certain rituals that conform to Van Gennep's threefold scheme.

Kikuyu initiation into adulthood involves a physical operation—circumcision for males and clitoridectomy for females. Days before the physical operation, the initiates go through a number of rituals designed to separate them from society and their old status and place them in close relationship to god. First, the initiates are adopted by an elder man and his wife; this event symbolically separates them from their own parents. Second, the initiates spend the night before the circumcision singing and dancing in an effort to solicit the guidance and protection of the ancestor-gods. Third, the initiates have their heads shaved and anointed, symbolizing the loss of the old status. And finally, they are sprayed with a mixture of honey, milk, and medicine by their adoptive parents in another separation ritual, which John Middleton and Greet Kershaw (1965) call the ceremony of parting.

As Van Gennep's theory suggests, the second (transition) phase of the Kikuyu initiation ceremony is a marginal phase filled with danger and ambiguity. The initiates undergo the dramatic and traumatic circumcision or clitoridectomy as a vivid symbolization of their

CROSS-CULTURAL MISCUE

Several weeks after the great tsunami disaster in December 2004, a female talk-show co-host on U.S. television made the following comment: "I was on my honeymoon in the Maldives Islands several weeks before the tsunami hit. I thank God for sparing me from that terrible disaster." Such a proclamation of faith in god is generally seen in the United States as perfectly legitimate, a devout, faith-based statement of her gratitude to god's infinite mercy. Who could possibly take issue with such a statement? Well, for starters we could cite all those tens of millions of people in the world who do not interpret every aspect of their lives as being directed by the purposeful hand of god. They would view the statement by this TV co-host as arrogant and self-serving, because they would see it as being dismissive of the one hundred seventy thousand plus people who died in the tsunami, and who god, by implication, did not deem sufficiently worthy of being spared from that terrible disaster. To cite this cross-cultural miscue is not to suggest that the TV co-host should not have made what, for her, was a sincere statement of faith. However, she should have been aware of how her statement might be heard in other parts of the world by good, religious, well-meaning people like herself, who just happen to have a different view of how god works in their everyday lives.

soon-to-be assumed responsibility as adults. Both male and female initiates are physically and emotionally supported during the operation by their sponsors, who cover them with cloaks as soon as the operation is completed. Afterward, the initiates spend four to nine days in seclusion in temporary huts (*kiganda*), where they are expected to recover from the operation and reflect upon their impending status as adults.

The third and final phase of Kikuyu initiation rituals involves the incorporation of the initiate (with his or her new status) back into the society as a whole. At the end of the seclusion period, the new male adults have certain ceremonial plants put into the large loops in their earlobes (a form of body mutilation practiced during childhood), symbolizing their newly acquired status as adult men. This phase of incorporation (or reintegration) involves other rituals as well. The men symbolically put an end to their transition stage by burning their *kiganda*; their heads are again shaved; they return home to be anointed by their parents, who soon thereafter engage in ritual intercourse; they ritually discard their initiation clothing; and they are given warrior paraphernalia. Once these incorporation rituals have been completed, the young people become full adults with all of the rights and responsibilities that go along with their new status.

Rites of Solidarity

The other type of communal cult is directed toward the welfare of the community rather than the individual. These *rites of solidarity* permit a wider social participation in the shared concerns of the community than is found in societies with predominantly shamanistic cults. A good example of a cult that fosters group solidarity is the ancestral cult, found widely throughout the world. Ancestral cults are based on the assumption that after death, a person's soul continues to interact with and affect the lives of her or his living descendants. In other words, when people die, they are not buried and forgotten but rather are elevated to the status of ancestor-ghost or -god. Because these ghosts, who are viewed as the official guardians of the social and moral order, have supernatural powers, the living descendants practice certain communal rituals designed to induce the ancestor-ghosts to protect them, favor them, or at least not harm them.

Like many of their neighboring cultures in northern Ghana, the Sisala believe that the ancestor-ghosts are the guardians of the moral order. All members of Sisala lineages are subject to the authority of the lineage elders. Because the elders are the most important living members of the group, they are responsible for overseeing the interests and harmony of the entire group. Though responsible for group morality, the elders have no direct authority to punish violators. The Sisala believe that the primary activity of the ancestor-ghosts is to punish living lineage members who violate behavioral norms. To be specific, ancestor-ghosts are thought to take vengeance on any living members who steal from their lineage mates, fight with their kin, or generally fail to live up to their family duties and responsibilities. Eugene Mendonsa (1985: 218–19) describes a specific case that graphically illustrates the power of ancestral cults among the Sisala:

> At Tuorojang in Tumu there was a young man named Cedu. He caught a goat that was for the ancestor of his house (*dia*), and killed it to sell the meat. When the day came for the sacrifice, the elders searched for the goat so they could kill it at the *lele* shrine. They could not find it, and asked to know who might have caught the goat. They could not decide who had taken the goat, so they caught another and used it for the sacrifice instead. During the sacrifice, the elders begged the ancestors to forgive them for not sacrificing the proper goat. The elders asked the ancestors to find and punish the thief. After the sacrifice, when all the elders had gone to their various houses, they heard that Cedu had died. They summoned a diviner to determine the cause of death, and found that Cedu had been the thief. The ancestors had killed him because he was the person who stole the goat that belonged to the ancestors.

This case illustrates the Sisala belief in the power of the ancestor-ghosts to protect the moral order. When a breach of the normative order occurs, the elders conduct a communal ritual petitioning the ghost to punish the wrongdoer. As with other aspects of religion, the anthropologist is not concerned with whether the diviner was correct in determining that Cedu died because he stole the goat. Instead, the anthropologist is interested in the communal ritual and its immediate social effects: it restored social harmony within the lineage and served as a warning to others who might be thinking of stealing from their lineage members.

Ecclesiastical Cults

The most complex form of religious organization, according to Wallace, is the *ecclesiastical cult*, which is found in societies with state systems of government. Examples of ecclesiastical cults can be found in societies with a pantheon of several high gods (such as traditional Aztec, Incas, Greeks, or Egyptians) or in those with essentially monotheistic religions, such as Buddhism, Christianity, Islam, or Judaism. Ecclesiastical cults are characterized by full-time professional clergy, who are formally elected or appointed and devote all or most of their time to performing priestly functions. Unlike shamans who conduct rituals during times of crisis or when their services are needed, these full-time priests conduct rituals that occur at regular intervals.

In addition, these priests are part of a hierarchical or bureaucratic organization under the control of a centralized church or temple. Often, but not always, these clerical bureaucracies are either controlled by the central government or closely associated with it. In many

---

rites of solidarity Any ceremony performed for the sake of enhancing the level of social integration among a group of people.

ecclesiastical cults Highly complex religious systems employing full-time priests.

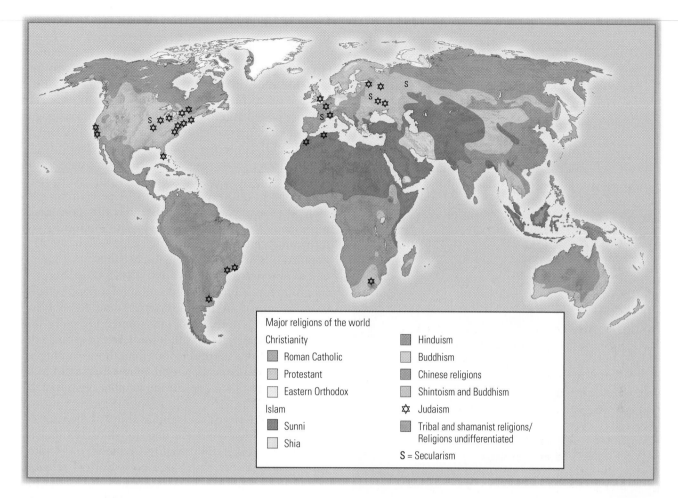

Major Religions of the World

ecclesiastical cults, the prevailing myths and beliefs are used to support the supremacy of the ruling class. In fact, it is not unusual for the priests to be part of that ruling class. Because of this close association between the priesthood and the politico-economic institutions, women have not traditionally played very active roles as priests. This is another important difference between priests and shamans, for at least as many women as men are practicing shamanism throughout the world. Even in modern, complex societies, women are particularly active as mystics, channelers, palm readers, astrologers, and clairvoyants.

In societies with ecclesiastical cults, a clearly understood distinction exists between laypersons and priests. Laypersons are primarily responsible for supporting the church through their labor and their financial contributions. The priests are responsible for conducting the religious rituals on behalf of the lay population, either individually or in groups. Whereas the priests serve as active ritual managers, the lay population participates in rituals in a generally passive fashion. Because the members of the lay population have little control over religion, they become spiritually dependent on the priests for their ritual/supernatural well-being.

Although ecclesiastical cults have enormous control over people's lives, they have not wiped out other forms of religion. Inuits, many of whom have converted to Christianity, for example, may continue to consult a shaman when ill; Africans from Tanzania often still worship their ancestors despite being practicing Roman Catholics; and in our own society, many people have no difficulty consulting a palmist, a psychic, or an astrologer even though they adhere to one of the large, worldwide, monotheistic religions.

We certainly do not need to go very far from home to see examples of ecclesiastical organizations. The United States, for example, has hundreds of religious denominations and approximately a quarter of a million separate congregations. Most people in the United States think they understand the nature of religious institutions around them, but there are probably more misconceptions and stereotypes about religion than about any other area of American life. Most people would be surprised to learn that church membership in the United States has grown, not declined, steadily over the last several hundred years. According to Roger Finke and Rodney Stark (2005: 23), only 17 percent of the population in 1776 claimed church membership; by

Rabbi Naamah Kelman, the first female rabbi to be ordained in Israel, is a full time religious specialist who works within a hierarchical organization.

Table 14.2 Number of Adherents of Major World Religions	
Religion	**Number of Adherents (millions)**
Bahai	7.5
Buddhist	375
Christian	2106
Roman Catholic	1105
Protestant	369
Orthodox	218
Anglican	79
Independent	416
Hindu	851
Jewish	15
Muslim	1283
New Religionists	107

SOURCE: *World Almanac and Book of Facts 2006*, p. 721.

the start of the Civil War, it had grown to 37 percent; by the mid-1920s, it had leaped to 58 percent; and by the early 1990s, 69 percent claimed church affiliation. According to a Gallup Poll conducted in 2003, 65 percent of adults in the United States claimed to be a member of a church or synagogue. Thirty-two percent of those polled said they attended church or synagogue at least once per week, while 58 percent claimed to attend at least once per month (Newport 2004).

In answer to the question, "How important would you say religion is in your life—very important, fairly important, or not very important?" 61 percent said religion was "very important." Although this percentage represents the average response, some interesting patterns emerged for certain subgroups within the U.S. population. For example, religion becomes more important to Americans as they get older; Blacks constitute the subgroup for whom religion is most important; religion is more important to conservatives and Republicans than to liberals and Democrats; women are more religious than men; people with lower levels of formal education tend to be more religious than those with higher levels of formal education; and Southerners tend to be more religious than people living in other regions of the country.

North Americans also tend to think of their society as being much more secular than religious. But in comparison with other industrialized nations, the United States places a very high value on organized religion. Public opinion polls dating back to the early 1980s show that approximately 60 percent of the adults in the United States acknowledge affiliation with a formal religious organization, as compared to 5 to 20 percent of adults from various western European countries. This explains why in many areas of the United States—particularly outside of major urban areas—new neighbors are often greeted with the question, "And what church do you belong to?" And, the separation of church and state notwithstanding, religion plays an important role in modern politics in the United States to the extent that voters want to see visible evidence of the faith of their leaders. According to a Pew survey, for every U.S. citizen who thinks that politicians should talk less about religion, there are two who think politicians should talk about it more (Brooks 2004).

Any attempt to measure religious participation in the United States is difficult at best. For example, it is not easy to define the terms *religion, denomination,* or even *Christianity.* Should Christianity be viewed as a single religion? Should we, instead, divide Christianity as practiced in North America into two major categories: liberal Christianity, on the one hand, and conservative, fundamentalist, evangelical Christianity on the other? Or should we be guided by the *Encyclopedia of American Religions* (Melton 1999), which lists more than a thousand different Christian religious organizations in North

The Islamic religion is the fastest growing organized religion in the United States, as illustrated by the Islamic Center of Greater Toledo located in a cornfield in the heartland of America.

© Peter Yates/CORBIS

America? Moreover, because there is no one major denomination, all denominations in the United States are minority denominations.

Nevertheless, thanks to two recent national surveys of religion in America (the Pluralism Project at Harvard University in 1997 and the American Religious Identification Survey conducted at City University of New York in 2001), we can get a reasonable understanding of religious affiliation and practice in the United States. The findings can be summarized as follows:

- Roman Catholicism is the largest single religious group, comprising 24 percent of the adult population (60 million).

- Anglicans, Eastern Orthodox, and Protestant churches, comprising some 220 denominations, represent 36 percent of the adult population (94 million people).

- Approximately 1.5 percent of the population is Jewish.

- The Islamic religion is the fastest-growing organized religion in the United States.

- The percentage of adults identifying with a particular religious group dropped from 90 percent in 1990 to 81 percent in 2001.

- The fastest-growing group in the United States is composed of those who do not identify with any specific religion; this group went from 14.3 million in 1990 to 29.4 million in 2001.

Since the elimination of national quotas by the Immigration Act of 1965, the United States has become,

without question, the most religiously diverse country in the world. In addition to the many Native American religions, Christian denominations, and branches of Judaism, the United States is now the home of many Muslims, Buddhists, Hindus, Bahais, Sikhs, Scientologists, and Rastafarians—among others. The religious landscape has become increasingly diversified over the past four decades, and it has not been confined to major urban areas such as New York, Chicago, Detroit, and Los Angeles. Makeshift Hindu temples and Muslim mosques are springing up in such unlikely places as Pawtucket, Rhode Island; Salt Lake City, Utah; and Raleigh, North Carolina. Diana Eck (2002) in her book *A New Religious America: How a "Christian Country" Has Become the World's Most Religiously Diverse Nation*, reminds us that the U.S. Navy now has Islamic chaplains, Los Angeles is the home of more than three hundred Buddhist temples, and there are more Muslims in the United States than Jews, Presbyterians, or Episcopalians. How the United States will deal with its growing religious complexity—particularly in light of the September 11 attacks—is one of the major challenges facing the nation in the twenty-first century.

Some observers have noted that people in the United States tend to harbor misconceptions concerning the ethnic affiliations of certain religious groups residing within their borders. As Barry Kosmin and Seymour Lachman (1993) have reported from their extensive survey of religion in America, most Americans of Irish descent are not Catholic, most Asian-Americans are Christian, most American Muslims are not Arabic, and most Arab-Americans are not Islamic.

Anthropology and the U.S. Supreme Court

Anyone traveling through rural Pennsylvania, Indiana, or Ohio is likely to see bearded men in black hats driving horse-drawn buggies and women wearing long dresses reminiscent of the nineteenth century. These people, seemingly so out of place in today's world, are the Old Order Amish, one of the oldest and most visible religious minorities in the United States. Amish society is characterized by several cultural themes to which they strongly adhere. First, the Amish strive to separate themselves from the world to the extent that they avoid worldly goods, practice strict endogamy, and even refrain from entering into business partnerships with non-Amish. Second, they place high value on adult baptism and the acceptance of the many social obligations that such baptism symbolizes. Third, the Amish maintain a highly disciplined church community. Fourth, they maintain the purity of their church community by excommunicating, or shunning, any erring members. Fifth, the Amish live their lives in harmony with the soil and nature. (See Chapter 2 for more on Amish culture.)

© Dennis MacDonald/PhotoEdit

In the early 1970s, the Amish were involved in a legal battle with the state of Wisconsin that went all the way to the U.S. Supreme Court. The central issue revolved around whether the state's compulsory education law violated the free exercise of religion of the Amish. Holding the religious belief that their church communities should be separate from the world, the Amish raise their children to be members of a self-sufficient community that rejects many of the values and physical trappings of mainstream society. The Amish argue that if they are required to send their children to public high schools, their self-sufficient church communities will be destroyed in a generation or two.

In its landmark decision in *Wisconsin v. Yoder*, the U.S. Supreme Court ruled that for the state to require Amish parents to send their children to public school beyond the eighth grade was a violation of their constitutional rights. By agreeing with the Amish argument, the Court exempted the Amish from compliance with the state's compulsory education law on the grounds of their religious beliefs. In rendering its decision, the Court drew

GLOBALIZATION OF WORLD RELIGIONS

In much the same way that markets have been globalizing over the past decade, the revolution in information and communications has had far-reaching effects on the various ecclesiastical religions of the world. For much of the twentieth century, most North Americans identifying with a particular religion adhered to a fairly straightforward set of religious beliefs and practices. People practiced Islam, Christianity, Buddhism, or Judaism, and it was relatively easy to predict what set of beliefs they held. As we begin the new millennium, however, many people are practicing a hodgepodge of beliefs. It has been reported (Lamont-Brown 1999) that as many as 40 million people in Japan are now practicing "new religions," which involve blending the two major religions in Japan (Buddhism and Shintoism) with elements of Confucianism, shamanism, animism, ancestor worship, Protestantism, and Catholicism. Traditional world religions, and even denominations of Christian religions, are cross-pollinating at a rapid rate. As one observer (Miller 1999: 1) has noted:

> Jews flirt with Hinduism, Catholics study Taoism, and Methodists discuss whether to make the Passover seder an official part of worship. Rabbi Zalman

Schachter-Shalomi, a prominent Jewish scholar, is also a Sufi sheik, and James Ishmael Ford, a Unitarian minister in Arizona, is a Zen sensei, or master. The melding of Judaism with Buddhism has become so commonplace that marketers who sell spiritual books, videotapes, and lecture series have a name for it: "JewBu."

It is difficult to tell if this cross-fertilization of religious beliefs and practices will be a short-term phenomenon or a more long-term, permanent condition of the world's ecclesiastical religions. In any event, it is causing a fairly serious dilemma for the leaders of world religions who see this intermingling as a threat to their very identity.

Not only are people blending elements of more than one religion, but decades of Christian proselytizing are actually changing the geographic distribution and centers of power in some world religions such as Christianity. Over the course of the past half century, Christianity has experienced a major shift in power and influence from the long-established churches of Europe and North America to the so-called "Global South" (Africa, South America, and South Asia). For decades, European Christian churches have been losing membership and have faced considerable difficulties recruiting priests. Christian church membership in the developing world, however, has been booming during this same period. For

heavily upon the testimony of John Hostetler, an anthropologist who served as an expert witness at the lower level court proceedings. In fact, as one observer (Rosen) commented:

> A close reading of the Supreme Court opinion clearly demonstrates that the anthropological testimony in this case may well have been indispensable to the Court's assertion that enforcement of the school attendance law would have had an unusually harsh effect on the entire community of Amish people. (nd: 20)

Hostetler argued that to require Amish teenagers to attend high schools that fostered such radically different social and religious values would have subjected them to great psychological harm. The conflicting values between mainstream schools and Amish church communities would have caused considerable alienation between Amish parents and their children. Central to Hostetler's argument is the anthropological theory of the integrated nature of a culture. Hostetler was able to convince the Court that Amish culture is an organic whole, the parts of which are intimately interconnected. More specifically, he pointed out the close interconnection between Amish religion and the Amish people's daily communal life.

Basing much of its decision on Hostetler's anthropological testimony, the Court concluded:

> Aided by a history of three centuries as an identifiable religious sect and a long history as a successful and self-sufficient segment of American society, the Amish in this case have convincingly demonstrated the sincerity of their religious beliefs, the interrelationship of belief with their mode of life, the vital role that belief and daily conduct play in the continued survival of Old Order Amish communities and their religious organization, and the hazards presented by the State's enforcement of a statute generally valid to others.

Because of the closeness of fit between Hostetler's testimony and the Court's decision, it seems safe to conclude that this landmark case might well have had a different outcome had Hostetler not used his anthropological insights as an expert witness.

Questions for Further Thought

1. In what ways is Amish society different from mainstream U.S. society?
2. What is the anthropological theory concerning the integrated nature of a culture, and how does it apply to this case study?
3. What social function of religion (discussed earlier in this chapter) would have been disrupted had this case been decided differently?

---

example, whereas there were 10 million Christians in Africa in 1900, there are more than 360 million today. South America now boasts 560 million Christians while South Asia has 313 million (Steinmetz 2004). In fact, Christianity has become so widely practiced in the "godless" country of China (approximately 50 million adherents) that Chinese authorities in June 2006 pulled *The Da Vinci Code* off movie screens nationwide as a concession to Chinese Catholic groups.

Not only are religious beliefs being blended, but the age of globalization has also seen certain religious ideas and practices working their way into the secular world of international business. For tens of generations, Indians from all segments of society have sought guidance from mystics and astrologers who claim to predict the future by analyzing numbers or studying the alignment of the stars and planets. But today, there is growing evidence that these traditional supernatural practices are being used in the offices of multinational corporations to help with decisions concerning strategic planning, mergers, and hiring. Some Indian mystics are specialists in vaastu (similar to the Chinese belief in feng shui), which seeks to ensure good fortune by means of proper interior design. It is not at all uncommon for Indian high-tech corporations to hire such mystic specialists to review architectural plans prior to the construction of new corporate facilities. Film producers in Bollywood (India's counterpart to Hollywood) often seek the advice of numerologists, who claim that one's destiny is largely determined by numbers and their configurations, before making a final decision on a film's title or date of release. A person's astrological signs may even be a factor in whether a person is hired. The line between science and supernatural beliefs is becoming increasingly blurred (Lakshmi 2004).

In some countries the nonreligious changes occurring in the global economy are bringing about fundamental changes in their own traditional religious practices. To illustrate, although Indians have practiced yoga for centuries, many middle-class Indians, whose twenty-first-century jobs are putting increased pressure on their time, feel that the practice of traditional yoga is too complex and time consuming. Today, followers of Swami Ramdev practice a form of "yoga lite" with twelve thousand of their closest friends in Jawaharlal Nehru Stadium in New Delhi, India. By concentrating on breath control, which is only one aspect of traditional yoga, the Swami claims that practitioners of his "yoga made easy" will remain healthy in mind and body. This is a very appealing message for people caught up in the pressures of the twenty-first-century global economy (Kumar 2005).

We have heard a good deal in recent years about outsourcing of manufacturing and even high-tech jobs from Canada and the United States to India. Less known,

© Grzegorz Galazka/CORBIS

Cardinal Bernardin Gantin represents a part of the world that is growing rapidly in the number of people practicing Catholicism.

however, is that due to a shortage of priests in North America, local Catholic parishes are sending Mass Intentions (requests for masses said for a sick relative, the remembrance of deceased kin, or a prayer offering for a newborn) to India. Catholic priests in India (who have more time than North American priests and need the money) are now conducting the masses on behalf of North American Catholics after receiving the requests via e-mail (Rai 2004). Thus, here is a dramatic illustration of how, in this age of globalization, we are not only outsourcing jobs to India, but also our religious rituals.

RELIGION: CONTINUITY AND CHANGE

By examining the various functions of religion, it is quite clear that religion is a conservative force within a society. In a general sense, religions support the status quo by keeping people in line through supernatural sanctions, relieving social conflict, and providing explanations for unfortunate events. Moreover, some of the major world religions, through both philosophical convictions and political interpretations, have tended to retard social

change. To illustrate, orthodox Hindu beliefs, based on the notion that one's present condition in life is based on deeds from past lives, have had the effect of making people so fatalistic that they accept their present situations as unchangeable. Such a worldview is not likely to bring about major revolutions, or even minor initiatives for change. Likewise, on a number of issues facing the world's population, Catholicism has taken highly conservative policy positions. For example, the 1968 papal decree by Pope Paul VI opposing all forms of artificial birth control makes it very difficult for developing nations to bring their high population growth under control. Conservative Muslims in a number of countries have taken a strong stand against the introduction of new values and behaviors, particularly from the Western world. The Islamic government of Bangladesh issued a warrant for the arrest of feminist writer Taslima Nasreen for blasphemy because of her statement that the Koran (the Islamic holy book) needs to be revised to better protect women. Nasreen's writings, like those of Salman Rushdie, provoked a religious decree calling for her death (Weiner 1994).

Religion, however, has also played a major role in global social change over the past several decades. For example, the Catholic church, allied with the Solidarity Movement, played a pivotal role in bringing about the downfall of the communist government in Poland in 1989. By burning themselves alive on the streets of Saigon during the 1960s, Buddhist priests in Vietnam played a powerful role in stimulating antiwar sentiments in the United States, which eventually led to the withdrawal of U.S. troops. In South America during the 1970s and 1980s, a militant form of Catholicism known as *liberation theology* merged Catholic theology with activism for social justice for the poor. Catholic priests and nuns, often without the support or approval of their own church authorities, engaged in various projects designed to help the poor raise themselves from the lowest echelons of society. Because these liberation theologians were often at odds with government and church officials, many lost their lives because of their activism.

Closer to home, African American churches in the United States, with their strong theme of the struggle against bondage and oppression, have long played a role in social change. Well before the civil rights movement of the 1960s, Black churches served as headquarters and rallying places for protestors and community activists. Prior to the abolition of slavery, churches served as stations on the Underground Railroad, which helped slaves travel undetected from the south to the north. More-

---

liberation theology A form of Catholicism found throughout South and Central America in which priests and nuns became actively involved in programs for social justice for the poor.

over, the Black Muslim movement in the United States, with its strict dietary prohibitions and behavior codes, has been a force for social change by fostering the idea of autonomous African-American communities. Thus, for the past 150 years, African-Americans have used the moral authority of their churches and mosques to push for racial justice and social change.

Under certain circumstances, religion can play an important role in transforming a society. At times, certain societies have experienced such high levels of stress and strain that the conservative functions of religion could not hold them together. Instead, new religions or sects have sprung up to create a new social order. A number of different terms have been used in the literature to describe these new religious forces of social change, including *nativistic movements*, found among American Indians; *cargo cults*, found in Melanesia; the *separatist Christian churches* of southern Africa; *mahdist movements* in the Muslim world; and *millenarian movements* found in Christian areas of the world.

All of these religious movements, with their aim of breathing new life and purpose into the society, are called *revitalization movements* by Anthony Wallace (1966). The common thread running through them is that they tend to occur during times of cultural stress brought about by rapid change, foreign domination, and perceived deprivation. Because these three conditions are often, but not always, associated with colonialism, many revitalization movements have appeared in societies that have been under colonial domination.

Despite considerable differences in the details surrounding various revitalization movements, Wallace suggests that most follow a fairly uniform process. Starting from the state of equilibrium (in which change occurs, although slowly, and individual stress levels are tolerable), a society is pushed out of equilibrium by forces such as conquest and social domination. These conditions lower the self-esteem of an increasing number of individuals and place them under intolerable stress. People become disillusioned, and the culture becomes

---

nativistic movements   A religious force for social change found among Native Americans.

cargo cults   Revitalization movements in Melanesia intended to bring new life and purpose into a society.

separatist Christian churches   Small-scale churches that break away from the dominant church to gain greater political, economic, social, and religious autonomy.

mahdist movements   A term used to describe revitalization movements in the Muslim world.

millenarian movements   Social movements by a repressed group of people who are looking forward to better times at a specific time in the future.

revitalization movements   Religious movements designed to bring about a new way of life within a society.

---

disorganized (with higher crime rates and a general increase in antisocial behavior, for example). When the social fabric deteriorates sufficiently, revitalization movements are likely to appear in an effort to bring about a more satisfying society. Some movements call for a return to the better days of the past; others seek to establish a completely new social order.

Revitalization movements have been found in many parts of the world, but nowhere have they been more widespread and better documented than among Native American groups. The tragic suffering of American Indians since their earliest contact with Europeans has resulted in a number of revitalization movements, including the movement among the Seneca Indians headed by Handsome Lake, several versions of the Ghost Dance, and the Peyote cults found among the Plains Indians. In recent decades, these religious revitalization movements have been replaced by more secular/political efforts to reclaim Indian land, resources, and dignity through legal action, political activism, and civil disobedience.

One of the earliest Native American revitalization movements was started by Handsome Lake (Parker 1913; Deardorff 1951). By the year 1800, the Seneca Indians of New York State had fallen upon hard times. They had lost much of their land to Whites, who held them in contempt because they were on the losing side of the French and Indian War. The Seneca were confined to reservations, and their numbers had been severely reduced by European diseases such as measles and smallpox. Once a proud nation of warriors, hunters, and traders, the Seneca by the start of the nineteenth century were defeated, dehumanized, and demoralized. Alcoholism became rampant, and conflicts and accusations of witchcraft increased.

From this state of cultural disorganization came a prophet—Handsome Lake—who was visited by God in a vision and told to stop drinking and start a new revitalizing religion. The deity warned that the Seneca would suffer a great catastrophe (such as fire, destruction, and death) if they did not mend their ways. Most of the prescriptions set down by Handsome Lake constituted a new set of moral principles and rules of behavior. Followers of the new religious movement were expected to stay sober, be peaceful, and lead pure and upright lives.

Handsome Lake instituted a number of other important cultural changes as well. For example, he urged his followers to adopt European agricultural practices involving both men and women working in the fields. In terms of the Seneca family, he emphasized the priority of the conjugal unit of man and wife over the matrilineage. Divorce, which had always been common in traditional Seneca society, was no longer permitted. Thus, Handsome Lake's revitalization movement led to far-reaching cultural changes. The Seneca became models of sobriety, their family structure was altered, they initiated new farming practices, and they changed the traditional division of labor between men and women.

The last several hundred years witnessed a number of religious revitalization movements, but it is also possible to find such movements in today's world of cell phones, space probes, and the Internet. In the late 1990s, the economy of Indonesia, due largely to the widespread corruption of the Suharto government, went into major crisis. Banks failed, companies went bankrupt, unemployment soared, and there was a mass exodus of foreign investment from the country. The general Indonesian population, suffering from widespread poverty even before the financial meltdown, experienced extreme hardship and economic stress.

In this environment of economic crisis, Indonesia's Muhammadiyah Islamic organization emerged as a new form of religious revitalization. According to Habib Chirzin, a leading figure in the organization, Islam is the answer to Indonesia's crisis. The decades of the 1980s and 1990s saw the Indonesian economy grow rapidly, due largely to foreign investment. But the rapid economic growth caused many people (and their government) to lose their moral compass. The result was that corruption and cronyism became the order of the day. The Muhammadiyah, with approximately 30 million members, wants to reinstate the basic principles of Islam—devotion to God and community self-help—as the most effective way of recovering from the economic crisis that is gripping its people. The organization, which operates 130 universities, thirteen thousand schools, and 750 medical clinics, is beginning to re-energize its communities by encouraging a number of local self-help initiatives, including health care programs, food kitchens, child care, and job programs. By focusing on education and encouraging people to help themselves and one another, they are revitalizing the basic principles of Islam and, at the same time, building a broader base of economic development that is less dependent on foreign capital and less susceptible to government cronyism (Fuller 1999).

Not all revitalization movements coexist comfortably with national government systems. One recent millenarian group in the United States that had a tragic confrontation with the federal government was the Branch Davidians in Waco, Texas, who were led by David Koresh. According to Michael Barkun (2000), the deadly shoot-out between federal agents and the Branch Davidians, and the subsequent fire that killed many sect members, resulted from a number of miscalculations by federal agents. The single most costly error was that the U.S. government failed to take the religious beliefs of Koresh and the Branch Davidians seriously. Rather than appreciating that their religious beliefs were deeply held and sincere, the government agents treated the Branch Davidians as delusional "wackos from Waco." The group was defined as a cult of brainwashed followers, while David Koresh was seen as the egomaniacal cult leader obsessed with nothing more than his own personal gains.

Because Koresh believed that the Branch Davidians would be delivered from their enemies and achieve total salvation here on earth, the use of force by the federal agents played directly into the hands of the Branch Davidians. According to Barkun (2000: 335), the various government assaults on the compound with tanks and helicopters, "when taken from a millenarian perspective, [although] intended as pressure, were the fulfillment of prophecy." Barkun concludes that the tragic loss of life *might* have been avoided if the federal agents had been willing to wait them out and avoid a show of force.

RELIGIOUS CHANGE IN THE AGE OF GLOBALIZATION

Much has been written in the last several decades about a worldwide shift toward religious fundamentalism. In the 1990s, Benjamin Barber (1996) posited that globalism (modernism) and tribalism (antimodernism) would be the two major, and diametrically opposed, forces competing with one another in the twenty-first century. He referred to globalism by the term *McWorld*, which encompasses expanding world markets, global integration, homogenizing world cultures, and faith in science and technology on steroids. At the opposite polarity, Barber spoke of "Jihad," an antimodern force that sees an ideological struggle among cultures, tribes, and religions. Whereas McWorld seeks global integration, Jihad seeks to focus on the local community and the preservation of traditional customs, values, and religions. Barber's formulation of the polarizing forces of McWorld versus Jihad is similar to that developed several years later by Thomas Friedman (1999), who spoke of the "Lexus and the olive tree."

Religious fundamentalists (i.e., those jihadists interested in protecting the olive trees in their own backyards) feel threatened by an increasingly modern, scientific, secular world. They want to separate themselves from twenty-first-century modernists, whose original religious principles, they believe, have been corrupted through neglect and compromise. The use of the Islamic term *jihad* (meaning struggle) or the reference to olive trees (native to the Middle East) should in no way suggest that religious fundamentalism refers only to Islamic fundamentalism. In fact, religious fundamentalism refers to any group that purposefully chooses to separate itself from the larger religious group from which it arose. They seek to separate themselves from both foreign religions and compromised versions of their own religion. Thus we see Islamic fundamentalists who, rejecting foreign and modern ideas, advocate a return to Islamic culture, strict principles based on Islamic law (shariah), a literal interpretation of the Koran, and close fellowship among Muslims. Likewise, Christian funda-

In countries like Iran, the notion of religious nationalism makes no attempt to separate church and state.

mentalists, wanting to return to an earlier and less corrupted form of their own religion, insist on interpreting scripture as infallible, historically accurate, and literally true. Moreover, like any other form of religious fundamentalism, Judaic fundamentalists see themselves as distinct from the corruptions of the modern world and hold their own sacred scriptures as divinely inspired, infallible, and unchangeable. What all fundamentalist groups have in common is that they all draw *most* of their converts from among members of their own religion, a religion which, the fundamentalists claim, has strayed from its original principles and practices.

Christian Fundamentalism

The rise of fundamentalism among Christian churches in the United States, despite conventional wisdom, is *not* a phenomenon associated with globalization over the past several decades, but actually has been progressing in an evolutionary fashion over the past several centuries. If we look at just the sixty-year period between 1940 and 2000, we see a dramatic decline in "market share" (i.e., relative membership) among the mainline denominations (United Methodists, Episcopal, Presbyterian) and a concomitant increase in market share among the evangelical churches. To illustrate, during this six-decade period, the United Methodists lost 56 percent membership, the Presbyterian church (USA) lost 60 percent, and the Episcopalians lost 51 percent; during the very same period the Southern Baptists gained 37 percent, the Church of God in Christ gained 1,292 percent, and the Pentecostal Assemblies of the World gained a whopping 2,375 percent (Finke and Stark 2005: 246).

Not only have fundamentalist Christian churches shown dramatic growth in the United States in the last century, but fundamentalist religions (and their accompanying faith-based agendas) are playing an increasingly important role in the political affairs of the United States. The presidential election of 2004—one of the closest and most contentious in recent history—was won primarily on the ability of the Republican Party to mobilize its Christian religious base in the southern and midwestern states. In the aftermath of the 2004 election, most political observers pointed to a cultural divide (or perhaps more aptly, a "religious divide") in the United States to explain the election results. The issues that swung the election in favor of George W. Bush were those issues of *personal* morality held most stridently by fundamentalist Christian religious groups. These issues include opposition to abortion rights, same-sex marriage, and embryonic stem cell research. But in addition to these hot-button issues, the issue of presidential leadership was also framed in religious terminology. When speaking to voters in the heartland, President Bush made statements such as "I carry the word of God," "I pray to be as good a messenger of His will as possible," and "I trust God speaks through me" (Suskind 2004: 51). Clearly, he was communicating to his religious supporters that (a) he knew what the will of God was and (b) that God's will was being carried out through the president's domestic and foreign policies. For many voters in the Republican base, who judged the worth of both candidates on such criteria as character, certainty, fortitude, confidence, and proximity to God, there was no question as to which candidate was the stronger leader. In much the same way that an evangelical preacher would never question Holy Scripture, a true political leader would never deviate from the course (even in the face of evidence suggesting that things were not going well), provided, of course, that the policy was seen as having divine backing. According to this way of thinking, any

Rollin Riggs/The New York Times/Redux

The merging of religion and nationalism is not just something occurring in certain Middle Eastern countries. On July 4, 2006, this *Statue of Liberation Through Christ* was consecrated at a fundamentalist church in Memphis, Tennessee, as a way of demonstrating their belief that Christianity is the foundation of American society.

candidate who questioned the validity of the war in Iraq (or the war in Vietnam a generation earlier) would be the spitting image of Doubting Thomas. Such a candidate would be denounced as both faithless and unpatriotic, and consequently a poor leader during trying times. Thus, the presidential election of 2004 was described as "the most important election of our lifetime" largely because, for the first time in recent history, religious ideas played a central role in determining the outcome.

Islamic Fundamentalism and Religious Nationalism

An extremely significant trend in global religion today is what is called *religious nationalism*. This movement, which can be found in countries that represent a

> *religious nationalism*   A phenomenon that is occurring in many parts of the world today in which traditional religious principles are merged with the workings of government.

number of different religious traditions, rejects the idea that religion and government should be separate. Instead, religious nationalism calls for an absolute merging of traditional religious beliefs with government institutions and leaders. With the collapse of the former Soviet Union and the communist bloc, many nations are beginning to reject the secular solutions that were so prevalent during the Cold War years. Instead, they are increasingly embracing a fundamentalist religious state that does not tolerate nonbelievers.

Nowhere is religious nationalism more evident than in the Middle East. Islamic nationalism—perhaps the most visible form of religious nationalism—combines fundamentalist religious orthodoxy with contemporary political institutions. The alignment of Islam with contemporary political Arab nationalism stems from the 1967 Arab–Israeli war. Israel's thorough humiliation of Syria, Egypt, and Jordan in just five days left many Arabs feeling that there was something very wrong in the Arab world. From the late 1960s onward, many Arabs have restructured their sense of nationalism within the religious framework of Islam. Their religion has become a vibrant source of national identity as well as an alternate solution to their political, economic, and military problems. By the early 1980s, Islamic nationalism was experiencing some significant victories over the non-Arab, non-Islamic world. For example, Hezbollah forced the United States from Beirut, the Israelis were driven out of Lebanon, and Russia finally limped out of Afghanistan. As Islamic nationalism flexed its muscles, it sent a clear message to others both in the Arab world and beyond: Islam is a powerful force and can be mobilized to challenge what it sees as foreign influence and oppression.

In the late 1970s, the pro–American shah of Iran was overthrown by the fundamentalist Islamic revolution headed by Ayatollah Khomeini. That revolution, condemning the United States as the "great Satan," has spread throughout other parts of the Islamic world. This form of religious nationalism rejects the individual freedom of expression and political choice so highly valued in the West. Islamic nationalism also represents a rejection of the often-exploitive government and economic systems (such as capitalism and democracy) that Middle Eastern peoples have endured over the decades.

Many Middle Eastern government *leaders* have succumbed to Western influence because cooperating with Europe and the United States has made them personally wealthy. To their rank-and-file citizens, the royal families in countries such as Saudi Arabia and Kuwait appear to be pawns of the West. In these countries, religious nationalism (the merging of Arab political identity with the Islamic religion) goes beyond fighting the infidels abroad; it also extends to their own leaders at home—a type of domestic jihad. Indeed, terrorist attacks in Saudi Arabia (directed at the ruling royal family and their Western allies) have increased dramatically in the last several years. In its more extreme form, religious nationalism, which takes on the character of a religious war, can pose a real threat to the rest of the world. Secular nationalistic movements, such as those found in Western democracies, have goals and objectives with certain imposed time limitations. For example, secular nationalists promise their followers that if they do certain things now, they will live for a long time in a peaceful world. Religious nationalism, on the other hand, promises its followers endless rewards; for example, if you martyr yourself in the struggle against the infidels, you will immediately enter paradise and stay there forever. That, needless to say, poses some real challenges for those defined as infidels.

RELIGIOUS CHANGE AND TECHNOLOGY

Although religious evangelists have used the radio to convert nonbelievers to Christianity, it wasn't until the 1970s that television greatly increased their capacity to gain converts, raise funds, and spread their influence. In fact, television was such a powerful medium that many televangelists became superstars, with their own broadcasting empires, news exposure, and political influence. Evangelists such as Jerry Falwell, Billy Graham, Oral Roberts, Pat Robertson, and Robert Schuller recruited by promising personal salvation, material success, and improved physical health. Their messages resonated particularly well with those who were poor, undereducated, underemployed, sick, elderly, and fearful of crime, changing sexual values, and anything foreign. Through their on-air fundraising many televangelists have built multimillion-dollar media empires. During the 1980s, however, scandals destroyed the reputations of several well-known televangelists. Jim Bakker, head of the PTL ("Praise the Lord") Club was sent to prison for financial improprieties when he tried to exploit the faith and charity of his viewing audience. Some cynical observers suggested that PTL was an acronym for "Pass the Loot."

Meanwhile in Baton Rouge, Louisiana, Evangelist Jimmy Swaggart made a tearful confession to his TV audience that he would be leaving the pulpit temporarily due to an "unspecified sin," which turned out to be soliciting the services of a prostitute. While these scandals resulted in a temporary reduction in viewership, televangelism remains popular into the twenty-first century.

As we have seen in previous chapters, the information revolution in general, and the Internet in particular, are having enormous effects on our economic, social, and political lives. How will information technology affect our religious lives? Although it is too early to answer this question definitively, we are already seeing a rapidly growing number of religious organizations posting their own websites and chat rooms. It is now possible to spread your own religious ideas cheaply, instantaneously, and all over the world. In much the same way that radio and television extended the reach of religious ideas, the Internet is accelerating the notion of religion no longer being confined to the walls of a church. Are we headed for a new type of "churchless religion" in which cyber-churches and virtual congregations replace the face-to-face interaction found in traditional churches, mosques, synagogues, and temples?

As with so many aspects of life today, the Internet brings together people who share common religious traditions. We saw in Chapter 9 the proliferation of websites in recent years devoted to dating (and matchmaking) specifically designed for a variety of demographics, including Indians, Russians, Chinese, or Latinos, among others. But we also find religious-specific matchmaking websites as well. For example, Jewish singles can log onto Jdate.com, Christians can visit Christiansingles.com, while Eharmony.com appeals to those of a more "new age" religious persuasion. There is even a boutique website called Dharmadate.net, designed for the approximately 5 million Buddhists living in the United States. ∎

Summary

1. Although all cultures have supernatural beliefs, these beliefs take widely varying forms from society to society. It is often difficult to define supernatural belief systems cross-culturally because different societies have different ways of distinguishing between the natural and the supernatural.

2. The anthropological study of religion does not attempt to determine which religions are better than others or which gods are able to work the most miracles per unit of time. Rather, cultural anthropologists concentrate on describing the various systems of religious belief, how they function, and the degree to which they influence human behavior.

3. Religion differs from magic in that religion deals with big issues such as life, death, and god, whereas magic deals with more immediate and specific problems. Whereas religion asks for help through prayer, magic is a direct attempt to control and manipulate supernatural forces.

4. Witchcraft and sorcery are two types of supernatural belief systems that cause harm to people. Whereas sorcery involves the deliberate attempt to cause people misfortune through the use of certain material substances, witchcraft is an inborn and generally involuntary capacity to work evil.

5. Religion performs certain social functions. It enhances the overall well-being of the society by serving as a mechanism of social control, helping to reduce the stress and frustrations that often lead to social conflict, and intensifying group solidarity.

6. Religion also performs certain psychological functions such as providing emotional comfort by

helping to explain the unexplainable and helping a person cope with the stress and anxiety often accompanying illness or misfortune.

7. Following the scheme suggested by Wallace, there are four distinctive patterns of religious organization: individualistic cults, shamanistic cults, communal cults, and ecclesiastical cults. These four types of religion vary roughly with increasing levels of socio-economic complexity; individualistic cults are associated with food-collecting societies and ecclesiastical cults are found in highly industrialized societies.

8. The most basic level of religious organization is the individualistic cult, characterized by an absence of religious specialists. The vision quest of certain Native American cultures is an example of a religious practice of an individualistic cult.

9. Shamanistic cults involve the least complex form of religious division of labor. Shamans are part-time religious specialists who, it is believed, help or cure their clients by intervening with the supernatural powers while in an altered state of consciousness.

10. Communal cults involve groups of ordinary people who conduct religious ceremonies for the well-being of the community. Examples of communal cults are the rites of passage (such as circumcision ceremonies) found widely throughout sub-Saharan Africa and the ancestral cults that function to foster group solidarity among members of a kinship group.

11. Ecclesiastical cults, which are found in societies with state systems of government, are characterized by full-time professional clergy who are usually organized into a hierarchy.

12. Revitalization movements—religious movements aimed at bringing new life and energy into a society—usually occur when societies are experiencing rapid cultural change, foreign domination, or perceived deprivation. Revitalization movements have taken a number of different forms, including nativistic movements, cargo cults, and millenarian movements.

13. Religion has played an important role in global social change through liberation theology (whereby Catholic priests and nuns work for social reform and justice for the poor) and religious nationalism (whereby religious beliefs are merged with government institutions).

14. A significant trend in global religion today is the rise of religious fundamentalism and religious nationalism. Found most prominently in the Islamic world, religious nationalism aims to merge traditional religious beliefs with contemporary political institutions.

Key Terms

animatism	imitative magic	myths	Satanists
animism	individualistic cults	nativistic movements	separatist Christian churches
cargo cults	liberation theology	polytheism	shamanistic cults
communal cults	magic	religion	shamans
contagious magic	mahdist movements	religious nationalism	sorcery
covens	mana	revitalization movements	vision quest
cult	millenarian movements	rites of passage	Wicca
ecclesiastical cults	monotheism	rites of solidarity	witchcraft

Suggested Readings

Anderson, Robert. *The Ghosts of Iceland.* Belmont, CA: Wadsworth, 2004. This ethnography examines various spiritual movements in contemporary Iceland. Drawing heavily upon participant-observation, Anderson spent time with spirit mediums, observed and recorded conversations between the living and the dead, and participated in group séances.

Eck, Diana. *A New Religious America: How a "Christian Country" Has Become the World's Most Religiously Diverse Nation.* San Francisco: Harper, 2002. An eye-opening examination of the growing religious diversity in the United States in the twenty-first century.

Finke, Roger and Rodney Stark. *The Churching of America, 1776–2005: Winners and Losers in Our Religious Economy.* New Brunswick, NJ: Rutgers University Press, 2005. This updated analysis of the development of religious organizations in the United States from 1776 to 2005 treats the nation's religious environment as an extension of the free market economy. Both mainline churches and "upstart sects" have competed for "market share" over the course of the nation's history.

Kamenetz, Rodger. *The Jew in the Lotus.* San Francisco: Harper, 1995. Illustrating the trend of theological borrowing among practitioners of world religions,

Kamenetz takes the reader on his personal journey as a Jew who finds spiritual renewal in the Buddhism of the Dalai Lama.

Lattas, Andrew. *Cultures of Secrecy: Reinventing Race in Bush Kaliai Cargo Cults.* Madison: University of Wisconsin Press, 1998. By taking an ethnographic approach, Lattas explores one form of the religious revitalization movement, the cargo cults, by showing how the Kaliai of Papua New Guinea have blended their traditional myths with imported folklore and Christian stories.

Lehmann, Arthur C., James E. Myers, and Pamela Moro, eds. *Magic, Witchcraft, and Religion: An Anthropological Study of the Supernatural*, 5th ed. Boston: McGraw-Hill, 2001. This comparative reader takes an anthropological approach to the study of religion, both familiar and exotic.

Sanders, Andrew. *A Deed Without a Name: The Witch in Society and History.* Oxford: Berg, 1995. A comprehensive yet readable study of witchcraft, drawing on contemporary and historical case studies from medieval Europe to African tribal societies to contemporary North America. The author suggests that the process of labeling witches is similar in all societies, both now and in the past.

Wallace, Anthony F. C. *Religion: An Anthropological View.* New York: Random House, 1966. An old yet still-valuable analysis of the anthropology of religion that discusses some general theories, the structure, goals, functions, and ritual processes of religion from a cross-cultural perspective.

Art

Glass sculptures by Dale Chihuly float in a canal in Venice, Italy.

CHAPTER

15

ARTISTIC EXPRESSION IS one of the most distinctive human characteristics. No group of people known to cultural anthropologists spends all of its time in the utilitarian pursuit of meeting basic survival needs. In other words, people do not hunt, grow crops, make tools, and build houses purely for the sake of sustaining themselves and others. After their survival needs are met, all cultures, even technologically simple ones, decorate their storage containers, paint their houses, embroider their clothing, and add aesthetically pleasing designs to their tools. They compose songs, tell riddles, dance creatively, paint pictures, make films, and carve masks. All of these endeavors reflect the human urge for self-expression and aesthetic pleasure. It would be hard to imagine a society without art, music, dance, and poetry. As the study of cultural anthropology reminds us, artistic expression is found in every society, and aesthetic pleasure is felt by people everywhere (Coote and Shelton 1992).

WHAT IS ART?

For centuries, people from a variety of disciplines—including philosophers, anthropologists, politicians, art historians, and professional artists themselves—have proposed definitions of *art*. George Mills has suggested that "definitions (of art) vary with the purposes of the definers" (1957: 17). To illustrate, the artist might define art in terms of the creative process, the politician's definition would emphasize the communicative aspects of art that could mobilize public opinion, the art historian or knowledgeable collector would focus on the emotional response art produces, and the cultural anthropologist might define *art* in terms of the role or function it plays in religious ceremonies. Nevertheless, despite these diverse definitions, any definition of *art*, if it is to have any cross-cultural applicability, must include certain basic elements:

1. The artistic process should be creative, playful, and enjoyable and need not be concerned with the practicality or usefulness of the object being produced.

2. From the perspective of the consumer, art should produce some type of emotional response, either positive or negative.

3. Art should be *transformational*. An event from nature, such as a cheetah running at full speed, may be aesthetically pleasing in that it

What We Will Learn

- How do anthropologists define the arts?

- What are the various functions of art in society?

- How do music and dance reflect other aspects of a culture?

 Click!

For interactive exercises and study aids, Go to **www.ichapters.com**; enter the author name and select your text, then click the Study Help tab to purchase the following online resources:

- **ThomsonNOW** for chapter-specific online tutorials, quizzes, and a personalized study plan

- **Anthropology Resource Center** for interactive maps, modules, videos, and the Applied Anthropology site

- **Thomson Audio Study Products** for a brief overview of the major chapter themes and to test your knowledge with quiz questions

transformational The quality of an artistic process that converts an image into a work of art.

367

In parts of Polynesia, full-body tattooing is considered a significant form of art.

© Bob Krist/Corbis

evokes a strong emotional response, but it is not art. It becomes art only when someone transforms the image into a painting, dance, song, or poem.

4. Art should communicate information by being representational. In other words, once the object of art is transformed, it should make a symbolic statement about what is being portrayed.

5. Art implies that the artist has developed a certain level of technical skill not shared equally by all people in a society. Some people have more highly developed skills than others because of the interplay of individual interests and opportunities with genetically based acuities.

Centuries of debate by reasonable people have failed to produce a universally agreed-upon definition of *art*. Although we will not presume to establish a universal definition, it will be useful, for the purposes of this chapter, to suggest a working definition of *art* based on the five elements just listed. Thus, art is both the process and the products of applying certain skills to any activity that transforms matter, sound, or motion into a form that is deemed aesthetically meaningful by people in a society.

By using these five features, we can include a wide variety of artistic activities in our definition of *art*. In all societies people apply imagination, creativity, and technical skills to transform matter, sound, and movement into works of art. The various types of artistic expression include the graphic or plastic arts—such as painting, carving, weaving, basket making, and sculpting out of clay, metal, or glass; the creative manipulation of sounds and words in such artistic forms as music, poetry, and folklore; and the application of skill and creativity to

body movement that gives rise to dance. It should be pointed out that these three neatly defined categories of artistic expression sometimes include forms that are not familiar to Westerners. Westerners usually think of graphic and plastic arts as including such media as painting and sculpture, but in the non-Western world people may also include the Nubians' elaborate body decoration (Faris 1972), Navajo sand painting (Witherspoon 1977), and the Inuits' body tattooing (Birket-Smith 1959). Moreover, sometimes activities that in our own society have no particular artistic content are elevated to an art form in other societies. The Japanese tea ceremony is an excellent case in point.

It is also possible for these different types or modes of art to be combined in creative ways. In 2005, the Columbia (South Carolina) City Ballet staged a beautifully choreographed performance entitled "Off the Wall and Onto the Stage: Dancing the Art of Jonathan Green." In this brilliantly conceived marriage of painting with music and dance, each dance selection either started or ended with a painting by African-American painter Jonathan Green, whose colorful paintings portray life among the Gullah people of coastal South Carolina. The Gullah people portrayed in Green's paintings, complete with meticulously replicated costumes, came alive on stage through the medium of ballet and modern dance. Thus, by combining the art forms of painting, dance, and music, audiences were able to experience a more complete image of the Gullah people and their rich cultural traditions.

Every society has a set of standards that distinguish between good art and bad art or between more and less satisfying aesthetic experiences. In some societies, such as our own, what constitutes good art is determined

This painting, *Sea Swing*, was one of many paintings by artist Jonathan Green which was combined with dance and music by the Columbia (SC) City Ballet in their 2005 performance entitled "Off the Wall and Onto the Stage."

largely by a professional art establishment comprising art critics, museum and conservatory personnel, professors of art, and others who generally make their living in the arts. Although other societies may not have professional art establishments, their artistic standards tend to be more democratic in that they are maintained by the general public. Thus, the decoration on a vase, the rhythm of a song, the communicative power of a dance, or the imagery of a painting are subject to the evaluation of artists and nonartists alike.

DIFFERENCES IN ART FORMS

As Chapter 2 pointed out, the term *primitive* has fallen out of fashion when referring to societies that are radically different from our own. When associated with art, however, the term has had greater staying power. Despite numerous attempts by some art historians to disassociate themselves from the term, it retains some legitimacy. This reluctance to eliminate the use of *primitive* was expressed in H. W. Janson's *History of Art:*

> Primitive is a somewhat unfortunate word.... Still, no other single term will serve us better. Let us continue, then, to use primitive as a convenient label for a way of life that has passed through the Neolithic Revolution but shows no signs of evolving in the direction of "historic" civilizations. (1986: 35)

This attitude about the "primitive" nature of non-Western art is reflected in the way such art is looked upon in Europe and the United States. For example,

Western art is displayed in museums and galleries with the name of the artist prominently featured. When we visit exhibitions of African or Polynesian art in Western museums, however, the artist is not identified by name. Instead, the viewer is given a rather elaborate description of where the piece comes from, the materials and techniques used to make it, the function it performs, how it might reflect other aspects of the local culture, and the name of the Western collector who purchased it. According to Sally Price (2001: 102–03), this practice of identifying the collector rather than the artist is a not-so-subtle way of saying that the value of the art object is determined more by who bought it than by who made it. Despite such attempts by art historians to perpetuate the use of the term *primitive*, it is not used in this book because of its misleading connotations of both inferiority and evolutionary sequencing. Instead, the term *small-scale* is used to describe egalitarian societies with small populations, simple technologies, and little labor specialization.

Having disposed of the term *primitive*, we can now proceed to look at some of the major differences in art forms between small-scale and complex societies (this discussion is developed in much fuller detail by Anderson [2003]). One difference stems from the general lifestyles and settlement patterns found in these logically opposite types of societies. Because small-scale societies tend to be foragers, pastoralists, or shifting cultivators with nomadic or seminomadic residence patterns, the art found in these societies must be highly portable. It is not reasonable to expect people who are often on the

© Layne Kennedy/Corbis

In complex societies, artistic standards are defined by full-time specialists such as philosophers, curators, art professors, and professional critics—many of whom are associated with institutions such as the Art Institute of Chicago.

move to develop an art tradition comprising large works of art such as larger-than-life sculptures or large painted canvases. Instead, art in small-scale societies is limited to forms that people leave behind on rock walls or cliffs or forms that they can take with them easily, such as performing arts (song, dance, and storytelling); body decoration, such as jewelry, body painting, tattooing, and scarification; and artistic decorations on practical artifacts such as weapons, clothing, and food containers.

Another significant difference between the art of small-scale societies and complex societies stems from their different levels of social differentiation (that is, labor specialization). As societies began to develop increasingly more specialized roles following the neolithic revolution (about ten thousand years ago), some segments of the population were freed from the everyday pursuits of food getting. The subsequent rise of civilizations was accompanied by the emergence of full-time specialists, such as philosophers, intellectuals, literati, and aesthetic critics, whose energies were directed, among other things, at distinguishing between good art and bad art. The standards of aesthetic judgment have become much more explicit and elaborately defined by specialists in more complex societies. To be certain, aesthetic standards exist in small-scale societies, but they are less elaborate, more implicit, and more widely diffused throughout the entire population.

A third major contrast arises from differences in the division of labor. As a general rule, as societies become more specialized, they also become more highly stratified into classes with different levels of power, prestige, and wealth. The aesthetic critics responsible for establishing artistic standards in complex societies are invariably members of the upper classes or are employed by them. Thus, art in complex societies becomes associated with the elite. Not only are those who set the standards

often members of the elite, but art in complex societies often is owned and controlled by the upper classes. Moreover, in some complex societies, art both glorifies and serves the interests of the upper classes. In contrast, because small-scale societies are more egalitarian, art tends to be more democratic in that all people have roughly equal access to it.

In addition to these three fundamental differences, we often see art in small-scale societies embedded to a greater degree in other aspects of the culture. To be certain, we can observe connections between art and, say, religion in our own society. But in small-scale societies, art permeates into many other areas of culture. In fact, because art is such an integral part of the *total* culture, many small-scale societies do not even have a word for art. That is, because art pervades all aspects of peoples' lives, they do not think of art as something separate and distinct. One such example, sand painting as practiced in Navajo culture, is as much religion, myth, and healing as it is art. According to Dorothy Lee, Navajo sand paintings are created as part of a ceremony that

> brings into harmony with the universal order one who finds himself in discord with it.... Every line and shape and color, every relationship of form, is the visible manifestation of myth, ritual and religious belief. The making of the painting is accompanied with a series of sacred songs sung over a sick person.... When the ceremonial is over, the painting is over too; it is destroyed; it has fulfilled its function. (1993: 13)

In some parts of the world, it is possible to see how the political system of a society can be reflected in its art. Anthropologist Christopher Steiner (1990) has shown how one form of artistic expression—body decoration—reflects the different political structures in Melanesia

The art form of sand painting among the Navajo of New Mexico is intimately connected to their traditional systems of healing and religion.

© Emil Muench/Photo Researchers, Inc.

and Polynesia. As mentioned in Chapter 8, a prominent form of political leadership in Melanesia is big men. In the absence of permanent political offices or hierarchies, big men earn their authority by working hard to attract a large number of followers. Because big men can lose their followers, the system of political leadership in Melanesia is a very fluid one, always subject to change. In Polynesia, on the other hand, leadership is based on centralized chiefdoms with permanent (usually hereditary) authority. The differences in political structure of these societies are reflected in their forms of bodily adornment. Melanesians decorate their bodies with paints—a temporary medium that can be washed away or lost in much the same way that a big man can lose his high status if he loses support of his followers. By way of contrast, Polynesians use tattoos, a permanent form of body art, reflecting the more centralized and permanent nature of political authority. Thus, to distinguish themselves from commoners, Polynesian chiefs use tattoos, a particularly appropriate form of body decoration that reflects both the high status and the permanency of their hereditary offices.

THE FUNCTIONS OF ART

To gain a fuller understanding of art, we must move beyond our working definition to an examination of the roles art plays for both people and societies. The very fact that artistic expression is found in every known society suggests that it functions in some important ways in human life. The two different approaches to functionalism taken by Malinowski and Radcliffe-Brown can be instructive for our analysis of the functions of art. As mentioned in Chapter 4, Malinowski tended to empha-

size how various cultural elements function for the psychological well-being of the individual. Radcliffe-Brown, in contrast, stressed how a cultural element contributes to the well-being or continuity of the society. Although we will examine the various functions of art for both the individual and society, Radcliffe-Brown's more structural approach will be emphasized.

Emotional Gratification for the Individual

Quite apart from whatever benefits art may have for the total society, it is generally agreed that art is a source of personal gratification for both the artist and the viewer. It would be hard to imagine a world in which people engaged only in pursuits that met their basic survival needs. Although people devote most of their time and energy to meeting those needs, it is equally true that all people derive some level of enjoyment from art because it provides at least a temporary break from those practical (and often stressful) pursuits. After the crops have been harvested, the African horticulturalist has time to dance, tell stories, and derive pleasure from making or viewing pieces of art. Likewise, as a diversion from their workaday lives, many Westerners seek gratification by attending a play, a concert, or a museum. No doubt, it was this personal gratification one derives from art that prompted Richard Selzer to comment that "art . . . is necessary only in that without it life would be unbearable" (1979: 196).

The psychologically beneficial functions of art can be examined from two perspectives: that of the artist and that of the beholder. For the artist, the creative process permits the release of emotional energy in a very concrete or visible way—that is, by painting, sculpting, writ-

CROSS-CULTURAL MISCUE

George Burgess, an art major at a Canadian university, invited Kamau, his Kenyan roommate, to his family home in Toronto for the Christmas holidays. While in the downtown area, George suggested that they go to the local art museum to see a new exhibition of abstract expressionists from the 1940s. While looking at an abstract painting by Jackson Pollock, Kamau asked George what it meant. George threw up his hands and said cheerfully, "That is the beauty of abstract art; it can mean anything you want it to mean." In a puzzled tone, Kamau inquired, "Then why did he make it?" George could not understand why Kamau didn't appreciate this classic piece of abstract expressionism.

George did not realize that different cultures have different ideas about what art is and what function it should perform. Art in Kenya, and in many parts of Africa, is much more public in nature than it is in North America. African artists tend to emphasize both conveying a message to the audience and demonstrating the function of the piece of art for the life of the community. In contrast, the Western artistic tradition that George was studying at the university places much more importance on the individual expressiveness and creativity of the artist. This cross-cultural misunderstanding occurred because Kamau failed to appreciate the highly individualistic nature of the artist in Western society, and George failed to understand the African tradition of the artist explicitly communicating to the audience.

ing a play, or performing an interpretive dance. Artists, at least in the Western world, are viewed as living with a creative tension that, when released, results in a work of art. This release of creative energy also brings pleasure to the artist to the extent that she or he derives satisfaction from both the mastery of techniques and the product itself.

From the perspective of the viewer, art can evoke pleasurable emotional responses in several important ways. For example, works of art can portray events, people, or deities that conjure up positive emotions. The symbols used in a work of art can arouse a positive emotional response. The viewer can receive pleasure by being dazzled by the artist's virtuosity. These pleasurable responses can contribute to the mental well-being of art viewers by providing a necessary balance with the stresses in their everyday lives.

However, it is also possible for art to have the opposite effect by eliciting negative emotions. The artistic process, if not successful from the artist's point of view, can result in increased frustrations and tension. Moreover, any art form is capable of eliciting disturbing or even painful emotions that can lead to psychological discomfort for the viewer.

Social Integration

In addition to whatever positive roles it may play for the individual, art functions to help sustain the longevity of the society in which it is found. As functionalist anthropologists remind us, art is connected to other parts of the social system. One need only walk into a church, synagogue, or temple to see the relationship between art and religion. Moreover, art has been used in many societies to evoke positive sentiments for systems of government and individual political leaders. In this section we will explore some of the ways in which art contributes to the maintenance and longevity of a society.

Through various symbols, art communicates a good deal about the values, beliefs, and ideologies of the culture of which it is a part. The art forms found in any given society reflect the major cultural themes and concerns of the society. To illustrate, prominent breasts on female figures are a major theme in much of the wood sculpture from West Africa. This dominant theme reflects a very important social value in those West African societies: the social importance of having children. Somewhat closer to our own cultural traditions, much of the art in Renaissance Europe reflected many of the religious themes central to Christianity. Thus, certain forms of graphic arts function to help integrate the society by making the dominant cultural themes, values, and beliefs more visible. By expressing these cultural themes in a very tangible way, art ultimately functions to strengthen people's identification with their culture by reinforcing those cultural themes.

The intimate interconnectedness of art and religious life is well illustrated in Bali (Indonesia), a culture with a long and rich tradition of dance and music. The large number of ceremonies that occur annually on the Bali-Hindu calendar involve elaborate displays and performances designed to attract the gods and please the people. Various life cycle events such as births and funerals are celebrated by special orchestras with music and dance. Some musical instruments, thought to be the gift of the gods, are considered so sacred that they can only be displayed, not actually played. According to one Balinese expert, "Music and dance are spiritual musts. The arts are an invitation for the gods to come down and join the people. There is a very physical contact with the unseen, with the ancestors . . . that makes the people in the village very happy" (Charle 1999: 28).

Art helps to strengthen and reinforce both social bonds and cultural themes. For example, cultural values are passed on from generation to generation using the media of song and dance. As part of the intense education in African bush schools, various forms of dance are used to teach proper adult attitudes and behaviors to those preparing for initiation. The role of music in education is well illustrated by Bert, Ernie, Kermit, and the other characters of *Sesame Street*, who sing about values such as cooperation, acceptable forms of conflict resolution, the fun of learning, and race relations. Music also can be used to solidify a group of people. Any history of warfare would be woefully incomplete without some mention of the role that martial music played to rally the people together against the common enemy.

Social Control

A popular perception of artists and their works in the Western world is that they are visionary, nonconformist, and often anti-establishment. Although this is often the case in contemporary Western societies, much art found in other societies (and indeed in our own Western tradition in past centuries) functions to reinforce the existing sociocultural system. For example, art can help instill important cultural values in younger generations, coerce people to behave in socially appropriate ways, and buttress the inequalities of the stratification system within a society. We will briefly examine several ways that the arts can contribute to the status quo.

First, art can serve as a mechanism of social control. Art historians generally recognize that art has a strong religious base, but they have been less cognizant of the role art plays in other cultural domains. A notable exception has been Roy Sieber (1962), an art historian who has demonstrated how wooden masks serve as agents of social control in several tribal groups in northeastern Liberia. It was generally believed by the Mano, for example, that the god-spirit mask embodied the spiritual forces that actually control human behavior. The death of a high-status man was marked by carving a wooden death mask in his honor. A crude portrait of the deceased, the death mask was thought to be the ultimate resting place of the man's spirit.

Through the medium of these pieces of art, the spirits were thought to be able to intervene in the affairs of the living. Specifically, the masks played an important role in the administration of justice. When a dispute arose or a crime was committed, the case was brought before a council of wise and influential men who reviewed the facts and arrived at a tentative decision. This decision was then confirmed (and given supernatural force) by one of the judges, who wore the death mask, concealing his own identity. Thus, in addition to whatever other functions these artistically carved masks may play among the Mano, they serve as mechanisms of social control within the criminal justice system.

Art also plays an important role in controlling behavior in more complex societies. In highly stratified societies, state governments sponsor art for the sake of instilling obedience and maintaining the status quo. In some of the early civilizations, for example, state-sponsored monumental architecture—such as pyramids, ziggurats, and cathedrals—was a visual representation of the astonishing power of both the gods and the rulers. Most people living in these state societies would think twice before breaking either secular or religious

This bronze head of Lenin, the largest in the world, located in the city of Ulan-Ude, Russia, is a piece of art commissioned by the communist government to evoke positive feelings about one of its founders.

rules when faced with the awesome power and authority represented in these magnificent works of art.

Preserving or Challenging the Status Quo

By serving as a symbol for social status, art also contributes to the preservation of the status quo. To one degree or another, all societies make distinctions between different levels of power and prestige. As societies become more highly specialized, systems of stratification become more complex, and the gap between the haves and the have-nots becomes wider. Power is expressed in a number of different ways throughout the world, including the use of physical force, control over political decisions, and accumulation of valuable resources. One particularly convincing way to display one's power is symbolically through the control of valuable items in the society. The accumulation of practical objects such as tools would not be a particularly good symbol of high prestige because everyone has some and because one hardly needs an overabundance of everyday practical objects to meet one's own needs. The accumulation of art objects, however, is much more likely to serve as a symbol of high prestige because art objects are unique, not commonly found throughout the society, and often priceless.

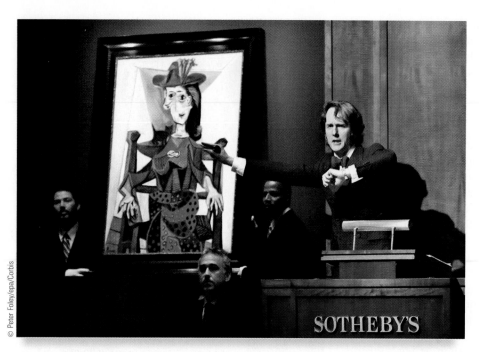

© Peter Foley/epa/Corbis

Picasso's "Dora Maar Au Chat" sold recently for $95 million at Sotheby's auction house. Because many pieces of western art bring very high prices, they can serve as very visible symbols of social status for the upper classes.

This association of art with status symbols is seen in many societies with ranked populations. For example, virtually all of the art in ancient Egyptian civilizations was the personal property of the pharaohs. The high status of the hereditary king of the Ashanti of present-day Ghana is symbolized by a wide variety of artistic objects, the most important of which is the Golden Stool. In the Western world, many public art galleries are filled with impressive personal collections donated by powerful, high-status members of society (Getty, Hirshhorn, and Rockefeller, among others).

Not only is art a force for preserving the status quo, it is often used in just the opposite way, as a vehicle of protest, resistance, and even revolution. There are a number of instances of artists who, through their own artistic media, attempted to raise the consciousness of their oppressed countrymen in order to bring about changes in the political and social structure. For example, Marjorie Agosin (1987) documented the case of the Chilean *arpilleristas* who told the story of political oppression on scraps of cloth. These courageous artists were considered such a threat to the established government that they were eventually banned in their own country. Also in Chile during the Pinochet regime, local artists painted murals under the cover of night depicting scenes of government oppression, only to have them removed by the military police the next morning.

Perhaps one of the most influential forms of art used for social change is what has come to be known as *liberation theater*. Based on the philosophies of Franz

Fanon, Eric Fromm, and Paulo Freire, liberation theater was started in the 1960s by Augusto Boal in Peru. Boal was one of the first to suggest that effective political theater (used to bring about change) should not focus on the plot, the dialogue, or the quality of acting, but rather on the involvement of the audience in the creation and the performance of the play itself. Boal developed the now-legendary method that he called the liberation theater workshop. Working with experienced theater people, oppressed people from local communities participate in workshops that may last for several days. Through a series of experiential techniques they are exposed to the language of theater, which includes elements such as body movement. Participants are then invited to write their own scenarios portraying oppression from their own lives, which are then acted out by professional actors. Only the oppressive scenario is acted out, not its resolution. After seeing the scenario played out, participants are then asked to offer possible resolutions to the scenarios, and if they wish, they may play it out themselves by taking over the role from the actor. Thus, through the medium of theater, Boal was training locally oppressed people to assume the protagonist role, offer solutions to the situation, and discuss strategies for change. As Boal (1979: 122) himself wrote, "The theater is not revolutionary in itself, but it is surely a rehearsal for the revolution."

Some works of art make strong political or social statements without being as overtly revolutionary as liberation theater. A recent (2004) work entitled "The Passion of Andy" by ceramic artist Russell Biles is a case in point. The work consists of five separate ceramic pieces portraying various characters from *The Andy Griffith Show*, a popular TV series from the 1960s. Andy Taylor (played by Andy Griffith) was the beloved sheriff

liberation theater A type of theatrical production using high levels of audience participation and aimed at bringing about social change.

This five-piece series entitled "The Passion of Andy" is one artist's commentary on contemporary U.S. society.

of Mayberry, a fictitious small town in the southeastern part of the United States, which was the epitome of small-town Christian values (faith, love, and compassion). Andy, the soft-spoken, sensible town sheriff who embodied the principle of "love thy neighbor," was the town hero and role model, because his faith in the inherent goodness of his neighbors always prevailed, even in adverse times. Artist Biles makes his twenty-first-century sociopolitical commentary by placing Mayberry characters in contemporary U.S. society.

According to Biles, "The virtues that once sanctified Sheriff Andy now instigate his downfall through the hands of misguided faith." The first of the five pieces (subtitled "Compassion") portrays characters Howard and Floyd, who have "come out of the closet," sitting for their same-sex wedding photo. The second piece (subtitled "Son of God") depicts the fatally wounded Sheriff Andy with his arms in "crucifixion" position being supported by his shocked deputy, Barney Fife. The shape of the bloodstain on Andy's shirt (near his heart) is vaguely reminiscent of the face of Christ, and his belt is unbuckled, representing the unleashing of the wrath of the Bible Belt. Andy, the metaphorical savior,

has been assassinated by an irate local who cannot forgive Andy his final act of love and compassion: performing the same-sex marriage of Howard and Floyd. In the third piece (subtitled "Vengeance and Grace") we find the lovable but anxiety-ridden Aunt Bee seated in an armchair with a lapful of empty prescription drug containers, clearly a political statement about the high cost of medicine for the elderly and the ineffective prescription drug legislation passed by Congress in 2004. Seated on the arm of Aunt Bee's chair is Opie with a revolver sticking out of his belt and an expression of determination to avenge the death of his father. The controversial war in Iraq is the subject of the fourth piece in the series (subtitled "Faith"), which portrays Gomer Pyle as a double amputee in a wheelchair being pushed by his cousin Goober, a staunch supporter of the war and an employee of Wal-Mart. And finally, the fifth piece (subtitled "Salvation") shows Mayberry's two most socially dysfunctional characters, Otis the town drunk and Ernest, who had occasional violent tendencies, seated on a park bench contemplating their salvation in the twenty-first century. Otis, now on the wagon, has become a painter of religious figures (such as Jesus and Andy) on black velvet, while Ernest is having his antisocial behavior controlled with mind-altering prescription drugs. The rehabilitation of both men is Biles's way of reminding the viewer that, as children of God, everyone is entitled to forgiveness and redemption. When these five pieces entitled "The Passion of Andy" (an obvious reference to the 2004 Mel Gibson film entitled *The Passion of the Christ*) are viewed together, they make a number of powerful social/political statements about how far American society of the twenty-first century is removed from the fantasy world of Mayberry of the 1960s.

Graphic and Plastic Arts

Graphic and plastic arts include a number of forms of expression and a wide variety of skills. Although the Western notion of *graphic* and *plastic arts* usually refers to painting, sculpture, print making, and architecture, the anthropological definition also includes such art forms as weaving, embroidery, tailoring, jewelry making, and tattooing and other forms of body decoration. In some societies, one form of art, such as wood carving, may be highly developed, and others, such as painting or metal-working, may be nonexistent.

The analysis of these art forms is further complicated because different cultures use different materials and technologies depending, in part, on what materials are available locally. Whereas Native Americans of the Northwest Coast are well known for their carvings of wood, other cultures may use horn, bone, ivory, or soapstone. In some small-scale societies, the nature of people's ceramic art is determined by the availability of locally found clays. Often the level of technology influences whether a culture uses metals such as gold, silver, and bronze in its art traditions.

Cross-Cultural Variations

Not only do different art traditions draw on different materials, techniques, and media, but the nature of the creative process can also vary cross-culturally. To illustrate, in the Western tradition, the practice of commissioning a piece of art is quite common. For a fee, portrait artists use their creative talents to paint realistic (and usually flattering) likenesses of their prominent clients. However, it is not likely that a client could commission an Inuit artist to carve a walrus from a piece of ivory. According to the Inuit notion of the creative process, that would be much too willful, even heavy-handed. Whereas the Western artist is solely responsible for painting the canvas or molding the clay in a total act of will, the Inuit carver never forces the ivory into any

uncharacteristic shapes. The Inuit artist does not create but rather helps to liberate what is already in the piece of ivory. Edmund Carpenter describes the Inuit's notion of the role of the artist:

> As the carver holds the unworked ivory lightly in his hand, turning it this way and that, he whispers, "Who are you! Who hides there!" And then: "Ah, Seal!" He rarely sets out to carve, say, a seal, but picks up the ivory, examines it to find its hidden form and, if that's not immediately apparent, carves aimlessly until he sees it, humming or chanting as he works. Then he brings it out: seal, hidden, emerges. It was always there: he did not create it, he released it; he helped it step forth. (1973: 59)

Of all of the various forms of art found in the world, the graphic and plastic arts have received the greatest amount of attention from cultural anthropologists. This is understandable because until recently the analysis of the plastic and graphic arts was the most manageable. Until the recent development of such data-gathering technology as sound recorders, motion pictures, and camcorders, analysis of music and dance was difficult. The graphic and plastic arts, however, produced objects that are tangible and can be removed from their cultural contexts, displayed in museums, and compared with relative ease. Moreover, a painting or a sculpture

© Nikreates/Alamy

Art comes in many forms, some utilitarian, others not. Here a man weaves a rug in Rajasthan, India.

graphic arts Forms of art that include painting and drawing on various surfaces.

plastic arts Artistic expression that involves molding certain forms, such as sculpture.

has a permanence of form not found in music, dance, or drama.

MUSIC

We often hear the expression "music is the universal language." By this people mean that even if two people do not speak each other's language, they can at least appreciate music together. But like so many popular sayings, this one is only partially true. Although all people do have the same physiological mechanisms for hearing, what a person actually hears is influenced by his or her culture. Westerners tend to miss much of the richness of Javanese or Sri Lankan music because they have not been conditioned to hear it. Whenever we encounter a piece of non-Western music, we hear it (process it) in terms of our own culturally influenced set of musical categories involving scale, melody, pitch, harmony, and rhythm. And because those categories are defined differently from culture to culture, the appreciation of music across cultures is not always ensured. To illustrate this point, Mark Slobin and Jeff Titon tell a story about a famous Asian musician who attended a symphony concert in Europe during the mid-nineteenth century:

> Although he was a virtuoso musician in his own country, he had never heard a performance of western music. The story goes that after the concert he was asked how he liked it. "Very well," he replied. Not satisfied with this answer, his host asked (through an interpreter) what part he liked best. "The first part," he said. "Oh, you enjoyed the first movement?" "No, before that!" To the stranger, the best part of the performance was the tuning up period. (1984: 1)

Ethnomusicology

The cross-cultural study of music is known as *ethnomusicology*, a new field involving the cooperative efforts of both anthropologists and musicologists (Nettl and Bohlman 1991). Although the field is quite young, ethnomusicology has made rapid progress lately because of the recent developments in high-quality recording equipment needed for basic data gathering. Slobin and Titon (1984) have identified four major concerns of ethnomusicology:

1. *Ideas about music:* How does a culture distinguish between music and nonmusic? What functions does music play for the society? Is music viewed as beneficial or harmful to the society? What constitutes beautiful music? On what occasions should music be played?

2. *Social structure of music:* What are the social relationships between musicians? How does a society

J. Harp/Robertstock.com

Ethnomusicologists would be interested in studying both the music of this Ukrainian andura player and how that music reflects the wider culture of which it is a part.

distinguish between various musicians on the basis of such criteria as age, gender, race, ethnicity, or education?

3. *Characteristics of the music itself:* How does the style of music in different cultures vary (scale, melody, harmony, timing)? What different musical genres are found in a society (lullaby, sea chantey, hard rock, and so on)? What is the nature of musical texts (words)? How is music composed? How is music learned and transmitted?

4. *Material culture of music:* What is the nature of the musical instruments found in a culture? Who makes musical instruments and how are they distributed? How are the musical tastes reflected in the instruments used?

As these areas of interest indicate, ethnomusicology is concerned with both the structure and techniques of music and the interconnections between music and other parts of the culture. Yet, during the course of cross-cultural studies of music, ethnomusicologists have been torn between two approaches. At one extreme,

ethnomusicology   The study of the relationship between music and other aspects of culture.

Avoiding Cultural Extinction Through Craft Industries

In recent decades, anthropologists have become increasingly concerned by the rapid disappearance of indigenous cultures through-out the world. Small-scale (indigenous) societies are facing mounting pressures from both government and industry to develop the areas they inhabit. In many cases, the land rights and human rights of people whose traditional lands are being bulldozed are being sacrificed to various development programs. Anthropologists have contributed their expertise to a growing number of advocacy organizations formed to protect and empower these vulnerable and largely marginalized cultural groups. One such organization, Cultural Survival, founded by anthropologist David Maybury Lewis, helps indigenous people gain title to their land and avoid exploitation by outsiders. By providing information and serving as advocates, Cultural Survival supports endangered groups by

helping them develop new sources of revenue, adapt to changing times, and shape their own futures (see Chapter 16 for more information).

One of the ways Cultural Survival empowers indigenous populations is by organizing local craft enterprises to revitalize indigenous crafts and generate much-needed cash for the local community. The Cultural Survival Tibetan Rug Weaving Project, founded in 1990, is an excellent example of such a craft project. The project's original goal was to generate funds for the half million Tibetan refugees living in India and Nepal. Since its inception, the Tibetan Rug Weaving Project has built and funded a school for refugee children in Nepal and two in India, sponsored food supplement programs for five refugee schools, funded the construction of a computer classroom in Nepal, and sponsored the shipment of two containers of text-

they have searched for musical universals—elements found in all musical traditions. At the opposite extreme, they have been interested in demonstrating the considerable diversity found throughout the world. Bruno Nettl describes this tension: "In the heart of the ethnomusicologist there are two strings: one that attests to the universal character of music, to the fact that music is indeed something that all cultures have or appear to have . . . and one responsive to the enormous variety of existing cultures" (1980: 3).

All ethnomusicologists—whether their background is in music or cultural anthropology—are interested in the study of music in its cultural context. Alan Lomax and his colleagues (1968) conducted one of the most extensive studies of the relationship between music and other parts of culture. Specifically, Lomax found some broad correlations between various aspects of music and a culture's level of subsistence. Foraging societies were found to have types of music, song, and dance that were fundamentally different from those of more complex producers. By dividing a worldwide sample of cultures into five different levels of subsistence complexity, Lomax found some significant correlations. For example, differences emerged between egalitarian, small-scale societies with simple subsistence economies and large-scale, stratified societies with complex systems of production (see Table 15.1).

These are just some of the dimensions of music that Lomax was able to relate to different types of subsistence. This monumental study, which required large samples and extensive coding of cultural material, was

open to criticism on methodological grounds. The difficulties involved in such an approach help explain why ethnomusicology has made considerably greater gains in the analysis of musical sound than in the study of the cultural context of music. Nevertheless, the efforts of Lomax and his associates represent an important attempt to show how music is related to other parts of culture.

DANCE

Dance has been defined as purposeful and intentionally rhythmical nonverbal body movements that are culturally patterned and have aesthetic value (Hanna 1979: 19). Although *dance* is found in all known societies, the forms it takes, the functions it fulfills, and the meanings attached to it vary widely from society to society. In some societies, dance involves considerable energy and body movement, whereas in other societies it is much more restrained and subtle. Because the variety of postures and movements the human body can make is vast, which body parts are active and which postures are assumed differ from one dance tradition to another. In some African societies (such as the Ubakala of Nigeria), drums are a necessary part of dance, whereas in others (such as the Zulu) they are not. Dancing alone is the

dance   Intentional, rhythmic nonverbal body movements that are culturally patterned and have aesthetic value.

books from the United States to Tibetan refugee schools in Nepal and India (Walter 2003).

From an aesthetic perspective, the Tibetan Rug Weaving Project consists of 250 designs that encompass traditional weaving patterns as well as some inspired by the modern world. In recent years, the Tibetan weavers have taken on an adjunct project called Gaon Naksha, whereby they create their own free-form, spontaneous designs representing their life experiences. Only the purest of hand-carded and handspun wool from Tibet is used in the project's rugs, and the dyes are all traditional vegetable dyes. Most of the rugs, which come in qualities ranging from 60 to 150 knots, are made to order.

In 1998, the Tibetan Weaving Project undertook its first project in Tibet itself, rather than working exclusively in India and Nepal where the refugees are located. By using proceeds from rug sales, the Tibetan Weaving Project initiated a reforestation project in eastern Tibet, which, as of 2004, had planted more than four hundred thousand seedlings and established extensive fruit orchards in the region. Thus, the Tibetan Weaving Project, sponsored by Cultural Survival, is helping to preserve Tibetan culture, both in Tibet and among the substantial Tibetan refugee population in India and Nepal.

Questions for Further Thought

1. Should anthropologists contribute their time, energy, and expertise to organizations like Cultural Survival, or should they try to remain neutral by focusing on basic research efforts?

2. What types of other crafts projects does Cultural Survival sponsor to help indigenous peoples maintain the integrity of their cultures? (Find the Cultural Survival website by using any search engine.)

3. By using the same website mentioned in question 2, explore issues of concern to Cultural Survival other than craft-related ones.

Table 15.1 Comparison of Music from Egalitarian Societies and Stratified Societies

Egalitarian Societies/Simple Economics	Stratified Societies/Complex Economics
Repetitious texts	Nonrepetitious texts
Slurred articulation	Precise articulation
Little solo singing	Solo singing
Wide melodic intervals	Narrow melodic intervals
Nonelaborate songs (no embellishments)	Elaborate songs (embellishments)
Few instruments	Large number of instruments
Singing in unison	Singing in simultaneous intervals

expected form in some societies, but in others it is customary for groups to dance in circles, lines, or other formations. Yet, whatever form dance may take in any culture, it remains a persuasive form of communication which blends body movements with both emotions and cognition. As Judith Hanna (2005: 11) reminds us, "Both dance and verbal language have vocabulary (locomotion and gestures in dance), grammar (ways one movement can follow another), and semantics (including symbolic devices and spheres for encoding feelings and ideas)."

Moreover, the relative value of dance as an art form varies widely from one society to another. To illustrate, the government of the small country of Cuba supports dance in a number of visible ways, making Cuba one of the great dance nations of the world. For example, Cuba is the venue for a number of important international dance festivals, and in fact, many world class dancers come to Cuba to study dance. The professional dancers of the Ballet Nacional de Cuba enjoy high status at home and international acclaim when performing abroad. And free dance education is available to any child from kindergarten through university. Now, compare this high level of public promotion of all forms of dance in Cuba with the situation just ninety miles to the north in the United States. The overwhelming majority of adults in the United States have never attended a fully staged ballet, a contemporary dance performance, or even a ballroom dance competition. Despite the fact that the physical conditioning required of professional dancers often exceeds that of other professional athletes, dance in the United States is generally thought of as a female, or an effeminate, profession. And despite the recent popularity of several reality-based dance shows on television (*Dancing with the Stars* and *So You Think You Can Dance*), an enormous amount of time and energy of

Dancers from the world renowned Cuban National Ballet rehearse at Madrid's Albeniz Theater. As an art form, ballet is taken much more seriously in Cuba than it is in the United States.

government officials (from the courts to officials in the National Endowment for the Arts) is expended trying to determine if certain dance forms are too sexual, involve too much nudity or semi-nudity, or if the distance between dance partners is inappropriately close (Hanna 2005).

Functions of Dance

As with other forms of artistic expression, the functions of dance are culturally variable. Dance is likely to function in a number of different ways both between and within societies. Dance often performs several functions simultaneously within a society, but some functions are more prominent than others. To illustrate, dance can function psychologically by helping people cope more effectively with tensions and aggressive feelings; politically by expressing political values and attitudes, showing allegiance to political leaders, and controlling behavior; religiously by various methods of communicating with supernatural forces; socially by articulating and reinforcing relationships between members of the society; and educationally by passing on cultural traditions, values, and beliefs from one generation to the next.

Dance and Other Aspects of a Culture

Lomax and his colleagues (1968) demonstrated quite graphically how dance is connected to other aspects of a culture. Specifically, their research shows how dance reflects and reinforces work patterns. By examining more than two hundred films, they were able to find a number of similarities between work styles and dance styles. The Netsilik Eskimos (Inuit) provide an interesting—and not atypical—example. For the Netsilik, dancing consists of solo performances that take place during

the winter in a large communal igloo. Lomax (1968: 226–227) describes the dance in considerable detail:

> One after another, the greatest hunters stand up before the group, a large flat drum covered with sealskin in the left hand, a short, club-like drumstick in the other. Over to the side sit a cluster of women chanting away as the hunter drums, sings, and dances. The performer remains in place holding the wide stance used by these Eskimos when they walk through ice and snow or stand in the icy waters fishing. Each stroke of the short drumstick goes diagonally down and across to hit the lower edge of the drum and turn the drumhead. On the backstroke it strikes the other edge, reversing the motion, which is then carried through by a twist of the left forearm. The power and solidity of the action is emphasized by the downward drive of the body into slightly bent knees on the downstroke and the force of trunk rising as the knees straighten to give full support to the arm on the upstroke. The dance consists largely of these repeated swift and strong diagonal right arm movements down across the body.

Many of the postures and motions found in Netsilik dance are the very ones that are necessary for successful seal hunting in an Arctic environment. The Netsilik seal hunter may wait patiently and silently for hours over a hole in the ice before a seal appears. When it does, the hunter's harpoon flies instantly and powerfully in a single stroke diagonally across the chest. Thus, the stylistic movements found in Netsilik dance are essentially identical to those found in their everyday hunting activities. The qualities of a good hunter—speed, strength, accuracy, and endurance—are portrayed and glorified in dance. In other words, as part of their leisure activity, hunters, through the medium of dance, re-dramatize the essentials of the everyday subsistence activities that are so crucial for their survival.

Another example of how dance is often combined with other aspects of a culture is *capoeira*, a combination of dance, acrobatics, and martial arts originating in the state of Bahia in Brazil. In the Brazilian city of Salvador, for example, capoeira is as popular a pastime among youngsters as basketball is for their inner city counterparts in New York, Philadelphia, or Chicago. This high-energy activity, which for Bahians is as much of a way of life as a recreational sport, has been described as "a fight like a dance (and) a dance like a fight" (Samuels 2001). Two capoeira "players" engage in spectacular high kicks, spins, cartwheels, and back flips, all the while coming within inches of each other's rapidly moving appendages and other body parts. Those players who fail to keep their heads up, their eyes open, and

capoeira   A combination of dance, martial arts, and acrobatics originating among Brazilian slaves of the sixteenth century.

their concentration focused on what they are doing are likely to have their heads pounded by someone else's rapidly and powerfully moving foot or hand. This stunningly frenetic form of movement is often accompanied by singing and chanting by capoeira group members, and by music from drums, tambourines, and a traditional stringed instrument called a *berimbau*.

It is generally believed that capoeira originated with the African slaves brought to Bahia by the Portuguese in the 1500s. Because these slaves were forbidden to fight or defend themselves, they developed capoeira as a surreptitious martial art disguised as a dance form. Some have suggested that the capoeira movements, whereby only the hands, feet, and head ever touch the ground, were developed so as to avoid dirtying the dancers' white religious clothing, very similar to the clothing worn by present-day capoeirista. While capoeira is both a dance form and a martial art, it involves strong emotional, mental, and spiritual dimensions as well. Always a group activity, capoeira is about dialogue, camaraderie, and bringing people together. Moreover, because it teaches discipline, self-esteem, and personal control, capoeira has been a source of self-confidence and inspiration for those descendants of slaves who continue to face poverty, violence, and discrimination in the twenty-first century.

Capoeira as an art form has received considerable attention in North America and indeed throughout the world. For example, the world renowned group, Dance Brazil, which combines capoeira with modern dance and the Samba, has played to appreciative audiences at Lincoln Center in New York and the Kennedy Center in Washington, D.C. And capoeira is gaining an increased presence among mainstream Americans as well. As Lauren Miller (2006: 28) reminds us, the dance form has appeared in feature length films such as *Lethal Weapon* and *Cat Woman*, commercials for Dockers and

the Mazda Protégé, and has even been incorporated into fitness programs offered by Crunch Gym. Moreover, for those interested in the serious study of capoeira, the tourist industry now offers an increasing number of packages designed exclusively to study the art form and attend authentic performances.

VERBAL ARTS

Creative forms of expression using words are found in all societies of the world. In Western societies—which place a great deal of emphasis on the written form—one might immediately think of the common literary genres of the novel, the short story, and poetry. Western societies also have a strong tradition of unwritten verbal arts, which are often subsumed under the general heading of *folklore*. In preliterate societies these unwritten forms are the only type of verbal art that exists. Although the term *folklore* is a part of everyday vocabulary, it has eluded a precise definition. Alan Dundes has attempted to define *folklore* by listing a number of forms that it might take. Recognizing that this is only a partial listing, Dundes includes the following:

> Myths, legends, folktales, jokes, proverbs, riddles, chants, charms, teases, toasts, tongue-twisters, and greeting and leave-taking formulas (e.g., see you later alligator). It also includes folk custom, folk dance, folk drama (and mime), folk art, folk belief (or superstition), folk medicine, folk instrumental music (e.g., fiddle tunes), folksongs (lullabies, ballads), folk speech (e.g., slang), folk similes (e.g., blind as a bat), folk metaphors (e.g., to paint the town red), and names (e.g., nicknames and place names).

Capoeira, a form of dance combined with acrobatics and martial arts, is a popular pastime in the Brazilian state of Bahia.

folklore   Unwritten verbal arts that can take a variety of forms, such as myths, legends, proverbs, jokes, and folktales.

Folk poetry ranges from oral epics to autograph book verse, epitaphs, latrinalia (writing on the walls of public bathrooms), limericks, ball bouncing rhymes, finger and toe rhymes, dandling rhymes (to bounce the children on the knee), counting-out rhymes (to determine who will be "it" in games), and nursery rhymes. The list of folklore forms also contains games, gestures, symbols, prayers (e.g., graces), practical jokes, folk etymologies, food recipes, quilt and embroidery designs, . . . street vendors' cries, and even the traditional conventional sounds used to summon animals or to give them commands (1965: 2).

This list is neither comprehensive nor exhaustive, but it does give us some idea of the wide range of verbal arts that have been, or could be, studied by cultural anthropologists. Even though we could focus on any of these forms of verbal art, our discussion will concentrate on the forms that have received the greatest amount of attention from anthropologists: myths, legends, and folktales.

Myths

As mentioned in Chapter 14, myths are specific types of narratives that involve supernatural beings and are designed to explain some of the really big issues of human existence, such as where we came from, why we are here, and how we account for the things in our world. In other words, they are stories of our search for significance, meaning, and truth.

The relationship between the artistic expressions of myth and other aspects of a culture is well illustrated by the myths of creation found among the Yanomamo of Venezuela and Brazil. According to Napoleon Chagnon (1983), the Yanomamo have two separate creation myths: one for men and one for women. Both myths illustrate two fundamental themes of Yanomamo culture: fierceness and sexuality. According to the myth of male creation, one of the early ancestors shot the moon god in the stomach with an arrow. The blood that dripped from the wound onto the ground turned into fierce men. The blood that was the thickest on the ground turned into the most ferocious men, and the blood that was more spread out turned into men who engaged in more controlled violence. Nevertheless, the fierceness of the Yanomamo people today is seen as a direct result of the early violence described in the male creation myth.

According to the other creation myth, which attempts to account for the beginning of Yanomamo women, the men created from the blood of the moon god were without female mates. While collecting vines, one of the men noticed that the vine had a wabu fruit attached to it. Thinking that the fruit looked like what a woman should look like, he threw it to the ground, and it immediately turned into a woman. The other men in the group, struck with intense feelings of lust, began

copulating frantically with the woman. Afterward, the men brought the woman to the village, where she copulated with all of the other men of the village. Eventually, she gave birth to a series of daughters, from whom descended all other Yanomamo women. This highly sexual account of the creation of women is certainly consistent with everyday Yanomamo life, for as Chagnon reminds us, "Much of their humor, insulting, fighting, storytelling, and conceptions about humans revolve around sexual themes" (1983: 94).

It is generally thought in the Western world that myths, such as those of the Yanomamo, are characteristic of small-scale, non-Western, preliterate peoples. The entire history of Western civilization, particularly since the Enlightenment, has witnessed what Belden Lane (1989) has described as a demythologization—a steady rejection of myth and illusion as we "progress" toward science, rationality, and critical insight.

Yet even the highly reason-oriented West is not without its mythology. How else can we account for the enormous popularity in recent years of the works of Joseph Campbell on mythology, the proliferation of seminars and books based on Jungian psychology, and such futuristic mythological figures as Luke Skywalker and Obi-Wan Kenobi? We continue to learn a great deal about living from myths, and indeed much of our scientific Western culture has been molded by the power of myth, an art form that continues to have relevance for both Western and non-Western societies alike.

Folktales and Legends

Other forms of verbal arts include legends and folktales, both of which are secular in nature, are set in the world after creation, and are instructive. *Legends* are told as if they were true, but often are only partially true or not at all true. They often attempt to explain the establishment of local customs, the movement of populations from one land to another, or the traits of folk heroes. The legend of George Washington confessing to having chopped down the cherry tree is an example of a well-known, and often told, legend in the United States. *Folktales*, by way of contrast, have no particular basis in history and exist largely for the purpose of entertainment.

Because most folktales have a moral, they play an important role in socialization. Particularly in societies without writing, folktales can be significant in revealing socially appropriate behavior. The heroes and heroines who triumph in folktales do so because of their admirable behavior and character traits. Conversely, people who behave in socially inappropriate ways almost

legends   Stories aimed at explaining local customs; legends may or may not be based on historical facts.
folktales   Stories from the past that are instructive, entertaining, and largely secular in nature.

always get their comeuppance. To illustrate, tales with very strong social messages are told to Dahomean children in West Africa around a fire (Herskovits 1967). Usually held at the compound of an elder, these story-telling sessions are designed to entertain, provide moral instruction for children, and develop the children's storytelling skills by encouraging them to tell tales of their own. Despite the very different settings, a story-telling session among traditional Dahomeans is quite similar to parents reading "Jack and the Beanstalk" or "Cinderella" to their children in front of the fireplace.

Folktales can be seen as an art form from two per-spectives. Like written works of literature, folktales are creative expressions that can be analyzed in terms of plot, character development, and structure, even though the original author or authors may have been long forgotten. In much the same way that literary critics have analyzed the structure and meaning of Western literature (such as poetry and prose), the literary and artistic structure of folklore in both complex and small-scale societies can be analyzed. For example, Dell Hymes (1977) has demonstrated how the folklore narratives of the Native American Chinooka people of Oregon and Washington were highly organized in terms of lines, verses, stanzas, scenes, and acts. According to Hymes,

> A set of discourse features differentiates narratives into verses. Within these verses, lines are differen-tiated, commonly by distinct verbs.... The verses themselves are grouped, commonly in threes and fives. These groupings constitute "stanzas" and, where elaboration of stanzas is such as to require a distinction, "scenes." In extended narratives, scenes themselves are organized in terms of a series of "acts." The elaborate structures of these folk narratives allow us to regard them and similar texts as legitimate works of art. (1977: 431)

In addition to the artistic structure, artistry is pres-ent in the telling and retelling of folktales. Even though the basic elements of the original tale cannot be changed, the tale teller retains the right to embellish and dramatize the story as he or she sees fit. The rhythm of the storyteller's utterances, the dramatic emotions expressed, and the use of nonverbal gestures all possess an artistic content of their own. Chagnon reminds us that in Yanomamo folklore a certain amount of artistry is involved in the telling:

> Some of the characters in Yanomamo myths are downright hilarious, and some of the things they did are funny, ribald, and extremely entertaining to the Yanomamo, who listen to men telling mythical stories or chanting episodes of mythical sagas as they prance around the village, tripping out on hallucinogens, adding comical twists and nuances to the sidesplitting delight of their audiences. Everybody knows what Iwariwa did, and that part cannot be changed. But how he did it, what minor gestures and comments he

made, or how much it hurt or pleased him as he did it is subject to some considerable poetic license, and it is this that is entertaining and amusing to the listener. (1983: 93)

Jokes and Humor

While it is true that there are no known cultures that lack a sense of humor, it is also true that what is laugh-able varies enormously from one culture to another. In some cultures, like the British and North American, humor is used in business meetings and, in fact, business presentations often start with a humorous anecdote. However, in other cultures, such as Germany or Japan, business is considered no joking matter. To illustrate, it is not unusual at international business conferences, particularly in Asia, to hear the interpreter say, "The American is now telling a joke. When he finishes, the polite thing to do is to laugh." Often jokes are told in an international business context when, in fact, it is inap-propriate to use humor in such situations. But, even if humor is appropriate, the meaning of the joke or humorous story is frequently lost because it doesn't translate well from one language to another.

Jokes are difficult to understand because they con-tain a good deal of information about the culture of the joke teller. In order to "get" the joke, the listener must understand these pieces of cultural information and how they are combined to make something funny. The long-standing joke in the United States about lawyers is a case in point. "Why do lawyers not have to worry about sharks when they vacation at the beach?" The answer: "Professional courtesy." In order to appreciate the humor, the listener would have to know several pieces of *cultural* information about the United States: (a) that sharks have been known to attack Americans while swim-ming, (b) that lawyers in the United States, like sharks, have the reputation of preying on people, and (c) that members of some professions in the United States give special considerations to other members of their profes-sion. And, assuming the listener did understand these culture-specific pieces of information, he or she would still need to appreciate the idea that people in the United States find humor in ridiculing an entire profession of people. Asians, however, with their strong tradition of Buddhism and Confucianism, place a high value on politeness and face-saving for others and would find little to laugh about in this type of sarcasm or parody.

Humor tends to be so culture-specific that it is usually a good entrée into understanding the culture of the joke teller. Jokes, in other words, tell you a good deal about what is valued in a particular culture. To illustrate, there is a contemporary joke in the United States about the attractive young woman who asks the old man, "Would you like super sex?" His response, "I think I'll take the soup," reflects the generally negative stereotypes that most Americans have concerning the

Anthropologist-Turned-Detective Finds Stolen African Statues

In 1985 Monica Udvardy, a cultural anthropologist from the University of Kentucky, was conducting field research among the Mijikenda people on the Kenya coast. During the course of her research, Dr. Udvardy took a photograph of a local man standing in front of two traditional wooden statues (known as vigango) erected to appease the ancestor spirits and to honor and protect his two deceased brothers. When anthropologist Udvardy returned several months later to give the man a copy of the photo, he told her that the two statues in the photo had been stolen and asked for her help in trying to locate them. Before leaving Kenya, Dr. Udvardy searched curio shops in some of the tourist oriented towns in hopes of finding the purloined statues, but never did located them.

Then, fourteen years later in 1999, while attending the African Studies Association meetings in

Philadelphia, Dr. Udvardy was startled to see one of the missing statues in a slide presentation given by Linda Giles on some of the artifacts from the Museum at Illinois State University. Anthropologist Udvardy, with the collaboration of Ms. Giles, then began to research how the statue made its long journey from the coast of Kenya to the museum at Illinois State University. In the process of their sleuthing, the two scholars tracked down 294 other vigango located in nineteen museums in the United States, among which was the second stolen statue from the 1985 photograph.

It was determined that most of these 294 vigango were brought into the United States by a single art dealer from Los Angeles, who claims to have purchased the statues legitimately from tourist shops in Mombasa, Kenya. He then sold these statues to private collectors and to

---

elderly; that is, that they have no interest in sex, are hard of hearing, or are so mentally diminished that they don't know the difference between soup and sex. While Americans like to joke about getting old, people from many parts of Asia, Africa, and South America have the highest regard for the elderly. Thus, any attempt to be funny at the expense of the elderly would not only be not humorous, it would be offensive.

So, here is yet one more reason why you should stay awake in anthropology class. Knowing something about the *art of humor*, wherever it may be found, requires that you know as much as possible about the cultural values, beliefs, and assumptions of the people telling the joke. Knowledge of other cultures is absolutely essential if we are to understand: (a) why people in other cultures are laughing, (b) what type of joke is appropriate in that culture, (c) what social situations are appropriate for a particular type of humor, and (d) when someone in another culture is laughing *with* you or *at* you.

FILM: A RECENT ART FORM

When Americans think of film as an art form, instinctively they imagine American filmmaking legends such as Steven Spielberg, Robert Altman, and Francis Ford Coppola. However, many countries in all parts of the world have long and rich traditions of filmmaking as an art form. For example, Ingmar Bergman in Sweden, Sergei Eisenstein in Russia, and Akira Kurosawa in

Igloolik Isuma/CTV/The Kobal Collection

The film *Atanarjuat: The Fast Runner,* by Inuit filmmaker Zacharias Kunuk, was shown in theaters around the world and received the award for "best first feature film" at the Cannes Film Festival in 2001.

Japan have all made a number of world-class films during the twentieth century. The continent of Africa (from Cape Verde to Cape Horn) as well possesses a rich tradition of filmmaking; since 1981 it has supported its own annual international film festival in Mogadishu, Somalia, exclusively for African films. The latest territory to receive critical acclaim for filmmaking is Nunavut, the new homeland of the Inuit people carved out of the landmass of Canada in 1999 (see Chapter 7). Up until the twenty-first century, the only connection between the Inuit people and filmmaking was Robert Flaherty's

museums for as much as $5,000 each. The most generous interpretation of the art dealer's behavior is that he had no idea of the cultural and religious significance of these vigango, which, he claims, he was buying and selling as nothing more than works of art. But no self-respecting Mijikenda adult would ever erect a statue to the spirits in honor of their dead relatives, and then sell it off for money. This would be as absurd as a person in the United States ripping the headstone from the grave of their deceased mother and selling it to get a little extra cash. Anyone who understands the cultural significance of vigango in Mijikendo society would immediately realize that such a statue, being sold in a tourist shop in Mombasa, would have had to have been stolen.

In February 2006, the National Museums of Kenya requested that museum officials in Illinois return the vigango to the original family owners in eastern Kenya. Since the original photograph, coupled with Dr. Udvardy's investigations, provided solid evidence that the statue had been stolen, museum officials agreed to return the supernatural statue to its rightful owners. Negotiations are under way with the Hampton University Museum in Virginia where the second stolen statue in the photograph presently resides. Here, then, is yet another example of how original anthropological fieldwork, along with years of sleuthing and investigating, has led to the solution of a real-life societal problem—namely, the return of stolen sacred objects to their rightful owners (Lacey 2006: 4).

Questions for Further Thought

1. Is this incident of stolen artifacts becoming part of a museum's permanent collection a rarity, or is it fairly common?
2. Should those museums that have vigango as part of their holdings return them to the Mijikenda people of East Africa?
3. Does the government of Kenya have a responsibility to prevent the sale and exportation of vigango statues or other similar spiritual artifacts?

documentary *Nanook of the North,* a silent film about the Inuit, made in 1922. Eight decades later an Inuit filmmaker named Zacharias Kunuk, using all Inuit actors and crew, made a feature-length film in the native language of the Inuit (Inuktitut). The film, *Atanarjuat: The Fast Runner,* while providing a great deal of ethnographic insights into traditional Inuit culture, is more than just another documentary about a vanishing way of life. Based on an ancient Inuit folk epic, *Atanarjuat* uses Inuit actors to tell a powerful and compelling story in the ancient words of their traditional language. Shot over a period of six months, the film captures the movement of the seasons, which so thoroughly influence Inuit daily life. Capturing on camera a number of different hues of black and white, Kunuk manages to reveal complex psychological motives behind the actions of his mythical characters, whose story up until now had always been conveyed in oral tradition. *Atanarjuat* won the "best first feature film" award at the Cannes International Film Festival in 2001, just two years after the founding of the Inuit self-governing territory.

While Hollywood studios have been making big budget films for decades, filmmakers in Mumbai, India (colloquially known as "Bollywood"), have made far more films than Hollywood over the decades and have won the hearts and minds of a much larger audience. Not only are Bollywood films devoured by a potential audience of a billion people at home, but also by the millions of overseas Indians living in the United States,

Aamir Khan Productions/The Kobal Collection/ Singh Sachdevc, Hardeep

Far more people see films made in Bollywood (India) than those made in Hollywood (California).

the United Kingdom, Europe, the Middle East, and elsewhere. These films have been dubbed into a number of different languages, including French, Russian, and Mandarin Chinese. They are watched by Iraqis and Iranians, Dominicans and Haitians, and even Pakistanis. In short, they provide the primary form of entertainment for probably half of the world's population.

The popularity of Bollywood films rests on their story lines, which have been called "pre-cynical" (Mehta 2004). Unlike their Hollywood counterparts that tend to be edgy and ambiguous when dealing with such topics

CROSS-CULTURAL MISCUE

Some anthropologists (Geertz 1973) have suggested that various forms of game playing can be considered as art forms. It has been argued that games such as baseball or football are a kind of art because they involve performances that combine the experiences of the performers and the audience. If we follow this line of thought, we can look at the "art of baseball" as it is performed in North America and in Japan.

In recent decades, an increasing number of Major League Baseball players from North America have signed contracts to play in Japan. Many unsuspecting American ballplayers think that if they can pitch, field, or hit a baseball effectively at home, they will be equally successful playing in the Japanese league. Although America's pastime is played according to the same rules in Japan, the values, attitudes, and behaviors surrounding the game as it is played in these two countries are worlds apart.

At the heart of the differences between baseball in these two cultures is the concept of *wa*, translated as "group harmony" (Whiting 1979). Baseball players in the United States—not unlike people in other sectors of American life—emphasize individual achievement. American ballplayers are constantly vying with one another for the most impressive set of statistics. Those with the best stats can demand the highest salaries. If management fails to meet their demands, the better players are likely to refuse to show up for spring training.

In contrast, Japanese ballplayers are expected to put the interest of their team above their own personal interests. Because it is assumed that the Japanese manager is always right, any disagreement with a manager's decision is a serious disruption of the team's *wa*. In the Japanese view, *wa* is the most important factor in having a winning team.

Robert Whiting documents a number of cases of North American ballplayers who had considerable difficulty adjusting to the radically different behavior expected on Japanese teams. Many Western ballplayers, despite their own personal success on the field, often found themselves being traded because their very individualistic (and typically American) behavior was seen as damaging the team's *wa*. The American players who have been successful in Japan have understood the importance of *wa*. Thus, if they want to perform well in the art of baseball, even these high-priced professional athletes will need to understand cultural differences.

and dance numbers. Even though many Americans have heard of these Indian-made films, few have actually seen one, unless they happen to be Indians living in the United States. For most Americans, these films are too corny, illogical, and Pollyanna-like for the coffee house crowd and certainly too sedate for American males, who prefer to watch things being blown up. Even though Indian films are very popular among the several million Indian-Americans living in the United States, it remains to be seen if Bollywood will make as much of an inroad into mainstream U.S. cinema as Indian engineers and computer scientists have made into Western technology industries.

ART: CONTINUITY AND CHANGE

Like all other aspects of culture, the various forms of expressive arts (graphic and plastic arts, music, dance, verbal arts) are subject to both internal and external forces of change. Anyone who has ever taken a course on the history of twentieth-century American art, for example, will know that unique schools of painting (with their own distinctive styles, materials, and themes) emerge, become prominent, and eventually die out and become part of history. To illustrate, the ashcan school (Edward Hopper, Arthur Davies) of 1908–1918 featured scenes of urban realism; the 1920s and 1930s witnessed the Art Deco style, characterized by straight lines and slender forms; abstract expressionists during the 1940s such as Jackson Pollock and Willem de Kooning emphasized spontaneous personal expression over more conventional artistic values; minimalism, popular in the 1950s, emphasized pure, simple, and reduced forms; and, finally, the pop art of Andy Warhol and Roy Lichtenstein used images from mass media, advertising, and popular culture in ironic ways. In the early centuries of American art, painting styles and approaches were relatively stable, often lasting a number of decades. In the absence of high-speed transportation and communication technology, different artistic traditions were not able to diffuse very rapidly. The late twentieth century, however, witnessed many more changes than occurred in the two previous centuries.

Rapid and dramatic changes occurred in the art world even before the term *globalization* became fashionable. Nowhere is this truer than in the area of glass sculptural art over the last forty-five years. In the early 1960s, advances in small furnace technology—along with the pioneering efforts of Harvey Littleton in the United States and Erwin Eisch in Germany—brought the art of glassmaking out of the factory and into the artist's studio. In a little more than four decades, many new techniques of glass blowing, casting, constructing, and lampworking diffused rapidly throughout the world.

American artist Dale Chihuly (see chapter opening photo) traveled to Venice in 1969, Venetian master Lino Tagliapietra traveled to the Pilchuk School of Glass

as love, family, and patriotism, Indian films are melodramatic and always celebrate true love, courage, devotion to country, and, above all, motherhood. Moreover, every Bollywood film is a musical lasting up to three and a half hours, with as many as a dozen "big production" song

outside of Seattle, and the influential Czech glass artists Stanislav Lebenski and Jaraslava Brychtova traveled all over the world. This frenzy of cross-fertilization since the 1960s has produced a worldwide art movement that now numbers more than five thousand studio glass artists. The Venetians, continuing their centuries-old tradition of glasswork, have produced new glass superstars such as Lucio Bubacco and Laura Diaz de Santillana; the long and rich Czech tradition of glass art, started by the late Stanislav Lebenski, is being carried on by Jan Frydrych, Petr Hora, Stepan Pala, and Zora Palova. In the United States, the torch first lit by Harvey Littleton has been passed to a new generation of world-class artists including Dante Marioni, William Morris, and Keke Cribbs. But glass art has also taken hold in other, less likely parts of the world. For example, world-class glass art is being made in Sweden (Bertil Vallien), England (Colin Reed and Tessa Clegg), Hungary (Zoltan Bohus and Maria Lugossy), Poland (Anna Skibska), Japan (Kyohei Fujita and Hiroshi Yamano), and Australia (Brian Hirst and Giles Bettison).

The growth of the glass art movement over the last four decades is noteworthy not only for its scale and global distribution, but also because of its prominence in the art world and in the marketplace. The Glass Art Society was formed in the United States in 1971, followed by the Japan Glass Art Society in 1972 and the British Artists in Glass in 1976. The 1970s and 1980s witnessed a substantial number of international glass conferences in England, Czechoslovakia, the United States, and Australia. Commercial galleries devoted exclusively to art glass began to appear in the early 1970s, and new publications emerged, including *Glass Art Magazine,* the *Corning Glass Review,* and *Neues Glas.* With the dissemination of this information about glass came a rapid and spectacular increase in demand for quality works of glass art. To illustrate, at the beginning of the twenty-first century, single pieces of glass art (which would fit on an ordinary end table in one's living room) by contemporary artists such as Lino Tagliapietra or William Morris sell for $60,000 and upward. Larger pieces by these same artists (such as Chihuly chandeliers or Morris's life-sized pieces from his "Man Adorned" series) retail for between $300,000 and $500,000 apiece.

The magnitude of the growth of the glass art field since the 1960s is perhaps most dramatically illustrated by one of the leading figures in the field, Dale Chihuly. In addition to being one of the pioneers behind the glass art movement, Chihuly has been the movement's visionary and entrepreneur for the past forty years. To illustrate, in 1996 Chihuly orchestrated "Chihuly over Venice," a festival that involved placing a number of his brilliantly colored chandeliers over the canals of Venice, as a symbolic gesture of appreciation for the five-hundred-year-old tradition of Venetian glass making. In the typical Chihuly style of international collaboration, these larger-than-life installations were actually

A sculpture entitled "Wolf Crest Hat," by Preston Singletary, a Native American glass artist.

fabricated in glass factories in Finland, Ireland, Mexico, Venice, and Seattle. Since his Venetian extravaganza in 1996, Chihuly has produced other major installations in cities around the world, for museums and corporate headquarters.

The possibilities in the twenty-first century for quick and widespread cultural diffusion, and the accompanying cross-fertilization of artistic traditions, are increasing. Art exhibits today travel around the world rather than remaining in galleries or museums for centuries on end as they did in the past. Similarly, in the area of music, both rock stars and symphony orchestras go on world tours, performing in front of audiences all over the globe. It is not unusual today for Celine Dion to perform in South Africa, the Chicago Symphony to perform in Bangkok, or the Dixie Chicks to perform in Copenhagen. And, it is not just Western music that is being exported and diffused to other parts of the world; there is considerable flow in the opposite direction. In recent decades we have seen recording artist Paul Simon collaborate with Ladysmith Black Mambazo, a singing group from South Africa, and Sting record fusion music with Cheb Mami from Algeria. Perhaps an even less likely union is the collaboration between Jaz Coleman, lead singer for the British rock group Killing Joke, and Maori singer and poet Hinewehi Mohi. According to anthropologist Renata Rosaldo, "Cultural artifacts flow between unlikely places, and nothing is sacred, permanent, or sealed off" (Jenkins 2001: 89).

Nowhere in the art world has this "flow between unlikely places" been more startling than in the recent merging of Muslim-American culture in the United States with the genre of hip-hop music. One such rap band from Chicago, MPAC, uses typical rapper dress (baggy pants and oversized T-shirts), hip-hop beats and instrumentation, and even the assertively confident strutting around the stage so characteristic of contemporary hip-hoppers. But their lyrics are strictly religious, focusing on the forgiveness of sins, proclamations of faith, and "there being no god but God." Curse words (or any type of off-color language) are absent, female concert-goers almost all wear head scarves, and soft drinks are sold, not alcohol. Thus, Muslim-Americans, through the medium of music, are developing creative ways of adapting to life in the United States, fusing with other cultures and traditions, and showing potential converts that Islam can be both empowering and cool (Abdo 2004).

Many cultures that used to be relatively isolated are today linked to the rest of the world through mass media, tourism, and the Internet. Some social scientists fear that today's fiercely competitive consumerism will quickly obliterate the various artistic traditions of many small-scale societies. As younger generations are exposed to different art forms from other parts of the world, there may not be a sufficient number of people to carry on the traditional art forms. Young people from Bolivia, for example, may be so enamored with Eminem or U2 that they will lose interest in learning how to play the traditional flute. To be certain, there is reason to be concerned that traditional art forms in small-scale societies may be globalized out of existence.

As was mentioned earlier in this chapter, the island of Bali, in Indonesia, has had a long and rich tradition of the performing arts that permeates the everyday lives of its citizens. Dance and music in Bali are interwoven into the total fabric of Balinese culture. Participation in the arts is so widespread in Bali that some observers have suggested that everyone in Bali is an artist. Although this is perhaps overstating the case, it would not be an exaggeration to say that most Balinese are influenced by the traditional forms of music and dance in Bali. And because Bali has become a hub of tourism in recent decades, it is feared that much of this traditional dance and music will be cheapened, or changed beyond recognition, by making it available to tourists. Expressing such fears more than a century ago, some nineteenth-century Dutch colonialists proposed making Bali an artistic museum so as to preserve its traditional art forms. Sukarno, the first president of Indonesia, considered Bali to be the center of Indonesian culture and took specific steps during his administration to protect it from tourism.

Although the vulgarization of these art forms would be disastrous, there is reason to believe that (perhaps because of its interconnectedness to other parts of the culture) these Balinese art forms have traditional resilience and staying power. Despite the fact that Bali is now the home of world-class hotels and its own Club Med, Balinese artists have always had a capacity to absorb features of other artistic traditions and make them their own. According to local legend, some elaborate (and sacred) musical instruments were introduced into Balinese society by foreign sailors as early as 1,200 years ago. This propensity to incorporate outside artistic themes and techniques into their own Balinese traditions is further explained by Indonesianist Suzanne Charle (1999: 28):

> The *kecak* dance—the "classic" monkey dance in which scores of men chant the syncopated rhythm— was, in fact, commissioned by Walter Spies, a German artist who lived here in the 1930s and based his dance on older Balinese forms. In turn, his kecak has been reworked time and again, most recently as "Body Cak," a wildly popular collaboration between . . . the director of the arts college and Keith Terry, a California artist.

In addition to this knack for collaboration, present day Balinese are making deliberate efforts to preserve their traditional arts. In precolonial times, Indonesian art was nurtured and sponsored by the royal palaces. After the ruling elites were deposed in 1949, traditional art forms, although somewhat repressed, survived the socialist regime of Sukarno and the chilling effects of the anticommunist government of Suharto.

Today, art supporters in Bali are stepping forward to ensure the survival of traditional art forms. Private art dealers are using their own money to fund public museums; world-class dancers, who have performed all over the world, are spending their retirement years teaching young children the intricacies of Balinese dance; and professors from the College of Indonesian Arts are documenting the rural dances that were near extinction, while their students are actually going to these remote regions of the country to study with the local dance masters. Thus, owing to both considerable flexibility and a strong desire to maintain their aesthetic traditions, it appears that traditional arts in Bali will remain intact well into the future.

And finally, sometimes new art forms or art institutions are diffused into a culture because they resonate with already existing cultural values. A case in point is the recent success of the TV show produced in Mumbai, India, called *Indian Idol*. Following closely the format of its predecessor, *American Idol*, the Indian show winnows out thirty thousand musical hopefuls to identify its finalists, all of whom compete for stardom and recording and film contracts. With its rapidly developing economy, rising middle class, and a long tradition of competition and entrepreneurialism, India is a likely country to embrace their own local version of *American Idol*. But, because India is also the world's largest democracy, many Indians believe that it is possible to become a star on merit and talent, because, after all, the winner is determined by a popular vote of the viewers, not some elitist group of musicians or media executives. Thus, *Indian Idol* has gained such large audiences precisely because it taps into a basic Indian sentiment: that democracy (the voice of the people) will trump elitism and favoritism and that talent will be recognized on its own merits, irrespective of family connections (Sengupta 2006: 4). ■

Summary

1. Although there is no universal definition of *art*, for purposes of this chapter we have defined *art* as the process and products of applying certain skills to any activity that transforms matter, sound, or motion into a form that is deemed aesthetically meaningful to people in a society. The creative process of making art should be enjoyable, produce an emotional response, be transformational, convey a message, and involve a certain level of skill on the part of the artist.

2. The forms of artistic expression discussed in this chapter include the graphic and plastic arts (such as painting, sculpting, and weaving), music, dance, and verbal art (such as myth and folklore).

3. Rather than using the term *primitive* to refer to certain types of art, we use the term *small-scale,* which refers to essentially egalitarian societies with small populations, simple technology, no written language, and little labor specialization. In contrast to the art found in small-scale societies, the art of more complex societies is more permanent, has more elaborate and explicit standards of evaluation, and is associated with the elite.

4. Art contributes to the well-being of both the individual and the society. For the individual, art provides emotional gratification to both the artist and the beholder. From a social perspective, various forms of art strengthen and reinforce both social bonds and cultural themes, promote social control, and serve as a symbol of high status, particularly in complex societies.

5. Ethnomusicologist Alan Lomax suggests that the music traditions found in small-scale societies differ from those of more complex societies in that the former are characterized by more repetitive texts, slurred articulation, little solo singing, nonembellished songs, few instruments, and singing in unison.

6. Like other forms of art, dance takes a number of different forms and functions. Moreover, dance is intimately connected to other aspects of culture, as illustrated by Brazilian capoeira, a dance form with ties to religion, martial arts, and social commentary.

7. Verbal art includes myths, legends, jokes, and folktales. Myths tend to involve supernatural beings; legends may be based on historical events; and folktales are secular in nature. Like other forms of art, the verbal arts are intimately connected to other aspects of a culture, as illustrated by the Yanomamo myth of creation.

8. Like all other aspects of culture, forms and styles of art change over time. Despite the Internet and the information revolution (which has accelerated the sharing of art across cultures), cultures do not appear to be surrendering their unique forms of artistic expression.

Key Terms

capoeira	folklore	legends	transformational
dance	folktales	liberation theater	
ethnomusicology	graphic arts	plastic arts	

Suggested Readings

Anderson, Richard L. *Calliope's Sisters: The Role of Art in Human Thought,* 2d ed. Upper Saddle River, NJ: Prentice-Hall, 2003. Examining such issues as the origin of art, the nature of art, and the role of art in human affairs, Anderson explores the philosophy of art in ten diverse cultures, including the San, Inuit, Yoruba, Aztec, and Japanese.

Dissanayake, Ellen. *Homo Aestheticus: Where Art Comes From and Why.* Seattle: University of Washington Press, 1995. A thought-provoking book that argues that art was central to human evolutionary adaptation. Drawing on her experiences in a number of different parts of the world, the author shows how song, dance, drama, and the visual arts help people define their cognitive world.

Hanna, Judith L. *To Dance Is Human: A Theory of Nonverbal Communication.* Austin: University of Texas Press, 1979. A comprehensive ethnological treatment of dance as a significant part of culture. It is particularly strong in drawing on various forms of dance throughout the world to illustrate how this artistic form functions within religious, political, and social institutions.

Hatcher, Evelyn P. *Art as Culture*, 2d ed. Westport, CT: Bergin and Garvey, 1999. An excellent introduction to the field of anthropology and art, this book looks at the correlation between the level of complexity of a culture and its art forms.

Lomax, Alan. *Folk Song Style and Culture.* Washington, DC: American Association for the Advancement of Science, 1968. A classic study of musical styles around the world and how they relate to other aspects of culture.

Nettl, Bruno, et al. *Excursions in World Music*, 3d ed. Upper Saddle River, NJ: Prentice-Hall, 2000. This excellent introduction to world musical traditions, which divides the world into ten major culture areas, examines such topics as musical styles, history, genres, social contexts, and instrumentation.

Titon, Jeff Todd, et al. *Worlds of Music: An Introduction to the Music of the World's Peoples.* New York: Simon & Schuster, 1996. An introductory survey of music in various parts of the world, including Native America, Africa, Indonesia, eastern Europe, Japan, and India. The book contains a number of case studies written by ethnomusicologists with firsthand knowledge of the music and culture of a number of peoples of the world.

Culture Change and Globalization

An early dawn view of the modern city of Hong Kong with a traditional Chinese junk in the foreground.

CHAPTER

16

ONE NEED NOT be a scholar of cultural change to notice that cultures have been changing more rapidly with each passing decade. In contrast to our hectic existence, the everyday lives of our grandparents seem simple and slow moving. Today, many people are overwhelmed by how quickly their cultures are changing. In 1971, Alvin Toffler coined the term *future shock*, which he defined as the psychological disorientation resulting from living in a cultural environment that is changing so rapidly that people feel they are constantly living in the future. In the first decade of a new millennium, Toffler's notion of future shock rings truer than ever before.

Cultural change occurs at such an accelerated pace today that it is often difficult to keep up with the latest developments. The recent revolution in transportation and electronic communications has made the world seem smaller. Today, it is possible to travel to the other side of the earth on an SST (supersonic transport airplane) in about the same time it took our great-grandparents to travel thirty miles using a horse and carriage. Via satellite we can view instant transmissions of live newscasts from anywhere in the world. Indeed, the global exchange of commodities and information is bringing the world's population closer to the notion of living in a global village. Because of this rapid and dramatic increase in our capacity to interact with people in other parts of the world, the likelihood of cultures diffusing (or spreading) has increased dramatically in recent decades.

This apparent shrinkage in the cultural world has led some observers to wonder whether the discipline of cultural anthropology will lose its subject matter. Such people argue that it will be just a matter of years before all of the cultures of the world have been homogenized into a single culture, leaving the discipline of anthropology without a field of study. If one takes a very traditional view of anthropology—the idea that its sole purpose is to document the cultural and biological features of isolated, indigenous people—then the future of the discipline indeed holds little promise. It is certainly true that exotic cultures (untouched by the modern world) are hard to find today.

In the twenty-first century, however, only a handful of cultural anthropologists are studying the quickly diminishing number of pristine cultures that continue to exist. The research interests and activities of the

What We Will Learn

- How do cultures change?

- What are some obstacles to cultural change?

- In what ways do civilization and industrialization threaten the cultures of indigenous populations?

- Do planned programs of economic development always benefit the local people?

- What is globalization, and how does it affect the cultures of the world?

▶ Click!

For interactive exercises and study aids, Go to **www.ichapters.com**; enter the author name and select your text, then click the Study Help tab to purchase the following online resources:

- **ThomsonNOW** for chapter-specific online tutorials, quizzes, and a personalized study plan

- **Anthropology Resource Center** for interactive maps, modules, videos, and the Applied Anthropology site

- **Thomson Audio Study Products** for a brief overview of the major chapter themes and to test your knowledge with quiz questions

discipline have adapted to the realities of a changing world. The fact that former food-collecting societies are now involved in market economies and consumerism should not lead us to conclude that all cultural differences are disappearing. Even though some of the obvious differences among cultures may be decreasing, there is little evidence to suggest that the world is becoming a cultural melting pot. Despite rapid cultural change, there will certainly be enough cultural diversity to keep anthropologists occupied well into the future.

In a very real sense, any ethnographic description of a specific group of people is like a snapshot at one particular time. If the ethnographer conducts a restudy of the same group five years later, it is likely that a number of cultural features will have changed. Some cultures (usually small-scale, preliterate, and technologically simple societies) tend to change slowly. Modern, complex, highly industrialized societies tend to change much more rapidly. Whatever the rate of change, however, we can be sure of one thing when dealing with cultures: nothing is as certain as change.

If we require proof of this basic maxim, we need only turn to the 1902 edition of the Sears, Roebuck mail-order catalogue, republished in 1969. Glancing through the pages, one is struck by the vast changes that have taken place in our material culture over the last century. Because of its comprehensiveness, the catalogue, in the words of Cleveland Amory, "mirrors the dreams and needs of Americans at a time when life was less complex than it is today" (1969: Introduction). In other words, it provides a near-total inventory of our material culture at the turn of a bygone century. Today, many items in the 1902 catalogue—such as horse-drawn plows, patent medicines, and high-top leather shoes—can be found only in museums. Other items in the 1902 edition still exist as part of our material culture but in drastically altered form, such as sewing machines, windmills, men's toupees, and lawn mowers.

We can learn much about the attitudes and values of our early twentieth-century ancestors from the material goods these people surrounded themselves with. For example, the catalogue advertised a substantial number of books on palmistry, astrology, and hypnotism. Many were "self-help" books that came in very handy in rural areas. Nearly a quarter of the book section was devoted to family bibles. Another dramatic illustration of the magnitude of changes that have occurred in U.S. culture is the three-page section devoted to the advertisement of corsets and bustles designed to rearrange or accentuate certain features of the female anatomy. On nearly every page of the catalogue, we are reminded of the vast cultural changes, both material and nonmaterial, that have occurred in U.S. society since the early 1900s.

As mentioned in Chapter 2, cultural change is brought about by both internal and external factors. Internal factors include inventions and innovations, and

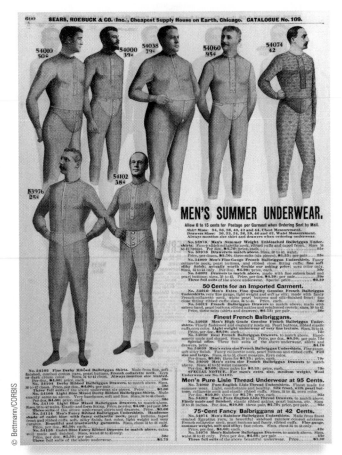

A page from the Sears catalogue advertising men's summer underwear during the early 20th Century.

external factors include cultural diffusion and borrowing. Although diffusion is responsible for the greatest amount of cultural change, it is important to examine both processes of change in greater detail.

INVENTIONS/INNOVATIONS

Any new thing, idea, or behavior pattern that emerges from within a society is an *invention*. Some inventions are very deliberate and purposeful, while others are unconscious and unintentional. Ralph Linton, one of the most prominent scholars of cultural change in the twentieth century, has suggested that over the long run, the unconscious inventor has had a greater impact on cultural change than has the conscious inventor. The unconscious or accidental inventor contributes to cultural change without being driven by an unmet societal need or even realizing that she or he is making a contribution. As Linton puts it, "Their inventions are, as a rule, of little individual importance, but they loom large in the aggregate" (1936: 311).

invention   New combination of existing cultural features.

These numerous unintentional inventors often go unnoticed and unrewarded, even though they may be making a very significant cumulative contribution to their culture. (An example of an unintentional invention—which actually had an important impact—was the scientist at 3M who, while trying to invent a very strong adhesive, failed and produced instead a very weak adhesive that was ideal for Post-it notes.) Most often, it is the deliberate, intentional inventor who is recognized and rewarded. From our own recent history, Eli Whitney was sufficiently motivated by the need to produce more cotton to invent the cotton gin, Jonas Salk discovered the polio vaccine to eradicate a crippling disease, and hundreds of other inventors have come up with new discoveries, gadgets, and ideas because they wanted to do something better or more efficiently.

There is a good deal of truth in the adage "Necessity is the mother of invention." Often, an invention is developed because there is a pressing need for it. Linton (1936) relates the case of an invention that occurred around the year 1900 on the island of Hiva Oa. A man from the neighboring Gilbert Islands took up residence on Hiva Oa, married a local woman, and became a fisherman. It soon became apparent to him, however, that theft of outrigger canoes was rampant on the island. Motivated by the desire to avoid having his own boat stolen, he invented a new type of outrigger canoe with a detachable outrigger. By removing the outrigger assemblage, he could safely leave the canoe on the beach unattended. Within a short time, this new detachable outrigger almost totally replaced the previous model because there was a perceived need for this particular invention.

For years, social scientists have tried to discover which people tend to become inventors or innovators. (It should be pointed out that innovation and invention are not the same thing, for it is possible to be an innovator without being an inventor. Innovators are the first people to adopt or use a new thing or idea.) Why do some people invent new things, ideas, and behavior patterns, whereas most do not? And once something is invented, why are some people quicker than others to adopt the invention? A number of interesting theories have been set forth. Some (Tarde 1903; Smith 1976; Rogers 1983) have suggested that both inventors and innovators tend to be *marginal people* living on the fringes of society. Not bound by tradition or convention, these marginal people can see problems and their solutions with a fresh perspective. Louise Spindler summed up this position when she noted that "Innovators are often 'marginal men,' who are, for a variety of reasons,

somewhat divorced from the core of their culture and thus more free to create" (1984: 15).

Everett Rogers's (1983) research suggests that innovators and early adopters are most likely to come from upper-class, wealthy, and well-educated segments of society. He goes on to speak of a basic paradox whereby the people who most need the benefits of an innovation are generally the least likely to adopt it. Rogers illustrates this paradox by looking at the adoption of contraception in developing countries. Citing his own research, Rogers (1973) notes that elite families, which already had small numbers of children, were the most receptive to using contraceptives, whereas lower-status (poorer) families, which averaged between five and six children apiece, were the most resistant.

Other theorists tend to take a more psychological approach by looking at the effects of child-rearing on innovative personalities. Everett Hagen (1962), for example, holds that innovators are most likely to come from families with excessively demanding fathers or from families with weak fathers and nurturing mothers. In his classic studies on achievement, David McClelland (1960) found that early training in the mastery of certain skills often leads to entrepreneurial success. As interesting as many of these theories are, we still lack a definitive understanding as to why some people are innovators and others are not. An idea may appear to be sound, a technological invention may appear to be efficient, or a new behavior may appear to make sense, and yet it will not be adopted by a particular group of people. The problem, of course, is that innovation is influenced by a multitude of variables—some social, some cultural, and others psychological—and certain variables are operating in some situations but not in others.

DIFFUSION

In addition to changing as a result of inventions and discoveries, cultures change through the process of cultural *diffusion*: the spreading of a thing, an idea, or a behavior pattern from one culture to another. As important as inventions and discoveries are to cultural change, the total number of inventions in any given society is generally quite small. In fact, Linton (1936) estimates that no more than 10 percent of all of the cultural items found in any culture—including our own—originated in that culture. If every culture had to rely solely on its own inventions, human progress over the centuries would indeed be slow. Cultures have been able to develop rapidly because the process of diffusion has enabled humans to pool their creative/inventive resources.

marginal people Non-mainstream people who are at the fringes of their own culture.

diffusion The spreading of a cultural trait (that is, material object, idea, or behavior pattern) from one society to another.

General Patterns of Diffusion

Because diffusion plays such a prominent role in cultural change, it is appropriate to examine this process in some detail. Even though cultural diffusion varies from situation to situation, a number of generalizations about the process are worth mentioning.

Selectivity

The process of diffusion is selective in nature. When two cultures come into contact, not every cultural item is exchanged between them. If that were the case, there would be no cultural differences in the world today. Instead, only a small number of cultural elements are ever diffused from one culture to another. Which cultural item is accepted depends largely on the item's utility and compatibility with already existing cultural traits. For example, it is not very likely that men's hair dyes designed to "get out the gray" will diffuse into parts of rural Africa where a person's status is elevated with advancing years. Even when an innovation is consistent with a society's needs, there is still no guarantee that it will be accepted. For example, most people in the United States have resisted adopting the metric system because they see no particular advantage to taking the time and effort to learn it. The societal benefit of adopting the metric system would be that U.S. citizens would be able to interface with the rest of the world more efficiently.

According to Rogers (1983), the speed with which an innovation is adopted—or whether it is adopted at all—usually is affected by whether it is seen to be superior to what already exists, is consistent with existing cultural patterns, is easily understood, can be tested on a trial basis, and has benefits that are clearly visible. This process of selective diffusion is evident in the area of religious ideas and practices. As mentioned in Chapter 14, in recent years a number of religions have experienced cross-pollination of ideas. One of the more popular Eastern religions in North America today is Buddhism. In many parts of the United States, Christians and Jews of all varieties are forming *sanghas,* or small communities, for the purpose of practicing Buddhist meditation. Even though the number of Jews and Christians engaging in certain Buddhist practices does not exceed a million people, the numbers are not insignificant. Most of them, however, have not embraced Buddhism totally. Most do not adhere to the complex and esoteric Buddhist theology but instead focus on certain techniques that aid concentration and relieve stress. For example, from Zen Buddhism, practiced most in Japan and China, North American adherents have taken meditation, breathing, and stilling the mind, whereas from Tibetan Buddhism they have adopted visualization and chanting. In a world that is becoming increasingly fast-paced and stressful, it is not surprising that Westerners are turning to those aspects of Buddhism that stimulate spirituality as well as provide relief from the tensions of everyday life. Thus, by accepting some aspects of Buddhism but not others, a growing number of Westerners serve to remind us that diffusion is indeed a selective process.

Reciprocity

Diffusion is a two-way process. We should not assume that cultural items diffuse only from technologically complex societies to simpler societies. The anthropological record from many parts of the world clearly shows that cultural traits are diffused in both directions. European contact with Native Americans is a case in point. Even though Europeans introduced much of their culture to Native Americans, the Europeans nevertheless received a number of cultural features in return, including articles of clothing such as ponchos, parkas, and moccasins; medicines such as quinine, pain relievers, and laxatives; and food items such as corn, beans, tomatoes, squash, yams, avocados, and the so-called "Irish" potato. Westerners tend to assume that most diffusion occurs from West to East. Yet, as Bestor (2000) reminds us:

> James Dean, baseball, Coca-Cola, McDonald's, and Disneyland have all gone over big in Tokyo. Yet Japanese cultural motifs and material—from Kurosawa's *The Seven Samurai* to Yoda's zen and Darth Vader's armor, from Issey Miyake's fashions to Nintendo, Playstation, and Pokémon—have increasingly saturated North American (and indeed the entire world's) consumption habits and popular culture.

Modification

Once a cultural element is accepted into a new culture, it may undergo changes in form or function. Pizza is a good example of how a cultural item can change form as it diffuses. Pizza, which diffused from Italy to the United States in the late nineteenth century, has been modified in a number of significant ways to conform to American tastes. It is unlikely that its Italian originators would recognize a pizza made of French bread, English muffins, or pita bread and topped with pineapple, tuna fish, or jalapeño peppers.

Sometimes the reinterpretation process involves a change in the way an item is used. While living in Kenya, this writer observed a stunning example of functional reinterpretation. The Maasai of Kenya and Tanzania practice the custom of piercing their earlobes and enlarging the hole by inserting increasingly larger round pieces of wood until a loop of skin is formed. Rather than using pieces of round wood for this purpose, one group of Maasai was observed using Eveready flashlight batteries obtained from the United States. In this case, the form of the batteries was the same, but the function definitely had been reinterpreted.

In some contemporary societies we see a partial diffusion of an item into another culture. For example,

The pizza pie has made a number of changes in form as it diffused from Italy to the Americas in the early 1900s.

The production of multimillion-dollar luxury yachts has been diffused to the PRC, even though they are not sold in that socialist country.

the Kingship Marine Company of southern China manufactures multimillion-dollar yachts for export but not for domestic consumption. Luxury personal yachts measuring several hundred feet in length have not been embraced by mainland Chinese for several reasons. Chinese, schooled as they are in outward modesty, are not attracted to conspicuous consumption. Also, with widespread tax evasion and dubious dealings for contracts, many of the new Chinese entrepreneurs do not want to bring attention to their wealth or their lifestyles. Moreover, cruising about the China Sea in a $12 million yacht is hardly in keeping with the communist ethic of "to each according to his/her need" (Bradsher 2004).

Likelihood

Some parts of culture are more likely to be diffused than others. As a general rule, items of material culture are more likely candidates for diffusion than are ideas or behavior patterns. For example, a traditional farmer in Senegal is more likely to be convinced of the advantages of using a bulldozer over a shovel for moving dirt than he is of substituting Shintoism for his traditional form of ancestor worship.

Variables

There is reason to believe that diffusion is also affected by a number of important variables: the duration and intensity of contact, the degree of cultural integration, and the similarities between the donor and recipient cultures. Although we know a good deal about the process of diffusion, social scientists are not able to predict with certainty when and where diffusion will take place.

ACCULTURATION

The concepts of diffusion and acculturation have some things in common; in fact, *acculturation* is a special type of diffusion that takes place as a result of sustained contact between two societies, one of which is subordinate to the other. Thus, both diffusion and acculturation involve cultural change as a result of contact with another group. But whereas diffusion involves a single trait or a complex set of traits, acculturation involves the widespread reorganization of one or both cultures over a short period of time. Both the dominant and subordinate culture may experience changes, but the subordinate culture always changes more dramatically. Acculturation can have a variety of consequences. The subordinate culture could become extinct, it could be incorporated as a distinct subculture of the dominant group, or it could be assimilated (blended) into the dominant group. But whatever form it may take, acculturation is *forced* borrowing under conditions of external pressure.

The extent of the external pressure put on a subordinate culture varies considerably from one accultura-

acculturation   A specific form of cultural diffusion in which a subordinate culture adopts many of the cultural traits of a more powerful culture.

tion situation to another. Some cultural anthropologists (Mead: 1956) have described situations of acculturation in which the subordinate culture has freely chosen to emulate the culture of the dominant society. At the other extreme, we find examples of excessive coercion, such as the Spanish conquest of Mexico, which involved the brutal exploitation of the local population by both the Spanish government and the Catholic church.

We should bear in mind that not all anthropologists agree on how to interpret the levels of coercion to which subordinate people are subjected. Some anthropologists (Diamond 1960; Bodley 1999) feel strongly that there is no such thing as voluntary acculturation. They hold that there are simply different degrees of force and coercion. As Stanley Diamond has stated, "Acculturation has always been a matter of conquest ... refugees from the foundering groups may adopt the standards of the more potent society in order to survive as individuals. But these are conscripts of civilization, not volunteers" (1960: vi).

At the "free choice" end of the spectrum are the Manus of the South Pacific as described by Margaret Mead (1956). When Mead first studied the Manus in the late 1920s, the people lived in stilt houses over the lagoons, had no system of writing, wore simple grass skirts, and lived in extended family groups. When she returned to restudy the Manus in the 1950s, Mead found a culture that was actively and intentionally seeking education and a place in the modern world. During the intervening quarter of a century, the Manus had been exposed to hundreds of thousands of American soldiers who had passed through the Admiralty Islands during World War II. The Manus had been exposed to large doses of American technology as well. The American armed forces had built roads, houses, and runways with the help of Manu labor. Mead claims that the Manus emulated the Americans not only because the Americans had an impressive array of technology but also because they treated the Manus with greater respect than had earlier contacts. So complete was the transformation

in a mere quarter of a century that Mead spoke of the Manus as having given up their old lives for new ones.

Whereas most previous studies of rapid cultural change had been quick to point out the deleterious effects on the affected culture, Mead's restudy of the Manus suggests that rapid cultural change need not be disruptive. Mead claimed that if the local people were willing participants in the change, the disruptive effects of change would be minimal, however rapidly the change might occur. Even though Mead may have overestimated the Manus' willingness to participate in the acculturation process and underestimated the disruptive effects on their lives, the Manus nevertheless serve as an excellent example of acculturation with little coercion.

Sometimes people voluntarily become acculturated because they believe that the adoption of certain technologies or behaviors will increase their adaptation to the environment. A case in point is the extensive cultural change that resulted from the rapid adoption of snowmobiles by the reindeer-herding Skolt Lapps of Finland. According to Pertti Pelto (1973), the first snowmobile was introduced into Finland in 1962, and nine years later fifty-eight of the seventy families under study (83 percent) owned at least one snowmobile.

Traditional Lapp culture had always placed considerable emphasis on transportation systems and mobility. The seminomadic Skolt Lapps had adapted to their

The Skolt Lapps adopted snowmobiles in the 1960s to help them become more efficient reindeer herders.

© Christophe Boisvieux/Corbis

CONTEMPORARY ISSUES

If You Really Want to Help Disaster Victims, First Understand Their Culture

On November 6, 1977, the dam above Toccoa Falls, Georgia, broke and sent a wall of water traveling at 120 miles per hour through the campus of the Christian and Missionary Alliance College located below the dam. Before the waters receded from the one-hundred-acre campus, thirty-nine members of the campus community had lost their lives. Federal disaster workers were quickly dispatched to provide assistance with housing, insurance claims, and trauma counseling. Although the survivors did avail themselves of the housing and insurance assistance, federal disaster relief personnel were stunned to find no interest in the psychological services offered by the grief counselors. Despite the enormous death and destruction suffered by the members of this religious community, the survivors were not suffering from post-traumatic stress disorders nor were they in need of grief counseling over the loss of friends and colleagues. Owing to their shared faith in god, survivors did not need psychological counseling to help them understand how god could have caused so much harm. Rather they were enveloped in love, gratitude, and optimism, because their friends and neighbors had now joined their maker. This surely was a time to rejoice rather than wallowing in one's own sense of personal loss.

© Philip Wallick/Corbis

As this scenario illustrates, some thirty years ago disaster relief personnel in Toccoa Falls failed to understand the basic religious beliefs of the people they were trying to help. Unfortunately, in the twenty-first century, well-meaning, but short-sighted, disaster relief workers are making the same culturally naïve decisions. Within days of the December 2004 tsunami in South Asia, American mental health workers were arriving in Sri Lanka and Indonesia offering counseling for the victims of post-traumatic stress disorder. They were operating on the assumption that people all over the world respond similarly to the traumas of war, torture, terrorism, and natural disasters. They never stopped long enough to ask themselves an absolutely basic question: that is, can well-intentioned outsiders provide meaningful assistance by providing counseling services in times of crisis? To be certain, tens of thousands of Sri Lankans were traumatized by the tsunami and its aftermath, but psychological counseling, either individually or in groups, is not the answer. People from many different cultures in the world are not best served by expecting them to engage in debriefing sessions aimed at expressing their emotions and reliving the trauma as vividly as they can. Disaster assistance personnel must first understand a number of things about the cultures of the victims they are attempting to serve, such as: What is their indigenous concept of mental illness? Who are the traditional healers in the community and what role do they play in restoring mental health? Is emotional self-disclosure even considered to be helpful for restoring mental health? And, if it is, to whom can one safely disclose one's emotions? And, what role do supernatural beliefs play in the mental health process?

It has been found that for people in many parts of the world—including Albanian Kosovars from the Balkan conflict and South Asians left homeless by the tsunami—Western-style therapy is not what the victims needed most. Like the residents of Toccoa Falls, Georgia, these disaster victims rejected therapy and instead appreciated much more such practical assistance as job training and housing. Whereas mental health practices in the West are based on confronting one's emotions through self-disclosure, such an approach has little meaning in some other cultures. If non-Westerners are grieving over the loss of family members, they feel that getting a job or having their house rebuilt is a far more effective antidepressant than talking about their grief to a total stranger.

Disaster relief organizations such as the International Red Cross, Oxfam, and FEMA (the Federal Emergency Management Agency) are Western bureaucratic organizations with clearly defined roles and statuses, values, and cultural assumptions. More frequently than not, these organizations provide disaster assistance to victim populations that have quite different values, beliefs, and cultural assumptions. In fact, the cultural differences between relief agencies and the people they serve may not only be different, but diametrically opposite in such areas as ways of coping with crisis, gender role relationships, linguistic style, dietary patterns, notions of privacy, supernatural beliefs, family relationships, and attitudes about accepting assistance. We cannot assume, in other words, that what constitutes an appropriate course of action from the agencies' perspective would necessarily be appropriate from the victims' perspective. Thus, in order to achieve maximum success in the delivery of disaster assistance, it is vital that relief organizations understand their own cultural assumptions as well as those of the people they are trying to help.

environment by maintaining two separate households: the nucleated villages, which they inhabited during the winter, and the calving and fishing grounds they inhabited during the spring. From these seasonal homesteads, the Lapp herders traveled intensively, rounding up their herds. Their concern with transportation as a key to successful adaptation was expressed in songs and folklore, in recreational activities (such as reindeer races), and in courting and marriage rituals. As Pelto reports, "Personal mobility, it was told to me again and again, is a main characteristic of the successful reindeer man: 'You have to be able to get around'" (1973: 55). Thus, it is not difficult to understand the fascination that the Skolt Lapps had with the snowmobile: it provided them with a technological quantum leap in efficient mobility. In the process of adopting the snowmobile for reindeer herding, however, the Skolt Lapps experienced far-reaching changes in both their technology and their sociocultural patterns.

LINKED CHANGES

Chapter 2 introduced the concept that cultures are more than the sum of their parts. Rather, cultures are systematic wholes, the parts of which are, to some degree, interconnected. If cultures truly are integrated wholes, it would follow that a change in one part of the culture would be likely to bring about changes in other parts. In other words, most changes that occur in cultures tend to be *linked changes*. The introduction of a single technological innovation may well set off a series of changes in other parts of the culture. This proposition can be illustrated by looking at one such innovation—television— which was introduced into U.S. society during the 1950s. When the TV set, a part of our technological system, replaced the radio as the major form of electronic communication in U.S. households, it had far-reaching consequences for other nontechnological parts of the culture, such as family interaction, the political process, and religious institutions.

Without question, the advent of television has altered the behavior of the American family. Before television became widespread, dinnertime provided an occasion for family members to have face-to-face interaction with one another. With the coming of television and the TV dinner, however, parents and children began spending dinnertime interacting with the "electronic cyclops" rather than with one another. Campaign politics has never been the same since the arrival of television. Whereas Truman and Dewey conducted their presidential campaigns largely from the back of railroad cars in 1948, subsequent candidates were brought into our homes via television advertisements and televised debates.

Today's candidates for public office need to pay as much attention to such variables as lighting, clothing, and makeup as they do to the substantive issues in the campaign. In the area of organized religion, evangelism has been greatly enhanced by television. One can legitimately question whether Billy Graham would have had such a lucrative ministry, Oral Roberts would have had a university named after him, or Jim Bakker would have served time in federal prison if television did not exist.

A more contemporary example of linked cultural changes is provided by the boom in cell phone usage that has occurred not only in the West but throughout the world. A mere fifteen years ago, anyone using a cell phone on the streets of Chicago would, in all likelihood, have been a wealthy investor who was calling his stockbroker on a mobile phone the size of a gallon container of milk. Today, however, it seems as though there are more people than not walking the streets of our cities with a mini-phone pressed to their ear. One change linked to the cell phone has been the increase in auto accidents caused by multitasking Americans wanting to make business calls or chat with friends while driving to work. This problem is being addressed by state laws prohibiting the use of handheld phones while driving, but two new problems have been identified in some urban areas in the United States: "pedlock" and "pedrage," pedestrian variations of traffic gridlock and road rage (Belson 2004). Accurate statistics are not available, but there is abundant circumstantial evidence to suggest that in some U.S. cities there has been a dramatic rise in automobile accidents caused by inattentive pedestrians talking on their phones. In fact, the New York City Department of Transportation has initiated alertness

The increased use of cell phones by inattentive pedestrians on busy streets has led to a significant rise in auto accidents.

linked changes   Changes in one part of a culture brought about by changes in other parts of the culture.

campaigns warning cell phone–toting pedestrians of the dangers of not paying attention when crossing the streets. In addition to the dangers involved, the sidewalks of cities such as New York are losing some of their civility. In pre–cell phone days, crowded rush-hour sidewalks were reasonably easy to navigate because most people were looking where they were going and were able to negotiate oncoming pedestrians or those wanting to pass. Today, however, with their minds elsewhere, cell phone–using pedestrians bump into other walkers, confuse others with their public conversations, and accidentally hit other pedestrians with their unrestrained hand gestures. These developments raise an important question: Just how aware are we of the negative social consequences of our signing a one-year contract with a cell phone company offering us five thousand "anytime" minutes per month?

OBSTACLES TO CULTURAL CHANGE

In every culture there are two opposing sets of forces: those promoting the status quo and those promoting change. At certain times the forces of conservatism are in control, but at other times the forces of change are in ascendancy. These two sets of forces are really two sides of the same coin. People are motivated to change their culture by a host of factors, including the desire for prestige, economic gain, or a new, more efficient way of solving a problem. There are also certain barriers to cultural change that are important to understand, particularly if one works as a change agent. Some of the more prominent change-retarding factors are discussed in the following sections.

Cultural Boundary Maintenance

An important mechanism for preventing cultural change is the creation and maintenance of *cultural boundaries* that distinguish people from the members of other groups. Sometimes these boundaries are physical to the extent that most or all of the people live in close geographic proximity. The more physically isolated a group is, the less susceptible it is to cultural diffusion. A culture does not need to be physically remote from other cultures, however, to avoid, or at least retard, cultural change. Rather, a culture can maintain its distinctiveness by imposing certain cultural boundaries that strengthen and glorify its own cultural traditions and discourage cultural borrowing from other groups. Aspects of culture such as language, eating habits, clothing, folklore, and humor are used to both emphasize a culture's uniqueness and to exclude outsiders.

cultural boundary maintenance The practice of cultural groups keeping themselves separate from other cultural groups.

CROSS-CULTURAL MISCUE

The scene is a small grocery store operated by a Korean couple in a predominantly African-American neighborhood in Los Angeles. David, a thirty-two-year-old African-American father of three, enters the store, as he has many times in the past, to buy a quart of milk. He greets the proprietor, Mr. Kim, with an enthusiastic "What's happening?" and proceeds to strike up a conversation with Mr. Kim. David inquires about Mr. Kim's family, tells him a slightly "off-color" story, and is generally quite willing to share with the store owner various details of his own life. During David's monologue, however, Mr. Kim says hello but remains quiet and seemingly uncommunicative. As he is leaving the store, David can't help thinking how unfriendly, impolite, and perhaps even racist Mr. Kim seems to be.

Here again is yet another example of a cross-cultural misunderstanding brought about by two radically different communication styles (see Chapter 6 for a more detailed discussion of linguistic style). African-Americans and Korean-Americans have very different ideas as to how to communicate politeness and respect. According to Benjamin Bailey (1997), Koreans engage in "restraint politeness," which involves respecting other people's privacy by remaining low-key, quiet, and non-intrusive. African-Americans, by way of contrast, engage in what Bailey calls "involvement politeness," wherein the best way to show respect is by engaging other people in conversation, asking questions, bantering, and generally showing interest in their lives. Thus, because both men failed to understand these vital differences in communication style, David interpreted Mr. Kim's "restraint politeness" as rude and unfriendly, while Mr. Kim interpreted David's "involvement politeness" as loud, boisterous, and disrespectful of his privacy. This unfortunate cross-cultural encounter (which is played out daily between African-Americans and Korean-Americans in Los Angeles) could have been avoided had David and Mr. Kim been familiar with some of the basic research literature from the field of anthropological linguistics.

Language

Perhaps no other part of culture is more unique to a group than its language. As discussed in Chapter 6, language is more than merely a system for sending and receiving messages. It is also highly reflective of a people's ethos or worldview. In other words, language is an embodiment of the people's values. If a group of people want to remain culturally separate, the way to do it is to use their own language exclusively, forbid the use of other languages, and discourage outsiders from speaking their language. Perhaps the most dramatic expression of linguistic exclusiveness takes the form of battles

The sharing of food and eating habits are a cultural barrier to contact with other cultural groups.

revolving around national language policy. The selection of Hindi in India or Swahili in Tanzania as a national language can be seen as an attempt to assert a particular cultural tradition while excluding others. Closer to home, the Quebec language law and the recent referendum on establishing a French-speaking state are examples of the use of language as a mechanism of cultural boundary maintenance.

Clothing

In large part because of its high visibility, clothing is another important symbol of group identity used to distinguish "us" from "them." To maintain their own unique cultural identity, people (particularly when away from home) are likely to wear their own ethnic or national dress. Africans wearing brightly colored kente cloth, Kuwaiti men wearing a headdress (*ghotra*) and white robe (*thobe*), or American motorcycle riders wearing black leather jackets are all expressing their cultural identity. Sometimes feelings run high about the meanings conveyed by ethnic dress. For example, a man from the Swiss-German section of Switzerland who was married to a German woman refused to allow his seven-year-old son (who was half German) to wear *lederhosen*, a distinctive type of leather pants from southern Germany, because he wanted to make sure that everyone would recognize his son as Swiss and not German (personal communication).

Eating Styles and Food

Eating customs are another critical dimension of ethnicity that can serve as a cultural barrier to contact with other groups. In most cultures, if not all, eating is a highly social activity. What foods are eaten, in what manner, how often, and particularly with whom are all factors that vary from one culture to another. Every culture uses the sharing of food in one way or another to maintain social ties and group solidarity. A good illustration is Hindu India, where people are strictly forbidden from eating with members of other castes. In some societies the communal aspects of eating are emphasized to a far greater degree than they are in the United States. For example, Amharic speakers from Ethiopia not only eat food from a common basket but on special social occasions will actually put the food into one another's mouths rather than in their own. Moreover, by creating and maintaining certain food taboos, cultures set themselves apart from other cultures that do not recognize such prohibitions.

Relative Values

Sometimes people resist changes in their culture because the proposed change is not compatible with their existing value system. Change agents (such as overseas development workers or Peace Corps volunteers) often fail to understand why some people are so resistant to certain changes and don't seem to comprehend the advantages of the change. People from a particular culture may refuse to participate in an agricultural improvement project not because they do not understand the likely outcome of the project but because the change would bring about a situation that would be less desirable (according to their values) than the status quo.

An example of relative values serving as a barrier to cultural change comes from South America (Ferraro 2006: 165). A U.S. timber company harvesting wood in a remote area of the rain forest was experiencing difficulties recruiting labor from among the local Indian communities. In an attempt to attract laborers away from its main competitor (a German company), the U.S. firm invested heavily in housing for its employees, offered considerably higher wages than its competitor, and guaranteed the workers a salaried forty-hour work week (the Germans paid their workers by the hour). Yet despite these economic advantages, the majority of workers continued to work for the German firm. The explanation for this apparently irrational behavior on the part of the Indian workforce is that what might be valued by workers in Detroit is not what appeals to Indian workers in the South American rain forest. For the Indian workers, flexibility of their time was more important than housing or high wages. Under the system used by the German firm, which paid an hourly wage rather than a forty-hour-per-week salary, the workers were able to take time off to participate in festivals and ceremonies without fear of losing their jobs.

Cultures as Organic Wholes

The functional interrelatedness of the parts of culture—as discussed in the preceding section—serves as a conservative force discouraging people from cultural change. After a number of generations of adapting to their environments, many small-scale societies are in a state of equilibrium. That is, solutions to most societal problems have been worked out (albeit imperfectly), and a balance of social relationships has been established between various members of the group. To change one part of such a culture is likely to threaten existing social and economic relationships. To illustrate, Alan Beals (1962) cites the classic case of Gopalpur, a village in South India, which for centuries has used farming techniques that do not produce high yields. The introduction of modern technology, pesticides, chemical fertilizers, and modern irrigation systems would, in all likelihood, lead to increased agricultural productivity. But by adopting these new farming techniques, the local farmer would jeopardize significant social and economic relationships. As Beals explains:

> At every step, the farmer wishing to improve his agricultural practices must weigh the claims of the new method against the known economic and social benefits of the traditional method. To purchase improved agricultural equipment, the farmer must sever his traditional relationship with the Blacksmith and Carpenter. This is more than an economic relationship. Not only are the Carpenter and Blacksmith neighbors and friends, but they have religious functions that make their presence essential on such occasions as births, marriage, and death. (1962: 79)

As Beals demonstrates, accepting changes in one part of a culture (such as agricultural technology) is likely to bring about undesirable changes in other parts of the culture (such as social and religious relation-

ships). By refusing to adopt new farming technology, the rural farmer is not necessarily reacting in an ultraconservative way but instead is taking a broader view of the situation.

CULTURAL SURVIVAL OF INDIGENOUS PEOPLE

In recent years, cultural anthropologists have become increasingly concerned with a particular type of cultural change—namely, the rapid disappearance of indigenous populations of the world. An *indigenous population* refers to a group of people who (a) are original inhabitants of a region, (b) identify with a specific, small-scale cultural heritage, and (c) have no significant role in the government (see Bodley 1999: 4). Classic examples of indigenous people are the small-scale cultures in Asia, Africa, and the Americas that came under the influence of the colonial powers during the past several centuries.

Many anthropologists are concerned about the survival of these indigenous people not because they form the subject matter of much anthropological research, but because their disappearance raises some basic human rights issues. A growing number of cultural anthropologists feel strongly that indigenous populations over the past several centuries have been negatively affected by the onslaught of civilization. Cultural patterns—and in some cases the people themselves—have been eradicated as a direct result of civilization's pursuit of "progress" and economic development.

indigenous populations The original inhabitants of a region who collectively wield little political power, and whose cultures and ways of life are threatened by the forces of economic development.

AP/Wide World Photos

If the Shasta Dam, located in Northern California, is elevated by 18 feet (as proposed), the last remaining sacred sites of the Winnemem Wintu Indians will be destroyed.

The industrial revolution in nineteenth-century Europe was "revolutionary" to the extent that it led to explosions in both population and consumerism, which in turn had drastically negative effects on indigenous people. The technological efficiency of the industrial revolution resulted in a quantum leap in population growth. To illustrate, before the industrial revolution it took 250 years for the world's population to double, whereas by the 1970s it took only thirty-three years (Bodley 1999). At the same time that populations were exploding in the industrializing world, there was a corresponding growth in consumerism. If economies were to grow and prosper, production had to be kept high, which could be accomplished only if people purchased and consumed the products of industry. In order to meet the needs of a growing population with ever-increasing desires to consume, people needed to control and exploit natural resources wherever they might be found.

A major motivation for the colonization of the non-Western world was economic in that the natural resources found in Asia and Africa were needed to fuel European factories. The so-called scramble for Africa, which was initiated when the leaders of Europe set national boundaries in Africa at the Conference of Berlin in 1884, was thought to be a "civilized" and "gentlemanly" way of dividing up the continent's natural resources for the industrializing nations of Europe. Unfortunately, the rights of indigenous populations were not protected. In many cases, land and resources needed by the indigenous people were simply appropriated for use by the colonial powers. Landless populations were forced to become laborers, dependent on whatever wages the colonial governments and businesses wished to pay. Native resistance to this systematic exploitation was usually met with force. In some cases, large segments of the population were killed directly or died

from European diseases. In other less severe situations, indigenous people were economically exploited, systematically kept at the lowest echelons of the society, and forced to give up their land and traditional identities.

Specific examples of the demise of indigenous populations are all too common in the literature (Burger 1987; Bodley 1999). The tragic annihilation of the population of Tasmania in the nineteenth century is one of the more dramatic examples. Through the use of military force and heavy-handed missionary efforts, not only was the aboriginal culture of Tasmania eliminated, but the people themselves were literally exterminated, many by deliberate killings, because the White settlers wanted the land for sheepherding. Similarly, around the turn of the nineteenth century, the Germans administered their "protectorate" in southwest Africa (currently Namibia) on the principle that native populations should give up their land for European use. When the indigenous Herero people refused, the Germans made good on their threats to wage a war of extermination, justifying their military actions on the basis of social Darwinism and White supremacy.

But we need not go to the far corners of the earth to find tragic examples of the exploitation of native people. The litany of atrocities committed against Native Americans in the name of progress and manifest destiny dates back to the earliest European settlements. The massacre of the Pequot in Connecticut in 1637 and the massacre of the Sioux at Wounded Knee in 1890 are just two examples from U.S. history. More recently, examples of the demise, or potential demise, of indigenous cultures in the United States are far less violent but devastating nevertheless. To illustrate, a small tribe of 125 Native Americans currently are threatened with having their last remaining ancestral land flooded by a proposed expansion of the Shasta Dam in northern California. The Winnemem Wintu Indian tribe is no stranger to having their lands swallowed up in the name of water conservation. When the Shasta Dam was first constructed in the 1930s, Winnemem ancestral lands along the McCloud River were lost to the reservoir. Some 183 corpses were exhumed from their traditional graveyard and reburied, while tribal members watched their homes being destroyed. The plan now is to elevate the height of the dam by eighteen feet, thereby inundating most of the remaining twenty sacred tribal sites. If even one site is destroyed, the symbolic circle of connection between it and the remaining nineteen sites will be broken, which would make the practice of Winnemem religion difficult at best. The project, if approved, is not scheduled to begin until 2010, but the loss of their remaining ancestral sites would deprive the tribe of one of its major mechanisms for maintaining its tribal identity. One enterprising Winnemem, an ardent opponent of the proposed dam expansion, is making and selling T-shirts to his fellow tribesmen with the inscription "Homeland Security: Fighting Terrorism Since 1492" (Murphy 2004).

Anthropologists believe that the Brazilian Amazon shelters the largest segment of the world's remaining isolated populations. In recent years, the most dramatic examples of the degradation of indigenous people have come from this area, where Indians are being swept away by the relentless movement of colonialism and economic development. To illustrate, during the 1960s, an Indian village in Brazil was attacked by a gang of gunslingers allegedly hired by a large Brazilian corporation that wanted the Indians off the land. Shelton Davis (1977) described the Massacre at Parallel Eleven, in which hired hit men attempted to wipe out the village and its inhabitants by throwing dynamite from a low-flying airplane. During the 1970s, the threats to indigenous people, though not quite so blatantly genocidal, were no less devastating. By building roads through the Amazonian frontier, the Brazilian government introduced diseases such as influenza and measles to the indigenous people of the region. By the beginning of the 1990s, tens of thousands of gold prospectors had invaded the territory of the Yanomamo, extracting millions of dollars' worth of gold from the land and leaving the Yanomamo ravaged by disease. In a feeble attempt to protect the indigenous Yanomamo, the Brazilian government ordered the destruction of 110 airstrips built by the gold miners on Yanomamo land. But the miners circumvented the government's efforts to destroy their airstrips by using helicopters, which do not require landing strips—an indication of just how difficult it is to protect indigenous people from the onslaught of the industrial world (Brooke 1990).

Cultural anthropologists have not only been documenting the demise of indigenous people, but many have also been using their specialized knowledge to help these endangered cultures survive. In one of the most urgent forms of applied anthropology, a number of cultural anthropologists in recent years have contributed to the efforts of Cultural Survival, Inc., a nonprofit organization based in Cambridge, Massachusetts, that supports projects on five continents designed to help indigenous people survive the changes brought about by contact with industrial societies.

Founded in 1972, Cultural Survival works to guarantee the land and resource rights of tribal people while supporting economic development projects run by the people themselves. As part of their work with Cultural Survival, cultural anthropologists have conducted research on vital cultural issues, served as cultural brokers between the indigenous people and government officials, and published literature informing the public about the urgency of these survival issues. To help support its work, Cultural Survival holds semi-annual bazaars in Cambridge selling high-quality arts and crafts made by the indigenous people they are trying to protect. Given the ever-increasing number of indigenous populations that are facing cultural extinction—including the Ju/'hoansi of southern Africa, the Sherpas of Nepal,

and the Kurds in the Middle East—it is likely that cultural anthropologists will continue to apply their expertise to help these people avoid cultural extinction. (For a detailed description of one of Cultural Survival's projects, see the Applied Perspective on "Avoiding Cultural Extinction Through Craft Industries" in Chapter 15.)

CHANGE AND DEVELOPMENT

Today's world can be roughly divided into two broad categories of countries: the haves and the have-nots. This dichotomy is sometimes characterized as the industrialized versus the non-industrialized world or the developed versus the undeveloped. There is considerable disagreement as to the reasons for these differences, but no one can deny the vast differences in material wealth between the richest nations (such as Canada, Switzerland, the United States, and Japan) and the poorest nations (such as Chad, Mozambique, Ethiopia, and Bangladesh). In terms of comparative income, Canada's per capita income is 170 times higher than Mozambique's, and the average U.S. citizen earns approximately 178 times more money as the average Ethiopian. Enormous disparities can also be seen in non-economic measures. To illustrate, the life expectancy is seventy-seven years in Norway but only forty-seven years in Burkina Faso. The infant mortality rate in Mali is 168 per one thousand live births, whereas in Finland it is only 6.

How did the modern world become so uneven in terms of economic development? A number of social scientists have offered differing interpretations, but they usually boil down to one of two competing theories.

The income of the average Canadian is 170 times greater than that of this man from Mozambique, Africa.

One broad theory explains these vast differences in economic development in terms of the inherent sociocultural differences found between the rich and the poor, the developed and the undeveloped. Often called *modernization theory*, this model is based on a dichotomy of traditional versus modern that serves not only as an attempted description of reality but also as a planning strategy for bringing about economic development in undeveloped nations. The modern nations are associated with high levels of technology, industrialization, urbanization, formal education, efficient bureaucratic governments, strong market economies, precise reckoning of time, religious pluralism, low birth and death rates, upward mobility based on merit, rapid change, planning for the future, and a decline in the extended family. Traditional nations, on the other hand, have fewer of these characteristics. This modernization theory assumes that in order for undeveloped nations to become developed, they must engage in activities that would make them more like the developed nations. In short, they need to become more modern. The process of economic development would occur through the mechanism of foreign aid from the wealthy nations to the undeveloped nations.

The modernization theory includes many of the same assumptions as the *culture of poverty* notion set forth by Oscar Lewis (1966). Some groups, Lewis argued, remain poor because they are crippled by certain cultural features, passed from generation to generation, that perpetuate poverty. The only way to break the cycle of poverty is to change their culture (that is, their ideas, values, material possessions, and behaviors). In other words, this theory blames poverty on the poor by suggesting that some countries are poorly developed because of their cultural characteristics, which they pass on to their children.

The other major theory regarding the disparities between rich and poor has been called the *world systems theory*. According to this theory, the rich and poor nations of the world are not fundamentally different because of innate cultural features but rather because of how they have operated within the world system. The wealthy countries of the world have achieved high levels of development by exploiting other regions, plundering their natural resources, using their people as cheap sources of labor, and dominating their markets. As mentioned previously in this chapter, in 1884 at the Conference of Berlin, European powers carved up the entire continent of Africa. The French took large parts of west Africa; the British controlled Nigeria, the Gold Coast, Kenya, Uganda, and the Rhodesias; the Portuguese got Angola and Mozambique; and the tiny country of Belgium took control of the mineral-rich Congo, an area seventy-six times larger than itself. These nineteenth-century industrializing nations of Europe used these colonies for their plantations and mining operations, exploited cheap African labor, exported some of their own excess populations to the colonies, and then sold many of their finished products back to the Africans they claimed to be helping.

Whereas Europeans actually took political control over their colonies, the United States chose to establish commercial influence through its corporations, mostly in Central and South America. Whether we are talking about corporate imperialism or outright colonialism, however, the consequences were the same. The exploitation of people and resources by the dominant powers impeded economic growth of the subordinate nations. Thus, according to the world systems theory, economic development is not the result of an enlightened or progressive population but instead occurs when one group purposefully increases its own wealth at the expense of others.

As we begin the twenty-first century, the period of colonialism has all but ended. Spain and Portugal relinquished control over their South American colonies in the nineteenth century. The 1960s witnessed large numbers of African colonies winning their independence. However, turning over the reins of government to local people has not necessarily resulted in complete autonomy. By a process known as *neocolonialism*, the wealthy (former colonial) nations continue to exercise considerable political, economic, financial, and military power over the less developed nations. By virtue of their economic dominance, the industrialized nations control the international markets of the commodities they buy from the *less developed countries (LDCs)*. That is, the industrialized world determines the price on world markets of Ghanaian cocoa, Bolivian tin, and Kenyan coffee. The wealthier nations also lend capital to the less developed nations, which has the effect of turning them into perpetual debtors. Debt can be a major form of control, with the

---

modernization theory   The theory that explains economic development in terms of the inherent sociocultural differences between the rich and the poor.

culture of poverty   An interpretation of poverty that suggests that poor people pass certain cultural features on to their children that tend to reinforce and perpetuate poverty.

world systems theory   An attempt to explain levels of economic development in terms of the exploitation of the poor by the rich nations of the world, rather than in terms of innate socioeconomic characteristics of each.

neocolonialism   The economic, political, and military influence that developed nations continue to exert over less developed countries, even though the official period of colonization ended in the 1960s.

less developed countries (LDCs)   Countries that have a relatively low gross national product (GNP) and low annual family income.

These Vietnamese Buddhist monks walk past a huge inflatable
Pepsi can in Ho Chi Minh City. Many multinational corporations,
such as PepsiCo, have more assets than the countries in which
they operate, which gives them enormous control over those
governments and their economies.

creditors calling many of the shots. Moreover, with the
debtor nations obliged to pay considerable interest payments, they never seem to have enough surplus capital to
invest in building their own economic infrastructure.

The maintenance of the wide gap between rich and
poor nations is also caused by the increasing power and
influence in recent years of *multinational corporations*. In
some cases multinational corporations directly exploit
LDCs, as with the Firestone Rubber Company in Liberia
or the United Fruit Company in Central America. More
often, however, multinational corporations tend to exploit LDCs simply by doing business as usual. These
multinational corporations have assets and power that
far exceed those of most of the governments of the de-

multinational corporations   Large corporations that have
economic operations in a number of different countries
throughout the world.

veloping world. To illustrate, approximately one-third
of the world's assets are controlled by the hundred
largest multinational corporations. More specifically,
the revenue generated by Wal-Mart (United States) is
roughly equivalent to the GNP of Belgium; British Petro-
leum (United Kingdom) is the size of Denmark's; and
Mitsubishi (Japan) generates revenues roughly the size
of Israel's GNP. Put yet another way, General Electric
Corporation (with capital assets roughly equivalent to
the GNP of Thailand) has more assets than more than a
hundred different independent countries in the world
today. Any single multinational corporation may engage
in a wide variety of commercial activities, including transportation, manufacturing, and advertising. No matter
how they make their profits, one thing is certain: most
of the corporate profits go back to the home country
rather than staying in the developing nation. Furthermore, when a multinational manufacturing firm decides
to open a plant in another country, you can be certain
that it will exert considerable influence over the government of that country.

The modernization approach to economic development suffers from several ethnocentric assumptions.
First, modernization theorists assume that all people in
the world ought to gladly embrace all of the economic,
cultural, and social changes inherent in "becoming
modern." Second, proponents of modernization theory
clearly overestimate the extent to which some non-
Western people resist modernization, in large part because they ignore the many creative adaptations these
people have made for centuries. Third, and perhaps
most important, modernization theorists assume that
traditional people will be better off if they become modern. Because becoming modern is progressive, it is
thought, it must be good. Modernization theorists assume that the advantages of becoming modern—such as
increased income, better health, and a higher standard
of living—are universally beneficial. Even though becoming modern also involves giving up one's traditional
culture, modernization theorists see it as a small price to
pay in exchange for the obvious benefits. We now consider this last point in greater detail.

The present debate in development anthropology
revolves around the question of whether raising income
levels and standards of living always has a positive effect
for all parties concerned. Modernization theorists would
answer this question affirmatively, but a number of studies over the past several decades have strongly suggested
that economic growth and development do not always
improve people's lives. Some have even suggested that
economic progress (as defined by rising wages, increased
GNP, and so on) actually has lowered the quality of life for
many non-Western people. Despite the best intentions of
international development agencies, multimillion-dollar
foreign aid projects have often resulted in greater poverty,
longer working hours, overpopulation, poorer health,
more social pathology, and environmental degradation.

APPLIED PERSPECTIVE

Environment and Development in Central Honduras

Anthropologists have been involved in economic development projects sponsored by national and international organizations for decades. Unlike most other social scientists involved in development projects (economists, political scientists), cultural anthropologists contribute grassroots knowledge about the end-users of the development schemes. Problems facing development projects such as reforestation, agricultural reform, educational programs, or disease control are as likely to be sociocultural as technological. Over the decades, successful projects have taken into consideration the sociocultural realities of the people whose lives are to be "developed." And conversely, it is likely that many projects have failed because of insufficient attention to local cultures, languages, and social relationships.

© Michel Szulc-Krzyanowski/The Image Works

The field of development anthropology has been around long enough to know, in general terms, what works and what does not when designing programs of planned change. It would be overstating the case to suggest that an anthropologically informed project that takes into consideration local cultural realities is bound to succeed. But it

would not be unreasonable to hold that any project ignoring local cultures is very likely to shoot itself in the foot. It is, therefore, stunning to read about a development project initiated in the 1990s that completely avoided addressing the major issues of development anthropology. Applied anthropologist William Loker (2000) describes a $25 million project in Central Honduras designed (allegedly) to create sustainable development while at the same time protecting the environment.

The El Cajon Watershed Renewable Natural Resource Program was designed to help very poor people who had been displaced a decade earlier by the construction of a large dam controlled and operated by the national electrical authority. Although the planning documents said all of the right things, the implementation was quite another story. First, because there was no anthropological input, the project administrators knew little about the local culture, attitudes, or local organizations. Project plans called for active participation by local people and close coordination with local nongovernmental organizations (NGOs). Yet, owing to a lack of interest, a lack of

Contrary to conventional thinking, many of the anticipated benefits of economic development have turned out to be illusory or downright detrimental. Attempts to engage non-Western people in programs of planned economic development often result in an increase in diseases in several significant ways. First, many of the new, more modern lifestyles that people adopt result in a marked increase in diseases associated with the industrialized world. For example, Charles Hughes and John Hunter (1972) and Ian Prior (1971) found that rapid cultural change was followed by dramatic increases in diseases such as diabetes, heart disease, obesity, hypertension, gout, and high blood pressure in areas where these conditions previously had been unknown. Second, certain bacterial or parasitic diseases tend to increase precipitously in areas experiencing rapid cultural change. To illustrate, the construction of dams and irrigation systems in the Sudan as part of the Azande development scheme created ideal breeding conditions for the snail larva that causes schistosomiasis, one of Africa's most deadly diseases. And third, health problems in the developing world are further aggravated by the rapid urbanization that often accompanies economic development. People crowding into cities looking for employment receive greater exposure to contagious diseases, which are made even worse by poor nutrition and unsanitary living conditions.

Programs of economic development often lead to people making changes in their dietary habits. In some cases, these dietary changes are voluntary to the extent that some new foods, associated with powerful outsiders, are status symbols. But more often than not, dietary changes occur because of circumstances associated with the objectives of the economic development that are beyond the control of the local people. For example, in an attempt to develop more cash crops (which help to raise wages and bring in foreign exchange capital), non-Western people often divert time and energy from growing their normal subsistence crops. The result is that they spend much of their hard-earned cash on foods that are both costly and nutritionally inferior in order to feed their families.

This was the case among Brazilian farmers who had changed from growing food crops to growing sisal, a cash crop used in making rope (Gross and Underwood 1971). Although they were spending most of their income on purchasing food, they were unable to provide adequate nutrition for their families. The study showed that the children of sisal workers were particularly at risk because most of the food went to the adults in order to maintain the strength needed for their strenuous work. Daniel Gross and Barbara Underwood showed how the children of sisal workers, owing to their caloric deficiencies, experienced slower growth rates in

good information, or both, neither of these proposed goals was successfully carried out.

But perhaps even more damaging to this expensive, but potentially beneficial, project was the apparent lack of consideration for some basic issues of development. The dual objectives of the project—sustainable economic development for local people *and* protecting the environment—are often at odds with each other. The literature is filled with examples of how conflicts exist between economic development and protecting the environment, yet program planners never addressed this issue or its implications for project activities. Instead of considering how environmental and development goals could be made compatible, administrators embarked on a tree-planting project without considering its potential effects on the social or natural environment. After interviewing the forestry engineer responsible for carrying out the tree-planting project, Loker discovered that the most basic questions had not been answered. For example, what trees should be planted, by whom, and for what purpose? How should trees be integrated into the already existing agricultural system? On whose land should the trees be planted, and who will own them? The fact that none of these questions had been answered prior to the start of the project indicated to Loker a shameful lack of forethought about the project on the part of the administrators.

Experience shows that if environment/development projects such as this one in Honduras are to be successful, the local people and their institutions must be understood, appreciated, and built into the fabric of the program. After all, it is the local people for whom the project is designed to provide economic benefits, and it is these very same people who will interact with the environment, leading to positive or negative outcomes. Yet the lack of anthropological involvement in all stages of this project (planning, implementation, and evaluation) was a glaring oversight. As Loker concludes, "Haven't they read Murray's (1987) article on reforestation in Haiti?" (Murray's highly successful work on reforestation in Haiti was discussed in Chapter 4.)

Questions for Further Thought

1. What were the two primary goals of the El Cajon Watershed Renewable Natural Resource Program in Honduras?
2. Is it possible to promote economic development without harming the environment?
3. What would the planners of this poorly executed project have learned had they read about the work of Gerald Murray in Haiti (see the Applied Perspective in Chapter 4 of this book)?

their physical development. In addition to physical retardation, improper nourishment can lead directly to a reduced mental capacity and a lowering of one's resistance to infection.

Not only do people who are caught up in economic development often eat less food, but they also eat food that is worse for them than their traditional diets. Often these foods, purchased rather than homegrown, are low in minerals, vitamins, fiber, and protein while being high in sugar, sodium, and saturated fats. The lack of vitamins and minerals leads to increases in nutritionally related diseases and the lack of protein causes kwashiorkor (protein malnutrition), the leading cause of death in Africa and other parts of the developing world. The marked increase in sugar consumption by non-Western people has led to a rapid and dramatic deterioration of dental health (Bodley 1999).

The United States is now beginning to experience some of the adverse health effects of these changes in dietary habits. With nearly two of every three North Americans overweight, obesity may soon replace smoking as the leading cause of preventable death. While the United States has taken economic development, production, and consumption to greater lengths than any other nation in history, the country also serves as a model for the developing world, which is on the same track to "progress." As hard as it may be to comprehend,

obesity in poor countries is also becoming a major health issue. Referring to the explosion of obesity worldwide as "globesity," the World Health Organization (WHO) reports that obesity increased from 200 million

AP Images

A 22-year-old woman weighing about 330 pounds rests after performing a dance to mark the founding of a club for obese people in Beijing, China. Increased affluence and China's one child policy is leading to an alarming rate of obesity in the younger generation.

to 300 million people in the five years between 1995 and 2000. This recent phenomenon of "plump poverty" is the result of a variety of factors: as people stop producing their own food and enter the world of wage employment, they are forced to purchase foods high in starch, sugar, and fat; because food is becoming more plentiful and affordable, restaurants are super-sizing their portions; with more women entering the work-force, there is a greater demand for convenient (and usually, fattening) foods; cheap sugar is another contrib-uting factor to the worldwide pandemic of obesity; and the obesity problem is further aggravated by a severe reduction in physical exercise.

It is possible to show how economic development programs have had deleterious effects on sizable seg-ments of the target populations. Not only is health negatively affected, but other unfortunate (and usually unanticipated) consequences occur. The natural envi-ronment is often degraded, families break down, social problems increase, and support systems disintegrate. In most cases, economic development brings with it higher productivity, lower prices for goods and services, and a rising standard of living; however, higher productivity eventually may lead to fewer jobs due to automation or outsourcing. Automobiles in developing countries get increasingly better and more affordable; but as autos become more desirable, roads get clogged with traffic, air pollution increases, and people waste more time in traffic jams. Economic development stimulates higher living standards, but stress, anxiety, and clinical depres-sion become more prevalent. E-mail is cheap and fast, but users must deal with hundreds of spam messages each day. Cell phones are convenient, but cell phone owners are virtually never out of contact with the office. SUVs may be cool and very macho, but they produce more traffic fatalities, increase a nation's dependency on Middle East oil, and are the newest twenty-first-century symbol of the principle of "power without responsibil-ity." Biotechnology may increase people's life expec-tancy, but it also may leave them dependent on costly synthetic drugs.

To be certain, there are segments of non-Western populations that benefit from programs of economic development, but large numbers or even the majority wind up worse off than they would have been if the development efforts had never been initiated. To point out these negative consequences, however, is not to suggest that we should abandon foreign assistance pro-grams or stop trying to increase people's access to mate-rial resources. These negative results occur most often when development programs are introduced without the full participation and understanding of the people they are designed to help. The target populations need to control their own resources and define their relation-ship to the changing economy. But in addition to includ-ing the local people in the planning and administration of the programs, it is absolutely imperative for program

planners to fully understand the dimensions of the local cultures. If we take seriously the notion of the systemic nature of culture, then we must assume that a change in one part of the system is likely to bring about changes in other parts of the system. It is only when development planners understand the nature of those parts, and how they are interrelated, that they can anticipate what some of the negative consequences may be and thus take steps to mitigate or avoid them.

GLOBALIZATION AND WORLD CULTURES

As we have tried to show throughout this text, the total discipline of anthropology looks at humans, wherever they may be found, from earliest prehistory up to the present. Because of the enormous time frame it has carved out for itself, anthropology is able to observe both long-term and short-term sociocultural trends. To illustrate, because archaeologists have looked at cultural development over the last several million years, they have been able to identify some major cultural trends or transformations, such as the neolithic revolution, the rise of urban societies, and the industrial revolution. Cultural anthropologists, who focus on contemporary cultures and societies of the world, are constantly look-ing at more recent, and by definition, more short-term sociocultural trends and developments, such as world immigration patterns since 1945, the rise of religious fundamentalism, and the increasing gap between the rich and the poor throughout the world over the last three decades.

Because anthropologists have identified these re-cent trends, they are often asked to prognosticate about where these trends will lead humankind into the future and what effects they will have on the human condition. Anthropologists, like members of any other profession, have no special powers of prediction. They cannot tell us, with any degree of certainty, what the global cultural mosaic will look like at the end of the twenty-first cen-tury. What anthropologists are able to do, however, is to document the recent trends and changes, and then predict how things might be, *provided these changes con-tinue on their present course.* How the world actually looks ninety years from now will depend on certain natural phenomena (over which humans have little control, such as earthquakes) as well as certain purposeful actions taken by people and their governments. In any event, it is impossible to predict how either will affect current sociocultural trends. The best we, as anthropologists, can do is to describe the current recent trends so as to enable reasonable people in the future to (a) reinforce those beneficial trends and (b) take action to slow down or re-verse those more deleterious trends.

By far the most significant recent trend over the last several decades has been the rapid cross-national inte-gration known as globalization, a term which has become one of the most overused and poorly understood words in the English language. As pointed out in Chapter 8, globalization involves the worldwide trend toward open markets, deregulation, and privatization of services formerly provided by governments. To be certain, there have been interconnections between countries and cultures for centuries that have had far-reaching implications for culture change through diffusion. But when the Berlin Wall came down in 1989, the world began to change in some dramatic ways. Forces were unleashed that are having, and will continue to have, profound effects on all cultures of the world. Cultural anthropologists, whether they are studying large industrialized societies or small-scale foragers, cannot afford to ignore both the magnitude and the speed of this process called globalization.

It is generally agreed that globalization is not just a passing trend but rather is a worldwide phenomenon that has replaced the Cold War system. From 1945 until the late 1980s, the nations and cultures of the world were compartmentalized into two major camps: the communist bloc and the free world. However, with the demise of world communism, so powerfully symbolized by the physical dismantling of the Berlin Wall, the world is experiencing (at a very rapid pace) a new type of integration of markets, technology, and information that is oblivious to both national and cultural borders. This post–Cold War globalization is driven by free-market capitalism and the idea that the more a country opens up its markets to free trade, the healthier its economy will become. The economics of globalization involve lowering tariff barriers while at the same time privatizing and deregulating national economies. The North American Free Trade Agreement (NAFTA) and the European Union are two examples of the recent globalization of markets. In a global economy, goods and services from all over the world will make their way into other cultures. At the same time that world trade barriers are falling, there is a concomitant revolution going on in the world of information technology. In the mid-1980s only a handful of people in the world could operate a computer. Today, computers are nearly as common in the home as radios were in the 1940s. Moreover, with the help of digitization, fiber optics, satellite communication, and the Internet, people are now able to communicate with one another instantaneously. During the Cold War days, grandparents in Pennsylvania would have had to wait several weeks to see a photograph of a new grandchild born in Istanbul. Today, however, a photo of the new baby can be taken on one's cell phone in Istanbul and sent via e-mail to the grandparents on the other side of the globe in a matter of minutes. In short, these revolutionary developments in information processing are greatly facilitating the exchange of ideas across national and cultural boundaries.

Various countries have responded to this information revolution in different ways, some positively and

© Alain Nogues/CORBIS SYGMA

The fall of the Berlin Wall in 1989 marked the symbolic beginning of our present period of globalization.

others negatively. India and Saudi Arabia provide stark contrasts in terms of their responses to globalization. To illustrate, Bangalore, India, with its abundance of highly educated computer scientists, engineers, and software designers, has become the new Silicon Valley and call center for many Western corporations. Indians are using their technical expertise, the Internet, global teleconferencing, and e-mail to provide a wide variety of services to the rest of the world. With the opening up of world markets, India over the past fifteen years has ridden the wave of globalization by creating millions of high-tech, well-paying jobs. By way of contrast, Saudi Arabia, which has given the world al Qaeda, has militantly opposed democracy, science, and the empowerment of women and intellectuals. Rather than putting its resources into scientific education, Saudi Arabia has produced "madrasses," Islamic fundamentalist schools where young men memorize and recite passages from the Koran. Viewing globalization as a threat to Islam, graduates of these madrasses are using the Internet and e-mail to export anger and form communities of hate.

Earlier chapters have pointed out a number of examples of the recent growth in global integration. Anyone who is even vaguely aware of current events will be aware of the outsourcing of not only manufacturing jobs abroad, but also more highly skilled jobs such as accounting, software development, and even human organ replacement. In Chapter 13 we looked at how certain U.S.-based multinational corporations (Microsoft and Yahoo!) have assisted the Chinese government in suppressing Chinese dissidents on the Internet and how they prevented a possible nuclear war between India and Pakistan in 2002. And, in Chapter 14 we showed how not only jobs, but in fact, our religious rituals are being outsourced from Catholic parishes in the United States to Catholic priests in India. There is certainly no shortage of examples of this growing global interconnectedness:

- Major league baseball and football teams have their preseason games in Europe and Japan.

- In 2003, according to a survey of the International Franchise Association, 56 percent of all U.S. franchise operators (e.g., Burger King and Dunkin Donuts) were in markets outside the United States as compared to 46 percent three years earlier (Tahmincioglu 2004).

- Coca-Cola sells more of its products in Japan than it sells in the United States, even though Japan has only half the population of the United States.

- The environmental organization Greenpeace originated in Vancouver in the early 1970s and now has offices in more than thirty countries.

- In the twenty years between 1980 and 2000, the percentage of the world's population that traveled internationally more than tripled from 3 percent to 11.3 percent.

These and other facts and figures suggest the dimensions of this movement toward greater global integration, but we often don't fully comprehend how intimately we ourselves are connected to the rest of the world. Barbara Garson (2001) gives us a glimpse into the international money marketplace by tracing a small sum of money she personally invested in the Chase Manhattan Bank as it travels around the globe. Along the way, she interviews people whose lives are affected by this initial bank deposit. To illustrate, she learned that Chase loaned some of her money to Caltex, a U.S. petrochemical company, to build an oil refinery in Thailand. Initial opposition to the oil refinery on the part of the Thai government was overcome when Caltex spent some of Garson's money for campaign contributions to U.S. politicians who lobbied the Thai government to relent on its opposition to the refinery. Another part of Garson's deposit was used to bribe a Thai government official. Once the opposition was eliminated, still more of Garson's money was used to build the refinery, which, in

As yet one more leading indicator of rapid globalization, more than half of all U.S.-based franchises are now located in other parts of the world, as is this KFC restaurant in Shanghai, China.

fact, as government officials had originally argued, damaged the environment and displaced both local fisherman and farmers. Eventually, due to an economic downturn, the refinery was shut down, thereby putting a number of Thai oil workers out of work. By both tracing the flow of money, and its impact on the lives of real people around the world, Garson was able to demonstrate how her own small investment in a U.S. bank account had enormous and immediate implications for people on the other side of the world.

The globalization phenomenon itself is a dynamic process, because markets for both labor and products do not stay the same for long periods of time. To illustrate, during the 1980s and part of the 1990s, large numbers of highly trained engineers and technicians from India took jobs in the United States, particularly in the high-tech center of Silicon Valley. During this period, Indian engineers had a comfortable living, lived in California suburbs, and began the process of Americanization. During the mid- to late 1990s, however, with India developing high-tech industries of its own, many of the

After working in Silicon Valley, many Indian engineers are returning to India to make even higher salaries and live in California-style gated communities.

Indians living in the United States returned to India, took even higher paying jobs with Indian high-tech firms, and reestablished their California-style neighborhoods in cities such as Bangalore. Moreover, an increasing number of U.S. graduates from American universities are now choosing to take their first job in India's software, informational technology, and business-process outsourcing industries, rather than stay in their own country. Thus, the so-called "brain drain," which saw vast numbers of highly trained Indians emigrating to the United States in the 1980s, has now reversed itself a mere two decades later.

The long-term effects of globalization on the cultures of the world have yet to be fully realized. Some suggest that globalization will eventually lead to the formation of a single global culture (Jameson 1990). They argue that the rapid flow of money, commodities, and information to every corner of the world, if allowed to continue unchecked, will tend to eradicate cultural differences. An unfettered free enterprise system, open markets, advertising, and the free flow of information, it is suggested, will force local people to abandon their traditional values, ideologies, and preferences. For those who predict cultural homogenization, the case of the Kalahari Ju/'hoansi, discussed in Chapter 7, provides an excellent example of how the introduction of new commodities and ideas can radically transform a culture.

In recent years, however, an alternative view has emerged to suggest that globalization, rather than totally changing cultures, can stimulate local cultures to redefine themselves in the face of these external forces. In other words, local cultures, although eventually changing some features, will reaffirm much of their uniqueness while entering into a dialogue with global forces. In one such case, Rosalva Aida Hernandez Castillo and Ronald Nigh (1998) have examined the effects of globalization on a local group of Mam (Mayan-speaking) coffee growers in Chiapas, Mexico. Of all Latin American countries, Mexico—as a full participant in NAFTA—

is up to its eyeballs in globalization. In terms of agriculture, the Mexican government has brought about a number of reforms designed to (1) discourage collective agriculture while encouraging individual agricultural entrepreneurs, (2) encourage cash crops over basic food crops, and (3) increase overall agricultural productivity for world trade purposes.

Despite the national efforts to transform more traditional types of communal agriculture, in 1988 the Mam started their own organic coffee growers' cooperative, which combined modern technologies with a deliberate reaffirmation of traditional values. With more than 1,200 members and annual export revenues of more than $7 million, the Mam cooperative sells its organically grown gourmet coffee all over the world, has acquired a coffee processing plant, and is planning to build an instant coffee production facility. By any standards one might choose, the Mam cooperative is a highly successful global player. Yet they have not earned their success at the expense of their traditional values, which include participatory democracy, equity, environmental protection, and the use of traditional organic farming methods rather than reliance on chemical fertilizers. The Mam have used the same communication technology that has exposed people to Big Macs and iMacs for the purpose of strengthening, not weakening, their traditional cultural values. They have used promotional trips to international trade fairs, the telephone, e-mail, and the Internet to link up with indigenous people and ecologically conscious consumers in other parts of the world. In fact, their corporate marketing image, a curious blend of old and new, emphasizes that their coffee is organically grown by socially responsible descendants of the Mayans. Clearly, such an image combines their traditional identity with a brand of coffee that appeals to a specific market of gourmet coffee drinkers from Tokyo to New York. These contacts and experiences have enabled the Mam organic coffee growers to reinforce many traditional values, accept some new ones from the rest of the world, and essentially reinvent or redefine their traditional culture instead of forsaking it.

So, despite all of the examples of global integration—from lowering of tariff barriers to the widespread acceptance of Levis, Big Macs, and e-mail—cultural anthropologists should not have to fear running out of a sufficient number of cultures to study. It is certainly true that some languages and cultures are becoming virtually extinct, but at the same time other cultures and ethnic groups are experiencing a resurgence. It is important to recognize that states, formed by coalescing a number of ethnic entities together, also have the tendency to eventually come apart. The best contemporary example of this is the Soviet Union, established in 1945 from fifteen constituent republics (e.g., Armenians, Azerbaijanians, Belarussians, Estonians, Georgians, Kazakhs, Latvians, Lithuanians, Moldovans, Russians, Tajiks, Turkmen, Ukrainians, and Uzbeks). When this strongly centralized

Technology, such as the iPod, tends to spread more easily than other aspects of culture such as ideas, beliefs, and ideologies.

CROSS-CULTURAL MISCUE

Sometimes well-intentioned but short-sighted environmental sanitation programs can go awry when the planners are not sufficiently aware of local cultural realities. Through various types of foreign aid programs, U.S. technicians have made major efforts to introduce sanitary latrines into many developing countries. Although most North Americans do not regard latrines, or outhouses, as the height of sanitation, they do represent a significant advance over some traditional ways of disposing of human waste. Latrines built by U.S. technicians are fashioned after outhouses found in some rural areas of the United States; they are inexpensive wooden structures with a raised seat perforated by several holes. However, this latrine design is not particularly well received in other parts of the world. George Foster relates an incident from El Salvador:

> Several years ago a coffee planter, interested in the welfare of his employees, built a latrine for each house according to the standard American model. He was upset when his employees refused to use them. Finally an old man offered a suggestion. "Patron, don't you realize that here we are squatters?" ... Latrines with raised seats seem to cause constipation among people who customarily defecate in a squatting position. (1973: 103)

federal union collapsed in 1991, all fifteen constituent republics, with their own distinctive languages and cultures, became independent nations. Also during the 1990s, Czechoslovakia split into the Czech and Slovak Republics, and francophone Quebec Provence came dangerously close to declaring its independence from the rest of Canada.

Thus, it seems unreasonable to expect that the world, through the process of globalization, is moving relentlessly toward a single, benevolent, culturally homogeneous nation-state. News media every day report cultural differences throughout the world, with each group operating from its own unique cultural heritage and narrowly shared values and interests. The overwhelming power of any single nation-state—whether we are talking about the United States, China, India, or even the European Union—is insufficient to change the rest of the world into its own image. At the turn of the millennium, the United States was unquestionably the most influential power (politically, economically, militarily, and culturally) on earth, and yet its attempt to spread its influence to the rest of the world has largely backfired. Its attempts to open trade relationships with other nations, to spread democracy throughout the world, and to diffuse its popular culture to every corner of the earth has met with considerable resistance. Even though some

Austrians may appreciate the convenience of being able to drink a tall latte at a Starbucks in Vienna, they have no interest in becoming culturally indistinguishable from residents of Seattle.

If the many cultures of the world are not homogenizing into a single mega-culture, then what would be the most sensible foreign policy strategy for interacting with the rest of the world? Rather than deliberately trying to eradicate cultural differences, a more workable approach would be some type of *multiculturalism*—that is, an official policy that recognizes the worth and integrity of different cultures at home and abroad. Such an approach, which we have seen operating effectively in Switzerland and Canada, requires the basic anthropological understanding that culturally different people are not inherently perverse or immoral. Rather, it is possible to live together in peaceful coexistence, provided we understand the logic of culturally different people and are willing to negotiate with them in good faith and without exploitation.

At the very least, multiculturalism requires an awareness that people from other cultures, who do not share

multiculturalism A public policy philosophy that recognizes the legitimacy and equality of all cultures represented in a society.

Some of our closest allies, such as Italy, have very different ideas about what is the proper size of an automobile. While many in the United States aspire to own a large SUV, people in Rome prefer the Smart Car.

our cultural assumptions, probably do not sympathize with some of our behaviors, ideas, and values. For example, living within a culture that highly prizes individualism, most middle-class North Americans see themselves as strong, competitive, assertive, and independent achievers. People from a more collective value orientation, by way of contrast, view North Americans in far less flattering terms as self-absorbed, greedy materialists with hardly a shred of altruism. Many Americans are proud of the fact that they are sufficiently motivated by their value of individualism to achieve power, fame, and fortune to work seventy hours per week so as to be able to afford payments on their $75,000 Hummer. Many Swedes, however, look at this "admirable" behavior of a thirty-something lawyer from Chicago as being selfish and dismissive of others. Working seventy hours per week translates, for them, to less time spent with one's family and fewer social activities, which could lead to a more balanced life and a healthier society. Moreover, working so hard to be able to afford a Hummer is particularly antisocial because driving this cousin to the military assault vehicle increases the cost of gasoline, destroys the environment quicker than a more conventional automobile, and essentially makes the statement that my vehicle, while keeping me and my children safe in the event of an accident, will, in all likelihood, kill you and your children. So, here are two radically different perceptions of the same behavior, one by Americans and one by Swedes. We are not arguing here that Americans need to give up their individualism or their high value placed on seventy-hour work weeks. Nor are we suggesting that Americans agree with the typically Swedish interpretation. What is important, however, is that we learn to recognize the perceptions of other people, the reasons behind those perceptions, and their right to

own their perceptions without unsolicited help from us to change them.

We do not need to travel to exotic parts of the world to see that some of the closest allies of the United States, with their long, rich traditions of democracy, liberty, and individualism (such as France, the United Kingdom, and the Netherlands), have real differences with the United States on a wide variety of issues. To illustrate, in addition to the volatile topic of the war in Iraq, these issues include the environment, the role of government in society, family values, capital punishment, labor relations, domestic spying, religion in government, campaign finance, coping with terrorism, corporate corruption, the role of the United Nations, the banning of land mines, gun control, fuel efficiency of cars, the right to bear arms, preemptive warfare, free trade, public education, global warming, and executive compensation, to mention some of the more obvious concerns. To be open to seeing the logic inherent in someone else's position on societal issues is neither foolish nor unpatriotic. The reason that this author, and indeed most anthropologists since the nineteenth century, have insisted on looking at "the rationality of another culture within its proper cultural context" is because it will enable us to better understand that culture, and when we reach this greater understanding, we will be in a position to interact with them more rationally and more humanely. In other words, we will be less likely to misinterpret what they are saying and thinking, and in the process, will enable *us and them* to more effectively meet our personal and professional objectives. Operating in a globally interconnected world in the twenty-first century should not be a zero-sum game, whereby if we are to meet our objectives, others have to fail at meeting theirs. Thus, the rationale behind a multicultural approach to the rest of the world is that it can lead to a win-win situation.

The alternative to multiculturalism is a world that is fragmented into many ethnic enclaves: self-absorbed, provincial, fearful, uncooperative, militant, suspicious, and mean-spirited. In such a world, it becomes increasingly difficult to achieve what every group, irrespective of size, wants: namely, security, prosperity, and freedom. There are no people in the world, to this author's knowledge, that actively seek to have their houses blown up by suicide bombers, to live in abject poverty, or to be tyrannized.

Multiculturalism (understanding and acceptance of culturally different people) remains the best hope for enabling all people to get the security, prosperity, and freedom they crave and deserve. And yet, multiculturalism should not be seen as a totally selfless and altruistic philosophy. Rather, it should be seen as a "win-win" opportunity. The value of multiculturalism is poignantly captured by Kishore Mahbubani (2005: 203–04) in the following parable:

> There was a farmer who grew award-winning corn. Each year he entered his corn in a state fair, where it won a blue ribbon. One year, a newspaper reporter interviewed him and learned something interesting about how he grew it. The reporter discovered that the farmer shared his seed corn with his neighbors. "How can you afford to share your best seed corn with your neighbors when they are entering corn in competition with yours each year?" the reporter asked. "Why sir," said the farmer, "didn't you know? The wind picks up pollen from the ripening corn and swirls it from field to field. If my neighbors grow inferior corn, cross-pollination will steadily degrade the quality of my corn. If I am to grow good corn, I must help my neighbors grow good corn."

The point of this simple tale is this: the only way we can be safe and prosperous is if we enable our neighbors to be safe and prosperous. ∎

Summary

1. Although the rate of change varies from culture to culture, no culture remains unchanged. The two principal ways that cultures change are internally through invention and externally through diffusion.

2. Inventions can be either deliberate or unintentional. Although intentional inventors usually receive the most recognition, over the long run, unintentional inventors have probably had the greatest impact on cultural change. Because they are not bound by conventional standards, many inventors and innovators tend to be marginal people living on the fringes of society.

3. It is generally recognized that the majority of cultural features (things, ideas, and behavior patterns) found in any society got there by diffusion rather than invention. The following generalizations can be made about the process of diffusion: cultural diffusion is selective in nature, it is a two-way process, it is likely to involve changes in form or function, some cultural items are more likely candidates for diffusion than are others, and it is affected by a number of important variables.

4. Acculturation is a specialized form of cultural diffusion that involves forced borrowing under conditions of external pressure. Some anthropologists have described situations of acculturation in which the nondominant culture has voluntarily chosen the changes, whereas others claim that acculturation always involves some measure of coercion and force.

5. Because the parts of a culture are to some degree interrelated, a change in one part is likely to bring about changes in other parts. This insight from cultural anthropology should be of paramount importance to applied anthropologists, who are often involved directly or indirectly with planned programs of cultural change.

6. Among the barriers to cultural change are the following: some societies maintain their cultural boundaries through the exclusive use of language, food, and clothing; some societies resist change in their culture because the proposed change is not compatible with their existing value systems; and some societies reject change because they are unwilling to disrupt existing social and economic relationships.

7. In recent years cultural anthropologists have become increasingly concerned with the rapid worldwide disappearance of indigenous people—those small-scale societies that originally inhabited a region. Endangered indigenous populations include the Yanomamo of Brazil, the Kurds of the Middle East, and the Ju/'hoansi of southern Africa.

8. Planned programs of change have been introduced into developing countries for decades under the assumption that they benefit the local people. But a number of studies have shown that although some segments of the local population may benefit, many others do not.

9. The forces of globalization (intensification of the flow of money, goods, and information) that have occurred since the late 1980s have made the study of cultural change more complex. In some cases, globalization may be responsible for an accelerated

pace of change in world cultures. In other situations, the forces of globalization may stimulate traditional cultures to redefine themselves.

10. The twenty-first-century world is so intimately interconnected that money invested in a U.S. money market account directly touches the lives of farmers in Zimbabwe, factory workers in Thailand, and certified public accountants in Brazil.

11. Because the cultures of the world are not homogenizing down to a single mega-culture, the best strategy for coping with the world is through multiculturalism, a philosophy based on understanding and respecting cultural diversity wherever it may be found.

Key Terms

acculturation	indigenous population
cultural boundaries	invention
culture of poverty	less developed countries (LDCs)
diffusion	

linked changes	multinational corporations
marginal people	neocolonialism
modernization theory	world systems theory
multiculturalism	

Suggested Readings

Bodley, John H. *Victims of Progress*, 4th ed. Mountain View, CA: Mayfield, 1999. This important book examines the sometimes disastrous effects of westernization and industrialization on tribal societies. Bodley discusses the high price small-scale societies pay for "progress" and the role that Western institutions play in this cultural devastation.

Clifford, James. *Routes: Travel and Translation in the Late Twentieth Century*. Cambridge, MA: Harvard University Press, 1997. Whereas in the past anthropologists traveled to remote areas to study relatively isolated cultures, today Clifford finds cultures colliding with one another. Clifford examines diasporic people, unexplored Western influences on indigenous people, and the effects of globalization on those cultures traditionally studied by anthropologists.

Kottak, Conrad P. *Assault on Paradise: Social Change in a Brazilian Village*. New York: McGraw-Hill, 1998. A readable and highly personal account of changes occurring in Arembepe, a fishing village in Brazil. The book chronicles the cultural changes that have occurred between his initial fieldwork in 1962 and 1998.

Lewellen, Ted C. *The Anthropology of Globalization: Cultural Anthropology Enters the Twenty-first Century*. Westport, CT: Greenwood (Bergin and Garvey), 2002. By drawing upon many timely ethnographic examples, this readable book examines the process of globalization (the increased flows of commerce, finance, culture, and ideas) from the perspective of small-scale societies.

Pelto, P. J. *The Snowmobile Revolution: Technology and Social Change in the Arctic*. Menlo Park, CA: Benjamin/ Cummings, 1973. A study of sociocultural change documenting how a single technological device, the snowmobile, brought about vast economic and social changes among the reindeer herding Skolt Lapps of Finland.

Rogers, Everett M. *Diffusion of Innovations*, 5th ed. New York: Simon & Schuster, 2003. The first edition of this book was published in 1962, and this latest edition covers research on cultural diffusion spanning nearly five decades. This is the best of the books on the important, yet little researched, topic of social change.

Sachs, Jeffrey. *The End of Poverty: Economic Possibilities for Our Time*. New York: Penguin, 2005. Sachs proposes a nine-step program that he claims will eliminate world poverty by 2025. He focuses on the 1 billion poorest people in the world who are trapped in a cycle of disease, physical isolation, lack of capital, environmental stress, inadequate education, and political instability.

Strathern, Andrew, and Pamela Stewart. *Collaboration and Conflicts: A Leader Through Time*. Fort Worth, TX: Harcourt College Publishers, 2000. This life history of Ongka, a leader among the Kawelka people of Papua New Guinea from a time before contact with the outside world up to the year 2000, chronicles the enormous changes that have taken place in a small-scale society over a single lifetime.

References

Abdo, Geneive. 2004. "Muslim Rap Finds Its Voice." *Chicago Tribune* (June 30): 1.

Adams, Bert, and Edward Mburugu. 1994. "Kikuyu Bridewealth and Polygyny Today." *Journal of Comparative Family Studies* 25(2): 159–66.

Agar, Michael H. 1996. *The Professional Stranger*. 2d ed. San Diego: Academic Press.

Agosin, Marjorie. 1987. *Scraps of Life: Chilean Arpilleras*. Toronto: William Wallace Press.

Amadiume, I. 1987. *Male Daughters, Female Husbands*. London: Zed Books.

American Anthropological Association. *www.aaanet.org*.

American Anthropological Association Statement on Race. *www.aaanet.org/stmts/racepp.htm*.

American Medical Association. 2002. *www.ama-assn.org/ama/pub/category/4867.html*.

American Religious Identification Survey. 2001. New York: City University of New York.

Amory, Cleveland. 1969. *Introduction: The 1902 Edition of the Sears, Roebuck Catalogue*. New York: Bounty Books.

Anderson, Richard L. 2003. *Calliope's Sisters: The Role of Art in Human Thought*. 2d ed. Upper Saddle River, NJ: Prentice-Hall.

Ardrey, Robert. 1968. *The Territorial Imperative*. New York: Atheneum.

Associated Press. 1999. "Group Wedding in Kuwait Helps 28 Couples Defray High Costs of Getting Married." *AP Worldstream* (December 5).

Baba, Marietta. 1986. "Business and Industrial Anthropology: An Overview." *NAPA Bulletin* 2, National Association for the Practice of Anthropology (a unit of the American Anthropological Association).

Bailey, Benjamin. 1997. "Communication of Respect in Interethnic Service Encounters." *Language and Society* 26(3): 327–56.

Bakhshi, Vicki. 1999. "Gender Inequality Persists Without Exception." *Financial Times* (July 12): 4.

Balzer, Marjorie. 1993. "Two Urban Shamans." In *Perilous States: Conversations Amid Uncertain Transitions*. G. Marcus, ed., pp. 131–64. Chicago: University of Chicago Press.

Bamberger, Joan. 1974. "The Myth of Matriarchy: Why Men Rule in Primitive Society." In *Women, Culture and Society*. Michelle Zimbalist Rosaldo and Louise Lamphere, eds., pp. 263–80. Stanford, CA: Stanford University Press.

Barber, Benjamin. 1996. *Jehad and McWorld*. New York: Ballantine Books.

Barfield, Thomas. 1993. *The Nomadic Alternative*. Englewood Cliffs, NJ: Prentice-Hall.

Barker, Holly. 2004. *Bravo for the Marshallese: Regaining Control in a Post-Nuclear, Post-Colonial World*. Belmont, CA: Wadsworth.

Barkun, Michael. 2000. "Millennialists and the State: Reflections After Waco." In *Conflict and Conformity: Readings in Cultural Anthropology*. 10th ed. James Spradley and David McCurdy, eds., pp. 332–40. Boston: Allyn & Bacon.

Barnes, Sandra T. 1990. "Women, Property, and Power." In *Beyond the Second Sex: New Directions in the Anthropology of Gender*. Peggy Reeves Sanday and Ruth G. Goodenough, eds., pp. 253–80. Philadelphia: University of Pennsylvania Press.

Barnard, Alan. 2000. *History and Theory in Anthropology*. Cambridge, U.K.: Cambridge University Press.

Barrett, Richard A. 1991. *Culture and Conduct: An Excursion in Anthropology*. 2d ed. Belmont, CA: Wadsworth.

Barrett, Stanley. 1996. *Anthropology: A Student's Guide to Theory and Methods*. Toronto: University of Toronto Press.

Basso, Keith H. 1970. "'To Give Up on Words': Silence in Western Apache Culture." *Southwestern Journal of Anthropology* 26(3): 213–30.

Bates, Daniel. 2001. *Human Adaptive Strategies: Ecology, Culture, and Politics*. 2d ed. Boston: Allyn & Bacon.

Beals, Alan. 1962. *Gopalpur: A South Indian Village*. New York: Holt, Rinehart and Winston.

Beals, Ralph L., Harry Hoijer, and Alan R. Beals. 1977. *An Introduction to Anthropology*. 5th ed. New York: Macmillan.

Beattie, John. 1960. *Bunyoro: An African Kingdom*. New York: Holt, Rinehart and Winston.

———. 1964. *Other Cultures: Aims, Methods, and Achievements in Social Anthropology*. New York: Free Press.

Beckerman, Stephen, and Paul Valentine. 2002. *Cultures of Multiple Fathers: The Theory and Practice of Partible Paternity in Lowland South America*. Gainesville, FL: University Press of Florida.

Beebe, James. 1995. "Basic Concepts and Techniques of Rapid Appraisal." *Human Organization* 54(1): 42–51.

Behar, Ruth. 1993. *Translated Woman: Crossing the Border with Esperanza's Story*. Boston: Beacon Press.

Belson, Ken. 2004. "No, You Can't Walk and Talk at the Same Time." *New York Times* (August 29): 4.

Benedict, Ruth. 1934. *Patterns of Culture*. Boston: Houghton Mifflin.

———. 1946. *The Chrysanthemum and the Sword*. Boston: Houghton Mifflin.

Benet, Sula. 1976. *How to Live to Be a Hundred: The Lifestyle of the People of the Caucasus*. New York: Dial Press.

Bensman, Joseph, and Arthur Vidich. 1987. *American Society: The Welfare State and Beyond*. rev. ed. South Hadley, MA: Bergin and Garvey.

Berger, Joseph. 2005. "Noo Yawkese? Forget About It. The Dialect Today is Global." *New York Times* (January 30).

Berman, Russell A. 2004. "Differences in American and European Worldviews." *Commentary* 117(2): 73.

Bernard, H. Russell. 1988. *Research Methods in Cultural Anthropology*. Newbury Park, CA: Sage Publications.

———. 1998. *The Handbook of Methods in Cultural Anthropology*. Walnut Creek, CA: AltaMira Press.

Berreman, Gerald D., and Kathleen M. Zaretsky, eds. 1981. *Social Inequality: Comparative and Development Approaches*. New York: Academic Press.

Besteman, Catherine and Hugh Gusterson, eds. 2005. *Why America's Top Pundits Are Wrong: Anthropologists Talk Back*. Berkeley: University of California Press.

Bestor, Theodore. 2000. "How Sushi Went Global." *Foreign Policy* 121 (November/December): 54–63.

Betzig, Laura. 1988. "Redistribution: Equity or Exploitation?" In *Human Reproductive Behavior: A Darwinian Perspective*. Laura Betzig, M. B. Mulder, and Paul Turke, eds., pp. 49–63. Cambridge: Cambridge University Press.

Bird, S. Elizabeth, and Carolena Von Trapp. 1999. "Beyond Bones and Stones." *Anthropology Newsletter* 40(9) (December): 9–10.

Birket-Smith, K. 1959. *The Eskimos*. 2d ed. London: Methuen.

Bishop, Naomi H. 2002. *Himalayan Herders*. Belmont, CA: Wadsworth.

Blount, Ben B. 1995. *Language, Culture, and Society: A Book of Readings*. 2d ed. Prospect Heights, IL: Waveland.

Blunt, Peter. 1980. "Bureaucracy and Ethnicity in Kenya: Some Conjectures for the Eighties." *Journal of Applied Behavioral Science* 16(3): 336–53.

Boal, Augusto. 1979. *Theater of the Oppressed*. London: Pluto Press.

Boas, Franz. 1911a. *Handbook of American Indian Languages*. Bureau of American Ethnology. Bulletin 40.

———. 1911b. *The Mind of Primitive Man*. New York: Macmillan.

———. 1919. "Correspondence: Scientists as Spies." *The Nation* (December 20): 797.

Bodley, John. 1999. *Victims of Progress*. 4th ed. Mountain View, CA: Mayfield.

———. 2000. *Anthropology and Contemporary Human Problems*. New York: WCB/McGraw-Hill.

Bohannan, Paul, and Philip Curtin. 1988. *Africa and Africans*. Prospect Heights, IL: Waveland Press.

Bonvillain, Nancy. 2001. *Women and Men: Cultural Constructs of Gender*. 3d ed. Upper Saddle River, NJ: Prentice-Hall.

Borden, Teresa. 2004. "In Chiapas, Cola Is King." *Atlanta Journal Constitution* (April 14): F-1.

Bowen, Elenore Smith. 1964. *Return to Laughter*. Garden City, NY: Doubleday.

Boyd, Robert S. 2003. "A Case of He Wrote, She Wrote." *The Charlotte Observer* (May 25): 7A.

Bradsher, Keith. 2004. "The Ultimate Luxury Item Is Now Made in China" *The New York Times* (July 13): 1-A.

Brady, Ivan. 1991. "The Samoan Reader: Last Word or Lost Horizon?" *Current Anthropology* 32(4) (August–October): 497–500.

———. 1998. "Two Thousand and What? Anthropological Moments and Methods for the Next Century." *American Anthropologist* 100(2): 510–16.

Brettell, Caroline B., and Carolyn Sargent. 2005. *Gender in Cross-Cultural Perspective*. 4th ed. Upper Saddle River, NJ: Prentice-Hall.

Brewer, Jeffrey D. 1988. "Traditional Land Use and Government Policy in Bima, East Sumbawa." In *The Real and Imagined Role of Culture in Development: Case Studies from Indonesia*. Michael R. Dove, ed., pp. 119–35. Honolulu: University of Hawaii Press.

Brooke, James. 1990. "Brazil Blows Up Miners' Airstrip, Pressing Its Drive to Save Indians." *New York Times* (May 23).

———. 2005. "For Mongolians, E is for English, F is for Future." *New York Times* (February 15): 1.

———. 2005. "Here Comes the Japanese Bride, Looking Very Western." *New York Times* (July 8): A-4.

Brooks, David. 2004. "A Matter of Faith." *New York Times* (June 22): A-23.

Brooks, Geraldine. 1990. *Wall Street Journal* (October 10): A16.

Brown, Donald E. 1991. *Human Universals*. New York: McGraw-Hill.

Brown, Judith. 1970. "A Note on the Division of Labor by Sex." *American Anthropologist* 72: 1073–78.

Buckley, T. 1993. "Menstruation and the Power of Yurok Women." In *Gender in Cross-Cultural Perspective.* Caroline B. Brettell and Carolyn F. Sargent, eds., pp. 133–48. Englewood Cliffs, NJ: Prentice-Hall.

Burger, Julian. 1987. *Report from the Frontier: The State of the World's Indigenous Peoples.* London: Zed Books/Cultural Survival Report 28.

Burns, John F. 1998. "Once Widowed in India, Twice Scorned." *New York Times* (March 29): A1.

Burton, M. L., L. A. Brudner, and D. R. White. 1977. "A Model of the Sexual Division of Labor." *American Ethnologist* 4: 227–51.

Byatt, A. S. 2002. "What Is a European?" *New York Times Magazine* (October 13): 46–51.

Callender, Charles, and Lee Kochems. 1983. "The North American Berdache." *Current Anthropology* 24: 443–70.

Campbell, Bernard G. 1979. *Mankind Emerging.* 2nd ed. Boston: Little, Brown.

Campbell, Lyle. 1999. *Historical Linguistics: An Introduction.* Cambridge, MA: MIT Press.

Candy, Dana. 2002. "Lifting Veil for Photo ID Goes Too Far, Driver Says." *New York Times* (June 27): A16.

Carneiro, Robert. 1970. "A Theory of the Origin of the State." *Science* (August 21): 733–38.

Carpenter, Edmund. 1973. *Eskimo Realities.* New York: Holt, Rinehart and Winston.

Carsten, Janet. 2004. *After Kinship: New Departures in Anthropology.* Cambridge: Cambridge University Press.

Carvajal, Doreen. 1998. "Better Living Through Sorcery." *New York Times* (October 26): E1.

Casagrande, Joseph B. 1960. "The Southwest Project in Comparative Psycholinguistics: A Preliminary Report." In *Men and Cultures: Selected Papers of the Fifth International Congress of Anthropological and Ethnological Sciences.* Anthony F. C. Wallace, ed., pp. 777–82. Philadelphia: University of Pennsylvania Press.

Cassel, John. 1972. "A South African Health Program." In Charles C. Hughes, ed. *Make Men of Them.* Chicago: Rand McNally.

Chagnon, Napoleon A. 1983. *Yanomamo: The Fierce People.* 3d ed. New York: Holt, Rinehart and Winston.

———. 1992. *Yanomamo: The Last Days of Eden.* 5th ed. San Diego: Harcourt Brace Jovanovich.

Chambers, John, ed. 1983. *Black English: Educational Equity and the Law.* Ann Arbor, MI: Karoma Publishers.

Chambers, Keith, and Anne Chambers. 2001. *Unity of Heart: Culture and Change in a Polynesian Atoll Society.* Prospect Heights, IL: Waveland.

Chambers, Veronica, et al. 1999. "Latino America: Hispanics Are Hip, Hot, and Making History." *Newsweek* (July 12): 48.

Chance, Norman A. 1990. *The Inupiat and Arctic Alaska: An Ethnography of Development.* Fort Worth: Holt, Rinehart and Winston.

Charle, Suzanne. 1999. "A Far Island of Cultural Survival." *New York Times* (July 25, section 2): 1, 28.

Childe, V. Gordon. 1936. *Man Makes Himself.* London: Watts.

Chomsky, Noam. 1972. *Language and Mind.* New York: Harcourt Brace Jovanovich.

Chura, Hillary. 2006. "A Year Abroad (or 3) as a Career Move." *New York Times* (February 25): B-5.

Cipollone, Nick, Steven Hartman Keiser, and Shravan Vasishth, eds. 1998. *Language Files: Materials for an Introduction to Language and Linguistics.* 7th ed. Columbus: Ohio State University Press.

Clifford, James. 1997. *Routes: Travel and Translation in the Late Twentieth Century.* Cambridge, MA: Harvard University Press.

Coates, Melissa. 2005. "Trends in Degrees and Dissertations in Anthropology." *Anthropology News* 46(4): 9.

Cohen, Eugene N., and Edwin Eames. 1982. *Cultural Anthropology.* Boston: Little, Brown.

Cohen, M. N., and G. J. Armelagos, eds. 1984. *Paleopathology at the Origins of Agriculture.* New York: Academic Press.

Cohen, Ronald, and Elman R. Service, eds. 1978. *Origins of the State: The Anthropology of Political Evolution.* Philadelphia: Institute for the Study of Human Issues.

Cohen, Theodore F. 2001. *Men and Masculinity: A Text Reader.* Belmont, CA: Wadsworth.

Coleman, Richard P., and Lee Rainwater. 1978. *Social Standing in America.* New York: Basic Books.

Collier, Jane F., and J. Yanagisako, eds. 1987. *Gender and Kinship: Essays Toward a Unified Analysis.* Stanford, CA: Stanford University Press.

Collins, John J. 1975. *Anthropology: Culture, Society and Evolution.* Englewood Cliffs, NJ: Prentice-Hall.

Collins, Robert J. 1992. *Japan-Think, Ameri-Think.* New York: Penguin.

Condon, John. 1984. *With Respect to the Japanese: A Guide for Americans.* Yarmouth, MA: Intercultural Press.

Connelly, Marjorie. 2005. "Advisory: Travel Notes." *New York Times* (July 17).

Cooke, Benjamin G. 1972. "Nonverbal Communication Among Afro-Americans: An Initial Classification." In *Rappin' and Stylin' Out: Communication in Urban Black America.* Thomas Kochman, ed., pp. 32–64. Urbana: University of Illinois Press.

Coontz, Stephanie, Maya Parson, and Gabrielle Raley, eds. 1999. *American Families: A Multicultural Reader.* New York: Routledge.

Coote, Jeremy, and Anthony Shelton, eds. 1992. *Anthropology, Art, and Aesthetics.* Oxford: Clarendon Press.

Council of the American Anthropological Association. 1971. *Statement on Ethics: Principles of Professional Responsibility.* May (as amended through November 1976).

Counts, David. 1995. "Too Many Bananas, Not Enough Pineapples, and No Watermelon at All: Three Object Lessons in Living with Reciprocity." In *Annual Editions: Anthropology, 95/96.* Elvio Angeloni, ed., pp. 95–98. Guilford, CT: Dushkin.

Counts, G. S. 1925. "The Social Status of Occupations: A Problem in Vocational Guidance." *School Review* 33 (January): 16–27.

Cowan, Betty, and Jasbir Dhanoa. 1983. "The Prevention of Toddler Malnutrition by Home-Based Nutrition Education." In *Nutrition in the Community: A Critical Look at Nutrition Policy, Planning, and Programmes.* D. S. McLaren, ed., pp. 339–56. New York: Wiley.

Cronk, Lee. 1989. "Strings Attached." *The Sciences* (May–June): 2–4.

Dahlberg, Frances. 1981. "Introduction." In *Woman the Gatherer.* New Haven, CT: Yale University Press.

Daly, Emma. 2005. "DNA Test Gives Students Ethnic Shocks" *New York Times* (April 13): A-18.

D'Antoni, Tom, and Alex Heard. 1998. "Subway Spirits." *New York Times Magazine* (October 25): 23.

Darian-Smith, Eve. 2004. *New Capitalists: Law, Politics, and Identity Surrounding Casino Gaming on Native American Land.* Belmont, CA: Wadsworth.

Dash, Eric. 2006. "C.E.O. Pay Keeps Rising, And Bigger Rises Faster." *New York Times* (April 9): 5.

Davis, Kingsley, and Wilbert Moore. 1945. "Some Principles of Stratification." *American Sociological Review* 10 (April): 242–49.

———. 1988. "Wives and Work: A Theory of the Sex-Role Revolution and Its Consequences." In *Feminism, Children, and the New Families.* Sanford Dornbusch and Myra Strober, eds., pp. 67–86. New York: Guilford Press.

Davis, Shelton H. 1977. *Victims of the Miracle: Development and the Indians of Brazil.* Cambridge: Cambridge University Press.

Deardorff, Merle. 1951. "The Religion of Handsome Lake." In *Symposium on Local Diversity in Iroquois Culture.* W. N. Fenton, ed. Washington DC: Bureau of American Ethnology, Bulletin 149.

Dellios, Hugh. 2004. "Altered Corn Ignites Furor in Mexico." *Chicago Tribune* (April 24): 1.

Dembo, Richard, Patrick Hughes, Lisa Jackson, and Thomas Mieczkowski. 1993. "Crack Cocaine Dealing by Adolescents in Two Public Housing Projects: A Pilot Study." *Human Organization* 52(1): 89–96.

DeVita, Philip R., ed. 1992. *The Naked Anthropologist: Tales from Around the World.* Belmont, CA: Wadsworth.

———. 2000. *Stumbling Toward Truth: Anthropologists at Work.* Prospect Heights, IL: Waveland Press.

DeVita, Philip R., and James D. Armstrong. 1993. *Distant Mirrors: America as a Foreign Culture.* Belmont, CA: Wadsworth.

Diamond, Jared. 1987. "The Worst Mistake in the History of the Human Race." *Discover* (May): 64–66.

———. 1995. "Easter's End." *Discover* (August).

———. 2001. "Death of Languages." *Natural History* (April): 30.

Diamond, Stanley. 1960. "Introduction: The Uses of the Primitive." In *Primitive Views of the World.* Stanley Diamond, ed., pp. v–xxix. New York: Columbia University Press.

Dissanayake, Ellen. 1995. *Homo Aestheticus: Where Art Comes From and Why.* Seattle: University of Washington Press.

Domhoff, G. William. 1990. *The Power Elite and the State: How Policy Is Made in America.* New York: DeGruyter.

———. 1998. *Who Rules America?* Mountain View, CA: Mayfield.

Donitsa-Schmidt, Smadar, Ofra Inbar, and Elana Schohamy. 2004. "The Effects of Teaching Spoken Arabic on Students' Attitudes and Motivation in Israel." *Modern Language Journal* 88(2) (Summer): 217–28.

Donnelly, John. 2006. "Study Suggests New HIV Infections Have Peaked." *Charlotte Observer* (March 3): 8A.

Dorjahn, Vernon. 1959. "The Factor of Polygyny in African Demography." In *Continuity and Change in African Cultures.* William R. Bascom and M. J. Herskovits, eds. Chicago: University of Chicago Press.

Downs, James F. 1971. *Cultures in Crisis.* Beverly Hills: Glencoe Press.

Dreifus, Claudia. 2001. "How Language Came to Be, and Change: A Conversation with John McWhorter." *New York Times News Brief* (October 30).

Dresser, Norine. 1996. *Multicultural Manners: New Rules of Etiquette for a Changing Society.* New York: Wiley.

Dundes, Alan. 1965. "What Is Folklore?" In *The Study of Folklore.* Alan Dundes, ed. Englewood Cliffs, NJ: Prentice-Hall.

Durkheim, Emile. 1933. *Division of Labor in Society* (G. Simpson, trans.). New York: Macmillan.

———. 2001. *The Elementary Forms of Religious Life* (Carol Cosman, trans.). Oxford: Oxford University Press (orig. 1912).

Dyson-Hudson, Rada, and Neville Dyson-Hudson. 1980. "Nomadic Pastoralism." *Annual Review of Anthropology* 9:15–61.

Dyson-Hudson, Rada, and Eric A. Smith. 1978. "Human Territoriality: An Ecological Reassessment." *American Anthropologist* 80: 21–41.

Eck, Diana. 2002. *A New Religious America: How a "Christian Country" Has Become the World's Most Religiously Diverse Nation.* San Francisco: Harper.

Edgecomb, Elaine L., and Tamra Thetford. 2004. "The Informal Economy: Making It in Rural America." FIELD (The Microenterprise Fund for Innovation, Effectiveness, Learning, and Dissemination), a program of the Aspen Institute.

Eggan, Fred. 1950. *Social Organization of the Western Pueblos.* Chicago: University of Chicago Press.

Ehrenreich, Barbara. 2001. *Nickel and Dimed: On (Not) Getting By in America.* New York: Metropolitan Books.

Eller, Jack David. 2006. *Violence and Culture: A Cross-Cultural and Interdisciplinary Approach.* Belmont, CA: Wadsworth.

Ember, Carol R. and Melvin. 2005. "Explaining Corporal Punishment of Children: A Cross Cultural Study." *American Anthropologist* 107(4): 609–19.

English-Lueck, January 2002. *Cultures @ Silicon Valley.* Palo Alto, CA: Stanford University Press.

Ennis-McMillan, Michael C. 2001. "Suffering from Water: Social Origins of Bodily Distress in a Mexico Community." *Medical Anthropology Quarterly* 15(3): 368–90.

———. 2002. "A Paradoxical Privatization: Challenges to Community-Managed Drinking Water Systems in the Valley of Mexico." In *Protecting a Sacred Gift: Water and Social Change in Mexico.* Scott Whiteford and Roberto Melville, eds., pp. 27–48. La Jolla, CA: Center for U.S.-Mexican Studies, University of California at San Diego.

———. 2005. *A Precious Liquid: Drinking Water and Culture in the Valley of Mexico.* Belmont, CA: Wadsworth.

Ensminger, Jean, ed. 2002. *Theory in Economic Anthropology.* Lanham, MD: Rowman and Littlefield.

Errington, Frederick, and Deborah Gewertz. 1987. *Cultural Alternatives and a Feminist Anthropology: An Analysis of Culturally Constructed Gender Interests in Papua New Guinea.* Cambridge: Cambridge University Press.

Esber, George S. 1977. *The Study of Space in Advocacy Planning with the Tonto Apaches in Payson, Arizona.* Doctoral dissertation, University of Arizona.

———. 1987. "Designing Apache Homes with Apaches." In *Anthropological Praxis: Translating Knowledge into Action.* Robert M. Wulff and Shirley J. Fiske, eds., pp. 187–96. Boulder, CO.: Westview Press.

Etzioni, Amitai. 1993. "How to Make Marriage Matter." *Time* 142(10) (September 6): 76.

European Commission. 2005. "Europeans and Languages." *Eurobarometer,* September.

http://europa.eu.int/comm/public_opinion/archives/ebs/ebs_237.en.pdf

European Space Agency. 2004. News release (February 17).

Evans-Pritchard, E. E. 1940. *The Nuer.* Oxford: Oxford University Press.

Everett, Margaret. 1998. "Latin America On-Line: The Internet, Development, and Democratization." *Human Organization* 57(4) (Winter): 385–93.

Fabrikant, Geraldine. 2002. "G.E. Expenses for Ex-Chief Cited in Filing." *New York Times* (September 6).

Farb, Peter. 1968. "How Do I Know You Mean What You Mean?" *Horizon* 10(4): 52–57.

Faris, James C. 1972. *Nuba Personal Art.* Toronto: University of Toronto Press.

Ferguson, B. 1984. "Re-examination of the Causes of Northwest Coast Warfare." In *Warfare, Culture, and Environment.* R. Ferguson, ed., pp. 267–328. New York: Academic Press.

Ferguson, R. Brian. 1995. *Yanomami Warfare: A Political History.* Santa Fe: School of American Research Press.

———. 2003. *The State, Identity, and Violence: Political Disintegration in the Post-Cold-War World.* New York: Routledge.

Ferguson, Charles A. 1964. "Diglossia." In *Language in Culture and Society: A Reader in Linguistics and Anthropology.* Dell Hymes, ed., pp. 429–39. New York: Harper & Row.

Ferraro, Gary. 1976. "Changing Patterns of Bridewealth Among the Kikuyu of East Africa." In *A Century of Change in Eastern Africa.* William Arens, ed., pp. 101–13. The Hague: Mouton Publishers.

———. 1983. "The Persistence of Bridewealth in Swaziland." *International Journal of Sociology of the Family* (Spring): 1–16.

———, ed. 2004. *Classic Readings in Cultural Anthropology.* Belmont, CA: Wadsworth.

———. 2006. *The Cultural Dimension of International Business.* 5th ed. Upper Saddle River, NJ: Prentice-Hall.

Fetterman, David M. 1989. *Ethnography: Step by Step.* Newbury Park, CA: Sage Publications.

Fink, Paul J. 2002. "Fink! Still at Large: Hikikomori Syndrome and Social Withdrawal." *Clinical Psychiatry News* 30(9): 25.

———. 1992. *The Churching of America, 1976–1990: Winners and Losers in Our Religious Economy.* New Brunswick, NJ: Rutgers University Press.

Finke, Roger, and Rodney Stark. 2005. *The Churching of America, 1976–2005: Winners and Losers in Our Religious Economy.* New Brunswick, NJ: Rutgers University Press.

Finkelstein, Marni. 2005. *With No Direction Home: Homeless Youth on the Road and in the Streets.* Belmont, CA: Wadsworth.

Fish, Jefferson M. 1995. "Mixed Blood." *Psychology Today* 28(6) (November-December): 55–58, 60, 61, 76, 80.

Fisher, Roger, Bruce Patton, and William L. Ury. 1981. *Getting to Yes: Negotiating Agreement Without Giving In.* Boston: Houghton Mifflin.

Forde, Daryll. 1967. "Double Descent Among the Yako." In *African Systems of Kinship and Marriage.* A. R. Radcliffe-Brown, and Daryll Forde, eds., pp. 285–332. London: Oxford University Press (orig. 1950).

Fortes, M., and E. E. Evans-Pritchard. 1940. *African Political Systems.* London: Oxford University Press.

Foster, George M. 1967. *Tzintzuntzan: Mexican Peasants in a Changing World.* Boston: Little, Brown.

———. 1973. *Traditional Societies and Technological Change.* 2d ed. New York: Harper & Row.

Fox, Robin. 1967. *Kinship and Marriage: An Anthropological Perspective.* Baltimore: Penguin Books.

Frank, Thomas. 2004. *What's the Matter with Kansas?* New York: Henry Holt and Company.

Freedman, Maurice. 1979. *The Study of Chinese Society: Essays by Maurice Freedman.* Stanford, CA: Stanford University Press.

Freeman, Derek. 1984. *Margaret Mead and Samoa: The Making and Unmaking of an Anthropological Myth.* New York: Penguin.

Freilich, Morris, Douglas Raybeck, and Joel Savishinsky, eds. 1990. *Deviance: Anthropological Perspectives.* South Hadley, MA: Bergin and Garvey.

French, Howard W. 2006. "In a Richer China, Billionaires Put Money on Marriage." *New York Times* (January 24): A-4.

Fried, Morton H. 1967. *The Evolution of Political Society: An Essay in Political Anthropology.* New York: Random House.

Friedl, Ernestine. 1978. "Society and Sex Roles." *Human Nature* 1(4): 68–75.

Friedl, John, and John E. Pfeiffer. 1977. *Anthropology: The Study of People.* New York: Harper & Row.

Friedman, Thomas L. 1999. *The Lexus and the Olive Tree.* New York: Farrar, Straus, and Giroux.

———. 1999. "Senseless in Seattle." *New York Times* (December 1): A23.

———. 2002. "India, Pakistan, and G.E." *New York Times* (August 8): 13.

———. 2004. "Small and Smaller." *New York Times* (March 4): A-29.

Fromkin, Victoria, Robert Rodman, and Nina Hyams. 2002. *An Introduction to Language.* 7th ed. Boston: Heinle.

Fujita, Mariko, and Toshiyuki Sano. 2001. *Life in Riverfront: A Middle-Western Town Seen Through Japanese Eyes.* Belmont, CA: Wadsworth.

Fuller, Graham. 1999. "Islam Is the Answer to Indonesia's Crisis." *New Perspectives Quarterly* (Summer): 32–33.

Galanti, Geri-Ann. 1991. *Caring for Patients from Different Cultures: Case Studies from American Hospitals.* Philadelphia: University of Philadelphia Press.

Gallup Organization. 1988. "Geographic Knowledge Deemed Vital, But Many Lack Basic Skills." *Gallup Report* (277): 35.

Gardner, R. Allen, and Beatrice T. Gardner. 1969. "Teaching Sign Language to a Chimpanzee." *Science* (August 15): 664–72.

Garfinkle, H. 1956. "Conditions of a Successful Degradation Ceremony." *American Journal of Sociology* 61: 420–24.

Garson, Barbara. 2001. *Money Makes the World Go Around.* New York: Viking.

Geertz, Clifford. 1973. *The Interpretation of Cultures.* New York: Basic Books.

———. 1983. *Local Knowledge: Further Essays in Interpretive Anthropology.* New York: Basic Books.

———. 1984. "Distinguished Lecture: Anti Anti-Relativism." *American Anthropologist* 86 (June): 263–78.

Gibbs, James L. 1963. "The Kpelle Moot." *Africa* 33(1).

Gibson, Christina, and Thomas S. Weisner. 2002. "'Rational' and Ecocultural Circumstances of Program Take-up Among Low-Income Working Parents." *Human Organization* 61(2)(Summer): 154–66.

Gilbert, Dennis. 2003. *American Class Structure in an Age of Growing Inequality: A New Synthesis.* 6th ed. Belmont, CA: Wadsworth.

Glossow, Michael. 1978. "The Concept of Carrying Capacity in the Study of Cultural

Process." In *Advances in Archaeological Theory*. Michael Schiffler, ed., pp. 32–48. New York: Academic Press.

Gmelch, George. 1994a. "Lessons from the Field." In *Conformity and Conflict*. 8th ed. James P. Spradley and David McCurdy, eds., pp. 45–55. New York: HarperCollins.

———. 1994b. "Ritual and Magic in American Baseball." In *Conformity and Conflict*. 8th ed. James P. Spradley and David McCurdy, eds., pp. 351–61. New York: HarperCollins.

Goldberg, David T. 2001. *The Racial State*. Malden, MA: Blackwell.

Goldschmidt, Walter. 1979. "Introduction: On the Interdependence Between Utility and Theory." In *The Uses of Anthropology*. Walter Goldschmidt, ed. Washington, DC: American Anthropological Association.

Goldstein, Melvyn C. 1987. "When Brothers Share a Wife." *Natural History* 96(3): 39–48.

Goode, William J. 1963. *World Revolution and Family Patterns*. New York: Free Press of Glencoe.

Goodenough, Ward H. 1956. "Componential Analysis and the Study of Meaning." *Language* 32: 195–216.

Goodnough, Abby. 2005. "Survivors of Tsunami Live on Close Terms with the Sea," *New York Times* (January 23): 8.

Gorer, Geoffrey, and John Rickman. 1949. *The People of Great Russia*. London: Cresset.

Gough, Kathleen. 1959. "The Nayars and the Definition of Marriage." *Journal of the Royal Anthropological Institute* 89: 23–34.

Gouldner, Alvin. 1960. "The Norm of Reciprocity: A Preliminary Statement." *American Sociological Review* 25: 161–78.

Gray, J. Patrick, and Linda Wolfe. 1988. "An Anthropological Look at Human Sexuality." In *Human Sexuality*. 3d ed. William H. Masters, Virginia E. Johnson, and Robert C. Kolodny, eds. Cambridge, MA: Addison Wesley.

Gray, Robert F. 1960. "Sonjo Brideprice and the Question of African 'Wife Purchase.'" *American Anthropologist* 62: 34–57.

Grindal, Bruce. 1972. *Growing Up in Two Worlds: Education and Transition Among the Sisla of Northern Ghana*. New York: Holt, Rinehart and Winston.

Grobsmith, Elizabeth S. 1989. "The Relationship Between Substance Abuse and Crime Among North American Inmates in the Nebraska Department of Correctional Service." *Human Organization* 48(4): 285–98.

———. 1992. "Applying Anthropology to American Indian Correctional Concerns." *Practicing Anthropology* 14(3) (Summer): 5–8.

Gross, Daniel, and Barbara A. Underwood. 1971. "Technological Change and Caloric Costs: Sisal Agriculture." *American Anthropologist* 73(3): 725–40.

Gudeman, Stephen, ed. 1999. *Economic Anthropology*. Northampton, MA: Edward Elgar.

Guru, Gopal, and Shiraz Sidhva. 2001. "India's Hidden Apartheid." *Unesco Courier* 54(9) (September): 27–29.

Gusterson, Hugh, and Catherine Besteman. 2005. "While We Were Sleeping." *Anthropology News*, 46(4): 31.

Hagen, E. 1962. *On the Theory of Social Change*. Homewood, IL: Dorsey Press.

Hall, Edward T. 1969. *The Hidden Dimension*. Garden City, NY: Doubleday.

———. 1983. *The Dance of Life: The Other Dimension of Time*. Garden City, NY: Anchor Press/Doubleday.

Hanna, Judith Lynne. 1979. *To Dance Is Human: A Theory of Nonverbal Communication*. Austin: University of Texas Press.

———. 2005. "Dance Speaks Out on Societal Issues." *Anthropology News*, 46(4): 11–12.

Hardin, Garrett. 1968. "The Tragedy of the Commons." *Science* 162: 1243–48.

Harkin, Michael. 1998. "Whales, Chiefs, and Giants: An Exploration into Nuu-chah-nulth Political Thought." *Ethnology* 37(4): 317–32.

Harner, Michael J. 1973. "The Sound of Rushing Water." In *Hallucinogens and Shamanism*. Michael J. Harner, ed., pp. 15–27. New York: Oxford University Press.

Harris, Grace. 1972. "Taita Bridewealth and Affinal Relations." In *Marriage in Tribal Society*. Meyer Fortes, ed., pp. 55–87. Cambridge: Cambridge University Press.

Harris, Marvin. 1968. *The Rise of Anthropological Theory*. New York: Thomas Y. Crowell.

———. 1977. *Cannibals and Kings: The Origins of Culture*. New York: Random House.

———. 1979a. "Comments on Simoons' Questions in the Sacred Cow Controversy." *Current Anthropology* 20: 479–82.

———. 1979b. *Cultural Materialism: The Struggle for a Science of Culture*. New York: Random House.

———. 1979c. "The Yanomamo and the Cause of War in Band and Village Societies." In *Brazil: Anthropological Perspectives: Essays in Honor of Charles Wagley*. M. Margolis and W. Carter, eds., pp. 121–32. New York: Columbia University Press.

———. 1984. "A Cultural Materialist Theory of Band and Village Warfare: The Yanomamo Test." In *Warfare, Culture, and Environment*. R. B. Ferguson, ed., pp. 111–40. Orlando: Academic Press.

———. 1990. "Potlatch." In *Annual Edition: Anthropology, 1990–91*. Elvio Angeloni, ed., pp. 88–93. Guilford, CT: Dushkin.

———. 1999. *Theories of Culture in Postmodern Times*. Walnut Creek, CA: AltaMira.

Harris, Marvin, and Orna Johnson. 2003. *Cultural Anthropology*. 6th ed. Boston: Allyn & Bacon.

Harris, M., and E. B. Ross, eds. 1987. *Food and Evolution: Toward a Theory of Human Food Habits*. Philadelphia: Temple University Press.

Hart, C. W. M., and Arnold R. Pilling. 1960. *The Tiwi of North Australia*. New York: Holt, Rinehart and Winston.

Hart, C. W. M., and Arnold Pilling, and Jane Goodale. 1988. *The Tiwi of North Australia*. 3d ed. New York: Holt, Rinehart and Winston.

Hatch, Elvin. 1985. "Culture." In *The Social Science Encyclopedia*. Adam Kuper and Jessica Kuper, eds., p. 178. London: Routledge and Kegan Paul.

Hatcher, Evelyn P. 1999. *Art as Culture*. 2d ed. Westport, CT: Bergin and Garvey.

Hawkes, K., and J. O'Connell. 1981. "Affluent Hunters? Some Comments in Light of the Alyawara Case." *American Anthropologist* 83: 622–26.

Hayward, Fred M., and Laura M. Siaya. 2001. *Public Experience, Attitudes, and Knowledge: A Report of Two National Surveys About International Education*. Washington, DC: American Council on Education.

Hecht, Michael L., Mary Jane Collier, and Sidney Ribeau. 1993. *African American Communication: Ethnic Identity and Cultural Interpretation*. Thousand Oaks, CA: Sage Publications.

Hecht, Robert M. 1986. "Salvage Anthropology: The Redesign of a Rural Development

Project in Guinea." In *Anthropology and Rural Development in West Africa*. Michael M. Horowitz and Thomas M. Painter, eds., pp. 13–26. Boulder, CO: Westview Press.

Heider, Karl. 1979. *Grand Valley Dani: Peaceful Warriors*. New York: Holt, Rinehart and Winston.

Hellinger, Daniel, and Dennis Judd. 1991. *The Demographic Facade*. Pacific Grove, CA: Brooks/Cole.

Herdt, Gilbert. 1981. *Guardians of the Flutes: Idioms of Masculinity*. New York: McGraw-Hill.

Hern, Warren M. 1992. "Family Planning, Amazon Style." *Natural History* 101(12): 30–37.

Hernandez, Daniel. 2003. "A Hybrid Tongue or Slanguage?" *Los Angeles Times* (December 27): A-1.

Hernandez Castillo, Rosalva A., and Ronald Nigh. 1998. "Global Processes and Local Identity Among Mayan Coffee Growers in Chiapas, Mexico." *American Anthropologist* 100(1): 136–147.

Hernandez Licona, Gonzalo. 2000. "Labor Market Transitions in Mexico: The Evolution of Household Businesses During Economic Crises." Paper delivered at conference on "Consequences of Financial Crises on Income: Distribution and Poverty in Latin America." Sponsored by ITAM (Instituto Tecnologico Autonomo de Mexico), May 19–20, 2000.

Herskovits, Melville. 1967. *Dahomey: An Ancient West African Kingdom*. Volume 1. Evanston, IL: Northwestern University Press (orig. 1938).

———. 1972. *Cultural Relativism: Perspectives in Cultural Pluralism*. New York: Vintage Books.

Hickerson, Nancy P. 1980. *Linguistic Anthropology*. New York: Holt, Rinehart and Winston.

Hildebrand, Peter. 1982. "Summary of the Sondeo Methodology Used by ICTA." In *Farming Systems Research and Development: Guidelines for Developing Countries*. W. W. Shanner, P. F. Philip, and W. R. Schmehl, eds., pp. 289–93. Boulder, CO: Westview Press.

Hill, Kim, Hillard Kaplan, Kristen Hawkes, and Magdalena Hurtado. 1985. "Men's Time Allocation to Subsistence Work Among the Ache of Eastern Paraguay." *Human Ecology* 13: 29–47.

———. 1987. "Foraging Decisions Among Ache Hunter-Gatherers: New Data and Implications for Optimal Foraging Models." *Ethology and Sociobiology* 8.

Hockett, C. F. 1973. *Man's Place in Nature*. New York: McGraw-Hill.

Hodge, Robert W., Donald J. Treiman, and Peter H. Rossi. 1966. "A Comparative Study of Occupational Prestige." In *Class, Status, and Power: Social Stratification in Comparative Perspective*. 2d ed. Reinhard Bendix and Seymour Martin Lipset, eds., pp. 309–21. New York: Free Press.

Hoebel, E. Adamson. 1960. *The Cheyennes: Indians of the Great Plains*. New York: Holt, Rinehart and Winston.

———. 1972. *Anthropology: The Study of Man*. 4th ed. New York: McGraw-Hill.

Hostetler, John, and Gertrude Huntington. 1971. *Children in Amish Society: Socialization and Community Education*. New York: Holt, Rinehart and Winston.

Howard, Beth. 1991. "Ape Apothecary: Self-prescribing Chimps Lead Researchers to Nature's Medicine Cabinet." *Omni* 13: 30.

Howell, N. 1986. "Feedbacks and Buffers in Relation to Scarcity and Abundance:

Studies of Hunter-Gatherer Populations." In *The State of Population Theory*. D. Coleman and R. Schofield, eds., pp. 156–87. Oxford: Basil Blackwell.

Hudson, Valarie, and Andrea M. den Boer. 2004. *Bare Branches: The Security Implications of Asia's Surplus Male Population*. Cambridge, MA: The MIT Press.

Hughes, Charles C., and John M. Hunter. 1972. "The Role of Technological Development in Promoting Disease in Africa." In *The Careless Technology: Ecology and International Development*. M. T. Farvar and John P. Milton, eds., pp. 69–101. Garden City, NY: Natural History Press.

Hull, Cindy. 2005. "Information Mapping Survey Reveals Email Writing Skills Vital to Job Effectiveness." *Information Mapping Inc.*, Waltham, MA (August 2).

———. 2007. "From Field to Factory and Beyond: New Strategies for New Realities in a Yucatecan Village." In *Globalization and Change in 15 Cultures: Born in One World, Living in Another*. George Spindler and Janice Stockard, eds., pp. 172–98. Belmont, CA: Wadsworth.

Humphrey, Caroline. 1999. "Shamans in the City." *Anthropology Today* 15(3) (June): 3–10.

Hunt, Linda M., Jacqueline Pugh, and Miguel Valenzuela. 1995. *What They Do Outside the Doctor's Office: Understanding and Responding to Diabetes Patients' Strategic Adaptations of Self-Care Behavior*. Paper given at the meetings of the Society for Applied Anthropology, Albuquerque, NM, April.

Hymes, Dell. 1977. "Discovering Oral Performance and Measured Verse in American Indian Narrative." *New Literary History* 8(3): 431–57.

Igoe, Jim. 2004. *Conservation and Globalization: A Study of National Parks and Indigenous Communities from East Africa and South Dakota*. Belmont, CA: Wadsworth.

Isaac, B. 1990. "Economy, Ecology, and Analogy: The !Kung San and the Generalized Foraging Model." In *Early Paleoindian Economies of Eastern North America*. B. Isaac and K. Tankersley, eds., pp. 323–35. Greenwich, CT: JAI Press.

Jackson, Bruce, and Edward Ives. 1996. *The World Observed: Reflections on the Fieldwork Process*. Urbana: University of Illinois Press.

Jameson, Frederic. 1990. *Postmodernism, or the Cultural Logic of Late Capitalism*. Durham, NC: Duke University Press.

Janson, H. W. 1986. *History of Art* (revised by Anthony F. Janson). New York and Englewood Cliffs, NJ: Harry Abrams and Prentice-Hall.

Jehl, Douglas. 1999. "Arab Honor's Price: A Woman's Blood." *New York Times* (June 20): 1.

Jenkins, Henry. 2001. "Culture Goes Global." *Technology Review* 104(6): 89.

Johnson, Bradley. 2005. "What Blogs Cost American Business." *Advertising Age* (October 24).

Jonaitis, Alldona, ed. 1991. *Chiefly Feasts: The Enduring Kwakiutl Potlatch*. Seattle: University of Washington Press.

Jones, Maggie. 2006. "Shutting Themselves In." *New York Times Magazine* (January 15): 46–51.

Jordan, Cathie, Roland Tharp, and Lynn Baird-Vogt. 1992. "Just Open the Door: Cultural Compatibility and Classroom Rapport." In *Cross-Cultural Literacy: Ethnographies of Communication in Multiethnic Classrooms*. Marietta Saravia-Shore and Steven F. Arvizu, eds., pp. 3–18. New York: Garland.

Jorgensen, Danny L. 1989. *Participant Observation: A Methodology for Human Studies*. Thousand Oaks, CA: Sage Publications.

Kaplan, David, and Robert Manners. 1986. *Culture Theory*. Englewood Cliffs, NJ: Prentice-Hall.

Kasarda, John D. 1971. "Economic Structure and Fertility: A Comparative Analysis." *Demography* 8(3): 307–18.

Kaslow, Amy. 1995. "Helping Women Seen as Boosting World Prosperity." *Christian Science Monitor* (August 24): 1.

Katzner, Kenneth. 1975. *The Languages of the World*. New York: Funk & Wagnalls.

Keefe, Susan E. 1988. "The Myth of the Declining Family: Extended Family Ties Among Urban Mexican-Americans and Anglo-Americans." In *Urban Life: Readings in Urban Anthropology*. 2d ed. George Gmelch and Walter Zenner, eds., pp. 229–39. Prospect Heights, IL: Waveland Press.

Keenan, Elinor. 1974. "Norm-makers, Normbreakers: Uses of Speech by Men and Women in a Malagasy Community." In *Explorations in the Ethnography of Speaking*. Richard Bauman and Joel Sherzer, eds., pp. 125–43. London: Cambridge University Press.

Keesing, Roger. 1992. "Not a Real Fish: The Ethnographer as Inside Outsider." In *The Naked Anthropologist: Tales from Around the World*. Philip DeVita, ed., pp. 73–78. Belmont, CA: Wadsworth.

Kelly, David. 2005. "'Lost Boys' Cast Out of Polygamous Enclaves," *Charlotte Observer* (June 19): A-23.

Kelly, Robert L. 1995. *The Foraging Spectrum: Diversity in Hunter-Gatherer Lifeways*. Washington, DC: Smithsonian Institution Press.

Kendall, Laurel. 1996a. "Korean Shamans and the Spirit of Capitalism." *American Anthropologist* 98(3): 502–27.

———. 1996b. *Getting Married in Korea: Of Gender, Morality, and Modernity*. Berkeley: University of California Press.

Kent, Susan. 1996. *Cultural Diversity Among Twentieth-Century Foragers: An African Perspective*. Cambridge: Cambridge University Press.

Khazanov, Anatoly M. 1994. *Nomads and the Outside World*. 2d ed. Madison: University of Wisconsin Press.

Kilbride, Philip L. 1997. "African Polygyny: Family Values and Contemporary Change." In *Applying Cultural Anthropology: An Introductory Reader*. Aaron Podolefsky and Peter Brown, eds., pp. 201–08. Mountain View, CA: Mayfield.

Kirby, David. 2004. "Party Favors: Pill Popping as Insurance." *New York Times* (June 21): E-1.

Kirsch, A. T. 1985. "Text and Context: Buddhist Sex Roles/Culture of Gender Revisited." *American Ethnologist* 12: 302–20.

Kluckhohn, Clyde. 1949. *Mirror for Man: Anthropology and Modern Life*. New York: Wittlesey House (McGraw-Hill).

Knauft, B. 1987. "Reconsidering Violence in Simple Human Societies: Homicide Among Gebusi of New Guinea." *Current Anthropology* 28: 457–500.

Kohls, L. Robert. 1984. *Survival Kit for Overseas Living*. Yarmouth, ME: Intercultural Press.

Kolenda, Pauline M. 1978. *Caste in Contemporary India: Beyond Organic Solidarity*. Prospect Heights, IL: Waveland.

Kosmin, Barry A., and Seymour Lachman. 1993. *One Nation Under God: Religion in Contemporary American Society*. New York: Crown.

Kottak, Conrad P. 1998. *Assault on Paradise: Social Change in a Brazilian Village*. New York: McGraw-Hill.

———. 2004. *Cultural Anthropology*. 10th ed. Boston: McGraw-Hill.

Krajick, Kevin. 1998. "Green Farming by the Incas?" *Science* 281: 323–29.

Kramer, Cheris. 1974. "Folk Linguistics: Wishy-Washy Mommy Talk." *Psychology Today* 8(1): 82–85.

Krause, Elizabeth. 2005. *A Crisis of Births: Population Politics and Family-Making in Italy*. Belmont, CA: Wadsworth.

Krauss, Clifford. 2004. "When the Koran Speaks, Will Canadian Law Bend?" *New York Times* (August 4): A-4.

———. 2006. "Years Into Self-Rule, Inuit Still Struggle." *New York Times* (June 18): 4.

Kroeber, Alfred L., and Clyde Kluckhohn. 1952. *Culture: A Critical Review of Concepts and Definitions*. Papers of the Peabody Museum of American Archaeology and Ethnology 47(1).

Kuczynski, Alex. 2004. "A Lovelier You, with Off-the-Shelf Parts." *New York Times* (May 2, sect. 4): 1.

Kumar, Hari. 2005. "India's Harried Elite Now Turns, and Twists, to Yoga Lite." *New York Times* (February 1): A-4.

Kuper, Hilda. 1986. *The Swazi: A South African Kingdom*. 2d ed. New York: Holt, Rinehart and Winston.

Kurtz, Donald V. 2001. *Political Anthropology: Paradigms and Power*. Boulder, CO: Westview Press.

Kutsche, Paul. 1997. *Field Ethnography: A Manual for Doing Cultural Anthropology*. Upper Saddle River, NJ: Prentice Hall.

Kuznar, Lawrence. 1996. *Reclaiming a Scientific Anthropology*. Thousand Oaks, CA: Sage Publications.

Labov, William. 1972. *Sociolinguistic Patterns*. Philadelphia: University of Pennsylvania Press.

Lacey, Marc. 2004. "Tribe, Claiming Whites' Land, Confronts Kenya's Government." *New York Times* (August 25): A-1.

———. 2005. "Victims of Uganda Atrocities Follow a Path of Forgiveness." *New York Times* (April 18): 1.

———. 2006. "The Case of the Stolen Statues: Solving a Kenyan Mystery." *New York Times* (April 16): 4.

La Fontaine, Jean. 1963. "Witchcraft in Bagisu." In *Witchcraft and Sorcery in East Africa*. J. Middleton and E. Winter, eds., pp. 187–220. New York: Praeger.

Lakshmi, Rama. 2004. "Factory Orders Dropping? Astrologer Is Go-to Guru for Struggling Corporate Executives." *The Washington Post* (July 4): A-17.

Lamont-Brown, Raymond. 1999. "Japan's New Spirituality." *Contemporary Review* (August): 70–73.

Lamphere, Louise. 1974. "Stategies, Conflict, and Cooperation Among Women in Domestic Groups." In *Women, Culture, and Society*. Michelle Zimbalist Rosaldo and Louise Lamphere, eds. Stanford: Stanford University Press.

Lane, Belden C. 1989. "The Power of Myth: Lessons from Joseph Campbell." *The Christian Century* 106 (July 5): 652–54.

Lanier, Alison. 1979. "Selecting and Preparing Personnel for Overseas Transfers." *Personnel Journal* (March): 160–63.

Laumann, Edward O., John Gagnon, Robert T. Michael, and Stuart Michaels. 1994. *The Social Organization of Sexuality: Sexual*

Practices in the United States. Chicago: University of Chicago Press.

Lave, Jean, and Etienne Wenger 1991. *Situated Learning: Legitimate Peripheral Participation.* Cambridge: Cambridge University Press.

Lee, Dorothy. 1993. "Religious Perspectives in Anthropology." In *Magic, Witchcraft, and Religion: An Anthropological Study of the Supernatural.* 3d ed. Arthur C. Lehmann and James E. Myers, eds., pp. 10–17. Mountain View, CA: Mayfield.

Lee, Richard B. 1968. "What Hunters Do for a Living, or How to Make Out on Scarce Resources." In *Man the Hunter.* Richard B. Lee and Irven DeVore, eds., pp. 30–48. Chicago: Aldine-Atherton.

———. 2003. *The Dobe Ju/'hoansi.* 3d ed. Belmont, CA: Wadsworth.

———. 2007. "The Ju/'Hoansi at the Crossroads: Continuity and Change in the Time of AIDS." In *Globalization and Change in 15 Cultures: Born in One World, Living in Another.* George Spindler and Janice Stockard, eds., pp. 144–71. Belmont, CA: Wadsworth.

Lee, Richard B., and Richard Daly, eds. 1999. *The Cambridge Encyclopedia of Hunters and Gatherers.* Cambridge: Cambridge University Press.

Lee, Sharon M. 1993. "Racial Classifications in the United States Census: 1890–1990." *Racial and Ethnic Studies* 16(1)(January): 75–94.

Lehmann, Arthur C., and James E. Myers, eds. 1993. *Magic, Witchcraft, and Religion.* 3d ed. Palo Alto, CA: Mayfield.

Lehmann, Arthur C., James E. Myers, and Pamela Moro, eds. 2001. *Magic, Witchcraft, and Religion: An Anthropological Study of the Supernatural.* 5th ed. Boston: McGraw-Hill.

Leighton, Dorothea, and Clyde Kluckhohn. 1948. *Children of the People.* Cambridge: Cambridge University Press.

Lenski, Gerhard E. 1966. *Power and Privilege: A Theory of Social Stratification.* New York: McGraw-Hill.

di Leonardo, Micaela. 1991. *Gender at the Crossroads of Knowledge: Feminist Anthropology in the Postmodern Era.* Berkeley, CA: University of California Press.

Lepowsky, Maria. 1990. "Big Men, Big Women, and Cultural Autonomy." *Ethnology* 29(1): 35–50.

Lévi-Strauss, Claude. 1969. *The Elementary Structures of Kinship.* Boston: Beacon Press.

Levy, Dany. 2004. "Chickspeak." *The New York Times Magazine* (August 22): 18.

Lewellen, Ted C. 2002. *The Anthropology of Globalization: Cultural Anthropology Enters the Twenty-First Century.* Westport, CT: Greenwood (Bergin and Garvey).

Lewis, Oscar. 1952. "Urbanization Without Breakdown." *Scientific Monthly* 75 (July): 31–41.

———. 1955. "Peasant Culture in India and Mexico: A Comparative Analysis." In *Village India: Studies in the Little Community.* McKim Marriott, ed., pp. 145–70. Chicago: University of Chicago Press.

———. 1966. "The Culture of Poverty." *Scientific American* (October): 19–25.

Lewis-Williams, J. D., and T. A. Dowson. 1988. "The Signs of All Times: Entoptic Phenomena in Upper Palaeolithic Art." *Current Anthropology* 29(2): 20–45.

Linton, Ralph. 1936. *The Study of Man.* New York: Appleton-Century-Crofts.

Lloyd, Marion. 1999. "Affirmative Action Dispute Leads to Violence at a Top Medical School in India." *Chronicle of Higher Education* (April 23): A58.

Loker, William M. 2000. "Sowing Discord, Planting Doubts: Rhetoric and Reality in an Environment and Development Project in Honduras." *Human Organization* 59(3): 300–310.

Lomax, Alan, et al. 1968. *Folk Song Style and Culture.* Washington, DC: American Association for the Advancement of Science.

Low, Setha M. 1981. *Anthropology as a New Technology in Landscape Planning.* Unpublished paper presented at the meetings of the American Society of Landscape Architects.

Lowie, Robert. 1963. "Religion in Human Life." *American Anthropologist* 65: 532–42.

Lundgren, Nancy. 2002. *Watch and Pray: A Portrait of Fante Village Life in Transition.* Belmont, CA: Wadsworth.

Luo, Michael. 2006. "Preaching the Word and Quoting the Voice: An Evangelist Thrives in Manhattan by Embracing the City and Identifying with Its Culture." *New York Times* (February 26): 28.

Lutz, William D. 1995. "Language, Appearance, and Reality: Doublespeak in 1984." In *Anthropology: Annual Editions 95/96.* Elvio Angeloni, ed. Guilford, CT: Dushkin.

MacFarquhar, Emily. 1994. "The War Against Women." *U.S. News and World Report* (March 28): 42–48.

Macionis, John J. 2001. *Sociology.* 8th ed. Upper Saddle River, NJ: Prentice-Hall.

Madigan, Nick. 2005. "After Fleeing Polygamist Community, an Opportunity for Influence." *New York Times* (June 29): A-14.

Mahbubani, Kishore. 2005. *Beyond the Age of Innocence: Rebuilding Trust Between America and the World.* New York: Public Affairs.

Malinowski, Bronislaw. 1922. *Argonauts of the Western Pacific.* New York: Dutton.

———. 1927. *Sex and Repression in Savage Society.* London: Kegan Paul.

———. 1944. *A Scientific Theory of Culture.* Chapel Hill, NC: University of North Carolina Press.

Mandelbaum, David G. 1970. *Society in India.* Vol. 1. Berkeley: University of California Press.

Marett, Robert. 1914. *The Threshold of Religion.* London: Methuen.

Marksbury, Richard A., ed. 1993. *The Business of Marriage: Transformations in Oceanic Matrimony.* Pittsburgh: University of Pittsburgh Press.

Marshall, Donald S. 1971. "Sexual Behavior on Mangaia." In *Sexual Behavior: Variations in the Ethnographic Spectrum.* Donald S. Marshall and Robert Suggs, eds., pp. 103–62. New York: Basic Books.

Marshall, Lorna. 1965. "The !Kung Bushmen of the Kalahari Desert." In *Peoples of Africa.* James Gibbs, ed., pp. 243–78. New York: Holt, Rinehart and Winston.

Marx, Elizabeth. 1999. *Breaking Through Culture Shock: What You Need to Succeed in International Business.* London: Nicholas Brealey Publishing.

Marx, Karl. 1909. *Capital* (E. Unterman, trans.). Chicago: C. H. Kerr (orig. 1867).

Matloff, Judith. 1998. "Russian Hard Times a Boon to Native Peoples." *Christian Science Monitor* (November 20): 7.

Mauss, M. 1954. *The Gift* (I. Cunnison, trans.). New York: Free Press.

Maybury-Lewis, David. 1992. *Millennium; Tribal Wisdom and the Modern World.* New York: Viking Press.

McClelland, D. C. 1960. *The Achieving Society.* New York: Van Nostrand.

McGee, R. Jon. 1990. *Life, Ritual and Religion Among the Lacandon Maya.* Belmont, CA: Wadsworth.

McGlynn, Frank, and Arthur Tuden, eds. 1991. *Anthropological Approaches to Political Behavior.* Pittsburgh: University of Pittsburgh Press.

McGrath, Charles. 2006. "The Pleasures of the Text." *New York Times Magazine* (January 22): 15–19.

Mead, Margaret. 1928. *Coming of Age in Samoa.* New York: Morrow.

———. 1950. *Sex and Temperament in Three Primitive Societies.* New York: Mentor (orig. 1935).

———. 1956. *New Lives for Old.* New York: Morrow.

Meek, Charles K. 1972. "Ibo Law." In *Readings in Anthropology.* J. D. Jennings and E. A. Hoebel, eds. New York: McGraw-Hill.

Meggitt, Mervyn. 1977. *Blood Is Their Argument.* Palo Alto, CA: Mayfield.

Mehrabian, Albert. 1981. *Silent Messages.* 2d ed. Belmont, CA: Wadsworth.

Mehta, Suketu. 2004. "Bollywood Confidential." *New York Times Magazine* (November 14): 60ff.

Melton, J. Gordon. 1999. *The Encyclopedia of American Religions.* Detroit: Gale Research.

Mencher, Joan P., and Anne Okongwu, eds. 1993. *Where Did All the Men Go? Female-Headed/Female-Supported Households in Cross-Cultural Perspective.* Boulder, CO: Westview.

Mendonsa, Eugene. 1985. "Characteristics of Sisala Diviners." In *Magic, Witchcraft, and Religion: An Anthropological Study of the Supernatural.* Arthur C. Lehmann and James E. Myers, eds., pp. 214–24. Palo Alto, CA: Mayfield.

Merton, Robert K. 1957. *Social Theory and Social Structure.* Glencoe, IL: Free Press.

Michael, Robert T., John Gagnon, Edward O. Laumann, and Gina Kolata. 1994. *Sex in America: A Definitive Survey.* Boston: Little Brown and Company.

Michrina, Barry P., and Cherylanne Richards. 1996. *Person to Person: Fieldwork, Dialogue, and the Hermeneutic Method.* Albany: State University of New York Press.

Middleton, John. 1965. *The Lugbara of Uganda.* New York: Holt, Rinehart and Winston.

Middleton, John, and Greet Kershaw. 1965. *The Kikuyu and Kamba of Kenya.* London: International African Institute.

Middleton, John, and David Tait, eds. 1958. *Tribes Without Rulers: Studies in African Segmentary Systems.* London: Routledge and Kegan Paul.

Miller, Barbara D. 1993. "Female Infanticide and Child Neglect in Rural North India." In *Gender in Cross-Cultural Perspective.* Caroline Brettell and Carolyn Sargent, eds., pp. 423–35. Englewood Cliffs, NJ: Prentice-Hall.

Miller, Lauren. 2006. "Selectively Importing Candomble: Through Americans' Capoeira Pilgrimages to Brazil." *Anthropology News* 47(5): 28.

Miller, Lisa. 1999. "The Age of Divine Disunity," *Wall Street Journal* (February 10): B1.

Mills, C. Wright. 1956. *The Power Elite.* New York: Oxford University Press.

Mills, George. 1957. "Art: An Introduction to Qualitative Anthropology." *Journal of Aesthetics and Art Criticism* 16(1): 1–17.

Mincer, Jillian. 1994. "How Schools Shortchange Girls." *New York Times* (January 9, Education Life section): 27.

Miner, Horace. 1953. *The Primitive City of Timbuctoo.* Philadelphia: American Philosophical Society.

Moller, V., and G. J. Welch. 1990. "Polygamy, Economic Security, and Well-Being of Retired Zulu Migrant Workers." *Journal of Cross-Cultural Gerontology* 5: 205–16.

Montagu, Ashley. 1972. *Touching: The Human Significance of the Skin.* New York: Harper & Row.

Montana, Cate. 1999. "Tribe That Killed a Whale: Allies Say Traditions Not Wrong, Just Different." *Indian Country Today* (May 24).

Moock, Joyce L. 1978–79. "The Content and Maintenance of Social Ties Between Urban Migrants and Their Home-Based Support Groups: The Maragoli Case." *African Urban Studies* 3 (Winter): 15–32.

Moody, Edward J. 1993. "Urban Witches." In *Magic, Witchcraft, and Religion: An Anthropological Study of the Supernatural.* 3d ed. Arthur C. Lehmann and James E. Myers, eds., pp. 231–37. Mountain View, CA: Mayfield.

Morgan, Lewis H. 1871. *Systems of Consanguinity and Affinity of the Human Family.* Washington, DC: Smithsonian Institution.

———. 1963. *Ancient Society.* New York: World (orig. 1877).

Morin, Richard, and Megan Rosenfeld. 1998. "With More Equity, More Sweat." *Washington Post* (March 22): A1.

Moynihan, Colin. 2004. "City of a Thousand Handshakes." *New York Times* (May 22): A-13.

Mulder, Monique B. 1988. "Kipsigis Bridewealth Payments." In *Human Reproductive Behavior: A Darwinian Perspective.* Laura Betzig, Monique B. Mulder, and Paul Turke, eds., pp. 65–82. Cambridge: Cambridge University Press.

———. 1992. "Women's Strategies in Polygynous Marriage." *Human Nature* 3(1): 45–70.

Murdock, George. 1945. "The Common Denominator of Cultures." In *The Science of Man in the World Crisis.* Ralph Linton, ed., p. 124. New York: Columbia University Press.

———. 1949. *Social Structure.* New York: Macmillan.

———. 1967. "Ethnographic Atlas: A Summary." *Ethnology* 6(2): 109–236.

———. 1968. "The Current Status of the World's Hunting and Gathering Peoples." In *Man the Hunter.* Richard B. Lee and Irven DeVore, eds., pp. 13–20. Chicago: Aldine-Atherton.

Murphy, Dean E. 2004. "At War Against Dams, Tribe Turns to Old Ways." *New York Times* (September 14): A-13.

Murphy, R. F., and L. Kasdan. 1959. "The Structure of Parallel Cousin Marriage." *American Anthropologist* 61: 17–29.

Murray, Gerald F. 1984. "The Wood Tree as a Peasant Cash-Crop: An Anthropological Strategy for the Domestication of Energy." In *Haiti—Today and Tomorrow: An Interdisciplinary Study.* Charles R. Foster and Albert Valdman, eds., pp. 141–60. Latham, NY: University Press of America.

———. 1986. "Seeing the Forest While Planting the Trees: An Anthropological Approach to Agroforestry in Rural Haiti." In *Politics, Projects, and People: Institutional Development in Haiti.* Derick W. Brinkerhoff and J. Garcia-Zamor, eds., pp. 193–226. New York: Praeger.

———. 1987. "The Domestication of Wood in Haiti: A Case Study in Applied Evolution." In *Anthropological Praxis.* Robert Wulff and Shirley Fiske, eds., pp. 223–40. Boulder, CO: Westview Press.

Mwamwenda, T. S., and L. A. Monyooe. 1997. "Status of Bridewealth in an African Culture." *Journal of Social Psychology* 137(2): 269–71.

Nagourney, Adam. 2006. "Politics Is Facing Sweeping Change Via the Internet." *New York Times* (April 2): 1.

Nakao, Keiko, and Judith Treas. 1990. *Occupational Prestige in the United States Revisited: Twenty-Five Years of Stability and Change.* Paper presented at the annual meetings of the American Sociological Association.

Nanda, Serena. 1990. *Neither Man nor Woman: The Hijras of India.* Belmont, CA: Wadsworth.

———. 1992. "Arranging a Marriage in India." In *The Naked Anthropologist.* Philip DeVita, ed., pp. 137–43. Belmont, CA: Wadsworth.

Nash, Jesse W. 1988. "Confucius and the VCR." *Natural History* (May): 28–31.

National Center for Health Statistics (Centers for Disease Control). www.cdc.gov/nchs/hus.htm.

National Opinion Research Center. 1996. "General Social Surveys, 1972–1996: Cumulative Codebook. Chicago: National Opinion Research Center.

Navarro, Mireya. 2005. "A Minder to Mind Your Manners," *New York Times* (August 14): 9-1.

———. 2006. "Families Add 3rd Generation to Households." *New York Times* (May 25): 1.

Nelson, Richard. 1993. "Understanding Eskimo Science." *Audubon* (September/October): 102–09.

Nettl, Bruno. 1980. "Ethnomusicology: Definitions, Directions, and Problems." In *Music of Many Cultures.* Elizabeth May, ed., pp. 1–9. Berkeley: University of California Press.

Nettl, Bruno, and Philip V. Bohlman, eds. 1991. *Comparative Musicology and Anthropology of Music.* Chicago: University of Chicago Press.

Nettl, Bruno, et al. 2000. *Excursions in World Music.* 3d ed. Upper Saddle River, NJ: Prentice-Hall.

Newman, Katherine S. 1988. *Falling from Grace: The Experience of Downward Mobility in the American Middle Class.* New York: Free Press.

———. 1999. *No Shame in My Game: The Working Poor in the Inner City.* New York: Knopf.

Newport, Frank. 2004. "A Look at Americans and Religion Today." *The Gallup Organization,* March 23, www.gallup.com/poll/content/default.aspx?ci511089&pg52.

Oberg, Kalervo. 1960. "Culture Shock: Adjustments to New Cultural Environments." *Practical Anthropology* (July/August): 177–82.

Oliver, Douglas. 1955. *A Solomon Island Society.* Cambridge, MA: Harvard University Press.

O'Meara, Tim. 1990. *Samoan Planters: Tradition and Economic Development in Polynesia.* Fort Worth: Holt, Rinehart and Winston.

Onishi, Norimitsu. 2004. "A Crash Course in Tradition for Modern Korean Brides." *New York Times* (June 25): A-4.

Ortiz, Sutti, and Susan Lees, eds. 1992. *Understanding Economic Process.* Lanham, MD: University Press of America.

Ortner, Sherry. 1974. "Is Female to Male as Nature Is to Culture?" In *Women, Culture, and Society.* Michelle Zimbalist Rosaldo and Louise Lamphere, eds., pp. 67–88. Stanford, CA: Stanford University Press.

Ottenheimer, Harriet. 2005. *The Anthropology of Language: An Introduction to Linguistic Anthropology.* Belmont, CA: Wadsworth.

Ottenheimer, Martin. 1996. *Forbidden Relatives.* Champaign: University of Illinois Press.

Pachon, Harry P. 1998. "Buenos Dias California." *UNESCO Courier* (November): 31–32.

Pape, Robert A. 2005. *Dying to Win: The Strategic Logic of Suicide Terrorism.* New York: Random House.

Paredes, J. Anthony. 1992. "'Practical History' and the Poarch Creeks: A Meeting Ground for Anthropologists and Tribal Leaders." In *Anthropological Research: Process and Application.* John Poggie, Billie R. DeWalt, and William W. Dressler, eds., pp. 209–26. Albany: State University of New York Press.

Parker, Arthur C. 1913. *The Code of Handsome Lake, the Seneca Prophet.* Albany: New York State Museum Bulletin, No. 163.

Parker, Patricia L., and Thomas F. King. 1987. "Intercultural Mediation at Truk International Airport." In *Anthropological Praxis.* Robert Wulff and Shirley Fiske, eds., pp. 160–73. Boulder, CO: Westview Press.

Parkin, Robert. 1997. *Kinship: An Introduction to Basic Concepts.* Malden, MA: Blackwell.

Parkin, Robert, and Linda Stone. 2004. *Kinship and Family: An Anthropological Reader.* Malden, MA: Blackwell.

Parrenas, Rhacel Salazar. 2001. *Servants of Globalization: Women, Migration, and Domestic Work.* Stanford, CA: Stanford University Press.

Parsons, Talcott. 1951. *The Social System.* New York: Free Press.

Parsons, Talcott, and E. Shils. 1952. *Toward a General Theory of Action.* Cambridge, MA: Harvard University Press.

Patten, Sonia. 2003. "Medical Anthropology: Improving Nutrition in Malawi." In *Conformity and Conflict: Readings in Cultural Anthropology.* 11th ed. James Spradley and David McCurdy, eds., pp. 405–14. Boston: Allyn & Bacon.

Peacock, James L. 1986. *The Anthropological Lens.* Cambridge: Cambridge University Press.

———. *The Anthropological Lens: Harsh Light, Soft Focus,* 2nd ed. New York: Cambridge University Press, 2002.

Pelto, Pertti J. 1973. *The Snowmobile Revolution: Technology and Social Change in the Arctic.* Menlo Park, CA: Benjamin/Cummings.

Plattner, Stuart, ed. 1989. *Economic Anthropology.* Stanford, CA: Stanford University Press.

Plotkin, Mark. 1995. "Through the Emerald Door." In *Annual Editions: Anthropology 95/96.* Elvio Angeloni, ed. Guilford, CT: Dushkin.

Pluralism Project at Harvard University. www.fas.harvard.edu/pluralism/.

Polanyi, Karl. 1957. "The Economy as Instituted Process." In *Trade and Market in the Early Empires.* Karl Polanyi, Conrad Arensberg, and Harry Pearson, eds., pp. 243–70. New York: Free Press.

Porterfield, Elaine. 1999. "How to Throw a Good Potlatch: Just Add Whale." *Christian Science Monitor* (May 25): 2.

Prestowitz, Clyde. 2003. *Rogue Nation: American Unilateralism and the Failure of Good Intentions.* New York: Basic Books.

Price, Sally. 2001. *Primitive Art in Civilized Places.* Chicago: University of Chicago Press.

Price, T. Douglas, and James A. Brown. 1985. *Prehistoric Hunter-Gatherers: The Emergence of Cultural Complexity.* Orlando: Academic Press.

Prior, Ian. 1971. "The Price of Civilization." *Nutrition Today* 6(4): 2–11.

Pristin, Terry. 2002. "Behind the Legal and Private Worlds of the Veil." *New York Times* (August 11): L4.

Pruzan, Todd. 2005. *The Clumsiest People in Europe: Or, Mrs. Mortimer's Bad-Tempered*

Guide to the Victorian World. New York: Bloomsbury.

Pryor, F. L. 1977. *The Origins of the Economy: A Comparative Study of Distribution in Primitive and Peasant Economies.* New York: Academic Press.

———. 1986. "The Adoption of Agriculture." *American Anthropologist* 88: 879–97.

Rai, Saritha. 2004. "Short on Priests, U.S. Catholics Outsource Prayers to Indian Clergy." *New York Times* (June 13): 13.

Ramanamma, A., and U. Bambawale. 1980. "The Mania for Sons: An Analysis of Social Values in South Asia." *Social Science and Medicine* (14): 107–10.

Raphael, D., and F. Davis. 1985. *Only Mothers Know: Patterns of Infant Feeding in Traditional Cultures.* Westport, CT: Greenwood Press.

Rasmussen, Knud. 1927. *Across Arctic America.* New York: G. P. Putnam's Sons.

Rathje, William L. 1989. "Rubbish!" *Atlantic Monthly* 67(6): 99–109.

Rathje, William L., et al. 1992. "The Archaeology of Contemporary Landfills. *American Antiquity* 57: 437–47.

Read, Margaret. 1960. *Children of Their Fathers: Growing Up Among the Ngoni of Nyasaland.* New Haven, CT: Yale University Press.

Real, Terrence. 2001. "Men's Hidden Depression." In *Men And Masculinity.* Theodore F. Cohen, ed. Belmont, CA: Wadsworth.

Renaud, Michelle L. 1993. "We're All in It Together: AIDS Prevention in Urban Senegal." *Practicing Anthropology* 15(4): 25–29.

———. 1997. "Applied Anthropology at the Crossroads: AIDS Prevention Research in Senegal and Beyond." *Practicing Anthropology* 19(1): 23–27.

Reynolds, Simon. 1998. *Generation Ecstasy.* Boston: Little Brown.

Richards, Audrey I. 1960. "The Bemba— Their Country and Diet." In *Cultures and Societies of Africa.* Simon and Phoebe Ottenburg, eds., pp. 96–109. New York: Random House.

Richtel, Matt. 2004. "For Liars and Loafers, Cell Phones Offer an Alibi." *New York Times* (June 26): A-1.

Rickford, John R. 1999. "Suite for Ebony and Phonics." In *Applying Anthropology: An Introductory Reader.* 5th ed. Aaron Podolefsky and Peter J. Brown, eds., pp. 176–80. Mountain View, CA: Mayfield.

Riding, Alan. 2004. "Babel, A New Capital for a Wider Continent." *New York Times* (May 2): 3.

Robben, Antonius, and Carolyn Nordstrom. 1995. "The Anthropology and Ethnography of Violence and Sociopolitical Conflict." In *Fieldwork Under Fire: Contemporary Studies of Violence and Survival.* Carolyn Nordstrom and Antonius Robben, eds., pp. 1–23. Berkeley, CA: University of California Press.

Roberts, John M. 1967. "Oaths, Autonomic Ordeals, and Power." In *Cross-Cultural Approaches: Readings in Comparative Research.* Clellan S. Ford, ed. New Haven, CT: HRAF Press.

Robinson, Linda. 1998. "Hispanics Don't Exist." *U.S. News and World Report* (May 11): 26.

Roesch, Roberta. 1984. "Violent Families." *Parents* 59(9) (September): 74–76, 150–52.

Rogers, Everett M. 1973. *Communication Strategies for Family Planning.* New York: Free Press.

———. 1983. *Diffusion of Innovations.* 3d ed. New York: Free Press.

———. 2003. *Diffusion of Innovations.* 5th ed. New York: Simon and Schuster, 2003.

Rohner, Ronald P., and Evelyn C. Rohner. 1970. *The Kwakiutl: Indians of British Columbia.* New York: Holt, Rinehart and Winston.

Rohter, Larry. 2004. "Learn English, Says Chile, Thinking Upwardly Global." *New York Times* (December 29): H-3.

Romanucci-Ross, Lola. 1995. *Ethnic Identity: Creation, Conflict, and Accommodation.* 3d ed. Walnut Creek, CA: AltaMira.

Rooney, James F. 1961. "Group Processes Among Skid Row Winos." *Quarterly Journal of Studies of Alcohol* 22: 444–60.

Rosaldo, Michelle Zimbalist. 1974. "Women, Culture, and Society: A Theoretical Overview." In *Women, Culture, and Society.* Michelle Zimbalist Rosaldo and Louise Lamphere, eds. Stanford, CA: Stanford University Press.

Rosen, Lawrence. (no date). *The Anthropologist as Expert Witness.* Mimeographed paper on file with the Applied Anthropology Documentation Project at the University of Kentucky.

Rosenfeld, Gerry. 1971. *Shut Those Thick Lips: A Study of Slum School Failure.* New York: Holt, Rinehart and Winston.

Rosenthal, Elisabeth. 2003. "Bias for Boys Leads to Sale of Baby Girls in China." *New York Times* (July 20): 1.

Ross, M. H. 1986. "Female Political Participation." *American Anthropologist* 88: 843–58.

Russell, Diana. 1990. *Rape in Marriage.* Indianapolis: Indiana University Press.

Ryu, Charles. 1992. "Koreans and Church." In *Asian Americans.* Joann Faung Jean Lee, ed., pp. 162–64. New York: New Press.

Sahlins, Marshall. 1968. "Notes on the Original Affluent Society." In *Man the Hunter.* R. B. Lee and I. DeVore, eds., pp. 85–89. Chicago: Aldine.

———. 1972. *Stone Age Economics.* Chicago: Aldine-Atherton.

Salopek, Paul. 2004. "Southern Seas: The New Wild West." *The Charlotte Observer* (September 5): P-1.

Salzmann, Zdenek. 2003. *Language, Culture, and Society: An Introduction to Linguistic Anthropology.* 3d ed. Boulder, CO: Westview.

Samovar, Larry A., and Richard E. Porter. 1991. *Communication Between Cultures.* Belmont, CA: Wadsworth.

———. 2002. *Intercultural Communication: A Reader.* 10th ed. Belmont, CA: Wadsworth.

Samuels, Shayna. 2001. "Capoeira," *Dance Magazine* 75(12): 66–70.

Samuelson, Paul, and William Nordhaus. 1989. *Economics.* 13th ed. New York: McGraw-Hill.

Sanday, Peggy R. 2004. *Women at the Center: Life in a Modern Matriarchy.* Ithaca, NY: Cornell University Press.

Sapir, Edward. 1929. "The Status of Linguistics as a Science." *Language* 5: 207–14.

Scarce, Rik. 2005. *Contempt of Court: A Scholar's Battle for Free Speech from Behind Bars.* Lanham, MD: AltaMira Press.

Scheper-Hughes, Nancy. 1989. "Death Without Weeping." *Natural History,* October.

Schlegel, Alice. 1990. "Gender Meanings: General and Specific." In *Beyond the Second Sex: New Directions in the Anthropology of Gender.* Peggy R. Sanday and R. G. Goodenough, eds., pp. 21–41. Philadelphia: University of Pennsylvania Press.

Schusky, Ernest. 2002. *Manual for Kinship Analysis.* 2d ed. Lanham, MD: Rowman and Littlefield.

Schwartz, Barry, Hazel Marcus, and Alana Snibbe. 2006. "Is Freedom Just Another Word for Many Things to Buy? *New York Times Magazine* (February 26): 14–16.

Schwartz, John. 2006. "Archaeologist in New Orleans Finds a Way to Help the Living." *New York Times* (January 3): D-1.

Scrimshaw, Susan C. M. 1976. *Women's Modesty: One Barrier to the Use of Family Planning Clinics in Ecuador.* Monographs of the Carolina Population Center. pp. 167–83.

Scrimshaw, Susan, and Elena Hurtado. 1987. *Rapid Assessment Procedures for Nutrition and Primary Health Care: Anthropological Approaches to Improving Programme Effectiveness.* Los Angeles: UCLA Latin America Center Publication.

Scudder, Thayer. 1999. "The Emerging Global Crisis and Development Anthropology: Can We Have an Impact?" *Human Organization* 58(4): 351–64.

Seabrooke, Kevin, ed. 2002. *The World Almanac and Book of Facts.* New York: World Almanac Education Group.

Seattle Times. 2004. "Reviving California's Native Languages." (July 12): A-6.

Selzer, Richard. 1979. *Confessions of a Knife.* New York: Simon & Schuster.

Sen, Amartya. 2001. "The Many Faces of Gender Inequality." *New Republic* (September 17): 35–40.

Sengupta, Somini. 2006. "India's 'Idol' Recipe: Mix Small-Town Grit and Democracy." *New York Times* (May 25): A-4.

Service, Elman R. 1966. *The Hunters.* Englewood Cliffs, NJ: Prentice-Hall.

———. 1975. *Origins of the State and Civilization.* New York: Norton.

———. 1978. *Profiles in Ethnology.* 3rd ed. New York: Harper & Row.

Sharff, Jagna W. 1981. "Free Enterprise and the Ghetto Family." *Psychology Today* (March).

Sheets, Payson D. 1993. "Dawn of a New Stone Age in Eye Surgery." *In Archaeology: Discovering Our Past.* 2nd ed. Robert J. Sharer and Wendy Ashmore, eds., Mountain View, CA: Mayfield.

Sheflen, Albert E. 1972. *Body Language and the Social Order.* Englewood Cliffs, NJ: Prentice-Hall.

Shenk, Mary. 2006. "Models for the Future of Anthropology." *Anthropology News* 47(1): 6–7.

Shostak, Marjorie. 1983. *Nisa: The Life and Words of a !Kung Woman.* New York: Vintage Books (Random House).

Sieber, Roy. 1962. "Masks as Agents of Social Control." *African Studies Bulletin* 5(11): 8–13.

Simpson, George E., and J. Milton Yinger. 1985. *Racial and Cultural Minorities: An Analysis of Prejudice and Discrimination.* 5th ed. New York: Plenum.

Singer, Merrill. 1985. "Family Comes First: An Examination of the Social Networks of Skid Row Men." *Human Organization* 44(2): 137–42.

Sklar, Holly. 2004. "Don't Outsource Workers, Bring in CEOs." *Charlotte Observer* (April 29): 9-A.

———. 2005. "Are CEOs Earning Their 54% Pay Increase?" *Charlotte Observer* (May 15): 2-D.

Slobin, Mark, and Jeff T. Titon. 1984. "The Music Culture as a World of Music." In *Worlds of Music: An Introduction to the Music of the World's Peoples.* Jeff T. Titon et al., eds., pp. 1–11. London: Collier Macmillan Publishers.

Smith, Anthony D. 1976. *Social Change: Social Theory and Historical Processes.* London: Longman.

Smith, Craig S. 2005. "Abduction, Often Violent, a Kyrgyz Wedding Rite." *New York Times* (April 30): 1-A.

Smith, Dorothy E. 2000. "Schooling for Inequality." *Signs: Journal of Women in Culture and Society* 25(4): 1147–51.

Smith, E. A. 1983. "Anthropological Applications of Optimal Foraging Theory: A Critical Review." *Current Anthropology* 24: 625–51.

Smith, Susanna. 1995. "Women and Households in the Third World." In *Families in Multicultural Perspective*. Bron Ingoldsby and Susanna Smith, eds., pp. 235–67. New York: Guilford Press.

Spain, Daphne, and Suzanne M. Bianchi. 1996. *Balancing Act: Motherhood, Marriage, and Employment Among American Women*. New York: Russell Sage Foundation.

Spindler, George and Janice Stockard, eds. 2007. *Globalization and Change in 15 Cultures: Born in One World, Living in Another*. Belmont, CA: Wadsworth.

Spindler, Louise S. 1984. *Culture Change and Modernization*. Prospect Heights, IL: Waveland Press.

Spradley, James. 1970. *You Owe Yourself a Drunk*. Boston: Little, Brown.

Stack, Carol. 1975. *All Our Kin: Strategies for Survival in a Black Community*. New York: Harper & Row.

Statistical Abstract of the United States. 2006. www.census.gov/prod/www/statistical-abstract .html, Table 13 (Resident Population by Sex, Race, and Hispanic Origin Status, 2000–2004).

Stavans, Ilan. 2003. *Spanglish: The Making of a New American Language*. New York: Rayo (HarperCollins).

Steiner, Christopher B. 1990. "Body Personal and Body Politic: Adornment and Leadership in Cross-Cultural Perspective." *Anthropos* 85: 431–45.

Steinmetz, David. 2004. "World Christianity: Under New Management." *Charlotte Observer* (July 12): 11-A.

Stenning, Derrick J. 1965. "The Pastoral Fulani of Northern Nigeria." In *Peoples of Africa*. James Gibbs, ed., pp. 363–401. New York: Holt, Rinehart and Winston.

Stephens, William N. 1963. *The Family in Cross-Cultural Perspective*. New York: Holt, Rinehart and Winston.

Stille, Alexander. 2003. "Experts Can Help Rebuild a Country." *New York Times* (July 19): A15 and A17.

Stockard, Janice E. 2002. *Marriage in Culture*. Fort Worth, TX: Harcourt College Publishers.

Stocking, George W. 1983. *Observers Observed: Essays on Ethnographic Fieldwork*. Madison: University of Wisconsin Press.

Stone, Linda. 2000. *Kinship and Gender: An Introduction*. Boulder, CO: Westview.

Strathern, Andrew, and Pamela Stewart. 2000. *Collaboration and Conflicts: A Leader Through Time*. Fort Worth, TX: Harcourt College Publishers.

Strathern, Marilyn. 1984. "Domesticity and the Denigration of Women." In *Rethinking Women's Roles: Perspectives from the Pacific*. Denise O'Brien and Sharon Tiffany, eds., pp. 13–31. Berkeley: University of California Press.

Strauss, Murray A. 2001. "Physical Aggression in the Family: Prevalence Rates, Links to Non-Family Violence, and Implications for Primary Prevention of Societal Violence." In *Prevention and Control of Aggression and the Impact on Its Victims*. Manuel Martinez, ed., pp. 181–200. New York: Kluwer Academic/ Plenum Publishers.

Struck, Doug. 2006. "Warmer Weather Melting Arctic." *The Charlotte Observer* (March 26): 17–18A.

Strum, Philippa. 2002. *Women in the Barracks: The VMI Case and Equal Rights*. Lawrence, KS: University Press of Kansas.

Sturtevant, William. 1964. "Studies in Ethnoscience." *American Anthropologist* 66(3) (Part 2): 99–131.

Suggs, David N., and Andrew Miracle, eds. 1993. *Culture and Human Sexuality: A Reader*. Pacific Grove, CA: Brooks/Cole.

Sullivan, Thomas J., and Kenrick Thompson. 1990. *Sociology: Concepts, Issues, and Applications*. New York: Macmillan.

Sundkler, Bengt. 1961. *Bantu Prophets of South Africa*. 2d ed. London: Oxford University Press.

Suskind, Ron. 2004. "What Makes Bush's Presidency So Radical Even to Some Republicans Is His Preternatural, Faith-Infused Certainty in Uncertain Times." *New York Times Magazine* (October 17): 44–51, 64, 102, 106.

Takahashi, Dean. 1998. "Doing Fieldwork in the High-Tech Jungle." *Wall Street Journal* (October 27): B1.

Tahmincioglu, Eve. 2004. "It's Not Only the Giants with Franchises Abroad." *New York Times* (February 12): C-4.

Talmon, Yohina. 1964. "Mate Selection in Collective Settlements." *American Sociological Review* 29: 491–508.

Tannen, Deborah. 1990. *You Just Don't Understand: Women and Men in Conversation*. New York: Morrow.

———. 1994. *Talking From 9 to 5*. New York: William Morrow and Company.

Tarde, Gabriel. 1903. *The Laws of Imitation* (Elsie Clews Parsons, trans.). New York: Holt.

Taylor, Brian K. 1962. *The Western Lacustrine Bantu*. London: International African Institute.

Terry, Don. 1996. "Cultural Tradition and Law Collide in Middle America." *New York Times* (Dec. 2): A-10.

Thernstrom, Melanie. 2005. "The New Arranged Marriage." *New York Times Magazine* (Feb. 13): 35–41.

Thomson, David S. 1994. "Worlds Shaped by Words." In *Conformity and Conflict*. 8th ed. James P. Spradley and David McCurdy, eds., pp. 73–86. New York: HarperCollins.

Tierney, John. 2003. "Letter from the Middle East." *New York Times* (October 22): A-4.

Tierney, Patrick. 2000. *Darkness in El Dorado: How Scientists and Journalists Devastated the Amazon*. New York: Norton.

Tiger, Lionel, and Robin Fox. 1971. *The Imperial Animal*. New York: Holt, Rinehart and Winston.

Titon, Jeff Todd, et al. 1996. *Worlds of Music: An Introduction to the Music of the World's Peoples*. New York: Simon & Schuster.

Tollefson, Kenneth D. 1995. "Potlatching and Political Organization among the Northwest Coast Indians." *Ethnology* 34(1): 53–73.

Treiman, Donald J. 1977. *Occupational Prestige in Comparative Perspective*. New York: Academic Press.

Trichur, Rita. 2004. "Muslims Divided Over Whether Shariah Belongs in Ontario Arbitration Law." *Community CustomWire* (August 22) (Item: CX2004235U7973).

Truzzi, Marcello. 1993. "The Occult Revival as Popular Culture: Some Observations on the Old and the Nouveau Witch." In *Magic, Witchcraft, and Religion: An Anthropological Study of the Supernatural*. 3d ed. Arthur C. Lehmann and James E. Myers, eds., pp. 397–405. Mountain View, CA: Mayfield.

Turnbull, Colin. 1981. "Mbuti Womanhood." In *Woman the Gatherer*. Frances Dahlberg, ed., pp. 205–19. New Haven, CT: Yale University Press.

Tylor, Edward B. 1958. *Origins of Culture*. New York: Harper & Row (orig. 1871).

———. 1889. "On a Method of Investigating the Development of Institutions: Applied to Laws of Marriage and Descent." *Journal of Royal Anthropological Institute* 18: 245–69.

United Nations. 1995. *The World's Women 1995: Trends and Statistics*. United Nations, Gender Empowerment Measure, 2002. http://humandevelopment.bu.edu/dev _indicators/show_info.cfm?index_id=230& data_type=1

United Press International. 2001. "Parents Hang Inter-Caste Lovers in India." August 7.

Urdang, Stephanie. 2001. "Women and AIDS: Gender Inequality Is Fatal." *Women's International Network News* 27(4) (Autumn): 24.

U.S. Census Bureau. 2002. *Statistical Abstract of the United States*. Table no. 53. P. 782.

Van Esterik, Penny. 1989. *Beyond the Breast–Bottle Controversy*. New Brunswick, NJ: Rutgers University Press.

Van Gennep, Arnold. 1960. *The Rites of Passage*. Chicago: University of Chicago Press (orig. 1908).

Vanneman, Reeve, and L. W. Cannon. 1987. *The American Perception of Class*. Philadelphia: Temple University Press.

Van Willigen, John. 2002. *Applied Anthropology: An Introduction*. 3d ed. South Hadley, MA: Bergin and Garvey.

Vincent, Joan. 1990. *Anthropology and Politics: Vision, Traditions, and Trends*. Tucson: University of Arizona Press.

———. 2002. *The Anthropology of Politics: A Reader in Ethnography, Theory, and Critique*. Malden, MA: Blackwell Publishers.

Wagner, Gunter. 1949. *The Bantu of North Kavirondo*. London: Published for the International African Institute by Oxford University Press.

Wallace, Anthony F. C. 1966. *Religion: An Anthropological View*. New York: Random House.

Walter, Chris. 2003. "Weaving a Future for Tibetan Refugees: Tibetan Rug Weaving Project." *Cultural Survival* 27(2) (June 15).

Ward, Martha C. 1971. *Them Children: A Study in Language Learning*. New York: Holt, Rinehart and Winston.

———. 2002. *A World Full of Women*. 3d ed. Boston: Allyn & Bacon.

Wardhaugh, Ronald. 2001. *An Introduction to Sociolinguistics*. 4th ed. Oxford: Blackwell.

Ware, H. 1979. "Polygyny, Women's Views in a Transitional Society, Nigeria 1975." *Journal of Marriage and the Family* 41(1): 185–95.

Weber, Max. 1946. *From Max Weber: Essays in Sociology* (Hans Girth and C. Wright Mills, trans. and eds.). New York: Oxford University Press.

———. 1958. *The Protestant Ethic and the Spirit of Capitalism*. New York: Charles Scribner's Sons (orig. 1904).

Weiner, Annette. 1976. *Women of Value, Men of Renown*. Austin: University of Texas Press.

Weiner, E. 1994. "Muslim Radicals and Police Hunt Feminist Bangladeshi Writer." *Christian Science Monitor* (July 26): 6.

Weismantel, Mary. 1995. "Making Kin: Kinship Theory and Zumbagua Adoptions." *American Ethnologist* 22(4): 685–709.

Weller, Christian E., Robert Scott, and Adam Hersh. 2002. "The Unremarkable Record of Liberalized Trade." *Economic Policy Institute, www.epinet.org* (October).

Whelehan, Patricia. 1985. "Review of *Incest: A Biosocial View* by Joseph Shepher." *American Anthropologist* 87: 677.

White, Benjamin. 1973. "Demand for Labor and Population Growth in Colonial Java." *Human Ecology* 1(3): 217–36.

White, Leslie. 1959. *The Evolution of Culture.* New York: McGraw-Hill.

Whitehead, Neil L., and R. Brian Ferguson. 1993. "Deceptive Stereotypes About Tribal Warfare." *Chronicle of Higher Education* (November 10): 48.

Whiting, John W., and Irvin L. Child. 1953. *Child Training and Personality: A Cross-Cultural Study.* New Haven, CT: Yale University Press.

Whiting, Robert. 1979. "You've Gotta Have 'Wa.'" *Sports Illustrated* (September 24): 60–71.

Whyte, M. K. 1978. *The Status of Women in Preindustrial Societies.* Princeton, NJ: Princeton University Press.

Wilk, Richard. 1996. *Economies and Culture: Foundations of Economic Anthropology.* Boulder, CO: Westview.

Williams, Florence. 1998. "In Utah, Polygamy Goes Suburban." *Charlotte Observer* (February 28): G3.

Williams, Thomas R. 1969. *A Borneo Childhood: Enculturation in Dusun Society.* New York: Holt, Rinehart and Winston.

Wilson, Monica. 1960. "Nyakyusa Age Villages." In *Cultures and Societies of Africa.* Simon and Phoebe Ottenberg, eds., pp. 227–36. New York: Random House.

Witherspoon, Gary. 1977. *Language and Art in the Navajo Universe.* Ann Arbor: University of Michigan Press.

Wittfogel, Karl. 1957. *Oriental Despotism: A Comparative Study of Total Power.* New Haven, CT: Yale University Press.

Wolf, Arthur. 1968. "Adopt a Daughter-in-Law, Marry a Sister: A Chinese Solution to the Incest Taboo." *American Anthropologist* 70: 864–74.

Wolf, E. 1964. *Anthropology.* Englewood Cliffs, NJ: Prentice-Hall.

Wolf, Margery. 1972. *Women and the Family in Rural Taiwan.* Stanford, CA: Stanford University Press.

Wood, Julia T. 1994. "Gender, Communication, and Culture." In *Intercultural Communication: A Reader.* 7th ed. Larry Samovar and Richard Porter, eds., pp. 155–65. Belmont, CA: Wadsworth.

The World Almanac and Book of Facts. 2006. New York: World Almanac Education Group.

World Bank Atlas. www.web.worldbank.org/wbsite/external/data statistics.

Wulff, Robert, and Shirley Fiske, eds. 1987. *Anthropological Praxis: Translating Knowledge into Action.* Boulder, CO: Westview.

Xinhua News Agency. 2001. "16,000 Dowry Death Cases Pending In Indian Courts." June 11.

Ya'ari, Ehud, and Ina Friedman. 1991. "Curses in Verses." *Atlantic* 267(2): 22–26.

Yardley, Jim. 2005. "Fearing Future, China Starts to Give Girls Their Due." *New York Times* (January 31): A-3.

Yellen, John. 1990. "The Transformation of the Kalahari !Kung." *Scientific American* (April): 96–104.

Index